GW00832930

A
History of Plymouth

Llewellynn Jewitt

Originally published 1873

This edition published 2001 by
Edward Gaskell publishers
6 Grenville Street
Bideford
Devon
EX39 2EA

isbn 1-898546-42-8

A History of Plymouth

Llewellynn Jewitt

Subscribers Edition
Number
....
of
100

Printed and bound by
Lazarus Press
Unit 7 Caddsdown Business Park
Bideford
Devon
EX39 3DX

Lazarus Press
Bideford
Devon

A
HISTORY OF PLYMOUTH

BY
LLEWELLYNN JEWITT, F.S.A.,
ETC., ETC.,
Author of "The Life of Josiah Wedgwood"; "Grave Mounds and their Contents"; "Life of William Hutton"; "Domesday Book of Derbyshire"; "Chatsworth," etc., etc., etc; and Editor of "The Reliquary Quarterly Journal and Review," etc.

ILLUSTRATED WITH WOOD ENGRAVINGS

1873.
LONDON:
SIMPKIN, MARSHALL & Co., STATIONERS' HALL COURT.
PLYMOUTH:
W.H. LUKE, BEDFORD STREET.

2001.
EDWARD GASKELL PUBLISHERS
6 GRENVILLE STREET
BIDEFORD
DEVON EX39 2EA

TO HIS ROYAL HIGHNESS

ALBERT EDWARD, PRINCE OF WALES, K.G.,

ETC., ETC., ETC.,

THIS HISTORY OF THE ANCIENT AND LOYAL

BOROUGH OF PLYMOUTH,

OF WHICH HIS ROYAL HIGHNESS HOLDS THE OFFICE OF

LORD HIGH STEWARD,

IS,

BY HIS MOST GRACIOUS AND SPECIAL PERMISSION,
DEDICATED WITH THE MOST PROFOUND FEELING OF RESPECT
AND WITH EARNEST PRAYERS FOR HIS LONG
LIFE AND HAPPINESS,
BY HIS MOST FAITHFUL AND DEVOTED
SERVANT,

LLEWELLYNN JEWITT

INTRODUCTION

In presenting this volume to the world, it is right, at the outset, to say a few words as to its origin and the reasons which have induced its preparation. In fact, as the volume itself professes to be a History of the Town of Plymouth, so, I conceive, this "Introduction" ought to be, in spite of tautology, a history of this History. This, very briefly, I proceed to lay before its readers, and as my work commences its records with the earliest periods of the annals of Plymouth, so this Introduction shall, as it ought, begin with the first attempt to collect materials for its preparation.

Some years before his death, the late Mr. Nettleton, the well known bookseller of Plymouth, commenced the collection of materials towards a history of that borough, without however, I believe, having any view to arranging them for publication. His collection mainly consisted of various notices of Plymouth from different histories of Devonshire, and other sources, copied out into a series of volumes; extracts from town records; copies of charters, etc.; and a list of Mayors arranged in years, under which he had, here and there, made entries of events that had occurred. At Mr. Nettleton's death this collection passed, by purchase, in to the hands of Mr. W. H. Luke, who some time afterwards placed it in my hands as the nucleus of a "History of Plymouth"; I then arranged to prepare for him. On going through the volumes I found but little beyond the mayoral annals and copies of documents that would be of value for the plan of my work, but, fortunately, I had large collections of my own, which fell in remarkably well with them. I determined for the first portion of my work, to adopt, with modifications, Mr. Nettleton's plan of mayoral annals and to add to it, from every source that might prove available, records of events, year by year, and to bring these down to the hour of publication. This I have done, and the annals, as I have prepared them, form a large and important part of my present volume. To this I have prefixed a brief historical notice of the locality so as to carry the history back to pre-historic times, and so render that part of my work as complete as circumstances would allow.

The remainder of the volume I have devoted to a history and description of the town and of its various public buildings, its religious establishments, fortifications, manufactures, institutions and attractions, and of places of interest in its neighbourhood.

Thus the work is entirely original, and I can safely say that no trouble, pains, or expense, have been spared to make it worthy of the great and growing town whose history it is intended to illustrate.

At the time of my first undertaking the preparation of this work, no "History of Plymouth" had ever been published, or was in preparation, or even thought of. The field was therefore entirely clear, and my announcement was as follows:–

"It has long been a matter of surprise that a town of such magnitude and importance as Plymouth no history has as yet been written; and that, beyond the information contained in guide books, which have from time to time been issued, there is literally nothing known publicly, of its early history or of the different events which have occurred in connection with it. It is strange, and is indeed a serious reproach to the town, that while almost every other borough in the kingdom – nay, almost every parish and market town – has had its history chronicled and made as imperishable as goodly folio, quarto, or octavo volumes can make it, that of Plymouth should have remained so long unwritten, and consequently, unknown, not only to its own inhabitants, but to the world at large. It has been the aim of the Editor of the present work, so far as in him lies, to remove this reproach from the town, and to produce a history, so far as available information will admit, which shall be worthy of itself, fit to find a place in the library of the topographer and the historian, and make its way into the hands of every inhabitant of the place."

The first portion of the present volume was at once put to press and was proceeded with as rapidly as the nature of the work, and the other engagements of myself and of the publisher, would allow. When about one half of the entire work was actually printed off, another so called "History of Plymouth" was, much to my surprise, announced as ready for publication, and was at once issued. It has not, however, affected my work or my labours in the slightest degree, and I am well content – nay, only too ready – to let the two, be side by side for careful comparison and stand the test of public criticism. On the total disregard of literary etiquette by its compiler, who, while a work long announced, and actually passing as rapidly as circumstances would allow through the press, attempted to forestall it by one of his own, it is not *worth* my while to remark. If he can reconcile it to his own conscience, well and good – I am content. My own and only feeling is that, in a large town like Plymouth, there is "room enough for all," and I heartily congratulate the town, that, instead of having no written History at all, it has now the advantage of having two, which, so far from interfering with each other, may well stand side by side on the library shelf.

It remains only for me to say, that after a long but unavoidable delay, my "History of Plymouth" is at last presented to the public. It may have (and doubtless has) faults, and errors may here and there have crept in, but these, if pointed out to me, I shall hope to rectify in a future edition. I trust, however, it may be found to be, what it has been my wish to make it, a work worthy of Plymouth and of Plymouthians, and one which may be referred to with confidence by all into whose hands it may fall.

To those kind friends who have aided me with information – and I am proud to feel and to know that in the town I lived in for years and love so well, and with whose literary and scientific institutions I was so intimately connected, I have many friends – I beg to tender my warmest thanks.

LLEWELLYNN JEWITT
The Hall, Winster,
Derbyshire
January 1st 1873.

CONTENTS.

LIST OF ILLUSTRATIONS

PLATES

WOOD ENGRAVINGS

Lazarus Press
Bideford
Devon

HISTORY OF PLYMOUTH

CHAPTER I

PRE-HISTORIC PERIOD — ADVANTAGES OF SITUATION— THE DAMNONII — THE SILURES — THE BELGIC-GAULS — THE IBERIAN SETTLERS— PHŒNICIAN TRADERS — TYRIAN AND GADITANIAN VESSELS CROSS TO DEVONSHIRE FOR TIN — THE CASSITERIDES — MERCHANTS OF MASSILIA TRADE FOR TIN — THE ROMANS DISCOVER THE TRADE — DWELLINGS OF THE ANCIENT BRITONS — ENCOUNTER BETWEEN CORINÆUS AND GOGMAGOG ON THE HOE AT PLYMOUTH — DRAYTON'S POLYOLBION — ANCIENT BRITISH REMAINS AT MOUNT BATTEN — CAVE AT STONEHOUSE — KENT'S CAVERN AT TORQUAY.

The early history of any town which possesses the slightest claim to antiquity is, naturally, involved in mystery, and is so obscure as only to be arrived at by the most careful and painstaking research. It is natural that it should be so, and that all attempts to fix a date to its foundation must in a great measure be presumptive. Plymouth certainly is no exception to this general rule, and it would be little more than speculation to attempt to fix even an approximate period to its first foundation. Dating back to prehistoric times, the town no doubt owes its origin to its admirable situation as a harbour, and its desirable position at the confluence of two such important rivers as the Plym and the Tamar, and to the commanding altitude of some of its native heights.

Possessing all the advantages of situation both land-ward and sea-ward, with fertile and well-watered land, abundant woods and grazing grounds – the delight of the hunter – with natural rock fortresses on its most pregnable side, and heights which commanded an uninterrupted view of the surrounding country for many miles, the site where stands the present and important town of Plymouth – the "Metropolis of the West" – was just the one to be chosen by the early inhabitants of this island whereon to found a colony; and this they evidently did at a very early period of this, their prehistoric existence. That this place *was* inhabited by the Ancient Britons is abundantly proved by remains of that people which have been exhumed, and that they held maritime connection with foreign states is also placed beyond reasonable doubt.

In this period, the district was inhabited by the *Damnonii*, a race which spread itself over this county and the adjacent one of Cornwall. The *Silures,* a race of Iberians whose first colony was probably brought over by the Phœnicians, occupied the Scilly Islands, and gradually extended themselves over Cornwall and this part of Devonshire, but were ultimately supplanted by the Belgic-Gauls who drove them from their settlements and their mines, in this district whence they migrated and took refuge among the mountains of South Wales.

The Silures were of Iberian origin, and were probably brought over as miners by the Phœnicians, who had for a long time traded with the inhabitants of this district for tin. The Iberians themselves do not appear to have been distinguished in navigation, but their knowledge of this art must in some parts of Spain have been materially advanced by their contact with the Phœnicians, who had permanent settlements among, and were mixed with, the Iberian people. William Von Humboldt has shown that names of places compounded of *ura*, which in the Basque or Euskarian signifies *water*, are of common occurrence in the Peninsula and Iberian part of Gaul, but not elsewhere: such names are Asturia, Iburia, Ilurbiba, etc. The country of the Astures and that of the Silures were separated from each other by the waters of the Bay of Biscay and the British Ocean, and as the former seem to have derived their name from *asta* a rock, and *ura* water, so may the latter have owed theirs to *ura* water with a Basque prefix *sal, zal,* or *soloa*, (a meadow.) We are moreover, as has been remarked, by no means compelled to restrict the observation of Tacitus altogether to the Silures, or to the district to which in his days they were confined, the Silures perhaps being named, as a more distinguished tribe, *gens nobilissima.* The Scilly Isles themselves, so familiar to the Phœnician voyagers from Gades, may not improbably have possessed an Iberian population, which their still existing name of Scilly may indicate. The passage in Solinus in which the "*insula Silura*" separated by a stormy channel from the coast of the Damnonii is probably correctly taken as applying to these islands; Dionysius Periegetes (A.D. 290) a better authority than Solinus, and who appears to preserve the views of the eminent Eratosthenes, expressly declares that the inhabitants of the Cassiterides or as he calls them the "Hesperides whence tin proceeds" to be descendants of the Iberians. Priscianus in his Latin paraphrase of this passage follows Dionysius almost literally – "*Hesperides, populus tenuit* *arcis fortis Iberi.*" In Strabo's description of the inhabitants of the Cassiterides he used language almost identical with that in which he described the manners of some of the people of the south of Spain, the dress of both being said to comprise a black mantle *sagum* or *lœna*. The Bastelani of whom this is related, were a mixed race partly Iberian and partly Phœnician, and there is much reason to suppose that the same was the case with the inhabitants of the Cassiterides. The Phœnicians were remarkable for the facility with which they mingled with other races, and as the object of their voyages to Britain was the trade in metals and particularly tin, nothing seems more probable than that they should have induced a colony of Iberian miners, probably of mixed Phœnician and Iberian stock, to settle in the south-west of the Island. The evidence on this subject, though on no one point decisive, is of the cumulative kind, and the legitimate conclusion seems to be the admission of an Iberian settlement in the south-west of Britain, to which in particular the principal tribe of Silures is to be traced.*

It was through the Phœnicians of course – Phœnicia being the greatest maritime state of the ancient world – that Britain was first known to Greece and Rome, and that part of Britain which was first made known was the coast of Cornwall and Devonshire from which the tin, procured by the Phœnicians was got. Tyrian ships had probably crossed to the shores of Britain, and there is no doubt that Gaditanian vessels from Tarshish traded here for tin as early probably as the time of Solomon, (about a thousand years before Christ,) and doubtless before the time of the prophet Ezekiel, who, speaking of Tyre, says "Tarshish was thy dealer, by the abundance of all riches; with silver, iron, *tin*, and lead, they furnished thy markets."† Herodotus (450 B.C.) speaks of the Island Cassiterides (the Scilly Islands) as the place from whence tin was brought, and where ancient workings have been discovered. It is said by Strabo that the Phœnicians possessed the exclusive trade for tin with the people of the Cassiterides, and they were so jealous of their trade that a Gaditanian vessel being tracked by a Roman ship for the purpose of discovering the country from whence tin was obtained, the master run his vessel ashore, rather than allow them to discover his route. Later on the Carthaginians shared the trade, and they and the Phœnicians to some extent settled and mixed with the inhabitants of Cornwall and Devon. In the sixth century (B.C.,) the merchants of Massilia traded here for tin. It seems that the primeval tinners of Cornwall carried that metal to the Island (Mount's Bay,) where they met the Phœnicians, etc., and bartered it with the foreign merchants. The Romans discovered the country of tin some few

*Crania Britannica

†Ezekiel xxvii, 12.

years before the invasion, and the metal obtained by them was no doubt taken to Narbon, whilst that obtained by the Greeks was taken to Massilia. At the time of the subjugation of Britain by the Romans, the people of the western district were nomadic, and subsisted by their cattle and by their trade in tin, and it would appear that not only were they compelled to cultivate the soil for their conquerors, but to work the lead and tin mines for their profit and advantage.

The dwellings of the Britons, resembling those of the Gauls, were circular huts constructed of boards, of wicker-work, and reeds, and covered with straw thatch. Their towns or colonies, were simply a number of these huts placed together and surrounded by felled trees or by a roughly piled wall and a ditch. Under the pressure of the Roman invasion these defensive precautions were strengthened and made more important. Remains of these hut circles and towns are to be found on Dartmoor and other places in Devonshire, and doubtless one or two of such huts formed the first nucleus of what afterwards became a colony of the Britons, and has grown into the present large and important town of Plymouth.

It is traditionally said that on the Hoe at Plymouth, of which I shall have to speak in a later chapter, a deadly conflict took place between the Corinæus and Gogmagog, after the arrival of the Trojans. Of this supposed encounter old Michael Drayton, after graphically describing the wanderings of Æneas and his son Ascanius after the destruction of Troy, and the death of Brute, his causing the death of his parents, his leaving Italy and his subsequent discovery of the Isle of Albion, thus writes:*–

"For Albion sailing then, th' arrived quickly here,
O! never in this world men half so joyful were;
With shouts heard up to Heaven, when they beheld the land,
And in this very place where Totnes now doth stand,
First set their gods of Troy, kissing the blessed shore
Then, forraging this Ile, long promis'd them before,
Amongst the ragged Cleeues those monstrous Giants sought;
Who (of their dreadful kind) t'appall the Troians, brought
Great *Gogmagog*, an Oake that by the roots could teare:
So mightie were (that time) the men who lived there:
But, for the vse of Armes he did not vnderstand
(Except some rock or tree, that comming next to hand
Hee raz'd out of the earth to execute his rage)
Hee challenge makes for strength, and offereth there his gage.
Which, *Corin* taketh vp, to answer by and by,
Vpon this sonne of Earth his vtmost power to try.
All, doubtful to which part the victorie would goe,
Vpon that loftie place at *Plimmouth* call'd the *Hoe*,

*Polyolbion Canto 1

Those mightie Wrastlers met; with many an ireful looke
Who threatened, as the one hold of the other tooke;
But, grappled, glowing fire shines in their sparkling eyes.
And, whilst at length of arme one from the other lyes,
Their lusty sinewes swell like cables, as they strive:
Their feet such trampling make, as though they forc't to drive
A thunder out of earth; which stagger's with the weight;
Thus, eithers vtmost force vrg'd to the greatest height.
Whilst one upon his hip the other seekes to lift,
And th'adverse (by a turne) doth from his cunning shift,
Their short-fetcht troubled breath a hollow noise doth make,
Like bellowes of a Forge. The *Corin* vp doth take
The Giant twixt the grayns; and voyding of his hould
(Before his combrous feet he well recover could)
Pitcht head-long from the hill; as when a man doth throw
An Axtree, that with sleight delivered from the toe
Rootes vp the yeelding earth; so that his violent fall,
Strooke *Neptune* with such strength, as shouldred him withall;
That where the monstrous wanes like Mountaines late did stand,
They leap't out of the place, and left the bared sand
To gaze vpon wide heaven; so great a blowe it gaue.
For which, the conquering *Brute* on *Corineus* braue
This horne of land bestow'd, and markt it with his name:
Of *Corin, Cornwall* call'd, to his immortal fame."

Camden* speaking of the same supposed encounter says: "I shall take liberty just to mention the fabulous combat of Corinæus with the giant Gogmagog here, in a line or two of the Architrenius concerning our giants."

"Hos avidum belli robur Corinæus Averno
Præcipites misit, cubitis ter quatuor altum
Gogmagog Herculea suspendit in aëra lucta,
Antheumque suum scopulo detrusit in æquor,
Potavitque dato Thetis ebria sanguine fluctus,
Divisumque tulit mare corpus, Cerberus umbram."

"These savage monsters, train'd to war and blood,
Dash'd Corinæus to the Stygian flood.
Aloft in air tall Gogmagog he bore,
And flung the Giant from his rocky shore,
While Ocean feasted on his wasted gore.
His corpse twelve cubits length the waves o'erspread,
And his soul flitted to the infernal dead."

This tradition is interesting as carrying down to our own day the remembrance of the conflicts, which took place between the natives of this Island and their invaders.

*Britannia, 1607.

In the neighbourhood of Plymouth, Celtic remains are somewhat abundant. This is more especially the case on Dartmoor where hut circles, tumuli, and many other remains are to be seen. At Mount Batten, Plymouth, some highly interesting remains of this period have been found. These consist chiefly of ancient British coins of different types. The principal discovery of these coins was made in the year 1832, and other coins have since then, at various times been found on the spot. They have principally been brought to light in the process of quarrying, when they have slipped down with the surface soil.

These coins, which are among the most important antiquities yet found at Plymouth or in its neighbourhood, and which show incontestably, its occupation by the Celtic race, are as follows, and other examples are shown on plate II.

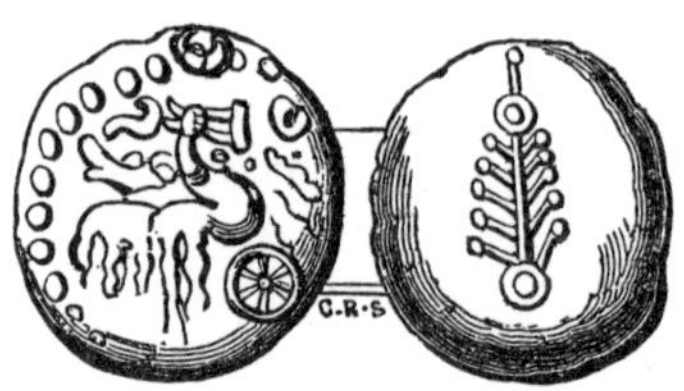

Obv. – Rude horse to the right; above, a figure derived from the arms of Victory; in front, a ring ornament; below, a wheel; below the horse's head, a small cross; the whole surrounded by a circle of pellets placed at some little distance apart.

Rev. – Convex; a branch or wreath springing from an annulet, and having another small annulet near its point.

The type of this coin which is of gold, is considered by Mr Evans to be peculiar to the West of England, and its date is supposed to be comparatively late – probably of the time of Tiberius. It is engraved, Evans pl. C fig 4; Num. Jour., vol. 1 pl. fig. 7; Hawkins pl. 1 fig. 6; and Ruding pl. A fig. 80.

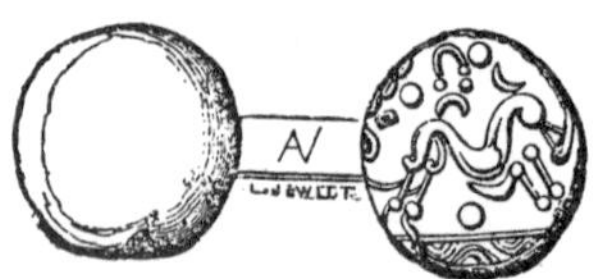

Obv. – Convex; and quite plain.

Rev. – Tail-less horse galloping to the right; above, a reversed crescent and a horse-shoe-formed figure terminated with pellets derived from the arms of Victory, pellets, etc.; over the horse's head a kind of crescent and an annulet; below, a pellet; behind the horse, a semicircle, etc.

This remarkably fine coin is in my own cabinet. It is of gold and has been engraved in the Archaeological Journal.

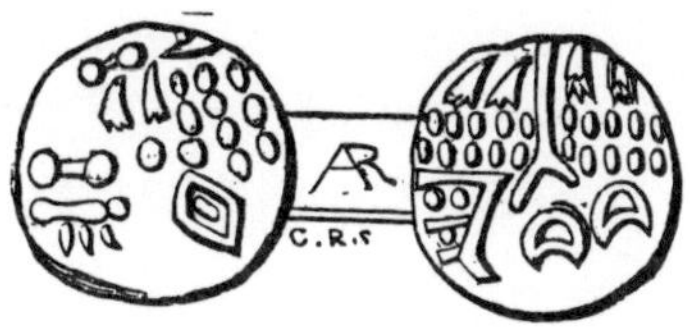

Obv. – Extremely disjointed and almost imperceptible figure of horse, with pellets, etc.

Rev. – Rude portions of a laureated bust.

This coin is of silver, it is very similar in type to those given by Borlase, as having been found at Karn Bre in Cornwall in 1749.

The remainder of the coins which have been found at Mount Batten are principally, of the class which, differing from the usual British and Gaulish series, appears to be in some way peculiar to the Channel Islands. The examples engraved are selected from those in my own cabinet and that of Mr. Cuff.

In a naturally formed cave in Stonehouse first discovered in 1776, some remains of extinct animals were, at a later period found, along with flint implements belonging to the Celtic period. This again, proves the occupation of the spot where the "Three Towns" now stand, by those early races. A somewhat similar cave, but which had the advantage of a more careful and scientific examination, was discovered some years ago at Torquay. In this cave remains of extinct species of bears, hyaenas, lions, and tigers were dug up from beneath a stalagmitic floor of considerable thickness, and along with them was found a human skeleton; the stalagmatic floor having been broken up to form the slabs of the cist, in which it was placed. Intermingled with these bones were found flint knives, and arrow and spear-heads, bone implements and fragments of Celtic pottery. There were also ashes and masses of decomposed animal and vegetable matter, remains of fire and of feasts, and heaps of flint pebbles and flakes of flint in different stages of manufacture, which all clearly showed that the cave had formed the workshop, and probably the residence, of some of the primeval inhabitants, where they prepared the implements of the chase and of fishing.

The mixture of the human remains with those of savage beasts must be accounted for by the stalagmitic floor having been broken up.

Many other traces of British occupation of Plymouth and its neighbourhood besides those alluded to, including some traces of stone circles near Cawsand, have been noticed, but these will be sufficient to show that its foundation is coeval with the earliest period of which there is any evidence of man inhabiting this country.

CHAPTER II

THE ROMANO-BRITISH PERIOD — ROMAN ROADS — IKNEILD STREET — ROMAN COINS — BRONZE IMPLEMENTS — MOULDS FOR CASTING BRONZE BLADES — SPEAR HEADS — ROMAN POTTERY.

Under the Romans, although there is no evidence of Plymouth being a place of note – for, not lying on one of their roads it could not, certainly, have been a Station – it was, doubtless, occupied by that warlike people, and probably was much used as a port for the shipment of the merchandise of the western district as well as a place for fishing.

The principal British roads in Devonshire were the following. The ancient-British way, the Ikneild-street, was the principal road, and passed through the whole length of the county from north-east to south-west on its way to the tin mines of Cornwall. A second road ran from the mouth of the Exe to the great camp at Woodbury, from whence it passed to Streetway-head, where it joined the Ikneild-street. A third road left Exeter and proceeded by Cleeve-hill, and ultimately fell into the road from Crediton to Exeter. A fourth appears to have joined Molland, Bottreaux, and some British settlements with Exeter. From Molland another road ran to Seaton, and others have been traced in different parts of the county. Of these the Ikneild-street was the only one which came near Plymouth, and is therefore the only one of which it is necessary to speak. It enters Devonshire from Dorsetshire, a little to the east of Axminster and to the right of the turnpike road, then proceeds with it by Kilmington and Shute-hill to Dalwood-down, where it bears away from it on the left, for the sake of keeping the ridge of the hill, which it does till it gradually descends by Honiton Church to the house called the "Turk's Head," where it crosses it and runs direct to the large camp called Hembury Fort, which was very probably a British post on it; from thence it ran by Lay-hill, Colstocks, Tallwater, Tallaton-common, and Larkbeare near Whimple to Streetway-head, being still known in this part of its course by the name of the Old Taunton-road. Here the ancient trackway is lost, but it probably continued nearly in the line of the present turnpike road to Exeter, which was certainly the principal town of the Damnonii (though we may not perhaps adopt the conjecture of Mr. Polwhele, that it is exactly delineated on a Damnonian coin.) It crossed the Exe at a ford a little below the present bridge, which ford was the site of the ancient bridge, and ran through St Thomas's by the Causeway, now a nursery, to the village of Alphington, so over Haldon, leaving Ugbrooke where there is a strong British camp, on the right. Some way beyond this it bore off again from the present turnpike road at Sandygate, and passing by Kings Teignton crossed the Teign below Newton Abbot, by a ford still called Hackneild-way; then leaving another British camp on its left, went over Ford-common, and again joined the modern road to Totnes, which we may fairly conclude to have been a British town, both from its being celebrated in the tales of our old historians, not only as the spot where Ambrosius and Uter Pendragon, but even where Brute himself landed, (and, whatever we may think of the matter of fact, it proves the idea of these early writers as to the traditionary antiquity of the place,) but also from the evident bend to the east which the line of the road makes in order to pass through it.* From this place the road passed on by Brent to Plympton-St.-Mary near Plymouth, and thence, it is conjectured, by way of an old circular camp near Borrington, to a ford across the Tamar, probably near to the present village of Tamerton.

Situated so near the Ikneild-street it is more than probable that a branch way connected Plymouth – then, as has been shown, used as a port for the shipment of tin and other articles, and as a fishing station – with that main road, and thus placed it in direct communication with Cornwall on the one hand, and with *Isco* (Exeter) and the road system of the whole of the country, on the other.

But few remains of the Romano-British period have been found in the neighbourhood of Plymouth, but what have been discovered are very decisive as to its occupation by that people. Roman coins have, however, from time to time been found in Plymouth and on the surrounding heights, some of which are in my own cabinet. Bronze weapons of the late Celtic or early Roman periods have also been found in the neighbourhood; and at South Brent, within about ten miles of Plymouth, the remarkably fine bronze spear head here engraved was found a few years ago, along with several other remains of the same period. With the spears were found some pieces of bronze tube which, it has been suggested, may have been used as ferrules at the lower end of the shaft. The spear here engraved, measured 14 inches in length, and 2½ inches in breadth at its broadest part. It was, as will be

*Lysons.

seen, barbed, and the rivets which had attached it to the shaft were perfect. The barbed form of these curious weapons (which were found at a spot called the "Bloody Pool," now merely a swampy hollow on the verge of Dartmoor) is very unusual in England, only very few other examples having come to light. They are conjectured to have been fishing-spears. All the examples found in the "Bloody Pool" were broken into three pieces. Within the blades is a kind of core, apparently not metallic, which is interesting as showing the mode of casting.*

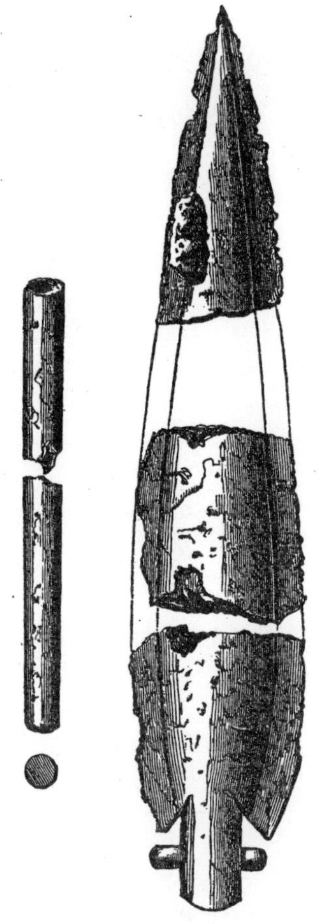

Of Roman pottery but very few examples are noted as having been found at Plymouth. They consist of portions of cinerary urns, and of various other vessels, with here and there a fragment of a mortarium. A few small pieces of Samian ware have also, it is said, been dug up. What have been found however, fragmentary though they have been, are significant as showing, with the coins and other remains, that the locality was inhabited by the invaders.

*It will be interesting while giving this passing notice of bronze implements, to note the discovery in Devonshire of those extremely rare relics of the bronze period, stone moulds for the casting of blades of bronze. They are of extreme interest, as showing incontestably, the manufacture in Devonshire, and within some twenty miles of Plymouth of metal blades of a form rarely found except in Ireland. These moulds which are engraved on plate III, were found at Knighton. Two pair were found: each mould was formed of two pieces which when found were placed together as when adjusted for casting: they separated when removed from the drift-sand and gravel in which they lay. These unique moulds are formed of a strong micaceous schist, similar to that found in Cornwall, and are very heavy: the pair weighing about twelve pounds. Some remarkable bronze weapons were also discovered at Tallaton in 1867, and are engraved on plate IV. Other weapons of bronze have also been found at Winkleigh, Worth, and other places in Devonshire, and are most important for purposes of comparison. Those found at Winkleigh and Worth are engraved on plate V. An excellent and highly interesting account of these discoveries and of other bronze relics discovered in Devonshire, is given by Mr. C. Tucker, F.S.A., to whom the world is indebted for so many important archaeological discoveries, in the "Archaeological Journal," vol. xxiv, page 110, *et seq*. To the Council of the Royal Archaeological Institute we are indebted for the loan of the engravings on plates III, IV and V, which were executed to illustrate Mr. Tucker's paper, to which we have alluded.

PLATE II

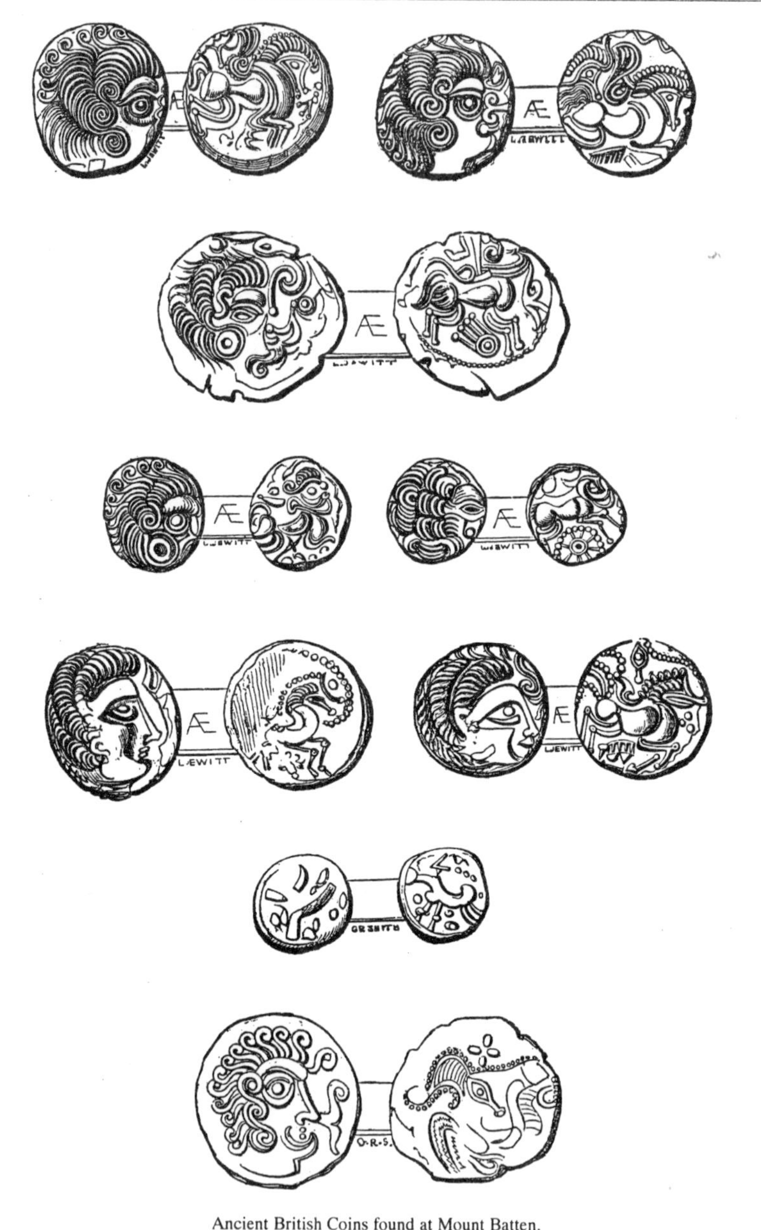

Ancient British Coins found at Mount Batten.

Stone Moulds for casting Bronze Weapons, found in Hennock Parish.

PLATE IV

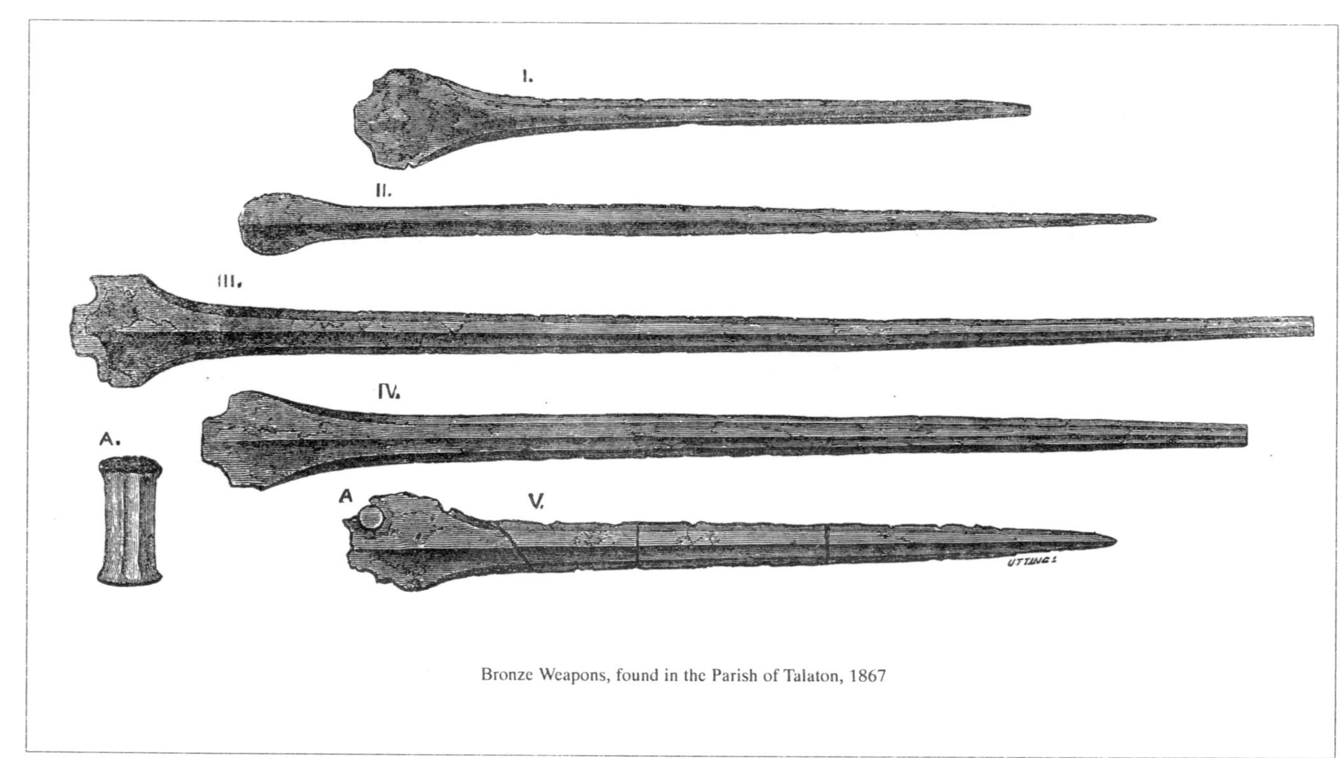

Bronze Weapons, found in the Parish of Talaton, 1867

PLATE V

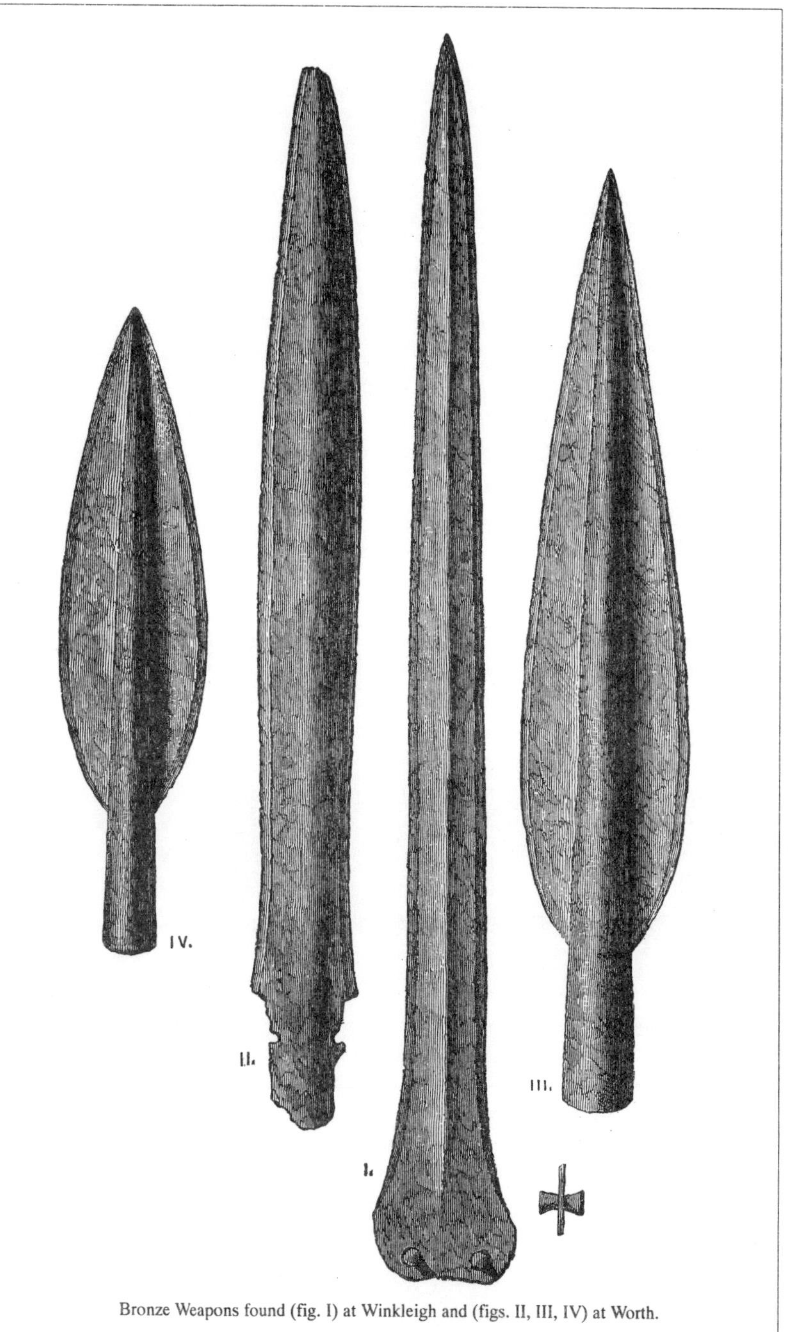

Bronze Weapons found (fig. I) at Winkleigh and (figs. II, III, IV) at Worth.

CHAPTER III

DISCOVERY OF A CEMETERY AND OTHER REMAINS AT STAMFORD HILL — MR. SPENCE BATE'S ACCOUNT OF THE DISCOVERY — BRONZE MIRRORS — BRACELETS — ARMLETS — FIBULÆ — POTTERY — GLASS VESSELS — RINGS — IMPLEMENTS OF IRON, ETC.

One of the most important discoveries of antiquities ever made in the neighbourhood of Plymouth, was made in the early part of the year 1865, when a cemetery of considerable extent was laid bare, and a large number of highly interesting relics found. Of this curious discovery, Mr Spence Bate, who superintended the excavations, has furnished the following detailed account: –

"In the spring of 1865, in order to remove all interference with the range of the guns in the New Forts erected on Stamford-hill, the engineer found it necessary to cut away the slope between it and the sea. In doing this the excavators came upon sundry evidences of the remains of an ancient burial ground. The hill on which it stands consists of slate, and is situated between the broad bay of Plymouth Sound on the west, and an arm of the sea that is known as Catwater, the estuary of the river, on the east. On the north the land projects to some distance, and ends in a bluff hill of limestone, known as Mount Batten; between which and the hill on which the grave-yard stands, is a low grass plane, that previously to the erection of the Breakwater, was occasionally flooded at high spring tides. On the east of Fort Stamford, (being portions of the same, rather than a separate hill,) another mass of limestone stands; on the south is the high land of Staddon Heights.

The graves generally were about four to four and a half feet deep, one foot of which consisted of soil; the remaining three were excavated in the partially disintegrated surface of the natural rock. They were mere hollow excavations, having the walls sharply cut sometimes, but this appears to have been the more evident where the soft slaty rock was present. The bottoms of the excavations were the deepest towards the centre, and they were filled in with the debris which had been taken out of them, together with numerous large rough weather-worn blocks of limestone, that must have been purposely brought from some of the neighbouring limestone hills.

The formation of the slope had been proceeded with for some time, and the workmen stated that they occasionally found bones and pieces of earthenware. It was only, however, when they found some bronze articles, for which they anticipated getting a few shillings in exchange, that they reported the discovery to Captain Moggridge, the engineer officer in charge of the Fortification Works. Immediately the circumstance was known, I was made acquainted with the facts, and proceeded to watch as far as practicable the progress of the exploration. The graves were very numerous, their longitudinal axis lying mostly in a direction east and west. There were evidences however that this was not invariably the case, for in several instances they broke one into another; and in one case a grave appeared to have been associated with others at right angles. When I first arrived, four graves had been partly exposed in section, out of which some human bones, two bronze armlets, a bronze fibula, and some pottery had been previously taken. After my arrival some more human bones were found, which evidently formed portions of at least three human bodies, as were also several isolated molars of the pig, several pebbles from the sea beach mostly of one size, and fragments of glass, together with a vase of coarse ware. Upon opening one grave we found at the bottom a bronze mirror in tolerably perfect condition, and some traces of decomposed bones. A bronze fibulæ was also found in this grave by a workman. In other places the workmen discovered the handles of two bronze mirrors; two bronze bracelets of different formations; a dagger or knife in its bronze sheath; and portions of a bronze cup and some fibulæ. There were also found fragments of many kinds of vases, of more or less perfect pottery ware; portions of human skeletons; and a considerable quantity of iron in a decomposed state, but showing traces of their being parts of some kind of implements.

Of *Bronze Mirrors* the first that was found was seen lying flat at the bottom at the eastern extremity of a grave. It was nearly circular in form, being, imperceptibly, without measurement, longer in one diameter than another, the shortest diameter being probably the vertical axis, when in use. The front or polished surface of the mirror was turned downwards; the back, which was upwards, was the best preserved, and was ornamented with a considerable quantity of scroll engraving. The pattern consists of three circular figures, the two bottom ones being larger than that which I take to be the central top one. Although each circular scroll differs from the others, they are evidently figured upon one general plan; the lines within, being segments of circles of various sizes, form crescents with various modifications Some portions of the engraving in order to give solidity to its character, were filled in with numerous striated spots, consisting of three lines one way and three lines at right angles to them. The entire surface of the mirror was surrounded by a narrow border or rim, which was formed of a separate piece and folded over the margin. This specimen was damaged in many parts, particularly upon the under surface and some of the edge was entirely eaten away, but where the rim was preserved, the plate was not only in good preservation, but not even oxidized, retaining the bright colour of the bronze as perfectly as when, probably, in use by its ancient possessor. With this specimen no handle was found, but a second example (of which the small portion remaining is sufficient to show it to be its duplicate in form,) has the handle still attached to it. The handle is cast in one piece in the form of a loop, having been made by folding one half back against the other, and securing them in that position by a band, the two free ends being spread out to hold the mirror, which is received in a groove and supported on each side by a scroll work of bronze, of much of which, although lost, the impression still remains upon the plate. The greater diameter of the mirror is eight inches, that of the handle of the duplicate specimen, which is supposed to be of the same size as the missing handle, is four inches.

A second handle of a more finished character was also found. It consists of an oval ring, the longest diameter being at right angles to the vertical axis; a shaft which is grooved at each end and doubly so at the middle; and at the extremity opposite to the handle a grooved flange, into which the mirror was secured by rivets. No trace of the plate which belonged to this handle has been found, and the difference of form together with the different style of execution seen in the details of some of what little engraving is present on the flange of the handle, demonstrates that this mirror must in its complete state have varied considerably from that previously described.

The length of this handle is six inches and the detail of the engraving is made up with small uniform notches, while that of the preceding one consists of short lines placed by threes, alternately arranged at right angles with each other. I am informed by Mr. Evans that these mirrors are rare, and that only a single specimen with engraved back has previously been found. This was in the county of Bedford, and is now preserved in the museum of the county town. I know not whether that example is as large as the Plymouth specimen, but those generally found, do not exceed three or four inches in diameter.

Chapter III

Bracelets – The next objects of interest which have been obtained from these explorations, are a series of bronze bracelets; three of those found being of one form, and one of another. We will describe the most numerous first: – these were formed of solid bronze, flattened upon the internal and rounded upon the external surface; they opened by a hinge in the middle, which was made by the insertion of a tongue into a deep notch or groove, and secondly a rivet on which the two halves swung.

It is not exactly clear what kind of clasp secured them when shut, two of them had one kind whereas the third evidently differed.

From the position of the rivets, it appears that the two shut by the projection of a central piece of wire that was caught with a spring clasp, much as we find it in bracelets of the present day: the third has a tongue very similar to that of the hinge, but smaller, and this probably was also caught by a spring. The external surface of these bracelets was ornamented by embossed markings of a running scroll that looked like a series of the letter S folded into each other successively; the rounded portion formed by the bottom of one S enclosing the top of the succeeding, is raised and perforated by two deep holes placed side by side; these holes are in some few places still filled by a dull red bead as at one time, I have no doubt, were all the rest. The material of which the beads were formed, I am not quite certain of. It may have been jasper, as suggested to me by a friend, although from its appearance under a lens I am inclined to think that they may have been made out of the slag or waste material left in the pots after the melting of the bronze, which is often of a deep red colour. I am informed by Mr. Evans, that specimens in which are beads of this description are rare if not unique.

The second form of bracelet, of which we have but two specimens, is much more slender and almost without ornament. Five embossed bands of which the centre one is the largest, ornament the middle, which is the shortest part of the bracelet; there appears to be no fastening, and the bracelet is evidently formed on the principle of a spring that yields to the pressure of the hand as it is forced on the wrist.

Fibulæ: – Three specimens of fibulæ were found; two in an injured, and one in a tolerably perfect state. These brooches which are of bronze are of cruciform shape, the upper end at which the pin is attached having a bar fixed at right angles with the upright part. The lower end is widened into a plate that gradually thins from the front to the extremity, at which the pin clasps, which it does by means of the plate being curved so as to form a secure lodgment for it. The pin in one brooch appears to have been attached to its position by being several times twisted round the bar. It is thus made secure, and, as well, receives an elastic character which renders it doubly firm when fixed. In both the others the cross piece at the top is flattened and turned up at the extremities and a bar is fixed between the two extremities; passing through a hole is a pin that is rivetted at each end; round the bar, on each side of the pin, wire is closely twisted, which gives an ornamental finish to the brooch as well as serving to keep the pin in its place. The flattened portion, which is bent to receive the pin is perforated in one specimen with three holes, each encircled by a single grooved line. This specimen has lost a portion of the cross-bar, but this appears to have borne some relation to its early history, in as much as that a small plate of bronze still remains secured to the shaft of the fibula by two rivets, and a hole in the plate shews where a rivet formerly secured the cross-bar. This, I think, clearly demonstrates a fracture and repair during the period of its use; the length of these fibulæ is about two inches and a half.

Dagger. – A small dagger or knife in a bronze sheath was also dug out by one of the workmen; the blade of the dagger is still within the sheath, but although the guard is of bronze, yet I am inclined to believe that the blade may have been of iron, from the circumstance of there being a ferruginous rust, at the entrance, as well as visible through a crack in the sheath. The point that remains of the spill that was inserted into the handle, shews that it also was of iron. The form of the knife may probably be suggested from the outline of the sheath. It is four inches long, and about three-quarters of an inch broad, nearest the hilt, from whence the sides run parallel to nearly two-thirds the length, when they gradually narrow to the point; one side doing so more rapidly than the other, thus suggesting that one side of the blade possessed a cutting, and the other a safe, edge. The sheath is formed of two pieces of bronze plate, one being broader has its edges folded so as to enclose the smaller. A small loop of flattened wire is secured by three rivets to the margin of the handle, which thus enabled the implement to be secured to a belt. The whole of this (as of all the workmanship in bronze) is made by means of rivets, fold and castings; no evidences of solder being apparent in any part of this or other article.

A *Bronze Cup*, or rather portions of one, were found by the workmen: the fragments consisted of the bottom and a part of the rim only; the bottom is about an inch and a quarter across, and the arch of the rim shews the top of the cup to have been about three inches in diameter: the edge of the rim is slightly turned out, a circumstance that is suggestive of a flowing or waved outline to the sides, which were very thin; a fact that accounts for the destruction of the cup.

Some fragments of a *glass vase, or bowl*, were thrown out of one grave: they are of a beautiful amber colour, the surface being only slightly encrusted with that prismatic colouring which so frequently corrodes glass that has been long buried in the earth. The fragments that were recovered, are the bottom of a basin, a portion of the side, and a part of the rim. The bottom is about two inches and a half across, from which the base passes out in a nearly horizontal line, until it has reached the approximate diameter of five inches; it then gradually ascends to the probable height of four or five inches, and as gradually increases in size until it has reached the diameter of six inches, then it is finished by a hollow rim, formed by the folding of the edge outward, and back upon itself.

The lower portion of the vase is ornamented with a series of raised lines radiating from the base, but which instead of passing directly to the circumference, run diagonally outwards, as if they were the result of lines formed during the time the plastic material revolved on its axis. Although in many parts the workmanship shews crudeness in execution, yet the vessel as a whole must have exhibited an elegance of appearance, that is suggestive of the idea that it must have been the property of an individual of some pretention among his fellows, particularly when we compare it with the quality of the pottery found in the same locality.

Pottery.– With but a single exception all the ware that has been procured from this cemetery was in a fragmentary state, nor is this wholly to be attributed to the carelessness of the excavators, although, no doubt in some measure it is due to the fact of the excavations having been carried on by men working for a contractor under government. They thus were compelled to pursue their regular labour assiduously, and were not permitted the time necessary to remove such fragile relics with safety from their position in the graves.

The ware of one of the bowls, of black pottery, is coarse. It stands upon a circular ring which is about three inches in diameter. From the ring the bottom of the vase extends on each side until the diameter is about five inches; the sides then rise inwardly, then gradually curve outwardly, and terminate in a small rim at about four inches from the base. There is a small round depression upon the inside, near the upper edge, corresponding with a similar depression upon the outside, from which latter a groove passes as far as the broken edge. This marking is suggestive of a small horizontal handle having been situated in this portion; but if so, there was no corresponding handle at the opposite extremity of the basin, since the two fragments together complete more than half the diameter of the vase.

A second black vase was found by Capt. Moggridge. This is of much finer ware than the previous one, and much more slender in texture, it is also of more elegant shape though formed on the same general design. The ring at the bottom is about three inches in diameter, the centre of which is deeply excavated, corresponding with a convex elevation on the inside. From the ring at the bottom the sides extend either way until the diameter is about seven inches, they then rise slightly inwardly, and then gradually curve outwardly to the edge where they terminate without any embossed edge at a height of about three inches from the bottom.

Of a third black bowl or vase, one small fragment alone had been recovered, but this is enough to shew that the design was the same as the previous ones. The substance was a little stouter than the last, but less so than the first, and it differed from both in having a double embossed rim all round the middle of the sides. This like the two previous examples, is of very dark, almost black, ware, not only on the surface, but throughout the substance, a circumstance that I think must be due to the character of the clay, of which the vessels were made, and not attributable to the muffling of the furnaces during the process of baking.

Another example, a very small vase, of a less darkened surface than the two previously described specimens, Capt. Moggridge was fortunate enough to save, in a perfect state from the uplifted axe of the excavator. The bottom is flat, and about an inch and a half in diameter, from which it gradually rises outwardly until just above the middle, from which point it rounds more suddenly inwards to form a constructed neck just beneath the edge of the mouth, which turns outward. The diameter of the mouth is about three and a half inches; and the vase is about four inches in height.

The next vase is one to which I attach value, from the circumstance of having made out and figured its entire form from the character of the neck only; afterwards finding a part of the sides and the bottom I was enabled to establish the correctness of my figure. The form of this vase is much like the last described, from which it differs in having a more sudden curving below the neck. It also stands higher. The utensil is also larger, the diameter of the bottom being about four inches; of the body of the vessel at its greatest width, about seven inches; of the mouth, about three inches; the height about eight inches and a half. It is of red clay.

The next vase to which I draw attention, differs in form from the others, and has evidently attained a higher degree of external finish; unfortunately but few fragments have been recovered, but these are sufficient to establish its full form. It is composed of hard-baked clay, of a coarse character; the general colour is red, but in some places the external surface is blackened, probably owing to the muffling of the kiln during the process of baking. Its height is about four inches and a half; and it stands upon a circular bottom of about three inches in diameter, which raises the vessel from the ground about an inch. The bottom of the vase within is flat, the sides gracefully rounding outwards, then inwards, and again outwards to the mouth, the diameter of which is about six inches, – being in fact the widest part of the vessel, and overhanging the body of the vase about three-quarters of an inch. The external surface is ornamented at the edge of the rim by an embossed ring; about an inch below by a second, but less raised ring; beneath which point, the swelling part of the vessel is covered by a number of short engraved notches, placed in lines vertical to the base.

Two vessels, apparently intended for holding water, were found: the first was a plain earthenware bottle, made of very soft, friable yellow ware. The body of the vessel was nearly circular, having a flat ringed base and a narrow neck. This when found was standing perfect as to form, but was so much fractured, that it was impossible to remove it, except in fragments. The height of the vessel, which had portions of the neck broken off, was about eight inches, and its diameter about six inches. Another vessel was found of the same general form as the preceding, but somewhat larger. It is made of a light yellow friable ware; it probably stood about 12 inches in height, and its diameter at its greatest circumference was probably about eight inches. The rim round the mouth was reversed, having a hollow between it and the neck of the bottle: the outer surface of the rim was surrounded by a concave ring; and beneath the rim the remains of a handle exist, the opposite extremity of which was no doubt attached to the upper portion of the body of the vessel.

The only other piece of pottery of sufficient importance to describe, appeared to have been part of a drinking cup in yellow clay. Its sides were perpendicular to its flat base, and ornamented by a double embossed line traversing the circumference on a level with the lower extremity of the handle. Assuming this to be the case, the cup probably stood about five inches in height, and its circumference, taken from a continuation of the preserved segment, could not be less than four inches and a half, so that it was nearly as broad as high, and probably held about a pint of water.

The iron implements were mostly in too decomposed a condition for us to arrive at any positive conclusion, as to their uses. Some appear to have been the remains of blades of knives; some were probably the tangs of knives that were driven into the handles, and the remains of the wood, deeply stained with ferruginous rust still clinging to them, support this hypothesis. Some, of which a considerable number were taken from one spot, might have been the armed points of arrows, or the umbone and studs of a buckler. They consisted generally of an irregularly shaped nodule of iron from which a point of sharp tongue projected; there are many other pieces of irregular form.

About a hundred feet distant from these graves, whilst cutting in a direction towards the sea, the labourers came upon a solitary grave of similar character to the rest, out of which they procured three or four fragments of iron, four of which upon being put together, were found to be the remains of a pair of scissors, resembling in shape, and being about one-half the size of, modern sheep-shears.

The others were parts of a knife. The point was curved forward, one edge of the blade was very sharp, the other, while forming the back of the knife, was thick and safe. With the last implements, parts of three bronze rings were found. The longest was faced with three circular discs, the middle one being much greater in diameter than the other two, the lateral ones being of smaller dimensions and of one size; the centre one is ornamented by an embossed ring round the margin, by two oval longitudinal nodules in the middle and by three circular ones on each side, of which the central nodule is the largest. The small circles on each side are deep, and when found, where partially filled with a white material. They appear as if they were formed for the purpose, and probably once held, each a bead. In each of these the white substance which remained, may have been the remains of cement used to secure them in their places. The ring, which is now somewhat flattened, was evidently intended as an ornament to be worn on the finger.

The second ring is smaller than the previous one; its face is merely a flattened exterior of itself, and is ornamented by two rows of short vertical lines enclosed within engraved margins. The ring of which only a portion has been recovered, appears to have been too small to have been worn on the finger, even of a female, and the circumstance of the face being at right angles with the sides, suggests that it may have been used for other purposes than a finger ring.

A small portion of a third ring was also found, but not sufficient to enable any certain ideas to be formed of its character. The fragment consists of a small wire, flattened at one extremity, the sides of the whole being closely ribbed.

"Upon the completion of the work necessary for the fortifications, I applied for permission to make further search. In this way I have been enabled to proceed more cautiously, and to obtain a clearer idea of the position of the relics found in relation to each other. Undoubtedly the remains appear to be very heterogeneously mingled together, but still I think the following may be relied upon, as being an approximation to their relation to each other. The blocks of weather-worn limestone, which appeared in the first instance to be so irregularly placed, I ascertained by tracing the circuit of the walls of the graves when it was practicable to do so, to have been placed originally as a wall, within which the corpse was placed in a sitting posture. It is probable that some of the stones were also employed for the purpose of covering in the body.

"The reason why ornaments and objects of value were buried with the dead has never been clearly established. The few things that are found interred, militate altogether against the idea which Caesar has affirmed to be the case with the inhabitants of ancient Britain – that all their wealth was buried with them; even if we suppose that the inhabitants of a Roman colony had so far adopted the customs of the people among whom they had settled, as to have copied their mode of interment. Judging from these explorations, the opinion at which I have arrived is, that it was customary to bury with the body, either from feelings of affection or otherwise, all the objects which the individual had possession of, at the time of death, or during the sickness that preceded it.

"It is in this way that I can account for, not only the existence of ornaments and vessels of value, but trace a reason for the presence of pebbles from the shore as well as the tooth of the pig, all of which I assume to have been objects of amusement to the child from whose grave I took them. In the solitary grave the discovery of finger rings, a knife, and scissors, indicate that it was the burial place of a female, but why it was separated so distinctly from the rest, there is at present no means of ascertaining; but that it was intentional, I think may be accepted from the circumstance that a cutting in the rock was found to exist between it and the other graves, which from its appearance and character, the engineer officer assures me must have been originally intended as a drain.

"I offer these suggestions merely as ideas that occurred to my mind as I prosecuted the research, which at present must be considered in an unfinished state, inasmuch as there appears to be a very considerable extent of ground that has yet to be explored."

CHAPTER IV

THE NORMANS, ANGLO-SAXONS, AND DANES — DOMESDAY BOOK — MEMBERS OF PARLIAMENT FIRST RETURNED — VESSELS FOR THE ROYAL FLEET — DISPUTES WITH THE PRIOR OF PLYMPTON — PLYMOUTH RAVAGED BY PIRATES — EDWARD THE BLACK PRINCE AT PLYMOUTH — SIEGE OF CALAIS — IMPRESSMENT OF SHIPS — TRANSIT OF PILGRIMS — INCURSIONS BY THE BRETONS — THE FIRST CHARTER OF INCORPORATION ETC., ETC.

During the Anglo-Saxon period, Plymouth, at first frequented as a fishing station, gradually rose into a place of note as a settlement of that people. By the Saxons it was called *Tameorwerth*, which name it continued to hold until, after the Norman conquest, it was changed to *Sutton* or *South Town*. It was named Tameorworth "according to St. Indractus, in his life, as being situated at the conflux of the river Tamar on its approach to the sea." By the Saxons, probably a place of worship, and doubtless many residences were erected. That Tameorworth became a place of considerable resort for fishing, etc. among the Saxon settlers, and that it must have been tolerably fully inhabited, there are abundance of circumstances to show, and various relics of the period have, from time to time, been found in the course of excavations, both in and around the present town.

Late in the eighth century, the Danes landed in England, and, not many years afterwards, made their way into Devonshire and Cornwall, which district they are said to have inhabited for some years from 786. In 878, Hubba the brother of Halfden, landed at Appledore, but was defeated with the loss of his standard. In 897, the Danes were again in Devonshire, which from this time downwards, was frequently the scene of their incursions. Although no remains which can be assigned to the Danish invaders, have been recorded as found at Plymouth, it is more than probable that the place was for a time peopled by them, and some earthworks which existed not many miles distant, have been said to be of Danish origin.

Chapter IV

Devonshire was one of the last districts to submit to Norman rule, and some two years after the King himself had marched against Exeter and subdued it, the Saxons again rose and attempted to repossess themselves of that city, but were defeated with great slaughter. In this struggle the Saxons resident about Plymouth no doubt took an active part with their brethren, and were long ere they submitted entirely to the yoke of the Conqueror.

In the Domesday-Book, compiled in the year 1086, Plymouth (as *Sutone*) is described as being held by the King in demesne.

The town was afterwards divided into the town of Sutton Prior, the hamlet of Sutton Valletort, and the tithing of Sutton Ralph – a part of it having been granted by the Crown to the Norman family of De Valletort, while the greatest part belonged to the Priory of Plympton. From this time the place rapidly increased, and in the thirteenth century began to send members to Parliament.

In 1287, a fleet of ships, 325 in number, and commanded by the brother of the King, is stated to have anchored at Plymouth.

In 1292, the first members were returned to Parliament.

In 1298, the members of Parliament for the town were William de Stoke and Nicholas le Rydeley. In the same year, Plymouth furnished one ship to the King's fleet. Exmouth, Teignmouth, Looe and Fowey each also provided one, and Dartmouth two.

In 1305, William Bredon and John Austin were returned as members of Parliament.

1307. – "About the commencement of the reign of Edward II, great disputes arose between the Prior of Plympton and the King, respecting certain rights and immunities claimed by the former, but always contested by the Crown. At length by a writ issued from the Exchequer in 1313, a jury was summoned to examine the various claims, and determine the differences between the Prior and the king. By their decision the Prior was confirmed in the exercise of various privileges and particularly that of granting leases of houses as lord of the fee, the assize of bread and beer, a ducking stool and pillory, and the right of fishery of the waters from the entrance of Catwater to the head of the river Plym. In the reign of Edward the Third, 1327, the manor came in to the possession of the Earl of Cornwall. The claims advanced by the Earl occasioned new disputes, which were settled by the decision of a special jury."

1310. – Sir John de Caunton having been appointed captain and governor of the fleet, letters were sent to the authorities of Plymouth and other ports, stating that the King supposed they were aware that Robert Bruce his traitor and enemy had broken the truce and was in arms, and that he intended to proceed in person to Berwick-on-Tweed against his enemies, and that he therefore required the use of their navy. Each port was therefore desired to provide one or more ships of war well manned. In this year Robert de Sopere and William Smith were the members of Parliament for this town.

1313. – Thirty of the largest and best ships were ordered to be provided by the ports between Plymouth, Shoreham and other places, and were placed under command of Sir William de Montacute. It is believed in this year that John Austyn and William Byrd were the members of Parliament.

1314. – "A monastery of White Fryars or Carmelites was licensed at Plymouth, by H. Stapledon at the instance of the King."

1324. – "In consequence of the masters and crews of some ships of the royal fleet which the ports of Lyme, Weymouth, and Poole had been ordered to send to Plymouth by the middle of June, having quitted those places in contempt of the King's commands, other large ships were directed to be equipped and dispatched to Plymouth to supply the deficiency. A priest was sent to Plymouth to survey the ships, and to see that they were properly manned and furnished with stores. On the 16th July, the King appointed Sir John de Cromwell, admiral of the sea coast and captain of his mariners and sailors in his service proceeding to Gascony."

"Accurate information of the size, officers, and crews of ships is obtained from the instructions that were issued to Sir John Deverye, a priest, who was sent to survey the fleet at Plymouth and Southampton and in the other western ports, destined for Guienne in 1324. He was to see that the vessels were well found in rigging, anchors, ropes, cables, and other necessary articles, and that they were manned with good crews in the following proportions: –

A ship of	240 Tons	...	...	...	60 Mariners.
"	200 "	...	...	...	50 "
"	160 to 180	...	...	...	40 "
"	140 "	...	...	...	35 "
"	120 "	...	...	...	28 "
"	100 "	...	...	...	26 "
"	80 "	...	...	...	24 "
"	60 "	...	...	...	21 "

Every ship of 180 tons and upwards was to have one master and two constables, and those of 160 tons and less, one master and one constable, who were to be included in the number of the crew. Deverye was ordered to consult with the good people of the ports as to the bridges, clayes and "rafteux." When a sea port from which a ship was required for the king's service was too poor to furnish it, the neighbouring towns were ordered to contribute for the purpose: thus in 1310, when the inhabitants of Dartmouth declared that they were unable to maintain a ship and its crew, orders were sent to the people of Totnes, Brixham, Portlemouth, and Kingsbridge, to assist those of Dartmouth on the occasion. Similar commands were sent to Plympton, Modbury, Newton-Ferrers and Yalmouth (qu. Yealme-mouth) to assist the inhabitants of *Sutton*."

1337. – On the 26th February in this year, the western fleet was directed to assemble at Plymouth, victualled for 13 weeks, and the sheriffs of the southern and western counties were commanded to see that the ships were properly equipped and fitted with clays and bridges for receiving horses.*

1339. – On the 20th May, another squadron of "pirates" consisting of 18 galleys and pinnaces, burnt 7 ships belonging to Bristol, and some other vessels in the port of Plymouth. The enemy was however, gallantly resisted by the inhabitants, above 89 of whom were killed, and the French are said to have lost 500 men. Two days afterwards they renewed the attack, burnt all the ships in the harbour and many houses, but a large force having arrived, the enemy suddenly left Plymouth on the 25th and went to Southampton, where they burnt two ships.

1340. – Members of Parliament, John Bernard and John Byrd. "No year was more memorable in the naval History of England than 1340. Early in January, Edward the Third formally assumed the title and arms of King of France, and resolved to maintain his right by force of arms. Parliament was adjourned in consequence of the absence of the Duke of Cornwall, Guardian of England. Among others, the sailors of the western ports engaged to furnish 70 ships of 100 tons and upwards each, and as far as they could at their own expense, the council finding the remainder of the money. Richard, Earl of Arundell's commission as admiral of the western fleet was issued on the 20th February."

1347. – When Edward the Third laid siege to Calais, he received the assistance of 700 ships from the sea ports of his dominions. The following extract from the list will show the relative importance of the ports specified at that time: –

London	...	...	25 Ships...	662 Mariners
Bristol	...	...	24 " ...	608 "

*Rot. Scot 484.

Portsmouth	...	...	5 "	...	96 Mariners	
Plymouth	...	...	26 "	...	603	"
Fowey	...	...	47 "	...	770	"
Yarmouth	...	...	43 "	...	1905	"
Dartmouth	...	...	31 "	...	757	"
Hull	...	...	16 "	...	466	"
Ilfracombe	...	...	6 "	...	79	"
Milford	...	...	2 "	...	24	"
Cardiff	...	...	1 "	...	51	"
Swansea	...	...	1 "	...	29	"
Carmarthen	...	...	1 "	...	16	"
Mersey (Liverpool)		...	1 "	...	6	"

1348.– In January 1348, forty ships were ordered to be provided by the western ports and to assemble at Plymouth, to carry to Bordeaux, the Princess Joan, the King's daughter, who was intended to be married to the eldest son of the King of Castile. In this same year, Edward the Black Prince landed at Plymouth from France, and dined with the Prior of Plympton. On the 14th March, Sir Reginald Cobham was appointed admiral of the western fleet, and orders were issued for impressing mariners to man the King's ships.

1354. – On the 10th July, the Prince of Wales was constituted Lieutenant of Gascony, but he was detained at Plymouth by contrary winds until 8th September, when he sailed with about 300 ships full of troops and stores, and arrived in the Gironde after a short passage.

1357. – "Edward the Black Prince having gained the ever memorable victory of Poictiers, in which 12,000 English defeated an army of more than 60,000 of the choicest troops of France, taking John, King of France, his youngest son, and a great number of noblemen prisoners, on his return, landed at Plymouth, and from thence went to Exeter, was received with the greatest testimonies of joy; the prince and his royal prisoners were nobly entertained at the expense of the mayor, and also by the mayor and citizens of Exeter, during their stay in that city, which was three days."*

1360. – Three ships and a "Crayer" of Plymouth, conveyed Constance Lady Knollys, 20 men at arms and 40 mounted archers and her suite to Brittany. The "Crayer" was a small merchant vessel, which seldom exceeded 60 tons in burden.

1362. – In June, ships were ordered to be found for the passage of the Prince of Wales who was created Duke of Aquitaine, to assemble at

*Jenkins

Plymouth by the 15th of August. The prince's voyage was however postponed until the following year, and the ships were afterwards ordered to be at that port by Easter-day in 1363.

1364. – On the 7th July, Sir Ralph Spigurnell was made admiral of the south, north, and western, fleets, and also appointed keeper of Dover Castle and warden of the Cinque ports. The right of passage over the river Tamar at Saltash in Cornwall, and an annuity of £20 was granted by the Prince of Wales, and confirmed by the King in August in this year, to the prince's porter, William Lenche, in consideration of his having lost an eye at the battle of Poictiers.[†]

1370. – Early in May, shipping and mariners were sent to Dartmouth, and every vessel in the Welch ports of from 12 to 40 tons ordered to proceed to Southampton, but ships above 40 tons were to go to Plymouth for the passage of the Duke of Lancaster and his troops to Gascony. Several vessels were also hired to convey an embassy to the King of Navarre in Normandy, and to bring some of his knights to England.

1371. – "Edward the Black Prince, being in a consumptive state, returned from France and landed at Plymouth. In his journey to London, he went to Exeter with the princess his wife and was joyfully received, but being in a very weak condition, he staid several days to recover his strength. During his stay, the prince and his suite were elegantly entertained at the expense of the mayor, at whose house he lodged till his departure from Exeter."*

In March every vessel of 100 tons and upwards, all vessels and boats called "Pikards", of 10 or more tons, in the Severn and Wales, Gloucester, Devon, and Somerset, except Bristol, were arrested and sent to Plymouth and placed under Admiral Sir Guy Byran.

1374. – Eight of the King's ships and other ships and barges being about to cruize on the western coast, sailors were ordered to be impressed to man them on the 28th January and 3rd February. An effort appears to have been made to increase the navy, for many of the northern ports furnished "a new barge" each, which vessels were directed to be manned and sent to Sandwich by the 16th March, and other barges were to proceed to Plymouth by that day, to serve in an expedition at sea. On the 12th May, 19 masters of ships from different ports were summoned to attend the King's council at Westminster for the purpose of giving information on maritime affairs. Every vessel of 40 tons and upwards in the northern, and 20 more tons in the western or watch ports, were directed on the 17th July, to rendezvous at Dartmouth and Plymouth by the 8th September, to convey the Earl of

†Faedera III, 741. *Jenkins.

Cambridge and an army to Brittany. In this year, Edward the Black Prince died, deeply lamented, at Richmond.

1377. – The French landed on several parts of the English coast and pillaged and burnt many towns, carrying off much booty and many prisoners. Amongst towns which suffered, were Plymouth and Dartmouth.

1378. – About Midsummer, the Duke of Lancaster left Southampton with 4,000 men at arms and 8,000 archers for Normandy, and finding the Earl of Salisbury and Sir John Arundell at Plymouth waiting for a wind to go to Brest for its relief, returned to the Isle of Wight, news having arrived that the French fleet had sailed. Arundell was sent with some troops to defend Southampton.

1381. – Ships were fitted out and an army raised to assist the King of Portugal against Spain, and the command was given to the Earl of Cambridge. The fleet left Plymouth and after a boisterous voyage, sailing by the wind and stars, arrived at Lisbon.

1385. – On the 8th January, ships were impressed and sent to Plymouth for an expedition to Portugal, and all Portuguese vessels, seamen, and property in the western admiralty were soon after ordered to be arrested.

In 1390, Plymouth was constituted a place of legal transit of pilgrims for crossing the channel to continental shrines, and was so favourite a place of resort with them, that considerable numbers not unfrequently took up their abode in the town and remained for some time.

In 1400, the French fleet having landed through contrary winds, destroyed much of the town and committed great ravages on the property of the inhabitants. A gale however springing up, some of their largest vessels were destroyed, and the invaders escaped with difficulty.

1402. – "This yere the Lord of Castell in Briteyn, landed within a myle of Plymmouth with a great companie, and lodged in the towne all that day and night, and the next day spoyled and robbed the sayde towne, and caryed away all that was therein, and returned again into their shippes."* – "Plimouth spoyled by the Bretons. The Bretons Amoritees, the Lord of Castell being their leader, invaded the towne of Plymouth, spoyled and brent it, and went their way free, but immediately the western navie under the conduct of William Wilford, Esq., in the coast of Briton, tooke fortie ships laden with yron, oyle, sope, and wine of Rochell, to the number of a 1,000 tunne, and in returning back again he brent 30 ships, and at Penarch the said William arrived with his men, and burned townes and lordships, the space of six leagues, and set the town of Saint Matthew on fire, and the mills about the said towne."† From this attack by the Bretons, the name of

*Grafton's Chronicle. †Stowe.

Breton or Briton-side is said to have been derived. Soon after this time the inhabitants by virtue of a patent from Henry IV, erected "a wall of stone and chalk with towers, fortresses, and other defences."

1412. – The inhabitants petitioned for a charter of incorporation with all necessary powers, but this was for a long time opposed by the Prior and Convent of Plympton, in whose hands the government of the town had hitherto been held. In 1416, Bishop Stafford granted an indulgence towards the erection of towers and other repairs.

1439. – In this year, a petition was again presented, and this time (the Priory of Plympton having previously agreed to relinquish the manorial rights, and, in return, to receive a yearly rent-charge,) was successful. The petition which is extremely curious and interesting, as being the first incorporation of the borough, is as follows. It is taken from the Rolls of Parliament of 18th, Henry VI: –

"Also a certain other petition was exhibited to the same Lord the King in the Parliament aforesaid, by the aforesaid Commons, for the Men of the Town of Plymouth, and other persons in the same petition, specified in these words: –

"Prayeth your Royal Highness, the Commons of your whole Realm of England, in your present Parliament assembled, that whereas the town of Sutton Pryor, and the tithing of Sutton Ralf, and parcel of the hamlet of Sutton Vautort, which town, tithing, and parcel are commonly called Plymouth, and a certain parcel of the tithing of Compton within the county of Devon, are situate so near the shore and sea coasts, and such a large and common arrival of ships and vessels, as well of enemies as others, is from time to time had in the port of the said town, tithing, parcels of the hamlet and of the tithing of Compton adjoining; that the town, tithing, and parcels aforesaid, have heretofore in the times of your famous progenitors been very often burnt and destroyed in many parts thereof, by reason of a defect of the inclosure of walling of the same. And also the inhabitants thereof have been despoiled of their goods and chattels by night and by day, and many of the same inhabitants have been carried away to foreign parts by the said enemies, and have been cruelly imprisoned until they have made fines and ransoms; and other evils, losses, and great inconveniences have in time past very frequently happened to the same town, tithing and parcels of the hamlet and tithing aforesaid, and much greater it is feared, will there happen hereafter, unless for the relief, fortification, and bettering of the town, tithing and parcels aforesaid, a proper remedy be very speedily provided. – Whereupon, the premises being considered, may it please your aforesaid

Royal Highness, by the consent and assent of the lords, spiritual and temporal, and the Commons of your Realm of England, in this present Parliament being, and by authority of the same Parliament for the resisting of the malice of your enemies there daily arriving, and the safety of the town, tithing, and parcels aforesaid, and that the inhabitants thereof, when the town, tithing, and parcels aforesaid, shall be strengthened, inclosed, and fortified, may the better, more quietly, and securely reside and dwell there, to ordain and establish, that the town, tithing, and parcels aforesaid be hereafter a free Borough Incorporate, of one Mayor and one perpetual Commonalty, and be for ever called "The Borough of Plymouth;" and that the same Mayor and one perpetual body in deed and name, and have perpetual succession, and that at all times hereafter they be called the "Mayor and Commonalty of the Borough of Plymouth," and be persons able and capable in the law to purchase to themselves their heirs and successors in fee and perpetuity, or for term of life or years, or in any other estate whatsoever, any lands, tenements, rents, reversions, possessions, and hereditaments whatsoever, of any persons whomsoever, and that they may have a common seal, and by the name of "the Mayor and Commonalty of Plymouth" may be able to plead and be impleaded in any of the courts whatsoever of you, your heirs and successors and others whomsoever, and before any judges whomsoever, and on any actions whatsoever. And that the borough aforesaid do always consist by the metes and bounds underwritten, (that is to say) between the hill called Wynrigge by the bank of Sourpool towards the north unto the Great Dyche, otherwise called the Grate Diche, and therefrom again towards the north to Stoke Damarle flete, and from thence by the shore of the same flete unto Millbrook Bridge inclusively, and from thence towards the east by the middle ditch of Houndescome unto Houndescome Bridge inclusively, and therefrom unto Thornhill Park exclusively, and from thence unto Lypston Bridge inclusively, and therefrom by the sea shore in continuation unto the Lare to the caae of Hyngstone, Fishtorre, and Eastking, and from thence unto the said hill of Wynrigge, as the metes and bounds on all sides erected and fixed more fully and openly shew.

"And that the aforesaid Mayor and Commonalty and their successors may have and hold the same borough to them, their heirs and successors aforesaid of you, your heirs and successors at fee farm, rendering therefore yearly forty shillings at the exchequer of you and your heirs, at the terms of Easter and St. Michael equally. And that the aforesaid Mayor and Commonalty, their heirs and successors may have authority to strengthen the borough aforesaid, and to inclose and incompass the same with stone walls, and to make anew and build towers in the same walls for the fortification and defence of the same borough, and also the same walls and towers lawfully and without punishment to fortify and embattle. And that it may please your Royal Majesty to create and appoint William Ketrich, one of the more honest and discreet men now dwelling within the metes and bounds aforesaid, to be Mayor of the borough aforesaid, who may continue to be Mayor of the borough aforesaid until the Feast of Saint Michael next coming, well and faithfully to rule and govern the same borough. And further may it please your aforesaid Royal Highness of your special grace by authority of the Parliament aforesaid, graciously to grant to the aforesaid Mayor and Commonalty, that every year on the Feast of Saint Lambert, Martyr and Bishop, they may elect a certain person out of themselves, who, according to their sound discretions, shall be the more fit and discreet, to be the Mayor of the same borough for one whole year, for the good and wholesome government of the same borough. And that on the Feast of Saint Michael then next following, they may appoint him to be Mayor of the same borough. And if the aforesaid William, by you created and appointed to be Mayor of the borough aforesaid, shall die before the Feast of Saint Michael now next coming, or if either his successors the future Mayors of the same borough, during his office of mayoralty shall die or unjustly or improperly rule and govern the same borough, for which the said Commonalty, for the utility of the same borough or of the republic, shall deem him worthy to be amoved from the same office, then the same Commonalty may have power to amove the said Mayor so offending from the office of Mayor, and another fit person out of themselves in the place of the Mayor so dying or offending, to elect to the same office, and appoint to be Mayor, and so as often as any Mayor of the borough aforesaid shall die, or shall unjustly or improperly rule or govern the same borough as aforesaid, And that such Mayor so anew elected and appointed, be Mayor of the same borough until the Feast of Saint Michael then next following, unless he shall act in like manner in the said office, for which he shall be worthy to be amoved from the same office. And that every one by the said Commonalty, hereafter to be elected to the said office of Mayor of the borough aforesaid and by the said Commonalty, on the Feast of Saint Michael, to be appointed Mayor of the said borough before he take upon himself the office of the said mayoralty, shall in the Guidhall of the borough aforesaid, take his Corporal Oath before the Commonalty thereof, and also before the Prior of Plympton for the time being, or in his absence, before the steward of his lands or household, if the same Prior or steward aforesaid will to be there present on the same Feast of Saint

Michael, before the hour of Eleven of the same Feast Day, but otherwise before the said Commonalty only, the presence of the said Prior or his steward for that turn not being further expected, well, faithfully, and indifferently to rule and govern the same borough. And also all and singular the articles, rents, and appointments in the present petition contained and specified, touching the Prior and Convent of Plympton, duly to observe, pay, and fulfil, whilst he shall so remain in the office of such mayoralty. And that every one in form aforesaid, to be appointed Mayor of the borough aforesaid, after the death or amotion of any Mayor thereof, shall before he take upon himself such office of mayoralty, take the like Corporal Oath as abovesaid, in the presence, place, form, and order, above limited, on a day which the Commonalty of the said borough shall then limit for that purpose, due warning being given to the Prior of Plympton, for the time being, at his Priory or to the Convent of the same Priory, in the absence of the said Prior, by the space of three days before the day so limited. And that the same Mayor and Commonalty, their heirs and successors, for the public good of the borough aforesaid, may have power from time to time, to make and create burgesses of the same borough as often as they shall please, by authority of the parliament aforesaid.

"And that the same Mayor and Commonalty may have and hold to them, their heirs and successors, by authority of this Parliament, all manner of lands, tenements, rents, services, the mills called the Surpool Mills, possessions, fairs, feasts, markets, courts, franchises, liberties, views of frankpledge, privileges, and other the temporal and secular profits and emoluments, which were, and now are belonging to the aforesaid Prior and Convent, as in right of their aforesaid, and within the limits, metes, and bounds aforesaid, and within the said Borough of Plymouth. Saving always and except and reserved to the aforesaid Prior and Convent and their successors, three messuages and three gardens to the same messuages adjoining, with their appurtenances, situate in the Borough of Plymouth aforesaid, one of which messuages is situate between a tenement of John Jaybien on the east side, and a tenement of John Snellying on the west, and land of the heirs of Roger Goold, and land of the aforesaid John Jaybien on the south, and the highway called Bilbury-street on the north; and another tenement lies between a messuage of Thomas Piers on the east, and a tenement of William Myleton on the west, and a garden of William Venour on the north, and the highway called Note-street on the south; and the third messuage is situate between a tenement of Vincent Hagge on the east, and the toft, late of John Piers on the west, and a tenement of Walter Whiteleigh on the north, and the highway called Stillman-street on the south. – Saving also and except and reserved to the same Prior and Convent, and their successors for ever as well, the advowson of the Church of Plymouth formerly called Sutton, which church they have and hold to their own use, as well the advowson of the vicarage of the same church, and the tythes, oblations, obventions, emoluments, things, rights, and profits whatsoever, to the same Church of Plymouth, in any manner whatsoever, belonging or appertaining. And that the aforesaid three messuages may be for ever, without the franchise, liberty, and jurisdiction of the said Mayor and Commonalty, and of the said Borough of Plymouth, and not parcels thereof.

"And that the said Prior and Convent and their successors, and their tenants of the messuages aforesaid, be in nowise hereafter chargeable, charged, nor taxed to any burden, payment, exaction, or imposition whatsoever, with the burgesses and inhabitants in the said Borough of Plymouth, but from the payment, exaction, or imposition of any burden by the said burgesses and inhabitants to be paid or borne, that they may be quit and discharged for ever. Saving also to the said Prior and Convent and their successors, the island called Saint Nicholas Island, and all their lands, tenements, and possessions, being within the parish of Maker, with all the appurtenances and commodities to the same belonging, and the profits and advantages whatsoever upon any of them hereafter happening or arising, of which island, lands, tenements, possessions, profits, and commodities, the aforesaid Mayor and Commonalty and their successors, or either of them, may in nowise intrude themselves. Provided always that if any felon or traitor shall fly into any place within the said three messuages and gardens, or shall remain there, that then it shall be lawful to the aforesaid Mayor and his servant and ministers of the said Borough of Plymouth, for the time being, to enter into the same messuages and gardens, and him, so to any place within the same messuages and gardens for the cause aforesaid flying, or there for the same cause remaining, to take, arrest, and to your Gaol, in the county aforesaid, to lead and carry. Provided also and ordained that the said Prior and Convent and their successors, and the ministers, servants, officers, and families of the said Prior and Convent, and of the same Prior and his successors, may freely come to the said Borough of Plymouth, and to every place within the metes, liberties, and jurisdiction thereof, with their waggons, carts, horse-loads, and carriages whatsoever, and with all the goods, chattels, victuals, and merchandizes of the aforesaid Prior and his successors, and of the servants, officers, ministers, and families of them and their successors, for the time being, and there sell their goods and chattels whatsoever, and buy other goods, chattels, and merchandizes there without any toll, custom, picage, panage, portage, murage, stallage, and other charges, exactions, impositions, and demands whatsoever, to the same Mayor and Commonalty or their successors, to be paid for any cause whatsoever, now being imposed or hereafter to be imposed, or by you or your heirs to be hereafter granted. – And that the same Prior and Convent and their successors and the ministers, families, officers, and servants of them and their successors, may be quit and discharged for ever within the said borough, and the precinct and jurisdiction thereof of the aforesaid tolls, exactions, and demands whatsoever to the same Mayor and Commonalty and their successors, and to the ministers of the same payable. – Provided also and ordained that neither the aforesaid Prior and Convent, nor their successors, nor their families, servants, officers, and men for the time being, shall in anywise for any cause whatsoever, be impleaded before the Mayor of the said Borough of Plymouth, nor his successors, nor before any ministers of the said mayor and Commonalty and their successors, nor shall be attached or imprisoned by their bodies, or distrained or attached by their goods and chattels, by any ministers, of the same Mayor and Commonalty or their successors, to answer any of your people, by virtue of any plaints, bills, matters, or causes affirmed or prosecuted, or to be affirmed before the same Mayor and his successors, or the ministers whomsoever, for the time being, of the said Mayor and Commonalty, nor by virtue of any presentments or indictments taken before the same Mayor and his successors, or before any officers, stewards, or bailiffs of the said Mayor and Commonalty and their successors, in any courts, views of frankpledge or hundreds held, or to be held within the borough aforesaid, but that from all jurisdiction, power, arrest, and coercion of the same Mayor and Commonalty and their successors, they be altogether exonerated, quit and exempt for ever. And that neither the said Prior and Convent, nor their successors, nor their families, servants, officers, and ministers, nor their men, or the tenants of the aforesaid three messuages, for the time being, may in anywise howsoever be distrained or compelled to do any suit at any courts, to be held before the said Mayor and his successors, or their ministers, within the borough aforesaid, nor at any views of frankpledge or hundreds, within the same borough. And if before the same Mayor and his successors, or any of the ministers of the same Mayor and Commonalty and their successors, for the time being, anything to the contrary of this ordination shall be done, proceeded or attempted against the aforesaid Prior and Convent or his successors, or their families, servants, officers, ministers, or men, or against the tenants of the aforesaid three messuages, for the time being, that then the process thereof shall in law be nought, and held as a process made *coram non judice.* And that the said Prior and Convent and their successors and their families, servants, officers, ministers, and their men, for the time being, may implead the said Mayor and Commonalty and their successors and the burgesses whomsoever of the borough aforesaid, for the time being, and other persons whomsoever, before you and your heirs, and in any of the courts whatever of you and your heirs, for any matter or cause whatsoever arising within the said borough, any franchise, liberty, and jurisdiction, by you or your heirs hereafter to be granted to the same Mayor and Commonalty or their successors notwithstanding. And further by the authority aforesaid, that it be ordained and established that the said Mayor and Commonalty and their successors for ever, shall render and pay to the said Prior and Convent and their successors in the Priory aforesaid, yearly from the Feast of Saint Michael the Archangel last past, £41 at four terms of the year, (that is to say) at the Feast of the Nativity of the Lord, Easter, the Nativity of Saint John the Baptist, and Saint Michael the Archangel, by equal portions, and if the same rent of £41, or any part thereof, shall be in arrear and unpaid to the aforesaid Prior and Convent or their successors, by the space of fifteen days after either of the terms of payment abovesaid, then it shall be lawful to the same Prior and Convent and their successors and their ministers, to distrain in the said Borough of Plymouth, and in the name of a distress, to take all the goods and chattels of the said Mayor and Commonalty and of the burgesses whomsoever of the same borough, and others therein residing and dwelling, found within the same borough, and the precinct thereof, and every part of the said goods and chattels whatsoever, and the distress so taken therefrom, to carry away, lead away, and impound, and retain in any place wheresoever they shall please, until of the rent so being in arrear, they shall be fully satisfied. And if it shall happen that the said rent or any part thereof shall be in arrear and unpaid by the space of six weeks, after either of the terms of payment abovesaid, or if the same Mayor and Commonalty, or any burgess of the borough aforesaid, or any other persons there residing and dwelling shall replevy any distress taken for the rent aforesaid, so being in arrear, or shall rescue the same, that then the same Mayor and Commonalty and their successors, shall pay and render to the aforesaid Prior and Convent and their successors 100s., in the name of a penalty, to be received as often as it shall happen that the said rent, or any part thereof shall be in arrear and unpaid by such space of six weeks, or the distresses so taken in form as aforesaid, shall be replevied or rescued.

"And if it shall happen that the said rent or any part thereof shall be in arrear and unpaid by the space of one quarter of a year, after either of the terms of payment abovesaid, that then the same Mayor and Commonalty and their successors, shall pay to the aforesaid Prior and Convent and their successors £10 in the name of a penalty, to be paid to them as often as it shall happen that the same rent or any part thereof shall be in arrear and unpaid by such quarter of a year, after either of the terms of payment abovesaid. And that it shall be lawful to the same Prior and Convent and their successors, to distrain within the same borough, and the precinct thereof in form abovesaid, as well for the said rent so being in arrear, as for the aforesaid 100s, and also for the aforesaid £10, payable in the name of a penalty in form abovesaid. And if it shall happen that the said rent, or any part thereof, shall be in arrear and unpaid by the space of one whole year, after either the terms of payment abovesaid, that then the same Mayor and Commonalty and their successors, shall pay and render yearly for ever to the said Prior and Convent and their successor in the Priory aforesaid, at the terms abovesaid, £20 beyond the said yearly rent of £41, and so in the whole £61, yearly for ever to be then paid. And if it shall happen that the same rent of £61, or any part thereof shall be in arrear and unpaid in form aforesaid, by the space of six weeks, after either of the terms of payment thereof, that then the same Mayor and Commonalty, their heirs and successors shall pay to the same Prior and Convent and their successors 100s., in the name of a penalty, to be had and received by the same Prior and Convent and their successors, as often as it shall happen that any part of the said rent of £61 shall be in arrear and unpaid by such space of six weeks. And that it shall be lawful to the same Prior and Convent, and their successors to distrain in form aforesaid, within the borough aforesaid, and the precinct thereof for the rent so being in arrear, and for the said 100s. payable in the name of a penalty. And further that it may be ordained and established by the authority aforesaid, that the said Prior and Convent and their successors may enjoy, have, and obtain all the aforesaid rents and penalties in form aforesaid, granted according to the manner, form, and condition above expressed, any statutes or ordinances to the contrary, made in anywise notwithstanding. And that by the same authority the writ of *fierifacias* of you and your heirs, at the prosecution of the said Prior and his successors, may issue out of the exchequer of you and your heirs, as often as to the same Prior and his successors, it shall seem expedient and fitting, to be directed to the Sheriff of Devon for the time being, commanding the same sheriff that he omit not by reason of any liberty, but that the same sheriff cause to be made and levied of the lands and chattels of the same Mayor and Commonalty, and of every burgess of the said borough, and others whomsoever residing and dwelling within the same borough, the monies which of the rents or penalties aforesaid, shall hereafter happen to be in arrear, and the same monies shall deliver to the aforesaid Prior for the time being, unless the same Mayor and Commonalty and their successors, shall show to the same sheriff sufficient acquittances, under the seal of the same Prior, of the payment of the monies so supposed to be in arrear. And although it may hereafter happen for any cause whatsoever arising, that the said Borough of Plymouth, or the said franchises, liberties, or possessions of the said Mayor and Commonalty or their successors or any part thereof, shall be taken or seised into the hands of you or your heirs, that notwithstanding such caption and seisin, such rents and penalties, in the form and condition aforesaid, be well and truly paid to the said Prior and Convent and their successors, at the terms and place aforesaid. Provided always that all the men and tenants of the said Prior and Convent and their successors, for the time being, may fully buy or sell within the said Borough of Plymouth and the precinct thereof, all and all manner of goods, chattels, wares, and merchandizes to their own proper use, without toll, custom, picage, panage, stallage, and murage, and that from all such exaction, imposition, and disquiet, in form aforesaid, they may be quit and discharged for ever.

"And moreover, whereas the Abbot of Buckland, in the county of Devon aforesaid, was seised in his demesne as of fee, and in right of his Church of the Blessed Mary of Buckland, of the Hundred of Roborough, with the appurtenances, within which Hundred, the aforesaid town of Sutton Prior, tithing of Sutton Raf, parcel of the hamlet and tithing of Sutton Vautort, and parcel of the tithing of Compton, which now make the aforesaid Borough of Plymouth, are, and from time whereof the memory of man is not to the contrary, were the parcels of the same Hundred. Now it may please your Royal Highness, by authority of the present Parliament, to grant and ordain that from henceforth the aforesaid Mayor and Commonalty, may have to themselves their heirs and successors for ever, all manner of such rights, liberties, franchises, jurisdictions, powers, hereditaments, and other profits whatsoever as the aforesaid Abbot hath or ought to have, within the precinct of the borough aforesaid, in any manner whatsoever, as in right of his church aforesaid. And that the aforesaid Mayor and Commonalty may have to themselves, their heirs and successors, their court to be held before the same Mayor in the Guildhall of the said borough, once in every month, where the same Mayor will appoint the same, and that in the same court all defaults, excesses, trespasses, articles, views of frankpledge, and all other things, which within the precinct of the said borough, may hereafter happen and be done, and which in any courts of the aforesaid Abbott, to be held within the Hundred aforesaid, ought to have been presented, amended, corrected, or punished in the court aforesaid, if the authority of the present Parliament had not existed, may hereafter be presented, amended, corrected, and punished before the said Mayor as aforesaid, in the like manner, and by the same ways, methods, and terms, as in the aforesaid court of the aforesaid Abbott, they ought, or have been accustomed to be presented, amended, corrected, and punished. And that all those, who by reason of their lands, tenements, or possessions, being within the precinct of the said borough, or by reason of their residence within the same precinct, have been bound to do, render, pay, or present, suit, service, payment, rent, certain or any other advantage whatsoever, to any of the aforesaid courts of the Abbott aforesaid, may hereafter for ever, do, render, pay, and present the same suit, service, payment, rent, and advantage to the aforesaid courts of the aforesaid Mayor and Commonalty and their heirs and successors. Saving always and reserved to the aforesaid Abbott and his successors, by the authority aforesaid, all their rights, franchises, liberties, commodities, jurisdictions, powers, hereditaments, and profits whatsoever in all the residue of his aforesaid hundred, being without the precinct of the borough aforesaid, as the same Abbott hath heretofore had, and ought to have the same. And may it please your Highness, by the authority aforesaid, to ordain that the aforesaid Mayor and Commonalty, their heirs and successors, for ever, render and pay to William, Prior of Bath, and his successors at Bath, in the county of Somerset, ten marks yearly, at the Feast of Easter and St. Michael the Archangel, by equal portions. And if it shall happen that the same annual marks, or any part thereof shall hereafter be in arrear, at either of the feasts aforesaid, that then it may be lawful to the same Prior of Bath and his successors, upon the whole of the borough aforesaid, by all the goods and chattels therein found, to distrain, and the distresses so taken, to carry and lead away wheresoever they shall please, and the same in their possession to retain until of all the arrearages of the aforesaid ten annual marks, together with all their cost and charges, which they shall have sustained by occasion of the non-payment thereof, they shall be fully satisfied. And that the same Prior and his successors, may have writs of *fierifacias* out of the exchequer of you and your heirs, directed to the Sheriff of Devon, and sufficient in law to levy of the lands and chattels of all the inhabitants of the said borough, all the monies which of the aforesaid ten annual marks shall hereafter happen to be in arrear, as often to the now Prior or his successors, it shall seem expedient or fitting. And whereas the aforesaid Prior of Bath, is now seised as of fee, and in right of his Church of the Apostles Peter and Paul of Bath, of the advowson of the Parish Church of Baunton in the county of Devon; that it be ordained by the authority of the present Parliament, that the aforesaid Abbott of the Church of the Blessed Mary of Buckland, may from henceforth have that advowson to him and his successors for ever. And that by the same authority it may be lawful to him and his successors, to appropriate the same church to themselves, and the same to their own use, to hold to them and their successors for ever, any statutes passed to the contrary, or that the aforesaid Priory of Bath, is of the foundation of your progenitors, or of your patronage in anywise notwithstanding. Saving always to the Prior of Bath and his successors, all his pensions and annuities, due out of the said church of Baunton or the rectory thereof. And that the aforesaid Abbott and his successors, servants, officers, family, tenants, and ministers of the same Abbott and his successors, may hereafter be exonerated and quit for ever of tolls, customs, picages, panages, portages, poutages, murages, and the charges, exactions, and demands whatsoever, to the aforesaid Mayor and Commonalty and their successors, hereafter payable for any merchandizes, victuals, or other things whatsoever, by the aforesaid Abbott and his successors, servants, officers, family, tenants, and the ministers of the same Abbott and his successors, within the borough aforesaid, and the liberty thereof, hereafter to be bought, sold, or in anywise provided any grants thereof, to the aforesaid Mayor and Commonalty, by you or your heirs, hereafter to be granted notwithstanding. Saving always and reserved to you, your heirs and successors, all your possessions, liberties, franchises, jurisdictions, courts, profits, hereditaments, escheats, forfeitures, and rights whatsoever, which in the present Act to the aforesaid Mayor and Commonalty, or to the other persons aforesaid in the same Act named, are not above specially and expressly granted."

"And which petition in the Parliament aforesaid, being read, heard, and fully understood, the same petition, by the advice and assent aforesaid, was thus answered: –

"The Kyng will that it be as desired by this petition, provided always that this present Act and Ordinance extende hem noght to the Manoir of Tremaiton, the Burgh of Saltayssh, to the Water of Tamer, nor to non other possessions, franchises, liberties, waters, fishynges, rentys, services, courtes, jurisdictions, offices, enheritances, forfaites, eschetes, other than other issues, profites, or commodities, the which Sir John Cornewaill, Lorde of Fannhope holdyth terme of his lyve, the reversion thereof to the King belonging.

When the inhabitants had thus succeeded in obtaining the royal licence and an Act of Parliament "which constituted them a Corporation, by the style of the Mayor and Commonalty of the Borough of Plymouth, the Prior and Convent, animated with a proper feeling, addressed a petition to Bishop Lacey, representing that it would be advantageous and commodious to convey to this municipal body, certain lands, tenements, franchises, fairs, markets, mills, rents, and services, which they had possessed therein, from time immemorial, and praying his consent to dispose of the same. On January 3rd, following, as bishop and patron, he directed a commission to the Archdeacon of Totnes, or his official, to hold an inquisition, and to report to him the verdict of the jury, which was done as is seen in their certificate, which states that the commission had been received on the day after its date, that on January 7th, the official, in the absence of the Archdeacon, held a public inquisition in the nave of the conventual church – the gates of the Priory and the folding doors of the church being thrown wide open for all comers to enter; that the jury, being sworn, found that the premises of the Priory, within Sutton Prior, had in part been burnt by a hostile descent from Brittany; that the yearly rental of the lands and tenements there was £8; of the courts, fairs, and markets 60s.; and the clear profit from the mills, something more than £10 yearly; that the offer by the Mayor and Corporation of the yearly fixed pension of £41, for the premises aforesaid, was deemed by the Prior and Convent, a satisfactory compensation, and that they were willing to except the same, and the jury concurred in recommending such alienation and sale, as being advantageous to the Priory. The fee-farm rent of £41, was in 1463 reduced to £29 6s. 8d., in consequence of the poverty of the town, (*Corporation Records*) and in 25 Henry VIII, 1533, was wholly discharged by Act of Parliament, and the parsonages of Ugborough and Blackawton, appropriated to the Prior and his successors in lieu thereof."

1439. – William Ketrich, "one of the more honest and discreet men now dwelling within" the proposed boundaries, was the first Mayor of Plymouth, being appointed to that office by the King, in accordance with the petition just given. He is said to have been a Yorkshireman. "He was a little squat man, remarkable for shooting with the strong-bow, and one of the greatest satires of the time. He gave at the feast of his mayoralty, a pye composed of all sorts of fish, flesh, and fowl, that could be gotten. It was 14 feet long, and 4 feet broad, and an oven was built on purpose for its baking." This circumstance gave rise to the saying – "as big as Ketherich's pie."

1440. – Walter Clovelly, Mayor. "Clovelly was nicknamed *goat's face*, for his extreme long beard, which he made a vow should never be cut or shaven, after the death of his wife. An instance of conjugal affection too rare to be met with in this depraved age."

"The tower of Saint Andrew's Church was built this year, at the expense of Mr. Thomas Yogge, a merchant of the town."

1441. – William Pollard, Mayor. "According to the prevailing humour of those days, he was conceitedly nicknamed, being commonly called *pull hard*, from his uncommon power and mastership in archery, few men being able to bend his bow, or to send an arrow within threescore paces of that distance, which he could, with ease, command."

1442. – John Shepley or Shipley, Mayor. "He was a man of exemplary character and great piety, by the anagrammatists of the age, called *sheeply* for his gentle and saint-like qualities. He was wont (says an ancient manuscript) to be likened unto King Harry; for that in mildnesse and meaknesse of heart, he had no compeere, saving his royalle and gracious master." "In this year, the King of Sicily's daughter was brought to Plymouth, and afterwards married to King Henry."

1443 and 1444. – William Nichols or Nycoles, Mayor. "He artfully detected a vile imposter, who pretended to be dumb, and that by no other means than seeming to pity him, and asking "how long he had been speechless?" to which the fellow unguardedly made answer "that he was born so!"

1445. – John Shepley, Mayor. The same who held the office in 1442.

1446. – John Facey, Mayor. Of this mayor it is recorded that "he struck the Town Clerk, as he sat upon the Bench, for addressing him without giving him his title of 'Worship', for which he was fain to compound with a good round sum; and he was called 'Worship Facey' ever after. He was remarkably cholerick, and would run the whole length of a street after the whorson boys as he called them, who took delight in flouting him as he passed."

1447. – John Carwinnick, Mayor. "Of whom we have no private memoir, but that he was a worthy magistrate. In this year, the Queen struck her aunt, the Duchess of Gloster, a box on the ear at court, and a little while after, the said duchess did penance, walking barefoot through the street, with a lighted taper in her hands, for sorcery."

1448. – John Facey again Mayor. When elected to the office for the second time, "he said they might as well have continued him the whole three years, and that would have saved the trouble of choosing him again."

1449. – John Paige, Mayor. "A man very strict in his office, insomuch that the least violation of the laws, as far as came within his jurisdiction, was punished with much rigour; he was a great devotee, never missed mattin or vesper, and took singular notice of those who absented from the mass on a Sunday. He had a rosary constantly in his pocket, and wore a silver crucifix continually beneath his band as a common appendage to his dress." The Duke of Clarence was this year at Plymouth.

1450 and 1451. – Stephen Chapman or Chepeman, Mayor. "He was a very rich man, and a lover of gain; of very mean origin, but most fortunate, and regarded as the wealthiest trafficker of his days. He was however a just magistrate."

1452. – Thomas Greyle or Gryll or Negle, Mayor. "A man of a merry heart, and a great lover of good cheer. A gallant man in his house, and goodly train, with good means for support thereof. He delighted in feasting his neighbours, and did much good to the poor." The King was this year at Exeter.

1452. – "The names of the xii psons that alwayes be of the Pvy Councell and Chyffe Men of the Burghe and Town of Plymouthe: –

Andrew Hillersdon, Esq., *Recorder*.
William Randell.

Thomas Gubb	Jacobus Horswell
Johes Gygporte	Wyllms Hawkyns
Johes Elyott	Thomas Clouter
Thomas Cyrte	Robtus Dyghton
Henricus Harvey	Johes Pers
Lucas Cok	Thomas Mills.

"The names of the xxiv Burgesses that be sworne to the Comon Councell within the Burghe of Plymouthe: –

John Thomas	Thomas Holwaye
Richard Lybbe	Robert Carswell
Henry Martyn	John Tasse
Robert Hampton	Wyllm Buller
Richard Guscot	Wyllm Wyk
Thomas Browne	John Body
John Brokyng	John Wyle
John Towsson	Wyllm Eggecomb
Wyllm Aysslegg	Stephen Burdon
John Mone	Wyllm Gibbons
—— Kinsman	John Cross
John Rolle	Richard Caunder."

1453 and 1454. – Vincent Patilysden, Mayor.

1455. – James Dernford or Samuel Dorniforde, Mayor. "This poor gentleman was taken in a fit at church, on the first day of his mayoralty. He however made shift to eat a fine Michaelmas goose afterwards at dinner, with this declaration, that he thought his illness at mass had given him a passing good stomach."

1456. – Vincent Patilysden again Mayor. "He first setting the example, the alderman and burgesses did wear, every Sunday, red roses in their hats as they went to church, to shew their loyalty to King Harry; but which, as they saw the York faction arising, they afterwards did prudently decline."

1457. – John Carnynnick, Mayor. "The mayor appeareth at church, with laced bonnet and buckles in his shoes." The French this year attacked Fowey, as they had done several times previously. The wife of Thomas Treffry gallantly repulsed them from her residence, Place House.

1458. – Thomas Greyle, (also called Tregell) again Mayor. "He gave a most noble feast at his in-swearing, at which he was honoured with the presence of several noble lords, knights, and ladies. A joust or tournament was held upon the Hoe. A pavilion was built at the mayor's expence, so large as to hold 400 people, and liquor given to the populace, so that it was for the time, a kind of jubilee."

1459. – William Yogge, Mayor. "A close thrifty man, proud of no exterior show, but much bent on amassing wealth. He would bear home his meat from the market with his own hand, and if any one told him it was unseemly in a man of his substance and a magistrate, he would say: 'T'were a sorry horse that would not carry his own provender.' "

1460. – John Pollard, Mayor. "A man of a taciturn and reserved bent, much given to silence, and in some sort, absent from himself. Regarded by some as being proud, but only such as knew him not. He was a strict honest man, a lover of justice and his word did fast bind him.

1461. – William Yogge again Mayor. About this time, a fort was built on each side of the harbour at Fowey.

1462. – John Paige, Mayor. "This year the mayor and the vicar had a great quarrel: the mayor insisted that particular prayers should be put up for the success of King Henry's arms against the rebellious Yorkists, which the vicar stubbornly refused, yet not unwisely. The mayor threatened to complain to the King, and the vicar defied him. Yet to shew that loyalty is not confined to any party, but him that ruleth; this very mayor in the same year, feasteth the Duke of Clarence, brother to King Edward IV, right royally, here in Plymouth, and drinketh long life and a prosperous reign to King Edward IV.

1463, 1464 and 1465. – John Rowland, Mayor. "A man of great interest and sway, and closely attached unto the House of York. He was chosen mayor more from fear and awe, than reverence and love, which office he held successive years, and was mayor again at the end of three years after. Sheep sent to Aragon in Spain, which increased, and did this nation much hurt."

1466. – Richard Bovey, Mayor. "A plain simple man, inoffensive in his manners and easy in his office; somewhat less of the stork than the log. While he was mayor, no one found fault with him, and when no longer such, nobody missed him. T'will be well (saith the writer) if no one of his successors leaveth a worse name behind him."

1467. – William Yogge, Mayor.

1468. – John Paige, Mayor.

1469. – John Rowland, Mayor. By an Act of Parliament passed this year, (in which was recited the charter of Henry VI,) upon the petition of the Prior of Plympton, and Mayor and Commonalty of Plymouth, by which it appears that inasmuch as the Borough of Plymouth was fallen into poverty and decay since the making of the former Act, and therefore not able to pay the said rent of £41 to the Prior of Plympton should pay the Prior of Plympton and his successors, but £29 6s. 8d. rent yearly at several days, with a clause of distress and several new penalties, and 20s. more yearly upon Simon and Jude Day, for the term of 41 years, and for non-payment, the Prior to have a writ to the sheriff to proclaim the Mayor, his rent-gatherers and receivers, to appear in the Court of Common Pleas and pay the rent, or be committed to the Fleet, but not to be troubled during the time of their offices, provided that the Mayor and Commonalty should have power to punish in any of the said three messuages, as in other parts of the said borough. Provided also that this Act be not prejudicial to any grant formerly made by the said King to the said Mayor and Commonalty.

1470. – William Yogge, Mayor. The Earl of Warwick and the Duke of Clarence, brother to Edward IV, and the Earls of Pembroke and Oxford, coming out of France, landed at Plymouth and dined with the mayor, proclaimed King Henry VI at the Guildhall, increased their number, and marched to London.

1471. – William Paige, Mayor. "King Henry let loose from the tower, and after six months, King Edward returning successfully to London, seizeth him again."

"Margaret of Anjou landed at Plymouth with her son Edward and a body of auxiliaries, chiefly French, on the same day as Warwick was defeated and slain."

1472. – Richard Bovey, Mayor.

1473. – Nicholas Heynstall or Henstock, Mayor.

1474. – Williams Paige, Mayor.

1475 and 1476. – Nicholas Heynstall or Henstock again Mayor.

1477. – John Pollard again Mayor

1478. – Nicholas Heynstall or Henstock fourth time Mayor.

1479. – William Rogers, Mayor.

1480. – Thomas Gregorthead or Graygorthand or Tregartha, Mayor.

1481. – Thomas Greswell, Grissell or Tresawell, Mayor.

1482. – Nicholas Heynstall or Henstock again Mayor.

1483. – Thomas Greyson, Mayor.

1484. – Pearse Craswell or Creswell, Mayor.

1485. – Thomas Tresawell, Mayor. "A sweating sickness began, and raged in England (at first, though afterwards it went beyond sea,) under the name of *Sudor Anglicus*, which reached Plymouth."

1487. – Nicholas Heynstall or Henstock, Mayor.

1488. – Perrin Earle, Mayor.

1489. – Thomas Greyson again Mayor.

1490. – Nicholas Heynstall again Mayor.

1491. – John Painter, Mayor.

1492 and 1493. – William Thickpenny, Mayor. The Guild in the following curious document, relating to the establishment of Church Ales on Corpus Christi Day, "seems to have been instituted in compliance with the power given to the Mayor and Commonalty by the charter, 9th July, 18 Henry VI": –

"For the honor of God and for thencressing of the benefittes of the Church of Seynt Andrewe, of Plymouth, it is agreed by the Mayre XII and XXIIII, sworne to the Councell of the Burghe of Plymouthe, that in the Feast of Corporis Christi, every warde of the said burghe shall from hensforthe, this the Xth day of June, make an *hale* yn the Parisshe Churche Yarde of Seynt Andrewe aforesaid. And every person of the said warde to bring with theym, except brede and drinke, such vytayle as the like best, and have there suche, and as many persons estraungers, as they thinke best of theyr frends and aquaynted men and women for thencressing of the said ale; paing for brede and ale as it cometh thereto in reckening for their dyners and sopers the same day, etc.

"*Item.* – It is agreed that every taverne of wyne and ale within the said burghe, to forbere theyr sale the same day, of theyr wyne and ale, for the wele of the said churche. Every person of the XII, upon payne of VIs.

VIIId., and every of the XXIIII, IIIs. IIIId., and every of the coiers, one pound of waxe or the value of the same, to the said churche's behoufe. And he or they doing the contrary, at the Mayer XII and XXIIII, is wylle to stonde in jupardye of his fredome, and to paye the said fyne, and every fyne or fynes or forfayte to be levyed by the Mayer, for the tyme being, within IIII days after the said feaste. And in his defaute to be levyed of his fee, and upon the audeyte thereof.

"*Item.* – The Mayre for the tyme being, allways in his owne warde, in the hale so made for him and his warde, etc., etc.

"*Item.* –That the XII and the XXIIII, aide and helpe the Mayre to levy the said paynes, forfayte at every yere and tyme therto called.

"*Item.* – That no person that shall goe about with the Shipp of Corpus Christi, bring no body there but him selfe to charge the Yle, (ale).

"*Item.* – That they make a reckening to every person for mete and drinke, and notte to pay at their leasure.

"*Item.* – That every ale from hensforthe, for the wealthe of the churche in tyme comyng be accomptabyll afore the Mayer the XII and the XXIIII, in the Gyldehall of the burgh aforesaid, and the debet of every of theym to be sett in the ligger of the said towne entred. And the said debet to be atte the Mayor XII and XXIIII, is disposition in every yere and tyme, for the wealthe of the said churche.

"*Item.* – That every freman is name be in tyme coming, entred in the said ligger

"*Item.* – That Alion borne outeward, be not freman in tyme coming, excepte the persons of Normandy, Gascon, Gyon, Irlond, Caleys, Berwyke, and the borders of the same being Englisshe.

"*Item.* – That all manner of wardeyns in tyme to come take their othe afore the Mayre in the Gyldehall, truly to doe their office.

"*Item.* – That this and all other articles contayned in the said ligger to be allways parcell of the Mayre's othe on Michelmas Day," etc., etc.

1494. – Thomas Bigport, Mayor. Wheat sold in Plymouth for 6d. a bushel, bay sale at 3½d per bushel, and herrings at 3s. 4d per barrel.

1495. – William Nichol, Mayor. The following is headed "An attested copy of a Bye-law made by the 12 and 24 relative to the imposition of persons refusing to take office: –

"An Act made by William Nycoll, Mayor of Plymouth, and by the Recorder of the same the 12 and 24 to be counsell of the said borough the 11th year of King Henry the 7th.

"*Item.* – It is enacted for them that refuse to be in office when they be chosen by the Mayor and Counsell of the Towne; that they so refusinge to be in the same office, to be putt by the Mayor, for the time beinge in the Hall, and to abide out the time that he or they so refusinge find surety, or they ... the said Hall to take the said office upon payne of £10, or more and larger sum as the case requires."

1496. – William Rogers, Mayor. "The Cornish men about Bodmin, rise, march to London, encamp on Blackheath, headed by the Lord Audley, and one Hammock and Joseph, who were defeated in June, 1497."

1497. – Thomas Tresawell, Mayor. "In September, Perkin Warbeck landeth at Whitsand Bay, in Cornwall, goeth to Bodmin, where making up a small army, he marcheth to Exeter and beseigheth it, but it bravely defended itself. At last King Henry coming with a great army, he submits, is put in the tower, where attempting another treachery, he was hanged at Tyburn."

1498. – John Painter, Mayor. Hay sold in Plymouth at 8s. 2d. per load.

1499. – John Slocombe or Wilcombe, Mayor. Wheat this year is said to have sold at 4s. per quarter.

1500. – William Boyle or Byle, Mayor.

1501. – Thomas Cross, Mayor. "The Princess Catherine of Spain landed at Plymouth, was married first to Prince Arthur, then to Henry VIII, who divorcing her, begat the quarrel between him and the pope, and was followed by a happy reformation." "She landed at Plymouth on Seynt Erkenweld's daye," and was accompanied by the Archbishop of Compostella and many great nobles. The unfortunate princess was handsomely entertained by the Corporation. She and the archbishop were lodged at the mayor's house in Notte-street – a house which seems to have been on considerable size and importance, in fact the best in the town. – Here she is said to have rested for a fortnight, and was then escorted by way of Tavistock, Okehampton, and Crediton,* to Exeter, on her way top London, where she was received with great honour and respect. "At Exeter, her residence was at the house of the dean. She rested here several days, then by short journies to London." She was married to Prince Arthur on the 6th November.

*"It is somewhat remarkable to find this line of road generally follwed by travellers to and from Plymouth, instead of the old Roman way by Ridgeway, Brent, Totnes, Teignmouth, and Haldon. We can only suppose that this older and more direct road had, like many of the Roman ways, been allowed to fall into comparative ruin; and that the road which ran by the great Abbey of Tavistock, the Castle of Okehampton, and the Bishop's Palace at Crediton, was favoured for the sake of the convenient halting places afforded at these several stations. It was by this road that Duke Cosmo of Tuscany travelled in the days of Charles II, and encountered Sir Coplestone Bamfylde hunting in great state on the moors between Tavistock and Okehampton. At Exeter the deanery was the usual headquarters of such illustrious travellers. There the Princess Catherine passed two nights, during the first of which, the noise of the weathercock on the spire of St. Mary Major's Church so much disturbed her, that it was taken down "for her greater content."

The house in Notte-street, said to be the one in which the Princess Catherine of Aragon was so well entertained by the mayor, is engraved above. It is one of the best remaining timber houses of its period, and is in excellent preservation, as is also another of the same period, likewise engraved above, which is still standing a little lower down in the same street. The appearance of these two houses is strikingly picturesque, and the whole of the details – the doorways, the windows, the barge-boards, the hip-knobs, the brackets, and indeed every part – are worthy of careful examination. They are each of them four stories in height; the upper story of each being gabled.

The Corporation of Plymouth this year appointed a master to teach grammar to the children of the town, at a salary of £10 a year, and lodging.

1502. – John Horsewell, Mayor. Prince Arthur died

1503. – John Painter again Mayor.

1504. – John Brewin or Breman, Mayor. "A dry summer, no rain from Whitsuntide to Michaelmas."

1505. - William Tregle or Trigle, Mayor. "In this yere the Duke of Burgoyne, father to Charles the V, emperoure, by force of wether landed on the south coste of England."

1506. – Thomas Tresawell, Mayor.

1507. – Simon Craswell or Carswell, Mayor.

1508. – John Painter, Mayor.

1509. – Richard Gewe, Mayor. "King Henry VII dieth at Richmond, April 21st, 1509. His son proclaimed under the name of Henry VIII, and is immediately married to his brother's relict."

In this year several noblemen and others embarked at Plymouth in four ships belonging to the King, and sailed for Cadiz, to assist the King of Aragon against the Spanish moors.

1510. – Walter Pollard, Mayor.

1511. – William Brooking, Mayor. "The Marquis of Dorset, Lords Howard, Broke, and Ferris, the Lord Willoughby and divers other noblemen, landed after six months' victorious warfare against the moors in Spain, with their archers." An expedition for the north coast of Spain, sailed from Plymouth. Two large ships were accidently burned in the harbour.

1512. – John Grisling, Mayor. In this year an Act for fortifying the town is said to have been passed. "In this yere the Lord Edward Howard, Lorde Admirall of England, was slayne on Saint Mark's Day, upon the coste of Brittany, the Kyng entered France and distressed the Frenchmen to take Tourenne and Tournay, and returned; but in the meantime, the Kyng of Scotts invaded England and was slaine with divers nobles and commons of Scotland by the Erle of Surrey, which after that, the Kyng did create Duke of Norffolke."

1513. – John Pound, Mayor.

1514. – William Brooking, Mayor.

1514. – John Painter again Mayor.

1516. – John Brewin, Mayor.

1517. – John Herford, Mayor.

1518. – William Randall, Mayor.

1519. – John Pound, Mayor. John Veysey, Bishop of Exeter, is said to have built part of the walls of Plymouth in this year, but probably it was in 1520, as next shown.

1520. – William Randall, again Mayor. On the 22nd September, Bishop Veysey granted an indulgence for 40 days to all true penitents, for assisting in building the walls and fortifications of the town.

1521. – Stephen Pors or Pearse, Mayor. The Emperor Charles V and the Queen of Aragon landed in England.

1522. – Thomas Bull, Mayor. The King of Denmark came into England, and landed at Plymouth.

1523. – John Bovey, Mayor.

1524. – William Brooking, Mayor. Hooker, one of the "Worthies of Devonshire," born.

1525. – John Pound, Mayor.

1526. – John Herford, Mayor.

1527. – Henry Brickham, Mayor. The sweating sickness raged in Plymouth and other parts of the country.

1528. – James Horswell, Mayor.

1529. – William Brooking again Mayor.

1530. – William Randall again Mayor. The celebrated Sir Richard Edgcumbe born at Stonehouse.

1531. – John Bigport, Mayor. "Navigation was now fairly afloat; ships were every year augmenting in size, and people began to see the importance of their harbours, which would require some care to be taken for their future preservation. Hitherto Sutton Pool, the Catwater, Millbrooke Lake, and Stonehouse Pool afforded ample accommodation for such ships as were sent to the blockade of Calais in 1346; but now, in 1531, the larger vessels required deeper water and greater space, and were not so easily managed for being careened, breamed, or repaired. Public attention began to be awakened to the necessity of, at least, paying some regard to the preservation of our harbours in their natural state. Petitions were sent from Plymouth, Falmouth, Fowey, Dartmouth, and Teignmouth, praying for an Act of Parliament for "amending the havens of these ports." These petitions stated "that formerly ships of 800 tons burthen could enter these harbours at low water; but that now (1531,) a ship of a hundred tons could scarcely enter at half tide;" and the prayer proceeded to state that these fillings-up arose from certain stream works, which occasioned great quantities of sand and gravel to be brought down, and to fill up the harbours. An Act of Parliament was accordingly passed in 1531, which provided that no stream works should, in future, be worked, unless "hatches" are provided to prevent the sand from being conveyed down by the rivers and into the harbours, and penalties are attached on offenders. It was also enacted that "any inhabitant" might give information and receive half the penalty etc. As this Act provided that "any inhabitant" might give information, it seems the stream workers managed to keep the inhabitants of the five towns above mentioned aloof from their operations."*

"William Strode of Newnham, in Plympton-Saint-Maurice, in the county of Devon, was imprisoned in the bishop's house at Exeter, upon suspicion of heresy, where he suffered great hardships; it is not ascertained how he was dealt with afterwards, but it is generally supposed he died in prison."

1532. – William Hawkins, Mayor. This gentleman was of the same family as the celebrated Admiral Sir John Hawkins.

1533. – Christopher Moore, Mayor. "In this year it was enacted that butchers should sell their beef and mutton by weight; beef for a 1/2d. the

*Captain Walker, Harbour Master.

pound, and mutton for 3/4d., which was thought a great advantage for the kingdom, but it turned out otherwise, for fat oxen were sold for 26s. 8d., fat sheep for 3s 4d., fat calves at same price, and a fat lamb, 1s. The butchers of London sold penny pieces of beef for the poor, each piece 21/2lb and sometimes 3lb for a penny; and 13 and 14 pieces for a 1s.; mutton 8d. the quarter, and 4s. 8d. for a cwt. of beef."

"By an Act of Parliament made in this year, upon a petition exhibited to the King in Parliament by the Mayor of Plymouth, it was ordained as the town was poor and in decay by reason of many costs and charges sustained, and not able to pay the said rent of £29 6s 8d. (*see page 58*) to the said Prior of Plympton; that the mayor should be discharged of the said rent, and in recompence thereof, the King did grant unto the said Prior to impropriate to him and his successors for ever, the advowsons of the churches of Ugborough and Blackawton; and the Vicar of Ugborough to be endowed with the parsonage house, garden and orchard, and £20 annuity out of the parsonage; and the Vicar of Blackawton to be endowed with the parsonage house, and orchard, and £16 yearly out of the parsonage. But this £29 6s. 8d. was only to be paid to the said Prior until those churches became void. And afterwards the church of Blackawton became void before the dissolution of monasteries, but the church of Ugborough continued until it came to King Henry the Eighth, by the act of dissolution. And then King Henry the Eighth, by his letters patent, dated 6th May, 36th of his reign, was pleased, at the request of the said Mayor and Commonalty, to release all the said rents and the arrerages thereof. All which commissions, inquisitions, Acts of Parliament, and charter, are recited in one exemplification before mentioned. (Now there is only 40s. rent, payable by the Mayor of Plymouth, yearly, out of the Borough of Plymouth)."

1534. – John Elliot, Mayor. "John Howe the last Prior of Plympton, with 20 of his brethren, subscribed to the King's supremacy on 5th August, this year."

1535. – James Horswell, Mayor. In 1535, another Act of Parliament passed, reciting that of 1531, for preserving the harbours in the west of England. The preamble states that "since the making of the said statute, the inhabitants of these port towns having little regard, respect, love, or affection to the amending and maintaining of the same towns, nor to their prosterity, as they are naturally bounden and obliged, have permitted the stream works to continue (1538) without any manner of suit commenced by the inhabitants thereof." It then provides that the penalty given to any inhabitant of the towns, who will sue for the same, shall now be given to "any of Her

Majesty's subjects who will sue for the same." It seems there was sufficient cause for complaint against the operations of these stream works in this locality; for Lelande, in his visit here about 1538, remarked, "After that, I passed over Plym river. I rode about half a mile by Tory Brook, whose color is always redde by the sande that it runneth on, and caryeth from the Tynne works with it, and so to Plympton Marie so called, because the church there is dedicate unto our Lady. Plympton Marie standeth not upon the Plym River, for it is distant almost half a mile from it; but it standeth by the Est Ripe of it, whereby the lower and first buildings of the Courte of the Priorie be almost cleve chocked with the sands that Torey bringeth from the Tynne works."

1536. – Thomas Bull, Mayor. A slight shock of an earthquake is stated to have been, this year, felt at Plymouth.

1537. – Thomas Clouter, Mayor.

1538. – William Hawkins again Mayor. The King established a councel for the west, at Tavistock.

John Howe, the last Prior of Plympton, subscribed to the King's supremacy, August 5th, 1534, and after governing the Priory nearly eighteen years, surrendered it to the Crown on March 1st, 30th Henry VIII. Attached to the surrender of this house is an impression of the common seal in red wax, representing Saint Peter with his keys, and Saint Paul with his sword, both seated. "For his subserviency he was gratified with the large annuity of £120, though, in the expectation of a dissolution of the Priory, he had been actively engaged in obtaining fines for long leases of its property, and in charging it with pensions. Retiring to Exeter College, Oxford, in January, 1545, the ex-Prior became a "sojourner" there.* He was still living in 1553.

"Amongst the leases of church property, made by Howe before the surrender, we find the following among the muniments and title deeds at Powderham Castle; the tithes of Wembury, leased for twenty-one years, to John Ryder of Wembury, for the rent of £40 13s. 4d., deducting £6 13s. 4d. towards the salary of the Incumbent; the tithes of Saint Budok to Thomas Withede and Robert Kemp for twenty-five years, rent £9; the tithes of Saint Julian of Maker, to Walter Shere, for twenty-five years, rent £11 6s. 8d.; of Maristowe and Thrusselton, to Edmund Langeford, for twenty-one years, rent £8; of Brixton, for twenty-one years, to Richard Chalons and Walter Shere, rent £30, deducting £6 13s. 4d. for the Incumbent's salary; the tithes of Plymouth to Richard Hoper, for twenty-one years, for £15; for the like terms to the same Hoper, the tithes of Egg Buckland, for £9; of Tamerton Follyett, for £10; and of Saint Martin's Chapel in Tamerton Foliot Parish, for

*Wood's Athen. Oxon., vol. 1. p. 568.

£13s. 4d.; the tithes of Sandforde, to Thomas Whitehede, for twenty-five years, rent £9 6s. 8d. deducting therefrom £6 for the Incumbent; the tithes of Saint Edward's of Shaugh, to Hugh Foster and Baldwin Heyle, for twenty-five years, rent £20, deducting therefrom £6 13s. 4d., for the resident curate; the tithes and oblations of Saint Thomas's (afterwards called Saint Maurice's) of Plympton East, with the exception of the tithe, garb and theaf, to Richard Chalons and Walter Shere, for thirty-five years, rent £11, out of which was to be deducted as a salary for the curate, £6 13s. 4d.; the tithes and oblations of All Saints at Plymstock, to Walter Shere and Christopher Hornebrooke for twenty-five years, rent £62, £8 of which to be deducted for the curate's stipend; the tithes, great and small, of Saint Mary's of Plympton, to Richard Chalons and Walter Shere for twenty-one years, rent £74, of which £16 to be deducted for the maintenance of two priests, viz: the parish priest and the (sacristan) sexton; the tithes of Saint Kew in Cornwall, to Richard Fortescue, Esq. and his son Humphrey for twenty-five years, sum £20," etc., etc.

1539. – Thomas Byrte, Mayor. Sir Francis Drake born. The patronage of the religious establishments in Plymouth, was given by the King to the Corporation. "A statute was made confirming the seizure and surrender of the abbies, in number 645, of which 28 were mitred abbots. 152 colleges were also suppressed and 129 hospitals. Their yearly value was £161,000 besides the money which arose from the materials of the houses, from plate, jewels, and church ornaments. Camden says the number of monasteries suppressed in England and Wales, was 643, colleges 90, chantries and free chapels 2,374, and 110 hospitals. From the above circumstance, the entire lordship of the Borough of Plymouth with the patronage of Saint Andrew's Church (previous to which, the Prior of Plympton was the sole impropriator) together with the hospital of White Friars, situated on the east part of the town, (Coxside) the hospitals of Grey Friars on the north side of Saint Andrew's Church, with the abbeys of Cistercian Friars, south and south-east of the above church, and everything appertaining to the above situations, fell by grant of King Henry VIII, into the hands of the Mayor and Commonalty, who enjoyed them with many other valuable appendages (some lost by lapse of time) to a late period."

1540. – John Thomas, Mayor. "This year a great ship of Portugal, laden with spice, was cast away at German Rock at Plymouth, much spoil made, and great inquisition, and divers imprisoned on that account." Between this time and the establishment of a royal dockyard in Hamoaze, wind-bound merchant ships took shelter in the estuary and supplies could be obtained."

"Plymouth in ancient times, does not appear to have been a desirable resting place for wind-bound mariners. The "Castel," or block-house, levying contributions, (which the citadel did until the beginning of the present century) within the limits of its jurisdiction. An old chronicler, who wrote in 1485, speaking of Cawsand Bay, describes it as 'an open road, yet sometimes affording succour to worst sort of sea farers, as not subject to comptrollment of Plymouth Fort. The shore is peopled with some dwelling houses and many cellars dearly rented for short usage, in saving of pilchards, at which time there flocketh a great concourse of sayners and others dependent upon their labours.' About this time (1540) there was only a single house at Mount Wise; green fields covering the site of Devonport and extending over the present dockyard, terminating on a point at the mouth of the present Camber, where the piled jetty still retains the ancient name of 'Froward Point.' There are some old oil-painted landscapes at Mount Edgcumbe House of the local scenery of the time, which display the house on Mount Wise, with Stoke Church in the distance, and the township, or village, of East Stonehouse on the sheltered side of Stonehouse Creek, above the present bridge."

1541. – Thomas Mylles Mayor.

1542. – James Horswell, Mayor. "One Ferrers, (George Ferrers) serving Plymouth in Parliament, this year being arrested on an execution by the Sheriff of London; he was fetched from the Counter, an Act made to free him of the debt, and the sheriff imprisoned in the Tower. – *Baker's Chronicle*. An Act was then passed to prevent the arrest of Members of Parliament.

1543. – Thomas Holloway, Mayor.

"The Sheriff's Receipt for the Fee-farm Rent of 40s.

"This Bill made the 10th day of October in the 35th year of our Sovereign Lord King Henry the Eighth, Wytnesseth that I, George Haydon, under-sheriff of Devonshyre the day of the ....have received of Thomas Holloway, Mayor of Plymouth, the sum of Forty Shyllyngs sterlynge of and for the fee-farms of Plymouth dewe unto our Lord the King on the Fest of Saynt Andrew, last past, in wytnyss whereof, I the said George Haydon, have subscribed my name, the day and year above written.

GEORGE HAYDON."

1544. – Thomas Clouter, Mayor. "About this time Marazion was burned by a party of marauding French, who did much damage along the coast."

1545. – William Randall again Mayor.

1546. – Luke Cock, Mayor. "At Plymouth was a Priory of White Friars, in the east part of the town, which was granted to Giles Iselham, 38 Henry VIII, (1546) as also a house of Grey Friars, founded in 7 Richard II."

1547. – John Elliot, Mayor. "In this yere was the fyrst insurrection in Cornwall, when one Bodye was slayne, and afterwards the commons were pacified by the gentylemen of the countrey, with small trouble, but yet many of the chyffe of the commons were hanged, drawn, and quartered."

1548. – Richard Hooper, Mayor. The admiral beheaded. "Insurrections general in the country, but Exeter, and the Castle of Plymouth, were valiantly defended, and kept from the rebels at the towne's expence – until Lord Russell and the King's army came. One rebel was burnt, others hung at Tyburn." The well-affected inhabitants took shelter in Saint Nicholas' Island.

1549. – Williams Weekes or Wykes, Mayor. During this mayoralty, the Cornish, Devonshire, and Somersetshire men began to rebel, and beseiged Exon, but were defeated. The rebels were repulsed from Plymouth, and one of them burnt at the town's expense.

"The four western counties, Dorset, Somerset, Devon and Cornwall, were distinguished in the important particulars of language, obstinacy in religion, climate, and remoteness from the metropolis. Many interesting changes had only recently been affected. The Reformation was not introduced in the quiet manner that it obtained in other counties. Our west-country spurned the book of Common Prayer as being *New English*, which so many could not understand, as they could neither read nor follow the services in English – Cornish a dialect of the Celtic, being their language. The rebellion of 1549, 3rd year of Edward VI, aptly styled in archives "Commocion Time," was one of violence and great bloodshed, as our annals confirm. The insurgents grew more daring, in proportion as mercy was offered them; and in their 10th article expressed their determination to have nothing to do with the English tongue, as follows: – 'We will have the Bible and all books of Scripture to be called in again. For, we are informed that otherwise, the clergy shall not of long time confound the heretics.'"

Bishop Lacey granted an indulgence for 40 days, on the 26th November this year, to all true penitents contributing *"ad novam fabricacionem fosse vil juxta eastium infra villam de Plymuth."* A similar indulgence having previously, in 1460, been granted by Bishop Stafford towards the erection of two towers and repairs of a causeway lately destroyed; *"per inimicos nostros de Britannia, jus defensione non solum ejusdem ville sed etiam patrie circumjacentis ac salvâ navium custodiâ ibidem applicatientium."*

1550. – John Kainsham, Mayor. The sweating sickness raged throughout England, and was very severe in this district.

1551. – Thomas Clouter, Mayor.

1552. – John Thomas, Mayor. Richard Edgecombe, Member of Parliament for Plymouth.

1553. – Luke Cock, Mayor. Roger Budophide and William Hawkins, Members of Parliament for Plymouth. "The Erle of Bedford, the Lord Fitzwaters with sondry other men of honor and also of worshippe, tooke shipping at Plymouth in the Queen's Majesties' shipes, and sayled into Spayn to Philipe, eldest son and here unto Charles V, emperoure, to thintent to wayte upon the said King Philipe, being then detyrmed to come into England; after this a nobleman of Spayne named the Marquis de las Navas, landed at Plymouth, where the Lord William Howard, Lord Highe Admiral of England, was with sondry of the Queen's Majesties' shippes, and received hym very honourably. The said Kyng Philipe landed at Southealmpton, and on Saint James his day then next following, was maryed unto the Queen's Highness at Wynchester." (The marriage took place in 1554).

This being the first year of Queen Mary's reign, a new charter was granted to the Borough of Plymouth. "By this charter, Queen Mary confirms the letters patent of King Edward the Sixth, King Henry the Eighth, King Henry the Seventh, and the Act of Parliament of King Henry the Sixth, and charter by the same King Henry the Sixth, the 25th July, 18th year of his reign, which charter is there recited, and by which it appears that these priviledges following be granted to the Mayor and Commonalty of Plymouth: –

"First – That the Mayor and Recorder be justices of the peace for the time being, and to hear and determine all offences within the borough, treason and felony excepted.

"Secondly – That the Mayor and Commonalty have and hold a guild of merchants within the said borough, with all that thereunto belongs, the same as the Mayor and Bayliffs of Oxford had done.

"Thirdly – To hold pleas in the Guildhall of all causes real and personal and mixt, and to hear and determine the same as the Mayor and Bayliffs of Oxford do, arising within the said borough.

"Fourthly – To have cognizance of pleas as the Mayor and Bayliffs of Oxford had, to be allowed in all the Queen's courts.

"Fifthly – To have the return and execution of all writs within the precinct of the borough, and that no sheriff, coroner, justice of the peace, bayliff, or any other minister of the King, his heirs or successors enter within the precinct of the said borough, to execute any process, rules for matters only, concerning the King, unless in default of the Mayor and Commonalty.

"Sixthly – That none of the burgesses there be returned in any juries of assizes, which should happen to be taken out of the borough, unless he had lands out of the borough.

"Seventhly – To choose a coroner within the borough as often as there should be one wanting, and swear him into that office.

"Eighthly – To have two fairs yearly, one upon Saint Matthew's Day, and the other upon Saint Paul's Day, and to continue three days after, and two markets every week, one Monday, the other Thursday; and to have within the precinct of the said borough, soccage, saccage, toll, tallage, infangtheft, outfangtheft, goods of felons and fugitives, outlaws or others, condemned or convict, and of felons of themselves happening, and to seize the same, without delivery or request.

"Ninthly – To have all fines, amerciaments, issues and redemptions, forfeited, assessed or adjudged within the said borough, and to levy the same to their own use, without any extracts out of the exchequer.

"Tenthly – That the Mayor and Commonalty and every of them and their servants and ministers, as well through the whole kingdom of England as by sea as far as the King's power was, should be free and discharged of tolls, murage, pontage, passage, stallage, lastage, keyage, pickage, panage, carriage, winage, anchorage, seawaige, strandage, chimmage, keelage, customs, impositions, and other charges whatsoever, and of all other exactions and customs of and for themselves their good and merchandizes any way to be paid."

1554. – John Ilcomb, Mayor. John Mallett and Richard Hooper, Members for Plymouth. "In this yere Thomas Gresham, Esq., the Queen's Majesties' agent and factor, retorned oute of Spaine and landed at Dartmouth in the monthe of February, with much treasor brought oute of Spaine, whereof some landed at Plymouthe, in merchant shippes, some at Dartmouth, and at other places.

The Spanish and other ambassadors entertaind at Mount Edgcumbe, by Sir Richard Edgcumbe.

1555. – John Ford, Mayor. Sir Thomas Knyvett and Roger Butockside, Members of Parliament.

1556. – Thomas Clouter, Mayor. Thomas Carew and John Yonge, Members. "Philip, King of Spain, landed at Plymouth, and dined with the Mayor and Corporation; the entertainment cost £300." "In this yere, the 7th day of June, was the warres proclaymed between the Ryalmes of England and France."

1557. – John Derry, Mayor. Humphry Speacot and Nicholas Slaning, Members. It is said that this is the year in which Philip, King of Spain, landed at Plymouth, and dined with the Corporation.

1558. – William Weekes, Mayor. "In this yere, the 12th day of April, was the peace proclaymed between the Realms of England, France and Scotlande."

1559. – Luke Cock, Mayor.

1560. – John Elliot, Mayor.

1561. – Edward White, Mayor. Another account says William Whitehaven. "William Lake was chosen but he dying the 10th Nov., Edward White was chosen instead of him."

The following payments, made this year by the Corporation, are highly interesting and curious.

"Extracts from the receipts and payments of the Receivours of the Mayor and Commonalty of the Borough of Plymouth, in the respective years mentioned in the margin.

		£	s	d
"1561. -	Item to my L. Busshoppe's players	0	13	4
	Item to Mr Fortescue's players	0	13	4
	Item to Mr Stidston for mendinge the foorde at Plymbridge	0	1	8
	Item to Mr Hawkins for moneye paide at Bristoll for inrollinge the Chartour ...	1	0	0
	Item to the Queen's players	1	0	6
	Item to a dinner given to the Lord Busshoppe	5	2	6
	Item to Mr Cook for the hier of his horse, when he rode to London	0	13	4
	Item for the Clocke with the charges in settinge uppe the same	6	13	4
	Item for takinge downe the howse in the churche yearde and for clensinge the same	0	6	8
	Item for a locke for the bulworcke door and for mendinge the school house door	0	3	4"

1562. – John Ford, Mayor. Sir Thomas Edmonds born at Plymouth. "At an early age, he appears to have been introduced to the court of James I, and speedily obtained the confidence of the King, being sent an ambassador to the Archduke of Brussels, and afterwards to France. On his recall from the latter appointment he became comptroller of the King's household, and afterwards treasurer, with the stewardship of the Marshalsea. He distinguished himself by his opposition to the views of the Catholic party. As a statesman he was able and polite, and his letters, which are preserved, show his ability as a writer." The following items are from this year's accounts of the Corporation: –

	£	s	d
Item to a Plumer for mendinge the lead in the Castell and Bulworcke	0	17	0
Item received for the rent of the Towne Mylles this yeare			
Item to a Helyar at the bulworcke	0	0	6
Item to cowpe for pynnynge the wall in the Castell	0	0	8
Item paid John Martyn for a dinner given to the Busshoppe's chancellor	1	5	4
Item paid for helynge stones for the Scholehowse ...			
Item paid to Mrs Lacye for a diner given to Sr Arthur Champnowne when he kept the Admyrall's Courte here	0	13	0
Item paide for the charges of fower men sent before the Comyssioners for the settinge furthe of him	0	2	6
Item given to Sir Parcvyall Hart's Plaiers	0	6	8

1563. – John Derry Mayor. Thomas Champernoun and William Periam, Members. The great massacre in France, at the marriage of the King of Navarre. A great plague in London. The following items are from the Corporation accounts of this year: –

	£	s	d
Item to the Erell of Warwicke ys pleers, the IX of June, for pleying	0	13	4
Item to the Mayor and Mr – with others for ryding to Plymton befor the comyssyon at the monster[s] ...	0	3	10
Item to the Queen's players	1	0	0
Item for a Throne for the towne	1	2	0
Item for the kayes of the Castell	0	1	11

1564. – Nicholas Stanning or Slaning, Mayor. The following are from the Corporation accounts of this year: –

	£	s	d
Item paid for carryinge of ten ordynance from the Haw, to Philipe Dingell ys howse … … … … … … … … … …	0	0	8
Item payed to the Erell of Worsetter's pleers … … …	0	13	4
Item payed for fatchynge of the ordinance from the Islonde …			
Item payed to John Waddon for a Maste for the Towne's Barge … … … … … … … … … … … … … … … … … …	0	6	8

1565. – Nicholas Pickford, Mayor. The following are from the Corporation accounts of this year: –

	£	s	d
Item paide for a dynner for Mr Southcote, Mr Shyverton, and Mr Gill syttinge in commyssion touchyn the dekaye of this towne, and other artycles touchyn the customer and controller … … … … … … … … …	0	10	0
Item paide for the passage of the 12 men that apered afore Sir Peter Carewe at Mounte Agcombe … … …	0	1	0
Item paide to 3 Brittons that were taken the 6th of January	0	2	0
Item paide to the foure boyes of Towne that played at the Mayor's … … … … … … … … … … … … … … … … …	0	5	0
Item paide to my Lord Munger's Pleyers … … … … …	0	13	4
Item paide to my Lord Hunsdon's Pleers … … … … …	0	13	4"

"There is a very long account of payments to workmen of all descriptions this year, and which evidently intimates that some large building was erected, and I am inclined to think it was the old Guildhall, because I observe charges for stone pillars, and this was the only building I can recollect where there were stone pillars used."

1566. – John Ilcomb, Mayor. The following interesting references to the Castle, to Minstrells, etc, occur in the Corporation accounts of this year: –

	£	s	d
Item paide to Players in the Churche upon Saint John is daye … … … … … … … … … … … … … … … … … …	0	6	8
Item paid to the Mynstrells and Dauncers uppon Maye daie for their dynners and drynkinge … … … … … …	0	6	8
Item paide for a dinner for the receivinge of the Quen'es Ambassador … … … … … … … … … … … … … … … …	1	0	0

	£	s	d
Item paide towarde the settinge fourth of Soldiours into Scotland … … … … … … … … … … … … … … … …	2	13	4
Item paied for mending the leades of the M'kett Cross	0	14	0
Item paied to Alse Lyell for my Lord Bushope's dynner	1	6	8
Item paied to the Cooke for the rostinge of the Meat	0	1	6
Item paied to Willm Flecher for fetheringe of ten Shiffe of Arrowes … … … … … … … … … … … … … …	0	8	8
Item paied for drynkinge when the ordynance was brought to the Hawe … … … … … … … … … … … …	0	2	8
Item paied to Mr Hawkins for fatchinge of the Ordynance from the Island to the Castell … … … … … … … …	2	0	0

"There is frequent mention made in this and preceding years of the expenses of repairing the pump; a thing of no small importance before the water was brought to the town."

1567. – William Hawkins, Mayor. "In this yere the Wache (Wake) on Mydsomer nyght was renewyead, which had not beene used in XX yeres before that tyme." The following are from the Corporation accounts of this year: –

	£	s	d
"Item, received of divers parsons inhabitinge with this Towne this yeare, not free … … … … … … … … … … …	3	1	4
Item recieved of Richard Filde of Plimpton, for his fyne for a forfeiture by him made, in sellinge of certeyne salt to a stranger this yeare and he himself a forryner also …	0	4	0
Item received of James Hampton for servinge of a wreyte that came from the Sheriff of the Shere, upon John Granger in breach of the liberties of the Towne … … …	0	3	4
Item paide to a man that broughte a letter from Mr Slannyinge concernygne the burgizes of the Parlyment	0	4	0
Item paide to one to cary the wryt that was indented to execs and to convaye hym to London … … … … … …	0	1	4
Item paid to Wm Flacher for trymynge of ten shevis of arrowes … … … … … … … … … … … … … … … … …	0	8	4
Item gave to the companny of Saint Budokes on May day	0	10	0
Item paide there to the Morysh Dauncers … … … … …	0	3	4

	£	s	d
Item paide for a breckfast for the Moryshe Dauncers pleers on May day… … … … … … … … … … … … …	0	5	0
Item paide to John Whyte of London for the Vicarage …	20	0	0
Item paide to Mr Slannynge for charges about the Vicarage … … … … … … … … … … … … … …			
Item paid to Wibber, Roberte, Kilburn and one more for dragging uppe of the planks for the gunnes … … … … … …	0	0	8
Item paide to Cawse and Crippe for drawing uppe of the Ordynance to the Hawe … … … … … … … … … … … …	0	1	0
Item paide for newe cuttinge of the Gogmagoge at the Hawe … … … … … … … … … … … … … … … … … …	0	0	8

"Several charges are inserted in this year's account for work upon the chaple."

1568. – Luke Cock, Mayor. "A regulation was this year made in the town for preventing ballast and filth from being thrown into Sutton Pool and other parts of the harbour; and a public functionary, named Robert Kilbourne, whose duty it was to "beat beggars out of the town," received for his service the handsome salary of ten shillings per annum." The following are taken from the Corporation accounts of this year: –

	£	s	d
"Item paid for a kaye for the Islande dore … … … … … …	0	1	4
Item paid for dressinge the Maye Pole … … … … … … … …	0	1	0
Item paid for rentinge of the Maye Pole… … … … … … … …	0	3	4
Item paid to the Morish Dawnsers on Maye day … … … …	0	4	0
Item paid to Kempe for the Maye Pole … … … … … … … …	0	3	4
Item paid to the Erle of Worcester's pleer … … … … … …	0	5	0
Item paid to Sir Harry Fortescue ys pleers … … … … … …	0	10	0
Item paid to Thoms Maynerde, of June, for charges about the benyfice … … … … … … … … … … … … … … … … … …	1	6	8

1569. – John Martin, Mayor. The new Conduit built by William Hawkins. The following are from the Corporation accounts of this year:

	£	s	d
"Item payed for mendynge the causse at Southside … …	0	8	0
Item payed for a rope for the bell upon the Hawe … … …	0	1	1

	£	s	d
Item payed to Feltwytt for 13 dayes to pulle downe the Ivey about the Castell Walles	0	6	6
Item payed at Stonehouse when Mr Maior and others met Mr Edgcomb aboute the Armour	0	0	8
Item paid for the dynner of Mr Edgcomb, Sir Arthur Champernowne, Knyght, Mr Strode, and other Commyssioners at the first Muster	0	19	4
Item payed to the souldioures that were sent into Irelonde	3	0	0
Item padyed to Robert Kylburn for one quarter, is wages, to beate the beggars out of town	0	2	6

"An account of the produce of the Tolls of the Market, from 1561, to this year: –

		£ s d	£ s d
1561. –	Market	1 12 0	7 2 7
	Shamells	4 15 4	
	Shamells	0 15 3	
1562. –	Market	1 10 0	6 17 10
	Shamells	4 8 10	
	Standings	0 19 0	

1563.	6 10 0	1567.	6 10 0
1564.	6 10 0	1568.	6 10 0
1565.	6 10 0	1569.	6 10 0"
1566.	6 10 0		

1570. – Gregory Cock, Mayor. The plague in Plymouth. "The first European settlers of Northern America, sailed from Plymouth, under Sir Humphrey Gilbert of Compton."

1571. – William Halloway or Holloway, Mayor. Sir Humphrey Gilbert and John Hawkins, (and afterwards John Hawkins and Edmund Tremain,) Members.

1572. – John Blyman or Blytheman, Mayor. "The Free School of Plymouth built, now known as the Corporation Grammar School; as also the quay on Southside from the Barbican northward, underneath the Castell, under full sea mark, in length 130 feet, and in breadth 44 feet." "On Whitsunday Eve, being the 24th May, Captain (afterwards Sir Francis) Drake, in the *Pascha* of Plimouth, of 70 tonnes, his admiral, with the

Swanne of Plimouth, 25 tonnes, vice-admiral, in which his brother John Drake was captain, having in both 73 men and boys, the eldest 50, all the rest under 30, so divided 47 on one, and 26 in the other, with victuals and apparel for a whole year, but especially having three dainty pinnaces made in Plimouth, taken asunder all in pieces and stowed aboard; set saile from out of the Sound of Plimouth, with intent to land at Nombre da Dios."

1573. – William Brooking, Mayor. "Captain (Sir Francis) Drake returned from his voyage on Sunday August 9, 1573, at what time the news of our captain's return brought unto his family, did so speedily passe over all the church, and surpasse their minds, with desire and delight to see him, that very few or none remained with the preacher, all hastening to see the evidence of GOD's love and blessing towards our Gracious Queen and countrey, by the fruite of our captain's labour and successe."

"On the 24th of May 1572, Sir Francis Drake and Thomas, his brother, sailed from Plymouth in two ships to attack the Spanish settlement in South America; they returned here on the 9th of August, 1573. It was on a Sunday, and so much were the people delighted, that they *left the preacher*, and ran in crowds to the quays with shouts and congratualtions. The quay "under the castell wall," whereof the southard adjoineth the Barbycan had just been built by the town for £141 3s 8d. (Yonge's M.S.) Its length was 130 feet, breadth 44 feet."

1574. – John Amadis, Mayor. Such a dearth, that wheat was £2 16s. a quarter; beef at Lammas 1s 10d a stone; 5 herrings so dear as 2d; bay salt never no dear, 6s. bushel; after harvest, wheat was 24s. per quarter, and so continued about a year.

1575. – Walter Peprill, Mayor. "Drake's success appears to have encouraged others to follow his example, for a Captain Oxenham left Plymouth in 1575, for the South Sea in a vessel of 140 tons burthen with a crew of 70 seamen. These small vessels appear to have carried one man for every two tons of measurement; that is, about ten times the number of men that are now found necessary."

1576. – John Illcomb, Mayor.

1577. – Gregory Maynard, Mayor. "Sir Francis Drake departs Plymouth on his voyage about the earth, 13th November, 1577, and having encountered a violent tempest, was obliged to return; the vessels composing his fleet, of which he was by the Queen constituted the Captain General, were –

The	Pelican	100 Tons	... ...	Admiral Drake
"	Elizabeth	80 "	... ...	Vice-Admiral John Winter
"	Marigold	30 "	... ...	John Thomas
"	Swan	50 "	... ...	John Chester
"	Christopher ...	15 "	... ...	Thomas Moche

The latter (Moche) was carpenter in Drake's former voyage."

"Drake having repaired the damages his fleet had suffered, again set sail from Plimouth the 13th Decr., 1557, on his voyage round the world." His own ship was the *Pelican.* Vessels were fitted out in Plymouth to trade from Guinea to the West Indies."

1578. – William Hawkins, Mayor. "The Governor's House and the Barbican builded."

"Sir Walter Raleigh joined Sir Henry Gilbert in the experimental establishment of a colony at Newfoundland. This endeavour failed, and Sir Walter returned to Plymouth." The Earls of Bedford and Northumberland and Lords Norton and Wharton, etc. visited Plymouth, and were entertained at the town's expense.

1579. – Gregory Cock, Mayor. The plague made sad ravages in Plymouth. It was "supposed to have been introduced with some cotton wool landed from a Smyrna ship, without being properly aired. Upwards of 600 fell victims to its ravages, and so general was the fear of its spreading, that the annual election of the mayor was held in the open air, on Catdown, at a distance from the scene of infection."

1580. – John Blithman, Mayor. The plague was so great in Plymouth, that this mayor was chosen on Catdown, 1600 persons died, a sign Plymouth was then but thinly peopled, and a small town.

"November 3, 1580, Sir Francis Drake returns from his voyage, and brought great treasure, the King of Spain seizeth the kingdom of Portugal, whose King came into England and lay awhile at Mount Edgcumbe."

"At Michelmasse came home Sir Francis Drake to Plymouth from the South Sea, and was round about the world two years and three-quarters, and brought home great store of gold and sylver in blockes, and was afterward in the same yere, for his good services in that behalf done, knighted. In this yere also, the south-west tower of the castell was newlie repaired, and covered with leade."

Sir Francis Drake returned from his voyage round the world, which had occupied him nearly three years. After a few days stay in Plymouth, he sailed for Deptford.

1581. – Sir Francis Drake, Mayor. He ordered a compass to be set up on the Hoe, which was there remaining in 1730. He also ordered that the regulation for the Corporation to wear scarlet robes should be observed. The plague again broke out in Plymouth, and continued several months, many of the inhabitants becomings its victims. The Queen dined on board the *Pelican*, at Deptford, with Sir Francis Drake.

"Sir Francis Drake was Mayor of Plymouth, and it is recorded that he 'set up the mariner's compass on the Hoe.' We must bear in mind that when Drake was mayor, the Town of Plymouth, small as it was, occupied the low shores of Sutton Pool, and that the Hoe then, as now, (although without the Citadel) afforded the best look-out position for all those interested about maritime affairs. Drake was a sharp and intelligent seaman, and must have done something more than is recorded in the Corporation Chronicles. Instead of merely setting up the mariner's compass on the Hoe, in 1582, I am of opinion he must have expended a part of his Spanish prize money in building a look-out house and place of shelter on the Hoe, where the compass, etc. was fixed; for I find that just 90 years after Sir Francis was mayor, there is this entry made in the Corporation accounts: "1672 – Sir F. Drake's compass on the Hoe repaired for £17 18s." What Drake did, in 1582, voluntarily, the Sutton Pool Company must now do by Act of Parliament. They are required to erect a tide wind and weather gauge for the information of mariners near the Barbican."*

1582. – Thomas Edmonds, Mayor. "Ale stakes put down, and signs set up; scarlet gowns first worn in Plymouth, by the Mayor and Court of Aldermen; the sluce made within the new keys; the spunging houses within the town put down. The market bushell made certain; double Winchester."

1583. – John Spark, Mayor. Sir Walter Raleigh engaged in prosecuting new discoveries, prevails on his friend, Sir Richard Grenville to join fortune with him, who sails hence to Virginia with 6 ships and 600 men. The result of this conjunction, was the discovery of Carolina and Virginia, in the year 1584, by two ships belonging to Sir Walter Raleigh and his company, commanded by Captain Philip Amidas and Captain Arthur Burlow. The account which these ships brought home of the country, its productions and inhabitants, induced the adventurers to endeavour the establishment of a settlement there." "The King of Portugal comes to Plymouth." Mr John White, of London, gave the Union Cup, value £13 6s 8d."

"Plymouth – A rate made for granaige and kaydidge within the borough aforesaid the xxth daie of September, in the xxvth yeare of the reigne of our Sovereigne Ladye, Queene Elizabeth, 1583.

*Captain Walker, Harbour Master.

"First. – It is agreed that every Merchante being no Townesman, shall pay for kaydage and granaige for every tonne	vj*d*
And if they lande or lade any Merchandize without the same, then to pay for every tonne	iiij*d*
And every Merchante that shall lade or unlade any merchandize, namely salt, and sold, shall pay for every tonne accompting xxiiij bushells to the tonne	j*d*
And every Merchante that shall lade or unlade any fardell of cloth, shall paye	j*d*
And for every paire of Cornish tyn	j*d*
And for every paire of Devonshire tyn	ob.
And for all kynde of graine as also beans and peas, shall pay for every tonne	ij*d*
And all inhabitants of the Towne, not being free, and using merchandizes, shall to paye for all merchandizes, as every is appoyntede to paye.	

1584. – Charles Brooking, Mayor. "The Queen undertakes the protection of the Hollanders. The Barbican stairs built; the Queen gives a rent of £39 10s 10d. for the maintenance of the Island. Sir Francis Drake goes for the West Indies, September 14th, with 24 ships and barks, 20 pinnaces, and 3,000 men. Sir Richard Grenville, Knight, departed from Plymouth with 6 shippes and barks, and 600 men.

"In September, 1584, Don Antonio, King of Portugal being driven out of his own kingdom by Philip, King of Spain, landed here from Lisbon, was entertained by the mayor, and proceeded on to Exeter."

"The Corporation claim a right, and appoint the Governor of Saint Nicholas' Island, and the Queen allows £39 10s 10d per annum as rent and for repairs. The old Barbican stairs were built. On the 14th September, 1585, this entry was made: "Sir Francis Drake sails for the West Indies with 24 ships, 20 pinnaces, and 3000 men, whom God preserve."

1585. – Thomas Ford, Mayor. Tobacco first brought into England. Henry Bromley and Christopher Harris, Members for Plymouth. "Sir Richard Grenville voyages to Virginia for Sir Walter Raleigh. April 9th. He departed from Plymouth with seven sayle, the chief men with him in command were Masters Ralph Layne, Thomas Candish (Cavendish), Jno.

Arundell, Master Stukely, Bremize, Vincent, Heryot, and Jno. Clarke. The General on his way home, took a rich loaden ship, of 300 tons, and arrived at Plymouth, 18th Sept., 1585. The first planting of Virginia on America."

"Sir Richard Granville, after his return from his expedition to Virginia, fixed his residence at Bideford, in the North of Devon, and brought with him an Indian, who was baptized in Bideford Church, by the name of Rawleigh, in honour of the brave and learned Sir Walter Rawleigh, Sir Richard Granville's kinsman and companion, on Sunday, March 26th, 1588. This Indian, however, did not live much above a year after, for he was buried in Bideford Churchyard, April 7th, 1589. He is entered in the parish Register, as a native of Wynganditoia."*

1586. – George Mainard, Mayor. Henry Bromley and Hugh Vaughan, Members for Plymouth. "Sir Francis Drake, General of Her Majesty, with 12 ships, sails from Plymouth, 3rd April, and burnt many of the King of Spain's ships, at Cadiz, that were preparing for the invasion, took a great carrick of 1,000 tons, laden with spices and brought her home." "Corn scarce through the kingdom, yet notwithstanding, by the help of God, the inhabitants of the town were sufficiently relieved. The judges come to see the town."

"On the 3rd of April, 1586, Drake left Plymouth, in command of 4 men-of-war, 12 merchant ships, with many small barks and pinnaces, to cruize against the Spaniards, on their own coasts. He greatly annoyed them, burning many ships and capturing 'a great carrick', of 1,000 tons burthen, laden with spices. The Spaniards were, at this time, preparing their Armada for the invasion of England. When Drake was cruizing against the Spaniards, (and just three days after Drake left Plymouth), the Mayor and Commonalty resolved that a Scottish ship, then lying in Sutton Pool and laden with rice, should be sold for the benefit of the poor! Whilst the Spaniards were sending forth their colonies and preparing their armaments, Plymouth, from its admirable hydrographical advantages and geographical position, was gradually brought into notice; for it was from Plymouth that the predatory expeditions of Drake, the Earl of Cumberland, Raleigh, Cavendish, and others took their departures."†

1587. – William Hawkins, Mayor. "Mary Queen of Scots beheaded. The Queen's fleet of 120 sail, under command of the Lord Howard, Sir Francis Drake, and Hawkins arrive at Plymouth. Went to meet the Armada July 21st; the following Sunday, appear before the harbour."

"Flemming the noted pyrate, although sought for, to be hung, as his companions Clinton and Pursser were, by order of Queen Elizabeth; yet such

*Watkins' History of Bideford, Svo, 1792. (see reprint Edward Gaskell *publishers*, Bideford 1993)
†Captain Walker, Harbour Master.

a friend was he to his country, that discovering the Spanish Armada, he voluntarily came to Plimouth, yielded himself freely to my Lord Admirall, and gave him notice of the Spaniards comming, which good warning came so happily and unexpectedly, that he had his pardon and a good reward."

1588. – Humphrey Fownes, Mayor. Miles Saunders and Reginald Nichols, Members for Plymouth. "Best beef 1d per lb. Christmas, 1588, wheat 2s 8d., barley 1s 8d., oats 11d; before the end, wheat 3s. to 4s 5d., rye 1s 6d., barley 1s. 6d. per bushell." "The Spanish Armada invades England and is destroyed." One account of this Armada says: –

"This yere Her Majestie's shippes, 2 pinnaces and 180 sail of merchant shippes, go in warlike manner to the Coaste of Spain, under the command and direction of Sir Jno. Norris, Kt. and Sir Francis Drake, Kt., Lords Generalls, they took diverse places of force in Spayne, but having a great sicknesse happening amongst theire men, they returned without enteringe into the Cytie of Lisbon, to which place theire chief bent was, yet entered they the subburbes and tooke it, and came to the gate of the cytie, where it was said the Right Honorable the Lord of Essex knocked with such instrument as he had in his hand." Another account says: –

"The Spanish Armada, or fleet, consisted of 132 sail of large ships, 20 caravals for conveying their artillery and stores, and 10 small vessels of six oars each, having on board 8,766 sailors, 2,088 galley slaves, 21,855 soldiers, and 3,165 pieces of cannon, (these were to be joined by the Prince of Parma, on their arrival off the English Coast, with 30,000 foot and 1,800 horse), set sail from Corunna; but meeting with a violent storm, were obliged to put back, notice of which being obtained by the English fleet, then cruizing at the mouth of the British Channell to intercept their passage, they returned into Plymouth, and thinking the danger over for that year, began to dismantle their ships; the Spaniard however, soon repaired their damages, and again set sail for the English Coasts; but being happily descried by Captain Winter, who commanded a small Scottish privateer, he hastened to Plymouth, and gave notice to the English commanders of the approach of the Spanish fleet. The contrary winds prevented the English fleet from coming out harbour, and the Spaniards proceeded up channell, (their fleet being drawn up in the form of a crescent,) and passing Plymouth, continued their voyage under a slow and easy sail in sight of the inhabitants, who were posted at the most accessible parts of the coast, to prevent their descent. The English, having with difficulty warped their ships out of Plymouth, followed them with a much inferior force, while the gentlemen of Devonshire greatly exerted themselves by fitting out all the ships they could procure, and hastening to join the English fleet, where they behaved themselves with the greatest intrepidity, and contributed highly to the success which followed. The Prince of Parma was prevented, by the vigilance of the English and Dutch squadrons, from joining the Spanish forces, in consequence of which, and meeting with several defeats, the Spaniards endeavoured to escape homewards round the north of Scotland and Ireland, where so many of their ships were lost, as out of the whole which left Spain, only 97 returned, and most of their crews were lost. The loss of the English was only one ship and about 100 men; thus the despotic designs of the Spanish Monarch to subjugate this nation and extirpate the Protestant religion was frustrated, through the providence of the Almighty, and the bravery of our ancestors. Among the Devonshire worthies, who distinguished themselves on this glorious occasion, were Sir Francis Drake, Sir Martin Gilbert, Sir Walter Raleigh, Sir Robert Carey, Knight, and Edward Fulford, Esq., then Sheriff for the County of Devon." And another account thus speaks: –

"This year the Spanish Armada appeared before Plymouth Sound, the Sunday before St. James' Day, in half moon form, lay too in sight of the Haw, and Mount Edgcumbe and Penlee Point for two days, and then made sail to the eastward. The Duke de Medina the Spanish Admiral, was so enraptured with the beauties of Mount Edgcumbe, that he parcelled it out for himself, in the division of lands. Sir Francis Drake sailed from the Sound, joined the Exeter ships, and the defeat soon ensued in the narrow seas.* There is a picture of their situation in Mount Egcumbe House."

On the 19th of July, says Macfarlane, one Fleming, a Scottish pirate or privateer, sailed into Plymouth with intelligence that he had seen the Spanish fleet off the Lizard. At the moment most of the captains and officers were on shore, playing at bowls on the Hoe. There was an instant bustle and a calling for the ships' boats, but Drake insisted that the match should be played out, as there was plenty of time both to win the game and beat the Spaniards. Unfortunately the wind was blowing hard in their teeth, but they contrived to warp out their ships. On the following day, being Saturday, the 20th of July, they got a full sight of the Armada standing majestically on – the vessels being drawn up in the form of a crescent, which, from horn to horn, measured some seven miles. Their great height and bulk, though imposing to the unskilled, gave confidence to the English seamen, who reckoned at once upon having the advantage of tacking and manoevering their lighter craft. At first it was expected that the Spaniards might attempt a landing at Plymouth, but the Duke of Medina adhered to the plan which had been prescribed to him, and which was to steer quite through the channel till

*Captain Cocke a native of Plymouth was killed in this fight.

THE SPANISH ARMADA
(From the Tapestry in the House of Lords; as engraved by the Society of Antiquaries.)

he should reach the coast of Flanders where he was to raise the blockade of the harbours of Nieuport and Dunkirk, maintained by the English and Dutch, make a junction with the Duke of Parma, and bring that prince's forces with him to England. Lord Howard (the Admiral) let his pass, and then followed in his rear, avoiding coming to close quarters, and watching with a vigilant eye, for any lucky accident that might arise from cross winds or irregular sailing. And soon a part of the Spanish fleet was left considerably astern by the main division, where the Duke of Medina kept up a press of sail, as if he had no other object in view but to get through the channel as fast as possible. He made signals to the slower ships to keep up, which they could not, and he still kept every sail bent. The *Disdain*, a pinnace, commanded by Jonas Bradbury, now commenced an attack by pouring a broadside into one of the laggards. Lord Howard, in his own ship, the *Ark Royal*, engaged a great Spanish galleon, and Drake, in the *Revenge*, Hawkins, in the *Victory* and Frobisher, in the *Triumph*, ranging up gallantly, brought into action all the galleons which had fallen astern. The Rear-Admiral, Recaldo, was with this division, and fought it bravely; but his lumbering ships lay like logs upon the water, in comparison with the lighter vessels of England, which were manageable, and in hand, like well-trained steeds. Before any assistance could come from the van, one of the great Spaniards was completely crippled, and another – a treasure ship with 55, 000 ducats aboard – was taken by Drake, who distributed the money amongst the sailors. The Duke of Medina hove to, till the slower ships came up, and then all of them, under press of sail, stood farther up the channel. This first brush gave great spirit to the English, and there were in it several encouraging circumstances. It was seen, for example, that the tall Spanish ships could not bring over the English without touching them: and the surer fire of the latter told with terrific effect on those huge ships, crammed with men – soldiers and sailors. Howard returned towards Plymouth, where he was to be joined by forty sail. In the course of the night one of the greatest Spanish ships was burned, purposely, it is said, by a Flemish gunner on board. It was a dark night with a heavy sea, and some of the Spaniards ran foul of each other, to their great mischief. On the 23rd, Howard, who was reinforced, and who had received into his division, Sir Walter Raleigh, came up with the whole Armada off Portland, when a battle began, which lasted nearly the whole day. The engraving we give of the Armada, of the ultimate fate of which we need give no further particulars, is copied from the Tapestry in the House of Lords, and is one of the best and most faithful representations extant. For its loan we are indebted to the courtesy of Messrs. Blackie, to whom we shall have occasion again to refer.

After the Armada had been defeated, Drake's Island was strengthened; and the old castle, while beetled over the Barbican, had seven small brass pieces placed on its platform, and Drake left Plymouth with an expedition to restore the King of Portugal – but without success."

SIR FRANCIS DRAKE
From a picture belonging to the Marquess of Lothian.

1589. – John Blithman, Mayor. "The town agreed with Sir Francis Drake to bring in the water of the River Meve, and gave him £200 in hand, and £600 for which he is to compound with the owners of the land over which it runneth." "April 18th – Sir John Norris and Sir Francis Drake sail from Plymouth with the King of Portugal, to endeavour to restore him, but could not; they came to the gates of Lisbon."

"The fifth voyage to Virginia, 1589. March 20th, three ships sayle from Plymouth, undertaken by Capt. John Whyte, Captains Spicer and Skinner, and five of the chiefest men were drowned, and the plantation of Virginia abandoned. Wheat 8s., rye 6s., barley 5s. 4d., in August, wheat 10s., rye 2s. 8d., barley 2s. 3d."

"This yere the north-west tower of the Castell was covered with leade, and 7 brass pieces was likewise planted upon the IV Castles. The gate at Cocksyde, which is to be shutte every night, was now made, and the great plateform by the gate at the Hawe, and the wall near the same conteyning 257 fote, was now newly made. Two demy-culverins and two whole culverins of iron mounted at the Barbican and bulwarks." "Don Antonio, illegitimate nephew of the king of Portugal, arrived at Plymouth with Sir Francis Drake. He lived as a refugee at Mount Edgcumbe. The plague still at Plymouth, the mayor being in consequence, again elected on Catdown."

1590. – Walter Pepperill, Mayor. "About this time divers platforms on the Hoe began to be methodized into a regular fortification, which was afterward the Fort of Plymouth." It is said that in this year, and not the preceding one, it was that the town agreed with Sir Francis Drake to bring in the water of the river Mewe or Meve, "which being in length about 25 myles, he with great care and diligence, effected and brought the river into the town the 24th day of April then next after. Presently after he sett in hand to build six great mills, two at Widey in Egg Buckland parish, the other four by the towne; the two at Widey and the two next the towne he fullie finished before Michaelmas next after, and ground corn with them."

1591. – John Spark, Mayor. "In December, 1590, Sir Francis Drake began on the rivulet, and brought it into the town 25 miles, the 24th of April following, and before Michaelmas he built six mills, two at Widey and four at the town, also divers conduits." "The Earl of Cumberland brings a rich carrick into Dartmouth; another account says Plymouth.' Provisions very dear this year; peas and beans in their cods 12s. a bushell; at Whitsunday, for a heifer that had newly calved £6 6s. 8d., *i.e.* 19 nobles.

"Copy of a petition to Queen Elizabeth from the Mayor and Inhabitants, touching the Fort then erecting here, 33, Elizabeth, 1591. –

"Most gracious Sovereign, we your Majestie's most humble subjects, being neither worthy of that most princely love, and gracious care, your sacred Majesty ever hath had of the good preservation both of our Towne, and of ourselves, nor yet being able to deserve the same, doe most humbly pray the Everlasting, everlastingly to continue your Majestie's most prosperous and flourishing estate. And whereas (most gracious Sovereigne) it hath been adjudged by men of good sufficiencie, that the finishing of the Fort here, will stand your Majesty, or any other that shall undertake to accomplish the same, at the least rate, viijc*li*; and that the intertaynement of a commander, with his band of 100 men, for the guard of the same, will amount unto little less than vijc*li* by the yeare. We your humble subjects in regard of your Majestie's service, and the preservation of our own libertie, will undertake as well to finish the Forte, at our own charges, as also to maintayne a well experyenced commander, with a sufficient garrison in the same, so it will please your Majestie to give unto us but viijc*li.* towards the perfecting of the same Forte, with some munition, artillerie, and powder, nowe at first, and to grant unto us the whole impost of the pilchards, with allowance of vjc*li* yearly, out of your customes here or elsewhere, towards the intertaynment of our garrison and commander, whom we most humblie crave maie be Mr Arthur Champernowne, your Majestie's servant, a gentleman well known to your Majesty and their honours, whom we desire to be under us commander, as well in respect that himself with his dearest friends and himself, are our nerest neighbours, whose sufficiencie in martial affaires is well known unto us; as also because he is both very neigh allyed unto the best of Devon and Cornwall, and likewise is well-beloved of them and the rest of our countrie, which said causes may be better means to draw the gentleman and countrie forces more speedy repair unto our succour (next under God and your Majesty,) depends the only preservation and defence of our Towne and ourselves, from the force and violence of an obstinate and forcible enemy, against whom the Fort can defend but itself, and not our Towne.

"Thus most humbly submitting our Towne, goodes, and lives unto your Majestie's due and most gracious consideration, we rest your Majesty, loyal and obedient, the Maior and poor inhabitants of the Town of Plymouth."

1592. – John Gear, Mayor. "The fort built on the Hoe Cliffs." Sir Francis Drake and Robert Bassett, Esq., Members for Plymouth.

1593. – John Phillips, Mayor. "The gallery was begun in the Old Church about this time. The cage of five new bells were cast for Plymouth Church in the Workhouse. Four gates set up in the town." "This yere the two judges of the circuit came hither to see the town and were honourably entertayned."

"A letter from the Lords of the Council to the Customers, and Officers of the Customs here, not to take entries until the impositions on pilchards be paid. –

"To all Customers, Comptrollers and all others, officers of the several Portes of Devon and Cornwall.

"Whereas we are sensiblie informed that the intended Fortifications at Plymouth, being thought verie requisit speedily unto our relief, in time of danger, whose and needful, for the better defence of the western parts of Devon and Cornwall, against any attempt to be made by the enemy, are of late greatly hindered and slack, by reason that the customs on pilchards was not paid the last year, at any other port than at Plymouth, as was meant and required by Her Majesty's commissioners, and other lords in this behalfe ernestlie writen; the strangers and others usualie repairing to such portes to take in their loading, where they might pass customs free, to the great prejudice of that Towne of Plymouth, and the hindrance of Her Majestie cruise in the .... of that country; for the better preventing whereof Her Majestie, having now granted to the finishing of this Fortification, under the great seall of this realm, the benefit of the customs of the pilchards of those western partes; we have thought it very expedient, hereby to require and charge you the Customers, and other the officers of the portes of Devon and Cornwall, verie strictlie in Her Majestie's name, not to take or suffer any entries of pilchards to be taken or made, at any the portes, breaks or places under your several jurisdictions until theis impositions be severally paid. But from time to time to use your best endeavours for the speedy collecting thereof, according to the tenor of the said grant, and other former, that this work may be speedily finished, to Her Majestie's good liking. So requiring you to take knowledge hereof by this bearer, and to see the premises duly performed at your peril; we bid you farwell. From the Court at Windsor Castle, the xxij day of August 1593. (*Signed*) – W. BURGHLY, ESSEX, HOWARD, RO. CECYLL, J. WILLEY, HUNSDON.

1594. – George Barnes, Mayor. "Sir Francis Drake and Sir John Hawkins went to the West Indies, with 33 sayle of shippes and pinnaces, and both died in the journey. Sir Nicholas Clifforde slaine. The fort which the Spaniards made at Croyden by Brest, taken and rased by Sir John Norris, Knight, Generall of the Armye."

The following is a letter from Sir Francis Drake, respecting some building near the Fort, 36, Elizabeth, 20th January, 1594. –

"After my verie heartie comendations unto you all, you shall understand that touching the matter between your Townes and Mr Strode, Mr Sparke hath done as much therein, as if many more of you had been there, could possibly have been done; for he hath not onlie stood in answeare of the cause at the Councill Board, but he also laboured all the cheife lords aparte, and yet upon examination of the matter, the lords said they saw no great reason to prohibit him to build upon his own lande, and to have the benefit of the lawe. Notwithstanding upon Mr Sparke's earnest allegations to the contrarie, their lordships considered to grant a comission to be directed unto the judges of .... to Sir John Gilbert, myselfe and some others, to the end we maie consider whether it be lawful and expedient to have any building between the two forts, and it be thought allowable, they are to lymitt how far into the water the same shall extend. For your other matter of the fort (which in my opinion) doth concerne you much neerer, doubt not but whilst I am here I shall stoppe itt, which in four or five days I shall be able to write you thereof more at large; and then if you sende some bodie up to sollicyte your suit in that behalfe, whilst Sir John Hawkins and myselfe are here together, I surely hope to get the government confirmed in the Towne; and soe in haste doe bid you hearilie farewell, from Dowgate, the 20th January, 1594.

Your assured lovinge friend,

FRAN. DRAKE."

1595. – James Bagg, Mayor. This year is especialy memorable in the annals of Devonshire by the death of its two greatest admirals, Sir Francis Drake and Sir John Hawkins, who both died of sickness and vexation in the course of their very unsuccessful expedition to Spanish America. Having previously given a portrait of Drake, we now below add that of Hawkins, who was as brave and good a seaman as Elizabeth or any other sovereign possessed.* He was father of another brave admiral, Sir Richard Hawkins. "The expedition under the Earl of Essex, for Cadiz; they sail from hence viz. Plymouth, in June, 1595." "This yere the Earl of Essex, my Lord Admirall and many other earls, knights, gentlemen, and others, took Cadiz in Spain, ryffled the town, and burnt some part of itt, also set on fyer a fleete of shippes, there ryding at anchor, whereof one was the Saint Phillip, Admyrall of Spayne, and brought away two of the Kinge's great shippes, viz. – the Saint Mathewe and the Saint Andrewe; also many were knighted by the Earle; and in this yere the Spannyards won Callys from the Frenche. Sir Ferdinando Gorges appointed captayne of the fort."

ADMIRAL SIR JOHN HAWKINS
From the "Heroolgia."

*For these portraits, from that truly admirable work the "Comprehensive History of England," we are indebted to the courtesy of Messrs. Blackie and Son. As we are also for that of the Spanish Armada. Of the "Comprehensive History of England," it is impossible too speak to highly. It is a truly admirable work.

1596. – Humphrey Fownes, Mayor. Wheat sold at 30s. per bushell, Plymouth measure; and barley, 12s. The gallery finished and the churchyard enclosed.

"The Maior and others of the Town's Men to the Towne's use, brought fower Shippes laden with rye out of Danske, to the great comfort and raleyffe, not onlye of the Town's people, but also of the counties of Devon and Cornwall, who came from the furthest parts of Devon for the same." "Sundrie parts of the town fortified with Barracks and the Gates made." "Wheat 10s., 12s., 15s.; barley 8s., 12. 6d.; oats 3s. 8d The Earl of Bath, by order from the council, fixed at Barnstaple a standard price. Any one selling above this price to suffer duress." – (Yonge's Diary).

"To all Christian people to whom this present wrytynge shall come. – The Maior and Commonaltie of the Borroughe of Plymmouthe send greeting; know ye vs the said Maior and Commonaltie for dyverse causes vs movynge to have bargayned, solde, assigned, sett over and departed with, and by theise presents do bargayne, selle, assigne, sett over and departe with to John Sparke of Plymmouthe, Merchaunte, and his assignes, all suche goodes, cattalls, and chattalls as sometyme were the proper goodes, cattalls and chattalls of William Sparke of Plymmouthe, Merchaunte, and by vs latelie seazed on as goodes forfeited, and soe to vs accrewynge by means that the said William Sparke was lately outelawed, and in that state yet standeth, together with all other righte, estate, title, and intereste of in and to the premises, and all deeds and wrytynges which concerne the same. To have and to holde to the said John Sparke, his executors and assignes, in as large and ample manner to all ententes as we mighte, oughte, or shoulde enjoyed the same if these presents had never been made. In witness whereof we the said Maior and Commonaltie have hereunto sett our Comon Seale. Dated the xiij daie of Julie, in the nyne and thirtyeth yere of the raigne of our Soueraigne Lady Elizabeth, by the Grace of Godd of Englande, France, and Irelande, Queene, Defender of the Faith."

1597. – John Trelawney, Mayor. Warwick Hele and William Stafford, Members for Plymouth. The conduit at Foxhole Quay built. "This yere Callys delivered agayne to the French King by composition, and all other towns which the Spannyards had in France. In Tiverton, 300 howses, and in Barnstaple, 30, burnt. Many soldiers shipped out of this port into Irelande."

1598. – John Blithman, Mayor. James Bagg and William Stallenge, Merchants, Members for Plymouth. "Martin White was elected mayor, but he dying, John Blithman succeeded him. This year our west country were apprehensive of the Spaniards, and therefore made gates, barricadoes, etc., and had 4,000 men and some horse, under command of the Earl of Bath."

"This yere a grete rebellyon in Irelande by the Earle of Tyrone, the Earle of Essex being there, but could not suppress them; many gallant gentlemen, knightes and others slayne, and fower hundred souldiers shipped from this port into Ireland." "The Earle of Bathe and his forces remayned here about three weeks, and were all lodged and entertayned to the great comforte and encouragement of the towne and country, who (if itt pleased God that the enemye should land) were then ready and willing to fighte."

The following letter relates to a bequest made to the town by Sir John Hawkins: –

"A letter from the Town Council to the Recorder, Mr Sergeant Hele."

"Right Worshipful, after our heartie commendation, Sir John Hawkyns, Knight, deceased, (as we understande) by his last will and testament, gave unto the poor of the Towne of Plymouthe, fiftie pounds in monie, and an annual rente of tenne pounds, issuinge and goinge out of his lands in Plymouthe, for ever. We understande also by Mr Hughe Vaughan, who is one of them that is putt in truste, to see the said will performed, that there shall be some course taken for the payment of the monie, and assurance to be given for the said annuytie, who wished us to appoint one to be unite with them this terme for the same. Whereupon we have appointed them this terme for the same. Whereupon we have appointed this bringer, Matthew Boys at attende theym therein, and withall, given him directions to take your worship's orders in all things, that he shall doe in that behalfe, whom we praie you likewise to aide and assist as the cause shall require, and we will reste moste thankful unto your worshipe for the same. So wishing your worshipe all healthe and prosperitie, most heartilie take our leave. Plymouthe the xxvth daie of January, 1598.

Your worship's loving friend,
JOHN BLYTHEMAN, Maior
of Plymouthe, and his brethren."

1599. – Richard Hitching's Mayor. "A new charter granted, the quondam Mayor to be justice of peace the following year." "This yere a petition was delivered to Her Majestie by the hand of Julius Caesar, one of the Masters of Request for the renewing of our charter, and that the Mayor should be of the quorum, and his immediate predecessor in office, justice of peace for the year following, with some other additions, which Her Majestie most graciouslye graunted, and willed it to be delivered to my Lord Keeper and Her Majestie's Attorney to draw the booke." "My Lord Maior's sonne, of London, named Anthony Mosley, bought a small number of hydes (within our liberties) of another Londoner, which our escheator seized, and uppon request made by sondrie of his friendes, being a townesman, he had his hydes again for the fyne of fyve poundes." "One Francis Parrott and Abraham Colmer, of London, Merchants, had likewise certayne gynger seized by the escheator, as forren boughte and forren solde, and uppon like entreatie, hadd it delivered backe for a fyne of tenne pounds."

"A great controversie risen through wrongs offered to the town by Mr Crymas's touching the river."

1600. – Thomas Pain, Mayor. "Twenty-two chests of Pope's bulls, pardons, etc. burnt in Plymouth Market-place, the 15th of December, by order from Her Majestie's High Commissioners for ecclesiastical purposes."

"This yere our charter was renewed with some farther addytions then were before contayned in the said charter, amongst which, the precedent Maior shall be a justice of the peace that yere next following his maioralty, and the Maior and Recorder for the time being to be of the quorum." The charter here alluded to, as granted by Queen Elizabeth, confirmed all the previous charters, and gave the following privileges: –

"Firstly – That the Mayor and Recorder, and last Mayor, if living, to be justices of the peace within the precincts of the said borough, and two of them, whereof the Mayor or Recorder be one, to enquire of, and punish all offences, except murder, felony, or any other matter which concerns loss of life or member, and that none other justice of the peace enter or meddle with any offences arising there.

"Secondly – To have all fines, forfeitures, amerciaments, and issues, lost or forfeited within the said borough, to their own use without let or accompt to be given.

"Thirdly – To have a prison and gaol there to keep such as should happen to be taken, attached, or apprehended for any offences, contempts or delinquencies, so that such prisoners as the Mayor, Recorder, or the Mayor's last predecessor could not reasonably deliver, might be delivered by the justices of assize according to the law.

"Fourthly – To make as many Burgesses as they should think fit, and the Mayor and Commonalty, or the major part of them, to meet together in the Guildhall and thereto counsel, confer and advise of all statutes, articles and ordinances, which might concern the said borough and good government thereof, according to their directions.

"Fifthly – That the Mayor and twelve of the chief Burgesses or Magistrates, or the major part of them, calling to them four and twenty more of the better and discreetest merchants or free inhabitants of the said borough, if they would be present with the assent of the Mayor and major part of the 12 Magistrates and merchants aforesaid, to have power to make such laws, statutes, ordinances, and constitutions, which in the discretions of them, or the major part of them, should be thought good, profitable, wholesome, honest, and necessary for the government of the said borough and inhabitants thereof, and for declaring in what manner and order they should behave and govern themselves, and otherwise for the better victualling of the said borough, and disposing or granting of the lands and hereditaments, granted or given or thereafter to be given or granted to the said Mayor and Commonalty, and all other things and causes concerning the said borough, state rights or intents therof, and the same laws to alter or confirm, if cause require, and to impose or levy such fines or penalties by corporal punishment or amerciament upon such deliquents as should break those laws, as they should think meet, and the same to levy by distress or actions of debt to their own use; so as the said laws and constitutions should not be contrary to the laws, statutes, customs, or rights of the realm of England.

"Sixthly – To choose and name officers, such and so many for the better government of the said borough, as they should think fit, as formerly they had done.

"Seventhly – That no foreigner, not being a burgess of the said borough, should sell any wares or merchandizes within the said borough other than in gross, or in the time of fairs and markets as they had formerly used, and the same merchandize and victuals not to be sold before they were placed and set in the public and usual places for buying and selling there.

"Eighthly – The said Mayor and his successors to be Clerk of the Market within the borough, and so and execute all things thereunto belonging as theretofore.

"Ninthly – The Mayor for the time being, to be escheater within the precincts of the said borough, during his mayoralty, and to do and execute all that belongs to the office, but to take his corporal oath before the old Mayor, for the well executing the offices of clerk of the market and escheator before he execute the said offices, as was formerly used in the same borough, so that no escheator might come there but in default of the Mayor.

"And all liberties, customs, privileges, immunities, etc., which the said Mayor and Commonalty have ever received, either by the grant of the former Kings, etc., or by whatsoever other lawful means, right, custom, use, prescription, or title theretofore held, used and accustomed."

1601. – William Parker, Mayor. "Smart's Quay built. A great East India carrick prize, sunk between the Island and main." "Sir Richard Hawkins returns from the South Sea, where he had been kept a prisoner eight or nine years by the Spaniards."

"This yere Sir Richard Luson went out of this harborough, the 13th of March, with VI of Her Majestie's shippes and two others made ready to followe, which did so, and on the 23rd of June, 1602, he arrived here with a carricke that he had taken, which came out of the East Indies, laden with commodities of that country, and in March followinge was sonke between the Island and the mayne."

1602. – John Martin, Mayor. The conduit at East Gate built and also that at the Barbican. "King James of Scotland, on the last day of March, 1602, was proclaimed at the Market Crosse here in Plymouth, to be King of England, which proclamation was read by Sergeant Hele, our late Queen's Sergeant-at-Lawe, and was proclaimed by John Luxton, our Town Clarke, at which time here was great triumphe with bonfires, gunnes, and ringing of bells, with other kind of musicke,"

1603. – Sir Richard Hawkins, Mayor. Sir Richard Hawkins and James Bagg, Merchants, Members of Parliament for Plymouth. The Plymouth Garrison expenses amounted to £2 16s. per diem, or £1,022 per annum.

1604. – Walter Mathews, Mayor. "This Mathews was servant to Sir Richard, as was his wife to the Lady Hawkins, who disdaining to sit below one that had been her maid, endeavoured to keep the upper hand, which the other attempting, the lady struck her a box on the ear. It made great disturbance, at length it was composed, and Sir Richard gave the town a house somewhere in Market-street for satisfaction."

"This yere the Maior buylded a newe cundict by the great tree at Brittayne-side, at his own costs and charges."

"Anno Domini 1604, was the greatest pestilence in London ever known or heard of by any man living. There died above 3,000 weekly. The pestilence reached to Exeter."

1605. – James Bagg – Mayor. "The King of Denmark cometh into England. The Guildhall of Plymouth built by the town and the Old Shambles." An Admiralty Court was held on the Barbican quay.

The erection of the Guildhall and the Flesh Shambles were commenced this year by the town. – "The charges of building the Guildhall and Flesh Shambles, and for redeeming of Thomas Sanders and Miles Waterford's two houses, by the Church Stile, amount in all to £794 8s 0d."

"The Guildhall was erected on arches, under which, and around the building, the butter and poultry market was held, and in an enclosed court behind it were collected the corn market and the vegetable market to the great annoyance of all passengers, there being on the market days scarcely a possibility of passing, and great was the clamour and dire the confusion that prevailed. But to return to the edifice, the Hall was ascended by a flight of seventeen steps, and hence arose a local bye-word – if any one was acting illegally either by the commission of any crime, or the incurrence of debt, it was said that he would soon ascend the seventeen steps. The open stair-case was in a tower which projected into the street and rendered it extremely narrow; over the landing place was a Council chamber, (which will be presently referred to,) and this was surrounded by a cupola containing a clock.

THE OLD GUILDHALL
As it existed at the end of the last century, (from an old view).

"On entering the Hall, at the western end of it were erected the seats for the Mayor and other Magistrates, and various members of the Corporation, and outside the bar the remainder of the Hall was left open for the inhabitants. At the eastern end of it another stair-case led to the Council chamber which was a small room partly over the Hall and partly in the tower. In this room, the deliberative meetings of the 12 and 24 took place, and here too, unfortunately were the archives of the corporate body kept in a place unfit for their preservation. Out of the Hall, at the western end was the entrance to the debtor's prison, and beyond it another apartment where criminals were confined, or detained prior to commitment for any heinous offence; below, and entered by the side of the steps were two dungeons, one called the *clink*, whose reputation has long survived its existence, and children are still told they shall be sent to the clink as a place of terror. The other prison was a low room for the confinement of all offenders, having free intercourse with the passers-by. Such was the "Old Guildhall" and its appendages. One custom that prevailed, on which some of the old inhabitants still love to dwell in their reminiscences of olden times, was this – the space under the Hall was duly cleaned after the market on Saturday evening, in order to prepare it as a fit promenade for all that was dignified and powerful in the corporate body on the Sunday morning, prior to their attendance at public worship. Here under each arch stood an halberdier with his ensign of office extended, whilst the dignified great ones paced up and down until the wonted signal was given for the procession to form itself." In 1800 the "Old Guildhall" was taken down. In the lapse of the two centuries, from time of its erection, "many eminent men must have made their appearance in the Old Guildhall, and some important events must have taken place: in that building, the contest between the Freeholders and the select body must have taken place at the Restoration in 1660; again, at the Revolution in 1688. And there was the Prince of Orange's declaration read in December, and it is recorded in the Corporation Books that Plymouth was the first town that declared for King William. We have to lament, that at its demolition in 1800, more care was not taken of the papers and documents belonging to the corporate body, for large piles of papers were indiscriminately thrown into heaps prior to their removal to the Mayoralty House in Woolster-street, which was temporarily used as a Guildhall, and a great many documents were then lost to the body, although some of them still remain in the hands of individuals."*

1606. – William Downame, Mayor. An extreme dearth of corn. Hay was sold this present winter in some places 2s 6d for 32 lb. The price of hay, taking into account the value of money, was extremely high, £8 14s per ton, or nearly the value of three fat bullocks, in 1643." The snow this winter was greater than before known at Plymouth.

"April 4th 1606, there came down a commission from London, directed to Sir William Strode, Sir Richard Champernowne, Sir Warwick Heale, Sir Amys Bonvile, Sir John Aclande, Knights; Mr Seamor, High Sheriff of Devon; Mr Pole, Mr William Walrond, Dr Edward Prideaux, Mr Richard Reynell, &c., Esquires; and to any two of them, to inquire what lands the recusants in Devon stood seized of, and also for the levying of the arrearages of all such fines as are behind and unpaid in Queen Elizabeth's time."

*South Devon Museum.

"The 22nd April, being Easter Tuesday, there came down from London a proclamation, the effect whereof was that all such ships as were of South Britain should carry a red cross; the North part a white cross. The red cross was Saint George's cross, and the white, Saint Andrew's cross. These were to be respectively displayed in the fore-top. These two crosses united were to be borne in the main-top by the subjects of Great Britain. Could we but personify the Union Jack, what feelings of degredation must we ascribe to it at that period, – pirates and Algerine corsairs in the channel, and our tars kept out of their pay and poisoned with bad victuals! The poursuivants were sent with the proclamations to the different ports."

1607. – Robert Trelawney, Mayor. "A prodigious snow fell. March, 1607. – This winter last past hath been such an extreme one for frosts, as no man living ever doth remember, or can speak of the like."

"May 31st. – The first settlers of New England, (Puritans) more than 100 in number sailed from Plymouth in two ships, and landed at the mouth of the river Kewnebec, then called the Sagadahoc, Aug. 11th, on the north-east coast of America. The spot they selected for a residence was on Parker's Island, where they raised a fortification called Fort Saint George. They brought two natives from England with them, who procured them a cordial welcome from the different tribes. In the December following, the ships sailed for England, leaving 45 persons but their hard fare, the severity of Kewnebec winter, the burning of their store, and the death of their president, Popham, so discouraged them, that with the next vessel which arrived, they all returned to England. So rose and fell the first colony on this coast, within the compass of a year."*

1608. – Thomas Sherwill, Mayor. "An extreme dearth of corn happened this year, by reason of extreme frosts (as the like were never seen) the winter going before, which caused much corn to fall away; so that many did sow barley where their wheat was sown before, thinking their wheat would never come to good. This year were very many tempestuous winds."

1609. – John Battersby or Buttersby, Mayor. "Extreme west causeth the price of all kinds of corn to be somewhat high, although great plenty – the like seldom seen – in ground which by reason of much wet weather, was much hurt; scarce any corn saved this year without great hurt. All kind of corn did grow in stack, and much cast away and spoiled. Oats were obliged to be turned some four or five times, before it could be saved." – (Yonge's Diary).

1610. – Thomas Fownes, Mayor.

1611. – John Trelawney, Mayor.

*Nettleton's M.S. Collection.

1612. – John Waddon, Mayor. The following document is interesting as giving the names of the major part of the Corporation, which, at this time, consisted of the Mayor "and the Twelve and Twenty-four." –

"XXIIII die Auguste, 1612. – It was ordered by the Mayor and his brethren and the XXIIII in the Guidhall assembled, that Mr Fowell elected Town Clarke for this borough, shall holde the same in as ample manner as Matthewe Bays, (or Boys) late used and helde the same notwithstanding any acte, order or decree heretofore made to the contrarie: –

Jno. M. Docke	John Waddon, Maior
Nicholas Sperwill	John Blytheman
John Trelawney	William Hitchins
Thomas Wolridge	Rowland Brandsforth
James Bayg	Robert Trelawney
William Gill	Robert Rawlyn
Walter Mathew	John Crobell
Thomas Sherwill	Jno. Buttersby
Nicholas Blake	Jno. Clement
John Bound	William Mall
The sign X of John Jope	William ....
Richard Breamlin	Leonard Pomeroy
Abraham Colmedy	John Predio

William Precy

1613. – John Scobbell, Mayor. A great snow at Plymouth. "The Devonshire gentry and tradesmen rode and walked in company for protection, to the metropolis. The judges rode the circuit on horseback, and one of them was censured for being so ill attired, that he looked more like a clothier than a judge. Sir Simonds D'Ewes himself rode to London from Coxden Hall, near Axminster, in 1613, and attributes his safe arrival in the metropolis to God's goodness, for he had *one servant only* with him. A principal member of the Corporation of Lyme was allowed 6s 8d. a day when travelling; 4s a day when in London. A Member of Parliament had about £10 allowed him for his residence and travelling."

The charter of King James, dated the 4th Nov., in this year, is a recital of Queen Elizabeth's charter in the same words, and a confirmation of the same, and of the charters of Queen Mary, Edward VI, Henry VIII, Henry VII, and Henry VI, and grants no further privileges to the borough.

1614. – John Clement, Mayor. John Glanville and Thomas Sherwill, Members for Plymouth. "December 16th. – This day the ministers of this diocese were called before the Bishop of Exon, who read letters from the Archbishop, the effect of which were that every minister should exhort his parishioners to continue together the Sabbath day, and not to wander to other preachers, who have better gifts than their own pastors, but should content themselves with the word of God read, and homilies. (2) – That all should kneel at the receiving of the Sacrament. (3) – To declare unto their parishioners that it is not necessary to have the word preached at the Sacraments." – (Yonge's Diary).

1615. – Abraham Colman, Mayor. The foundation of the Hospital, west from the steeple, laid, called the Workhouse, or "Hospital of the Poor's Portion."

1616. – Robert Trelawney, Mayor. "October. – A man at Littleham in Devon, was murdered in his house by four of his neighbours coming to rob him. They having killed him, set his house on fire and burned him in his house; all his body was consumed and burned, except that side where he was wounded, which was neither burned, not his clothes scorched with any fire, a wonderful judgement of God against murder."

1617. – Thomas Sherwell, Mayor. "Poconitas, an American Princess, arrives at Plymouth." "She afterwards dies in England; her child was taken charge of by Stuckeley." – (Smiths, Virginia).

This year at the beginning of April, Sir Walter Ralegh sailed from the Thames, on his last, and truly unfortunate expedition. His fleet consisted of seven vessels, the aggregate burthen of which was 1,215 tons. At Plymouth he was joined by four more vessels under the respective commands of Captains Sir John Ferne, Lawrence Kenys (the explorer of 1596, and faithful friend of Ralegh in the Tower years), Wollaston, and Chudleigh. A carvel and two fly-boats also joined him at Plymouth. One of the latter was commanded by a man whose name, Bayley, is one to be branded with every oprobrioum, as a deserter, a false swearer, and a rascal of the worst kind. In this disastrous voyage, Ralegh was made the victim of treachery, and met with many losses and troubles, one of the greatest of which was the death of his son, who fell gallantly fighting, at the hands of the Spaniard Erinetta, who beat him down with his musket.

The following is a copy of the grant of Sutton Pool, by Prince Charles for 21 years, at a yearly rent £13 6s 8d.

"This Indenture made the six and twentieth day of November, in the year of the reign of our Sovereign Lord James, by the grace of God of England,

Scotland, France and Ireland, King, Defender of the Faith, etc., that is to say of England France and Ireland the fifteenth, and of Scotland the one and fiftieth, between the most excellent Prince Charles, Prince of Wales, Duke of Cornwall and of York, and Earle of Chester, of the one part, and John Sparke and John Howell of Plymouth, in the county of Devon, Esqres., of the other part, witnesseth that the said most excellent Prince, for and in consideration of the yearly rent, or sum hereafter in these present specified, and for divers other causes and considerations His Highness thereunto moveing, hath granted, and to farm lett, and in and by these presents doth grant, and to farm lett, unto the said John Hawken and John Howell, all that the Water and Pool of Sutton, in the countye of Devon, parcel of the possessions of His Highnesses Duchie of Cornwall, together with the profits of the same hereafter in these presents particularly mentioned; that is to say anchorage and keyladge of every shipp entering within the said poole or touching land there, mesurage or busheladge of every shippe entering within the poole aforesaid, freighted with any kind of corn or grain, malt, cole, salt, or such like, and unladed there, lashadge of every shipp unladed within the poole aforesaid, the fyne of twelve pence yearly upon every fish-boat taking fish as coming into the said water and poole, and pottage, to weete all such fynes of fish as shall be agreed for by and between the said .... and the said John Sparke and John Howell, or their assigns, and also all sumes of money and other fees, duties and profits to or for the said anchorage, keyladge, measurage or busheldge, lashadge, fines or fisher-boats and pottage due, and payable or belonging and appertaining thereunto, (expected, and out of this present demise, always reserved to the said most excellent Prince and his heirs, all prisadge, butteradge, wrecks of sea and customes, goods of pyrates and all other goods and merchandizes forfeited, and all maritimall jurisdictions within the water and pool aforesaid, and all other profits whatsoever, issuinge or cominge of or by reason of the said water and pool of Sutton not hereinbefore particularly demised,) to have and to hold the said water and pool of Sutton, the said anchoradge, keyadge, measureage or bushelage, lashage, fines for fish-boats, pottage, and other the fees and dutyes to the premises thereinbefore mentioned, to be demised, together with all and singular their appurtenances (except before excepted) to them, the said John Sparke and John Howell, their executors, administrators, and assigns, from the feast of Saint Michael the Archangel, last past before these present, for and during the terme of one and twentie years, from thence next ensuing, fully to be complete and ended; yielding and paying therefore yearly, and the said John Sparke and John Howell for themselves, their heirs, executors, administrators, and assigns, do hereby covenant, promise, and agree to and with the said most excellent Prince, his heirs and assigns, to pay for the premises hereby demised yearly, for the said term of twenty-one years, the yearly rent or sum of £13 6s 8d: of good and lawful money of England, to be payed to His Highness's receivor of the Duchy of Cornwall for the tyme being, or his deputy to His Highness's use att two usual feasts or terms of the year, that is to say att the feasts of the Annunciation of our Lady the blessed Virgyn Mary, and Saint Michael the Archangel, by even and equal portions. Provided always that if the said yearly rent or sum of £13 6s 8d., shall be behynde, and unpaid in parte or in all by the space of eight and twentie days, next over or after any of the feasts or days of payment, whereon the same is limited and appointed to be payed in manner aforesaid, that then, and from thenceforth, itt shall and may be lawful to, and for the said most excellent Prince, his heirs and assigns, with the premises hereby demised, and every part and parcel thereof, wholly to re-enter, and the same to have agayne, enjoy and reposses, as in his and their former state, anything herein contayned to the contrary there of in anywise notwithstanding. And the said John Sparke and John Howell for themselves, their heirs, executors, administrators, and assigns, do hereby covenant promise and agree to and with the said most excellent Prince, his heirs and assigns, that they the said John Sparke and John Howell, their executors, administrators and assigns, during the terms hereby granted, shall not doe or wittingly or willingly suffer any act or thing whereby the haven in the water and poole aforesaid or the channel in the river there, may in any sort be stopt, impaired or dampnigfied. In witness whereof to one part of these presents remaining with the said John Sparke and John Howell, the said most excellent Prince hath caused His Highness's great scale to be put thereunto, and to the other part of these presents remaining with the said Prince His Highness, the said John Sparke and John Howell have put their hands and seales the day and year first above written."

1618. – Nicholas Sherwell, Mayor. On the 21st of June, Sir Walter Ralegh, one of the worthiest of Devonshire's most worthy of sons, and one of the worst treated and unfortunate of men, returned from his ill-fated expedition. His ship, the *Destiny*, arrived alone. Some had deserted him, others were parted from him by storms, and had, like poor Captain Pennington's been seized. Sir Walter moored her in the harbour and instantly sent her sails on shore. Lady Ralegh hastened to Plymouth to meet her husband, and that mournful meeting – mournful through the loss of their son, and the other disasters of the voyage – and many matters of business connected with his fleet kept him in Devonshire for two or three weeks. In the second week of July, Sir Walter and his wife and Captain Samuel King, one of his officers, left Plymouth for London. They had however but proceeded some twenty miles, to near Ashburton, on the skirts of Dartmoor, when they were met by Sir Lewis Stukeley, Vice-Admiral of Devon, who said to Ralegh, "I have orders to arrest both you and your ships." They therefore, with Stuckeley, returned to Plymouth, where Stuckeley appears to have busied himself much more about his own profit, from the equipments, etc., of the *Destiny*, and her cargo, than about the custody of the admiral. "For nine or ten days, Sir Walter remained at the house of Sir Christopher Harris at Plymouth. Two or three of them passed without his ever setting eyes on his custodian. Those days were filled with many anxious thoughts about the future; and to his own anxieties and forebodings were added those of a fond wife, and a faithful servant, whose one common care was to see him in safety from the pursuit of his enemies. Under the pressure of their alarms and entreaties, Ralegh empowered Captain King to hire a barque that would carry them to France.

SIR WALTER RALEIGH
From the print in his History of the World; Edition of 1677.

King did this, and made the vessel ride at anchor in Plymouth harbour, out of gunshot of the fort. At midnight the two men went out in a boat, for the purpose of embarking. But Sir Walter was now in a great strait., The anxious pleadings of his wife were opposed to the dictate of his own judgement. On reaching Plymouth, his pledge to return was but half redeemed. *She* thought only of the life that was so precious to her. *He* had to think of duty and of fame. When the boat was within a quarter of a mile of the French ship, he determined to return. Next day he sent orders that she should continue to lie in readiness for another night or two; but no further effort was made to go on board of her." On the 23rd July, the Privy Council wrote to Stukeley, that their lordships would listen to no more excuses of delay. – "We command you upon your allegiance, that, all delays set apart, you do safely and speedily bring hither the person of Sir Walter Ralegh, to answer before us such matters as shall be objected against him in His Majesty's behalf."

These peremptory orders reached Plymouth on the 25th of July, and on the same day, Stukeley, having previously sold the precious tobacco and other stores and cargo of the *Destiny*, set out with his noble prisoner for London, from Mr Drake's house, where he had been removed from that of Sir Christopher Harris. Weakened in health by over anxieties and troubles, Ralegh had made the acquaintance of a French physician in Plymouth of the name of Manourie, who he thought would be able to restore him to health and to beguile the tedium of the journey by conversation on chemistry and other genial subjects. He therefore engaged his services, but they were turned to account against him by Manourie accepting, as well, from Stuckeley, the office of spy. Presently, Ralegh and his wife set their eyes for the last time on their much-loved Sherborne; then in its full summer beauty. He passed near enough to the park to note the growth of his plantations, and to think of the hopes, now blighted, with which every improvement there had been bound up. – "All this" he said "was mine, and it was taken from me unjustly."

The first night was passed before reaching Sherborne, at the house of Mr Horsey; and the next, close to that place, either at Sir Edward Parhams or at his sons. The following day was continued to Salisbury, where, to gain time, Ralegh simulated illness. The time so gained he purposely devoted to writing a true, and most valuable statement of the matters at Guiana, which he did "with all the old vigour of intellect which neither the anguish of past bereavements, nor the fear of sufferings to come, was able to cloud." From Salisbury the journey to London was at length continued, Ralegh arriving at his house in Broad-street on the 7th August, and on the 10th he made his final and fatal entrance into the Tower of London. On the 29th of October he was beheaded, and with the fall of the axe, fell one of England's noblest sons, and of her best and most worthy of men.

1619. – Thomas Fownes, Mayor. A fleet sailed hence for Algiers.

1620. – Robert Rawling, Mayor. John Glanville, Recorder, and Thomas Sherwell, Merchant, Members for Plymouth. "Sir Richard Hawkins is going to sea with twenty sail of ships; viz: six of the King's ships, (two of 300 tons, 28 guns, 250 men; one of 200 tons, 24 guns, 250 men; two of 200 tons, 22 guns, 200 men, each,) and fourteen ships of the merchant of London. (Sir Robert Mansell afterwards took the command.) It is reported they go against the Turks of Algiers. They lay about there all winter and next spring, and concluded a truce for English merchants. James I proposed that the different Christian powers should unite to destroy the great piratical haunt, Algiers, and burn the ships there."

This year is especially memorable in the annals of Plymouth, by the sailing hence of that faithful band of puritans, the "Pilgrim Fathers," who sought on a foreign land that peace and liberty, which was denied to them in their own country. At the time when "the severities used against the Nonconformists had continued to increase, and when the ports of England were so closely watched that the victims could obtain the privilege of banishment, only at the risk of death or imprisonment, a congregation of Brownists, with their pastor, John Robinson, had effected their escape from England to Leyden. But they soon found that Holland was not their congenial home. The climate was unsuited to them, the mechanical occupations which they had to follow were unwelcome to them who had been accustomed to agriculture, and with the language and manners of the Dutch they could not become familiar. Though their country had cast them out, still they were, and would be, Englishmen; and they resolved to make, if they could not find, an England of their own – a country where they could follow their own mode of life, and above all, where they could worship God according to the dictates of their own conscience. Even their children and posterity were to be English, speaking the language of their fathers, and living under the dominion of the mother country; and from this patriotic feeling, they rejected the kind offers of their Dutch landlords, who would have defrayed the expenses of the enterprise and accompanied them to their distant place of settlement. Virginia was the place of their selection, because it was within the pale of English rule, but still sufficiently remote for the purposes of safety; and having obtained the permission of the Virginia Company in London, they made preparations for their departure by converting their scanty property into a common stock, and hiring two small vessels, the *Speedwell* of 60, and the *May-flower* of 180 tons. "We are well weaned," they said, "from the delicate milk of our mother country, and inured to the difficulties of a strange land. The people are industrious and frugal. We are knit together as a body in a most sacred covenant of the Lord, of the violation whereof we make great conscience, and by virtue whereof we hold ourselves straitly tied to all care of each others' goods, and of the whole. It is not with us as with men whom small things can discourage." Such were those Pilgrim Fathers of the New World, who, with such defective means, but heavenly and heroic purpose, embarked upon an enterprise a bold as that of Cortez and Pizarro – and with what a nobler termination!

Every step of this adventure, which forms so important an epoch in English History, is worthy of attention, although we must dismiss the subject with a brief and passing notice. After they had resided above ten years in Leyden, the first embarkation commenced in 1620. Of Robinson's congregations which numbered about 300 persons, only a minority could, in the first instance, set sail, owing to the smallness of the vessels; but these were to act as the pioneers of the enterprise, and were to be followed by Robinson and the rest, as soon as a settlement had been effected in Virginia, that had now obtained the name of New England. In that minister's parting harangue, there was a liberality and greatness of sentiment seldom accorded by popular report to these early puritans, and which all parties of Christians in the present day would do well to study. "The Lord has more truth yet to break forth," he said, "out of His Holy Word. I cannot sufficiently bewail the condition of the reformed churches, which are come to a period in religion, and will go, at present, no further than the instruments of the reformation. Luther and Calvin were great and shining lights in their times, yet they penetrated not into the whole counsel of God. The Lutherans cannot be drawn to go beyond what Luther saw; and the Calvinists, you see, stick fast where they were left by that great man of God. I beseech you remember it –'tis an article of your church covenant — that you shall be ready to receive whatever truth shall be made known to you from the written word of God." The vessels sailed in the first instance from Holland to England; but, after a short stay there, the *Speedwell* being declared unserviceable, the *May-flower* alone held onward in its course, freighted with 101 passengers, consisting of men, women, and children; and, after a voyage of 63 days, they landed at that part of the American Coast, on which they founded the Towns of Plymouth and Boston. Such was the foundation of the United States of America! A huge mass of dark grey granite was the ground on which they first set foot as they landed; and before the Town Hall of Plymouth it is now planted, as a great national monument of the "Pilgrim Fathers," the founders of the American Republic. Sick and exhausted with the fatigues of the voyage, they fell upon their knees as soon as they had reached the shore, and blessed the God of Heaven who had brought them in safety through perils and tempests, after which they proceeded to draw up the political constitution under which they were to live together as a community. It was as brief and simple as the germ of a great national contract could be, for it was in the following words: – "In the name of God, amen; we whose names are underwritten, the loyal subjects of our dead sovereign King James, having undertaken for the glory of God, and advancement of the Christian faith, and honour of our King and country, a voyage to plant the first colony in the northern parts of Virginia, do, by these presents, solemnly and mutually, in the presence of God and one of another, covenant and combine ourselves together into a civil body politic, for our better order and preservation, and furtherance of the ends aforesaid; and by virtue hereof to enact, constitute, and frame such just and equal laws, ordinances, acts, constitutions, and offices, from time to time, as shall be thought most convenient for the general good of the colony. Unto which we promise all due submission and obedience."

It was on the 6th of September, 1620, that this devoted band sailed from Plymouth. By break of day on the 9th of the following November, they had made Cape Cod in Newfoundland, and on the lst day of the year they all landed at a place which in grateful commemoration of our town – *the last town which they left in their native land* – they called New Plymouth. The coast upon which they landed was bleak, barren, and unhealthy; but this proved the only defence of these helpless adventurers against the tribes of wild Indians, who had no temptation to settle near such an uninviting spot. The rigours of an American winter, against which they were so ill prepared, came on, and in three months half the band of emigrants had perished, so that scarcely fifty survived. But though the *May-flower* returned to England in the following spring, not one of the survivors would avail himself of the opportunity to quit that strand of graves and sickness. On the contrary they founded their little town of Plymouth, elected a new governor in the room of the former one who had died, and opened a friendly intercourse with the nearest tribe, of whom they became the allies against their enemies, the Narragansetts. On the 9th of November, 1621, the *Fortune*, a small barque, arrived bringing 35 new settlers, and by the same vessel the first export of the colony was embarked for England, consisting of beaver-skins, and wood of various kinds, to the value of £500. But the *Fortune* was seized and plundered by a French privateer, just when she had neared the English Coast; and, to add to the difficulties of the colonists, a further arrival of destitute emigrants nearly destroyed the whole settlement with famine. Even when they were reduced to their last pint of corn, seven new colonists arrived to share it. Singularly enough even while the Plymouth brethren were thus destitute, the spirit of English commercial enterprise had directed its attention to New England; and new colonists arrived upon its shores, animated with a different spirit from that of the Pilgrim Fathers – men of whose crimes or idleness their own country had become weary, and whose chief motive of emigration was the hope of gain. From the scantiness of the means of support, an additional settlement was necessary, and this originated, in 1622, the founding of the State of Massachussetts. But these worthless additions, instead of being a help, were an incumbrance and a curse to their peaceful brethren; and their conduct toward the natives, in 1623, involved the whole colony in a war with the red hunters of the wilderness. While these events went onward, new bands of adventurers continued to arrive from the mother country, of a better character than the new colonists of Massachusetts, and while some were of the common file of industrious enterprise, and distinguished by the old-established English names of George, Thomas and Edward, there were others whose Puritan appelatives showed that they were of the same religious stock as the men of Plymouth; such as Elder Brewster, Manasseh Faunce, Christian Penn, and Experience Mitchel; Jonathan, Love and Wrestling, the sons, and Fear and Patience, the daughters of Elder Brewster. Stout of heart, and resolute in purpose were these comers, although the first step of their landing convinced them that this land of promise would also be one of "hope deferred." They were gladly welcomed by their old friends who had preceded them; but "the best dish we could present them with" one of them writes "is a lobster, or a piece of fish, without bread, or anything else, but a cup of fair spring water; and the long continuance of this diet, with our labours abroad, has somewhat abated the freshness of our complexion, but God gives us health." The reign of Charles I produced an immense accession to the population of New England, but, unfortunately, the new comers brought with them those religious differences, and that spirit of theological contention, which were so prevalent at that time in the mother country, and which culminated in disorder and confusion and warfare.

CHAPTER V.

ANNALS CONTINUED FROM THE YEAR 1620 TO 1680

1621. – John Bownde, Mayor. "The 10th day of January, 1621-2, there were seen by the minister of Plymouth, in Devon, and a French minister, then walking on the Hoe at Plymouth, three clouds in the air, which clouds seemed to come and meet together. At their meeting one of them brake, and gave a great noise, as if it had been a cannon. After, the second brake, and grave two sounds as of two cannons. Then the third brake, and gave a noise as if it had been the noise of cannons in a set battle, with a whistling in the air, as if bullets had been shot out of a piece. There was a thunderbolt seen at Plymouth to fall from thence into the ground, which weighed by report, VIIIlb. Sir Wm Strode who lived at Newnham, Plympton, had it."

"January – About the end of this month, the Earl of Oxford, the Earl of Essex and the Lord Chichester, with Sir Horatio Vere, were chosen to be of the king's council of war; which was the first council of war in England."

1622. – John Martin, Mayor. "A great scarcity of money throughout the kingdom, little or no employment for workmen; scarcely any person could depend on the receipt of any money due to him, the whole country impoverished. Tradesmen complain they cannot get work to employ themselves, so that many do offer to work for meat and drink only. Good livers cannot make any shift for money, as payments were at this time all made in silver and gold. The price of all things except corn was at a very low rate. In Exeter it is said there are 300 poor weavers, which go about the streets to crave relief by begging, because they can get no work, nor can the merchants sell the cloths when bought from them. The justices met this assizes 12th March, to consider of some course to set people at work, and to prevent an insurrection. Barley was this year, 5s 4d., and wheat at 8s. the bushel." "Order from the Earl of Bath from the Council, that all trained soldiers shall be ready at an hour's warning, Mr Drake's companies and regiment are appointed for Exon. Sir Edward Seymour for Plymouth; Sir

Wm Courtney and Sir Richd. Champernown for Dartmouth and Totnes; Sir Richd. Chichester for Ilfracomb." – (Yonge's Diary).

"*Benevolence.* – Two letters came down this month of April, directed to the Sheriff of Devon, for a benevolence of the laity towards the wars of the Palatinate, with command to deal with the substantial men, one by one, privately, and to return the names of such as obstinately refuse to give anything. The other letter was that the justices should call before them all clothiers, out of which, two of the most sufficient from every county, should be sent to London before certain commissioners, appointed to enquire the cause of the deadness of trade, and to settle a course to revive the trade of clothing beyond the seas which two clothiers so sent should deliver their opinions of the causes and reasons of the deadness of trade before the said commissioners, so that some course may be taken for some redress therein." – (Sir W Pole).

"*Benevolence.* – There was granted a benevolence by the justices of peace of this county, the 3rd of May, at Exon sessions. Mr Parker, High Sheriff gave £40; Sir Harry Roles, £40; Sir Wm Pole, £40; Sir T Drewe, £10; Mr Drake, £10; all the rest of the justices gave £4 a piece, except Mr George Chandler, who gave 40s."

1623. – Leonard Pomory or Pomersey, Mayor. John Glanville, Esq., recorder, and Thomas Sherwell, Merchant, Members for Plymouth.

1624. – Thomas Ceely or Seely, Mayor. "The States of Holland have now in Plymouth, 12 ships of 600 or 800 tons a piece, and 13 lesser ships, in all 25, which are bound for the Brazil. They carry with them ammunition, victuals and women and children to furnish those with victuals, and men which took Brazil. Great preparations are making to go for the recovery thereof, and divers of the nobility go in person." "An embargo on ships come down to Dartmouth, the merchants prohibited to carry away any fish out of the realm, but that it is to be reserved to furnish our navy, there being 60 sail of ships now preparing. – (in a letter from London from Mr Drake).

1625. – Nicholas Blake, Mayor. John Glanville, Esq., Recorder, Thomas Sherwell, Merchant, Members for Plymouth. "The King cometh to Plymouth to despatch a fleet. He calls a Parliament and finds great discontent, the Presbyterian interest prevailing so as to ferment the people. A great plague in Plymouth, of which 1,600 people died – some say 2,000."

"This yere the great plague raged in all this kingdom and of itt there died in this towne, in this yere, about 2,000! and a publick faste through the kingdom was proclaimed to divert God's judgement, which was observed solemnly every Wensdaye, and thereon the plague was stayed." "A press sent down into Devonshire to raise 300 men for Ireland; 500 oxen sent to Plymouth, for the victualling of our navy, and many mariners pressed, which are to be at Chatham, the 26th April." November, 1625. – There came a press into the country, at which time were up in Devon about 300 men; but for what service it is not known, but thought either to succour the estate of Holland, or to secure Ireland, or both."

"The King, Charles, came with his whole Court to Plymouth, and remayned here 10 days to give his fleete, that consisted of 120 sailes, and his army of 6,000 men, both under the command of Edward Lord Cecill, Viscount Wimbleton, theire despatch for Cadiz in Spayne, which they invaded." The following interesting document shows the expense to which the Town of Plymouth was put on occasion of this royal visit.

"Fees due to His Majesty's servants from the said Mayor, for his homage to His Majesty passing through his said towne the fiveteene day of September, 1625. –

	£	s.	d.
To the Gentlemen Ushers dayly Wayters …	5	0	0
To the Gent. Ushers of the Privy Chamber	5	0	0
To the S'jants at Armes … … … … … …	3	6	8
To the Knight Harbinger … … … … …	3	6	8
To the Knight Marshall … … … … … …	1	0	0
To the Gent. Ushers Quarter Wayters … …	1	0	0
To the Servers of the Chamber … … … …	1	0	0
To the Yeoman Ushers … … … … … …	1	0	0
To the Groomes and Pages … … … … …	1	0	0
To the Footmen … … … … … … … … …	2	0	0
To the fower Yeomen … … … … … …	2	0	0
To the Porters at the Gate … … … … …	1	0	0
To the S'jant. Trumpetters … … … … …	1	0	0
To the Trumpetters … … … … … … …	2	0	0
To the Surveyor of the Wayes … … … …	1	0	0
To the Yeoman of the fielde … … … …	0	10	0
To the Coachmen … … … … … … …	0	10	0
To the Yeoman Harbingers … … … …	1	0	0
To the Jester … … … … … … … … … …	0	10	0
Summ	£33	3	4

Received the some abovesaid, this 23rd of Septmebr, 1624, to the use of His Majesty's servants by mee.

THOS. KYNNASTON."

"A.D. 1625. – Exemp. 3rd day of May, the I of Charles. Thos. and Nic. Sherwell, erected, founded and established, the Hospitall of Orphan's Aid; granted all that message, tenement, and courtlage, between the Tower and Churchyard on the East, the lands of the said Sherwell's on the South, and the lands of the Mayor and Commonalty's part of the Almshouse, on the North; the same premises to be one Hospitall continuance for ever. One person to be head and called Governor; some other persons to be called Assistants; and 40 persons and under, and yet above the number of 3, which shall be poor persons for ever abiding there. The last Mayor shall be the 1st and modern Governor, to continue untill the death of the said Mayor, or choice of a new Mayor, which shall first happen, and so for ever. Four persons to be appointed as Assistants, and two to be Wardens, and four poor persons appointed to be the first poor perople to be relieved in the said Hospitall; such poor people to be removed at pleasure. Made a body corporate and politick, by the name of Governor, Assistants, Wardens and Poor People of the Hospitall of Orphans' Aid, within the Burroughe of Plymouth in the County of Devon; with the power to purchase, nothing to be done without the consent of the Mayor and Chief Burgesses, whereof the Mayor to be one, or the major part of them. The Grant etc. unto the said Governor and their successors for ever, of all that before recited house, and all those three messuages, courts, and gardens, and close of land, with the appurtenances, some time the lands of Brooking, since of Blythman, and then in the tenure of Jope, Blacksmith, and all that garden and orchard, with the appurtenances adjoining to the courtlage of the said Hospitall, lying West from the same two gardens, lying in Mud-street, in the tenure of Colmer, and all that messuage, tenement, etc. in Stilman-street, lately the lands of Fownes, another messuage lying in Southside, the lands of late Arthur Pollard, Esq., deceased, another messuage, tenement, and courtlage, in Southside, also the lands of Pollard, a close or parcell of land in a place called Lary, also called Pollard's lands, two closes of land, with barns, houses, and stables, in Egg Buckland called Awter's Well, 16 acres, also Pollards," etc., etc.

1626. – Thomas Sherwell, Mayor. John Glanvile, Esq., Recorder, and Thomas Sherwell, Merchant, Members for Plymouth.

1627. – Robert Trelawney, Mayor. Robert Trelawney dying the 7th December, Abraham Colman supplied the place that year.

"The charter of King Charles I, is dated the 3rd of March in this year. By this charter the King confirms the charters of King James, Queen Elizabeth, Queen Mary, King Edward VI, Henry VIII, Henry VII, and the Act of Parliament of Henry VI.

"And grants further that the Mayor and Commonalty or their successors, should not be troubled by the King, his heirs or successors, or his justices, sheriffs, escheators, bayliffes, or other officers for, or by reason of the premises.

"And commands also that neither the treasurer, chancellor or barons of the exchequer, or the justices, attorney general, or any other officers of his, or his successors, should grant out, or prosecute any writ, summons, *quo warranto*, or any process against the Mayor and Commonalty, or any of them for any cause, thing, matter, offence, claim, or usurpation, before the making of that charter.

"And the Mayor, Commonalty, or justices not to be troubled, hindered, or compelled to answer for any use or abuse of the liberties or privileges of the said borough –

"The King by these letters patent grants the same power unto them, and to two of the other most antient magistrates there, in degree and order of election, to be also justices of the peace within the said borough, and that they or any two of them, whereof the Mayor or recorder to be one, should have power to enquire of all felony's trespasses, evil deeds, and other delinquincies or articles committed, down, or perpetrated within the said borough, which any other justices of the peace without any county of this realm of England, might by the laws or statutes of this realm enquire of, except murder, felony, that which concerns loss of life or member, and to hear, determine, and punish the offences, according to the laws and statutes, as any other justices might do.

"But these justices are first to take their oaths of justices of peace before the Mayor there, and no justice of the county to inter-meddle within the borough."

"The misfortunes of King Charles I, had been the cause of great contention in the borough during the succeeding reign, and at length in 1684, (36th year of the latter reign) a *quo warranto* was brought against the Corporation, for some illegal proceedings against His Majesty in levying his dues, whereupon after some debate, the majority of the Corporation, or those which were convened by the Mayor, agreed to surrender their charters; and accordingly the same were surrendered to His Majesty at Windsor, who soon after in the same year, granted the Mayor and Commonalty a new charter upon a different plan to any of the former, but this charter became vacated by the charter of King William III, which was the last granted to Plymouth."

1628. – Nicholas Sherwell, Mayor. "The fleet goeth to the siege of Rochelle, sail from hence in September."

1629. – William Heal, Mayor. The following letter from the Council to the Mayor of Plymouth, is dated December 27th, this year: –

"Sir, – There being many bruits spread here of the preparations at sea, many by the French upon their coast, I hold it the dutie of my place to examine these reports, and to gain such certain knowledge of the truth, as I may be able to give His Majesty a good accompt thereof, which I shall the better doe, if besides forayne advertisements, on which I would not allone relye, I may be withall informed from those who drive the trades to and fro between coast and coast, that cannot but take notice of any understanding in this kind more than ordinarie. To this purpose I desire you should call unto you apart, (but with the least noise you can,) such as are lately returned from those post townes of France, especially in Brittanie, and inquire of them all particulars, which may serve for this discovery. Whereof when you have perfectly informed yourself, I shall entreat of you a speedy advertisement, and will assure you, your diligence herein will be an acceptable service to His Majestie, and deserve of me any requitall may lye in the way and power of your very loving friende, DORCHESTER."

1630. – John Pound, Mayor. "A great contested election for the choice of the Vicar of Saint Andrew's Church."

1631. – John Waddon, or Whaddon, Mayor. The bells new cast.

1632. – Philip Andrew, Mayor. Hele's Charity School said to have been founded.

1633. – Robert Trelawney, Mayor. "This yeare the King's fleet set forth with the first rate ship,. anchored in the Sound, the Earle of Linsay, commander."

1634. – John Martin, Mayor. This year the Mayor and Corporation determined upon the erection of a new church, (Charles' Church,) and took steps accordingly. Until this time, Saint Andrew's was the only church in the town. The following interesting extract from the "White Book" of the Corporation, will show the proposed division of the town for the two parishes: –

"Whereas this Borough of Plymouth, in the County of Devon, is so populous, and of late times so much increased, that the church here is unable to receive and contain a multitude of inhabitants thereof, who by reason, repair not to the church nor hear divine service on the Sunday, as they ought. And whereas the advancement and propogation of the honor and service of God, is and ought to be, the chiefest aim and end of all good magistrates and christians. And whereas some worthy and well devoted gentlemen our neighbours, have already exprest themselves liberal benefactors towards so good and religious a work. We the said Mayor, major part of the Magistrates and Common Council, within the said borough, assembled in the Guildhall thereof, for the advancement of God's glory, and for the furtherance of so needful and pious a work; do enact, constitute, order, and agree that (with the gracious licence and leave of His Majesty,) there shall be with all convenient speed, a new church erected and founded, within the Borough of Plymouth aforesaid, in and upon that piece or parcell of land called, or known by the name of the Coney Yard, now Gayer's Yard, lately dedicated and given us by John Hele, of Wembury, Esq., to that use. And we do further agree, that a petition be preferred to His Majesty for his royal assent thereunto, and grant that all that part and parcel of ground, messuages, houses, lands, and tenements, and of the inhabitants thereof, situate within the said borough, commonly called or known by the name of Looe-street Ward, Briton-side, Catdown and part of Vintry Ward and other messuages, land, and tenements within the said borough, bounded as follows, and contained inclusive within the said bounds, may be a parish distinct and independent by itself, and have parish rights for ever, viz: – from the Pump on the New Quay within the said borough, and up through Batter-street on the east side of the said street, and thence up Looe-street untill you come to the Pope's head, and thence down Buckwell-street on the east side thereof , untill you come to Bilbury Bridge, and thence to Hampton-street, and from thence to the higher end of Green-street, and thence through the King's highway that leadeth toward Plympton, untill you come to the bottom of Lipson-hill, on the east side thereof, and from thence along the sea-side and clift, untill you come to Friary Green, and from thence direct over the water and quay, untill you come to the Pump on the New Quay aforesaid; and that the Mayor and Commonalty of the said borough, and their successors for ever, may have the presentation and patronage thereof, and that His Majesty would be likewise graciously pleased to name the said parish and church. And we do further consent and agree that Sir James Bagg, Knight, a liberal benefactor towards the said work, shall present the said petition to His Majesty, according to his noble and free offer therein; which being obtained of His Majesty, we do further order, consent, and agree that the Mayor of the said borough for the time being, shall assemble and call together ourselves, and the most of the inhabitants within the said borough, to gather and receive our devotions, benevolences, and free will offerings towards the speedy perfecting and consummating of so pious and profitable a work; in true testimony whereof, we the said Mayor, &c., have hereunto subscribed our names."

Signed by ROBERT TRELAWNEY, and 30 others.

The following is the petition presented to the King, asking for leave to erect the New Church: –

"To the King's most excellent Majesty, the humble petition of the Mayor and Commonalty of the Borough of Plymouth, in the County of Devon, humbly sheweth. That whereas your Majestie's Borough of Plymouth, aforesaid, is so populous and of late times so much increased, that the church there* (though large and spacious,) is unable to receive and contayne a multitude of your Majesty's subjects, the inhabitants thereof, who by that means seldom repair to the church, or hear divine service on the Sunday as they ought. And whereas there is a willing and unanimous consent and concurrence among your petitioners, and several other able inhabitants within the said borough, (besides the devotion of some worthy gentlemen, our neighbours) for the raysinge of money towards the erecting and buildinge of a New Church, within the said borough, and a convenient plott of ground and place for that purpose already allotted, and a competent means and mayntenance intended for the endowment thereof in perpetuity. May it please your Majesty, out of your wonted piety, and princely grace and goodness, to give your royal assent and encouragement to the needful and pious work, and to grant that some convenient parte of the said borough and of the inhabitants thereof, may be assigned to repayre to the said church, and may be a parish and have parochial rights for ever. And that your petitioners and their successors, may from time to time for ever, have the presentation and patronage thereof, and that your Majesty will be likewise graciously plesed to name the said parish and church. And many poor soules who are now excluded (through numbers) from these publicque and divyne assemblies, shall blesse your Majesty, and your petitioners for ever bounde to pray for your Majesty's long life and happy regine over them."

1635. – Thomas Cramphorn, Mayor. "The first, or running, post between London, Exeter, and Plymouth, was established in 1635. It is interesting to read the very great charges incurred for sending letters from Lyme to Salisbury, London, Exeter, and the residences of great men, by a messenger. Sometimes a messenger was despatched to Chard, a distance of 12 miles, to find some one who would convey the letter to the metropolis. By an entry it appears the vicar of Lyme had £1 given him to take charge of a letter, the sending of which would otherwise have occasioned great cost." – (Yonge's Diary).

1636. – John Cawse, Mayor. The floods so great that boats might float in the street.

*St. Andrew's

1637. – Nicholas Sherwell, Mayor. "Contest arising between the vicar, Dr. Willson, and the bench, they go to law when a decree is made in Star Chamber, dividing the power of the Church between them."

1638. – William Heal, Mayor. A very great flood, boats were floated into the streets.

1639. – Robert Gubbs or Gibbs, Mayor.

1640. – William Birch, Mayor. Robert Trelawney, and John Waddon, Esqs., and afterwards Sir John Young, and John Waddon Esqs., Members for Plymouth.

"An Act for the confirmation of His Majesty's letters patent to the Town of Plymouth and for dividing the parishes and building a new church there, Anno Domini 1640.

"Whereas Queen Elizabeth of blessed memory, did heretofore grant unto the Mayor and Commonalty of Plymouth, in the County of Devon, the advowson of the vicarage of Plymouth aforesaid, and a certain portion of £8 yearly, issuing out of the said vicarage, after which the said Mayor and Commonalty enjoyed the said vicarage and pension for many years, till some question hath been made thereto by His Majesty, who by his letters patent, bearing date the 21st day of April in the 17th year of his reign, hath been pleased to grant, release and confirm the said vicarage and pension to the said Mayor and Commonalty and all arrears of the said pension, and because the said town is much increased of late, so the Parish Church is not capable of the inhabitants to heare divine service, His Majesty hath given licence to the said Mayor and Commonalty and their successors, to build a New Church within the said parish, and procure the same to be consecrated, and the said parish by certain bounds (by the said Mayor and Commonalty to be appointed) to divide; and to prefer two Vicars in the said churches, to the ordinary of the said place, to be presented and by him to be admitted; and that the said Mayor and Commonalty and their successors should have and enjoy the advowsons of both the said vicarages. And the said Mayor and Commonalty with His Majesty have undertaken to build the said New Church and to allow to a School Master for the education of the children there and youth £20 per annum; and to maintain an Hospital there, lately built for the use and relief of some poor persons there to be placed by the said Mayor and Commonalty; and His Majesty further granted that after such New Church built, and death or other avoidance of the present Incumbent, the respective Vicars of the said churches to be preferred, should enjoy and receive all the rights, obvensions, tythes, and profits belonging to the new vicarage, which shall arise and happen within the several and respective limits of the said parishes, as by the said letters patent more fully appeareth. Be it therefore (and for the encouragement of the said Mayor and Commonalty to proceed in the said work) enacted by authority of this present Parliament, that the said grant of His Majesty of the said advowson, pension and arrears be confirmed, and by this present Parliament made good, to the said Mayor and Commonalty and their successors, and that they shall have, hold and enjoy the said advowson and pension and arrears thereof in their hands, or by them received and to them granted, released and confirmed or mentioned to be granted, released and confirmed by the said letters patent of his said Majesty; that the said letters patent with the provisoes, alterations and savings in this Act, made and enacted, shall be of the same effect and validity, to pass, grant and convey the said advowson and premises to the said Mayor and Commonalty and their successors, as if the same were particularly and expressly by these presents enacted, granted and conveyed and not-recital, mis-recital or other fault or defect whatsoever in the said letters patent nothwithstanding. And notwithstanding that the same without help or aid of this Act, should or might be expounded to be void or ineffectual. And be it further enacted that the bounds of the said new parish shall be in manner following, viz: – from the sea and slipp at the New Quay, up Batter-street to Pope's head, and thence down Buckwell-street to Bilberry-street, and thence up Trevill-street to Old Town Gate or North Gate, and thence in the highway leading to the lower Wheaten Mills, and thence over the bridge in the highway leading to Maye's Cross, and thence in the highway up Justices-lane to the highway leading to Tavistoke, as far as the Parish of Plymouth goeth; all the houses, lands and grounds to the eastward of the said bounds and the limits of the Parish of Plymouth goeth; all the houses, lands and grounds to the eastward of the said bounds and the limits of the Parish of Egg Buckland and the sea, round to the said slip at the New Quay. And be it further enacted by the authority aforesaid, that from and after the death or other avoidance of the present Incumbent then as soon as the New Church shall be built and such division made of the said parish, the same division shall be effectual in law, and thenceforth there shall be in the said Parish of Plymouth, two vicarages and two Vicars to be appointed (that is to say) in each of the said churches, one, who shall severally and respectively serve in the cure in the said respective limits and bounds of the said parish. And the New Church to be built shall be called *Charles' Church* and the Vicars of the said churches hereafter to be preferred, shall have and enjoy the duties, rights, tithes and profits arising severally and respectively within the said bounds aforesaid to be appointed; each of them paying his tenths and first fruits proportionally to His Majesty; and the Vicar of the old Church, called St Andrew's, shall pay to the Mayor and Commonalty of Plymouth, a stipend of £8 yearly, with which the said vicarage stands charged, and the parishoners within the said several parts and bounds of the said parish, shall respectively, also have and receive all parochial rights in the said several limits and bounds, be liable to all charges for ornaments and repairations, and otherwise belonging to the respective church within the several bounds, in such manner as they now are to the present church there built; and the parishioners which shall happen to be in the respective bounds and limits aforesaid, shall be discharged of all charge of ornaments, repairations, and otherwise belonging to the said Old Parish Church, and in regard of the greatness of the said cure, and the multitudes of inhabitants in the said Parish of Plymouth. Be it further enacted that the said Vicars there be bound to residence in their several cures, and that no one person be capable to hold both the said vicarages jointly together, or either with any other church with cure. And it is further enacted that the Mayor and Commonalty may bring a *Quare Impedit* at the next avoidance of the said churches, or either of them, against any disturber that shall hinder them to present to either of the said churches, (that is to say) to the Old Church by the name of St Andrew's in Plymouth, and to the other by the name of the church in Plymouth, called Charles' Church, saving to all persons whatsoever, other than to His Majesty, his heirs and successors, all such right, title and interest to the said advowson and pension as they or either of them have or ought to have in the said advowson and pension, in such manner as if this Act had never been made anything to the contrary in anywise notwithstanding. Provided also that if the New Church be built before the vacancy of the now church, by the death of the present Incumbent or otherwise, it shall be lawful for the said Mayor, Chief Burgesses, and Common Council Men, with the assent of the Ordinary, to name, and at their own charge to maintain a preaching Minister in Holy Orders, to serve the cure within the said New Church, during the incumbency of the present Incumbent, and that the several inhabitants within the said several bounds, shall repair to and receive parochial and spiritual rights within the said New Church; and also it shall and may be lawful for the Mayor and Commonalty to nominate and maintain at their own costs and charges, any lecturer or lecturers or preaching Minister in Holy Orders, to preach the word of God to the inhabitants, in the now present Church of St Andrew's during the Incumbency of the present Vicar. – JOHN BROWN, Clere^{s}. Parliam^{s}."

1641. – Thomas Seeley, Mayor. Assessment on the inhabitants of Vintry Ward for Poll Tax, 1641. Sum total collected £201 15s 0d by James Debell, Anthony Skinner, and John Morrison, and signed and sealed by Sh. Clamady, John Harris, John Fownes, Frederick Howett, and Alexr. Maynard.

1642. – Philp Francis, Mayor. A conduit was built on the New Quay.

The latter part of this year, and the intervening time until the beginning of 1644, are among the most memorable and stirring in the Annals of Plymouth. During the whole of this year, the country had been embroiled and divided into deadly factions of Royalist and Parliamentarians, and in the dreadful scenes which were enacted, Devonshire was far from exempt. Plymouth declared, and was successfully held for the Parliament, while Exeter ultimately surrendered to the royalist army, and other towns and ports were taken and retaken, according to the vacillations of the fortune of war, by one or other parties, and suffered alike by each. In the commencement of these troubles, Plymouth, during the absence of its governor, Sir Jacob Astley, whom the King had appointed his Major-General of foot, was seized by the townsmen and strongly fortified for the Parliament, and the Earl of Ruthen was soon afterwards made governor; Sir Nicholas Carew having the command of the Fort and of Saint Nicholas Island. Various attempts were made by the royalist to get possession of this important post, but its defenders held it against all comers, even at the time when all the rest of the west was in the possession of the royal forces. Sir Ralph Hopton with his army appeared before Plymouth in December, 1642, but was driven from his quarters by the Earl of Stamford. In the following September, Colonel Digby was sent with a considerable force of horse and foot to blockade the town, and took up his quarters at Plymstock; the blockading army having batteries at Oreston and Mount Batten, and a guard at Hoo. In October, they planned an attack on the Fort of Mount Stamford, but in return, their guard at Hoo was defeated, as they were in several other skirmishes. Shortly afterwards, Prince Maurice with his whole army, advanced on the town, taking up his head-quarters, at Widey House, and stationing his army at Plympton, Plymstock, Causand, Egg-Buckland, Tamerton, etc. Mount Stamford was subsequently taken, and an attack was made on the Fort at Lipson. Colonel Wardlaw, Governor of Plymouth, then took possession of the Fort and Island of Saint Nicholas, with the castle and magazine, then under charge of the mayor, and placed them under approved parliamentary officers; the inhabitants took a solemn vow, and made protestation to defend the Towns of Plymouth and Stonehouse, and the fort and island, to the uttermost. This vow was set up, and registered in Parliament, and is given on a subsequent page. After much skirmishing on both sides, and a day of fast and humiliation being held, the siege was raised on Christmas Day, and a day of thanksgiving was at once appointed and observed.

In the following spring, April 1644, the royalist forces, under Sir Richard Grenville, again appeared before Plymouth, but were signally defeated by Colonel Martin, governor of the town, in an engagement at Saint Budeaux. Three days later the army again advanced on Plymouth, but again was repulsed, as it also was again in July, in which month, Colonel Kerr was made governor of the town. About this time Prince Maurice again attempted the capture of Plymouth, but again was unsuccessful, and left Sir Richard Grenville to continue the blockade. On the approach of the army under the Earl of Essex, Sir Richard abandoned the blockade, and Mount Stamford again fell into the hands of the garrison. In September, 1644, the King came in person before Plymouth, attended by Prince Maurice, and took up his head-quarters at Widey House; Prince Maurice's quarters being near Lipson, and the King's near Magdalen Fort; the town, of which Lord Roberts was then governor, was summoned by the King, on the 11th, to surrender, but refused; a council of war was then held by the King, and it was determined not to undertake an assault or a close siege. The King soon afterwards, with his army, marched from Plymouth, leaving the blockade as it had been before his arrival, in the hands of Sir Richard Grenville. After many changes and much skirmishing – forts being taken and retaken and changes being made, both in command of the beseigers and the beseiged – the blockade of Plymouth, which had been kept up so long, and so unsuccessfully, was finally abandoned, and the town returned to its former peaceful state.

The following is a contemporary account of some of the events connected with this memorable siege, which I insert here in preference to the following year, so as to give the narrative in a connected form. It is entitled:–

"A true narration of the most remarkable occurrences at the late Siege of Plymouth, from the 15th day of September, 1642, untill the 25th of December following. Attested from thence under the hands of several credible persons, together with an exact map and descriptions of the town and fortifications thereof, with the approaches of the enemy, as also the summons of the cavaliers to the mayor and governor of the said town, and Prince Maurice's warrant to the country, since the raising of the siege. –

Imprimatur JOHN WHITE.

London: printed by L.N., for Francis Eglesfield, and are to be sold at the sign of the Mary Gold, in Saint Paul's Churchyard, 1644."

The following is the narrative: –

"After Colonel Wardlaw, Commander-in-Chief, and Colonel Gould with the 600 men, shipt at Portsmouth about the 15th of September, for the relief of this town, had stopt in Torbay, and finding Dartmouth besieged, left 100 men there for the strengthening of that garrison; they arrived at Plymouth the last of September, which they found had been blockt up by some horse, so that no provisions were brought in from the country for six weeks before.

"After having refreshed the men, about 150 of them were mounted on horseback. The enemy had only one regiment of foot, (besides their horse) which was quartered at Plymstock, and kept a constant guard at Hue, close under Mount Stamford,* consisting of about 300 foot and a troop of horse. They intended (as we were informed) to attack this fort about nine days after our arrival. Upon which, on the 8th of October, we put over about 300 men before daybreak, in boats to Mount Stamford; and at break of day, fell on and surprized the enemy's guard at Hue, took Captain Howley, one ensign and 52 common soldiers prisoners, two colours and three barrels of powder, put the rest to flight, with loss only of two men on our side. About the same time some malignants were taken up in the town and sent up three of them to the Parliament.

"By this time, the King's forces had taken Dartmouth, and were on their march with their whole army, to sit down before Plymouth. Intelligence having been received that the enemy kept a guard of two troops of horse at Knackershole, (about two miles from our works) the 15th of October, we sallied out with our horse and 200 musquetiers, surprized that guard and had taken 20 or 30 prisoner, but about 16 of our horse, pursued the rest that fled so fast, that their orders for retreating could not overtake them, engaged themselves too far, and returning laiden with prey and prisoners, were overtaken by other troops of the enemy, who came from their quarters on Roborrow Down to answer the alarm, and were all taken except Major Searle, who charged through them and escaped. Lieutenant Chasing and 14 more were taken, but afterwards effected their escape out of prison and returned to us save only two or three. The King's forces being now arrived and stationed at Plympton, Plymstock, Cawsand, Buckland, and Tamerton, consisted of five regiments of horse and nine regiments of foot. The first manoeuvre they made was to bring overland from Yealme, 13 fisher's boats into Plunket Mills Bay, over against Prince Rock,† with an intention as we

*"So called from the Earl of Stamford, who was the Commander-in-Chief here after the Battle of Bradock Down, it was situated on some of the heights near Hue, but I have not been able to discover its remains (if any). There are however, evident marks of fortifications on Mount Batten, at the south-east of the present castle. I have since discovered that the remains are still visible, and that the situation is well known in that neighbourhood, and is still called Mount Stamford." Old MS Note.

†Here was a pretty large fort, immediately opposite to the arm of the river that goes up to Plunket Mills, the remains of which are still to be discovered by the unevenness of the ground."

conceived to land on Catdowne in the night, which they did not however attempt. They now set on Mount Stamford in good earnest, and on the 21st of October, in the night, they raised a square work within pistol shot of our Fort of Stamford, on the north-east side and from thence were drawing a line with half moons to surround the said fort and thereby to intercept any relief that might be sent to it. To prevent which, the same day we fell on the enemy in their new work, with all the disadvantage on our part that could possibly be imagined, exposing ourselves without any defence to an enemy within a strength, and assisted by their horse, who annoyed us much. We having no horse to assist us, nor could have, from our situation. After a long skirmish and diverse repulses, we at last gained their half moon, and after three hours hot fight, their close work; and in it Captain White and 50 others prisoners. In this fort was placed a guard that night, of 30 musquetiers, commanded by an ensign; by whose treachery or cowardice the enemy having attacked it in the night, the guard quitted the work to them, without giving any alarm to Mount Stamford, for which he was shot to death shortly after. This cost us a new labour next day, with far greater difficulty and danger than before; the enemy having their troops ready to second their guard in their new-regained work; which we however again made ours, after having sustained the loss on our part of Captain Corbet, who was shot in the forehead in the first onset, and three others of our captains were also wounded this day and the day before, and we had in both days, about 20 men killed and above 100 wounded. The King's forces lost six commanders, whose names were concealed from us, and many men besides those taken prisoners.

"After we had gained this work the second time, we slighted it, but to prevent the like approaches, Mount Stamford being small and very untenable of itself, much less to keep so large a circuit of ground as it was built to defend; we were necessitated to draw a line of communication both on the east and west side of the fort, to maintain a long ridge of ground, with half moons at each end of the line, which we defended several days, with extraordinary duty to our men and diverse skirmishes with the enemy, till the 3rd of November, when the enemy planted their batteries within pistol shot of our first, and on the 5th following, battered our work with 200 demi-cannon and whole culverine shot, besides other smaller cannon, that continually played on us, and flanked our line from Oreston-hill, by which means they made several breaches and killed the lieutenant and some gunners; the breaches we repaired in the night, thickening the rampart as much as the smallness of our work would admit, and strengthened the weakest places with wool sacks, the next day they continued their battery till noon with too much success, yet no considerable breach was made that day; but owing to their having received intelligence of the want of provisions and ammunition in the fort, about one of the clock, they attacked our half moons and line with horse and foot, where we had a sufficient guard, but tired with eight days' duty and long watching, after an hour's skirmish were forced to retreat from the half moons and breast work and were taken by the enemy's horse, who came on their backs. The captain of the fort having but seven men of six and thirty left to manage the guns, seeing himself thus surrounded by the enemy and no hopes of relief, of provisions or ammunition from the town; and upon examination, finding but two barrells of good powder, a small quantity of case shot and no provisions, and having held off the enemy some two hours, and given a sign to town, by hanging out a wift that he was in distress, and no relief coming. (The townsmen for some reasons which you shall hear anon, being unwilling to go over, and Colonel Gould's regiment were those that were put to the retreat and totally unfit to encounter the enemy's whole army, flushed with victory). The captain surrendered the fort about four o'clock, upon condition that he should march off with colours flying, matches lighted, bullet in mouth, and a demi-culverin the best in the work, with bag and baggage, and that the enemy should exchange the prisoners they had taken that day being about forty, for the like number of their prisoners with us, which the next day was effected accordingly; we are unwilling to make known by whose treachery, at least neglect, the fort was lost, for want of convenient quantities of ammunition and provision, (in the margin it was written that many insinuated that J.C. Mayor of the town,* was faulty;) whilst the enemy were busy about taking Mount Stamford, we had begun to raise a work upon Huestart,† where our men retreated after they were beaten from Mount Stamford, but being unfinished, and the same wearied men enjoyned to keep it till the next morning, (the townsmen refusing to go over) possessed with a fear of the enemy's horse, quitted that place also, which the enemy soon after took possession of, and have built a fort and diverse batteries there to hinder shipping from coming into the harbour, and others to shoot into the town, and at our wind-mill on the Hoe; but notwithstanding, they have done no harm to any ship or boat, that have passed in or out for these two months past, nor hath any shot of the many hundreds they have sent into the town from thence, done the least hurt to man, woman, or child, (except one woman hurt in the arm with a stone,) and but little to the houses, save that they shot off one vane of the wind-mill on the Hoe, which was presently new grafted; so that we find by experience that

*"John Caws was Mayor of the Town that year."

†"The peninsula, now called Mount Batten. Here are traces still left of many fortifications, and the building is so called from a Captain Batten, who erected it."

the loss of Mount Stamford, was the wonderful providence of God towards us, which had we kept, we must necessarily have lost the best of our strength in its defence; our ships being beaten out of Catwater before we lost Mount Stamford, by the enemy's cannon planted at Oreston, and on the other side from a battery under Mount Edgcumbe, from riding between the Island and the main, so that we were faine to take Mill Bay for sanctuary; nay rather the loss of it was advantageous to us, as it was a means of uniting our small strength for the defence of the town, and the offering an opportunity to us to seize upon the fort* and island, (the most considerable strengths in the defence of them, of which neglect of the authors of it, account may in due time be given to the Parliament; for in the very instant of the loss of Mount Stamford, while all men stood in doubt of the kingdom) which were then utterly destitute of provisions, ammunition, or any thing else necessary for issue, Colonel Gould by order of Colonel Wardlaw took possession of both these places, and afterwards settled stronger garrisons, with store of provisions and ammunition of all sorts in each of them, the securing whereof, and at the request of the well-effected of the town, of four deputy-lieutenants in them, of whose unfaithfulness to the State, the townsmen had great suspicion. By these means, the town which was before altogether divided, and heartless in its defence, became united and resolved to stick by us in defending it, partly out of fear, knowing that the fort and island would be goades in their sides, if the town should be surrendered; but more particularly from their being well-assured of our intention to defend the town to the last man, and of the resolutions formed by the officers, that when they could defend the town no longer, they would burn it to ashes, rather than the enemies of God and His cause should possess it; which resolution of theirs, they confirmed by joining with us in a solemn vow and covenant for the defence of the town. A copy whereof is annexed at the end of this relation. –

"The enemy thus possessed of Mount Stamford, accounting all now to be their own, sent a trumpet to us, with a summons to surrender; a copy whereof is also to be found at the end, which was answered by silence. The same day Mount Stamford was taken, the enemy made an attempt upon Lipson Work,† but was repulsed with loss.

"The 11th of November a party of horse and musquetiers were commanded out to Thorn-hill to guard in wood and hay, but they transgressed their orders, and pursued some of the enemy's horse to

*"This fort stood in the same situation that the Citadel does now, but was not so large, was built in 1593, and destroyed in 1666, when the present Citadel began to be erected." – Old MS Note

"†Part of the rampart of this fort is still to be seen, in a field adjoining the Turnpike road, (which appears to have been cut through part of it) on the left hand side going along down Lipson-hill. (above Lewis Jones's Turnpike Gate." – Old MS Note.

Knackershole killed a captain and some common troopers and took some prisoners; but staying too long, drew the main body of the enemy's horse upon them, and Major Leyton striving to make good their retreat was taken in the rear, after he had received five wounds.

"And now the enemy having refreshed their men, and secured their new gotten purchase, about the 16th of November sat down on the north-side of the town; we in the mean time were busied in mending some hedges, that had been pulled down between the works; the only line of communication we yet have; scarce defensible against the storming of horse; yet such places we must now resolve to defend upon equal terms with our enemies; for the works are at such a distance one from the other, and the grounds so uneven, that an enemy may in some places approach within the works, without any molestation from them. On the 28th of November the enemy planted a battery against Lipson Work, but could not approach within musket shot to better our works, on account of the deep valley between, so that at the end of three days battery, they had done little execution on our work. About this time, one Ellis Carkeet, a malignant mariner, was accused and taken up for tampering with Roger Kneebone, the chief gunner at Maudlin Work, to blow it up, the powder room being buryed in it, and he having the keys; but Kneebone after he had concealed it several days, God not suffering his conscience to give him rest, came and discovered it. Upon the apprehension of Carkeet, two notorious malignants, Henry Pitts a vintner, and Moses Collins an attorney, conceived to be privy to his treason, fled to the enemy. And upon the 3rd of December, (as we are credibly informed) the enemy guided by these two renegadoes with 400 musquetiers, three hours before daybreak, surprised our guard at Lairy Point, and in it three pieces of ordnance. The work is but a half moon, and the guard placed there only to give the alarm if the enemy should approach Lare Point over the sands, when the tide is out. By which means the enemy coming on under Lipson Work, (being a variable ground by reason of its steepness,) came on the back of our guard, and easily surprized it. The alarm being given to the town, at break of day, 150 horse and 300 musquetiers marched out to attack them, which the enemy at Mount Stamford perceiving, (for we fell on upon the south side of the hill, which was from the enemy's view) gave a signal to the main body of the enemy, who were at Compton all in arms; upon which Prince Maurice, and all the gallantry of his army, with four regiments of foot and five of horse, (having in the night made their way with pioneers) advanced under protection of their own ordnance and a hedge they possesst, (where we usually placed sentries, and where since we have built a work* under

*This is still to be discovered in a field to the eastward of the road, half way down Lipson-hill, at the first turning.

Lipson,) to the assistance of those, who in the night had surprized our guard. We were in hopes to have beaten off the enemy before Prince Maurice could come to their assistance, and therefore attacked them resolutely with horse and foot, but met strong opposition; and Captain Wansey a gallant man, charging at a gap which formerly he knew to be open, but now made up by the enemy, was unfortunately slain, which made our horse give ground, and were afterwards both horse and foot, put to an absolute rout for three fields together; at which time some of the enemy's horse mixt themselves with ours, and came within pistol shot of the walls, and were killed or taken. A stand being at last made upon the height of the hill above Lipson Work, and fresh men being drawn from several guards, and having encouraged our men, we held our ground for four hours. During which time, our ship at Lare Point seeing our guard were taken, entertained a parley with the enemy, and so stood neuter till we had beaten the enemy to a retreat, (for which some of them are in question for their life). The enemy sent a trumpet during this battle to summon Lypson Work, but was answered with a cannon, after it had been commanded to depart. In the mean time we having gotten a small Drake planted in the cross way, discharged it four or five times on the enemy's horse with good execution, and having given a signal by sound of drumm, when our several commanded places should fall on, the enemy began to give ground, and some 200 musquetiers of the trained bands of the town being come to our assistance, we sent a party of about 60 musquetiers to play upon their backs, which was no sooner perceived by Prince Maurice, but he commanded a retreat, which was followed so close by us, that it was little better than a hasty flight, for the greatest part retreating over the Lare, and not the same way they came on; their rear guard of horse of about 100 men being cut off from their way of retreat were forced into the mud between Lipson Work and Lare Point, and the horse were almost all taken or drowned when the sea came in, some of the riders by crawling through the mud hardly escaped; many of the enemy were killed in their retreat by our horse and foot, and by the ship at Lare Point, who then grew honest again; of the prisoners we took a captain-lieutenant of horse and one Langsford, once a priest, but now a captain, and about 30 common soldiers, 13 barrels of powder, two teams of horses with furniture, (by which they were drawing up our ordnance against us). Of ours the enemy took in our first retreat, Captain-Lieutenant Roe, Lieutenant Upton, Ensigns Crocker and Francis Rolles, and about 40 common soldiers, besides Captain Wansey, and about 12 others killed, and a 100 men wounded, some of whom are since dead. Colonel Gould had a horse killed under him and another shot, but he mercifully preserved. The Lord shewed himself wonderfully in our deliverance, for when the enemy had gained great advantages and were ten to one against us, yet was pleased by our handfull to drive them back another way than they came, for had they kept possession of the ground they had gotton that night, the next day they would have been masters of all Catdown, and then we must have quitted our outworks as useless to us, and have betaken ourselves to the Town Walls,* which then were not fully finished, and could not have been defended long. The same day the enemy with horse and foot assaulted Pennycomquick Work† and were repulsed with much loss. After this second repulse, they suffered us to be quiet (as usual,) for 15 or 20 days, in the mean time collecting together their routed troops, except one night they fell on upon a work we were raising under Lipson Work, called in the maps Lypson Mill Work, for the prevention of the enemy's incursions again that way, and partly slighted it, our guard there having quitted it without a shot; from this they were however suddenly beaten again, and the work re-edified. It were endless to recount the numerous skirmishes that daily past between us, sometimes about our cattle that strayed without our works, at other times to pass time by bravadoes and ambuscades, made by our guards to entrap the enemy. Prince Maurice now finding their battery against Lipson, and his intent to possess Lare Point successless, he began to make approaches against Maudlin Work, we in the mean time thick'ned that work within to make it proof, and finding they had planted their batteries within musquet shot of our work, we planted a platform close by Maudlin Work, and drew out a demy-cannon (which was taken in a prize that was going to the rebells in Ireland,) to counter-batterie against them, and intended to plant another if it had been needful. Upon the 18th of December the enemy began to batter, but by reason of our counter-batterie, which played constantly into their work through their ports, whereby their men could not stand safely by their ordance, we having the advantage of playing down upon them from the commanding ground; so that the enemy in two days had done us no harm with their battery. But on Wednesday night, the 20th of December, through the carelessness of the captain of the guard, that set out sentries, *perdue*, it being a wet and dark night, the enemy raised a square work with the help of the corner of a field, within pistol shot of

*I believe it is known by very few (if any) that there are still at this time remains of the Walls of this Town, but the present writer has traced a mound of earth, which formed a ditch before the wall from Old Town Gate to Gaskings Gate, of part of this mound a terrace in several gardens has been formed, and Huer's Row has evidently been built on it; the wall itself did not reach farther than the head of Little Church lane, and serves as the Northern Wall to several gardens there. The wall of the gardens etc., of the eastern side of Old Town street, was no doubt also part of the Town Walls, and before the building of Frankfort-place, might no doubt have been traced from Old Town Gate to Frankfort Gate." – Old MS Note.

†Pennycomquick Work or rather the vestige of it, forms a corner of a field above Pennycomquick Hill, at the cross roads there.

Maudlin Work, almost in a direct line between that and Pennycomquick, which if they had kept possession of, might have cut us off from the relief of that work, etc.; as soon as it was discovered by the guard at Maudlin the next morning, which consisted of about threescore men, they attacked the work in hopes to have regained it without any more help, but found it guarded with two or three hundred men, and so were fain to retreat until a reinforcement came from the town. Accordingly about nine o'clock, the horse and foot being got ready, we fell on upon their work, but were repulsed twice, and once after we had gained it; but our men being heartened with the assistance of some fresh men, and backed with most of the strength we could make, attacked it the third time, and took and slighted it. The prisoners taken on their side were one captain, Prince Maurice's trumpeter, and some few others, and killed near 100 men; there were taken of ours by the enemy, Lieutenant William Harwar, and two more surrounded by their horse in one place, and as many in another; we had 20 men killed, whereof Ensigne Grimes was one, and fourscore wounded, whereof Ensigne Samuel Horte and some others are since dead. Upon the enemy's retreat we could hardly dissuade our soldiers from falling on their works to gain their ordnance; but we had too few men to adventure upon so hazardous a design. The next day we could see the enemy preparing to draw off their ordnance, and on Christmas Day, the 25th of December, in the morning, they withdrew their guards; being the same day that Prince Maurice promised his soldiers they should be in Plymouth. That day Major-General Basset called to one of our officers that was a prisoner in their work, and told him that he thought God fought against them, and said if he could be persuaded that he was not in the right, he would hang himself at his door, before he would take up arms again in that quarrel. The day after the enemy had raised the siege, part of two of our works fell down, which might have endangered the loss of them, if they had continued their siege. The enemy now quarter at Tavistock and Plympton to refresh their men, and to recruit for a fourth siege, and for the present they block us up from provision, having driven all the cattle in the country before them, so that we cannot subsist long unless store of all sorts of provisions be sent us. But if we have a considerable supply of men, money and arms, for horse and foot, sent us with speed, by God's assistance we may be able to take the field, for all the country is inclined towards us, which opportunity we hope the Parliament will not neglect.

"One remarkable passage of God's providence to us, we must with all thankfullness remember and acknowledge; that after the town had been a long time strictly besieged, and no fresh victuals, either of flesh or fish could be had, whereby the poor people were great sufferers, there came an infinite multitude of pilchards into the harbour, within the Barbican, which the people took up with great ease in baskets, which not only refreshed them for the present; but a great many more were salted, whereby the poor got much money; such a circumstance never happened before. We cannot forget the humanity of the good women of Plymouth, not their courage in bringing out strong waters, and all sorts of provisions, in the midst of our skirmishes for the refreshing of our soldiers, though many were shot through the cloaths. We cannot omit mentioning that soon after our arrival here, Sampson Hele, Esquire, came on a message to the town from the Prince, to persuade the yielding of it up; but coming without drum or trumpet, he was constrained for this offence to give us £2,000 for the pay and cloathing of our soldiers, without which we could not possibly have subsisted so long.

"We had upon the loss of Mount Stamford, a day of humiliation, and upon God's delivering us at Lare Point, a day of thanksgiving, and another since the siege was raised.

"The chief commanders before us were Prince Maurice, the Earls of Marlborough, and Newport, the Lord Mohun, Sir Thos. Hele, Sir Edmd. Fortescue, Sir John Grenville, Sir Richard Cave, Sir James Cobourne, Sir John Digby, Sir Peter Courtney, Sir William Courtney, Lieut-General Wagstaffe, and Major-General Basset and divers other considerable persons, many of whom as well as of the common soldiers are either since dead or desperately sick. – Attested under the hands of

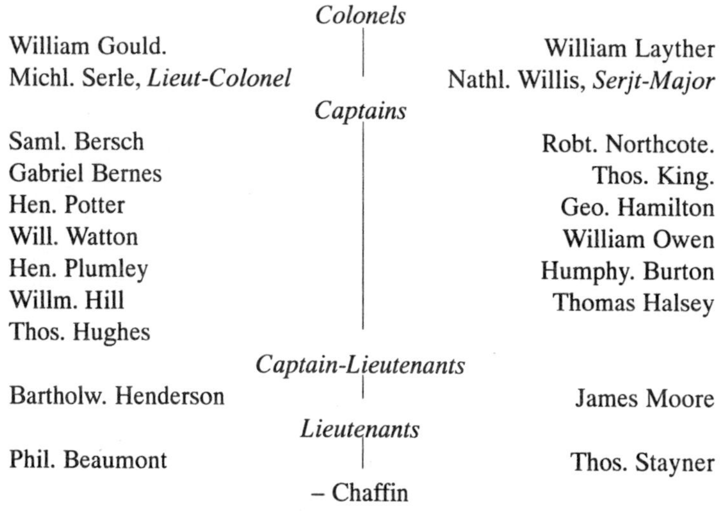

Colonels

William Gould.	William Layther
Michl. Serle, *Lieut-Colonel*	Nathl. Willis, *Serjt-Major*

Captains

Saml. Bersch	Robt. Northcote.
Gabriel Bernes	Thos. King.
Hen. Potter	Geo. Hamilton
Will. Watton	William Owen
Hen. Plumley	Humphy. Burton
Willm. Hill	Thomas Halsey
Thos. Hughes	

Captain-Lieutenants

Bartholw. Henderson	James Moore

Lieutenants

Phil. Beaumont	Thos. Stayner

– Chaffin

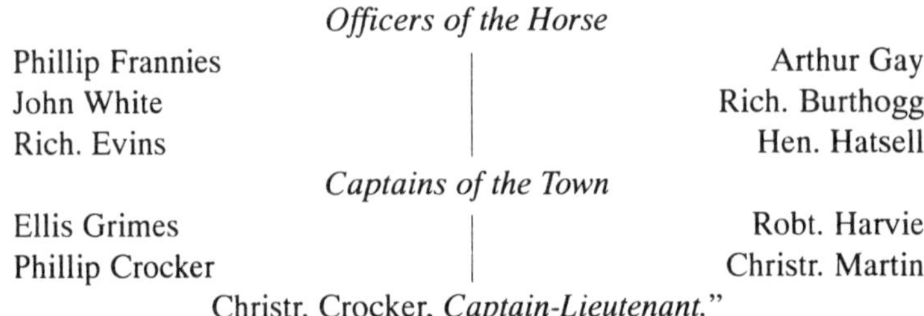

Officers of the Horse

Phillip Frannies	Arthur Gay
John White	Rich. Burthogg
Rich. Evins	Hen. Hatsell

Captains of the Town

Ellis Grimes	Robt. Harvie
Phillip Crocker	Christr. Martin

Christr. Crocker, *Captain-Lieutenant.*"

"The summons of the Cavaliers. – To the Mayor and Governor of the Town of Plymouth. That you may see our hearty desires of a just peace.

"We do summon you in His Majesty's name, to surrender the Town, Fort and Island of Plymouth, with the warlike provisions thereunto belonging, into our hands for His Majesty's use. And we do hereby assure you by the power derived to us from His Majesty, upon the performance hereof of a general pardon for what is past, and engage ourselves on our honour to secure your persons and estate from all violence and plunder. We have now acquitted ourselves on our parts, and let the blood that shall be split in the obtaining of these just demands (if denied by you) be your guilt. Given under our hands at Mount Stamford, the 18th day of Novr., A.D. 1643.

John Digby	Thos. Monke
Jno. Wagstaffe	Thos. Stucley
Jno. Arundell	Peter Killigrew
Jo. Downing	R. Prideaux
Thomas Basset	Wm. Arundell."
Jonathan Trelawny	

"Plymouth, 4th Novr., 1643. – It is this day ordered by the Council of War that this vow and protestation as followeth be openly published in the Assemblies by the Ministers of this Town to-morrow, being the 5th of Novr., 1643, and that it may be presented particularly to all officers and soldiers, inhabitants and strangers of the Towns and Garrisons of Plymouth and Stonehouse, the Fort and Island. And that especial notice be taken of all such as shall refuse to take the said vow and protestation which is as followeth. – I, A.B. in the presence of Almighty God do vow and protest that I will to the utmost of my power faithfully maintain and defend the Town of Plymouth and Stonehouse, the Fort and Island with all the outworks and fortifications to the same belonging, against all forces now raised against the said town, fort and island or any part thereof, or that shall be raised by any power or authority whatsoever, without the consent and authority of both Houses of Parliament, neither will I by any way or means whatsoever contrive to consent to the giving up of the said towns and fortifications aforesaid or any parcel of them, into the hands of any person or persons whatsoever, without the consent of both Houses of Parliament or of such as are authorized thereunto by them; neither will I raise or consent to the raising of any force or tumult; nor will I by any way or means give or yield to the giving any advice, counsel or intelligence to the prejudice of the said towns and fortifications, either in whole or part, but will with all faith, fully discover to the Mayor of Plymouth and to the commander-in-chief there whatsoever design I shall know or hear of hurtful thereunto; neither have I accepted any pardon or protection nor will accept any protection from the enemy, and this vow and protestation I make without any equivocation or mental reservation whatsoever, believing that I cannot be absolved from this my vow and protestation, and wishing no blessing from God on myself or my posterity, if I do not truly and sincerely perform the same. – SO HELP ME GOD."

"Prince Maurice's Warrant since the raising of the Siege. – "To the constables of Egg-Buckland, (and after notice taken of the publishing,) to the constables or tything men of Saint Budeaux, there to be published.–

"For as much as divers persons, disaffected to His Majesty's service, make their daily recourse into Plymouth, furnishing the rebells there with all manner of provision for man and horse, contrary to His Majesty's proclamation prohibiting the same, these are therefore to signify, that if any person, of what degree or quality, do ever presume to have any commerce or dealing with any in the said town, or take or carry with him any horses, oxen, kine, or sheep or other provision for man or horse into the said Town of Plymouth, for the relief of the rebells there, every such person and persons shall be proceeded against both in person and estate, as abettors of this horrid rebellion, and contemners of His Majesty's proclamation, according to the limitation of the Court of Wards in such cases provided; willing and requiring all mayors, justices of peace, bayliffs, constables and all others of His Majesty's officers and ministers, to cause this to be forthwith published in all churches, chapels, markets, or other places; whereby His Majesty's loving subjects may the better take notice hereof. – MAURICE."

" A continuation of the true narration of the most observable passages in and about Plymouth, from January 26th 1642, till this present, wherein you may observe how the Lord doth always work for that poor and remote garrison, together with the letter of Sir Richard Greenville, with the answer to it, as also the burning a book inclosed in his letter, by the hand of the common hangman; the book being intitled "The Iniquity of the Common

Wealth, with the discovery of a She Traitor," with the articles proved against her on oath at a Council of War. Published by authority."

"Plymouth being a town far remote, and the passage being by sea, an account of God's working (for Plymouth) against the enemy, cannot so speedily be given as might be wished and expected, besides the commanders, (being more desirous to serve their God and country, than to gaggle like hens on the laying of every egg,) are contented to be silent, until there is enough acted to fill up a relation; now therefore not willing that God's mercies should be stiffled, but published for His glory, and for the heartening of such as stand up courageously for the Lord against the mighty, this ensuing narration (as a continuation of the most observable passages in and about Plymouth,) is thought fit to be published.

"December 25th, 1643, our last ended: – and this begins January 26th, 1644, for in the interim, great care was taken and still is, to fortify the town, in pulling down hedges without our works, and repair the decayed and ruined outworks; in building new where they are wanting, and running breast works from work to work; two new works are made, two repaired that fell down December the 25th at night, the very night after the enemy removed the strait siege; and let not the world wonder, that we lay still a month without encounters when we had so many hedges to pull down, and three miles of ground to be new fortified against the enemy, besides the slighting of the enemy's works.

"If none of this had been needful to refresh such a tired and almost worn-out garrison, it being common in the winter for the poor soldiers to endure six or seven night's duty without relief, besides their bickerings and encounters with the enemy.

"But if the world knew what rubs against action hath lain in the way, it would not wonder the gallant garrison hath given no better account to Parliament, however take this narration for a truth, without questioning it, and bless God for this, and pray for them that are (by God's assistance) resolved to do more.

"January 26th 1644. – The enemy lying at Plympton and at Buckland and in other parishes in their quarters, sallied out and fell on some of our men that were about the country, but when we heard of it we drew forth our horse, Major Halsey, Commander-in-Chief fell upon the enemy in Tamerton, four miles from the town, when we took nine horses and nine prisoners and one slain.

"February 24th. – Captain-Lieutenant Chaffin was sent out with a party of horse, to fall upon the enemy's guard at Treniman's or Trenleman's Jump, four miles from the town, where we beat them of their guard and took 25 horses and one prisoner and lost but one horse.

"March 15th. – One of Colonel Gould's men and some others going into the country upon some occasion, the enemy came upon them and took the colonel's man (since redeemed,) and when the alarm came into the town, (Major Halsey, Commander-in-Chief,) we drew forth our horse and pursued our enemy to Treniman's Jump, where we fell on their guard and beat them out of their guard house, slew three of their men and took ten horses, six prisoners, two drums and nine muskets and lost not a man.

"March 20th. – Captain Lieutenant Chaffin, Commander-in-Chief, was sent out with a party of 60 horse, and fell upon the enemy's guard aforesaid, where we beat them out of their guard, and pursued them about a mile upon the Down towards Tavistock, and slew about ten men of them, and took ten prisoners, one captain, one lieutenant, one quarter-master and 30 horse, besides what was wounded of the enemy, and run away over the hedges forsaking their horses, and we lost but one horse and two men wounded, and so returned safe home to Plymouth.

"March 27th. – That unparalled (in respect to the west) Colonel Gould, departed this life, being called to Jesus Christ to have a crown of gold set on his head for his golden activity and fidelity and indefatigable patience, to help the Lord against the mighty in purging the Church and Common Wealth, being lamented of all but malicious malignants.

"By his death the affair of the town likely to be out of order, a commission was granted to the Mayor of Plymouth, Colonel Crocker, and Lieutenant-Colonel Martin, for the ordering of the affairs of the garrison until a commander-in-chief was sent down from the Parliament.

"The command of the island remaining in the hand of Captain Henry Hatsall, a captain of such known integrity, that though envious stomachs may rail against him, yet they cannot draw off the affections of the well-affected in Plymouth, from a high esteem of his approved valour and fidelity.

"The command of the fort is in the hands of Captain-Lieutenant Birtch, who intends to keep them, as they have signified to the Parliament for them, and none else, the garrison of both protesting the same constancy and fidelity.

"On April 16th, the Mayor of Plymouth and Colonel Crocker, having transferred the power they had from Colonel Wardlow unto Lieutenant-Colonel Martin alone, intelligence having been brought that the enemy (near 500) drew near us, and quartered at Saint Budeaux, two miles from Plymouth, (on Devonshire side,) Lieutenant-Colonel Martin sent about 600 commanded musquetiers with some horse to fall upon them, 17 colours being sent to face Plympton (a grand quarter of the enemy) in the mean time; but our forlorn hope of horse by mistake of the guides, went one way, and the body of foot another, notwithstanding our foot comeing up undiscovered, fell on the enemy and put them to flight; killed two of them, and took in Saint Budeaux Tower and in their flight, 44 prisoners, besides Lieutenant Cory (sometime servant to Sir Beville Greenville, Lieut-Colonel,) Porter's Ensign, three barrels of powder, 20 horse, and above 100 arms. Major Collings, Captain Vacey, of Tamerton, Captain Tavernon, hardly escaping by reason of the absence of our horse; most of these prisoners having taken the covenant and have taken up arms for us since.

"On April 19th, 200 musquetiers with some horse were commanded to fall on the enemy at Newbridge, in the way to Plympton, and the command was that our forlorn hope should not fall on until the relief was in sight, but disobeying the command, fell on them when the relief was a mile behind, yet they beat them from hedge to hedge, and one breast work on this side the bridge, but their powder being spent, and the greatest part of the enemy's forces at Plympton coming to the relief, our forlorn having spent their powder, they were compelled to retreat, but fairly without the loss of a man, two only being wounded.

"On April 21st, 40 foot sallied from Prince Rock to Pomphlet Mills, (a quarter of the enemy's) laying in a creek against Prince Rock, the enemy fled like hares, and our men took 16 foot, arms, one drum, five hogs, and five cows.

"As our forces have not been altogether idle and successless on the land, so have they not been loiterous at sea,* .... being removed, for our seaman at three several times, have fallen on the enemy's country and brought away 100 sheep.

"On April 25th, the packet boat took a bark laden with Irish cloth, tallow, hides, etc. And since this, another boat has taken a hoy laden with three butts of French wine, wherein were three grand Cornish cavaliers, and it is without exception that if our ships might have commissions to land men on the Cornish shore, we should not only help Plymouth to many necessaries, but also fill the Cornish hands so full with watching their own shores, that they would have little liberty, and less heart to fall on Devonshire or Plymouth. We cannot conceal what we have by our intelligences from the country: –

"First, we are informed that Shellam Grenville builds very much on Fitzford, (I hope castles in the air, or houses without foundation,) and boasts

*This blank is in the original MS.

of having Plymouth speedily, but garrison and Plymouth will not believe him.

"Second, that the said renegado Grenville hath seized on the Lord Bedford's estate, and Master Courtenay's estate, and sent him prisoner to Exon, making havoc of his goods and corn.

"Third, that the enemy endeavours all he can to raise forces to fall on Plymouth, and carry them eastward, threatening to hang such as refuse; and having pressed six in Lifton Parish, (according to which proportion, their whole number of pressed men will amount to 2,500 in the whole country,) they were compelled to send a guard with them to Exon.

"Fourth, that there were very lately expected 7,000 men to appear at Exeter, (as the cavaliers report,) but there appeared but 700, which so moved Sir John Berkeley's worship, that he pressed the constables, a fit reward for their activity.

"Fifth, that the generality of the country (notwithstanding the oath), are well affected to the Parliament, but want some to countenance them in the country, to cut the cavaliers's throats to free them of their iron bondage.

"Sixthly, that Arundel of Chiddock in Dorsetshire, a papist, is carrying his goods into Cornwall, and hath seized on the Lord Robert's children, and committed them to safe custody at Bodmin, this is confirmed once and again.

"Seventhly, that the Lords Mohun, Edgecombe, and Fane are returned from the feminine junto of Oxford.

"Eightly, that it is reported that the Queen is at Exon, where since her arrival, divers warrants have been issued out, to command the train bands to make their personal appearance, and to bring all fat cattle into the city, whereby it is likely they expect a siege.

"Ninthly, that the King's privy seals are abroad to make up £100,000, given (in words to His Majesty) for the recruiting of himself, and is destroying many by the perjured junto at Oxon.

"Tenthly, that the country is ordered to prepare three subsidies, which they cannot well digest, you may visibly see the misery of the county, let not the country patriots be forgetfull of that county that have expended £150,000 for their defence, let it not seem small that it sits in dust and ashes, like a widow looking for help, but none appears; you may see how God hath preserved the poor Garrison of Plymouth.

"On April 25th, the constable of Egg-Buckland was brought in hither, who had a warrant from Sir Thomas Hele, (not one of the wisest) requesting the appearance of his parishioners with the arms at Modbury, and for the providing new arms, (if they can get them) in the place of such as are wanted.

"It cannot be superfluous to give intelligence of God's gracious discovery of feminine malignants and traitors at Plymouth, one whereof is committed to the castle for holding correspondence with the enemy.

"The articles provided against her are, first that she sent suits of apparel to one Collins, a renegado of Plymouth, who endeavoured with Pike, his consort to betray the town, as in our former narration we have expressed.

"Second, that by message, she discovered to the enemy what quantity of powder was in the town.

"Third, that she invited the enemy to assault the town.

"Fourth, that she desired Major Harris (a cavalier) to quarter in her house (vizt.) when she was taken.

"Fifth, that she seconded her former invitation with intreaties, falsely informing him that the Protestant religion (since our Covenant) was decayed and breathing its last gasp in Plymouth.

"For the other virago, we shall let her sleep for a while, that her shame and doom may be the heavier.

"It is not to be omitted, to see how Providence watcheth over the town, for though ever since the gaining of Mount Stamford, the enemy hath daily continued shooting into the town; some days scores of great shot liberally spent, yet the hurt that they have done is but a trifle, and the people so far from being affrighted that they slighted it, being hardened, our boat going daily out into the Sound and Mill Bay under the mouth of the cannon, and within less than musket shot. It is worth knowing for imitation sake, that Colonel Gould hath much purged the garrison from swearers, drunkards and abominable livers; causing the town and garrison to be very careful in observing the Lord's day, days of humiliation, and to be frequently present at the ordinances of the Lord of Hosts.

"Here should follow Sir Richard Greenville's letter to Colonel Gould, together with the officers and soldiers now in the fort; but this letter doth not appear. The answer thereto is as follows.

"The answer of the Commanders of the Garrison to Sir Richard Greenville's letter: –

"Sir, – Though your letter meriting the highest contempt and scorn, which once we thought fit by our silence (judging it unworthy of our answer) to have testified; yet considering that yourself intend to make it publick, we offer you these lines that the world may see what esteem we have of the man, notorious for apostacy and treachery; and that we are ready to dispute the justness and equity of our cause in any lawful way, whereto the enemy shall at any time challenge us. You might well have spared the giving us an account of your dissimulation with the Parliament, we were soon satisfied, and our wonder is not so great that you are now gone from us, at the first, when we understood of your engagements to us, and to tell you the truth, it pleased us not so well to hear you were named to be governor of this place, as now it doth to hear you are in arms against us, accounting ourselves safer to have you an enemy abroad, than a pretended friend at home, being persuaded that your principles could not afford cordial endeavours for an honest cause.

"You tell us of the pretended Houses of Parliament in London, a threadbare scandal suck't from Aulicus, whose reward or bp. blessing you may chance to be honoured with for your court service, and how they make religion the cloak of rebellion, a garment which we are confident your rebellion will never be clad with; you advise us to consider the great charges we have been at, and the future charges we run ourselves into by making ourselves enemies to His Majesty, who more desires our good than we ourselves, and thence would have us propose conditions for peace.

"That we have been at great charges already we are sufficiently sensible, and yet resolve that it shall not any way lessen our affections to that cause, with which God has honoured us, by making us instruments to plead it against the malicious adversaries. If the King be our enemy, yet Oxford cannot prove that we have made him so. That His Majesty desires our welfare we can easily admit, as well as that it is his mishchievous counsellors so near him who render him so cruel to his most faithful subjects, and as for proposing conditions for peace, we shall most gladly do it, when it may advance the public service, but to do it to the enemies of peace though we have been thereto formally invited, yet hath it pleased the Disposer of All Things to preserve us from the necessity of it, and to support us against the fury of the enraged enemy. The same God is still our rock and refuge, under whose wings we doubt not of protection and safety, when the seducers of a King shall die like a candle, and that name, which by such courses is sought to be perpetual in honour, shall end in ignominy.

"For the want of money to pay the Parliament Soldiers, though it be not such as you would persuade us, yet certain we are, their treasury had now been greater and honest men better satisfied, but that some as unfaithful as yourself, have gone before you in betraying them, both of their trust and riches; whereas you remind us of the lost condition of our own town, sure it cannot be, you should be so truly persuaded of it, as they are of your personal, who subscribe themselves and so remain,

FRIENDS TO THE FAITHFUL."

1643. – John Cawse, Mayor. Fort Batten built. "It is remarkable that during the siege, when the inhabitants were in great want of provisions, a large quantity of pilchards came within the Barbican, so that the people could take them with case in baskets."

The following curious document is an agreement as to prices to be paid by the Master Shoemakers of Plymouth to their journeymen for various descriptions of work: –

"We whose names are underwritten, Master Shoemakers and Inhabitants of the Borough of Plymouth, upon a general meeting, and knowing the extraordinary charges that journeymen of our trade have put us unto, by a generall consent, doe between us absolutely conclude and agree that neither of us shall henceforth entertaine or receive any journeyman to work, unless it be upon the same conditions and usuall prizes, which heretofore they were accustomed to have. And further we doe also conclude and agree, that if any journeyman shall upon any pretended matter leave needlessly his said master, then none of us shall or will entertayne him into any of our works or services without the privity of his saide master, but by his consent from whom he so departed. Which said journeymen were formerly to have according to these prizes following, viz: –

First for French heele boots … … … … … … xij*d*
" for woodden heele boots … … … … … … x*d*
" for French heele shoos … … … … … … vi*d*
" for footing of French heele boots … … … viij*d*
" for wodden heele shooes & fale shooes … iiij*d*
" for playne shooes … … … … … … … … ij*d*

For the true performance of which said conditions and order we do each of ous bynd ourselves, our executors, administrators and assignes unto the other, theire executors and administrators in the full summe of five pounds of lawfull money of England. In witnes whereof we have each of us hereunder severally sett our hands this 17th day of Aprill, 1643.

Richard Randell.
Richard Dimery.
Roger Hooke.
Williame Webb.
Josiah Monyen.
Richard Morgan
John Kempe
Thomas Spry.

John Haythorne.
Jonathan Freythie.
John Lufe.
William Dundrich.
The mark (B) of
Christopher Burd.
Francis Lange.
Phillip Prouse.

"I, Francis Pavey of Plymouth, Notary and Tabellion Publique, doe certifie that the orders above written concluded on as abovesaid, were soe done really in the presense of me the said notary; witnes both hand and seale being requested so to doe.

PER ME FRANCISUM PAVEY,
Nori[ium] Pubc[ium] et Tabellionem,"

Endorsed – "The Shomakers' compants the 12th of Maye, 1643, being a rate for ther worke."

1644. – Justinian Peard, Mayor.

1645. – Bartholomew Nichols, Mayor. "The New Church called Charles' Church, in Plymouth, begun."

1646. – Christopher Ceely or Seeley, Mayor. This year the Mayor and Corporation leased the market with all tolls, rights and privileges for five years, to Christopher Ryder, gentleman, and Arthur Bickford, yeoman, both of Plymouth, at a yearly rental of £10.

"Proposed subscription to augment the yearly income of the Vicars of Saint Andrew and Charles, and also to provide a lecturer for Saint Andrew's at £80.

"We whose name are subscribed, doe promise quarterly to pay the respective sums by us severally underwritten, to such person or persons as shall be appointed by the maior of this borough to collect the same for and during the space of five years, from the 29th day of September last past, towards the maintenance of a lecturer, to preach once in the week, in the church of Saint Andrew, within this borough, as hath been accustomed, and towards the raisinge so much money as shall be needful to make the rent and profits belonging to the vicarage of Saint Andrew, £200 per annum, and the rent and profittes of the vicarage of Charles' Church £100 per annum, which we have thought good to undertake for the better incouragement of the ministers now living with us. And for the said lecturer it is agreed that he shall have £80 per annum. Plymouth, 3rd of November, 1646." (Here follows a very long list of persons who subscribed, with the amount of their subscriptions sett opposite their names).

1647. – Richard Evans, Mayor. "The Queen, Prince, etc., fly into France. The King brought to Westminster, where a High Court of Justice, as these villains called themselves, was erected."

1648. – Timothy Alsop, Mayor.

1649. – Oliver Ceely or Seeley, Mayor.

1650. – Robert Gubbes, Mayor.

1651. – Philip Francis, Mayor. "A war between the English and the Dutch, August 16th, 1652, Sir G. Askew and De Ruyter fight before Plymouth; General Blake beates them in divers fights, and at length, July 1653, our Immortal Monk beates them on their own coast, where the great General Tromp was slain."

In this year a Yarn Market that had used formerly to be held in the churchyard was revived, as is shown by the following extract from the Corporation Records: –

"January 31st, 1651. – Whereas there hath been antiently a Yarn Market weekly kept within this borough, (though for some late years intermitted,) it is this day in open sessions, upon due consideration thereupon had, and for divers good reasons then alledged, as well for the public good of the adjacent parts, as for the benefit of this place, ordered and hereby published and declared, that on Thursday, the 26th of February next, there be a Yarn Market kept within this borough, in the churchyard, between the hours of 10 and 12 in the forenoon, and so weekly on Thursdays, thenceforward to continue. And all persons who are concerned herein, may take notice that they may come and attend on the days and time and at the place aforesaid, and then and there buy and sell wool yarn as formerly, and have the weighing of the yarn free for one year next ensuing."

1652. – John Maddock, Mayor.

1653. – Richard Spurwell, Mayor. "Brave Penrudick, Graves, etc. rising for the king, were taken by perifidous Crook at South Molton in this county, and beheaded."

1654. – John Page, Mayor. Christopher Ceely or Seeley, Merchant, and William Yeo, Esq., Members for Plymouth. "The Almshouses on north side of Saint Andrew's Church built; known as the Old Church Twelves."

1655. – Christopher Ceely or Seeley, again Mayor. The Leather Hall built.

1656. – Justinian Peard, Mayor. John Maynard, Esq., Serjeant-at-Law, and Timothy Alsop, Merchant, Members for Plymouth. "Blake grown sickly, returns home, and in sight of this port dyeth, was embalmed, his bowells buryed here by the mayor's seat door; his corpse at Westminster among the Kings." Charles' Church consecrated by Dr. Gill, Bishop of Exeter.

1657. – William Jeffrey, Mayor. "The new Shambles in the midst of the Old Town-street built. The new Free School finished." Charles' Church was as appears from the following entry in the "Black Book" of the Corporation, finished building in this year. "1657, – In this yere was the New Church called Charles' Church finished, though long in building, and some disturbance by a paltry pretended churchwarden, etc., yett by God's goodness carried on, we hope to His glory."

1658. – Samuel Northcote, Mayor. Christopher Ceely or Seeley, Esq., and Timothy Alsop, Esq., Members for Plymouth.

1659. – John King, Mayor. "The mayor and several of the bench lost their places, for not renouncing the Covenant."

"In this year the Freemen of the town first voted at the election of Members of Parliament, which privilege had been refused them some time."

"King Charles II was proclaymed in Plymouth with great tryumphe, the cunditts running two days with wyne, and shortly after a curious present of rare wrought plate was presented to His Majesty by this Corporation, which was graciously accepted."

1660. – Oliver Ceely or Seeley, Mayor. John Allward, of Plymouth, for speaking treason beheaded, and his head set on the Guildhall.

"September 6th, 1660, peace between England and Spaine was proclaimed at Plymouth, and in the same month the Spanish Ambassador arrived at this town and was banquetted at the towne's cost." Two royal pieces of plate were presented to the King on his restoration.

It is stated that in this year a party of horse soldiers was ordered from the Garrison at Plymouth to dispossess the Rev. Arthur Gifford, or Giffard, B.D., who had been presented to the living of Bideford by Sir Bevil or Sir John Granville, Mr. Gifford was dispossessed of his living by the committee for plundering, or as it was termed, sequestration, of all the loyal and orthodox clergy, in the latter case, chiefly at the instigation of his curate or lecturer, William Bartlett. Concerning the manner of his ejection, Mr. Prince only says, "It was by force and violence against law and conscience." Dr Walker however, is more particular and informs us that "The old gentleman did not quietly give up his living, and therefore a party of horse was ordered to force him out of it by violence, which they did and used him barbarously, throwing dirt upon him and some spitting at him as he passed along the streets."

Calamy labours hard to disprove the charges alleged by Dr. Walker against the sequestrators, and particularly their assistant Bartlett, in the case of Mr. Gifford; concerning the manner of the latter's ejection, he says, "I have this account from some credible persons, who were then upon the spot. It seems after his sequestration he refused to resign, and having got a body of men into the parsonage house, which stands alone by itself, he undertook to defend it, and maintained possession. Upon this, a party of horse was ordered from the Garrison at Plymouth to dispossess him. The commanding officer came with his troop to Bideford in the evening, and resolving to execute his commission that night, rode up to the house, and found the door shut against him. He demanded entrance, and said he would use no violence if Mr Gifford and those within, would surrender themselves, otherwise he should be obliged to fire upon the house. Mr. Gifford finding the house beset, desired the liberty of conversing with the captain for which he had an opportunity given him at one of the windows of the house, they soon came to an agreement, Mr. Gifford and those within surrendered themselves prisoners; and my informants declare that Mr Gifford was conducted to the captain's lodgings without any abuse that they know of, offered by the way. The captain at length very civilly offered him the liberty of returning back to his own house, provided he would give him security for his forthcoming the next morning, which Mr. Gifford did, and the next day was carried by the same party of horse to Plymouth."

"Such is Dr. Calamy's circumstantial account, and evident partial softening of this iniquitous transaction; if any unbiased reader can, after a perusal of it, think that Mr. Gifford was very civilly treated, or that no manner of affront was offered to him, such reader I will be bold to say, must have the feelings of an inquisitor, and the christian charity of a republican fanatic. Dr. Calamy's informants he says, were credible persons, but he should certainly have mentioned their names, to judge what degree of credit was due to them. Upon this worthy confessor's ejection, the committee of robbers or sequestrators, put Mr. Bartlett into the possession of the rectory. He was an independent of the most violent stamp, and pursued Mr. Gifford with a spirit of persecution, for when the "Reverend and Pious Divine" says Mr. Prince, "would have served a small parish, called Westleigh opposite Bytheford, on the east side of the River Touridge, not for reward, but for what they would voluntarily contribute," (and Dr. Walker adds that he requested liberty to keep a school somewhere near the town,) such was the uncharitable zeal of that lordly independent preacher, William Bartlett, who by a prevailing rebellion had gotten into his parsonage and would not permit him so much as that. After this cruel treatment, Mr. Gifford retired to the house of his brother-in-law, Philip Harris Esq., Recorder of Great Torrington, where he lived privately and peaceably, expecting better times, which at length God was pleased to send again, upon the restoration of King Charles II, when Mr. Gifford returned unto his charge at Bideford, where he continued in peace and love with all good men unto the day of death, which was about eight years after.

"He was an able scholar, a constant and painful preacher, an orthodox divine, and a pious good man, he died at Bytheford, March 18th, 1668, and was buried in the parish church there, without any sepulchral monument."

1661. – William Allen, Mayor. "Commissioners regulate Corporations, turn out Mr. Hughes from being vicar, Mr. Allen from being mayor, etc.; Mr. William Jennens was put in by them, August 24th, and chosen by the Freemen, and served the year following."

1662. – William Jennens, Mayor. Dr. Ashton, chosen Vicar of Saint Andrew's.

"This mayor engaged the town in a law suit against my Lord Arundel for Sutton Pool, and after the fatal expence of £2,500 were cast, and lost the pool, which was worth £100 per annum, and had been in the town's hand many years."

"Those who refused to conform to the rights of the Church of England were silenced. Dr. Ashton, chosen Vicar of Saint Andrew's; George Hughes, father-in-law of the eminent Mr. Rowe, confined at Saint Nicholas' Island. About the same time Mr. Abraham Chear was also confined at the same prison." "The Workhouse revived."

The following curious entry by the mayor of this year, occurs in the Corporation Records: –

"1658 and 1659. – Whereas William Jefferie, above-named, assumes the honor of finishing the New Church, foulie aspersing myself the then churchwarden, whereas it is well known to the whole town I was under God, a main instrument to bring the saide church to be first preached in, without helpe from the said Jefferie, but to the contrary the worke obstructed by him, and others then in government, as to the other parte of his cronologie, let the proclaiming Richard (Cromwell) with acclamations be accompted as an instance of his rebellious affection to God, the King and his country, by advancing the continuance of succession to horrid rebels and rebellion. – William Jennens, Mayor, 1662 and 1663."

1663. – John Harris, Mayor. "Borough of Plymouth, 1663. – I do declare that I hold that there lyes noe obligation upon me or any other person from the oath, commonly called the Solemne League and Covenant, and that the same was in ittselfe an unlawful oathe, and imposed upon the subjects of this realme, against the known lawes and liberties of the kingdom. *Signed.* – John Harris."

"This declaration made and subscribed by John Harris, Merchant, Maior of Plymouth, in the Guildhall of the said burrough, the 29th day of September, 1663, being Michaelmas Day, at the time when he was sworne maior for the yeere, then next following, according to the Act of Parliament in that behalfe made.

"The above declaration was also then made and subscribed by William Jennens, Merchant. *Signed.* – William Jennens."

1664. – John Martin, Mayor. "Dr. Seth Ward, Bishop of Exeter, cometh his triennial visitation and consecrateth the New Church, by the name of Charles' Church."

1665. – William Harpur, Mayor. "The church-yard enclosed by Mr Schagell, Churchwarden."

"The royal Cittadell began to be built and carried far on this year, September 3rd, 1666."

1666. – George Strelley, Mayor. "The Guildhall new built." "The Dutch, while we were treating with them, and no navy at sea, came on our coast, burnt several navy ships at Chatham, and De Ruyter being Admiral, came on our western coast, and divers times anchored in the sound, but did no harm."

The following is the form of writ issued this year by the High Sheriff, John Kelland, Esq., to the Mayor of Plymouth, for the election of a Member of Parliament for that borough, in the room of Samuel Trelawney, Esq., deceased: –

"Devon. – John Kelland, Esq., High Sheriff of the county aforesaid.

"To the Mayor of the Towne and Burrough of Plymouth greetinge. By vertue of His Majesty's writt, to me directed, bearing date the twentyeth day of this instant moneth of September, for the continuinge of the Parlyament begaune and held at Westminster, the eighth day of May, in the thirteenth yeare of the raigne of Kinge Charles the Second, over England, etc., (his Majesty that now is,) and from thence by divers prorogacons until the three and twentyeth day of April last past; and from thence the said Parlyament being prorogued unto the eighteenth day of September last past, then and there holden. These are therefore to will and require you, that with all convenient speed after the receipt hereof, you do elect and chuse in the place and steed of Samuel Trelawney, Esq., late one of the burgesses chosen, appointed and returned according to the forme of the statute in that case made and provided, for your burrough, for this present Parlyament (in the Lower House for the Comonialtie of this kingdome of England) deceased, one other burgess for your said burrough, of the most discreet and sufficient, according to ye forme of the statute thereupon made and provided. Making first proclamation thereof of the daye and place for ye doing of the same. And that you summon and warne such person as you shall soe elect and chuse, to be forthwith at this present Parlyament in the said Lower House, for the said Comonialtie of the said kingdome, now sitting at Westminster. And that hee have full and sufficient power to doe and consent unto those things which then and there shall have to bee ordained for the good and safety of the Church and Kingdom; and also the you certify mee by your writing indented to be made betwixt mee of the one part and you of the other part, under your common seale or seales, (as usual in such cases) at the next county day to be holden at the Castle of Exeter, (being the sixteenth day of October next cominge) of your said election, and the name of such person, which you shall soe elect. And hereof you may not faile at your utmost perrills. Given under my seale of office, this six and twentieth day of September, in the xviijth yeare of the raigne of our said Souvraigne Lord Charles the Second, by the grace of God of England, Scotland, France and Ireland, King, Defender of the Faith, etc. Anno Domini 1666. – JOHN KELLAND, Vic."

1667. – Thomas Stutt, Mayor. "Peace with Holland, etc.; just upon the election of this man, Lambert, that arch rebell, brought prisoner to this island, Saint Nicholas."

1668. – William Symons, Mayor. "March, 1668, Cosmo de Medicis, Prince of Tuscany came to Plymouth, and after two days, travelled for London."

1669. – Daniel Barker or Booker, Mayor.

1670. – William Cotton, Mayor. This year the building of the Citadel having been completed, the King, with the Dukes of York and Monmouth, and a large retinue, on the 17th of July visited Plymouth to inspect it, and, of course, the town was put to considerable expense in fees to His Majesty and to his various retainers. The following account of these expenses is extracted from Deeble's MS.

	£	s.	d.
"Gave King Charles 150 pieces of gold	172	10	0
Purse to put it in	0	5	6
Ringers	2	0	0
King and Dukes' Footmen and Guards at the Fort	3	17	6
For making a Stage for His Majesty to stand on upon the New Quay	2	11	2
For removing timber and cleaning streets	1	11	6
Gentlemen Ushers daily waiting	5	0	0
Gentlemen Ushers Privy Chamber	5	0	0

	£	s.	d.
Serjeant at Armes	3	6	8
Gentlemen Ushers Quarter Waiters	1	0	0
Servers of the Chamber	1	0	0
Serjeants and Trumpeters	3	16	9
To the Pages of the Presence	0	10	5
Knight Marshalls	1	0	0
Knight Harbingers	3	6	8
Yeomen Ushers	1	0	0
Grooms of the Chamber	1	0	0
Footmen, Serjeants, Porter	3	0	0
Yeomen of the Month	2	0	0
Porters of the Gate	1	0	0
Coachmen	0	10	0
Surveyors of the Ways	1	10	0
Yeomen Harbingers	2	6	8
	£219	1	8"

"July 17th following, His Majesty, King Charles II, the Duke of York and the Duke of Monouth, came hither by sea, and lodged in the Old Fort, (the houses in the Citadell not finished) and returned as far as Dartmouth by sea." "Weights and measures of the town reformed, and the town bushel set up in the Market-place."

"A New Citadel having been built at Plymouth, His Majesty, King Charles II, came by water to view it, and on his return to London, taking Exeter in his route, he was received by the Mayor, Chamber, and Incorporated Trades, at the West Gate, and after the usual solemnities of presenting the city regalia, keys of the gates, etc., he was conducted to the Dean'ry where he lodged the night. During his stay, the Mayor, Aldermen and Members of the Common Council were admitted into his presence, and had the honour of kissing his hand. He also knighted the Mayor, Benjamin Oliver, Esq. The next morning he pursued his journey."*

1671. – Peter Schagell, Mayor. "Three new maces made for the Corporation. The water conveyed into the trennell of the Broad-street, and that which leadeth to Dung Key." "The compass new erected on the Hoe."

1672. – John Lanyon, Mayor. "The Exchange or Walk in the new Quay built. Sir John Skelton, Lieutenant-Governor of the Cittadell dyeth; Colonel Hugh Piper (afterward knighted) succeeds him. The debts of the town paid. The poor children clothed in red, maintained and set at work, in the Poors'

*Jenkin's Exeter, p. 177.

Portion. Houses of office made on the quays. The new Pounds built." "Sir Francis Drake's compass, on the Hoe, repaired for £17 18s." – *Corporation Records.*

1673. – Henry Webb, Mayor. "The Walk or Exchange on the Southside built, Lord Chief Justice Rainsford came to see the town. A fire engine with buckets, etc. brought to Plymouth."

The following account for the making of a suit and cloak for the Town Clerk is highly interesting and curious: –

"A Bill from Mr Henry Watts," (Town Clerk of Plymouth,) viz: –

	£	s	d
It. – For makeing a Sute and Cloake	00	16	00
It. – 11 yards of Serge at 4s. 4d. per yard	02	07	00
It. – For 3 yards of Florence Sarsnett	01	05	06
It. – Belly peeces, Coller, hookes and eyes	00	01	00
It. – Dyed Lining for ye Hose	00	03	06
It. – Ferrett Ribbin for ye Knees	00	01	00
It. – Pockets for Sute and Coate	00	01	06
It. – Silke to make it	00	03	00
It. – Galloone	00	01	03
It. – For pincking ye Lineing	00	05	06
It. – 2 yards 1/2 Fustian	00	02	11
It. – Stayes and Stifening for it	00	02	00
It. – 8 yards 1/2 of Bressel's Camblett	03	03	09
It. – 8 yards 1/2 Shalloone at 3s. 8d per yard	01	05	06
It. – For siseing ye Cloake and Vest	00	01	06
It. – Buckram and Stifening for ye Cloake	00	01	06
It. – 10 dozen Buttons	00	07	06
It. – One paire Stockings	00	06	06
It. – On peece and a halfe Ribbin	00	15	06
It. – For one Box	00	02	00
It. – For mending a Coate, and Silke	00	00	06
It. – Ribbin for a Shoulder Knott	00	02	06
It. – 1 dozen Buttons	00	00	06
1673, October 09th			
It. – For makeing a Vest	00	04	00
It. – 3 yards 1/2 Flowred Silk at 9s. 8d. per yard	01	11	06
It. – One yard of Sarsnett	00	08	06
It. – 2 yards 1/2 of Fustian	00	03	01
It. – 2 yards Callacoe for a Middle Lining	00	02	04

	£	s	d
It. – Silke and Buttons	00	02	02
It. – A Coller, Eyes and Galloon	00	01	00
It. – Stayes for it	00	01	06
It. – For siseing ye Vest	0	01	00
	£14	12	06
Received in part of this Bill at two severall payments ye summ of Eleaven Pounds,			
I say recd. in part	11	00	00
Rest to pay more	£03	12	06
Since, all pd."			

1674. – William Weekes, Mayor. "Lord Chief Justice North came to see the town."

1675. – John Dell, Mayor.

1676. – Andrew Horsman, Mayor. "August 1676, His Majesty and the Duke of York came by water to this town, staid two days, His Majesty touch't for the evil in our Great Church, dined at Mr. Edgcumbe's and returned by sea." While here, the King under a canopy of state in Saint Andrew's Church attended divine service and touched several persons for the King's evil. He dined at Mount Edgcumbe, and paid many visits in the neighbourhood.

"October 2nd, 1676, the Duke of Albemarle came to the town and with near 40 gentlemen attending him, were made free of our Corporation; Bishop Lamplugh made his triennial visitation. Judge James came to see the town, and lay at the mayor's. Dr. Ashton, Vicar of Saint Andrew's dying, Mr. Henry Greinsworth of Saint Udy in Cornwall succeeded."

1677. – William Tom, Mayor. About this time it appears the remains of the Castle were taken down or destroyed.

1678. – John Munyon, Mayor. The Barbican was rebuilt in this year.

1679. – James Hull, Mayor. "Mr Greinsworth our vicar, dying August 12th, great dispute arose about a successor, the rivals were Mr. John Gilbert, of Collumpton, recommended by the Bishop; Mr. Amos Crymes, of Exeter Colledge; Mr. Nicholas Claggett, of Saint Edmunds-Bury, recommended by Dr. Stillingfleet and Dr. Tillotson; and Mr. Honneck, preacher at the Savoy, but by reason of jarring they went not to election until November, in the mayoralty of Mr. William Symons."

"Charles' Almshouse at the head of New Church-lane now called Green-street built by the bounty of Mr. Lanyon and others, for 40 poor persons."

1680. – Wiliam Symons, Mayor. "When the competition lay between Mr. Claggett and Mr. Honneck, the Mayor and three Magistrates with eight Common Councell Men appeared for the former, eight Magistrates, and three Common Councell for the latter, but finding their party inferior they withdrew and putting in Caveats, we had a *Tryal Jus Patronatus*, where the election was made null, and the vicaridge suffered to lapse, and the Bishop collated it to Mr. John Gilbert above mentioned, who indeed proved a most worthy man, though Mr. Claggett was liked by most. From hence grew great anamosityes in the government, but indifferently composed by the next mayor."

CHAPTER VI

ANNALS CONTINUED FROM THE YEAR 1680 TO 1720.

1681. – Daniel Barker, Mayor. "Who was a prudent wary man, and endeavoured as much as possible to accommodate all the differences." "Mr. James Yonge was chosen churchwarden this year, of Saint Andrew's Parish, who rebuilt the gallery, painted it, set up the King's, Town's and Bishop's arms thereon, as also the picture of King Charles the Martyr, with pertinent inscription; made a new clock, paynted a very great part of the roof, built divers new seats in the chancell, and yet left his successor above £50 stock."

1682. – Peter Foot, Mayor. "June 1683, was discovered the damn'd fanatical plott, the design was to kill the King and Duke as they came from Haymarket, and set up the Duke of Monmouth, but were miraculously prevented. Several came in and confessed, as West, Lord Howard, Shepheard, Rumbold, etc. Others were taken and executed, Walcot Rowse, Bond and Hallaway, confest all at their execution, Lord Russell and Mr. Algernon Sidney, indirectly, but Sir Thomas Armstrong denyed all. Earl Essex cutt his throat in the Tower, my Lord Lansdown and Lady came hither. The Bishop made his triennial visitation; our contentions revived by the folly of this man, sett us anew into a flame, and at last broke the government in pieces, for influenced by Mr. Jennens, a crafty spightfull man, (the mayor being a pevish talkative idiot) studied all the ways of affronting the Common Councell, but chiefly by chusing a new way viz: – without the assistance of the Common Councell by the Magistrates; thus they chose William Martin and Joseph Webb, and immediately made the former a magistrate. This begat great regret, but soon after the fopp passing a judgement against the King in a tryal about the excise, he was called before the Councell, reprimanded, and the Attorney-General ordered to issue a *quo warranto* against the charter. This made the Common Councell quiet, knowing it were in vain to dispute about a government that would not long subsist."

1683 – William Martin, Mayor. "This man was chosen a magistrate in an unusual way, yet being loyal, was almost unanimously elected, but scarce had he sat three months before a *quo warranto* came against our charter, Mr. Mayor called us all together, and after some debate, it was put to the vote, and only Mr. Jennens, Mr. Cotton, Mr. Barker, Mr. Symons and Captain Cows opposed, the rest agreed to a surrender. Accordingly it was carryed up by the Mayor, his father, Mr. Pollexfen the Town Clerk, Mr. Horsman, Mr. Ackerman, Mr. Berry and servants, and surrendered to His Majestie at Windsor. Mr. Horsman and one of the serjeants dyed in London, and Mr. Mayor came away sick.

"June. – The new charter which His Majestie was pleased to grant us, arrived, was met at Ridgway by the Mayor, Governour and above 300 horse, brought to the Guildhall and there read over, then carried to the mayor's house, and a treat being provided, the King's, Duke's, etc. healths were drunk the Citadel, Island and ships in the harbour firing guns for near an hour, having all their flags flying; the Town Standard also met the charter at the Gate, and was carried by Lt. Deptford before it, till it was lodged; the bells rang all the while, at night abundance of bunfires, etc.

"Easter Day, my Lord Dartmouth arrived in Plymouth from Tangier, which he demolished, and brought off the garrison, etc.; left a company of foot here, and took with him those which were here in garrison before.

"In March, Sir J. Jeffery the famous loyal Lord Chief Justice, came Hither from Launceston Assize, lay at the mayor's, viewed the Cittadel and Mount Edgcumbe.

"The winter of this year proved very severe, east wind, frost and snow continued three months, so that ships were starved in the mouth of the channel, and almost all the cattle famished, the fish left the coast almost five months, all provisions excessive dear, and had we not frequent supply from the east, corn would have been at 30 shillings per bushel, above 130,000 bushels being imported hither, besides what went to Dartmouth, Fowey, etc."

"Lambert, that old rebel, dyed this winter on Plymouth Island, where he had been a prisoner 15 years and more."

The following are the documents, relating to the surrender of the old charters to the King, and the applying for their renewal: –

"To all Christian people to whom these presents shall come or any way concerne. The Maior and Cominalty of the Burrough of Plymouth, in the County of Devon, send greeting in our Lord God everlasting.

"Whereas the Maior, Magistrates and fower and twenty of this Burrough of Plymouth in Common Coucill, in the Guildhall of the borough aforesaid, lately assembled, did for severall great and weighty reasons, determine and resolve freely to grant, surrender, and yield upp unto His Most Sacred Majesty, Charles the Second, by the grace of God of England, Scotland, France, and Ireland, King, Defender of the Faith, etc., all and every the liberties, priviledges and franchises whatsoever, of and heretofore granted to and invested in the Maior and Cominalty of this Burrough of Plymouth; together with their charter and charters by which they are incorporated and endowed by his said Sacred Majesty, and all or any of his most royall ancestors, Kings and Queens of this realme. And in order thereunto, have also, now being in Common Council assembled, agreed and determined, from the great trust and confidence that they have and repose in William Martyn, Merchant, now Maior of the said borough, John Martyn, Esq., Andrew Horsman, Merchant, Edmund Pollexfen, Esq., Captain Stephen Ackerman and Robert Berry, Gentleman, (all of Plymouth aforesaid) to intrust and commit and hereby doe intrust and commit, into their custody and care, the charter and charters, and also the common Seale of this burrough or Corporation, to be carryed by them, or the major part of them, to London or elsewhere, in the kingdom of England. And doe hereby impower and authorize them or the major part of them, to sett or affix the same common Seale to any instrument or writeing, to be drawne and prepared and by them or the major part of them agreed unto or approved of, for the granting, conveying or passing over to any person or persons whatsoever, their goods and chattels; and also all or any the manors, messuages, mills, lands, tenements, kayes, advowsons, rents, services and hereditaments whatsoever, whereof the said Maior and Cominalty are now seised of any estate of inheritance, either in the right of the said Maior and Cominalty or any way in trust howsoever for any person or persons whatsoever, with all and singular their appurtenances. And further doe by these presents, impower and authorize the said William Martyn, now Maior of the said borough, and John Martyn, Andrew Horsman, Edmund Pollexfen, Stephen Ackerman and Robert Berry, or the major part of them, to put or affix the common Seale of the said burrough or Corporation to any instrument or writeing that shall be drawne and prepared, and by them, or the major part of them, consented to and agreed on, for the granting, surrendering and yielding upp unto His most Sacred Majesty, King Charles the Second, his heires and successors, all or any of their goods and chattels; and also all or any of the manors, messuages, mills, lands, tenements, kayes, advowsons, rents, services, and hereditaments; and all and every the liberties, priviledges and franchises whatsoever of and heretofore granted to and invested in the Maior and Cominalty of this Burrough of Plymouth and their predecessors; together with their Charter and Charters, by which they are incorporated and endowed by his said Sacred Majesty and all or any of his most royall ancestors, Kings and Queens of this realme; to have and to hold unto his said most Sacred Majesty, King Charles the Second, his heires and sucessors for ever. And moreover the said Maior and Cominalty, by these presents, doe fully and absolutely impower and authorize the said William Martyn and John Martyn, Andrew Horsman, Edmund Pollexfen, Stephen Ackerman and Robert Berry, or the major parte of them, to act, doe and consent unto any act, matter or thing whatsoever, which they or the major parte of them, shall think fit, reasonable, or convenient to be acted, done, performed or consented to, in, touching, or about, the premises, or in, touching, or about, the obtaining of any new charter or charters of incorporation, grant or grants, from his said most Sacred Majesty. And whatsoever the said William Martyn and John Martyn, Andrew Horsman, Edmund Pollexfen, Stephen Ackerman and Robert Berry or the major part of them shall act, doe, perform or consent unto, in, for or about the execution of the premises, they the said Maior and Cominalty, doe hereby promise, grant and agree to allowe of, ratifye, confirme, and abide by. And doe hereby declare and agree that the same shall bee to all intents and purposes as available and effectual in the law, as if the same were sealed, transacted and done in their presence in the Guildhall of the said burrough, by and with their consent, order and full approbation. In testimony whereof, the said Maior and Cominalty have hereunto sett or caused to be affixed, their common Seale, in the Guildhall of the burrough aforesaid. And the said Maior and Magistrates and Common Councill Men have hereunto severally subscribed their names. Given the fifteenth day of March, in the six and thirtieth yeare of the reigne of our now said Soveraigne Lord, Charles the Second, by the grace of God of England, Scotland, France and Ireland, King, Defender of the Faith, etc., Anno Domini 1683. – Wm. Martyn, (L.S.) Maior.

Michall Hoobe
Tho. Knottsford
Thos. Bound
George Orchard
Joseph Webb
Robert Berry
Andrew Mathews
Jno. Rogers
William Davis

Richd. Opie
John Allen
William Munyon
Richard Hingston
James Yonge
Peter Foote
John Martyn
John Harris
Will. Symons

Edmund Pollexfen	John Dell
Geo. Martyn	Andrew Horsman
Richard Cowes	Willm. Tom
Philip Wilcocks	John Munyon
Stephen Akarman	James Hull."

"To the King's most Excellent Majestie. The most humble petition of William Martyn, Maior of Plymouth, John Martyn, Andrew Horsman, Edmund Pollexfen, Stephen Ackerman and Robert Berry: – Most humbly sheweth that the Maior, Magistrates and fower and twenty of your Majesty's antient Borrough of Plymouth, in Common Council assembled, haveing determined to surrender into your royall hands all theire franchises, liberties, priviledges, together with their charter, have by an instrument under the common Seale of the sayd burrough, deputed and authorized us, your Majesty's dutifull and loyall subjects, to effect the same, as may be most conduceing to your Majesty's service and the good and well-being of the said Corporation, which your petitioners are very willing and most desirous to doe, in such manner as shall be best pleasing to your most Sacred Majesty. And forasmuch as a great part of the incomes of the said Corporation are (as your petitioners beleeve) held by antient usage and prescription or otherwise strengthened or supported by such other title, as may not be capable of a re-grant by a new charter. And for that the sayd Corporation is incumbered with great debts and some debts also due to the said Corporation, and the case and circumstances of the said Corporation are such as give your petitioners just cause to doubt that great prejudice will attend the inhabitants of the sayd towne, and especially the poore people thereof, in case of a generall surrender of all the lands, rights and priviledges of the said Corporation, wee your most humble petitioners doe therefore in all dutifull manner implore your Majesty to vouchsafe your princely compassion and favour to your said towne, and to pardon its past offences, and out of your abundant royall grace and bounty, to accept of a surrender of the whole governing part of the said Corporation, in such manner as is most conduceing to your Majesty's service. Wee only beseeching your royall favour that what is not usefull for your Majesty's service, but of great benefitt and advantage to the said towne may be preserved, wherein we most humbly pray your Majesty to signifie your royall pleasure in such manner, as your most Sacred Majesty, in your great wisdome, shall think fitt. And your petitioners as in duty bound shall ever pray, etc.

The following is the new charter granted by the King, but which was not afterwards fully recognised. –

Chapter VI

"Charles the Second, by the grace of God of England, Scotland, France and Ireland, King, Defender of the Faith, etc. To all to whom these our present letters shall come greeting. Whereas our Borrough of Plymouth, in our County of Devon, is an ancient burrough, and the Mayor and Commonalty of the said burrough have had, used and injoyed diverse libertys, franchises, pre-eminecys and hereditaments, as well by reason of diverse prescriptions, usuages and customes in the same burrough, time out of mind used, as by diverse Acts of Parliament and charters of severall of our predecessors, late Kings and Queens of England, to them heretofore granted. And whereas our beloved subjects, the late Mayor and Commonalty of the burrough aforesaid, have surrenderd unto to us all and singular their charters, franchises, libertys and priviledges whatsoever, which said surrender we have accepted, and by these presents do accept, and we att the humble petition and request of our well-beloved and very faithfull cozen and counsellor, John, Earle of Bathe, our Lieutenant and Governor of the royal Citadell and Borough of Plymouth, and desiring the bettering of the same burrough, and willing that from henceforth for ever hereafter, there may be had one certain and undoubted method or manner for keeping of the peace and good government of the people there; and that the said borough from henceforth for ever, may be and remain a burrough of peace and quietness to the terror of evil doers, and for the reward of good men. We at the humble petition of the said Earle of Bathe, and also of the said late Mayor and Commonalty of our Borough of Plymouth, for us, our heirs and successors, will, constitute, declare, ordaine and grant that the said Burrough and Towne of Plymouth shall be from henceforth for ever, a Free Burrough Incorporated, of one Mayor and one Commonalty perpetuall, and that the Burgesses of the said burrough and their successors, shall be from henceforth for ever, one body corporate and politick, by the name of the Mayor and Commonalty of the Burrough of Plymouth, and have perpetual succession, and be persons able and in law capable to have, purchase, and possess manors, lands, tenements, rents, reversions, libertys, priviledges, jurisdictions and hereditaments of what nature soever, and also goods, debts, creditts and chattels whatsoever; and also to give, grant, lease and assigne mannors, lands, tenements and hereditaments, goods, debts, credits and chattels, by the said name of the Mayor and Commonalty of the Borough of Plymouth, and by the said name to implead and to be impleaded; and that they may have a common Seale, which at their pleasure they may break, change and renew from time to time. And we will that the circuit, precincts and jurisdictions of the said borough, shall extend in length and breadth to such bounds and limits as the said Borough of Plymouth and the precincts thereof, time out minde, or att any time before the date of these presents, by any Act of Parliament, or otherwise have used, or ought to extend. And that it shall be lawful for the Mayor and Commonalty of the said borough and their successors, to make perambulations for the viewing and limiting their bounds and franchises, about, within and without the said borough in all places, lands, fields, tenements or royaltys, within the same burrough or County of Devon, att their will and pleasure. And we will that there shall be within the said burrough one of the Aldermen of the said borough, to be chosen as hereafter is mentioned, who shall be, and shall be called Mayor of the said burrough. And that there shall be twelve other Burgesses of the said burrough, to be chosen as hereafter is mentioned, besides the Mayor of the said burrough for the time being, viz: – Thirteene Capitall Liberi Burgeuses of the said burrough in the whole, who shall be, and shall be called Aldermen and Private Council of the said burrough; and that there shall be twelve other Liberi Burgeuses and inhabitants of the said borough, to be chosen as hereafter is mentioned, who shall be, and shall be called Assistants of the said borough; and that the Mayor, Aldermen and Assistants of the said borough for the time being, shall be, and shall be called by the Common Council of the said borough, and that Aldermen of the said borough shall be from time to time, aiding and assisting the Mayor of the said burrough in all causes, things and matters touching or concerning the said borough, and we assigne, nominate, constitute and make William Martyn, Esq., to be first Mayor of the said borough, from the date of these presents, until the Feast of Saint Michael the Archangel, next ensuing, and from the said feast until one other of the Aldermen of the said burrough, shall be chosen and sworn to the said office (a corporate oath in all things well and faithfully to execute the office of Mayor of the said burrough, before Hugh Piper, Kt. and John Martyn, Esq., or one of them, or two other Aldermen of the said burrough, being first to be taken by the said William Martyn). And we assigne, nominate, constitute and make the said Hugh Piper and the said John Martyn and Isaac Eillard, Merchant, Samuel Mordocke, Merchant, John Trelawney, of Ham, Esq., the said William Martyn, Thomas Stutt, Merchant, William Symons, Gent., Philip Andrew, Merchant, John Dell, Merchant, John Munyon, Merchant, James Hull, Merchant, and Lewis Stuckely, Esq., to be the first Aldermen of the said borough, during their respective natural lives, (their corporal oaths faithfully to execute the office or place of Aldermen of the said borough, being by them respectively first taken). And we assigne, nominate, constitute and make the said John Paige, junr, Philip Wilcocks, Stephen Acreman, Timothy Hamblyn, James Yonge, Robert Berry, George Orchard, John Rogers, Andrew Matthews, Nicholas Edgcombe, Walter Ingram, and Joseph Webb, to be first Assistants of the said burrough, during their respective natural lives (their corporal oath faithfully to execute the office or place of Assistant of the said burrough, being by them respectively first taken). And that it shall be lawful for the said Mayor, Aldermen and Assistants and their successors, to weare and use gownes, as they have antiently used and accustomed. And we will that there shall be in the said burrough one eminent man, who shall be, and shall be called Recorder of the said borough, to be nominated and chosen as hereafter is mentioned, which said Recorder shall have full power and authority by these presents to make and constitute from time to time his deputy. And we assign the said John, Earle of Bathe, to be the first Recorder of the said burrough during his natural life. And we will and command that the said John, Earle of Bathe, before he shall be admitted to the execution of the office of Recorder, and to the office and trust of *Justiciar* of the said borough, or to either of them, shall take the several oaths for the due execution of the said office and trust before Bernard Greenville, Esq., Hugh Piper, Kt., and Edmund Pollexfen, Esq., or any one or two of them, to whom we give power for administering the said oaths. And we grant to the said Mayor and Commonalty and their successors, that from henceforth for ever there shall be within the said burrough, a man skilful in the Laws of England, and who shall be a Barester, who shall be, and shall be called Deputy Recorder and Common Clerke of the said borough. And we will that the Recorder of the said borough and his successors, in all things and causes, in the Court of Records of the said burrough, as other courts held in the said burrough. And we assigne, etc. our well-beloved and very faithful cozen and chancellor, Christopher Duke of Albemarle and the said John, Earle of Bathe and our well-beloved and very faithful Charles, Lord Lansdowne, Richard Lord Arundel and the said Bernard Greenville and our beloved and faithful Edward Seamour, Bart., Jonathan Trelawny, Bart., Coplestone Bampfield, Bart., Richard Edgcombe, Kt. of the Bath, Nicholas Staming, Kt. of the Bath, and Bart., Arthur Tremaine, Edmund Tremaine, Richard Strode, Nicolas Courtney, the said Edmund Pollexfen, John Harris, Philip Lanyon and Henry Watts, Esq., and the said Mayor, Aldermen and Assistants, to be the first free Burgesses of the said burrough. And we will that there shall be in the said burrough, an honest and discreet man who shall be, and shall be called Coroner of the said burrough. And we assign etc., Thomas Paige, Gentlemen, to be the first

Coroner of the said burrough, to continue in the said office, during the good pleasure of the Mayor and Aldermen of the said burrough for the time being, or of the major part of them; and we will that the said William Martyn, Hugh Piper, Kt. and John Martyn (during their respective lives,) and also the Mayor, Recorder and Deputy Recorder of the said burrough, during such time as they shall continue in the said offices respectively, and after the death or removal of the said William Martyn, Hugh Piper, and John Martyn, or either of them from the office of Justice of the Peace, then and after such death or removal of either of them the last predecessor of every Mayor of the said burrough, then living for the time being, and his successors respectively, and after the death or removal of the said William Martyn, from the office of a Justice of the said burrough, the two oldest Aldermen of the said burrough, in degree and order of nomination or election within the said burrough, for the time being, for ever, shall be Justices of the Peace in the said burrough, and within the precincts and libertys thereof. And that the Mayor, Recorder, and Deputy Recorder, and other Justices in these presents nominated, and other Justices in the said burrough, for the time being as aforesaid, or any two or more of them (of whom we will that the Mayor or Recorder or Deputy Recorder of the burrough aforesaid, for the time being, shall be one,) shall have full power and authority to enquire of all felonies, trespasses and other articles whatsoever within the said burrough; so as nevertheless they proceed not to the determination of any murder or felony, (petty larcenies excepted) or of any other matter touching loss of life or member, without our special command. Nevertheless we will and grant that the Mayor, Recorder and Deputy Recorder, and other Justices in these presents nominated, and also the Justices of the Peace of the said borough for the time being, or any two or more of them (of whom we will that the Mayor or Recorder or Deputy Recorder shall be one,) shall and may enquire of all and singular melefactions, trespasses, offences and articles, and of all petty thefts and petty larcenies within the said burrough, and punish the same according to the laws of our realm. And we grant that the said Mayor and Commonalty shall for ever have Guildham Mercatoriam within the said burrough, with all things thereunto belonging, as the Mayor and Bayliffs of oure Towne and City of Oxon have or may or might have in all times past. And we further grant that the said Mayor and Commonalty for ever, shall and may have and holde in the Guildhall of the said burrough a Court of Record every Monday, in every week throughout the year, before the Mayor or his deputy of the said borough for the time being to be held, and that the Mayor or his deputy may hear and determine all pleas personal and mixt within the said burrough, in the same manner and forme, and by the same means as the Mayor and Bayliffs of the said City of Oxon, may or ought to hear and determine the like pleas within the said citty, by virtue of any grants or letters patents to the said Mayor and Bayliffs of the said citty, or to their predecessors granted, and by us, or our predecessors confirmed, or by virtue of any custome lawfully used in the said citty, and in such and in as ample a manner and forme, and by the like processes as hath been used and accustomed in the said burrough. And we will that the Serjeants-at-Mace of the said borough or either of them shall make and execute all juries, inquisitions, attachments, precepts, warrants and processes touching or concerning the said causes as shall be to them or him commanded according to the laws, and as in such like cases hath been used in any Court of Record in any other cittys, burroughs or towns incorporated within this our kingdome of England. And we grant unto the said Mayor and Commonalty and their successors, the return of all manner of writts and precepts and executions thereof, within the said burrough, so that no Sheriffe, Coroner, Keeper of the Peace, Bayliff, or any other of our Ministers, shall enter into the said borough or precincts thereof, to exercise or execute any thing in them, unless for things only touching or concerning us and our heirs or successors, or in defect of the Mayor and Commonalty aforesaid; and that Nullus Burgeuses of the burrough aforesaid shall be put or impannelled in any assizes or juries, which shall happen to be taken our of the said borough, unless he have lands, tenements or rents out of the said burrough, for which he ought to be put or impannelled in the said juries. And we will that the said Mayor and Commonalty have within the said burrough a prison and gayle, for the keeping all persons taken or attached within the said burrough for any felony, trespass or other contempt and offence whatsoever, done within the said burrough, as in time past hath been used. And we will that the Mayor and Aldermen of the said burrough, or the major part of them, (of whom the Mayor for the time being shall be one,) may for the common and public good of the said burrough, nominate, make, constitute and create from time to time, such and so many persons to be Liberis Burgeuses of the said burrough, as the said Mayor and Aldermen or the major part of them shall think fitt; and administer an oath upon the Holy Evangelists to the said Liberis Burgensibus, so to be chosen for their fidelity to the said burrough, and for their faithful doing all things which belongs to the place; and that the said Mayor and Commonalty or the major part of them, as often as shall to them seem necessary, may hold a convocation of the said Maior and Commonalty or the major part of them, in the Guildhall or other convenient place within the said burrough, and there treate, confer, consult and determine of the statutes, articles and ordinances of the said burrough, and touching and concerning the state and good government thereof. And we will that the Mayor, Aldermen and Assistants of the said burrough, being the Common Council thereof, or the major part of them (of whom the Mayor to be one,) shall have full power and authority to make, constitute and establish such laws, statutes, ordinances and constitutions whatsoever, which shall seem to them or the major part of them, good, profitable and necessary for the good government of the Mayor and Commonalty of the said burrough, and of all other officers, ministers, artificers, inhabitants and residents whatsoever, of the said burrough for the time being, and for the declaration and determination in what manner and order the said Mayor and Commonalty, and all merchants, officers, ministers, artificers and residents of the said burrough, and their factors, servants and apprentices shall behave and demain themselves in their offices, functions, misterys, wares, merchandizes, arts and business, within the said borough, and otherwise for the greater public good and common profit and good government of the said burrough; and also for the better preservation, government, disposition, leasing and setting of the lands, tenements, possessions, rents, reversions, hereditaments, goods and chattels of the said burrough, and to change and confirme the said laws, ordinances and constitutions according to their discretions; and impose such paines and penaltys by imprisonment, or by fines and amerciaments or either of them for not observing the said laws, ordinances and constitutions, and leavy the same by distress or action of debt to their own proper use, so as the said laws, ordinances, constitutions, imprisonments, fines and amerciaments be not repugnant or contrary to the laws, statutes and customs of our realm. And that they shall have power and authority yearly, in the moneth of September, to meet on Tuesday, next before the Feast of Saint Lambert the Martyr and Bishop, to nominate two of the Aldermen of the said borough, of whom one shall be Mayor the year following, and after such nomination it shall be lawful for the Mayor, Aldermen, and other Freemen of the said burrough or the major part of them, to choose one of the said two Aldermen to be Mayor of the said burrough. Provided always that no Aldermen of the said borough, without his assent, shall be nominated and chosen to the office of Mayor, who hath exercised the said office by election within the space of eight years then past, unless absolute necessity shall require it. And we will that he who shall be so yearly nominated and elected to be Mayor (having first taken his corporal oath for his well and faithful executing the said office,) shall have and exercise the said office during one whole year then next following, and until one other of the Aldermen of the said borough shall be elected and sworn Mayor of the said borough. And we will that if any Mayor of the said borough for the time being, shall happen to die or to be removed from the office, or if any person to be chosen to the said office shall refuse to take the said office upon him, that then and so often, and in every such case, it shall be lawful for the Aldermen of the said borough or the major part of them, to nominate two of the Aldermen of whom one shall be Mayor, until the Feast of Saint Michael the Archangell, then next following, as hereafter is expressed, and after such nomination of the two Aldermen, it shall be lawful for the Aldermen, Assistants and other Freemen or the major part of them, to elect one of the said two to be Mayor of the said borough, who shall exercise the said office until the Feast of Saint Michael the Archangell then next following, and until one other shall be chosen and sworn to the said office. And we will that the said Isaac Tillard shall be Mayor of the said borough, upon and from the Feast of Saint Michael next ensuing the date of these presents, for one year then next following, and until one other Alderman shall be chosen and sworn to the said office, if he shall so long live. And we will that as often as any of the Aldermen or Assistants shall happen to dye or to be removed or depart from his said office, it shall be lawful for the Mayor and Aldermen or the major part of them then surviving, one or more other de Liberis Burgensibus of the burrough aforesaid, in the place or places of the said Aldermen or Alderman, Assistants or Assistant so happening to dye or to be removed or to depart as aforesaid, to supply or fill up the said number of thirteen Aldermen and twelve Assistants, and is any Recorder shall happen to dye or to be removed or to depart from his office, it shall be lawful for the Common Council of the said borough or the major part of them, to nominate and elect an honest and discreet man, to be Recorder of the said borough, who shall have and exercise the said office by himself or by his sufficient deputy, being a Barester and learned in the Laws of England, taking first the corporate oaths to execute the said office, and the office and trust of Justice of the Peace within the said borough, before the Mayor of the said borough, to whom we give full power and authority to administer the said oaths. And if the Coroner shall happen to dye or to be removed or to depart from his office, it shall be lawful for the Common Councill or the major part of them, to nominate, elect and constitute another fit person of the said burrough, to be Coroner in his place. And we will that if any of the Aldermen who shall be nominated and elected to the office of Mayor, having notice of such election and nomination, shall refuse to take the oath for the execution of the office of Mayor of the said burrough, it shall be lawful for the Mayor and Aldermen or the major part of them, to tax and impose a fine or amerciament not exceeding two hundred pounds of lawful money of England upon every person so refusing. And if any de Liberis Burgensibus, who shall be elected to the place of Alderman, and having due notice or knowledge of such election, shall refuse to take upon him and exercise the said office or place, or to take the oath according to the use and custome of the said burrough, it shall be lawful for the Mayor and Aldermen or the major part of them, to impose or assess a fine or amerciament not exceeding one hundred pounds, upon every person so refusing, and if any de Liberis Burgensibus of the said burrough who shall be chosen to the office or place of Assistant, and having due notice or knowledge of the election, shall refuse to assume and exercise the same or to take the oath according to the custome of the said burrough, it shall be lawful for the Mayor and Aldermen or the major part of them, to impose a fine or amerciament not exceeding fifty pounds, upon every person so refusing. And for the better remedy in recovering the said severall sumes of money, fines or amerciaments, it shall be lawful for the Mayor and Aldermen or the major part of them, to impose a fine or amerciament not exceeding fifty pounds, upon every person so refusing. And for the better remedy in recovering the said severall sumes of money, fines or amerciaments, it shall be lawful for the Mayor and Commonalty of the said Borough of Plymouth aforesaid, to leavy and recover the same by distress of rent or otherwise, according to the due course of law, to the proper use of the Mayor and Commonalty and their successors. And we will that if the Mayor of the said borough shall happen to be so sick or to labour with any sickness, that he cannot attend the necessary businesses of the said burrough or that he shall goe out of the said burrough for any reasonable cause by the licence of the Aldermen or the major part of them, that then it shall be lawful for the said Mayor, so being sick or absent, to make and constitute one of the Aldermen to be his deputy, to continue in the office of Deputy Mayor, in the sickness or absence of the Mayor, which Deputy Mayor shall or may doe and execute all things in the sickness or absence of the Mayor, as fully and freely and in as ample manner and form as the Mayor might or could do if her were present. The Deputy Mayor first taking an oath before the said Mayor for the well and faithful execution of the office of Deputy Mayor. And we give full power and authority to the said Mayor to administer such oath to the Deputy Mayor. And we will that the Mayor and Aldermen or the major part of them, (of whom the Mayor to be one,) shall nominate, elect and constitute such and so many Serjeants-att-Mace and other officers and ministers whatsoever, within the said burrough, as they shall thinke fitt, who shall be sworn for the well and faithful execution of their offices, before the Mayor and Aldermen or any two of them, and shall have and exercise their said offices for one whole year then next following, at the will of the Mayor and Aldermen or the major part of them. And we will that the Mayor and Commonalty shall have in every weeke throughout the year, two markets viz. – on Monday and Thursday in every week, and in every yeare two faires, the one on the Feast of Saint Matthew the Apostle and Evangelist, and the other on the Feast of the Conversion of Saint Paul the Apostle, and by three days after each of the said feasts, together with toll, stallage, piccage and all and singular other profits, commodities and emoluments whatsoever, of and for the said markets or fairs belonging or appertayning. And we grant to the Mayor and Commonalty, a Court Leet and view of frankpledge of all the inhabitants and residents within the said burrough and precincts thereof, twice in the year, viz. – in the moneth next after the Feast of Saint Michaell the Archangell, and in the moneth next after the Feast of Easter, to be yearly held before the Common Clerk of the said burrough or his deputy; and all and whatsoever that appertaines to view of frankpledge and all amerciaments, fines, profits and commoditys belonging or appertaining to the said view of frankpledge. And that the Mayor and Commonalty shall for ever have, within the said borough and the precincts thereof, *Socam et Sacam, Tholl et Theam, Infangenthef, Outfangenthef*, chattels of felons and fugitives, of outlaws, and of persons howsoever condemned or convicted and of felons *de see* howsoever happening. And that they may putt themselves in seisin thereof without delivery or impeachment of us, our heirs or successors or of the ministers of us, our heirs or successors. And they shall have for ever all fines, recognizances or sumes of money thereupon due or forfeited or to be forfeited, amerciaments, issues and ransoms within the said borough and the precincts thereof. And to leavy and take the same by themselves and their ministers, and the same convert to the use of the Mayor and Commonalty without any estreats to be sent or returned thereof into our exchequer and without impeachment of us, our heirs or successors or of any other person whatsoever. And we will that the Mayor and Commonalty for the reparation and amendment of the keys, wharfs and barbicans, shall and may take and receive yearly within the said burrough and precincts thereof, all such sumes of money, for toll and custome as the Mayor and Commonalty or their ministers in time past have used and ought to take and receive. And we grant to the said Mayor and Commonalty, towards the necessary support, charge and cost of the said burrough and the poor thereof, that they shall or may have that part or moiety of the penalty of twenty pounds, due or payable to us, by virtue of an Act of Parliament, made in the seven and twentyeth year of the reign of the late Queen Elizabeth, for or concerning the carrying or conveying the water of the River Mew at Meavy, to or towards the Towne or Burrough of Plymouth aforesaid; and full power and authority to recover the same in our name, or in the name of the Mayor and Commonalty of the burrough aforesaid, by account of debt, bill, plaint or information, according to the tenor of the said Act of Parliament. And we will and grant to the said Mayor and Commonalty that from henceforth for ever, all the inhabitants and residents within the said burrough, shall doe and performe suit of mill to the mills of the said Mayor and Commonalty, situate and being within the said burrough, and shall grind their wheat, barley and grain to the said mills, as they have heretofore used or ought. And we grant that the said Mayor and Commonalty and their serjeants and ministers, as well throughout our realm of England, as by sea and elsewhere, within our power, shall be free, exonerated and acquitted for ever from all toll, murage, pontage, passage, stallage, kayage, piccage, panage, carriage, rivage, anchorage, scavage, strandage, chimage, terrage, keliage, custome, imposition, and of all other things whatsoever, and of all other payment, exaction and cutome of, or for themselves or any of them, or for the things, goods and merchandizes of them and any of them, to be payd in any wise howsoever. And we grant to the said Mayor and Commonalty that no foreigner who is not Burgeusis of the said burrough, shall sell or cause to be solde, any merchandizes or wares, within the said burrough or precincts thereof, other than in gross, unless only in the times of faires and markets, to be held or kept within the said burrough as hath been anciently used in the said burrough. And that noe foreigner or other person whatsoever, shall buy or sell any merchandizes, victuals or wares whatsoever, coming to the said burrough, before the same shall be brought to the said burrough, and from thence placed at the usual publicke places for buying and selling thereof. And we grant that the Mayor of the said burrough shall be Clerke of the Markett, within the said burrough and the precincts thereof, and shall doe and perform, or cause to be done and performed, all things belonging to the office of Clerke of the Markett, as in the said burrough hath been heretofore used and accustomed. And that the Mayor during his office shall be our Escheator, within the said burrough and precincts thereof, and so and execute all things belonging to the said office, first taking the oaths of Clerke of the Markett and Escheator before the old Mayor or Deputy Recorder or one other justice of the said burrough, to whom we grant authority to administer the said oaths; so that our Escheator of the County of Devon shall not intermeddle with any thing pertaining to the office of Escheator within the burrough, unless in defect of the said Mayor. And we grant that the Mayor and Commonalty shall for ever hereafter, have all the rights, libertys, franchises, jurisdictions, powers, hereditaments and other profitts whatsoever, whereof the Abbott of Bokeland, in the County of Devon, in time past, to weet, in the eighteenth year of the reign of King Henry the Sixth, was seised in his demesne as of fee and of right of his Church of the Blessed Mary of Bokleand, within the Burrough of Plymouth aforesaid, and the libertys and precincts thereof. And also a court once in every month, to be held before the Mayor in the Guildhall of the said burrough, when he shall please to assigne it, and that the Burrough of Plymouth and the inhabitants thereof for ever hereafter, shall be exempted and exonerated of, from and out of the Hundred of Rodborough, in the County of Devon aforesaid and the libertys thereof, in such and in as ample manner and forme, as by a certain Act of Parliament, made in the eighteenth yeare of King Henry the Sixth is enacted; by which act all the courts, suits and hereditaments, within the said Burrough of Plymouth and precincts thereof, were granted from the said Abbott to the Mayor and Commonalty of the said burrough and their successors. And we grant to the said Mayor and Commonalty full power and authority to purchase and possess any mannors, messuages, lands, tenements, rectorys, advowsons, tythes, rents, reversions, and other hereditaments whatsoever, as well of us and our heirs and successors as of any other person or persons whatsoever, the Statute of Mortmain or any other statute, act, ordinance or provision or any other matter, cause or thing to the contrary thereof, in anywise notwithstanding. And we grant to all persons, power and authority to give, grant, sell and alien any mannors, etc. to the said Mayor and Commonalty, the said Statute of Mortmain or any statute, etc. notwithstanding. Provided always and we reserve full power and authority to us, our heirs and successors, from time to time, any Mayor, Recorder, Deputy Recorder, Common Clerk, Coroner, and any Justice, Alderman or Assistant at our will and pleasure, by our letters under our signet and signe manuall from their said several offices respectively, to remove and declare them to be removed, who are and shall be thereby without any further process, really and to all intents and purposes whatsoever, and *ipso facto*, removed from their said several offices, anything to the contrary thereof in anywise notwithstanding, and within convenient time after such removal, other fitt person or persons into the said places and offices shall be elected, constituted and chosen in such manner, and by such person as in these presents is declared and expressed. And we will that noe Justice of the peace, in the County of Devon or any other county, shall intermeddle in any felony or in any things, causes, matters or articles whatsoever, to the office of Justice of the Peace, belonging within the said borough or precincts thereof, without our special mandate or commisison in that behalfe. And we will that the said Mayor and Commonalty shall have and enjoy all such gifts, grants, courts, prisons, libertys, priviledges, exemptions, franchises, acquittances, articles, immunitys and customes, as well in these presents and in any other charter or charters of us or our progenitors or ancestors, late Kings or Queens of England, as in any statute or Act of Parliament contained, granted, declared, specified or confirmed. And also all and singular franchises, priviledges, offices, officers, mannors, lordships, messuages, mills, waters, watercourses, catteracts, lands, tenements, rents, reversions, services, advowsons, viccarages and churches, rights of patronage and presentation to viccarages and to churches, wasts, hereditaments, borrough-customes, powers, tolls, marketts, market places, standings, kays, wharfs, small customes and dues or payments for rollage, kayage, wharfage and landliefe and dutys and payments of or for ale-weights and wine weights, libertys, creditts, debetts, rights, goods, chattels, real and personal uses, confidences, equitys of redemption, faires, courts, views of frankpledge, perquisites of courts, jurisdictions of courts, with correction or amending of bread and beer, exemptions, acquittances, immunitys, and customes. And also all other profits and emoluments, temporal and secular, heretofore lawfully granted to the late Mayor and Commonalty of the Burrough of Plymouth aforesaid, or by them or any of them by any name or name of Incorporation, or other legel means heretofore lawfully used, and which, by these presents, are not changed and altered. And we grant and restore to the said Mayor and Commonalty all authoritys, courts, jurisdictions, libertys, priviledges, franchises, acquittances and customes, so fully and freely as they or their predecessors in any times of any of our progenitors or ancestors, late Kings or Queens of England, have or ought to have, exercises, enjoyed or used the same before the surrender aforesaid. Provided always, and we reserve full power and authority of building and fortifying, for the safe keeping of the said burrough and harbour there, we paying a reasonable sume of money for houses or lands necessary for the fortification and building aforesaid. Provided always that these our letters patents, shall not be extended to grant to the said Mayor and Commonalty any lands, tenements, rents, services or hereditaments, parcell or our Dutchy of Cornwall or of our Honour of Trematon, but that our said dutchy and honour shall have and enjoy all their lands, tenements, rents, jurisdictions, services and hereditaments within the said burrough, in as ample manner and forme as they enjoyed or ought to enjoy the same at the time of the surrender aforesaid and not otherwise, which said authoritys, jurisdictions, libertys, priviledges, etc. are to be held of us, our heirs and successors as they were formerly held, and rendering and paying yearly such rents, services, sumes of money and demands as have been used and ought to be payed. And we will that these our letters patents shall be expounded, adjudged and interpreted in all courts and places whatsoever, most graciously and most benignly in favor and benefit of the Mayor and Commonalty of our said Burrough of Plymouth. In testimony whereof we have caused these our letters to be made patent. Witness ourselff at Westminster, the twenty-sixth day of June, in the thirty-sixth yeare of our reign."

1684. – Isaac Tillard, Mayor. "He was nominated in the new charter, to be the first mayor, and was a very good man, but lived not half his mayoralty; he dyed on Monday, 2nd February, 1685. King Charles II dyed, also near that time."

"Soon after the mayor, Timothy Hamlyn, his receiver, also dyed, a very good man. W. Martin succeeded in the mayoralty, by direction of my Lord Bath, and Mr. J. Paige made Alderman. A terrible cold winter; cattle dyed for want of fodder. Argyl landed in Scotland and Monmouth at Lyme this summer, many went to them but they were both routed, taken prisoners and beheaded."

"King James was proclaimed here February 10th, many new regiments levyed after Monmouth's rebellion. My Lord Bath had one of which Mr. Yonge was surgeon. A Parliament was called in May, and they of the bench chose among themselves, without Freemen or Freeholders, though both protested against it. August. – Mr. Davys and John Carkeet chosen Assistants. King Charles II, and the Mayor of Plymouth dyed the same day.

1685. – Samuel Madock, Mayor. August. – "The Bishop Lamplugh came for his triennial visitation; Lord Chief Justice Herbet followed him."

"His Majesty James II appointed a new Mayor, Recorder, Town Clerk, Coroner, 12 Capital Burgesses or Freemen, 24 Common Councillors and 26 Freemen; and also restored to the borough, all and every privilege hitherto enjoyed by the former Mayor and Commonalty before the surrender of the charter."

1686. – John Trelawney, Mayor. "A very worthy understanding gentleman, strove hard against the election to no purpose." "August. – Duke of Grafton came into Plymouth with six of the King's ships; the Queen of Portugal, daughter of the Duke of Newburg, going on here to Lisbon."

"Sir H. Piper, Lieutenant-Governour and Alderman dyed. Sir Nicholas Slanning made Governour, and Sir Philip Wilcocks, Alderman, John Tom, Assistant."

1687. – Thomas Stutt, Mayor. "This honest gentleman was mayor, 1667. About the time of his taking the charter, the Duke of Albemarle and his Dutchess, put in here in their voyage to Jamaica, where he went governour. He came not on shore although invited, and stayed some weeks.

1688. – William Symons, Mayor. "This man was twice mayor before. In November, the Prince of Orange with great force arrived at Torbay, landed and went to Exeter. King James' forces going over to the Pretender, His Majesty fled out of England, with the Queen and Prince of Wales. Prince of Orange proclaimed King in February. His declaration was read in the Guildhall and Cittadel in December, soon after which the Dutch fleet which brought him over, came into this harbour and wintered. War proclaimed against France."

1689. – Philip Andrew, Mayor. "Soon after this honest gentleman's election, four regiments of soldiers were sent here to embark for Ireland, and 400 ships wintered here, so that great infection happened, and above 1,000 people buryed in three months. Wm. Martin, Alderman, dyed; no great loss. The French appeared with a great fleet before our harbour, sailing eastward, where they beat us and the Dutch, before the Isle of Wight; we lost the aim of 70 guns, the Dutch lost six; King William then in Ireland. We apprehended the French might attack this harbour, made new forts, and kept in arms with good watching." "Christmas Day a great storm, the Henrietta and Centurian cast away here, and a Dutch man-of-war of 70 guns."

1690. – John Paige, Mayor. "In the gentleman's mayoralty happened nothing memorable, but that the Dock in Hamoaze was begun. That the 2nd Sept. and the end of it, a storm drove our grand fleet then on the coast, into this harbour, where the Coronation of 90 guns was sunk and men drowned, except 14, and the Harwich, of 70 guns, lost under Mount Edgcumbe." "Russell in the Brittania, Admiral of the red, Killigrew in the Duke, of the blew, here, as also the Sovereign,etc."

The following is an interesting letter written by the Mayor of Plymouth, John Paige, in 1690. It bears the Seal of the Corporation, and is addressed to John Trelawney, Esq., one of the representatives of the town in Parliament. this John Trelawny was the son of Robert Trelawny, who represented Plymouth in the Parliament of 1641, and who, from his loyalty, being a marked man, was impeached and imprisoned by that tyrannical Parliament for simply denying (as it is asserted, but never proved) "the right of the House to appoint a Guard for themselves without the King's consent." He was confined for more than a year in Winchester House, in Westminster, where he died in 1643, and his estates were confiscated, but afterwards restored to his son.

"Plymouth, 12 December, 1690.

"Honored Sr,

"I had your letter of the 9th instant with the Votes, for which I do most heartily thank you. I have communicated yours to as many of our Corporation as I have seen; we are all heartily glad you are indifferently well recovered, and hope in a little time to hear you are so well, that you will be able to be in the House to act there and in other places for the good of this poor Towne: we have had a letter from the good Lord of Bathe, of the 6th instant, about our fortifications, and this day we answered it, a Copy of wch I am promist to have, and am order'd to send it up to Coll^{l}. Grabvill and y^{r}self, that so you may see what is requested of my lord. I am likewise desired by all the Corporation to recommend the poor condition of our Towne to both of you, that so you may advise with my Lord of Bathe that he gett an Ord^{r} from their Maj^{ties} for the making those platforms and breastworks at their Maj^{ties} own charges, and that we may be supplied out of their Majties Magazines with great gunns and ammunition sutable; for had we monye, we could not here purchase fitt gunns and carriages that may be fitt for such service; this is heartily recommended to Coll^{l}. Granvill and y^{r}self (if possible) to get effected by my Lord of Bathe's directions, that so the gunns and other things may be sent downe with all expedition, that we may make some defence agst our potent enemies. Coll^{l}. Granville being out of Towne, I direct this wholy to you.

"Sir, y^{r} family at Ham were all very well yesterday.* * * *

"Tendring you and Coll^{l}. Granvill my true respects, I rest,

"Sr, yor Kinsman,

"and humble Servt,

"JOHN PAIGE, Mayor."

"For Jno Trelawny, Esq., Member of the Honorable House of Commons, Westminster."

(Frank).

1691. – John Martin, again Mayor. "This honest old gentleman was mayor once before. In August my Lord Chief Justice Holt came from

Launceston to see the town. September. – The Bishop, Sir Jonathon Trelawney made the triennial visitation, his first time." This Bishop Trelawny was translated to Exeter from Bristol. As Bishop of Bristol, he was one of the famous seven bishops committed to the Tower by King James, at which time he became the subject of the Cornish ballad, the burthen of which is still remembered: –

And shall Trelawny die?
And shall Trelawney die?
There's twenty thousand Cornish lads
Will know the reason why."

He died Bishop of Winchester, 1721, and was buried in the church of Pelynt, in Cornwall.

"Plymouth Dockyard. – This dockyard was formed in 1691, in the reign of William and Mary; in the year 1693, money was voted by the House of Commons for its completion. Previous to 1691 the master shipwright and artificers were borne on board one of Her Majesty's ships fitted for their reception."

1692. – John Munyon, again Mayor. "This man was a second time chosen mayor. Nothing memorable but fitting up an empty space in the New Quay, by which it became a very graceful square. Alderman Stuke or Stutt dyed this August." In this year the Fish Shambles were built.

1693. – Philip Willcocks, Mayor. "James Yonge and Robert Berry were in the Midsummer Sessions chosen Aldermen. Richard Zachary Mudge born; afterwards Vicar of Saint Andrew's in 1731."

1694. – James Yonge, Mayor. "December, the lord Cutts came to town, lay at his house. Three regiments quartered in town, to be embarked for the West Indies by this Lord. Alderman Dell dyed January, (no loss)." "June. – My Lord Marquis of Carmarthen, the son and heir to the Duke of Leeds, being Rear Admiral of the blew, came into port. In August, fitted up both benches by choosing John Rogers, Nicholas Edgcomb, William Munyon, and Mr. Thomas Pound, Aldermen; Thomas Burgoyn, James Bligh, Thomas Darracott, William Lovell, Benjamin Berry, and William Wyatt, Assistants." "The New Quay fitted up to the outside of the Slip, before Mr. Allen's house, and all new paved over." "In June this year, Mr. Fall, an officer of the broad Seal, being in town, and the people universally desirous to have the old charters, the mayor employed him in conjunction with Mr. Trelawney, one of the Aldermen and Burgess for the town, then in Parliament, and Robert Berry, who was Town Attorney and then going to London to endeavour a restitution thereof, but Berry hoping to be next mayor and to have the honor of getting the charter restored in his time and to do it for his own advantage, so embarrass'd the thing, that nothing was done, although Mr. Fall undertook to do it soon, effectually and cheaply, which sinister, proved to the ruin of the Church interest afterward."

1695. – Robert Berry, Mayor. "This man was an attorney, served the Town Clerk, by which he knew how to get the town's money, which he did to the purpose as may be seen in the audit books, where it appears he hath had vast sums for law charges, charters, etc. The benches being filled with such men as would not be accessary to his design, he goeth to London, and attempts to get our old charter restored, and framed such a body of men to fill the benches, as would be sure do as he would have them, but God defeated his project, for my Lord Bathe being put out of the government of the citadel and Lieutenant of the County and some of us approving the list of men the mayor had designed, he came home *re infecta* and spent the rest of his mayoralty dully and out of the good people's favour."

"Major General Trelawney was made governour in the room of my Lord Bath, this mayor put himself into the interest of that Earle to further his designs of getting the dues and revenues of the town into this hands, but all was frustrated for to oppose him who would have had Mr. Rogers succeed him, they chose John Munyon, at the end of this time, Sir Francis Drake got hands to a petition for the old charter, sent it up and by interest at court got one so called, out of which the mayor was excluded.

"This mayor declared that no obligation lay on him, or on any other person from the oath, commonly called "the Solemn League and Covenant," and that the same was unlawful and imposed upon the subjects against the laws and liberties of the kingdom." (*Signed by* John Harris and William Jennings). "King William's charter brought here by Sir Francis Drake, with 200 horse and trained bands."

The following is a copy of this new charter of the Borough of Plymouth, which being a remarkably interesting and important document, is here printed entire. -

"William the Third, by the grace of God, etc. To all to whom these our presents shall come greeting. We have seen certain letters patent under the great Seal of England, bearing date at Westminster the third day of March, in the third year of the reign of our most dear grandfather, Charles the First, late King of England, etc., made and granted to the Mayor and Commonalty of the Borough of Plymouth in these words, 'Charles by the grace of God, etc. To all to whom these present letters shall come greeting.' We have seen letters patent of our dear father, Lord James of England, Scotland, France and Ireland, King, Defender of the Faith, of blessed memory, made in these words, 'James by the grace of God, etc. To all to whom these present letters patent shall come greeting.' We have seen the letters patent of our dear sister Mary, late Queen of England, of a confirmation made in these words, 'Mary by the grace of God, etc. To all to whom these present letters shall come greeting.' We have seen letters patents of our dear brother the Lord Edward, of happy memory, late King of England, the Sixth, of a confirmation made in these words, 'Edward the Sixth by the grace of God, etc., and in the Lord of the Church of England, etc., supreme head. To all to whom these present letters shall come greeting.' We have seen letters patents of the Lord Henry the Eighth, King of England, our most dear father, made for a confirmation in these words, 'Henry by the grace of God, etc. To all to whom these present letters shall come greeting.' We have seen letters patents of the Lord Henry, late King of England, the Seventh, our most dear father, of a confirmation made in these words, 'Henry by the grace of God, etc. To all to whom these present letters shall come greeting.' We have seen a charter of the lord Henry, late King of England, the Sixth, made in these words, 'Henry by the grace of God, etc. To all and singular archbishops, bishops, abbotts, priors, dukes, earles, barons, justices, viscounts, provosts, ministers and all bayliffs and all faithful subjects greeting. Know ye that we by the lords spiritual and temporal, in our Parliament at Westminster, last abiding, and from thence to our Town of Reading adjourned, and at the special request of the Commons of our kingdom of England in the said Parliament, being for great and necessary and notable causes, us in the said Parliament especially moveing, by the request and authority of the said Parliament, the Town and Sutton Prior, the Tything of Sutton Raafe, parcel Hamlet of Sutton Vautort, and certain parcel Tything of Compton, in the County of Devon, our Borough of Plymouth for ever to be named and called, and that borough of one Mayor and one Commonalty for ever, at all times future to continue incorporated. And we have caused the said borough to be endowed of certain lands, tenements and other possessions, by the Mayor and Commonalty of the said borough and their successors for ever, to be possessed by authority of the said Parliament as in the Act of the said Parliament may more fully appear. Know ye that we especially observing how our aforesaid borough is situate near the shore and sea coast, and that by the said borough and inhabitants thereof upon that occasion, there may be necessary conveniency, not only for defence of the country, near the said borough and out liege people inhabiting there, but also for merchants, foreigners, natives and others, who may hereafter come there, to whom we are willing to shew favour, and also that our peace and other acts of justice and whatsoever do belong to peace and justice, may without further delay, damage or detriment, be firmly kept and performed, and hoping that if the Mayor and Commonalty of the borough aforesaid and their successors may enjoy greater liberties or priviledges than heretofore they have, they shall then think themselves more particularly and strongly obliged to exhibit and give those services, which they shall be able to perform and pay to us, our heirs and successors, and that they may be able, with the greater care and diligence, to perform their said services to us and our heirs, of our special grace, and from our certain knowledge and mere motion, we have granted, and for ourselves, our heirs and successors, by these presents do grant to the Mayor and Commonalty of the Borough of Plymouth aforesaid and to their successors for ever, that the Mayor and Recorder of the said borough for the time being, during the said term which they shall happen to be in their offices, and the last predecessor of the aforesaid Mayor then surviving and for the time being, and their successors and each of them, be our justices and justice to keep and preserve, and cause to be kept and preserved, our peace within the said borough and within the limits, precincts and liberties of the same, without any other mandate, commission or warrant from us, our heirs and successors, for that purpose to be had or obtained, and that the said Mayor and Recorder and last predecessor aforesaid of the Mayor of the borough aforesaid for the time being, and their successors or two of them, of whom the said Mayor or Recorder for the time being, shall be one, shall have full power and authority to enquire concerning any felonies, trangressions, misprisions, crimes and other deserts and any other articles whatsoever, within the borough aforesaid and limits and precincts and liberties thereof, made, done and committed, which before the Keeper and Justices of the Peace in any county of our kingdom of England, by the laws and statutes of the same kingdom, ought or may be enquired, nevertheless but that the Mayor and Recorder and last predecessor of the mayor of the said borough for the time being, and their successors or any of them, in any manner hereafter, do not proceed to the determination of any murder or felony or any other matter touching loss of life or limbs, within the borough aforesaid and limits, precincts and liberties thereof, without the special mandate of us, our heirs and successors. And we also grant to the Mayor and Commonalty of the Borough of Plymouth aforesaid and their successors, that the said Mayor and Recorder and last predecessor of the Mayor of the borough aforesaid for the time being, or two of them, of whom we will have the aforesaid Mayor or Recorder for the time being, and their successors hereafter for ever, to be one, shall have power, and may enquire into, hear, perform and determine, all and singular other crimes, transgressions, offences, failures and articles, which do belong to the offices of Justices of the Peace, within the borough aforesaid and the limits, precincts and liberties thereof, so fully, freely and absolutely and in such ample manner and form as any other Justices of the Peace of us our heirs and successors in any county of our kingdom of England by the laws and statutes of our kingdom of England or any of them may enquire, hear or determine and we will and command for ourselves, our heirs and successors, firmly by these presents that no Justices of the Peace, our heirs and successors, in the County of Devon, or in any other county or counties, for the time being, do of themselves in any manner hereafter intermeddle, nor any of them do intermeddle, for or concerning any felonies, things, causes, matters, failures or other articles whatsoever, belonging or appertaining to the office of a Justice of the Peace, within the said borough, limits, liberties or precincts of the same, upon any occasion issuing or happening. Moreover we will, and of our special grace, certain knowledge and mere motion, do grant for ourselves, our heirs and successors, to the aforesaid Mayor and Commonalty of the said Borough of Plymouth and to his successors, that they for ever have all and singular fines, issues, redemptions and amerciaments, lost and forfeited or to be lost and forfeited within the said borough, limits and precincts thereof, before the aforesaid Keepers of our Peace and of our heirs and our Justices and our heirs and before two of them, of which we will have the aforesaid Mayor or Recorder for the time being, to be one, appointed to enquire into, hear and determine felonies, transgressions and crimes aforesaid within the said borough and limits and precincts thereof, in whatsoever manner forfeited or to be forfeited from time to time, for the proper use and behoof of the Mayor and Commonalty of the said borough, with the impediment of us, our heirs and successors, or any of the officers of ministers of us, our heirs and successors, and without any account to be rendered thereof to us, our heirs and successors. And moreover we will for ourselves, our heirs and successors and by these presents, do grant to the aforesaid Mayor and Commonalty of the Borough of Plymouth and their successors, that the Mayor and Commonalty of the borough aforesaid for the time being, and their successors, may have for ever hereafter within the borough aforesaid, liberties and precincts thereof, a proper prison or goal, to keep all those who hereafter shall happen to be taken, attached or apprehended within the said borough and liberties thereof, for any felonies, trangressions or any other failures, contempts or offences there committed, as hath been in that case heretofore, within the said borough been used and accustomed, so as those being in the gaol aforesaid, who cannot reasonably be discharged by the Mayor, Recorder and last predecessor of the said Mayor of the borough aforesaid for the time being, according to the liberties and customs of the said borough, may be discharged by our Justices of the Peace, of our heirs or successors, appointed to deliver goals or take the assizes there, according to law and custom of our kingdom of England, and as formerly hath been accustomed. And further of our more abundant grace we will, and for ourselves, our heirs and successors by these presents, do grant to the aforesaid Mayor and Commonalty of the borough aforesaid and their successors, that the said Mayor and Commonalty of the borough aforesaid and their successors for the time being, from time to time, for the public good and common advantage of the said borough, shall and may make, constitute and create such and so many Freemen of the said borough, as shall seem most expedient to them or the major part of them, in the same manner and form as heretofore hath been used and accustomed in the said borough, and that the said Mayor and Commonalty of the said borough and their successors or the major part of them, as often as they shall think fitt and necessary, shall and may assemble together in the Guildhall of the said borough or any other convenient place within the said borough and hold the Assembly of the said Mayor and Commonalty or the major part of them, in all time to come, and in the same Assembly of the said Mayor and Commonalty or the major part of them, in all time to come, and in the same Assembly to treat of, debate, consent and determine of the statutes, articles and orders of the said Borough of Plymouth, touching and concerning the good management, state and government of the said borough, according to their sober discretions or the sober discretions of the major part of them. And further of our more abundant grace we will and by these presents, for ourselves, our heirs and successors, do grant to the aforesaid Mayor and Commonalty and their successors, that the Mayor of the borough aforesaid and his successors for the time being, the Twelve Capital Burgesses or Masters of the said borough, and those who from time to time hereafter, shall bear the major part of them, being met or assembled in the Guildhall of the said borough or other convenient place, calling to them four and twenty of the better and discreeter merchants or free inhabitants of the borough aforesaid for the time being, if they will be present with their consent or the consent of the major part of the said Mayor and Twelve Capital Burgesses or merchants or free inhabitants aforesaid, have and by these presents may have full authority, power and ability of granting, constituting and ordaining, making and appointing from time to time, such and such manner of laws, statutes, rights, orders and constitutions, as they or the major part of them shall think good, useful, wholesome, honest and necessary, according to their sober discretions, for the good management and government of the Mayor and Commonalty of the said borough, and of all other freemen, officers, ministers, burgesses, artificiers, inhabitants and residents of the borough aforesaid, and their factors, servants and apprentices, shall behave, manage and deport themselves in their office, functions, mysteries, merchandising, trafficking, trading and employment within the said borough and limits, liberties and precincts of the same for the time being, and which shall for the time being and which shall hereafter from time to time be, and otherwise for the better public good, common advantage and well government of the borough aforesaid and the victualling of the said borough, and also for the better preservation, government, disposing, setting the lands, tenements, possessions, reversions, hereditaments, given and granted or assigned or hereafter given, granted or assigned to the aforesaid Mayor, Commonalty and successors, and all other things and matters whatsoever of the borough aforesaid or touching or any way concerning the estates, rights and interests of the borough aforesaid; and the said laws, rights, orders and constitutions according to their sober discretions, as need shall require, to change them into better and more convenient and to confirm them; and what the Mayor of the borough aforesaid for the time being and the Twelve Capital Burgesses or Masters of the borough aforesaid, and the aforesaid merchants and inhabitants called to them as aforesaid for the time being, or the major part of them, as often as they shall constitute, make, ordain and establish such laws, statutes, rights, ordinances and constitutions in form aforesaid, to make, ordain, limit and provide such and such manner of punishments, penalties by imprisonment of body, or by fines and amerciaments, or by oath of them to and upon all offenders against such laws, institutions, rights, ordinances and constitutions, or any one or more of them, as to them, the said Mayor and Twelve Capital Burgesses or masters or merchants or inhabitants aforesaid or the major part of them, for the time being, shall seem more necessary, suitable and requisite and reasonable for the observation of the said laws, ordinances and constitutions, and that they may levy the said fines and amerciaments by distress or action of debt, as to them shall seem meet, and have them to the proper use and behoof of the aforesaid Mayor and Commonalty of the borough aforesaid and their successors, without the impediment or let of us, our heirs and successors, and without any account thereof to be made to us or our successors, all and singular which laws and ordinances, rights and constitutions so to be made as aforesaid, we will have to be observed under the penalties contained therein, so as such laws, ordinances, rights, constitutions, imprisonments, fines and amerciaments be not repugnant or contrary to the laws, statutes, constitutions or rights of our kingdom of England. And further we will, and by these presents, for ourselves, our heirs and successors, do grant that the aforesaid Mayor and Commonalty of the Borough of Plymouth and their successors, from time to time for ever, shall and may nominate and elect, constitute and appoint, such and so many officers and ministers whatsoever within the said borough, as to them the said Mayor and Commonalty or the major part of them, shall seem fit for the better government and common advantage and service of the said borough, and as heretofore in the said borough hath been used and accustomed. Moreover we have granted and by these presents, for ourselves, our heirs and successors, do grant to the aforesaid Mayor and Commonalty of the Borough of Plymouth and their successors, that no foreigner, who is not a Freeman of the said borough, do sell or cause to be sold any merchandize or wares within the said borough aforesaid, precincts and liberties thereof, otherwise than in gross, unless only at the times of fairs or markets to be held and kept in the said borough, as in the said borough hath anciently been used; and that no foreigner or any other whatsoever, do buy or sell any merchandize, victual or wares whatsoever, coming to the said borough aforesaid, before the said merchandize, victuals or wares be brought to the borough aforesaid, and there laid and deposited at certain public places, and usual for the buying and selling of such merchandize, victuals and wares. And further we have granted, and for ourselves, our heirs and successors, by these presents do grant to the aforesaid Mayor and Commonalty of the aforesaid borough and their successors, that the Mayor of the borough for the time being, for ever hereafter, be and shall be Clerk of the Market within the said borough, liberty and precincts of the same as heretofore in the said borough hath been used and accustomed, and that he shall and may do and execute or cause to be done and executed for ever, all and whatsoever doth belong to the office of the Clerk of the Market, and all and singular other deeds and things to be performed, which belong to the executing and performing the said office within the said borough, liberties and precincts of the same, as heretofore in the said borough hath been used and accustomed. Moreover we will, and for ourselves, our heirs and successors, do ordain and grant by these presents to the aforesaid Mayor and Commonalty of the borough aforesaid and their successors, during the term which he shall be in his office of mayoralty, be our Escheator, our heirs and successors within the said borough and liberties and precincts thereof, as heretofore in the said borough hath been used and accustomed, and that he do and execute and shall and may do and execute within the borough aforesaid, liberties and precincts of the same, all and whatsoever belongs to the office of Escheator there, as heretofore in the said borough hath been used and accustomed; and that the Mayor of the said borough for the time being, before he be admitted to the execution of the said office of Clerk of the Market and Escheator of the said borough, do take his corporal oath for the true and faithful executing and performing these offices of Clerk of the Market and Escheator, before the old Mayor and Commonalty of the said borough for the time being, or the major part of them, so as that any of our Escheators, our heirs and successors in our County of Devon, do not anyway intermeddle for anything which belongs to the office of Escheator within the said borough, nor presume to interpose in anyway hereafter unless defect of the Mayor of the borough aforesaid for the time being, as heretofore in time past hath been accustomed in the said borough. And moreover of our abundant special grace, and of our certain knowledge and mere motion, we have given, granted and confirmed and by these presents for ourselves, our heirs and successors, do give, grant and confirm to the aforesaid Mayor and Commonalty of the borough aforesaid Mayor and Commonalty of the borough aforesaid and their successors, all and singular markets, fairs, liberties, free customs, priviledges, franchises, immunities, executions, quittances and jurisdictions whatsoever, which the aforesaid Mayor and Commonalty of the said borough, by whatsoever name or names, incorporation or incorporations, or upon any pretence on incorporation whatsoever, have heretofore rightfully or lawfuly had, held, used or enjoyed by reason or pretence of any charters or letters patents heretofore made, confirmed or granted in any manner by us or any of our progenitors, or by any other lawful manner, rights, custome, use, prescription or title, heretofore lawfullly held, used or accustomed to be held and enjoyed by the said Mayor and Commonalty and their successors for ever, yielding there to us, our heirs and successors such, and such like manner of rents, services, sums of money, and demands, which on that account hath been heretofore wont to be due, and of right answered to us, our heirs and successors. Moreover we will and grant to the aforesaid Mayor and Commonalty of the borough aforesaid, that they have, hold, use and enjoy for ever all liberties, free customs, priviledges, authorities and acquittances aforesaid, according to the tenor of effect and those, our letters patents, without the let or impediments of us, our heirs or successors whatsoever. And our will is that the said Mayor and Commonalty of the borough aforesaid or any of them, nor any Freeman of the borough aforesaid be on the account of the premises, or any of them by us, our heirs, our justices, sheriffs, escheators, or other bailiffs or our ministers, our heirs or successors whatsoever hindered, molested, troubled or grieved or any ways disturbed. Moreover we will and grant to the aforesaid Mayor and Commonalty of the Borough of Plymouth aforesaid, that they have and shall have, these our letters patents under the Seal of England, in due manner made and sealed without fine or fee, great or small, to be thereupon in any matter rendered, made or paid to us in our Stamper Office or elsewhere for our use, notwithstanding the express mention of the true yearly value, or the certainty of the premises or any part of them, or of any other gifts or grants heretofore made by us or by any of our progenitors, to the aforesaid Mayor and Commonalty of the borough aforesaid, hath not in these presents been made or any statute, act, ordinances, proclamations, provision or restraints to the contrary thereof heretofore had, made, granted, ordered or provided, or any other thing, cause or matter whatsoever in anywise notwithstanding. In testimony whereof we have caused these our letters to be made patents, witness ourselfe at Westminster, the twenty-eighth day of February, in the three and fortieth year of our reign.' And we ratifying and being well pleased with the charters and letters aforesaid, and all and everything contained therein, do for ourselves, our heirs and successors, as much as in us lies, allow and approve the same. And to our beloved, the now Mayor and Commonalty of the borough aforesaid and their successors, by the tenour of these presents, do ratify and confirm as the charters and letters aforesaid, do reasonably in themselves evidence. In testimony whereof, we have made these our letters to be made patents. Witness ourself at Westminster, the fourth day of November, in the year of our reign of England, France and Ireland, the twelfth, and of Scotland the forty-eighth. Know ye that we being desirous to ratify the letters patents and charters above recited or mentioned, franchises, immunities, exonerations, gifts and grants and all other things whatsoever, in the same or any of them contained, have for ourselves, our heirs and successors, ratified, approved and confirmed the same to our now well beloved subjects, the Mayor and Commonalty of Plymouth aforesaid, and by these present do ratify, approve and confirm so fully, freely and intirely, in such ample manner and form, as if all and singular the things granted in the said letters patents, or mentioned to be granted, had been particularly in these presents expressed, recited or mentioned, although the same or any of them heretofore have not been used, or have been or are abused or discontinued and although the same or any of them have been or are forfeited or lost, yielding therefore to is, our heirs and successors, the same and such live services, rents, sums of money and demands, which on that account they have formerly paid, or of right ought to yield or pay. Wherefore we with and by these presents for ourselves, our heirs and successors, do firmly injoin, order and command that the aforesaid Mayor and Commonalty of the borough aforesaid and their successors, may have hold, use and enjoy, and shall and may fully and absolutely, have, hold, use and enjoy for ever, all the libertys, free customs, priviledges, authorities, jurisdictions and quittances aforesaid, according to the tenour of these our letters patents, without the lett or impediment of us, our heirs or successors, or of any officers or ministers of us, our heirs or successors whatsoever, ordering that the said Mayor and Commonalty of the borough aforesaid or their successors or any of them, be not on accompt of the premises or any thing thereof by us, our heirs or successors, our justices, sheriffs, escheators, or other bayliffs, or our officers, our heirs or successors whatsoever hindered, molested, troubled or grieved or any way disturbed, willing and by these presents requiring and commanding as well our treasurer, chancellor and barons of our exchequer at Westminster, and other justices and officers of us, our heirs and successors, as also our Attorney General for the time being, or any of them, and all other officers and ministers of us, our heirs and successors whatsoever, that neither they nor any of them, do not prosecute or continue, or do or cause to be prosecuted or continued, any writ or summons of *quo warranto* or any other writ, writts and our processes whatsoever, against the aforesaid Mayor and Commonalty of the borough aforesaid or their successors, or any one or more of them, for any causes, things, matters, offences, claims or usurpations or any of them, by themselves or their predecessors, or any of them duely claimed, used, held, had or enjoyed before the day of the execution of these presents. Moreover willing that the Mayor and Commonalty of the borough aforesaid, and their successors, by any one or more justices, officers or ministers aforesaid in or for the due use, clayme or abuse, of any other libertyes, franchises or jurisdictions within the borough aforesaid, the limits and precincts thereof, before the day of the making of these our letters patents, be not molested or hindered or be forced to render up them or any of them.

And whereas the aforesaid Lady Elizabeth, late Queen of England, by her foresaid charter or letters patents, bearing date at Westminster, the twenty-eighth day of February, in the three and fortieth year of her reign, hath for herself, her heirs and successors, granted to the Mayor and Commonalty of the Borough of Plymouth and their successors for ever, among other things, that the Mayor and Recorder of the said borough for the time being, during the time that they shall happen to be in their offices, and the last predecessor of the aforesaid Mayor then surviving, and for the time being, and their successors, should be justices of the late Queen, and every one of them should be her justice, her heirs and successors, for the keeping and preserving and causing the keeping and preserving of the peace in the said borough and within the limits, precincts and libertyes of the same, without any other mandate, commission or warrant from the said late Queen, her heirs and successors, to be therefore had and obtained. And that the said Mayor and Recorder and last predecessor of the said Mayor of the borough aforesaid for the time being, and their successors or two of them, whereof the said Mayor or Recorder for the time being, she would have to be one, should have full power and authority to inquire into any felonyes, transgressions, misprisons, crimes and other failures and articles whatsoever, made, done or committed within the aforesaid borough and limits, libertys and precincts therof, which before the Keepers and Justices of the Peace in any county of the kingdom of England, by the laws and statutes of the said ought or may be inquired into: yet so as that the said Mayor, Recorder and last predecessor of the borough aforesaid for the time being, and their successors or any of them, should not by any means then afterwards proceed to the determination of any murder or felony or any other matter touching loss of life or limbes within the burrough aforesaid, the limits, precincts or libertyes thereof, without special mandate of the said Queen, her heirs or successors. And the aforesaid late Queen have granted to the Mayor and Commonalty of the Burrough of Plymouth aforesaid and their successors, that the said Mayor and Recorder and last predecessor of the Mayor of the burrough aforesaid for the time being, or two of them, whereof she would have the aforesaid Mayor or Recorder for the time being to be one, and their successors, then for ever after, should and might enquire into, heare, accomplish and determine, all and singular other crimes, trangressions, offences, failures and articles, which did belong to the office of a Justice of the Peace within the said borough and the limits, precincts and libertyes thereof, soe fully, freely and absolutely and in such manner and forme as any other Justices of the Peace of the said Queen, her heirs or successors, in any county of the kingdom of England, by the lawes and statutes of the said kingdom or any of them, may or might enquire, hear or determine. And the said late Queen required for herself, her heirs and successors, firmly by the said letters patents, and commanded that none of her Justices of the Peace or any one of them, her heirs and successors, in the

County of Devon, or in any other county or countys for the time being, should any, way afterwards intermeddle for or concerning any felonyes, things, causes, matters, defects or other articles whatsoever, belonging or appertaining to the office of a Justice of the Peace, within the said burrough, limits, libertys or precincts thereof, for any cause whatsoever issueing or happening, nevertheless the said Mayor and Commonalty of the aforesaid Burrough of Plymouth, have shewn to us that the cause of the want of more justices there, (there being only three, to witt, the Mayor, Recorder, and last predecessor of every Mayor, which Recorder for the most part, inhabiteth out of the borough aforesaid, and the last predecessor of the Mayor, oftentimes by his business or affairs being hindered, is necessarily absent from the borough aforesaid,) diverse enormityes and inconveniences do arise, for oftentimes it happens by reason of the absense of some of these justices, that the sessions of the peace in the burrough aforesaid cannot be held in the usual times, but he delayed to the loss and prejudice of our subjects, who are obliged to make their appearance there or answer upon recognizance or otherwise; oftentimes also divers young men being by profession seamen and within the burrough aforesaid, being for small crimes and offences, commonly called petty theft and larcenys attached, have been sent to the common goale of the County of Devon, being distant forty miles or thereabout from the aforesaid burrough, where, among wicked people, they have soe accustomed themselves to wickedness, that they return unfitt for service; from whence also very great costs and troubles have ensued to our subjects, being obliged to give evidence there, and for the sending of the inhabitants of the burrough aforesaid thither to prison. And moreover, the said Mayor and Commonalty have most humbly petitioned us, that we would extend our royal favour and bounty, by the assigning and appointing more justices for the preserving of the peace within the burrough aforesaid and hearing and determining certaine felonyes, transgressions and offences, committed within the burrough aforesaid, and the adding of power to hear and determine small felonys and larcenys there to be committed. Know ye further, that we, considering the premises and being desirous to give a remedy in the premises, of our further special grace and from our certaine knowledge and mere motion have granted, and by these presents, for ourselves and successors, do grant to the aforesaid Mayor and Commonalty of the Borough of Plymouth aforesaid and their successors, that the Mayor and Recorder of the said borough for the time being, during the time which they shall happen to be in their offices, and the last predecessor of every Mayor of the said burrough for the time being, during one year after he shall have departed from his office of mayoralty, and also the two antientest Capital Burgesses of the burrough aforesaid, in degree and order of election, within the burrough aforesaid, for the time being, besides the aforesaid Mayor for the time being, and besides his aforesaid last predecessor, be justices of us, our heirs and successors, and each of them be justice of us, our heirs and successors, to keep and preserve, and to cause to be kept and preserved the peace of us, our heirs and successors in the said borough, and do all things there which do belong to the office of a justice, appointed to keep the peace in any county in England, by the laws and statutes of the kingdom of England, to be done and executed without any other command, commission or warrant from us, our heirs and successors, to be therefore had and obtained. And that the said Mayor and Recorder, and last predecessor of every Mayor of the borough aforesaid for the time being, and also the aforesaid two other most antient Capital Burgesses of the said borough, in degree and order of election within the borough aforesaid, as is aforementioned for the time being, or any two or more of them, of whom the Mayor or Recorder of the borough aforesaid for the time being, we will shall be one, have full power and authority to enquire concerning any felonyes, trangressions, crimes, and other offences and articles whatsoever made, had or committed within the said burrough and the libertys, precincts and limits thereof, which ought and may be enquired into before the Keeper and Justices of the Peace, in any county of our kingdom of England, by the laws and statutes of the said kingdom, so that they do not in any manner hereafter proceed to the determination of any murder or felony (little felonys or larcenys called in English, petty larcenys being excepted,) or of any other matter touching loss of life or limbs within the borough aforesaid, the limits, precincts and libertys of the same, without the special mandate of us, our heirs and successors. Nevertheless we will, and out intention is, and by these presents, for us, our heirs and successors, we grant to the aforesaid Mayor and Commonalty of the borough aforesaid and their successors, that the Mayor, Recorder, and last predecessor of the Mayor, and the aforesaid two other most antient Capital Burgesses of the borough aforesaid, in degrees and order of election, as is aforementioned for the time being, we will shall be one, shall and may for ever hereafter enquire of all and singular other crimes, trangressions, offences, failures and articles, and of all small felonyes or larcenys and inferior offences and crimes, commonly called petty thefts and petty larcenys committed or to be committed, and there happening within the borough aforesaid, the limits, precincts and libertys of the same, and all and singular the same to hear and determine; and the offender according to the laws and customs of our kingdom of England, with due punishment to correct, so fully, freely and absolutely, and in such ample manner and form, as any other Justices of the Peace of us, our heirs and successors, in any county of our kingdom of England, by the laws and statutes of our said kingdom or any of them, may and ought to inquire into, hear and determine and correct. And furthermore we will, and for ourselves our heirs and successors, firmly by these presents, do command that no Justices of the Peace of us, our heirs or successors, in our County of Devon, or in any other county or countys for the time being, intermeddle anyway hereafter, nor any one of them do intermeddle for or touching any felonys, things, causes, matters, failures or other articles whatsoever, belonging or appertaining to the office of a Justice of Peace within the said borough, limits, libertys and precincts therof, upon any cause arising or happening. And we will, and by these presents, for ourselves, our heirs and successors, do constitute and ordaine that all and singular the aforesaid most antient Capital Burgesses of the burrough aforesaid, in the degree and order of election as is before mentioned, as well present as future, being by these presents constituted to execute the offices of Justices of the Peace within the borough aforesaid, libertys, limits and precincts of the same, before they or any of them be admitted to the execution of the offices of Justices of the Peace there, they and every one of them shall take their corporal oath upon the Holy Gospel of God, well and faithfully to execute the office of Justices of the Peace within the borough aforesaid, the libertys and precincts thereof, in and through all things touching and concerning the said office; also they and every of them shall perform such oaths, as in that parte by the laws and statutes of the kingdom of England are provided, which are required to be taken by Justices of the Peace, before the Mayor of the said borough for the time being. To which Mayor of the borough aforesaid for the time being, we do by these presents, for ourselves, our heirs, and successors, give and grant full power, ability and authority in like manner to give and administer such oath from time to time, and this without any further warrant or any other commission, to be procured or obtained from us, our heirs or successors on that accompt. Notwithstanding express mention hath not in these presents been made of the true yearly value or of the certainty of the premises, or any of them or of other gifts or grants heretofore made by us or any of our progenitors or predecessors to the aforesaid Mayor and Commonalty of Plymouth aforesaid, or any statute, act, ordinance, provision, proclamation or restriction to the contrary thereof heretofore had, made, given, ordered or provided or any other thing, cause or matter whatsoever in any thing notwithstanding. In testimony whereof we have caused these our letters to be made patents, witness ourself at Westminster the third day of March, in the third year of our reign.

We, ratifying and well pleased with all and singular the franchises, libertyes, priviledges, quittances, immunityes, concessions and confirmations as aforesaid for ourselves, our heirs and successors, as much as in us lyes, do allow, approve and ratifye, and all and singular the franchises, libertyes, priviledges, quittances and immunityes aforesaid, to our beloved the Mayor and Burgesses or Magistrates in these presents hereafter named, and to the Mayor or Burgesses and Magistrates of the borough aforesaid and their successors, doe by these presents, grant and confirme, as the charters and letters patents aforesaid do reasonably testifye, and as the said Mayor and Burgesses of the said Borough of Plymouth or their predecessors, ever ought, could or should use and enjoy the franchises, libertyes, quittances and immunityes aforesaid, altho' the said Mayor and Burgesses of the same borough or their predecessors, have abused or not used the franchizes, libertyes, privileges, quittances and immunityes aforesaid or any of them. And forasmuch as we are given to understand, that on pretence of two instruments or witnesses, to which the common Seal of the Mayor and Commonalty of the borough aforesaid, hath by a combination of a few of the said borough been set and affixed, one of them bearing date the fifteenth day of March, in the thirty-sixth year of the reign of late Lord, King Charles the Second, our predecessor, of our happy memory; and the other of them, bearing date the seventeenth day of April, in the same thirty-sixth year of the reign of the said late King, Charles the Second, or either or one of them; and in the Court of Record of Chancery of the said late King inrolled, purporting to be a grant or surrender by the aforesaid Mayor and Commonalty of the said late King, his heirs and successors, of all and singular mannors, lordships, messuages, mills, suites of mills, lands, tenements, hereditaments, markets, fairs, market places, flesh-shambles, standings, wharfs, tolls, dutyes, town-customs, to be paid upon importing or exporting goods and merchandizes, dues on payments for rollage, package, kayage, wharfage and landleif dues, commonly called dues or payments of or for ale-weights and wine-weights, courts, profits, and perquisites of courts, mill-leats, waters, watercourses, weares, rents, reversions, advowsons of vicarages and churches, rights of patronage and presentations to the vicarages, wastes and all other statutes, rights, titles, interests, franchizes, libertyes, privileges, presentments, emoluments and hereditaments whatsoever, with the appurtenances of and in which the said Mayor and Commonalty then and at any time before, hath been anyway seized, possessed, estated, entitled or interested by the right of their Corporation, or in their corporate capacity, by any means whatsoever. And also purporting to be a grant by the aforesaid Mayor and Commonalty to the said late King, of all instruments, obligations, specialtys, and obligations whatsoever, wherein or whereby any person or persons then stood bound or obliged to the aforesaid Mayor and Commonalty of the Borough of Plymouth, in their corporal capacity, and sums of money thereon due and to be due, together with all debts, rents, sumes and sumes of money whatsoever, then due to the aforesaid Mayor and Commonalty by any person or persons whatsoever; and also purporting to be a grant, surrender and delivery of all and singular their charters, letters patents, incorporations, franchises, libertyes, privileges, powers, authorityes and immunityes whatsoever, at any time or times then before granted or held and enjoyed by the said Mayor and Commonalty, or by their or any of their predecessors, by any ways or means or by any name or names whatsoever. Also because, as well by reason of the aforesaid pretended grant and surrender, as by pretence or colour of a charter or letters patents of incorporation, made and granted or mentioned to be granted by the aforesaid late King, Charles the Second, after the date of the said instruments or pretended surrender, divers doubts, questions and controversyes have arisen, of and concerning the libertyes, franchises, customs, lands and possessions of the Mayor and Commonalty of the borough aforesaid, and also of and concerning the election and continuance of the officers of the borough aforesaid. Know yee therefore, that we graciously desiring the peace, tranquility and good government of the said borough and Commonalty and inhabitants of the same, and intending to take away and remove all the said doubts, questions and controversys in this case, have of our special grace, and our certain knowledge and mere motion, assigned, nominated, constituted and made, and by these presents, for ourselves, our heirs and successors, do assigne, nominate, constitute and make our beloved John Munyon, Merchant, to be the first and modern Mayor of the burrough aforesaid, to be continued in the same office to such time and in such manner and forme, as in the said burrough hath been accustomed and used before the day of the date of the aforesaid pretended grant or surrender, or either of them, or at any time before. And we have assigned, nominated, constituted and made, and by these presents, for ourselves, our heirs and successors, do assigne, nominate, constitute and make our beloved Francis Drake, Baronett, to be our first and modern Recorder of the borough aforesaid, to be continued in the said office during his natural life. And we have assigned, nominated, constituted and made, and by these presents, for ourselves, our heirs and successors, do assigne, nominate, constitute and make our beloved William Symons, Gent., William Cotton, William Tour, the aforesaid John Munyon, James Hull, Merchants, Peter Foot, Gent., Philip Wilcocks, John Warren, John Neel, Merchants, Thomas Knotsford, Apothecary, Richard Opie, William Munyon, Merchants, and Thomas Bound, Pewterer, to be our first and modern Capital Freemen or Masters for the borough aforesaid, to be continued in the said offices to such time, and in such manner and forme as hath been used and accustomed in the said borough, before the day of the date of the aforesaid pretended surrender, or any time before. And we have assigned, nominated, constituted and made, and by these presents, for ourselves, our heirs and successors, do assigne, nominate, constitute and make our beloved Edmund Pollexfen, Esq., to be our first and modern Common Clerke of the borough aforesaid, to be continued in the said office during his natural life. And we have assigned, nominated, constituted and made and by these presents, for ourselves, our heirs and successors, do assign, nominate, constitute and make our beloved Thomas Payne, Gent., to be our first and modern Coroner of the borough aforesaid, to be continued in the said office during the good pleasure of the Mayor and Capital Burgesses or Masters of the borough aforesaid. And we have assigned, nominated, constituted and made, and by these presents, doe, for ourselves, our heirs and successors, assigne, nominate, constitute and make our beloved Gregory Martyn, Apothecary, James Yonge, Chiurgeon, Joseph Webb, Merchant, Robert Berry, Gentleman, John Rogers, William Davis, Nathanael Yonge, Nathanael Dourish, Merchants, Samuel Allyn, Thomas Limbeare, William Cock, Mercers, Nicholas Gennys, Grocer, Thomas Darracott, Merchant, John Wallis, Mercer, Jonah Lavington, Apothecary, Samuel How, Brewer, James Cock, Robert Wilcocks, Merchant, Francis Hill, Robt. Hewer, Grocers, Samuel Harris, Woolen Draper, Robt. Cowne, Druggist, William Hurrill and John Simmones to be our first and modern Common Councellors of the borough aforesaid, to be continued in the same offices to such time, and in such manner and forme as in the said borough hath been used and accustomed before the day of the aforesaid pretended surrender, or at any time heretofore. And we have assigned, nominated, constituted and made, and do by these presents, for ourselves, our heirs and successors, assigne, nominate, constitute and make our beloved George Treby, Knight, Chief Justice of our Common Bench, Charles Trelawney, Esq., the aforesaid Francis Drake, William Courtney, William Davy, Walter Young, Baronets, John Elwill, Kt., Josias Calmady, George Parker, William

Harris, of Hayne, Arthur Tremayne, John Clobery, John Arscott, Martyn Rider, Courtney Croker, John Coplestone, Edward Fortescue, Nicholas Morris, Moses Gould, Henry Watts, Esq., Thomas Pyne and John Sprage, Doctors in Physick, George Lapthorne, Samuel Carkett, Philip Pentyre, Merchants, and John Vallack, Apothecary, to be the first and modern Freemen of the burrough aforesaid.

And further, out of our more abundant grace, and out of our certain knowledge and mere motion, we have given, granted, restored, confirmed, approved and ratifyed, and by these presents do, for ourselves, our heirs and successors, give, grant, restore, confirm, approve and ratify to the Mayor and Commonalty of the Borough of Plymouth aforesaid, and their successors, all and all manner of mannors, lordships, messuages, mills, suites at mills, lands, tenements, hereditaments, markets, fairs, market places, flesh-shambles, standings, wharfs, tolls, dues, dutys or town-customs, to be paid on importing or exporting goods and merchandizes, debts or payments for rollage, package, kayage, wharfage, and landlief, and debts commonly called debts or payments for or concerning ale-weights, wine-weights, courts, profits and perquisites of courts, mill leats, waters, watercourses, weares, rents, reversions, advowsons or vicarages and churches, rights of patronages and presentations to the vicarages, wastes and all other statutes, rights, titles, interests, franchises, libertyes, priviledges, profitts, emoluments and hereditaments whatsoever, with the appurtenances of and in which the said Mayor and Commonalty at the time of the aforesaid pretended surrender, or either of them, or at any time heretofore have been anyway seized, possessed, estated, intitled or interested by the right of their Corporation, or in their corporate capacity by any means whatsoever. And also all instruments, obligatory, specialtys and obligations whatsoever, wherein or whereby any person or persons at the time of the aforesaid pretended surrender, or either of them, or at any time before, stood bound or obliged to the aforesaid Mayor and Commonalty of the Borough of Plymouth in their corporated capacity, and sume and sumes of money by the same due, and to be due, and all other dues, rents, sume and sumes of money whatsoever due to the aforesaid Mayor and Commonalty, by any person or persons whatsoever. And all such and such like powers, prescriptions, libertyes, franchises, immunityes, jurisdictions, charters, letters patents, letters patents of incorporations, customes, profits, offices, officers, exemptions, quittances, wastes, voids, funds, commodities, emoluments, goods, chattels and hereditaments whatsoever, which and whatsoever by the letters patents, bearing date the third day of March, in the third year of the reign of the said late King, Charles the First, have been granted and confirmed, or mentioned to be granted and confirmed to the Mayor and Commonalty of the borough aforesaid or which the Mayor and Commonalty of the borough aforesaid or their successors, by whatsoever name or names of incorporation, before the said seventeenth day of April, in the aforesaid thirty-sixth year of the reign of our late Lord, King Charles the Second, have, had, used, held or enjoyed or occupied or ought or might have held, used or enjoyed, to themselves or their successors, by reason or pretence of the said several letters patents or any one of them, or any charters, grants or letters patents whatsoever by any of our progenitors or predecessors, late Kings or Queens of England, have been in any manner granted or confirmed before the seventeenth day of April, in the thirty-sixth year of the reign of our late Lord, King Charles the Second, or by any other legal manner, right or title, custome, use or prescription before the date of the presents, have been lawfully used, held, accustomed or enjoyed. And further we have given and granted, and by these presents do, for ourselves, our heirs and successors, give and grant unto the Mayor and Commonalty of the Borough of Plymouth aforesaid and their successors, all and singular instruments, obligatory, specialties and obligations whatsoever, wherein and whereby any person or persons, at any time after the aforesaid pretended grant and surrender, or either of them, and before the date of these our letters patents, stood bound or obliged to any person or persons taking upon themselves to be a body corporated or politick, by the name of the Mayor and Commonalty of the Borough of Plymouth, by pretence or colour of the aforesaid letters patents, made by the said late King, Charles the Second, and sume and sumes of money by them due, and to be due, and all other dues, rents, sume and sumes of money whatsoever due to the aforesaid persons, taking upon themselves to be a body corporate and politick, by the name of the Mayor and Commonalty of the Borough of Plymouth aforesaid, by any person or persons whatsoever.

Moreover we will, and by these presents do order and command, that the aforesaid Recorder, Capital Burgesses or Masters, Common Clerk, Coroner and Common Councillors of the borough aforesaid, by these presents nominated and appointed before they or any of them be admitted to the execution of their offices and trusts in the borough aforesaid, and all other solemn oaths and subscriptions required to be made by the laws and statutes of this our kingdom of England, before the aforesaid John Munyon; to which said John Munyon we do by these presents give and grant full power and authority to give, administer and require, the said several oaths and subscriptions. Willing moreover, and by these presents, for ourselves, our heirs and successors granting to the aforesaid Mayor and Commonalty of the burrough aforesaid and their successors, that these our letters patents, and the inrollment of them and all and singular the things continued therein, be and shall be good, firme, valid and effectual in the law, to the said Mayor and Commonalty of the borough aforesaid and their successors, in and by all things in any of our courts, and before any of our judges or justices whatsoever, or other officers or ministers of us, our heirs and successors, to be had and taken fully and amply as much as possible in favour and for the benefit of the said Mayor and Commonalty of the said borough aforesaid and their successors, towards and against us, our heirs and successors, notwithstanding the aforesaid pretended grant or surrender, or either of them or any thing in them, or any of them contained, and notwithstanding the not naming or not reciting, the ill reciting, or not fully or truly reciting the libertys, franchizes and premises by these presents before granted or confirmed, or any of them or any of our progenitors or predecessors, or any of them, or any other granted by us, or any other thing, cause or matter whatsoever to the contrary notwithstanding. In testimony whereof we have caused these our letters to be made patents. Witness ourself at Westminster, the eighth day of December in the eighth year of our reign. *Per pro de privato sigillo* – Pigott."

1697. – John Warren, Mayor. "Who was a perfect presbyterian and went to meeting every Sunday afternoon, yet a Parliament being called, exposed all their advantages and tricks which were many, it was carryed against the Regulator for Mr. G Trelawney and Sir John Rogers, against Mr. Parker and Mr. Calmady, who they set up 190 against 135. This so mortifyed the men and broke the credit of the party, that even the Regulator, Sir F. Drake, became quite confounded and never cared to concern himself in town matters from pure discontent. This mayor was a merchant and that's all. Of no knowledge in town affairs, or of any parts besides loading, by which the town suffered much, as it did by his successor also."

1698. – John Neal, Mayor. "Who was also a river merchant, and from ignorance in town usuages and justiceship, was so bewildered, that things went very uneasy, and all the care wanting that was necessary to cleanse it of dung. Beggars multiplied and the Corporation fallen into the lowest contempt. In this man's time four magistrates were chosen, Joseph Webb, W. Davys, S. Allen and Thos. Lymber, the two latter of that near model, so that in the short time of their charter, four of their upper bench dyed, viz., William Munyon, William Tom, William Cotton, and Thomas Knotsford."

1699. – Richard Opie, Mayor. "This gentleman was one of the 24 or Common Councillors in the old charter, and left out by the Earle of Bath and W. Martin in their new one, 1684, and restored in that of Sir F. Drake, but he abetted none of his arbitrary, sinnister, whiggish designers, nor followed the steps of his last predecessors, but made free as many churchmen as he could, by which he broke Jno. Warren's ballance, which displeased Sir F. Drake so that he abdicated the town, and came not near it in several years, doing us all the spite he could, without regard to his oath or the interest of his friends here, who suffered as much by his oppression as did his enemies. This year the Duke of Bolton was treated by the body."

1700. – Joseph Webb, Mayor. "This good man was a member in the two last charters and continued in this. His principles were just and he acted accordingly and quite broke the neck of the whig interest. The Parliament being dissolved, Mr. Gen. Trelawney and his brother, the brigadier, were both chosen, though opposed by all the power and tricks of the dissenters, whiggs and enemys of the church."

1701. – William Davys, Mayor. "Was a 24 or Common Councellman also in the two last charters, and so continued in this though he acted on the right side, like his three last predecessors. This yeare the brigadier dyed, and Mr. Woolcomb, of Petton, succeeded, and the Parliament being dissolved, and a new one called, the general and Mr. Woolcomb were chosen."

1702 – William Cock, Mayor. "A good churchman, and a tory, but of no parts nor temper; he was R. Berry's brother-in-law, who had now screwed himself in to the Town Clerk's chair, and proved as imperious and arbitrary as his master Pollexfen had before him. He governed this mayor, but nothing memorable happened this year."

1703. – Nicholas Gennys, Mayor. " A very honest good man. Some judges come to town in his time, and among them the famous Judge Price, who made that noble and bold English speech in Parliament, when the King had given his favourite Bentinck, Earl of Portland, a vast estate in Wales. Nothing else memorable happened this year, save that in November in a fearful tempest, the Eddystone Lighthouse was washed away; when Mr. Winstanley, who had expressed a wish to be in the building at such a period, perished in the stormy deep. Soon after the destruction of this fabric, the Winchelsea, a Virginiaman, the property of Sir John Rogers, Bart., of Plymouth, laden with tobacco for this port, was wrecked on those rocks in the night, and every soul lost." "The twelve Almshouses at Coxside, built for the widows of decayed mariners, at the expense of Col. Jory, native of the town; each widow has 25s. per month allowed." "Capts. Kirby and

Wade, of the Royal Navy, shot on the Hoe, pursuant to sentence of Court Martial, buried in lead coffins in Charles' Church Plymouth, under the pulpit."

The following document is highly interesting, showing the expense of the Plymouth Fishing Feast this year. The occasion of the fishing feast is as follows. The Mayor and Commonalty of the borough meet annually on a certain day, at the head-weir of the Plymouth Leat, in the Parish of Walkhampton, about nine miles distant from the town, and there drink, in *aqua pura*, to the memory of Sir Francis Drake, by whose munificence the fine stream of water with which the town is supplied, was brought a circuitous route of nearly 30 miles. After the performance of this ceremony, they return to Jump to dinner, and before they separate, the health of the intended mayor for the year ensuing, is generally proposed and drank. Expended at Jump.

		£	s	d		
Bought at Plymouth	Beef	0	5	0		
	Veal	0	2	6		
	Mutton	0	1	4		
	Collifloores and Lemons	0	0	8		
	Salt	0	0	3	—	£00 09 09
	6 Chickens	0	4	0		
	6 Ducks	0	4	0		
	2 Geese	0	3	0		
	Butter used in Ale and about ye Fish	0	4	0		
	18 Bottles of Sherry	1	16	0		
	6 Bottles of Canary and Fyall at 2s 6d	0	15	0		
	Syder in all	0	15	0		
	Beere	0	6	6		
	Bred and Cheese	0	2	6		
	Dressing of ye victualls	0	3	0		
	Brandy, Sugar, etc.	0	6	4		
	Six Bottles Syder more	0	1	6	—	£05 00 10
						£05 10 07
	Drunk after at ye Doore					
	Stale Beer and Sugar	0	0	10		
	Syder	0	1	0		
	Wyne	0	5	6	—	£00 07 04
						£05 17 11

Sept. ye 10th 1703

Recd. of Wm. Lovell, Five Pounds, Seaventeen shils. and Sixpence, ye full contents of this note, I say recd. £05 17 06

BENNIDICK REEFE

Spent at Nackershole £00 01 00

Total £05 18 06

1704 – Thomas Darracott, Mayor. "One whom we all thought honest, but he proved a shuffler, abetted the whiggs, encouraged Sir F. Drake to appear again, and on calling a new Parliament, he and R. Berry as very a k..... and hypocryte as could be, fell in with the wrong side, ousted Mr. Woolcomb, and endeavoured the same with Mr. G. Trelawney, but by tricks and overbearing returned Sir George Byng. I don't say elected him, for had the good voices of the one which they refused been admitted, and their ill ones refused, we had carried it. But they lived not long to go in their iniquity, both dying in the next mayoralty."

1705. – Jonah Lavington, Mayor. " A man of principles indifferent good, but his interest and want of courage made him much to the side of Sir F. Drake, by which means, upon the death of R. Berry, (who dyed this yeare) one that was no highflyer, but a trimmer great with Sir F. Drake, was made Town Clerk. He was as a man, more a gentleman, more a lawyer, and less a knave, than the other; but Reade, who we would have had chosen, would have set all right, upon a good and lasting foundation. He failed also in electing Aldermen, laying by Mr. John Blight after he had been chosen, under pretence of some defect in the form, and chose Hewer and R. Berry. This yeare dyed W. Symons, the oldest Alderman, and T. Darracott the preceding Mayor, neither of any loss to the town otherwise than that they made way for two scablers to be put into that bench. The death of Berry the Town Clerk, who had in all stations been fatal to the town, left room for Mr. Pengelly, a barrister, who by Sir F. Drake's tricks, the insinuations, the cowardice, and evil principles of others, was chosen, and now Sir F. Drake appeared among them on all occasions, with great vigour and spirit."

"It is remarkable that eleven Aldermen, had dyed since the new regulation by Sir F. Drake, John Munyon and Co., viz.: Wm. Symons, Wm. Cotton, Wm. Tom, John Munyon, Jas. Hull, Peter Foot, John Warren, Thos. Knotsford, Wm. Munyon, Thos. Lymber, Thos. Darracott, besides Mr. Phil. Willcocks who resigned, 1705, for dotage and poverty, and Thos. Bound, who abdicated 1700, because he was not chosen mayor, as he sat after Mr. Opie, and before Mr. Webb."

1706. – Samuel Allen, Mayor. "The election of this man was not the least mischief his predecessor's pusillanimity, trimming, or partiality produced, he was a creature of the Regulators and served his interest, and because of that, had been postponed in four preceding elections, being an older Alderman than W. Cock. He went constantly to church, weekdays as well as Sundays, but retained a spice of his education, which was presbyterian. His father was mayor at the Regulation, 1662, and turned out for nonconformity. Although a close frugal man, he kept a very generous mayoralty, few or none equalling him for goodness of meat and drink at his entertainments. This yeare dyed Samuel How, a 12th Alderman, and R. Berry and Robert Cowne chosen in." "The second Lighthouse on the Eddystone begun."

1707. – James Cock, Mayor. "A man who from very mean beginning, became master, owner and merchant adventurer; of good natural parts, indifferent with respect to parties generally, thought an honest man, though he shewed a byas to the wrong side sometimes. In his time, the body of the famous Sir Cloudesley Shovel was brought in here in the "Salisbury," lodged in the Citadel, and embalmed by Mr. Yonge, was then carryed to London, and interred in the Abbey of Westminster at the Queen's cost." "The body of Sir Cloudesley Shovel wrecked on the Scilly Islands, washed on shore at that place, was conveyed to the Plymouth Citadel, were it lay in state, till removed to the residence of his lady in Soho Square, London, and then buried in Westminster Abbey." "In this mayoraltie, the tower of Charles' Church in Plymouth, was begun to be built from the height of 20 foot, which 20 foot was built in the year 1652, or about that time." "This year the Parliament was dissolved, and we unanimously chose our last representatives, Mr. G. Trelawney and Sir G. Byng. This year the Bishop of Winchester visited the town, dined with the mayor; and this year an Act of Parliament was procured for employing and maintaining the poor, whereof Mr. Yonge was chosen first governour, and the Workhouse incorporated."

"A list of what charters, books and other things and papers in the Town's Trunk, taken this 6th October, 1707, from John Genny's last receiver, viz. –

"The old charter restored, granted by King William the Third; King Charles' first charter; Queen Mary's charter; King James' first charter; Queen Elizabeth's charter; King Charles' second charter; a confirmation of a charter by King James the First; exemplification of a charter by King James the First; a regulation of a charter from King Charles the Second, for the Newfoundland trade; a charter or grant from King Charles the First, for erecting of Charles' Church; Prince Charles' charter for Sutton Pool; King

Charles the Second's charter at his restoration; a copy of a charter granted to merchants trading to Spain and Portugal; a box with parchment interrogatories; Mr. Rich's abstract concerning the charter; a mortgage and another parchment writing concerning Sutton Pool; a bundle of parchments of weekly courts; a bundle of papers of inquisitions, copies of letters patents, etc.; 13 bundles of loose papers; five Acts of Parliament; seven old written town's books; the Black Book with a record of the mayors of the borough; two statute books; a book of Acts of Parliament; two covers of the Union Cup, which are at the mayor's; a bread table.

"Plymouth, ye 6th October, 1700.

"Then received of John Gennis, the late receiver, the Town Trunk with the above mentioned particulars.

By me, WM HURRILL."

"To the King's most excellent majesty. The humble petition of Jonathan Sparke, Esq., Philip Lamon, Gent., Thomas Caunter, Henry Brock, Richard Allen, John Allen, Gideon Allen, John Gubbs, Henry Martin, Henry Hopkins, Elizabeth Bartlett, Anne Mansfield, Catharine Cramporne, Adam Grills, Mary Bursh, Edith Mami, William Downing, in the behalf of themselves and other inhabitants of the Town of Plymouth; most humbly shews that whereas upon the erecting your Majesty's royal Citadel, now in hand, (upon the Howe of Plymouth, to which work tending much to the honour of your Majesty and the safeguard of the town and port there,) they have given all submission and obedience, though their particular losses are much concerned therein, their several lands being thereby laid waste and open, yet assuring themselves that your Majesty's just and royal intentions did no way tend to any particular prejudice of your petitioners, but that a fit compensation should be made unto them, your petitioners did formerly address themselves by petition to the Right Honourable the Earl of Bath, your Majesty's Governor of the said Town and Fort of Plymouth, for the repairation of their several losses sustained in the erecting of the said Citadel. And whereas his Lordship was thereupon pleased to refer the computation of your petitioners losses and damages thereby sustained to*.................. who thereupon have made a report of the same to his Lordship, (which said petition and report are hereunto annexed,) by which do appear that the damages which your petitioners have sustained have been very great. And we do also further represent to your Majesty that the inconveniences which thereby do accrue to ourselves and families are much greater by such a dissettlement, which we cannot possibly make up again in any other place. Your petitioners therefore most humbly pray that your

*Left blank in the copy.

Majesty would be pleased to take us and our families into your royal thoughts, and to assigne a fit and certain repairation for the same, equal to our particular losses and damages. And your petitioners shall ever, as they are most bound in duty, pray for your Majesty's prosperity and lengths of days, etc."

1708. – Robert Hewer, Mayor. "A zealous party man of the Regulator's side; did nothing; nor was anything done worthy of remembering, save that the New Church Steeple was carryed on very far by subscription. Dr. Blackett our new Bishop made his visitation, August 30th, against which time the new gallery for the boys in the Poor's Portion was built at the charge of the Guardians and Overseers." "Mr. W. Warren was elected Governour of the Workhouse; Mr Jas Blight chosen Alderman. A very severe winter, great dearth, etc., a mighty lightning and thunder, threw down one of the pinnacles of Saint Andrew's tower. Soon after (in August) Colonel Jory presented the church, with a ring of six fine bells."

1709. – James Bligh, Mayor. "An honest good principled man. Nothing of moment occurred in his time, but a visit to the town of Lord Chief Justice Parker and Bury." "In whose mayoralty, Joseph Jorey, Esquire, a great benefactor to this towne (by building and endowing Almshouses at Coxside and giving six very fine tuneable bells to Charles' Parish, in the late mayoralty of Mr. Hewer,) presented the Mayor and Commonalty with a very large double gilt mace; a larger and better hath not been seen." "The second Lighthouse on the Eddystone finished, which was erected by Mr. John Rudyerd, Silk Mercer of Ludgate Hill, London, and was constructed of stone and timber."

1710. – William Roche, Mayor. "A man of principles good enough, averse to the Regulator, and would have overset all that party had done, and restored the church interest, but being of a rash and headstrong temper, and with his brother, J. Read, having sinister aims, they discovered their designs, rejected the advice of wiser and much honester men, and alarmed the adverse party and were scandalously baffled." "Parson Martin of the New Church quitting that benefice, several appeared for it, but the mayor forbore long to elect, by which time the Corporation were divided, and great animosity grew on that account, at length he prefixed a day for choosing, and then a majority of the Aldermen and Common Councel went out of the town, but he went to the election, being but eight present, viz.: the Mayor, Justice Bligh, Mr Gennys, Aldermen John Read, Heal, Phil. Collins, John Webb, and John Fletcher, who then elected and chose Mr Hergo, a very good man every way, and the two justices refusing to open the chest to seal the presentation, it was forced, as once before, on the like occasion, 1680, in Mr Symons' mayoralty, and the other put in Caveats against his admission; it came to tryal before the Lord Bishop in Exeter, and the election voted good by the jury, accordingly Mr Hergo was instituted, but the generality of the town were so averse to him and the mayor, that by an illegal way chose and presented him, that they first turned him out of his office of mayor, by virtue of a power in the first charter of incorporation, and then sued him and Hergo, upon a *Quare Impedit*, but just as it was come to the time of the assize, the Bishop of Winchester who was formerly of his diocess, and Mr Hergo's friend, advised him to relinquish the benefice upon some consideration, which he did and Dr Moncton, of Liskeard, succeeded him in our new church. Roche, who was enough hated before, now was become odious to both partys, the torys for losing an opportunity by his folley and madness to have undone all that Sir Francis Drake had done to the advantage of the fanatics and whiggs in this town.

"N.B. – John Read, an attorney, and brother-in-law to Roche, governed this affair alone, and by ignorance, treachery, etc. lost all. Hergo was forced to quit, and Roche to bear the infamy and reproach (on record at Westminster and Plymouth) of having been guilty of such enormityes as forfeited his office. Never done before by 271 that preceded him in it."

The following interesting accounts refer to this affair:–

"Recd. of Mr. Wm. Roche, pursuant to a Rule of Court, made at Lammas Assizes, 1712, for the three old maces, which with £30 recd. of ye said Mr. Roche and Mr. John Webb, pursuant to ye said rule for cost, and which £30 hath been applyed towards paying the law charges in prosecuting the said Roche and Webb makes £71 11s 6d., in full of the said rule, £41 11s 6d.

"Paid several persons for watching in and about the Guildhall, after Mr. Roche's amovement from his office of mayoralty, in order to prevent ill-designing persons for attempting the town seale, £5 6s 8d.

"Paid Mr. Jno March for the old Corporation maces, which were unduly sold him by ye said Mr. Roche, £16 11s 6d.

"Paid ye Town Clerk and several others their charges for sending expresses to London from Exeter for a *Ne admittas* and several other charges at Exeter, before and after ye tryall of ye *Jus Patronatus*, £147 14s 6d.

"Paid Mr. Phillips and Mr Elford, their bill of cost in two actions of trover against Roche and Webb, for recovering the town regalia over and above £30, received from Roche and Webb, pursuant to a Rule of Court, £55 10s 6d.

"Paid their charges for motions for two *Mandamus* against Roche and Webb, commanding them to deliver up the towne regalia, and for ye writts and service and several other motions, etc., £51 11s 0d.

"Paid the ballance of their bills, relating to two *quo warrantos* against Mr. Cowne and Mr. Berry, for exercising the office of Mayor, £3.

"Paid Mr. Phillips the ballance of his bill for opinions before and after the said amotion, for copy of the act of incorporation and for fees and expences of ye tryall of ye *Jus Patronatus*, the sum of £52 6s 0d.

"Paid other charges relateing thereto, £7 3s 0d.

"1712. – Andrew Phillips

"Paid Mr Elford, etc., the ballance of their bills of cost at common law and chancery, in defending severall actions commenced by and for prosecuting Mr. Roche, for irregular levying a quarter's rent for ye shambles a little after his amovement from his office, the sum of £40 15s 0d.

"Paid Mr. Hull and others their bills in and about a *Quare Impedit* brought by the Mayor and Commonalty against ye Bishop of Exon and Hewgoe and for setting Dr. Muncton, Vicar of Charles' Parish, £87 6s 6d.

"Paid Mr Elford, etc., for moving for a *Mandamus* and other charges, to procure Mr Abraham Mangles sworn Churchwarden of Charles' Church, £14 9s 0d.

"Paid the ballance of their bills in prosecuting Mr Roche and Mr Webb, in the exchequer for a discovery of ye town charter, writings and regalia, and for delivering ye same up, £9 1s 6d.

"Paid them for several charges and expences about ye affairs, £10 12s 0d.

"1713. – William Hurrill. Recd of Mr Samuel Blatchford for two old Corporation maces, £14."

1711. – Robert Cowne, Mayor. "Was chosen the usual day, a tool and a fool. Dyed soon after, and was succeeded by B. Berry, who served the rest of the year, and having no house in town, lodged and kept the mayoralty at an house that was common for quartering strangers and selling punch and ale, to the great scandal of the office, but they stuck at nothing; seemed to regard neither the credit or welfare of the town, filled up the benches with men that were of mean and scandalous origin and behaviour, as if they had been sworn to chose the worst, and did many things contrary to the constitution or custom of the burrough, chose a mayor that did not inhabit, filled the benches with lawyers, and accepted the resignation of Webb a Justice."

"Guildhall, 30th August, 1711. At the election of a Vicar for Charles' Parish the candidates were as follows, viz.: Doctor Reynold, Mr. Walter Hugoe, Mr Thomas Samford, Mr George Derby, Mr George Mitchell, this election was strongly contested, and after awhile Mr Hugoe resigned, and on the 3rd, October 1711, the Rev. Charles Monkton, D.D., was elected the Vicar of Charles; his election took place by the votes of the Recorder, ten Aldermen and six Common Councilmen; it does not appear by this paper who the doctors were, but Mr Roche the Mayor, misconducted himself on this and so many other occasions that he was removed from his office."

1712. – Andrew Phillips, Mayor. "An attorney, in whose time nothing memorable happened, but the Bishop of Winchester coming to town, and being entertained by the Corporation. This year W. Davis and R. Opie dyed, Joseph Webb abdicated, and the whigg interest advanced."

1713. – William Hurrel, Mayor. "A man honest; more sense than money, much on the whigg side; made no figure. August 1st. – Our gracious Queen Anne dyed, and King George proclaimed the Thursday following in this town, and the whole kingdom quietly submitted, not one man appearing for the Pretender, although the whiggs had long reported he lay ready with an army and fleet. Grey School instituted." "John Rose stood in the pillory the 9th of April, 1713, being Easter Thursday; ye hangman stood by him all the tyme, being one hour at noon." "Dr. Mountney preacht at the New Church the 3 of May, and was inducted by the Canon Gilbert the 4, being Monday."

"The ratification of peace was exchanged between Great Britain and France, the 31 of March, at Utrich, (Utrecht) and the peace proclaimed at London, ye 5 day of May, being Tuesday, in the yeare 1713, and afterwards proclaimed at Plymouth, the 14 day of ye same about four a clock, being the Holy Thursday, at which time Martin's cundict, New Kay cundict, Pope's Head cundict, and Old Town cundicts run with wine and 21 guns fired at ye forte, in the mayoralty of Mr. Andrew Phillips, with several bonfiers and candles in great many houses with ringing of bells."

Memorandum. – "The peace proclaimed between Great Britain and Spain the nineth day of March, 1713-14, at the same placed that it was between Great Britain and France, with the usuall solemnityes, except wine runing in cundicts."

1714. – John G. Pike, Mayor. "Mr Edward Nickleson, Lieutenant of Curn^{ll} Goran's reidgement, stood in our pillory att Plymouth, the first day of Aprill, 1714, being East Thursday, from the houre of eleaven to ye hour of one, one houre his face towards the Guildhall, the other houre towards the church-style with his accusation writen upon a piece of paper fastened to his hatt, which words weare: – "God damn the Queen," and fined £20."

1715. – John Crabb, Mayor.

1716. – Abraham Joy, Mayor. "Wensday the 20 of March, 1716-17, Captain Dawson killed Lieutenant Butler, in Brigadier Stanwix's reidgement, by a stab a little above ye right pap, hee dyed imeadatly and the jury found it willful murder."

171. – John Beer, Mayor. But dying he was succeeded by Robert Hewer. Sir John Rogers, Bart., chosen Recorder.

1718. – Edward Deeble, Mayor. St. Martin's conduit rebuilt. "Itt begun to snow the 23 day of January at night, being Sunday, and continued almost till Tuesday morning, very great that theare was noe working till Friday, and a very hard frost for a long tyme besides, snow very often, and all things very deare, so that a halfe-peny rowle weidht just a crown-piece, and two turneps sold for a peny, and coals sold for forty shillings a quarter, and all theis things notwithstanding soe deare, was very bad in kinde." "A great thunder and lightning hapened the 3 day of March, being Thursday, about two o clock in the afternoon, caried away that pinicle of the tower that the cock stands on, and brauke in the church very much and brake a hole in the churchyard wall, oposite against Bishopp's house, which is to the east end and severall other strange things and yett noe person received damage, yett some with the surprize was strook down backward to ye ground."

1719. – William Bartlett, Mayor. "The clock and chimes given to Charles' Church by Colonel Jory." Bishop Blackburne came here ye 20 of July and confirmed some hundreds."

1720. – George Ridout, Mayor. "A Holoisbut (Halibut) brought in the markett from Carson, (Cawsand) was foare foot three inches long and two foot broad, wheare the firste fins ten inches more, and as clean and white a fish as could be seen, Mr. Bartlett, Mayor, oford 7s 6d., but next day was bought by Mr. Toulsha (Tolcher) Goolsmith for 5s. and was sent to London."

CHAPTER VII

ANNALS CONTINUED FROM THE YEAR 1720 TO 1800

1721. – John Fletcher, Mayor, who died the day after he was sworn in and was succeeded by John Elford. Hon. Wm. Chetwynd, and Hon. P. Byng, Members of Parliament. "March 22nd, Mr. Patt Byng and Mr. William Chettwin was chosen Members of Parliament at the Workhouse without opposition, Sir John Rogers declined the Munday before, upon which occasion was the greatest entertainment as ever was known in Plymouth, about 20 houses made provisions for meate and drink, and at the taverns, wine as plenty as smal beer, with ringing of bells, and at night was a bonfire on the New Key, wheare was two hogsheads of strong beare givein to the rabble."

1722. – Sir John Rogers, Bart., Mayor. "The Rev. John Gilbert, Vicar of Saint Andrew's, died. He was sent hither by the bishop, the town having let the time elapse for the election of a vicar. He was succeeded by the Rev. Wm. Stephens." "Mr Cannon Gilbert dyed ye 19 of January 1722, in ye 95 year of his age, being Vicar of Saint Andrew's in the 42 yeares and Canon of Exon 31 yeares of that tyme; was buried in the chancell ye 25 January, and being Fryday about 4 clock in the afternoon, ye pulpit and all the pews in mourning, likewise ye clark's seat, and a hearse stood over his grave, with 12 scuchings on itt. Fourteen ministers at ye funerall, six walkt before the corpse and eight bearers, hee had two funerall sermons precht ye Sunday after, one by Mr. Hicks, his curate, the other by Mr. Roberson of Buckland; the church was full."

1723. – Andrew Phillips, Mayor. "This year Sir Joshua Reynolds was born at Plympton, near Plymouth."

1724. – John Crabb, Mayor.

1725. – Samuel Brent, Mayor.

1726. – Benjamin Berry, Mayor. "A great opposition at this election, which lasted until 12 o'clock at night."

1727. – Edward Deeble, Mayor. Arthur Stert and George Treeby, Esqrs., and afterwards, in place of Treeby, the Hon. Robert Byng, Members of Parliament. "September 17th, a jury was chosen as usual to elect a mayor, 18 were for John Rogers and 18 for George Treeby. No mayor was then chosen. The dispute ran very high, the candidates drew their swords on each other, and bad consequences must have ensued from the mob, had they not been called off by a fire in Gasking-street. They met again next day, but could not agree, and the town was without a mayor from 17th September, to the 12th March following, when by virtue of a *Mandamus* from the court of the King's bench, John Rogers Esq., the son of Sir John Rogers, was chosen and sworn.

"Counsellor Martin sent an express to Sir Francis Drake, which arrived heare to Mr. Samuel Adis on Saturday morning att three a clock, of the King's death; the guns fired minitly and ye bell struck the same at the church. Sunday the bells rung at one a clock, and after a sermon, and the guns fired at the fort. Tuesday after, the proclamation came, and George the Second was proclaimed King by Mr. Baker, Town Clerk; he stood on a stool and read the proclamation first at the Guildhall, next upon the cross at the Shambles, then at New Key, and last at Martin's-gate, accompanied with fife, drums, and severall plaed on musick, with the whole Government almost, but was only one publick bonfire, and that on the New Kay, where was only the rable, but no appearents of any gentlemen nor one spoonful of drink given them; ye bells rung and the fort guns fired, this was in the mayoralty of Doctor Benjamin Bery. The King dyed in the 68 yeare of his age and ye 13 yeare of his rayne and almost universally lamented."

1728. – John Rogers, Mayor.

1729. – Samuel Allen, Mayor. Who died during his term of office and was succeeded by William or Luke Cock, mercer.

1730. – John Tapson, Mayor. "A grocer. An opposition; he was chosen Alderman by the Freemen." 10 bushells of wheat purchased for the Workhouse, cost £3 7s 3d.

1731. – John Whaddon, Mayor. The Rev. Wm. Stephens, Vicar of Saint Andrew's, died 16th March, and was succeeded by the Rev. Zachary Mudge.

1732. – Robert Hewer, Mayor. "Parson Stevins, (Rev. Mr Stephens) dyed March 16th, 1731-2, in the morning about eleaven clock, as is supposed in the gout in his stomach after about 10 days illness, the last sermon he preacht was of a Sunday, in the New Church, upon a subject of charity; he preacht the Wensday before in the Olde Church, being the 1st of March, upon the 11 chapter of ye Acts, the two last verses, upon charity, he was rector 9 yeares and in his 40 year of age. Parson Stevins had a funerall sermon preacht the 19 of March, being Sunday, by Parson Foster, upon the 3 chapter of the 2 Epistle of Tymothy and the 15 verse; he gave a very lardge inconium and nothing more than he deserved, hee being allowed as learned and fine a preacher as any of his age, and I never knew a man soo much lamented in all the course of my life. Many hundred people wept att his funerall sermon, and lamented by all that knew him. He was buried abute 8 or 9 o clock Saturday morning in the chancell, his uper bearers was six ministers and two walkt before the corps, the under bearrers had hatbands and gloves. Hee left his widdow with five small children and she with child with another."

"April 12th. – Stephen Woon and Benjamin Cruse was executed at Heavytree gallows, nigh Exon, for the murder of Mr John Pyke, Tyde Surveyor, about runing of brandy and was hanged in chains, the 14th January at Crabtree."

"April 15th. – The fifth bell in the Olde Church tower was new castt in the Workhouse, the weight of which is twenty-foure hundred grose and eighteen pounds, which is four pounds less than the old one, in the mearolty of Mr John Waddon, Land Surveyor and Thomas Cock and Mr Hering, Churchwardens. Cast by Mr Penitent and his father."

"August 23rd. – This day came on the election for a Vicar for Saint Andrew's Church, wheare one Doctor Burnett and Mr Zachariah Mudge was put up as candadates, and Mr Wadon, Mayor, after all the Government had struck, said there was fourteen struck for Doctor Burnett and fifteen for Mr Zachariah Mudge, but then Mr Mayor said that all the Government was not theare and talks of adjourning to the houses of two, which weare then sick in theare beds and one of them almost dying, but the opposite party said there was never any such custom, but only those that did not meet to the Guildhall, which caused a great dispute and the Black Book was sent for, and thare it appeared very plain it was to be decided by them only which appeared at the Guildhall and had most strokes of the electors thare, and then Mr Mayor declared Mr Zachariah Mudge, Vicar of Saint Andrew's Parish. A man admired by most of the town, but only a sett of men used all the arts and base tricks to set him aside; theare were severall other candadates sett up, but those trickers got them all to give up theare pretensions purely to put aside the said Mr Mudge, though a very deserving man both in lerning and moralls. For Mr Mudge was 7 Aldermen and 8 Common Counsell. For the Doctor 4 Aldermen and 9 others. The said Mr Mudge was inducted the 15 day of September, being Friday, just after the morning prayers, which was after this maner. Mr Bowden, ye Vicar of Charles' Parish and Mr Foster Elector (Lecturer) of Saint Andrew's and Mr Cocke and Mr Hering the two Churchwardens with a few others with Mr Mudge stood at the chancell doore, every body being com out of church, they lockt the doore and then they unlockt itt and let ye said Mr Mudge walk in, then lock the doore upon him, then he goes and made sum short prayer as is suposd to himself, itt being usuall att such tyme, then he went in the tower and struck several strokes on one of the bells and came out to the aforesaid gentlemen and ask them to walk into his church, when they walked in and signed the instrument hee brought from the bishop's court and the all that weare theare wisht him long life and happiness, then he invited them to drink a glass of wine to Morgan's after evening prayers, haveing no place of his own – mark, non signed it but they who let him in."

1733. – John Hellyer, Mayor. "A limner." "May 29th, the passage-boat at Saltash cast away, and 20 lives lost, nine of whom were of Plymouth."

1734. – Thomas Phillips, Mayor. "A mercer."

1735. – William Strong, Mayor. This gentleman dying during his mayoralty, was succeeded by Robert Herrer.

1736. – John Veale, Mayor. "An apothecary." "Elm trees planted round about the town, at Old Mills, Pennycomequick-hill, Frankfort-gate, etc. The old mayoralty house burnt on an assembly night."

1737. – Greenhill Darracott, Mayor. Arthur Stert and Hon. Robert Byng, and afterwards Charles Vanbrugh, Members of Parliament. "A picture of His Majesty set up in the Guildhall. An organ built in Saint Andrew's Church by James Parsons, and opened on Tuesday 22 November. The singing men of Saint Peter's Church, Exeter, attended on the occasion, and the vicar preached. The cupola rebuilt on the Guildhall. Chains on the New Quay fixed, the gift of Captain Dutour."

1738. – Henry Tolcher, Mayor. "Feast now discontinued. A great dispute arose in the election of members, which was adjourned from Guildhall to the Workhouse, where it lasted three or four days. J. Rogers and C. Vanbrugh, Esqrs., candidates. By the vast number of faggots, which came from the utmost parts of Cornwall, it was decided in favor of John Rogers, Esq., who took his seat, but the opposite party being dissatisfied, took a journey to London, where Freeholders' votes for members were declared invalid, by the House of Commons, whereupon Charles Vanbrugh, Esq. was declared, and sat member."

1739. – Edward Deeble, Mayor. Severe frosts this and the succeeding year.

1740. – John Whaddon, Mayor. Lord H. Beauclerc, Member of Parliament in room of Charles Vanbrugh, Esq. "The Spanish flag presented to the borough by Lord Vere."

1741. – Richard Gortley, (blind) Mayor. "Richard Gortley was a surgeon, who died, and was succeeded by Sir John Rogers, Bart., Recorder." Arthur Stert Esq. and Lord Vere Beauclerc, Members of Parliament.

1742. – Launcelot Robinson, Mayor. "A merchant. This mayor revived two yearly fairs, and moved the watch-house from the Guildhall to fish cage. About this time, a new altar piece by Mrs Ilbert, and velvet cloth and cushions for the communion table, were given to Saint Andrew's Church by Mrs Phillips."

1743. – Sir John Rogers, Mayor.

1744. – Edward Hoblyn, Mayor. "A very high tide on Freedom day Eve. The gentlemen carried out of the mayoralty house on mens' shoulders, boats and casks floated about the streets, fish-house beat down, quays shattered, and merchandize lost. The damage to the town alone computed at £3,000. In November, the King's bakehouse at Coxside consumed by fire, with many stores. December 31st, a soldier shot in the Citadel for desertion."

1745. – William (or Edward) Martyn, M.D., Mayor. "The town's water conveyed through leaden pipes from Old Town conduit to the Victualling Office. The bakehouse was rebuilt and enlarged. A new slaughter-house built close to the Garrison, and near the Barbican. The outworks of the Citadel repaired as well as the lower fort. The French prison at Old Mills burnt."

1746. – William Davis Phillips, Mayor. "The gutter which brought the town water into Old Town conduit, laid with moor stone." James Northcote, the painter, born at Plymouth.

1747. – Michael Nichols, Mayor. "A merchant. Pulpit cloths and cushions given to Saint Andrew's Church by Miss Penelope Archer. October 14th, a soldier shot in the Citadel for desertion. A cartel ship burnt at Catwater. A general election, Vere and Stert, Members." Arthur Stert Esq. and Lord Vere Beauclerc, Members of Parliament. "July, Thomas Smith, Esq. called by the seamen *Tom of Ten Thousand* when a lieutenant, was broke, on a complaint of the French ambassador, for obliging a French ship-of-war to lower her topsail to his ship, in Plymouth Sound; but by the King's order, was the next day made a Post Captain; he died in 1762."

1748. – John Ellery, Mayor. "An apothecary. Peace with France and Spain proclaimed at Plymouth, with great formality. The six bells of Saint Andrew's recast with additional metal into eight. Motto on the tenor bell. –

"Ego Sum Vox clamantis parate." Weight 4,493 lb. The tenor bell of Charles' Church recast at the same time. The foundry was at the back of the Workhouse." July 1st, Bishop Lavington's first visitation.

1749. – John Facey, Mayor. "The town's water carried to the Barbican for the purpose of watering the shipping."

1750. – James Richardson, Mayor. Capt. Saunders, Member of Parliament in room of Lord Vere Beauclerc. "This year Charles Saunders, R.N. elected M.P. He was recommended both by Lords Vere and Sandwich, and though neither a man of figure nor character, was readily accepted by the vile scoundrel Aldermen in places, and their lacquays the Common Council, – one half of both benches within a few years having made themselves *slaves and dependants* on the board of Admiralty by getting into places."

"Weights and measures reviewed throughout the town. Baptist meeting-house rebuilt and enlarged. Lord Anson made Lord High Steward of the borough in room of the late Prince of Wales. Sir J. Ligonier, Governor of Plymouth arrived August 29th 1751."

1751. – Robert Triggs, Mayor. A merchant. "The last eleven days of this mayoralty were superseded by the new style, when the 6th and 18th, were called the 17th and 29th September." "Dr Bidlake born at Plymouth."

1752. – John Drake, Mayor; who died during the terms of his office and was succeeded by Michael Nichols. "J. Drake chosen on a Sunday, owing to the new style, and appointed collector of customs. The horse pond below Frankfort-gate filled up, and two rows of trees planted on it. Rails, with gates and turnstiles erected on the Hoe down to the water-side, and from Denham's stairs over to Prout's house, towards the Victualling Offices. Butchers lane newly paved, and a gutter made to carry the water underground. Feasts at quarter sessions revived as formerly. The guard-house removed from fish cage to the back of Guildhall; in 1742 it was under the hall. The steps in Saint Andrew's Church, leading to the gallery, taken away. Mr. Drake died on Monday, 3rd September, 1753, and on Saturday following, Mr. Nichols was chosen to succeed him. Mr. Tolcher swore himself justice, at the same time having been refused by the Corporation as a non-inhabitant."

1753. – John Morshead, Mayor. "A merchant. In October, a prodigious quantity of mackrel taken at the very quay. Much counterfeit coin in circulation. The large mace taken from the mayor's house by the sheriff's officers for a neglect of citation to appear to a suit between the Corporation and Mr T Veal, about the limits of Sutton Pool. It was returned soon after.

A velvet cushion in Guildhall for the use of the mayor presented by Mr. Bewes' brother. Two rows of trees planted by the King's engineer from the top of Little Hoe-lane to the end of the walk on the Hoe, and a single row from the same place to Denham's stairs.* The water-house at the Higher mills rebuilt with stone, previously it was of wood. The New Quay paved and railed in, chiefly at the expense of the mayor. The roof on the Old Church tower new slated, and the battlements on the east and west sides opened."

1754. – Jacob Auston, Mayor. "A brewer. A petition for a turnpike road sent to the House of Commons by the town's members." Visct. Barrington and Samuel Dicker, Esq., Members of Parliament. "Sunday, December 16th, a dreadful thunderstorm, and on the 20th, news arrived that Mr. Veal has cast the town in the affair of Sutton Pool." At this time Plymouth had 54 ships that paid towards the Merchant Seamen's Hospital.

1755. – Thomas Bewes, Mayor. "Dec. 22nd, the Eddystone Lighthouse after sustaining the repeated attacks of the sea 46 years, was destroyed by fire, the attendants having a narrow-escape of their lives, being rescued from the two contending elements by some Cawsand fishermen. One of the keepers named Henry Hall, aged 94, while looking upwards at the flames, received a quantity of liquid metal into his stomach. This fact was corroborated after his decease, which occurred 12 days after, when on his body being opened, a solid piece of lead, weighing 7oz 5dr was found in his stomach. The large mace given by Col. Joseph Jory; one of the other maces, was to be carried before the mayoress. Entrenchment at Dock begun."

1756. – John Forrest, Mayor. Plymouth Dock (now Devonport) began to be fortified and barracks began to be built.

1757. – Anthony Porter, Mayor. June 1st, the foundation stone of the present Eddystone Lighthouse laid.

1758. – John Facey, Mayor. "May 18th, a young grenadier aged about 27, was shot at Plymouth for desertion; what is remarkable, being to receive 500 lashes by the sentence of a regimental court martial, he chose to appeal to a general court martial, who instead of confirming his former sentence, inflicted that of death. The young man suffered with great fortitude, having done nothing, he said, to offend his Saviour."

"September 14th, H.M. ships Kingston and Burford arrived at Plymouth from Louisbourg with the transports, having the Garrison of Louisbourg on board, under their convoy. His Majesty presented £500 to Captains Amherst and Edgcombe, who jointly brought the news of the taking of this important

*The steps at the head of the lane at the east entrance of Trinity Church.

fortress; and ordered a sum to each of these gentlemen to purchase a sword and ring."

1759. – James Richardson, Mayor. "The present Eddystone Lighthouse finished. Mr Smeaton has been very happy in his idea of its construction, nothing but an earthquake, it is conceived, will shake its stability. On the granite round the upper store-room, is this inscription. – "Except the Lord build the house, their labour is but vain that build it, Psalm cxxvii;" and over the east side of the lanthorn, "24th, August, 1759, *Laus Deo.*" It is stated to have been completed in 111 days, 10 hours. It is a round stone building, gradually decreasing in circumference from the base to a certain height, like the trunk of an oak, from which Mr Smeaton, its ingenious contriver (a self-educated architect), states that he took the idea.

"October 9th, the store vessel came into Plymouth from her moorings at the Eddystone, with all the workmen on board, the lighthouse then being entirely completed, under the direction of that excellent mechanic, Mr Smeaton, F.R.S., without the loss of one life, or any material accident." – *Annual Register*, 1759.

July 28th H.R.H. the Duke of York, sailed from Plymouth on board the *Hero* man-of-war, with Lord Edgcumbe, to join the fleet off Brest, he returned to Plymouth, October 13th, and left for London

"October 13th, H.R.H. Prince Edward Augustus, Duke of York, went on shore from the fleet then lying in Plymouth Sound in the evening in good health, and set out for Saltram, the seat of John Parker, Esq."

The following highly interesting "play bill" of a concert with the tragedy of Jane Shore between the parts; interspersed with songs, minuets, hornpipes, and comic dances, and ending with a farce, will show the state of public amusements in Plymouth in the middle of the eighteenth century. It contrasts very strongly and amusingly with the entertainments at the present day, as announced in the "play bills" of the now "Theatre Royal," and the explanatory note at its close is particularly curious. The entertainment took place at the Theatre in Frankfort-gate.

Chapter VII

At the New THEATRE, Franckfort-Gate

This present Thursday, being the 15th February 1759,

Will be a Concert of MUSICK,

Divided into several PARTS

Boxes 2s Pit 1s 6d Gallery only 6d

TICKETS to be had at Mr Thompson's at the Fountain Tavern in Pike Street; at Mr Perkin's at the Hawk Tavern near Foxhole Key; at the Printing-Office in Southside Street; and at Mr Pittard's Lodgings at Mr Jones's, next Door to the Star-Tavern in Southside Street.

The Curtain to be drawn up precisely at 6 o'Clock

Between the Parts of the CONCERT will be presented (*Gratis*) a TRAGEDY call'd

JANE SHORE

Containing, the Tyranny and Usurpation of the Duke of *Gloster*, then Lord Protector of the Realm. The Fate of Lord *Hastings*, the Lord Chamberlain of the Household, by the mistaken Jealousy of the Lady *Alicia*, whose fatal wiles brought on his death, and her own Destruction. The Distresses and lamentable End of the Unfortunate Fair One *Jane Shore*, (Concubine to King *Edward* the Fourth) who perish'd in a Ditch for want of Food: it being proclaim'd by Order of the cruel Duke, that whoever gave her Comfort, Food, or Harbour should die. With many other Historical beautiful Passages.

To Night, if you have brought your good old Taste,
We'll treat you with a downright English *Feast;*
A Tale which long since told in homely Wise,
Hath never fail'd of melting gentle Eyes.

Duke of Gloster	by	Mr Powell
Lord Hastings		Mr Pittard
Ratcliff		Mr Foster
Catesby		Mr Prigmore
Bellmour		Mr Drummond
Dumont		Mr Wood
Alicia	by	Mrs Powell
Jane Shore		Mrs Wood

With an Occasional PROLOGUE to be spoke by Mr PITTARD.

End of Act I. A Comic Dance, by Sig. TEREZA CALVI, and Sig BALBI, in the Characters of Harlequin and an Italian Peasant.

End of Act II. A SONG by Mrs Wood.

End of Act III. A Minuet by Sig MARIA SCOTTI, and Sig GEROLAMO PORLAVICINI

End of the Play, A SONG by Mrs WOOD

To which will be added a FARCE call'd

MISS in Her TEENS

Captain Loveit	by	Mr *Powell*
Fribble		Mr *Drummond*
Captain Flash		Mr *Wood*
Puff		Mr *Pittard*
Jasper		Mr *Foster*
Miss Biddy	by	Mrs *Wood*
Tagg		Mrs *Powell*

With an EPILOGUE on Every Body, to be spoke in the Character of No-body, by Mr FOSTER

End of the FARCE, a HORNPIPE

☞ Words cannot express our Acknowledgements from the Favours we have receiv'd from those Ladies, Gentlemen, and Others of this Town, Stonehouse and Dock, in favouring us with their Company on Thursday last at the New Playhouse at Franckfort-Gate; and it would have been a Pleasure to us had our Performance been more to the Audience Satisfaction; but we are very sensible, that the major Part of the Company came on purpose to help the Distress'd. And in Order to make amends for all past favours, I have been over to *Launceston*, to engage some of the best Performers belonging to the Company there; and I'm quite confident every Thing attempted next Thursday Night, will be entirely to the Audience Satisfaction, both in Playing, Dancing, and Singing; if not, I don't desire to have any more Favours from my Friends. I shall be at a great Expence (and am determined to spare none) in order to bring the Performers here, and I don't in the least fear, but I shall still meet with Encouragement from the Generous and Humane, which will always be gratefully acknowledg'd from their Ever Oblig'd Humble Servants, *Joseph* and *Maria Pittard*

No Persons whatsoever will be admitted behind the Scenes.

1760.– Robert Phillips, Mayor. Admiral Pocock, Member of Parliament in room of Samuel Dicker, Esq. "The *Ramilies* lost off the Bolt." "The *Conqueror*, a new 74, going out from Plymouth harbour was lost on the Island of Saint Nicholas; the crew and guns saved. The master and pilot were tried at a court martial, the former acquitted, but the pilot sentenced to be imprisoned for 18 months." – *Annual Register*, 1760. "February 15th, Admiral Boscawen returned to Plymouth with the fleet, much shattered in rigging, but the *Ramilies*, late Admiral Byng's flag ship, was lost, and all hands drowned except one midshipman and 25 sailors. When the gale came on, she made for Plymouth, but, the weather being hazy, she overshot the entrance into the Sound, and got embayed near the Bolt-head about 4 leagues from thence. She came to anchor, but her cables were not sufficient to hold her, and she drove upon the rocks called the Bolt-head, went to pieces and upwards of 700 souls perished."

"January 3rd, the body of a travelling jew, known by the name of Little Isaac was found murdered in a wood near Plymstock, since which Edward Jackson a militiaman, confessed that he met with this jew near to Plymstock, and after drinking a pint of beer together, they both went out, and after walking about two miles, the deceased stopt to rest himself, and putting a long stick he had in his hand behind his back to rest himself and his box on, Jackson took the stick from behind him and knocked him down, and when he was on the ground, gave him two more blows, which finished him. Then taking his watch out of his pocket, and some goods out of his box, he hid the box in the wood. When he offered some of the things for sale being asked how he came by them, he said he found them in a box, and would show it to Mr Sherenbeare, which he accordingly did, taking him into the wood where he had left it, and presently after, said his conscience troubled him and he confessed the murder."

"January 21st Admiral Hawke, arrived at Plymouth the 17th, waited on His Majesty, by whom he was received with particular marks of favour; His Majesty meeting him as he entered, and thanking him for the services he had done his country. His Majesty settled a pension of £2,000 a year on him for life, and the life of his two sons and the survivor of them."

"July, the sea flowed at Plymouth about 18 inches in two minutes, and immediately ebbed with the same rapidity, this extraordinary flux and reflux continued the whole day."

1761. – Michael Nicolls, Mayor. Viscount Barrington and Admiral Pocock, Members of Parliament. "July 31st, Plymouth. By an annual custom, the Right Worshipful the Mayor, many of the Corporation and several others rode out this day to the Head Weare, from whence this town is supplied with water, brought by a current of almost 20 miles, by the ever memorable Sir Francis Drake, who in the year 1581, was an inhabitant here, and mayor of the town, and as tradition has it, in the year 1590, when the water ran before his own door, dipped his scarlet gown therein for joy that he had obtained his desired end." – *Annual Register*, 1761.

"A young woman dressed in man's clothes was impressed at Plymouth, and sent to Captain Toby in this town (Leeds, October 20th). On her arrival she was committed to prison, but not liking confinement she disclosed her sex, and was discharged. She gives the following account of herself; that her name is Hannah Witney, that she was born in Ireland, had been a marine on board different ships for upwards of five years, and would not have disclosed herself if she had been allowed her liberty." – *Annual Register*, 1761.

1762. – John Morshead, Mayor. "The Barbican washed down, and two Messrs. Collier drowned. Colours of Moro Castle taken from the enemy, presented to the borough by Sir George Pocock. The Royal Naval Hospital opened." "October 30th, the fleet under Sir Charles Hardy and the Duke of York, arrived at Plymouth from the Bay, and on November 14th, sailed westward." "August 19th, a tremendous storm, the darkness exceeded that of the great eclipse in 1748, much resembling that which preceded the great earthquake at Lisbon. The hailstones measured from two to ten inches in circumference, killing fowl and even sheep, but the most surprising phenomenon was, the sudden flux and reflux in Plymouth Pool, exactly corresponding with the like agitation at the same place, at the same time of the great earthquake at Lisbon." – *Annual Register*, 1763

"Sept. 23rd, H.R.H. the Duke of York embarked at Plymouth for Lisbon, on board the *Centurian* man-of-war." "July 9th, The Royal Naval Hospital at Stonehouse opened." "October 30th, H.R.H. Prince Edward Augustus, Duke of York, Vice-Admiral of the blue, in command of H.M. Ship *Princess Amelia*, was on the 30th October, elected High Steward of the Corporation of Plymouth."

1763. – Jacob Austin, Mayor. "The conduit at Martyn's-gate demolished." Friary-gate taken down.

1764. – Thomas Bewes, Mayor. "The bridge at Stonehouse was begun to be built July 17th, 1764." "The *Dolphin* and *Tamar* under Byron, sailed from Plymouth to circumnavigate the Globe." The Duke of Gloucester and the Duke of York visited Plymouth.

"June 9th. – The galleon *Santissima Trinidada*, from the East Indies, arrived in Plymouth Sound. She is the largest and richest ship ever brought into the ports of England. She was loaded at Madras with a vast collection of foreign curiosities made by Governor Pigot, particularly wild beasts, most of which died on the passage, it being so very long, and the ship so very laboursome. One of those which has survived is a serpent, which is it is said 14 feet long, eats only once a month, and then changes its skin, and as some say, is quite harmless." "October. – Great disturbances at Plymouth and in many other parts of England, in consequence of the high prices of provisions. Petitions presented to Lord Halifax; a council was immediately called, and after examination of evidence his Majesty ordered his royal proclamation for the free importation of salted beef, pork and butter from Ireland, and a reward of £100 for discovering any unlawful combinations in the sale of provisions of any kind."

1765. – John Nicolls, Mayor. " A fire which happened lately at Plymouth was very near destroying the whole town and the Citadel, as the flames devoured all before it, till it came to within a thin partition only of 123 barrels of gunpowder, which had been landed from the eastward, and was reserved there till a French vessel bound to Guinea should call for it." "A soldier at Plymouth, servant to an officer of marines, being lately detected of theft, hanged himself, having first wrote to his master that his propensity for thieving was such that he could not restrain it, and therefore chose that method of putting a period to his life, rather than the more public one of dying on the gallows."

1766. – William Davis Phillips, Mayor. "The Princess Amelia landed here at Mount Edgcumbe. Streets and gutters begun to be paved; lamps set up; bathing-house finished and opened, May 12th, and the wooden spire of the New Church taken down; and the 20th of October, the ball and vane put up, the spire being finished." Captain Wallis in the *Dolphin* with two other ships sailed from Plymouth for a voyage round the World.

"*Mr Wildman of Plymouth* who has made himself famous through the West of England for his command over bees, being come to London, gave notice to Dr Templeman, Secretary to the Society for the Encouragement of Arts, &c., that he would pay him a visit in his bee dress. Several gentlemen and ladies were assembled at the doctor's. About five o'clock Mr Wildman came, brought through the city in a chair, his head and face almost covered with bees, and a most venerable beard of them hanging down from his chin. The gentleman and ladies were soon convinced that they need not be afraid of the bees, and therefore went up familiarly to Mr Wildman and conversed with him. After having staid for a considerable time, he gave orders to the bees to retire to their hive that was brought for them, which they immediately obeyed with the greatest precipitation." "October 8th. – Mr Wildman, whom we have before taken notice of, being sent for to wait on Lord Spencer, at his seat at Wimbledon, in Surrey, he attended accordingly, and several of the nobility and persons of fashion were assembled; the countess had provided three stocks of bees. The first of his performances was with one hive of bees hanging on his hat, which he carried in his hand, and the hive which they came out of in the other hand, which was to convince the earl and countess that he could take honey and wax without destroying the bees. Then he returned into the room, and came out again with them hanging on his chin with a very venerable beard. After shewing them to the company, he took them out upon the grass walk facing his lordship's window, where a table and cloth were immediately brought out, and he set the hive upon the table and made the bees hive therein; then he made the bees come out again and swarm in the air, the ladies and gentlemen standing amongst them, and no person stung by them. He made them go on the table, and took them up by handfuls, and tossed them up and down like so many peas, and made them go into their hive at the word of command. Near five o'clock in the afternoon he exhibited again with the three swarms of bees, one on his head, one on his breast, and the other on his arm, and then went in to his lordship, who was too much indisposed to see the former experiments; the hives which the bees were taken from were carried by one of the servants. He came into the room again, and came out with them all over his head, face and eyes, and was led blind before his lordship's window. He then begged of his lordship that he would lend him one of his horses, which was granted, and was brought out in his body cloaths. He then mounted the horse, with the bees all over his head and face (except his eyes), and breast and left arm, with a whip in his right hand, and the groom then led the horse backwards and forwards by his lordship's window for some time. He then took the reins in his hand and rode round the house. He then dismounted and made the bees march upon the table, and commanded them to retire to their hive, which they accordingly did, and gave great satisfaction to the earl, the countess and all the spectators." – *Annual Register*, 1766.

"December 16th. – The Society of Arts voted £100 to the famous Mr Wildman for his discoveries relative to bees."

1767. – Richard Beach, Mayor. "October 30th, the first stone of the new bridge at Stonehouse was laid." The Princess Amelia visited Plymouth.

1768. – Henry Tolcher, Mayor. Viscount Barrington and Francis Holburne, Esq., Members of Parliament. Captain Cook, in the *Endeavour*, sailed from Plymouth, August 26th, for a voyage round the World.

"February. – His Majesty's ship *Fame*, of 74 guns, which was driven on the rocks in Plymouth Sound and bilged, was weighed and buoyed off at high water by considerable quantities of casks, supplied from the Victualling Office there, and some small vessels being lashed to her. She is now in the Dock to undergo a repair, and which will make her as good a ship as at first. Had she remained on the rocks till the late stormy weather, it is said she must unavoidably have been beaten to pieces. We hear that a master, mate, and seven seamen remained on board the *Fame* during all the time of her distress, a good part of which time her hold and lower gun deck were full of water, and that for their good behaviour they will be rewarded with promotion." "October 26th. – This morning, about two o'clock, the Plymouth and Exeter stage-coach, which inns at the Bell Inn in Friday-street, London, was stopped in Belfond-lane, near Hounslow, by a highwayman, well mounted on a bay horse with a switch tail, who demanded the money of the passengers when the guard shot him dead with a carbine on the spot. He appears to be about 30 years of age, short in stature, but stout and well set, with a drab surtout coat on. He was carried to the Bell in the said lane, where he lies in order to be owned.

1769. – Samuel Peters, Mayor. "Stonehouse Bridge Gate opened March 5th." The Duke of Cumberland visited the town. "August 3rd, a duel was fought near Plymouth, by a captain and lieutenant of the marines, in which the latter was unfortunately killed. The duellists were inseparable companions, had been together all the day preceding and were very much in liquor. About three in the morning they came arm in arm to the barracks, when the deceased dropped down dead. The survivor who is committed to gaol is inconsolable for the loss of his friend, and protests he knows not how the affair happened." The *Kent*, guardship, blew up in Cawsand Bay.

"April 23rd, Rev. Mr Zachariah Mudge, Vicar of Saint Andrew's Plymouth, and Prebendary of Exeter, universally known by his writings, died, much lamented."

1770. – John Tolcher, Mayor. A considerable movement having been set on foot in the town for the paving, lighting and watching of Plymouth, an Act of Parliament was obtained and a Board of Commissioners appointed for the purpose of carrying out its provisions. The regulations laid down by the various committed are highly curious, and show how truly destitute the town must have been even of the most necessary conveniences for cleanliness and decency – the streets and pavements being the regular and recognised receptacles for all manner of filth and refuse. The regulations as to lighting were fixed as follows: – "That two hundred and fifty lamps be provided, which they apprehend may be procured upon the lowest and best terms at London or Bristol, and that a public notice be given to contract for mounting two hundred of them, agreeable to a pattern that shall be fixed on by a general meeting of the Commissioners. That the iron work whereto such lamps are to be fixed be of the following sizes, viz., that the main barr be three-quarters of an inch square, and the projection of each into the street to be regulated by the width of the street and the nature of the building whereto such lamps are to be fixed, and that at the time of their being put up, committees be chosen to see the business properly executed. That it appears to us a contract for such iron work, fixing up, maintaining and painting, will be the best method of doing it, and that public notice be given for contracting accordingly, which, from calculations made by us, we think may be effected for £110, supposing no lamps are given by the present owners, in which sum we mean the cost of 200 lamps, the mounting, iron work and painting. We also recommend that the size and quality of the wick, as well as the nature of the oyle, be such as is generally made use of in London, and that a contract be made for this purpose, such contractor undertaking to provide for the safe keeping of such lamps in the summer months, and to be answerable for all accidents happening by breakage, and that there be at least two principal contractors, who are to provide a sufficient number of hands for the more expeditious lighting such lamps every evening. – Geo. Leach, Geo. Winne, James Fox, Joseph Squire."

The following were the proposed regulations as to watching: – "That from Lady-day to Michaelmas there should be eight men at 8d each per night; one corporal at 12d per do. That from Michaelmas to Lady-day there should be eleven men at 9d each per night; one corporal at 12d per do. From Lady-day to Michaelmas the watch to sett from ten to four; from Michaelmas to Lady-day, to sett from ten to six. The watch to be stationed as follows: One at the mayor's door, and one under the Guildhall; to be relieved every hour. The remainder to be alternately patrolling the town; not less than three out at a time. To be armed with halberts as usual. Each patrol to have a bell to ring at proper distances and call the hour and weather. We are of the opinion there should not be less than four setts of watchmen and two corporals to watch in turn, the latter to have charge of the watch-house, coals and candles. The charge attending the above calculations is as follows:

	£	s	d
From Lady-day to Michaelmas the watch	59	17	0
" Michaelmas to Lady-day do.	81	8	0
For the use of the Guard-house			
2 quarter coals	1	6	0
12 pounds of candles	3	8	3
Ward	5	4	0
	£151	3	3

"We are further of the opinion there should be six men to ward every Sunday, and have fourpence each.

"Joseph Collier, John Bayly, Jacob Shaw, Austin Forrest, Peter Symons."

1771. – Diggory Tonkin, Mayor. Admiral Sir C. Hurd elected Member of Parliament. Saint Aubyn's Chapel at Devonport built. "January 15th. – A grand new dock was opened at Plymouth, and this day received the *Northumberland* man-of-war." "January 26th. – A man and three horses were found dead in the snow on Black Down near Tavistock."

1772. – Joseph Brent, Mayor. Captain Cook, commanding the *Resolution* and *Adventure*, sailed from Plymouth on the 13th July, for his second voyage round the world.

1773. – Robert Fanshawe, Mayor. Dr. Woollcombe, author of some important works, and a valuable contributor to "Risdon's Survey" and "Prince's Worthies," born in Plymouth.

1774. – Francis Rogers, Mayor. Viscount Barrington and Admiral Sir C. Hurd, Members of Parliament.

This year a disastrous and fatal attempt at diving, in a diving machine of his own invention, was made by a Mr Day in Plymouth Sound. Mr Day was a millwright in Suffolk, and having invented a diving machine and experimented with it in shallow waters, prevailed on Mr Christopher Blake, a man of fortune in his own country, to stake a large sum of money on his project, and to find the necessary means of making a large public trial of his skill. Plymouth Sound was fixed upon as the place of trial, and in the month of March following, a sloop was purchased of rather more than 50 tons burden. She was fitted by an eminent shipwright, in a way best adapted to answer the purpose of resisting the pressure of the water, and of containing a portion of air necessary for the support of the adventurer. A chamber was built in the vessel, in the strongest manner, with a valve just large enough to admit a man and to shut him in in perfect security. This chamber, which was fixed in the hold on four beams, and effectually secured on all sides, contained 75 hogsheads of air. The fore and after parts of the vessels were to be filled with water, admitted by cocks; 10 tons of lime-stones were placed in her hold, and 20 tons more were by ringbolts let into them, slung in two equal parts on either side. These bolts passed through lead pipes into the air chamber, where they terminated in screws, each of which had a nut and lever. The design of these was, that when they were unscrewed the bolts should slip through the pipe, and divest the vessel of the ballast fastened to them. By this means, it was thought, she would immediately rise to the surface of the water. On the 20th of June, Mr Day having provided himself with a hammock, a watch, a wax taper, a bottle of water and a biscuit or two, went on board his vessel; his patron and servant and two or three bargemen remaining in a boat near him. Having filled the fore and after parts of the vessel with water, he found she would not sink, and therefore desired more stones might be procured and thrown in. It was necessary to rip up some of the planks of the deck for this purpose, and then about twenty tons more of stones were thrown in before she sunk. When she began to descend, the self-devoted schemer retired to his chamber, shut the valve, and descended to the bottom, whence neither he nor the vessel ever again arose!

Mr Blake, the capitalist, was in close attendance in a barge, and the *Orpheus* frigate lay by, with orders to render every assistance. When the vessel containing Mr Day sank, the spectators observed a rippling and bubbling of the water, but this was all, and the surface instantly became quiet again. He had taken with him three buoys or floating signals, but none of these appeared, and doubts and apprehensions for his safety began to be felt. Mr Blake, however, remained for the stipulated time, twelve hours from the time of descent, and then applied for assistance. No trace, however, was ever obtained either of the diver or of his machine, although the Dockyard riggers were employed many days in the search. The spot chosen for the trial was in one of the deepest parts of the Sound, between Drake's Island and the Prince of Wales Redoubt, the depth being fully 28 fathoms of water.

"March 9th. – This day the royal assent was given to the Bill for paving, lighting and watching Plymouth, and for regulating the carmen and coal porters."

"June 7th. – The King has been pleased to order a charter to be made under the great Seal of Great Britain to re-incorporate the Borough of Saltash, in the County of Cornwall, by the name and title of "The Mayor and Free Burgesses of the Borough of Saltash," and to confirm to them and to their successors their ancient powers, authorities, liberties and privileges."

"July 4th. – At Plymouth the round-house of the *Kent* man-of-war suddenly blew up, and in its consequences exhibited a picture perhaps the most dreadful and shocking that it is possible for human nature to conceive. By the splinters of the deck in bursting between 40 and 50 brave fellows were (some of them) so terribly maimed as to have had their limbs taken off, or scorched so as to be deprived of their sight, whilst others again are flayed all over. There are now 35 of them patients in the Hospital at Plymouth, one having been since dead of two fractures, his arm and leg, he not surviving long after an amputation of the latter. It is remarkable no officer received any hurt, except Lieutenant Shea, of the Marines, who is slightly wounded. The accident happened in saluting the Admiral, by some sparks falling into an arm-chest, which stood on the after part of the poop and great cabin. A drummer who happened to be sitting on the lid of the chest was blown into the air, fell overboard, and was picked up by the *Albion's* boat, without receiving the least hurt. It is remarkable that out of the small squadron that sailed with Sir James Douglas, the *Egmont* sprung her foremast, the *Dublin* carried away her main and foretop mast yards and main topmast, the *Albion* a main topsail yard, the *Raisonable* a foretop mast, and the *Cerberus* ran on shore on Penlee Point."

"July 14th. – Captain Furneaux, of Swilly, near Plymouth, of His Majesty's sloop the *Adventure* who sailed from Plymouth the 31st of July, 1772, in company with Captain Cook, of H.M. sloop the *Resolution*, upon a voyage to make discoveries in the southern hemisphere, arrived at Spithead, having penetrated as far towards the south pole as the latitude of 67 deg. 10 min., and circumnavigated the Globe chiefly between the latitudes of 55 and 60, in which tract he met with much ice, but no land. the *Adventure* parted company with the *Resolution* on the 29th of November last off the coast of New Zealand. Capt. Furneaux brought with him a native of Otaheite, who was desirous of seeing the great King, and was afterwards presented to His Majesty."

"September 14th. – The *Charming Nancy*, with the lady of General Gage and 170 sick and wounded soldiers, arrived from Boston at Plymouth, all in great distress, though but 24 days on their passage. They sailed from Boston the 20th August, at which time nothing material had happened, except a notification being posted up, signifying that such inhabitants as were desirous of quitting Boston might give in their names to the Town Major, and receive a license so to do. This it was supposed was owing to the scarcity of provisions, by which General Gage was reduced to the necessity of supplying the people from the King's stores, or suffering them to perish. A few of the men came on shore, when never hardly were seen such objects! some without legs and others without arms and their cloaths hanging on them like a loose morning gown, so much were they fallen away by sickness and want of proper nourishment. There were moreover near 60 women and children on board, the widows of the men who were slain. Some of them too exhibited a most shocking spectacle, and even the vessel itself, though very large, was almost intolerable from the stench arising from the sick and wounded, for many of them were hardly cured yet. Two more transports were daily expected with invalids, who sailed from Boston with the above. It was a great hardship on this occasion, though perhaps the nature of the service cannot immediately relieve it, for the men to remain on board till an order from the War-office arrived for their debarkation, especially as the vessel was obliged to go up into Hamoaze to get in a new mainmast, from thence to proceed to the river with the invalids for their examination for Chelsea Hospital. As to the widows and orphans who came home in the above ship, a subscription was set on foot in four or five days after their arrival, by Messrs. Jardines, merchants at Plymouth, which by the 22nd amounted to £104, and next day was distributed at the Guildhall according to their several necessities."

1775. – Ralph Mitchell, Mayor. H.M.S. *Torbay*, 64 guns, burnt to the water's edge in Hamoaze.

1776. – Henry Tolcher, jun., Mayor. Captain Cook sailed from Plymouth on his third voyage round the World on the 12th of July.

Extensive natural caverns were this year discovered at Stonehouse, in the course of quarrying for stone; an account of them was written at the time by Dr. Geach.

1777. – Samuel White, Mayor. Carrington, the poet, born.

1778. – Joseph Freeman, Mayor. "Viscount Lewisham elected Member of Parliament, in the room of Viscount Barrington." "Water brought in pipes in Great George-street."

1779. – Thomas Blythe Darracott, Mayor. On the 15th August, "Hardy was cruising in the soundings when the French and Spaniards appeared off Plymouth; and some French frigates anchoring in Cawsand Bay captured a number of coasting vessels." "On the 16th the *Ardent*, 64, fell in with the enemy's fleet, and, mistaking it for the British, was surrounded and captured within sight of Plymouth." The fleet consisted of 60 or 70 ships of the line, with a "cloud" of frigates, sloops, fire-ships, etc.

"Plymouth, January 26th. – On Saturday night last, between the hours of 11 and 12, a man was discovered on the wall of the Dockyard, near the hemp-house. The watchman stationed there immediately fired, on which he jumped off, and although instantly pursued could not be found. The method he made use of to get on the wall was by means of a large fish hook, fastened to a small cord; this was thrown over the wall, by which means he hauled himself up; in his hand he took a small rope, with a basket fixed to it, in which was contained a pint bottle of gunpowder, some matches and a dark lantern; it was supposed he intended (when got on the wall) to pull these materials after him; a long piece of match was fastened to the bottle; and what is very remarkable, a window of the hemp-house was left open at the place he ascended. The scheme seems highly probably to have been concerted, as it happened on a very dark night, and when the yardmen were paid off, as on those nights they generally drink rather freely. Several of the people belonging to the hemp-house have been examined, but nothing has transpired to lead to a discovery."

"Order issued by the King of France respecting Capt. Cook. Paris, March 19th. – M. de Sartine, Minister of the Marine department, has wrote the following letter to all captains of armed vessels, etc.: – Captain Cook, who sailed from Plymouth in July, 1778, on board the *Resolution*, in company with the *Discovery*, Captain Clarke, in order to make some discoveries of the coasts, islands and seas of Japan and California, being on the point of returning to Europe, and as such discoveries are of general utility to all nations, it is the King's pleasure that Captain Cook shall be treated as a commander of a neutral and allied power, and that all captains of armed vessels, etc., who may meet that famous navigator shall make him acquainted with the King's orders on this behalf, but at the same time let him know that on his part he must refrain from all hostilities."

1780. – Jacob Shaw, Mayor. Sir Federick Leman Rogers, Bart., and Vice-Admiral Darby, Members of Parliament. "October, died Mrs. Bradshaw, formerly of Drury Lane Theatre. The circumstances of her death are worth recording. She had a few years ago adopted a young girl, but the uncommon care which she had taken of her education, and the fatal consequence which has attended the want of success of her adopted, make it now believed that she was really Mrs. Bradshaw's own daughter; for upon her return from France, she was engaged to dance at Plymouth; but whether from the length of the dance, the timidity of the performer, or the ill-nature or ignorance of the audience, she was hissed. The effect this misfortune had upon Mrs. Bradshaw was truly tragical. She fell into fits instantly, was conveyed home raving mad, and died a short time after." Mrs. Bradshaw herself had long been in the habit of appearing before Plymouth audiences. As far back as June, 1765, she played Mrs. Peachem in the "Beggar's Opera" and in July of the year, Fanny, in the "Maid of the Mill."

1781. – Joseph Austen, Mayor.

1782. – George W. Marshall, Mayor. The following is from the curious will of William Shackell, Esq., Governor of Plymouth, proved in the Prorogative Court of Canterbury, October 12th 1782. "I desire that my body may be kept as long as it may not be offensive, and that one of my toes or fingers may be cut off to secure a certainty of my being dead; I also make this further request to my dear wife, that as she has been troubled with one old fool, she will not think of marrying a second." The celebrated Dr Musgrave died in Plymouth.

"January 26th. – A cartel ship, with 300 French prisoners on board, part of the regiments of Aquitaine and Soissons, which were taken by Admiral Kempenfeldt, in clearing Mount Batten in Plymouth harbour, fell to leeward, missed stays, and drove upon the reef of rocks at the east-end of it. The poor unfortunate prisoners, who were but a moment before huzzaing in the highest spirits, were now sunk into the deepest distress, many of them wringing their hands as if on the point of perishing. Some that could swim reached the boats that had put off to their assistance. Six boys got out the yawl, and attempted to reach the shore, and the boat instantly staved. The next wave that succeeded cast the lads on the shore, who found means to crawl up the rocks and were saved. A cutter that attended the cartel got out all the boats, and with the assistance that instantly came from the shore took almost every man on board, not more than two or three being missing, who it was supposed in the hurry had slipped down between the boats." "July 13th. – This day the combined fleets of France and Spain were seen W.S.W. from the Lizard, distant about 13 miles."

1783. – John Arthur, Mayor. "April 1st. – 300 of the *Medway's* crew landed at North Corner with bludgeons, paraded up Fore-street, Dock, into Liberty Field, and there waited for the crew of the *Crown*. About an hour after, the crews of the *Crown* and *Vengeance*, near 800 men, landed to fight the *Medway's* people; but the crew of the *Medway*, finding they should be overpowered, dispersed and went on board their ship, which prevented a great deal of bloodshed. The quarrel originated from some of the *Medway's* people insulting the boatswain's wife of the *Crown*. Nothing here but fighting and rioting among the crews paid off." "April 5th. – The crew of the *Artois*, Captain Mc.Bride, mutinied, and threatened to unrig the ship; but the captain, on proper application, found means to quiet them, and on promising them redress they returned to their duty." The Somerset Militia and the Brecknock Militia, the one being encamped in the Brickfield and the other within the lines, fired on each other over the ramparts, and several were killed and wounded.

1784. – John Nicolls, Mayor. Captain Robert Fanshawe, R.N., Member of Parliament. January 31st. – An address from the mayor and inhabitants of Plymouth was presented to His Majesty upon the removal of the late ministry. In January an earthquake was felt in different parts of Devon and Cornwall. September 7th. – Thursday morning, at ten o'clock, the remains of Sir Eyre Coote, K.B., were landed at the jetty head in the Dockyard, the *Bombay Castle* firing 21 minute guns, the corps of marines forming a line to the gates, drums beating a point of war, colours flying, music playing a solemn dirge, the officers saluting the hearse as it passed. In Fore-street, two companies of Royal Artillery, the 39th and 40th Foot, received the body, forming themselves into divisions of six a breast, the grenadiers and light infantry taking the lead. They then proceeded through the Towns of Dock, Stonehouse and Plymouth and through the glacis to the gates of the Citadel, where the Lieutenant-Governor Campbell, received the body with every mark of respect. The two battalions and artillery formed on the Parade, before the Governor's house; the grenadiers and light infantry, in four divisions, escorted the hearse to the chapel, the troops presenting their arms, the drums beating and music playing; 19 minute guns were fired during this ceremony, and the body was deposited in the chapel with great solemnity and respect. The numerous crowd of spectators which attended, testified their regard to the memory of so great a man.

"September 6th. – Last night and this day our usual storm at this season of the year commenced with a violent gale at S.W., and has blown with incredible fury, accompanied with a most tremendous pitching sea. A boat with three men was overset in Hamoaze, and all perished. There were but two men-of-war in the Sound, who rode it out well."

1785. – Joseph Tolcher, Mayor. "April 2nd. – The winter season, from the first fall of snow on the 7th of October, 1784, to that which fell this day, lasted 177 days; and if we except about twelve days towards the end of January, the whole of this period was frosty or snowy, or both. September 5th. – A great storm which did considerable damage both at sea and land."

After much disputing and unpleasantness between the Vicar of Saint Andrew's and the inhabitants of Stonehouse, it was ultimately proved and agreed to that the Chapel at Stonehouse was a Chapel of Ease to Saint Andrew's.

1786. – Diggory Tonkin, Mayor. At Plymouth, on the 9th of March, 1786, His Royal Highness Prince William Henry, Duke of Clarence (Afterwards King William IV.), was initiated into the ancient and honourable Society of Free and Accepted Masons, Lodge No. 86, at the Prince George Inn and Tavern (Payne's), in Vauxhall-street, then one of the principal inns in the town.

"May 23rd. – His Royal Highness Prince William Henry accepted of the freedom of Plymouth, which was presented to him at Mr Winne's in a very elegant box, by the four senior Aldermen and Common Councilmen."

1787. – Robert Fanshawe, Mayor. "His Royal Highness Prince William Henry, Duke of Clarence (afterwards King William IV.) arrived here on the 27th of December, in the *Pegasus*, from America."

"Plymouth, December 27th. – The *Pegasus* frigate, from Cork, commanded by His Royal Highness Prince William Henry, arrived here. His Royal Highness, after visiting the Admiral and Commissioner of the Dock, took up his residence at Mr Winne's, an eminent merchant of this town. On his passage, His Highness experienced the effects of a very extraordinary phenomenon. A thunderstorm broke over the ship so violently as to tear some of the sails and shiver the mainmast, so as to render it necessary for a new mast to be supplied. The season of the year makes the circumstance memorable, and the more so as the storm was more tremendous on the north coast of France than at sea."

1788. – Peter Tonkin, Mayor. "Plymouth, January 5th. – Their Royal Highnesses the Prince of Wales and Duke of York arrived here on a visit to his Royal Highness Prince William Henry; viewed the Dockyard and Mount Edgcumbe and the Citadel, and after giving a ball at the Long Room returned to London. And in July, Prince William Henry in the *Andromeda*, sailed for America, accompanied by the most fervent wishes for his safe return from the inhabitants of this town, who had been so highly favoured by his presence; indeed, his politeness and attention will never be forgotten."

"Plymouth, January 14th. – Last Tuesday evening, at eleven, arrived here, in a coach and six, their Royal Highnesses the Prince of Wales and Duke of York, accompanied by Prince William Henry, who went to meet them. The concourse of people was astonishing, the illuminations splendid, and the demonstrations of joy on every countenance pleasing beyond expression. The carriage proceeded slowly through the town to lodgings prepared for the royal guests in Fore-street."

John Richards and William Smith, for the murder of Mr Philip Smith, clerk in the Dockyard, in 1787, were executed, and their bodies brought to Stoke, where they were gibetted opposite the churchyard. Smith's body remained there about seven years, and the other longer.

1789. – John Cooban, Mayor. This year Plymouth was visited by King George III and the Royal family. The following is an account of this visit: –

His Majesty, the Queen, with the three eldest princesses, Princess Royal, Augusta and Elizabeth, left Weymouth for Plymouth, Thursday, the 13th August, arrived at Exeter the same evening, and left for Plymouth on Saturday, the 15th, with their *Suite*, about nine in the morning, and about three in the afternoon reached Saltram House, the seat of Lord Boringdon, near Plymouth. Their arrival was announced by a royal salute. In the evening Saltram House was brilliantly illuminated.

Monday, August 17th. – Their Majesties and the Princesses left Saltram House about nine in the morning. At the entrance of the Town of Plymouth they were received under a triumphal arch by the Mayor and Corporation, and conducted to the bottom of Stonehouse-lane, where the Corporation took leave. About 11 they reached the Dock, where they were received by the troops in Garrison and saluted by a *feu de joie*. The cannon on the ramparts were fired, and were answered by another salute from the fort at Plymouth. Their Majesties alighted at Commissioner Laforey's in the Dockyard, where they were received by the Earls of Chesterfield, Chatham and Howe. After taking some refreshment the Royal family went on board the *Impregnable* of 90 guns, Admiral Sir Richard Bickerton. As their Majesties ascended the *Impregnable* a royal salute was fired, as well from her as from every other ship in the harbour and in the Sound. The Citadel and small forts paid the same respect. The *Lynx*, a Dutch ship-of-war, also dressed ship and saluted. Their Majesties stayed on board near an hour. As soon as their Majesties put off from the *Impregnable* the standard and Admiralty flags were hauled down, and in their stead, in less than a minute, the ship was dressed in all the variegated colours that the world could supply. A very handsome cutter, rowed by six fine young women, and steered by a seventh, all habited in loose white gowns, with nankin safeguards, and black bonnets, each wearing a sash across her shoulders of royal purple, with *Long live their Majesties!* in gold, accompanied the royal barge till it returned to shore. At half after three His Majesty, the Queen and Princesses left the Dock, and proceeded in state barges up Cattewater to Saltram, attended by an immense number of sloops, barges and boats, the forts, all the ships at anchor, and lastly all the guns in the park, saluting them as they passed.

Tuesday 18th. – This day the naval review took place. About eight in the morning His Majesty was rowed on board the *Southampton* on the Sound. At half after nine the *Southampton* got under weigh. The Duke of Richmond attended in his yacht. In a few minutes the first ship in the fleet appeared off Staddon Heights, steering due west, the wind east, with two points to the south, blowing a gentle breeze. When the King's ship had weathered Mewstone Point, she descried the whole of the fleet, and fired one gun. At this time the view was beautiful beyond description, there being above 100 different vessels, sloops, and yachts in motion, and the shore covered with spectators. The fleet formed in two separate lines of battle. Captain Mc.Bride, in the *Cumberland*, with three other ships, formed a line ahead, supposed for the enemy. Commodore Goodall, in the *Carnatic* formed the line with the other ships. As soon as he got up with the enemy's rear he engaged. The next ship passed to windward, and attacked the next ship ahead, and so till the rear ship of the British line was opposite the van of the enemy. When the *Southampton* came in full view of the fleet a general salute took place. After this ceremony was ended, and the captains having been introduced to His Majesty as he passed the line of battle, the dispositions were made for an action between the two divisions. The *Magnificent* had by this time joined the second line. After manoeuvering for some time upon different tacks, in order to bring each other to action, the engagement began with a most furious cannonade between the two commanders, the others speedily joined in the thundering festivity. In about a quarter of an hour, both fleets wearing westward, the first line gave way, and were furiously assailed by the second, and covered in their flight by Captain Mc.Bride, the Commodore. The people on shore conceived it was all over, but they were mistaken, for the French line (as it was called) wore upon the larboard tack, and faced the English with redoubled vigour. They continued until half past one, when they were a second time obliged to give way. His Majesty returned, highly pleased with his excursion, about half after three, under a salute of the fort, etc.

Thursday, August 20th. – His Majesty, unaccompanied by any of the Royal family, left Saltram, and went to Victualling Office to examine the state of the provisions. He ordered a cask to be opened and a piece to be taken out and sent to Saltram for his own tasting. He then visited the Lower Fort, the Citadel, the ramparts, the storehouse, and last of all the subterraneous works, the mines, etc., in which no person but the Duke of Richmond, Lord George Lennox (the Governor), and the Chief Engineer was permitted to accompany him. When he mounted the upper part of the Garrison, he was received by the Mayor and Corporation, the invalids, and a detachment of the South Devon Militia, their music playing "God save the King," and who attended him in his walk round the ramparts. When he came to the Governor's house the Mayor and Corporation were admitted to the royal presence, and a dutiful and loyal address was presented, and most graciously received. The Corporation had the honour of kissing hands. His Majesty left the fort, and proceeded by water to the Gun Wharf and surveyed the ordnance.

Friday, Aug. 21st. – Their Majesties visited Mount Edgcumbe. On their landing, sixteen young maidens dressed in white, preceded the royal pair, strewing roses, carnations and myrtles; and when they came to the steps that lead to the grand arcade, each maiden, on her knee, presented a curious flower to their Majesties, which was graciously received. The dinner and dessert were sumptuous and elegant. At six the King retired, and took water, accompanied by a large fleet of boats and barges, and was rowed through the Sound to Saltram.

Saturday, August 22nd. – The Royal family visited Maristow, the seat of Mr. Heywood, situated on the banks of the Tavy. The woods belonging to this gentleman extend nearly three miles down the river, in the most striking and romantic situations. Several new roads were cut through these woods for the accommodation of the royal visitors, who spent two hours in admiration of their beauties, and repeated their visit on Monday, the 24th. The two following days were spent in exploring the course of the Tamar. On Wednesday they landed at Cothele, an ancient seat of the Edgcumbe family, situated about 14 miles up the Tamar. Triumphal cars, with four wheels each, and two ponies, were provided to convey their Majesties and the Princesses to the castle, which stands on a proud eminence, about a quarter of a mile from the banks of the river. On their arrival at the outer gate 21 pateraroes were fired. After viewing the ancient curiosities of the castle, amongst which are the several pieces of old armour, and partaking of some refreshment, the whole party re-embarked and returned to Saltram at two in the afternoon, highly gratified by the novelty of the fresh-water navigation. The next morning they left Saltram on their return to Weymouth. Before His Majesty's departure he was graciously pleased to confer the honour of knighthood on Thomas Baynard, Esq., Captain of the *Impregnable,* who had the honour to steer his Majesty's barge in his excursions during his stay at this port."

1790. – Stephen Hammick, Mayor. Sir Alan Gardner and John Macbride, and afterwards Sir Alan Gardner and Sir Fred. L. Rogers, Members of Parliament.

1791. – George Wynne, Mayor. "March 7th. – A melancholy accident lately happened in the neighbourhood of Plymouth. Mr W Good and his daughter, crossing a ford in the Parish of Buckland Monachorum on one horse, the water being deep, the horse lost his footing, by which means the young woman fell off the horse, and the father, endeavouring to save his daughter, fell into the ford, and both were unfortunately drowned." The ferry at Torpoint established, and one of the piers at the entrance of Sutton Pool built.

1792. – William Creese, Mayor. On the 28th October, died Mr John Smeaton, the builder of the Eddystone Lighthouse, and one of the most accomplished engineers of any age. Mr Smeaton was born in 1724 at Ansthorpe, near Leeds, and was the son of an attorney of that place. His turn for mechanics and engineering displayed itself while he was yet a mere infant of four or five years old, and before he was fifteen he had made for himself an engine or lathe to turn rose-work, and had turned many snuff-boxes for his friends. In 1742 he was sent to London by his father to study for the law, but soon gave it up, and in 1750 he commenced business as a mathematical instrument maker. In 1751 he invented a machine for measuring a ship's way at sea, and two years later was elected F.R.S., and from that time frequently contributed to the Philosophical Transactions, receiving in 1759 the gold medal for his experiments in the powers of wind and water to turn mills. In 1755 the Eddystone Lighthouse built by John Rudyerd was burnt down, when the Earl of Macclesfield, President of the Royal Society, being applied to to recommend some one to undertake its reconstruction, named Mr Smeaton, who entered into the project with all his energy, and completed it, including all interruptions, in three years, nine weeks, and three days, from the time of the first stroke being given upon the rock – the time actually employed in the work being only 111 days and 10 hours. "This day (October the 9th, 1759)," he writes, "after innumerable difficulties and dangers, was a happy period put to this undertaking, without the loss of life or limb to anyone concerned in the work." In 1764 Smeaton was appointed one of the Receivers of the Derwentwater estates for Greenwich Hospital, an appointment which in 1777 he resigned in consequence of the increase of his engineering engagements. In 1785 Mr Smeaton's health began to fail, and in 1792 he was struck with the palsy, which in a few weeks carried him off. Shortly after his seizure he wrote: "I conclude myself nine-tenths dead, and the greatest favour the Almighty can do me (as I think) will be to complete the other part; but as it is likely to be a lingering illness, it is only in His power to say when that shall happen." Mr Smeaton was engaged in most of the engineering projects of his day, and his skill has never been surpassed.

1793. – Andrew Hill, Mayor.

1794. – William Symons, Mayor. Great mortality among the troops detained at this port for the West Indian expedition. The Hospital of White Friars converted into an hospital for the sick soldiers. The *Coquette* French frigate, a prize, accidentally burned.

1795. – Robert Fuge, Mayor. "Destructive fire in Plymouth. – December 16th. This evening, about five o'clock, a dreadful fire broke out in a sail-loft in Southside-street, belonging to Mr Douglas, sailmaker. In a few minutes the whole building was in flames. Every exertion was made to check its progress, but the lofts were filled with such inflammable materials as rendered every effort ineffectual. In addition to the sail cloth, rope, etc., belonging to Mr Douglas, the lofts of the premises were filled with a valuable cargo of bale goods, landed out of a Danish ship that was then under repair, to which the fire soon communicated, and the conflagration became terrible indeed. The flames presently extended to the houses on each side Mr Douglas's and they being occupied by people of the same profession, their lofts were also filled with the like inflammable materials, so that the fire became extremely alarming, and threatened destruction to the whole neighbourhood. It continued burning six hours with incredible fury, when by the great exertions of the inhabitants and the military, with the assistance of the Dockyard and Hospital engines, it was fortunately prevented from spreading further, but the three houses were entirely consumed. The loss is supposed to amount to £15,000. Many of the unfortunate sufferers are uninsured, and subscriptions are now open for their relief. It is a providential circumstance that the tide was flood at the time, or the fire would have communicated to the shipping in the pool, and probably in that case half the town would have been destroyed." The Marine Barracks built.

Chapter VII

As an illustration of the means of communication between Plymouth and Exeter at this period, the following extracts are made from advertisements in *The Exeter Flying-Post, or Plymouth and Cornish Advertiser* of December 3rd, 1795: "Hotel Assembly Room, Exeter, February 4th, 1795. The following carriages set out from Thompson's Hotel, Church yard, Exeter: Plymouth and Dock Diligence every morning at seven." "New London Inn, Exeter. The following carriages set out from the New London Inn, viz.: A Balloon Coach to Dock every morning at eight o'clock. Inside, 15s 6d. Outside, 8s. To the Old King's Arms Inn."

Considerable excitement prevailed in various parts of the kingdom, consequent on two bills introduced into Parliament for the preventing of seditious assemblies and the safety of the King and Government, and this was, as will be seen by the following, carried to great extent in this town:–

PLYMOUTH

At a MEETING of the Inhabitants of Plymouth and its Vicinity, convened by Public Notice, from the Worshipful the Mayor (in consequence of a requisition), and assembled at the Guildhall of this town, on the 30th day of November, 1795, for the purpose of considering the resolutions of a Meeting of the Inhabitants of Plymouth, Plymouth-Dock, and Stonehouse, held at the Long-Room, Stonehouse, on the 23rd inst, for the purpose of taking into consideration the propriety of petitioning against Two Bills pending in Parliament; the one for the Safety and Preservation of his Majesty's Person and Government; the other for the more effectually preventing Seditious Assemblies; a Motion being made that the printed resolutions of the said Meeting, at Stonehouse, be read, they were read accordingly; after which the following Resolutions were agreed to.

1. – That the Resolutions of the said Meeting at Stonehouse, being stated to be the Resolutions of the Inhabitants of Plymouth, Plymouth-Dock, and Stonehouse, We, as Inhabitants of Plymouth, think it proper to declare, that those Resolutions, as far as they relate to those two Bills, do not speak our sentiments.

2. – That, in particular, we see no just Ground for considering those Bills, either as subversive of the Principles of the Constitution, or as unnecessary; being Ourselves of Opinion that their Provisions are hostile only to the Licentious Abuse of our Constitutional Privileges, which Abuse calls aloud for a salutary Check, and that such Provisions are therefore friendly to a just, rational and honest liberty.

3. – That a petition from this Meeting, declaratory of its Sentiments, be presented to the House of Commons, praying that Honourable House to adopt such Provisions as to its Wisdom shall seem meet, for the Preservation of his Majesty's Person and Government, and the stability of our happy Constitution.

4. – That a Committee be appointed to prepare a Petition to the Honourable the House of Commons, on the principles of the above Resolutions, and that MR. SYMONS, MR. TONKIN, MR. HILL, MAJOR HAWKER, MR. CULME, MR. ROSDEW, MR. G. WOOLCOMBE, REV. MR. GANDY, MR. LEACH, MAJOR MONEY, MR. HARRIS, MR. CLEATHER, be a Committee for that Purpose.

5. – The Committee, having accordingly presented a Petition, Resolved That the same be adopted, and left on the Guildhall Table, till Wednesday next, at 4 o'clock in the afternoon, for the Signature of such Persons as may approve thereof, and that the same be then transmitted to Sir F.L. ROGERS and SIR ALAN GARDNER, Barts., the Members for this Borough, to be presented to the Honourable the House of Commons.

6. – That the Thanks of this Meeting be given to the Chairman for his Readiness in calling the Meeting, and his Manly and Impartial Conduct in the Chair.

7. – That the Thanks of this Meeting be given to Major Hawker, for bringing forward the above Resolutions.

8. – That the above Resolutions, signed by the Chairman, be printed and published in the Sun, Star, Courier, Sherborne, and Exeter papers.

ROBERT FUGE, Mayor, Chairman

1796. – Richard Burdwood, Mayor. Sir Frederick L. Rogers, Bart., and Francis Glanville, Members of Parliament. "September 24th. – Blowing up of the *Amphion* frigate in Hamoaze, Plymouth. The melancholy account of the blowing up of the *Amphion* frigate at Plymouth was received at the Admiralty from Sir Richard King, by which it appears that Capt. Israel Pellew, the first lieutenant, and 15 of the crew, out of 220, are the only survivors left to relate the dismal catastrophe. Capt. Swaffield, of the Dutch prize, is amongst the unfortunate victims. The accident happened at a quarter past 4 on Thursday afternoon (the 22nd), while the captain and his friends were at dinner. Captain Pellew is dangerously wounded. Every exertion that could be used was rendered by the ship's boats in the harbour." "October 10th, Plymouth. – The court martial which was held last Saturday on board the Admiral's ship *Cambridge*, to enquire into the cause of the loss of M.H. ship the *Amphion*, which blew up on the 22nd of last month in this harbour, after an examination of all the surviving crew, very honourably acquitted both the captain and officers of every idea of remissness or neglect upon that occasion. It must have been particularly gratifying to Captain Pellew, after the court martial was over, at the request made to him by the whole of the ship's company which survived this unhappy affair, that he would suffer them to be partners of his future fortune when he should obtain a ship, having so long sailed with him – one of the best testimonies this to the character of an officer." Capt. (afterwards Admiral) Israel Pellew, thus spoken of, was brother to Capt. (afterwards Admiral) Edward Pellew, who in the same year distinguished himself in saving the crew of the *Dutton*, as will be seen on the next page, and was afterwards created Viscount Exmouth. At the time of the blowing up of the frigate, Capt. Pellew and Capt. Swaffield were dining together on board along with the first lieutenant. They were seated together at the table, and the servant was just entering the cabin with a dish, when a sudden and violent shock threw them from their seats against the carlings of the upper deck. Capt. Pellew exclaimed, "The ship is blown up," and sprang to the quarter gallery. Looking forward, he saw the foremast carried up into the air. Next instant a block or spar struck him on the forehead, and knocked him senseless into the water. The lieutenant, who had closely followed him, was blown through the window, and taken up comparatively unhurt. About 300 perished. Captain Pellew remained in a critical state for some time, and ever afterwards bore the mark of the blow he had received. After a brilliant career he died 19th July, 1832, aged 73, and is buried in Charles's Church, where a tablet has been erected to his memory.

One of the memorable events of this year is the loss of the *Dutton*, East Indian transport ship, which on the 26th of January, while on her way to the West Indies with a part of the 2nd or Queen's Regiment on board, was driven through stress of weather into Plymouth. She had been out seven weeks, and had many sick on board. The gale increasing in the afternoon, it was determined to run for greater safety into Catwater; but the buoy at the extremity of the reef of Mount Batten having broken adrift unknown to the pilots, she ran on the shoal and carried away her rudder. Thus rendered unmanageable, she fell off and grounded under the Citadel, where, beating round, she lay rolling heavily with her broadside to the waves, and at her second roll threw all her masts overboard together. Sir Edward Pellew, of H.M. ship *Indefatigable* which was then lying in Hamoaze, and Lady Pellew were engaged to dine on that day with Dr. Hawker, the Vicar of Charles, who had become acquainted with Mr. Pellew, when they were serving together at Plymouth as surgeons to the marines. Sir Edward noticed the crowds running to the Hoe, and having learned the cause he sprang out of his carriage, and ran off with the rest. Arrived at the beach, he saw at once that the loss of nearly all on board, between five and six hundred, was inevitable, without some one to direct them. The principal officers of the ship had abandoned their charge, and got on shore just as he arrived on the beach. Having urged them, but without success, to return to their duty, and vainly offered rewards to pilots and others belonging to the port to board the wreck, for all thought it too hazardous to be attempted, he exclaimed, "Then I will go myself!" A single rope, by which the officers and a few others had landed, formed the only means of communication with the ship, and by this he was hauled on board through the surf. The danger was greatly increased by the wreck of the masts, which had fallen towards the shore; and he received an injury on the back, which confined him to his bed for a week, in consequence of being dragged under the mainmast. But disregarding this at the time, he reached the deck, declared himself, and assumed the command. He assured the people that every one would be saved, if they quietly obeyed his orders; that he would himself be the last to quit the wreck, but that he would run any one through who disobeyed him. His well known name, with the calmness and energy he displayed, gave confidence to the despairing multitude. He was received with three hearty cheers, which were echoed by the multitude on shore; and his promptitude at resource soon enabled him to find and apply the means by which all might be safely landed. His officers in the meantime, though not knowing that he was on board, were exerting themselves to bring assistance from the *Indefatigable*. Mr Pellowe, first lieutenant, left the ship in the barge, and Mr. Thompson, acting master, in the launch; but the boats could not be brought alongside the wreck, and were obliged to run for the Barbican. A small boat belonging to a merchant vessel was more fortunate. Mr. Esdell, signal midshipman to the port admiral, and Mr. Coghlan, mate of the vessel, succeeded at the risk of their lives in bringing her alongside. The ends of two additional hawsers were got on shore, and Sir Edward contrived cradles to be slung upon them, with travelling ropes to pass forward and backward between the ship and the beach. Each hawser was held on shore by a number of men, who watched the rolling of the wreck, and kept the ropes tight and steady. Meantime a cutter had with great difficulty worked out of Plymouth Pool, and two large boats arrived from the Dockyard under the directions of Mr Hemmings, the master-attendant by whose caution and judgment they were enabled to approach the wreck, and receive the more helpless of the passengers, who were carried to the cutter. Sir Edward, with his sword drawn, directed the proceedings, and preserved order, a task the more difficult as the soldiers had got at the spirits before he came on board, and many were drunk. The children, the women, and the sick were the first landed. One of them was only three weeks old, and nothing in the whole transaction impressed Sir Edward more strongly than the struggle of the mother's feelings before she would entrust her infant to his care, or afforded him more pleasure than the success of his attempt to save it. Next the soldiers were got on shore; then the ship's company; and finally, Sir Edward himself, who was one of the last to leave her. Every one was saved, and presently after the wreck went to pieces. Nothing could equal the lustre of such an action, except the modesty of him who was the hero of it. Services performed in the sight of thousands could not thus be concealed. Praise was lavished upon him from every quarter. The Corporation of Plymouth voted him the freedom of the town. The merchants of Liverpool presented him with a valuable service of plate. On the 5th of March following he was created a baronet, as Sir Edward Pellew, of Treverry, and received for an honourable augmentation of his arms a civic wreath, a stranded ship for a crest, and the motto, "Deo adjuvante Fortuna sequatur." This motto, so modest, and not less expressive of his own habitual feeling, was chosen by himself, in preference to one proposed, which was more personally complimentary." Sir Edward, who afterwards became an admiral, was in 1814 created Viscount Exmouth, of Canonteign. He died in 1833, and was buried at Christow, the parish in which Canonteign is situated, where an appropriate monument is erected to his memory.

1797. – Peter Tonkin, Mayor. William Elford, Member of Parliament, in room of Francis Glanville. Mutiny in the Dockyard.

Three marines were executed on the Hoe for mutiny. "Perhaps there never was so great a number assembled together in this neighbourhood before as there was to witness this, as the Hoe was literally full, and the military were calculated to be 10,000 men, as all the marines were sent on shore, and the inhabitants who were present were estimated at 4,000. Another marine received the first part of his punishment just before the execution. His sentence was 1,000 lashed and to be transported. He was an old man, but concerned in the mutiny. They were all Irishmen. Lee was a Protestant, and was attended from the Citadel cell through the west sally-port to the fatal spot by the Rev. R. Hawker. Coffey and Braning were of the Romish Church, and were attended by a priest of that persuasion. Their march from the Citadel to the Hoe was of the most awful kind ever witnessed. They were preceded by the Marine Band playing the Dead March in Saul, and each of the culprits had his coffin borne before him by four men, guarded by a strong party of foot and some of the Surrey Dragoons. They were allowed their own time for preparation for death. The firing party came very near; the culprits knelt each on his coffin. At the first fire two fell, but Lee remained until the reserve had almost all fired at him, until one came near and blew his brains out. After the execution the whole of the troops marched round them, so it was impossible for many to see the unfortunate men. They were tried in the Citadel Hospital by a military court. The witnesses were many, and some of them gave evidence in a clear and circumstantial manner respecting their assembling on Stonehouse-hill, with many others, and administering on oath to all that joined – it should rather be said caused them to take an oath – as a book was placed in the centre, and the form of the oath was – to be true and faithful to each other, to free themselves and the French prisoners, and not to stop until they overturned the Government of the kingdom. Lee was convicted of addressing them at one of the treasonable meetings, and assuring them that they would be joined by the crews of two line of battle ships then in harbour, as he and others had been on board for that purpose, but they did not then manifest any symptoms of discontent. Happily this alarming conspiracy was timely discovered by one of their party betraying them, and the first act of the commanding officer was depriving the whole battalion of their arms and accoutrements instantaneously, which was done by assembling all the officers which were at head-quarters, and which are generally very numerous, and going from room to room they collected all, and brought them to the guard-house."

"May 5th. – A melancholy accident happened this evening at Plymouth. Two young ladies, daughters of Mr. Shepherd, surgeon of the Dockyard, and another young lady of the name of Gregg, were playing on one of the ship's yards, which was at the mast-house to be repaired, when it gave way on a sudden, and the ladies not being able to extricate themselves, it rolled over them which occasioned the immediate death of the two first, who were most shockingly mangled, and the other had her leg broken. The eldest of the two sisters was about the age of fifteen, and the other only in her twelfth year."

"Bursting of a spring at Newton Ferrers. January 21st. This night, at 11 o'clock, a cottage at Newton Ferrers, a few miles from Plymouth, in which slept an industrious widow (cottager) and her two children, was overwhelmed by the bursting of a very large field and orchard on a hill above the cottage in Memblandlane. It totally destroyed the cottage and a barn, and suffocated the widow and her two children, who were found dead under a very great heap of earth, elm trees and cedar trees. A large chasm in the field above the cottage was found, out of which issued a rivulet of water. The farmers imagine that it was owing to the bursting of a spring that this melancholy accident occurred. The bodies were dug out on Monday, and Mr Whiteford, coroner for the southern district of Devon, took an inquisition, and the jury returned a verdict – "Accidental death."

The following singular death occurred here this year: – At Plymouth, after a long and painful illness, the Rev. Mr. Love, Rector of Hittersley. He was sitting up in his bed, and desired Mrs. Love to give him a sharp pen-knife to pare his nails. Suddenly he was seized with a rising of the lights and a suffocation in the throat. He forced his hands under both jaws to relieve himself, but part of the blade of the knife being above his grip, he separated the carotide artery and instantly bled to death. His wife and children were in the room at the moment of this unhappy accident."

1798. – Bartholomew Dunsterville, Mayor.

1799. – John Arthur, Mayor. Foundation stone of the new Market laid May 8th. Piers built at Sutton harbour.

1800. – Philip Langmead, Mayor. The old Guildhall taken down, and the present wretched one erected from the designs of Eveleigh.

CHAPTER VIII

ANNALS CONTINUED FROM THE YEAR 1800 TO 1871

1801. – Thomas Cleather, Mayor. Mutiny and riot in the Dockyard. The Lying-in Hospital founded.

1802. – John Clarke Langmead, Mayor. William Elford and Philip Langmead, Members of Parliament. Mr. Langmead was the first Mayor elected by the Freemen at large in Common Hall assembled. Act of Parliament obtained for embanking the Laira.

1803. – Edmund Lockyer, Mayor. Millbay-road opened.

1804. – James Elliot, Mayor.

1805. – John Hawker, Mayor. "March 22nd. – Died, Lord George Lennox, Governor of Plymouth, Colonel of the 28th Regiment of Foot, and only brother of the Duke of Richmond."

"April 10th. – Mr Eastlake, coroner for Plymouth, held an inquest on the body of John Rogers, who was stabbed by a woman in the left side, just above the heart, and died from internal haemorrhage in about an hour. The circumstances are nearly as follows: – The woman was called Betsy Barber and she cohabited with Rogers; but what is remarkable, her husband died the preceding day. The quarrel arose, it appeared, from the latter swearing she would go to her husband's funeral in white and blue; but he objected to it and said it was indecent. More words ensued, when she flew into a violent passion, rose up and committed the above rash action. The jury found a verdict of *Wilful Murder*, and she was committed to Exeter for trial at the next Assizes. The corpse of the husband of Barber and the corpse of Rogers were interred in the burial ground, side by side."

1806. – Thomas Lockyer, Mayor. Sir Thomas Tyrwhitt, Member of Parliament, in room of Philip Langmead, and afterwards Sir Charles Morice Pole and Sir Thomas Tyrwhitt elected Members of Parliament.

1807. – Thomas Eales, Mayor. Sir C.S. Pole and Sir Thomas Tyrwhitt, Members of Parliament.

1808. – Wm. Langmead, Mayor. Catwater moorings laid down by the Earl of Morley. "August 15th. Died at Modbury, near Plymouth, at the great age of 87, and in full possession of his faculties, Mr. William Rosdew, who for the last 50 years had lived a total recluse, denying himself not only the comforts, but almost the necessaries of life. By this extreme penury he had amassed a considerable property, a great part of which he most liberally distributed among his relatives before his death. He was a man of strict integrity, and, notwithstanding his love of money, scrupulously just in all his dealings. This extraordinary turn of a naturally strong mind is supposed to have arisen from a disappointment in his affections in an early period of his life."

In the latter days of 1807 and the first three or four months of this year, there were more than 160 days of successive rain at Plymouth.

1809. – Joseph Pridham, Mayor. The Public Dispensary in Catherine-street built. The proposed Plymouth Dock Police Bill – "a bill equally conspicuous for absurdity on the one hand and injustice on the other" – thrown out by the Commons.

A meeting held at the Guildhall, September 25th, "for the purpose of affording an opportunity to the inhabitants of joining in the general expression of joy on the approaching 25th of October, when his Majesty will enter into the 50th year of his reign, and to consider in what manner the day can be most properly celebrated." At this meeting, among other resolutions, it was determined that "the most proper mode would be for the Mayor, Corporation and inhabitants to attend Divine service, and to present a congratulatory address to his Majesty on the happy occasion; to have a public dinner at the Guildhall, and a ball in the evening at the Assembly Rooms; a bonfire on the Hoe; and an ox roasted whole and given to the populace and a display of fireworks."

"Thursday, 29th. – A grand dinner was given at the Guildhall by the Mayor, William Langmead, Esquire. Two of the rooms were completely filled by 150 persons at least, who sat down to dinner, amongst whom were, besides the Mayor and Commonalty, the Right Hon. Lord Boringdon, his Excellency Admiral Don Pasenal Ruis Hindobre, Governor of Monte Video, who arrived here in the *Prenava* Spanish frigate, Colonel Vianna; also the following officers of the *Portuguex*: Captain Josquin Simoza and Lieutenant Morles and Lona; also Captain Joaquin Moyda, of the Spanish ship *Carolina*, Generals Stephens, Thomas, and Mercer, Admirals Sutton, Kelly, and Kinnier, Colonels Cod, Hayne, and Langmead, etc., with the field officers of the regiments in garrison; also Mr J. F. Forlade, and many officers of the Portuguese cavalry and infantry. Lord Boringdon, for the Spanish officers, returned thanks to the company, and in the highest terms expressed their satisfaction. The most cordial harmony prevailed. The English, Spanish, and Portuguese colours were suspended in the hall. The band of the late Prince of Wales's Own Royal Volunteers by their airs contributed to enliven the scene."

1810. – Edmund Lockyer, jun., Mayor. The "Plymouth Public Library" founded at a public meeting held November 20th. The manufacture of earthenware commenced. Prince Lucien Buonaparte, with his family and *suite*, landed at the Victualling Office. First stone of the Theatre, Royal Hotel, etc., laid by the mayor.

1811. – George Bellamy, Mayor. The Theatre, Royal Hotel and Assembly Rooms built by the Corporation. The Laira embankment made.

1812. – John Arthur, Mayor. Sir Charles Morice Pole and Sir Benjamin Bloomfield, Members of Parliament. "Sir Charles Morice Pole, Bart., was a descendant of the ancient family of Pole, of Shute, in Devonshire, being great-grandson of Sir John Pole (the third baronet) and of Anne, youngest daughter of Sir William Morice, Knt., one of the Secretaries of State to Charles the Second. The father of Sir Charles was Reginald Pole, Esq., of Stoke Damerell, Devon, who married Anne, second daughter of John Francis Buller, Esq., of Morval, in the County of Cornwall. Charles Morice was born at Stoke Damerell, January 18th, 1757, was bred to the naval profession at the Royal Academy, Portsmouth, and first went to sea with Sir Edward Vernon in 1773. He performed gallant services, and ultimately became a Vice-Admiral, and was as a spontaneous mark of His Majesty's favour created a Baronet of Great Britain, August 18, 1801. He represented Plymouth in Parliament for several years. His integrity and ability gained the applause of his country. The virtues, goodness of heart and urbanity of his manners in private life, may be held up as worthy of general imitation."

The Plymouth Institution founded, in great measure through the exertions of Mr. H. Woollcombe. The meetings were at first held in the Public Library; afterwards in the Picture Gallery, Frankfort-place; and ultimately the Athenaeum was erected for its accommodation. Public Library in Cornwall-street, built from the designs of Mr. Foulston. Until this time the collection of books forming the nucleus of the Library were kept in a room at the Guildhall. The Free School in Cobourg-street built. The Plymouth Breakwater commenced August 12th.

1813. – Henry Woollcombe, Mayor. The Exchange in Woolster-street built. "August 23rd. – The new Theatre Royal opened this evening for the first time. There were 1,149 persons present, viz.: Boxes, 436; slips, 151; pit, 262; gallery, 300; Total, 1,149. The receipts were £152 14s." The cost of the pile of buildings was about £70,000. The plays were "As you like it" and "Catherine and Petruchio," the prices being to the boxes 4s., pit 2s. 6d., gallery 1s. "The doors to be opened at six, and to begin precisely at seven o'clock." A droll arrangement was made for keeping seats as follows: "Ladies and gentlemen are respectfully requested to send their servants to keep places at half-past five o'clock."

1814. – Sir Diggory Forest, Mayor. "The great Frost. – The Falmouth mail coach started from thence for Exeter; after having proceeded a few miles was overturned without material injury to the passengers. With the assistance of an additional pair of horses it reached the first stage; after which all endeavours to proceed were found perfectly useless, and the letters were sent to Bodmin by the guard on horseback. The Falmouth and Plymouth coach and its passengers were obliged to remain at Saint Austell. At Plymouth the snow was nearly four feet deep in several of the streets."

1815. – William Lockyer, Mayor. In July the *Bellerophon* dropped anchor in the Sound, having on board the Emperor Napoleon Buonaparte. Here he remained several days, and thousands upon thousands of visitors flocked to the place, and swarmed in boats of all kinds upon the Sound, surrounding the ship and doing their utmost to obtain a glance at the man who had so long been a terror to Europe, but who was now a prisoner of war. The Emperor frequently came on deck, and placing himself in the gangway gratified the curiosity of the crowd. Mr. Charles Lock Eastlake, then a young man of promise, and one of the most gifted of the many artist-sons of Plymouth, sketched the Emperor, and studied him so closely from his boat that he produced his celebrated picture, which is said to be the best and latest portrait ever painted of him. After being at Plymouth, Napoleon was transferred from the *Bellerophon* to the *Northumberland* and conveyed to his place of captivity, Saint Helena. Mr. Charles Lock Eastlake afterwards became Sir Charles, and was for many years President of the Royal Academy. The following is a contemporary account of the picture, copied from the *Plymouth Chronicle* of December 26th 1815: –

"Mr. Eastlake's grand picture of Buonaparte. – This work is executed on a canvas eight feet and a half by six feet. It represents Napoleon Buonaparte the size of life, as he presented himself at the gangway of H.M.S. *Bellerophon* when lying in Plymouth Sound, in the month of July 1815. He appears in his most usual attitude on that occasion, standing with his left foot on an inclined step, about two or three inches above the deck, which made him look rather taller than he really is. His height, which is exactly given, is about five feet six inches; his complexion is that brownish yellow so peculiar to the Corsicans, and mixing with his black beard produces what has been called in some descriptions "a clear bronze." His smile was always accompanied with a slight protrusion of the lips, and then without this smile, the corners of the mouth dropped down. The picture represents him with the first of these expressions, which in fact he was seldom without; there was always a slight degree of grief in the brows which seemed habitual, as his smile did not dissipate it. In his right hand he holds an opera glass, with which he from time to time surveyed the surrounding multitude in the boats below him. He most frequently appeared with his hat on, but took it off by way of salutation, on coming forward and again retiring; he wore a small tri-colour cockade in it, without any loop or button. His coat, cut in the French military fashion, is the uniform of a Colonel of Chasseurs, dark green, with red collar and cuffs and a red edging to the lappels, etc. Under the coat is displayed part of the Cordon of the Legion of Honour, of watered red silk. He wears likewise the star of the same order. Three small decorations are hung from the left lappel of his coat; the small cross of the Legion of Honour suspended by a red ribbon; the Order of the Reunion, by a blue; and that of the Iron Crown, by an orange one, with a green border. His small-clothes are whitish kerseymere, with a small gold buckle at the knee; white silk stockings and gold buckle in his shoe. Behind him, on his right, is Count Poniatowski, uncovered, in the uniform of *officer d'ordonnance* . This officer having been separated from Buonaparte sat to the artist for his portrait on board the *Saint George* at Plymouth. Behind Buonaparte, on his left, is Count Bertrand, seen in profile and also uncovered, in the uniform of a general officer. A marine is on guard at his post in the gangway, on Buonaparte's left. A sailor below has just removed the side rope (which hangs on his arm) from the ring, and is getting towards the main chains, where he always remained till Buonaparte retired; the other rope is hung over the hammock railing. An ensign, which is seen on the bulk-head, is supposed to have been used for an awning over the quarter-deck. The letter S on one of the hammocks indicates the starboard side of the ship."

This picture was exhibited "at the Picture Gallery, Frankfort-place, Plymouth," at an admission of a shilling from 23rd December, 1815.

To the Mayor, Mr. William Lockyer, during his term of office, a gold medal was presented by the Freemen of the borough, and has been regularly worn, attached to the gold chain of office, by the mayors of the borough ever since that time. On the obverse is a shield, bearing the arms of Plymouth, a saltire between four castles, beneath which on a ribbon is the borough motto: "*Turris fortissima est nomen Jehovæ.*" Surrounding the whole is a ribbon, with the inscription: "*Usurpatione depressi legibus restituti.* 17 March, 1803." On the reverse is the inscription in 16 lines: "The Freemen of Plymouth request your wearing this medal, to be returned at the expiration of your mayoralty, in honourable token of that inestimable branch of the British Constitution, Trial by Jury; by whose verdict their right to elect a chief magistrate for the borough was restored, after having been unjustly withheld for upwards of three centuries." On the exergue is the inscription: "Presented to Wm. Lockyer, Esq., in his mayoralty. 1st January, 1816."

1816. – Capt. Samuel Pym, Mayor. On removing the pulpit in Charles' Church during alterations, the leaden coffins containing the bodies of Capt. Richard Kerby and Captain Cooper Wade, who were shot in Plymouth Sound for cowardice in the action between Benbow and Du Casse, in 1702, were discovered. July 28th. – Lord Exmouth sailed from Plymouth to attack Algiers, and on the 5th of October passed up channel, having accomplished his object.

1817. – Thomas Miller, Mayor. His Royal Highness the Duke of Gloucester arrived in Plymouth, and the freedom of the borough was conferred upon him. The Grand Duke Michael arrived, attended by Sir William Congreve. The Marine-road at the foot of the Hoe formed by the poor during the severe winter; the funds raised by subscription. Two ships of war – the *Jasper*, sloop, and the *Telegraph*, schooner – wrecked in the Sound. Ebenezer Methodist Chapel built.

1818. – Capt. Richard Arthur, Mayor. The Athenaeum of the Plymouth Institution erected from the designs of Mr. Foulston. The first stone was laid on the 1st of May, by Mr. H. Woollcombe, and the building completed in February, 1819. Union-street completed.

1819. – George Eastlake, jun., Mayor. Sir William Congreve and Sir T. Byam Martin, Members of Parliament. The Freemen's dinner discontinued. Plymouth and Dartmoor Railway Company incorporated by Act of Parliament. The line authorised by this Act was from Prince Town to Crabtree, and the estimated cost of its construction was £27,783. The scheme was first projected and mainly carried out by Sir Thomas Tyrwhitt, the engineer being Mr. Stuart, the Superintendent of the Plymouth Breakwater. The Athenaeum opened in February. The Duke of Wellington visited Plymouth, and was presented with the freedom of the borough.

"Celebrated Miser. – February, 1819. Died lately at Notter, near Landrake, Devon, Lieutenant-Colonel O'Dogherty, of the Royal Marines, one of the most eccentric characters of England, who for more than 20 years occasionally visited Plymouth market on an old white horse, lean as Rosinante, whose lank appearance, combined with his own singular habiliments, formed together a spectacle of wretchedness fully equal to anything described of the celebrated Elwes. In his last visit to Plymouth, a few weeks since, he seated himself on the steps of the *Plymouth Telegraph* office to eat an apple. His dress then consisted of a dirty nightcap round his head, surmounted by the poll of an old hat without a brim, a rough waistcoat patched all over, greasy leather small-clothes, kept up by listing braces outside the waistcoat, with wads of straw round the bottom of his legs. In his hand he wielded a large hedge stick. Amidst all this seeming penury he possessed some very excellent freehold estates in the above parish, well stocked; yet he chose to quit the family mansion, and lived in a small cottage in the vicinity, without a pane of glass in the windows. He nightly entered it by a ladder, which he drew after him, and slept in a corner of one of the rooms on a wretched pallet."

1820. – Richard Jago Squire, Mayor. Sir W. Congreve and Sir T. B. Martin, Members of Parliament. An additional Act of Parliament passed for extending the Plymouth and Dartmoor Railway from Crabtree to Sutton Pool; the estimated cost of the additional works was £7,200. King George IV. proclaimed in the market-place, the Guildhall, etc., by John Anderson; great rejoicings on the occasion.

On the arrival of the welcome news of the acquittal of Queen Caroline, after the disgraceful trial she had undergone, the bells of Saint Andrew's Church were immediately rung, and in the evening the town was partially illuminated. The South Devon Militia, under Lord Rolle, at Plymouth. On the occasion of the coronation of King George IV. a grand procession of the Corporation, the military staff, the Freemasons, and others, attended Divine service in Saint Andrew's Church; and the charity children and others paraded the streets with a champion in armour at their head. Upwards of 5,000 persons dined in the market-place; also a grand dinner at the Royal Hotel, at which the mayor presided. A bonfire, consisting of 140 tar barrels and other inflammable materials, lit on the Hoe. The freedom of the borough conferred on Bishop Carey, on his first visitation. In September His Majesty King George the Fourth being off the land in his yacht, great preparations were made for his reception on landing, but contrary winds obliged him to put back to Milford Haven. The Custom-house on the Parade erected from designs by Mr. Laing.

"July 28th. – Died at Tolvan (Landrake), in the County of Cornwall, near Plymouth, Elizabeth, daughter of the late Colonel O'Dogherty (the miser alluded to on the previous page), of that place. Her death is supposed to be occasioned by the sudden shock she received about three weeks before on hearing of her cattle being impounded."

1821. – Edmund Lockyer, Mayor. The mayor erected a large pair of iron gates, with granite posts, at the east entrance to the Hoe. Lockyer-street opened, leading to the Hoe. General mourning on the occasion of the death of H.R.H. Duke of York. An additional Act of Parliament passed authorising deviations and alterations in the plan of the Plymouth and Dartmoor Railway, the estimated additional cost being £5,000. Mr. Hopkins, of Swansea, appointed engineer in place of Mr. Stuart, and under his plan the works were carried out. The "Plymouth Philosophical Society" held its meetings at the London Inn Assembly Room, Foxhole-street, Plymouth. The Royal Eye Infirmary established.

1822. – William Adams Welsford, Mayor. "September 23rd. – An immense concourse of spectators attended Saint Andrew's Church at nine o'clock in the morning to witness the first nuptials in that church under the new Act."

1823. – Captain Nicholas Lockyer, Mayor. April 12th – A new Act for paving and lighting obtained. The Crescent built. The new reservoir for supplying the Victualling Office with water from Plymouth Leat begun to be formed. Saint Andrew's Chapel, near the Royal Hotel, consecrated September 26th. An Oil Gas Company for lighting the town incorporated.

"The next presentation to the vicarage of Saint Andrew, in this borough, was sold by auction for £5,050. Mr Hatchard, the bookseller, of Piccadilly, was the purchaser," the Vicar, the Rev. J. Gandy, being then on his 83rd year.

The freedom of the borough presented to the Right Hon. George Canning, who attended at the Guildhall for that purpose on the 29th of October. The Patent of Freedom was presented in a box made of Breakwater marble, mounted with silver, and bore the Plymouth arms and the inscription, "The Freedom of the Borough of Plymouth to the Right Hon. George Canning, Secretary of State for Foreign Affairs, etc. Captain Nicholas Lockyer, R.N., Mayor, 1823."

General Mina, "the patriotic Spanish chieftan," landed here from the French brig of war, *Le Cuirassier* from Barcelona. The general had no sooner landed at the Western Pier than he was caught up by the people, conveyed to a carriage that was waiting, the horses of which were instantly taken out, and he was drawn by the populace to the Royal Hotel, and thence the same day, with his *suite*, took up his residence in Durnford-street.

Charles Buonaparte, Count de Messoens, son of Prince Lucien Buonaparte, with his wife (daughter of Joseph Buonaparte), and family, put into Plymouth through stress of weather, in the *Falcon*, American ship, and remained one night.

1824. – Edmund Lockyer, Mayor. The works for the new Laira Bridge commenced on August 4th. The Government reservoir for the Victualling Office completed, and filled for the first time, in the presence of the mayor, on the 31st of May.

On the first day of this year the Town of "Plymouth Dock" threw off not only its allegiance to its mother town, Plymouth, but officially took to itself the new name of "Devonport," the sanction by "letters patent" of the King (George the Fourth) having previously been obtained. As by this event Plymouth became dissevered from its Dock and a large part of its inhabitants, the following contemporary account of the proceedings will prove interesting: –

"Devonport. – On Thursday, the 1st instant, being the day chosen for changing the name of Plymouth-Dock to that of Devonport, it was celebrated as a day of general jubilee. The morning was ushered in by merry peals from the bells of the Parish Church and Dockyard Chapel, and although the appearance of the weather was lowering in the early part, yet before the procession moved from the Town Hall, the sun shone forth and gave additional life and brilliancy to the joyous scene.

About 10 o'clock, the company who were to form the procession being assembled, proclamation for changing the name of the town, preceded by a flourish of trumpets, was made by Mr. Rodd, the Town Clerk. The health of King George the Fourth was then given by the Chairman of the Committee, amidst the enthusiastic cheers of thronging inhabitants, accompanied by a second flourish of trumpets.

The procession being marshalled in the manner previously arranged, moved off in the following order:

Peace Officers to clear the way.
The Crown, mounted on a staff, and carried by an officer.
Four Silk Flags.
The Town Beadles, in handsome gold-laced purple cloaks and cocked hats,
bearing in their hands painted staves, inscribed with "Devonport,"
and surmounted by carved and gilded crowns.
Town Flag, with the word "Devonport," in large characters.
School-boys marching three and three, with
ten handsomely painted small flags.
Flags.

Devonport Amateur Band
Trumpeters
Flags
Mr. Wilmot, Sheriff-Officer, in the Sheriff's uniform, and a blue silk sash, with "Devonport for ever" in letters of gold.
Town-clerk, in a gown and cocked hat.
An elegant gilded figure of Fame, sounding a trumpet, attended on either side by a trumpeter.
The Chairman, supported on the right by T. Husband, Esq., the Resident Magistrate, and on the left by the High-Constable.
Churchwardens.
Overseers of the Poor.
Surveyors of the Highways.
Governor of the Workhouse, and Vestry Clerk.
Surveyor of the Street, and Assistant Overseer of the Poor.
Town Commissioners, walking two and two with white staves, decorated with laurel leaves.
Committee of Management, two and two, carrying white staves.
Flags.
Royal Marine Band.

A number of the respectable tradesmen and inhabitants of Devonport, three and three, followed, and the rear was closed by a flag, bearing the inscription "Devonport for ever."

The management of the procession was committed to Lieutenant Richardson and Mr. E. Lyne.

From the Town-Hall the procession passed into George-street, and on to the Government Parade. Whilst passing the Admiralty-house the band played *Rule Britannia*, and in front of the Government-house, *God save the King*. On reaching the southeast barrier the second proclamation was made. It then proceeded to the entrance of the town at Cumberland-street, where the ceremony of placing a pillar, with "Devonport" in gilded characters on it, took place, and the third proclamation was made. A few paces from this place was erected, opposite the Crown Hotel, a grand triumphal arch ornamented with laurel. "*Devonport*" in large capitals, as a transparency, formed the arch, and was surmounted by a profusion of evergreens and an elegant crown, formed of coloured lamps, which in the evening when lighted up presented a very brilliant object. Passing under the triumphal arch, the procession moved on to Saint Aubyn-street, and at the entrance into Fore-street, the fourth proclamation was made. At the north-eastern barrier the fifth proclamation took place. The procession then proceeded to the Parish Church, from the summit of whose ancient tower, which bore the Royal Standard, Mr. Rodd again proclaimed His Majesty's will and pleasure, which was distinctly heard by the large concourse of spectators assembled round the church.

On the return of the procession into Fore-street, proclamation was again made opposite the Dockyard gates; whence passing through Queen-street, the eighth proclamation was given at the Ordnance Gun Wharf gates, and repeated in the middle of the Town square: here the pageant had a very imposing appearance. In the centre of the shrubbery, on a high mast, waved a handsome Union Flag; and around it floated the numerous silk banners borne in the procession. From hence the procession next passed down King-street into Catherine-street, and when opposite the Market gates, proclamation was again made; thence proceeding up James-street, it turned into Pembroke-street, at the top of which the final proclamation was delivered, when the procession returned to the Town Hall, and the doors were thrown open to the public.

The Committee of Management having taken their places on the platform, the Chairman returned thanks to Lieutenant Richardson and Mr. Lyne, and all the persons who joined in the procession, for their attendance, and in conclusion proposed the national anthem, which the band immediately played, joined by the voices of the assembly, which had a very pleasing effect.

During the greater part of the day the shops were closed, and the town presented the appearance of a general holiday.

A most liberal supply of porter, given by the brewers, was freely distributed to the populace. Cakes and fruit had been previously given to the children who attended. In the Workhouse every individual was regaled with beef, plum-pudding, and strong beer. In the morning the Commissioners attended, and proclaimed a free pardon for the delinquents, who for various offences were confined within the walls of the house.

A sheep was roasted whole at Newpassage by Mr. Bone, of the Ferry Inn, and given to whoever chose to partake of it."

A dreadful hurricane occurred this year; twenty vessels sunk or dismasted in Catwater and several lives lost. In Sutton Pool a vessel was sunk and another much injured. The Breakwater much damaged. A singular and providential escape from death is recorded in connection with this storm. A vessel laden with cork was capsized at sea, and some of the crew washed overboard and lost. The master and a passenger, with two of the crew, being below, managed to reach the coal-hole, where they remained for several hours immersed in water up to their chins. The vessel, after having been drifted about for some time, struck on the Breakwater and receded;

again struck heavily on the Mole, when the hatches were knocked off, and the stones having penetrated the deck, held her firm. The crew, etc., crept out of their hiding place, and finding one of their flags in the hold, hoisted it as a signal of distress, which being observed by Mr. Eddy, pilot, of Cawsand, he succeeded in rescuing them, in great peril. The vessel soon after went to pieces.

1825. – William Henry Hawker, Mayor. The first stone of the new Laira Bridge laid on the 16th of March, by the Earl of Morley. "The Volunteers' colours deposited in Saint Andrew's Church, and unfurled on the mayor's entering."

An Act of Parliament "for the better paving, lighting, cleansing, watching and improving the Town and Borough of Plymouth, in the County of Devon, and for regulating the police thereof, and for removing and preventing nuisances and annoyances therein," was this year passed.

1826. – Captain Richard Arthur, R.N., Mayor. Sir William Congreve and Sir Thomas Byam Martin, Members of Parliament. The Race Course, Chelson Meadow, opened, and the Plymouth and Devonport Races established. The Royal William Victualling Yard commenced. The Rev. Dr. Hawker, Vicar of Charles' Church, died.

1827. – Captain Richard Pridham, Mayor. Sir T. Byam Martin and Sir William Congreve, Members of Parliament. The water supply much improved and increased. The small lead pipes by which the water was distributed through the principal streets were taken up, and replaced by iron ones of larger dimensions. The reservoirs adjoining the Tavistock-road were constructed in this and the following years; fire-plugs were fixed in the streets, and the whole placed under an improved management. The "Freemasons' Hall and Commercial Rooms" in Cornwall-street erected. The Laira Bridge opened on the 14th of July by H.R.H. the Duchess of Clarence, afterwards Queen Adelaide, and *Suite,* who were the first to pass over it. It was built from the designs of Mr. J. M. Rendell. The Camera Obscura fixed on the Hoe by Mr. Sampson. A large subterranean cavern, with water 43 feet in depth, discovered in the rocks at Stonehouse. The gibbet at Stoke taken down.

The Archdukes John and Charles sailed from Plymouth on the Sunday, and "precisely at the report of the first gun announcing their departure," says a quaint writer, "the officiating minister at Saint Andrew's came to the verse (37, Pslam cv.) 'Egypt was glad at their departing; for they were afraid of them.' "

1828. – Richard Freeman, Mayor. The foundation stone of the Royal Union Baths laid on the 29th July, by Sir Byam Martin, as proxy for His Majesty King William the Fourth. Foundation stone of Eldad Chapel laid. Charles' Chapel in Tavistock-place erected from the designs of Mr. Ball. Foundation stone of Triggs' Chapel, Morley-street, laid in January, which was opened in October. Don Miguel at Plymouth.

His Majesty King William the Fourth (the Duke of Clarence) visited Plymouth, and during his stay attended a meeting at the Athenaeum, when Mr. William Snow Harris (afterwards knighted) delivered a lecture illustrating and describing his newly invented lightning conductors, as applied to the preservation of ships.

Miss Foote, afterwards Countess of Harrington, played Miss Dorillon in "Wives as they Were and Maids as they Are," Lady Julia in "Personation," Moggy Mc.Gilpin in the "Highland-Reel," Lady Teazle in "The School for Scandal," and Zephryna in "The Lady and the Devil," at the Plymouth Theatre. Miss Foote was a native of Plymouth.

1829. – Captain William Furlong Wise, Mayor. The Duke de Chartres and *Suite* arrived at Plymouth, and staid at the Royal Hotel. Interior of Charles' Church restored.

1830. – Captain Nicholas Lockyer, Mayor. Britonside widened by taking down buildings near where Martin-gate stood, and in other parts. The Royal Union Baths opened on the 1st of May. November 9th, H.R.H. the Duke of Sussex elected Lord High Steward of the Borough, on the death of King George IV. The Barbican-house and gateway taken down. Charles' Chapel opened July 1st. Upwards of 3,000 Portuguese refugees arrived in Plymouth to avoid the tyranny of Don Miguel. The storehouses at Coxside were converted into barracks and the refugees provided for by the Portuguese Consul, and they were ultimately sent on to the Brazils. Mr. N. T. Carrington, the poet, died at Bath, September 8th.

1831. – Captain Aaron Tozer, Mayor. Sir Thomas Byam Martin and Sir George Cockburn, Members of Parliament. The Hon. Captain Elliott was an unsuccessful candidate. Much unpleasantness arose at the time of this election concerning the rights of new Freemen, who had purchased their freedom. James Northcote, R.A., the celebrated painter, died July 13th, aged 85. He left directions in his will for monuments to be erected in Saint Andrew's Church, Plymouth, to the memory of himself and of his brother, to be executed by Chantrey.

1832. – George Coryndon, Mayor. John Collier and Thomas B. Bewes, Members of Parliament – the first members under the then new Reform Bill.

For Parliamentary purposes, Devonport and Stonehouse were this year converted into a borough, and have ever since returned two Members of Parliament.

The freedom of the borough voted to Charles Lock Eastlake, R.A., President of the Royal Academy. The Mariners' Church opened. Ancient British coins discovered at Mount Batten. The Plymouth, Devonport and Stonehouse Female Penitentiary opened at Eldad.

On the 16th of March the Hoe became the scene of an immense public assemblage, uniting the Reformers of the Three Towns, who met to petition the House of Commons "to withhold its confidence and the public supplies from any minister who might not support unmutilated and unimpaired" the measure of Parliamentary Reform. The meeting was held in consequence of the resignation of Earl Grey on the question of Reform.

On the intelligence reaching Plymouth on the 12th of May that the "Reform Bill" had been thrown out of Parliament, "the shops were instantly half closed, flags were suspended from ships' masts and house tops, half mast high, and muffled bells rung, as expressions of the gravity of the event and the public dismay it induced." On the passing of the Reform Bill in June, the demonstrations were of a widely different character. The 27th of June was fixed upon for celebrating the event, when the public buildings and private houses were, with few exceptions, elaborately and artistically decorated with evergreens, flowers, silk banners, and flags of every description; splendid triumphal arches were thrown across the streets, and garlands gay and gorgeous were suspended from various eligible elevations." A procession of more than 10,000 persons, and more than a mile and a half in length, composed of trades of the town, distinguished by emblems, devices, models, and various emblematical designs, was formed, and carried innumerable flags, banners, and devices, and the whole of the Three Towns joined in hearty demonstrations of joy. The day following this demonstration the cholera broke out in Plymouth, and from its commencement to its close, no fewer than 1,798 cases and 696 deaths were reported. Medals were afterwards struck and presented to the medical men who had distinguished themselves during this terrible visitation.

On the 17th of October there was an extraordinary luminous appearance of the western hemisphere, which was taken to be a conflagration of the Dockyard.

1833. – William Hole Evens, Mayor. A valuable snuff-box (which was afterwards stolen) presented to Rev. John Hatchard for his exertions during the late visitation of cholera, and other testimonials presented to various surgeons and others. General Saldannah and several noted officers in Don Pedro's service, sailed from this port for Oporto. The brig *Erin* wrecked on the Breakwater. A tablet to commemorate the passing of the Reform Bill erected on the Hoe by means of a penny subscription. Foundation stone of the new Barbican pier laid. Lord John Russell and Lord Ebrington received the freedom of the borough, and were entertained, with others, at dinner.

In August, Plymouth was visited by H.R.H. the Duchess of Kent and H.R.H. the Princess Victoria, our present beloved Queen who landed at the Dockyard, and remained at the Royal Hotel, when an address was presented to them by the Corporation. During their visit the 89th Regiment was presented with new colours by H.R.H. the Princess Victoria.

1834 and 1835. – John Moore, Mayor. The mayor, by His Majesty's Order in Council, in accordance with the Municipal Reform Act, was authorised to continue in office till the 1st of January 1836. On the usual day, the Feast of Saint Lambert, 1835, for the choosing of the mayor, about twenty Freemen met in Common Hall, the mayor as usual taking the chair, when the clause of the Bill and the Order in Council were read. and the meeting dissolved. Mr. Moore consequently held the mayoralty from Saint Lambert's Feast, 1834, to the 1st of January, 1836.

"First tin coinage in this town took place in the hall in the Exchange, in Woolster-street, March 25th, 1834." Branch Bank of England opened May 1st. "May 28th. The Nunnery at Coxside broken up, and the sisterhood, who had been reduced to seven, all advanced in years, embarked on board the schooner *Minerva*, for Gravelines in France." The brig *Sarah*. bound for Quebec, got on shore at the back of the Breakwater and went to pieces. The freedom of Plymouth presented to Sir T. Fowell Buxton, M.P. The Old Town Conduit removed, and the sculpture, inscriptions, etc., built into the wall of the reservoir on the Tavistock-road.

Mr. John Ball, the painter, committed suicide by cutting his throat, in March this year. He was unmarried, and was aged 49, but had for some time "been in a deranged state of mind."

The Prince de Joinville visited Plymouth in the *Didon*, and with his *Suite* remained at the Royal Hotel.

"November 20th. – A meeting (the first) of the inhabitants of this town held in the Guildhall to take into consideration the expediency of constructing a railroad from Exeter to this port, in continuation of the Great Western and Bristol and Exeter Lines. The hall was crowded, and £20,000 was subscribed at its close."

On Saturday, December 26th, 1835, in pursuance of the statute, the first election of Town Councillors under the Municipal Reform Act took place in the respective wards, commencing at 9 a.m. and closing at 4 p.m. The first Corporation under the new Municipal Reform Act was as follows: – Mayor – Thomas Gill, Esq. Aldermen – Messrs. George Pridham, Wm. Eastlake, R. Bayly, W.H. Hawker, T. Gill, J.T. Fownes, W.H. Evens, R. Fillis, H. Knight, J. Collier, M.P., T.W. Fox, and C. Tolcher. Town Councillors. – *Frankfort Ward* – Messrs. J.C. Cookworthy, M.D., J. Whiteford, W. Jacobson, Colonel Elliot, F. Bone, and H.M. Gibson. *Drake's Ward* – Messrs. D. Derry, J. Shepheard, W. Prance, B. Aldham, G. Frean, and J.N. Tanner. *Charles' Ward* – Messrs. G. Coryndon, M. Duncan, J. Cleverton, W. Burnell, S. Rowse, and S. Derry. *Sutton Ward* – Messrs. W. P. Baldy, W.T. Harris, W.H. Hawker, W. Moore, J. Batten, and W. Kerswill. *Vintry Ward* – Messrs. J. King, T.W. Fox, W. Mortimer, T. Stevens, M.S. Grigg, and J. Chalker. *Saint Andrew's Ward* – Messrs. R. Freeman, W. Rendle, W. Baron, T. Gill, J. Lindon, and J. Moore.

Signor Bertolotto's exhibition of the Industrious Fleas opened in Plymouth, and caused a good deal of attraction.

1836. – Thomas Gill, Mayor, from January 1st to November 9th. James King, Mayor, from November 9th to November 9th, 1837. Mr. Gill took office under the Municipal Reform Act on the 1st of January, 1836, his predecessor, Mr. Moore, having filled it until that day. Mr. Gill's tenure of office was therefore a short one. He was succeeded in November by Mr. James King, who was elected mayor at the proper time fixed under the Municipal Reform Act. John Collier and Thomas B. Bewes, Members of Parliament; Sir George Cockburn an unsuccessful candidate. The "South Devon and East Cornwall Hospital and Plymouth Public Dispensary," in Sussex-place, erected from the designs of Mr. G Wightwick. The foundation stone laid on the 1st August, by the Rev. John Hatchard.

Charles Mathews, the celebrated comedian, died in Plymouth, and was buried in Saint Andrew's Church. He died on his 59th birthday. His funeral was attended by the Revs. J. Smith and B. Luney, Sir George Magrath, M.D., Mr. J.C. Cookworthy, M.D., and Mr. W. Snow Harris, surgeon, who conducted the funeral. The pall-bearers were Capt. Ross, C.B., J. Moore, Esq., Mayor of Plymouth, Capt. Hornby, C.B., Major Symons, Major Harvey Smith, and Col. C. Hamilton Smith. Mr. Charles Mathews, son of deceased, followed as chief mourner, accompanied by H. Gyles, Esq., Captain Tincombe, R.N., and Messrs. Franklin, Brady, Jacobson, and Wightwick, besides numerous other friends and admirers of the deceased, and the procession was closed with the carriages of Major-General Sir Willoughby Cotton and Admiral Sir William Hargood. The funeral service was performed by the Rev. J.C. Smith. Mathews died at his lodgings in Lockyer-street, where he had been remaining some time on account of his health.

"March 12th. – Calamitous fire in the Plymouth Citadel, at the residence of Fort-Major James Watson, in the south-west part of the Citadel, when Fort-Major Watson, with two of his daughters, fell a sacrifice to the devastating element. Their bodies were found together about an hour after the fire had been subdued."

July 4th. – The first Quarter Sessions for the Borough of Plymouth held under the provisions of the New Municipal Act, and the first appearance of the learned Recorder, William Carpenter Rowe, Esq. July 15th. – The new road leading from Plymouth to Saltash opened. July 16th. – A most alarming fire broke out about midnight in Treville-street, by which three houses, as well as Mr. Creagh's curriery, and a hatter's house behind, were burnt to the ground.

"August 2nd. – The ceremony of perambulating the bounds of the borough observed by the mayor and municipal authorities. The Members of the Council breakfasted with the mayor at his house, from thence started about 10 o'clock to go round the boundaries of the borough, attended by the sergeant-at-mace, constables, etc. On the return of the party, the mayor proceeded to the Barbican and Fisher's Nose, where he witnessed the landing of one of the Charity School boys, giving him the usual 'box under the ear' and a 'half-a-crown' to refresh his memory, if ever he should be called on to give evidence as to the bounds of the borough; from thence they proceeded to the Hoe, and returned to the Guildhall, when the 'Freedom Boys' had their usual glass of wine to drink the mayor's health, and a large bun to take home."

November 29th. – The town and neighbourhood visited by a very severe storm – the wind blowing terrifically from the south to west – several ships in the Sound and harbour parted their cables and dragged their anchors. One vessel, the *City of Edinburgh*, a fine barque, 400 tons, drifted towards the land; when within three cables' length the captain had the masts cut away. This relieved her; she brought up, and rode out the gale. Both the churches were injured. Charles' Church had a portion of the roof displaced, and 108 panes of glass broken, and most of the other public buildings were also injured. It was perilous to be in the streets – tiles, slates, bricks, and stones falling in every direction for more than a quarter of an hour.

A public meeting held for considering the establishing of a locomotive steam carriage on the public road from Plymouth to Devonport.

A daring attempt to escape from the borough gaol made by three prisoners.

The Borough of Devonport incorporated. The charter was received on the 8th of October by Mr. Abbott, the nominated returning officer, and having been produced to a public meeting next day was proclaimed round the town. Devonport was the first town to apply for a charter under the Municipal Reform Act.

The schooner *Alban* struck on the Breakwater in a gale of wind and subsequently took fire, and the whole cargo and vessel were completely destroyed. The captain's wife and child lost their lives under very distressing circumstances.

1837. – William Hole Evens, Mayor. John Collier and Thomas B. Bewes, Members of Parliament. Sir George Cockburn and the Hon. P. Blackwood, unsuccessful candidates.

This year the Town of Devonport, with Stoke Damerel, including Morice Town and Stoke, was incorporated by Act of Parliament, and became a municipal borough. It was divided by this Act into six wards, viz., Morice Ward, Saint Aubyn Ward, Saint John's Ward, Clowance Ward, Tamar Ward, and Stoke Ward, and is governed by a Mayor, 12 Aldermen, and 36 Councillors, with a Recorder, a Town Clerk, and other officers. The first Mayor was Edward Saint Aubyn, Esq., on which occasion the Corporation mace was presented by Sir John Saint Aubyn.

A heavy gale of wind, with fall of snow, occurred in February, by which very considerable damage was done to many houses in the town. The *Thetis* of Liverpool, struck on the Breakwater and became a total wreck. On the 25th February, the tide rose higher than it had done since the heavy gale of 1824, and the whole of the lower parts of the town and the Union-road were inundated, the water in many instances being several feet deep in the houses, and boats were used in the streets. Much damage was done to the Breakwater, and to the docks, quays, etc. A singular circumstance occurred this year. "A poor woman bought an old petticoat of a pawnbroker in Plymouth, and on reaching home found it was too long for her. She then began to alter it, and found in doing so no less than a hundred £5 notes stitched up in it."

"May 24th. – This being the birthday of the heiress presumptive to the throne, and the period when Her Royal Highness Princess Victoria attained her majority, was generally observed as a holiday. The bells of both churches rang a merry peal throughout the day. Flags were hoisted at the Guildhall and other public establishments. The Town Council of this Borough met and voted an address to Her Royal Highness. The day was closed with a display of fireworks on the Hoe. May 29th. – The King's birthday was observed with every demonstration of loyalty and attachment. The bells rang merrily throughout the day. In the evening fireworks were let off on the Hoe and also at Bovisand. June 9th. – The congratulatory address of the Town Council to Princess Victoria presented by a deputation, consisting of the Mayor, Recorder, and the two Members for the Borough, who were most graciously received.

June 21st. – The melancholy intelligence of the death of King William IV. was received at Plymouth by the *Brunswick* steamer at half-past 2 p.m., and the news becoming generally known, the tradesmen throughout the town partially closed their shops, the vessels in the port lowered their flags half-mast high, the 'minute gun' was fired from the shipping and the batteries, and the church bells tolled throughout the reminder of the day. Official communications were brought the same evening by the mail to the authorities of the port, at Devonport, announcing the demise of His Majesty. The Port Admiral immediately shifted his flag to the *Royalist*, lying in Hamoaze, and the Royal Standard was hoisted half-mast high on board the guard-ship and shipping in the harbour. Shortly after 5 o'clock p.m. the *Royal Adelaide,* which had been painted black (the news having arrived three hours before by the *Brunswick* steamer, allowed time for the preparation), with her yards topped up and down, commenced firing 72 'minute guns', being the number of years of His Majesty's life. This being concluded 30 minute guns were fired from the battery on Mount Wise, followed by 30 from the Citadel, and 60 from the battery in Mount Edgcumbe. Thousands of spectators were collected on Mount Wise, Devonport, and feelings of deep sorrow seemed to pervade the multitude universally. June 22nd. – The Royal Standard was hoisted full mast high on all the stations and ships in harbour in honour of the accession of Queen Victoria, and the *Royal Adelaide* fired a double royal salute in celebration of the event. The Citadel, the battery on Mount Wise, the battery in Mount Edgcumbe, and H.M.S. *Ringdove*, also fired royal salutes of 21 guns. The same morning a special meeting of the Devonport Board of Commissioners was held to decide the best mode of publicly recognising the authority of Her Majesty in that borough. A committee was appointed to carry out the proceedings. The inhabitants were invited to attend at the Town Hall at 5 p.m. A little before 6 p.m. a procession was formed in front of the hall.

When Mr. Rodd read the proclamation, the procession moved in the following order: – Standard Bearer; Constables of the Parish; High Constable; Beadles of the Borough; Clerk to the Board of Commissioners; Churchwardens; Board of Surveyors; Commissioners and Inhabitants of the Town, bearing white wands. At the Dockyard, the procession was met by the officers and workmen, and the same forms being gone through, the call of "God save the Queen" was responded to by hearty cheers. The same ceremonies were repeated at the Gun Wharf, Town Barriers, at Stoke Church, at Mount Wise, and in several of the principal streets." "June 23rd. – Her Most Gracious Majesty Victoria I. proclaimed in Plymouth. A procession, composed as follows, started from the Guildhall at 4 o'clock: – Two Police Officers; the Band; the Corporation Flag; the Superintendent of Police; two Inspectors; two Trumpeters on horseback; the Town Clerk on horseback; Surveyor to the Corporation; the Sergeants-at-Mace; the Mayor, Magistrates and Clergy, two and two; the Members of the Town Council, two and two; Inhabitants of the Borough, two and two; Policemen on both sides. The proclamation was read by Charles Whiteford, Esq., the Town Clerk, at the following places: – At the Guildhall, on the Parade, opposite the Post-office, centre of the Market, and corner of the Royal Hotel, followed by the loudest cheers, huzzas, and cries of 'Long live the Queen', emanating from the thousands who thronged the various quarters of the town, the band playing the national anthem. The weather was delightfully fine, and the streets through which the procession passed, appeared as a living mass."

"July 8th. – This being the day when the remains of the late Sovereign were interred at Windsor, it was observed here with great solemnity. Business was entirely suspended during the day, the shops and public establishments being completely closed, and a solemn knell was tolled from the various churches in the town. James King, Esq., the Right Worshipful the Mayor, and other Members of the Council, preceded by the Sergeants-at-Mace, carrying the maces, which were covered with crape, went in due form to Saint Andrew's Church, where Divine service was performed. An appropriate sermon was preached by the Rev. J. Hatchard from 46th Psalm. The church was crowded. The ceremony at the Jew's Synagogue on this mournful day was very impressive. This building was also crowded. At Devonport the day was observed with every mark of solemnity. The shops were universally closed, and every kind of business not absolutely necessary was suspended. At 11 o'clock a.m. the troops, consisting of the Royal Artillery and Royal Marines, the depôts of the 20th, 32nd, 36th, 37th, 43rd, and 99th Regiments were assembled at Mount Wise, where Divine service was performed in the open air by the Rev. H. Hennah, Chaplain of the Garrison, who preached from John xi. 11. The service commenced by the Marine Band playing the Dead March in Saul. The scene was one of the most sublime and impressive description. The troops were drawn up in the form of a hollow square, with their arms reversed. Major-General Ellice was present with his staff, and a number of the inhabitants also joined reverentially in the service. Divine service was also performed in the Dockyard Chapel in the morning by the Rev. Mr. Briggs, and at the other churches and chapels in the evening. Soon after 5 o'clock p.m. H.M.S. *Pembroke* lying in the Sound, commenced firing 30 minute guns, and was followed by the Citadel, Saint Nicholas' Island, the battery on Mount Edgcumbe, the platform on Mount Wise, and the *Royal Adelaide* guard-ship, firing 30 guns each – in all 180 guns. The troops in the Citadel paraded there, whilst the firing took place, resting on their arms reversed; those at Stonehouse, on the hill, whilst the guns of Saint Nicholas' Island were firing; and those at Devonport, on the Government Parade, during the firing at Mount Wise." July 9th. – A number of soldiers forming the left wing of the British Auxiliary Legion, serving in the Queen of Spain's cause, arrived in Plymouth.

August 16th – A public meeting of the inhabitants of the borough held to consider the propriety of presenting an address of congratulation to Her Majesty Queen Victoria, and also an address of condolence to the Queen Dowager. A committee was appointed, and addresses prepared and presented.

September 8th. – Freedom-day observed with all the ancient custom. The Members for the Borough, with the Mayor and Town Council, accompanied by a large number of the inhabitants in carriages and on horseback, visited the bounds of the borough, where the usual formalities took place.

1838. – George W. Soltau, Mayor. May 2nd – The Superintendent of Police's office in the Guildhall broken into early in the morning, when 17 sovereigns, two silver spoons, and other articles which had been placed in the office for safe custody were stolen. The superintendent's coat was also taken from the offices, but left on the premises behind the Guildhall. At a meeting of the Town Council held on the 16th May, in reference to the alleged robbery, and after a careful and minute investigation connected with the same, the Council were of opinion that no forcible entry on the premises were ever made; they therefore thought it their duty no longer to retain the

Superintendent of Police in their service. May 17th. – This being the day set apart for the celebration of the birth of Her Majesty Queen Victoria, was observed with all the demonstrations of loyalty. The morning was ushered in by the ringing of bells, etc., and the Royal Standard was hoisted at all the public establishments; the ships in port were also gaily dressed in colours. The troops in garrison, with the Royal Marines and Royal Artillery, assembled at Mount Wise in review order, and at 12 o'clock fired a *feu de joie*. The ships in commission also fired royal salutes. May 27th. – A fatal accident, attended with the loss of two lives, occurred on board the *Royal Adelaide*, guard-ship in Hamoaze, in consequence of the *Meteor* steamer running foul of her, by which the latter's spanker-boom was forced out of the saddle, and falling upon the deck so dreadfully wounded Mr. T. Lewis, mate, and Mr. J. Jones, quarter-master, that the latter expired on his way to the Naval Hospital, and the mate shortly after.

June 11th. – A private belonging to the 29th Regiment drummed out. The ceremony was performed in the presence of his comrades and a number of spectators. The regiment formed open line on the parade in the Citadel, and the culprit, having his facings cut from his regimentals, was led by one of the men, with a rope fastened round him, down the line to the Garrison gates, the drums beating the "rogue's march", and at the entrance of the barriers he was discharged from the corps as being unworthy to bear the name of a soldier.

Great rejoicings on occasion of the coronation of Her Majesty Queen Victoria. At the great state coronation banquet the salt-cellar presented by the Town of Plymouth to King Charles the First was used. "Among the mass of valuables in the Crown jewelhouse at the Tower, London, there are only two presents, both of which are from the County of Devon. The first is a wine fountain, three feet high, and used at the late coronation banquet, which was presented by the Corporation of Plymouth to Charles I.; the second, a saltcellar, model of the White Tower. It is about 18 inches high, a most splendid jewel, and was presented by the people of Exeter to William III."

"June 28th. – The celebration of the coronation of Her Majesty Queen Victoria was observed with every possible demonstration of loyalty in this town. The whole mass of the inhabitants appeared to be actuated with one spirit – a determination to display their attachment to the throne and loyalty to their Sovereign. The morning was ushered in by peals from the bells of both churches, which was continued at intervals throughout the day. The whole of the town was most tastefully decorated with flags of various descriptions, evergreens, ribbons, etc.; and at the various public buildings the Royal Standard was displayed. The tower of Saint Andrew's Church had a very imposing appearance, a line of flags having been extended from its summits to the tree in the churchyard. The Mayor, Magistrates, several Members of the Town Council, and many of the respectable inhabitants assembled at the Guildhall shortly after 10 o'clock, and at half-past ten proceeded to Saint Andrew's Church in due form, the mayor being preceded by the officers carrying the maces. The Rev. J.H.C. Borwell, the Corporation lecturer, read the prayers; and a sermon suitable for the occasion was preached by the Vicar, the Rev. J. Hatchard, text 1st Tim. ii. 1,2. Divine service was also performed at Charles' Church, Norley Chapel, and many other places of worship in the town. About 11 o'clock the children of the various schools, about 3,000 in number, assembled on the Hoe, and were arranged under the direction of Mr. Coath, who undertook the task by desire of the committee – their stations being according to the seniority of the respective schools. Their appearance on the Hoe, with their various banners, many of which were very splendid, having been provided expressly for the occasion, had a most animating and gratifying appearance. Thousands of persons were assembled on the spot to witness the proceedings. About 12 o'clock the mayor, accompanied by a number of gentlemen, having arrived on the Hoe, the children sang the national anthem, accompanied by the band. The procession was then re-formed in the following manner: – The Band; the Town Sergeants, with the three gold maces; the Mayor, in his robes, wearing the gold chain and other paraphernalia of office; the Magistrates; Gentlemen of the town, two and two; the Schools: Hele and Lanyon, Hospital of Poor's Portion, Grey School, Batter-street School, Free School, Ebenezer Sunday School, Salem-street Chapel School, Bethel School, Saint Andrew's Chapel School, Rehoboth School, West Hoe School, Eldad School, Charles' Chapel School, National School, Willow-street Chapel School, and Bible Christian School; many gentlemen aiding the masters by walking by the side of the children to protect them from the crowd. The procession proceeded from the Hoe, down Lockyer-street, through George-street, Bedford-street, Old Town-street, and on to the Market-gate in Drake-street, and though the whole line was densely crowded with spectators, nothing could exceed the good order manifested throughout. On entering the Market-gate each school was conducted to the tables appointed for it. The children being seated, grace was sang, the band playing the Old Hundredth Psalm. The children commenced their dinner, when the public were admitted to witness the interesting spectacle. The market was soon crowded, and every person seemed highly gratified with the manner in which the whole affair had been conducted, the tables being bountifully supplied with prime joints of roast and boiled beef, legs of mutton, bread, potatoes, etc., and in addition each child was allowed half-a-pound of plum-pudding. At the close, grace was sang; the Queen's health was given; the national anthem was again sung, and the children retired in due order to their respective schools. The children of the Orphan Asylum, Saint Andrew's Church Sunday School, Household of Faith, and Norley-street Sunday School, dined in the Market, though they did not join in the procession. While the young were dining in one part of the Market, 154 aged persons were regaled with good old English fare in another part, provided by the butchers, aided by some respectable inhabitants of the town, for the aged women in the Market, designated 'Basket Women,' and to such others as were provided with tickets by the subscribers. About 1 o'clock the bidden guests took their seats, and, shortly after, 15 superior dishes were placed before them, consisting of an excellent round, a rump, and other best cuts of beef, a large leg of pork, several legs and shoulders of mutton, etc., the whole with suitable vegetables being served up hot. Each person had half a pint of strong beer and a penny loaf. The first dishes being removed, 10 dishes of very excellent plum-pudding took their place, and each guest was supplied with a good slice. On the table being cleared 30 gallons of prime strawberries were divided among the happy group. An old woman 83 years of age, named Maria Higden, who had been upwards of 36 years a basket woman in Plymouth Market, presided on the occasion, and was supported on her right by another woman 90 years old. The vice-president was a man named Charles Spragg, 94 years of age. He had been 34 years in the employ of Messrs. Dickers and Warwick. The chair for the lady president was kindly lent by Mr. Paddon, and was said to be upwards of 200 years old. The united ages of those who partook of this benevolent repast (among whom were seven aged men) amounted to 9,424 years, averaging nearly 64 years. After singing the national anthem, and giving three times three cheers for their youthful Sovereign, the participators left the Market, gratefully acknowledging the kindness of their benefactors. Mr. James Cuddeford, butcher, was the originator of this spirited act, and the entire management devolved on him. The porters who worked on the Parade had a dinner provided for them, and those employed on Sutton Wharf were equally fortunate, dining together on the quay. Mr. Lindon gave the whole of the men in his employ a substantial dinner in one of his buildings. Messrs. Tanner, acted in a similar liberal spirit towards their workmen, by causing a dinner to be provided for them at Mr. Avery's White Lion Inn, in

Old Town. Mr. Eardley, of Bedford-street, gave the persons in his employ a dinner of roast beef and plum-pudding, and after the dinner a jug measuring five feet in circumference, and holding 14 gallons, was placed on the table, filled with prime strong ale, from which they all drank 'Health and long life to the Queen.' The residents of the Almshouses, under the management of the Workhouse, were given a sufficient sum to furnish them with a dinner; and the inmates of the Workhouse were feasted with a good dinner and a cup of strong beer to drink Her Majesty's health. The children of Hele and Lanyon's and Lady Roger's Schools had dinner provided for them on the occasion at their respective schools, the trustees not wishing them to dine in the Market; and the Baptist and Unitarian Sunday School children not joining in the procession were also regaled at the cost of the respective congregations. The men employed in Messrs. Stanford's Glass Manufactory at Millbay went in procession through the principal streets of the Three Towns in the following order: – A band of musicians; a banner, bearing on the one side the representation of the exterior, and the other the interior, of the Glass-House at Millbay; guards on horseback, bearing battle-axes made of twisted and cut glass; a royal crown of massive cut glass, ornamented with bead work, and imitation jewels of stained glass, placed on a cushion of crimson velvet, borne by a glass-maker; two boys bearing glass wands, surmounted by glass doves; a radiant star of richly cut glass, borne by a glass-worker, supported on right and left by boys bearing glass wands, surmounted by garlands of cut glass; a large globe of flint glass, threaded with pearl-coloured semi-transparent enamel, borne by a glass-worker, and supported on the right and left by boys bearing glass wands, surmounted by miniature crowns of cut glass; a glass barrel, surmounted by a cut glass drinking vessel and a crown, the barrel ornamented with stripes of milk-white enamel, borne by a glass-worker, and supported on the right and left by boys bearing glass wands, surmounted by glass feathers; a glass bellows, ornamented and enamelled, borne by a glass-worker, and supported on the right and left by boys bearing glass wands, surmounted by wreaths; a cut glass basket, richly ornamented and filled with flowers, borne by a glass-worker, and supported on both sides by boys bearing ornamental wands; a crown and sceptre, of richly cut glass, placed on a cushion of crimson velvet, and borne by a glass-worker, and supported as before; a glass globe, ornamented and supported as before; decanters and wine glasses, of superior festoon patterns, richly cut, and placed on a crimson velvet cushion, borne by a glass-worker, and supported by boys bearing ornamental wands. The men wore glass hats, which had a very imposing effect – a novelty never witnessed in Plymouth before. The procession was greatly admired. About 5 o'clock a large party of the most influential persons of the town, presided over by the Right Worshipful the Mayor, sat down to dinner at the Royal Hotel. A very brilliant display of fireworks on the Hoe closed the interesting proceedings of the day; many of the pieces were exceedingly brilliant, and the rockets were very fine. The Hoe was densely crowded for many hours. Several tradesmen and other inhabitants had very beautiful transparencies and illuminations on the occasion. Business was suspended during the whole day, and the town assumed gaiety seldom if ever equalled."

July 16th. – The *Sirius* steam-ship, Captain S.S. Mould, arrived in this port from New York; accomplished the passage in 15 days 12 hours, a distance of 3,200 miles; she brought the mail, containing about 3,000 letters and newspapers. July 30th. – A meeting of the burgesses of the borough held at the Mechanics' Institute, (897 burgesses said to be present) to protest against the very large and rapidly increasing expenditure of the Municipal Council, and that a daily police was inexpedient. Eight resolutions were passed condemning the acts of the Council, and urging extensive curtailment in expenditure.

August 4th. – A monument to the memory of the late comedian, Charles Mathews, erected in Saint Andrew's Church, from a chaste design in the Gothic style, furnished by Mr. Whightwick, executed by Mr. Brown, of Stonehouse. August 28th. – Meeting of the Town Council at the Guildhall, when the resolutions passed at a meeting of the burgesses held at the Mechanics' Institute, 30th July, was duly considered; occupying six hours and a half in discussion, which resulted in resolutions being passed expressing the Council's opinion, that there were no grounds for the apprehensions expressed, and that the abolition of the day police would not be productive of the saving contemplated; but was necessary for efficiency and good order. August 31st. – A grand display of fireworks in the Plymouth Market, by Mr. Hannaford. September 20th. – Funeral of Sir William Elliott, (who died in command of H.M.S. the *Royal Adelaide*) whose remains were interred in the burial ground attached to Maker Church; the highest military honours being observed.

"November 7th. – A distressing calamity took place in this port, by the upsetting of a boat in the Sound, when 20 men were drowned. This heart-rending affliction turned out to be very gloomy indeed, for not less than 49 children were left fatherless, and 16 widows bereaved of the assistance of their natural protectors. The unfortunate individuals were in the employ of the Government on the Breakwater works; it being their pay-day, nearly the whole of the men in the employment left the *Chatham* hulk in three pinnaces for Catwater, two of the boats starting a short time before the third, the wind blowing a gale from the S.W., and a strong sea running. Each of the boats had a lugg sail set; but unfortunately, just as the second boat neared the Cobler Buoy where the swell was very heavy from the conflux of the tides, she turned over, and every man in her was lost before assistance could be rendered. The accident was first seen at the Citadel. The moment the news was known at the Pier, two boats put off, one belonging to Messrs. Hawker, and the other to Messrs. Treeby, but were too late to render any aid. A public meeting was held in connection with this great calamity; a committee was formed, subscriptions were opened for the benefit of the bereaved, and the sum subscribed amounted to £1,375 7s. 10d." "November 27th. – H.M. ship *Inconstant* arrived from Quebec, and anchored in the Sound, having on board the Earl and Countess of Durham and their *suite*; Lord Durham arrived in this port from Canada, having resigned the post of Governor General. Public meetings were held both in Plymouth and Devonport, by requisitions to the mayors, when addresses of congratulation were drawn up and presented to the earl. – November 27th, 28th and 29th, very severe gales of wind experienced in this port, blowing violently from E to S. A schooner in crossing the Sound missed stays, and was obliged to let go her anchor just off the Citadel; she dragged her anchor and struck on the rocks, and in a few minutes was a total wreck. A brig also came into the port from the western end of the Breakwater about 2 p.m. at the most terrific part of the gale; she came to between the Island and the main and let go her anchor, but she unfortunately was not far enough to the west; she immediately drifted, proceeding gradually towards the shore, and in less than half an hour she was a wreck. She ran a-ground near the Rusty Anchor, only a few yards from the shore. One of the men in endeavouring to jump on shore lost his life. The *Harpy*, cutter, Mr. Grundy, chief officer, lying in Millbay, seeing the dreadful situation of the seamen put off with his boat's crew of four hands, and, succeeded in taking off the men, and landing them at Gill's Quay.

December 21st. – The Eddystone examined by Mr. Burgess, Engineer, and a member of Trinity Board, in consequence of a report having been circulated that the Stone had sustained great damage during the late storm, but it was found that it had not received the slightest injury.

1839. – Joseph Collier Cookworthy, M.D., Mayor. Great rejoicings in Plymouth on account of the marriage of the Queen.

Plymouth and the neighbourhood were this year visited with the cholera, which carried off a large number of the inhabitants. from the 15th of June, when the first case of cholera appeared, to the 24th of September, when the last was reported, the total number of cases in Plymouth alone was 1,805, and the number of deaths from cholera alone 702.

January 22nd. – An accident occurred in the Sound by which four persons lost their lives by the upsetting of a boat. There were five left Catwater in a boat on a gull shooting expedition, and when outside Bovisand pier the boat struck on a rock below the surface, and very soon sank; the youngest of the party, A.S. Stuart, clung to the mast of the boat, and was saved; the others were drowned.

May 31st. – A large Chartists' meeting on the Hoe. Mr. Petrie presided, and Mr. Richardson, a delegate from the National Convention, addressed the meeting, speaking for nearly two hours.

November 12th. – A public meeting of the inhabitants was held at the Guildhall to receive a communication from T. Gill, Esq., expressive of his intention to apply to Parliament to sanction the erection of a pier at Millbay.

1840. – J.C. Cookworthy, M.D., again Mayor. A destructive fire occurred in Devonport Dockyard.

January 5th. – The new steam-ship *President* was brought into this port by the Dublin Company's steamer *Royal William*, who fell in with her off the Start in a very disabled state. She was at that time one of the most stupendous pieces of naval architecture of the day, built on purpose to run between London and New York; she was on her way from London to Liverpool for her engines, machinery, etc., and being very light and having encountered a very heavy sea became unmanageable. She was placed alongside the *Sheer Hulk* in Hamoaze, and her damage repaired by the artificers of the dockyard. January 9th. – The Earl of Saint Germans met with an accident while on board the *President*, by falling down one of the hatchways. He was conveyed to the Admiral's house and shortly after left for Saint Germans.

"February 6th. – A public meeting convened by the mayor to take into consideration the most appropriate mode of celebrating the approaching marriage of Her Majesty the Queen. February 7th. – H.M. schooner *Skipjack*, Lieut. Wright, brought into this port the Portuguese brigantine *Ulysses*, slaver, with 529 slaves on board. She was captured off the Isle of Pines, after a chase of 12 hours. The master ultimately made for the shore, with the intention of running her high and dry, in which he partly succeeded. The master's name was Fernandez, a Portuguese, who escaped with 13 passengers, taking with him, as was ascertained by documents left on board, 8,000 dollars. The 500 slaves were landed and taken to the barracks; they were robust, muscular, and perfectly docile." "February 10th. – The Queen's nuptial day was observed in this borough with the usual demonstrations of loyalty which characterize the public rejoicings of its inhabitants. The day was observed as a general holiday. All business was suspended, but there were no processions on account of the unsettled state of the weather. Many large dinner parties were formed at the various hotels, when the toast of 'The Queen and Prince Albert, may God bless them,' was received with enthusiasm. The poor also were not forgotten. A sum amounting to nearly £200 was collected, and a committee of gentlemen formed for the purpose distributed to nearly 2,000 poor persons ample means of obtaining a good dinner on the auspicious day. Public buildings and many private houses were decorated with flags; the streets were crowded with the inhabitants and persons from the adjoining country. Mr. G. Polkinghorne, of George-street, Plymouth, Her Majesty's Confectioner, prepared the royal bridecake, which was cut up and presented to upwards of 800 persons on the marriage day. Devonport and Stonehouse also displayed their loyalty and attachment to their Sovereign on this joyous occasion in a similar way. The ships in the harbour were splendidly dressed with flags. In the evening H.M. ships *Impregnable* and *St. Joseph* were brilliantly illuminated, blue lights being exhibited from the ports, and greatly admired by the spectators who lined the shores." February 22nd. – A public meeting held at the Guildhall for an address of congratulation to Her Majesty on her marriage with His Royal Highness Prince Albert, which was agreed to, and the mayor requested to present the same in person.

April 22nd. – A rather indecorous proceeding at the Barbican. A man belonging to one of the mackerel boats lying in the Pool got drunk and made a disturbance. In consequence a policeman took him in custody, and was taking him to the station-house – but being overpowered the man was taken away and carried on board the boat. The policeman, fearing serious riot, sent to the mayor and the station-house. The mayor, with the superintendent and a body of police soon arrived. The mayor was told that they had rescued the prisoner, pointing out the boat he was in, when he, the superintendent and others of the police, got on board and demanded the man. Just as they got on board the crew hoisted the jib and the boat proceeded to sea. The mayor ultimately prevailed on the crew to put the boat back. The man and several others were afterwards brought before the magistrates and fined for their misconduct.

May 26th. – The foundation stone of Trinity Church laid by the Rev. J. Hatchard. According to arrangements, the Members of the Town Council, the subscribers to the building, and the clergy of the neighbourhood and others met the mayor and magistrates at the Guildhall, and walked in procession to the ground in Southside-street. After the proceedings were over, with a view to commemorate the gratifying event, the Rev. J. Hatchard was presented with an elegant and massive silver salver, a chaste silver tea service, and a richly bound quarto Bible, subscribed for by members of his congregation and other inhabitants of the town. The following inscription was engraved on the salver: "Presented to the Rev. John Hatchard, M.A., Vicar of the Parish of Saint Andrew, Plymouth, on the 47th anniversary of his birth, by various members of his congregation and other friends, to commemorate their approval of his ministry during the 16 years he has held that important office; of his unremitting exertions in all works of charity; and especially of his success in raising the funds for the building of Trinity Church." May 27th. – South Devon and East Cornwall Hospital opened.

June 27th. – The Commissioners appointed to enquire into the comparative advantages of the ports in the channel for a Packet Station arrived in this town, when a number of qualified persons gave evidence before them, showing the superiority of Plymouth over other ports as a rendezvous for steam packets intended to convey the Mediterranean and West India Mails.

September 1st. – The trawling sloop *Two Brothers*, of this port, seized by the officers of the *Busy*, having on board about a ton and a half of smuggled tobacco. September 10th. – The new Corn and Fish Markets opened. The Cattle Market this year removed from the back of the Market to the Tavistock-road, and the Market generally altered.

October 27th. – Great fire in the Devonport Dockyard. The first discovery was shortly after 4 o'clock (Sunday morning), when a policeman perceived flames issuing from the ship *Talavera*, then in dock under repair; he gave an alarm, but within a few minutes and before any effectual assistance could be brought, the ship was completely enveloped in fire from stem to stern. The alarm soon spread, the bell at the gate was rung as a notice to those employed in the establishment, and orders at first were given to allow no one to enter but the persons employed; but as the flames increased and the terror became greater, the gates were thrown open and assistance was readily rendered. The Dockyard engines were soon put in operation, but so intense were the flames that for some time the immense body of water had little or no effect. The engines belonging to the Marines,

Victualling Yard, Royal Hospital, and other Government places, and the soldiers of various regiments, with their engines, together with the Devonport and Plymouth engines, were soon on the spot. All the disposable police force of Plymouth was despatched to the yard as extra guards. Many thousands of persons entered the gates before 6 o'clock, and used every effort to assist the authorities. Fortunately the morning was very calm, scarcely a breath of wind blowing, and to this circumstance, aided by the immense body of water thrown from the engines and the admirable arrangements made, was the preservation of this establishment owing. From 6 o'clock it was clear that the volume of flames was decreasing, and the fire gradually sank, till at 8 o'clock, all danger might be said to be over, though the engines at that hour were in constant play. The *Talavera*, 74 guns, was literally burnt down; the *Imogene* frigate of 26 guns, was also totally burnt; the *Minden,* 74 guns, was greatly injured, being burnt from the bows to the fore chains, and inside her deck and beams as far as the main hatchway; also the Adelaide Gallery, nearly 200 feet in length, perished in the flames, and the fine old figure-heads, and other memorable relics were destroyed. The origin of the fire was not ascertained, but the opinion of the most competent judges was, that it was an act on incendiarism.

"October 30th. – The Directors of the Plymouth Company of New Zealand, to commemorate the sailing of their first ship from this port to their settlement of New Plymouth, gave a splendid entertainment to the nobility and gentry of the neighbourhood at the Royal Hotel." A very severe gale experienced in the autumn; the tide rose exceedingly high; most of the lower parts of the town were flooded. "The new tenor bell of St. Andrew's Church, cast by Meares, was put up on the 17th of July, this year; it weighed a quarter of a hundred weight less than the former one, which had been cast in 1748, and was cracked and rendered useless in 1839." St. Andrew's Church new roofed.

1841. – George William Soltau, Mayor. Thomas Gill and Viscount Ebrington, Members of Parliament. Alderman J. Johnson an unsuccessful candidate. The "British Association for the Advancement of Science," this year held its annual meeting at Plymouth and Devonport – called the "Plymouth Meeting" – under the Presidency of the Rev. Professor Whewell, F.R.S.; the Vice-Presidents being the Earl of Mount Edgcumbe, the Earl of Morley, Lord Eliot, Sir C. Lemon, Bart., and Sir T.D. Acland, Bart.; and the Local Secretaries, Sir W. Snow Harris, Col. Hamilton Smith, Robert Were Fox, Esq., and Richard Taylor, junr., Esq. The meeting commenced on the 29th of July, and ended on the 4th of August.

January 4th. – The members of the Natural History Society assembled for the first time, in their newly fitted-up rooms at the Royal Union Baths, Union-street. "January 9th. – A court martial held on board H.M. ship *San Joseph,* in Hamoaze, on George Hobbs, gunner of H.M. packet, *Pigeon.* The prisoner was arraigned on four charges – being drunk and disorderly, repeated drunkenness, insubordination and disobedience of orders, and for striking his superior officer, the master of the *Pigeon.* The prisoner pleaded guilty, and was sentenced to be hung on the yard arm of one of H.M. ships in Hamoaze."

"February 12th. – A very severe gale in the neighbourhood from the north-east, a heavy fall of snow during the night; from the drift, in many places travelling was completely put a stop to. The *Quicksilver* mail left at its usual time, a quarter-past nine; but at Smithalee, between Ridgway and Ivybridge, the coach was completely imbedded in snow – in many places it being eight or ten feet deep; after great difficulty the coach was extricated, and the mail bags were taken out. On information being conveyed to Mr. Marks, the Plymouth Postmaster, he proceeded to the spot in a coach and four, obtained the assistance of the road surveyor, and with the aid of seventy men, by the following morning, a road was cut through the drift, and the coaches were enabled to proceed. The mail due here at 4 o'clock on Saturday did not arrive till noon on Sunday. The bags were conveyed from Ivybridge on saddled horses. During the gale a Dutch barque, with a cargo of sugar and wool, was driven from her moorings at the western end of the Breakwater, and but for the energy and skill of John Eddy, a Cawsand pilot, the vessel would have been dashed to pieces on Penlee rocks. Most providentially for the lives of all on board, Eddy succeeded in running the ship on Cawsand beach. Also at the same time a Jersey packet working into the harbour ran on shore under the Citadel, but was got off shortly after, and in safety reached Millbay."

"February 22nd. – The first stone of the Lighthouse upon the western extremity of the Plymouth Breakwater laid by Admiral Warren, Superintendent of the Plymouth Dockyard. The time fixed for the ceremony was 12 o'clock, but owing to a dense fog the Admiral was prevented from reaching the Breakwater until nearly 3 o'clock, although he embarked in his yacht at 11 in the morning. After the necessary preparations were made, Admiral Warren and his party, and many of the inhabitants of Plymouth and its vicinity, who had been waiting on the Breakwater to witness the ceremony assembled round the site, when Mr. Stuart, the Superintendent Engineer, briefly explained the object of the Lighthouse, and that it was 28 years since the commencement of the Breakwater; that 3,362,727 tons of stone had been deposited there, and that the whole outlay did not exceed £1,200,000. The stone having been duly laid, Mr. Walker, the Queen's Harbour Master, proposed three cheers for the Queen and Prince Albert, which being heartily given, concluded the imposing ceremony." The foundation stone of the Devon and Cornwall Female Orphan Asylum, at the head of Lockyer-street, laid May 11th, by Sir Ralph Lopes, Bart. Mr George Wightwick was the architect. Collections made and blankets given to the poor in honour of the birth of the Prince of Wales, who was born in November this year. A new window and altar piece put up in St. Andrew's Church.

1842. – William Prance, Mayor.

1843. – Nicholas Lockyer, Mayor. Trinity Church, in Southside-street, erected. Plymouth visited by the Queen and the Prince Consort, who arrived in the Royal yacht. Her Majesty was escorted from the Dockyard through the Three Towns by the Mayors and Corporations, and addresses were presented from each of the Three Towns. Bonfires were lit on the Hoe.

1844. – Philip Edward Lyne, Mayor. Portland Chapel, in Portland-place, erected. The Western College, Radnor-place, established. Millbay pier opened. Baptist Chapel, George-street, built.

1845. – Benjamin Parham, Mayor. The Plymouth and Stonehouse Gas Light and Coke Company incorporated by Act of Parliament on the 30th of June, Christ Church, Eton-place, erected from the designs on Mr. Wightwick. The Grand Duke Constantine of Russia arrived at Plymouth, and was very cordially received by all the nobility and the authorities.

1846. – Thomas Hillersden Bulteel, Mayor. On occasion of Lord Ebrington becoming a Lord of the Treasury, an election took place, when he was opposed by Henry Vincent, who, however only obtained 188 votes. The Plymouth, Devonport and Stonehouse Cemetery Company established by Act of Parliament. The Cornwall Railway Company incorporated by Act of Parliament.

At 9 o'clock on Friday morning, August 21st, Her Majesty Queen Victoria arrived off the Port of Plymouth, the Royal yacht being signalled by the *Harpy* Revenue cutter. The Royal yacht, the *Victoria and Albert*, with the Royal Standard floating at the main, quickly hove in sight, followed by the *Fairy* and the *Black Eagle* Admiralty steamer. A Royal salute was fired from the *Caledonia* guard-ship in Hamoaze, and salutes were also fired from H.M.S. *Contest*, as well as from the Citadel and Mount Wise, and the batteries at Mount Edgcumbe. About 10 o'clock, the Royal yacht, with its precious freight, anchored safely at the moorings prepared for her in Barn Pool. Sir John West, K.C.B., Commander-in-Chief of this port and the other officers, at once proceeded to pay their respects to Her Majesty, and a guard of honour proceeded to Mount Edgcumbe, where every preparation had been made for Her Majesty's landing. Her Majesty however deferred her landing and that of H.R.H. the Prince Consort until the next (Saturday) morning. At half-past 1 o'clock, the Queen and the Prince Consort left the Royal yacht and went on board the *Fairy* for the purpose of making an excursion up the Saint Germans river to sight Port Eliot, the seat of the Earl of Saint Germans, and returned on board at half-past 5 and then proceeded up the Tamar to Cothele. At Cothele the Royal party landed and were conveyed through the grounds, and the old mansion of Cothele, Her Majesty remaining an hour in the house, and passing through and examining all the rooms. The Prince of Wales and the Princess Royal passed the afternoon at Mount Edgcumbe. The Mayor of Plymouth, Mr. Benjamin Parham, hastily summoned a special meeting of the Council. On the Saturday morning, shortly after 7 o'clock, the Prince Consort landed at Millbay pier and proceeded in the Royal carriage to Dartmoor where he inspected the Naptha Works, and then walked to Tor Royal House, from whence he returned to Millbay and so on board the Royal yacht. At 10 o'clock, the Queen and the two Royal children landed on Mount Edgcumbe and were received by the Earl and Countess and there remained enjoying the grounds till 12 o'clock, when they re-embarked to await the return of the Prince Consort, when they again landed, lunched at Mount Edgcumbe House with the Earl and Countess, and again went on board at 4 o'clock. At 5 o'clock, the Queen, the Prince Consort, and the Royal children went on board the *Fairy* yacht and steamed across the Sound, passed close up to the southern side of the harbour by Mount Batten, Turnchapel, and Oreston, where she moored to a buoy off Pomphlett Lake. The Queen and Prince then entered the yacht's cutter and were rowed under Laira Bridge by Chelson Meadow to the woods of Saltram, and then rejoined the *Fairy*, and, after nearing Catdown quarries and rounding the Bear's Head and Queen Anne's Battery, came close to the piers of Sutton Pool. Here the Royal party remained some time and then re-crossing the Sound, entered Millbay and then again went on board the *Victoria and Albert*. The Royal Marine Band played on board the *Victoria and Albert* during dinner, at the express desire of the Queen, the programme of music being her own selection. On Sunday morning the Royal party left Barn Pool for Guernsey, under Royal salutes from every available place. August 28th. – The Duke of Wellington arrived at Plymouth on an official visit, and remained at the Royal Hotel until the morning of the 30th.

1847. – James Moore, Mayor. Viscount Ebrington and Roundell Palmer, (afterwards Attorney-General) Members of Parliament. C.B. Calmady an unsuccessful candidate. Mr. Henry Woollcombe died February 14th, aged 70. The foundation stone of Union Congregational Chapel, in Courtenay street, laid in July, by David Derry, Esq.

1848. – William Burnell, Mayor. The new Post-office, erected from the designs of Mr. Arthur, opened in March. Eldad Chapel, now St. Peter's, licensed. The Cemetery, Pennycomequick, opened.

1849. – John Moore, Mayor. The South Devon Railway opened from Exeter to Plymouth, and thus placed in connection with all parts of the kingdom. The new prisons on North-hill completed at a cost of £12,500. Plymouth, with Devonport, Stonehouse, Stoke Damerel and the neighbourhood, was visited with the cholera, and the visitation was so violent, that from the 4th of July, when the first death occurred, to the 8th of November, when the last was registered, no less than 819 deaths from cholera occurred in Plymouth alone, while those in the adjoining towns were even a greater number. At this time, temporary cholera hospitals were erected in the Five Fields. The new Mechanics' Institution, Princess-square, erected from the designs of Messrs. Wightwick and Damant.

1850. – David Derry, Mayor. Saint Peter's Church, Eldad, commonly known as Eldad Chapel, consecrated. The Public Baths and Wash-houses, established principally through the exertions of Rev. W. Odgers, opened. On the 22nd of January, a public meeting was held in the Guildhall, at which the mayor presided, and Lord Ebrington, Lord Morley, Rev. W. Odgers, and others, took part in the proceedings. They afterwards visited the wash-houses, when about 300 poor women had tea and cake given them; after which they were shown the mode of heating the water, and the various conveniences for washing. They were allowed to occupy the wash-houses during the first week free of charge.

1851. – Alfred Rooker, Mayor.

1852. – Herbert Mends Gibson, Mayor. Charles John Mare and Robert Porrett Collier (afterwards Sir Robert Porrett Collier, Solicitor-General), Members of Parliament; Sir Roundell Palmer, G.T. Braine, and Bickham Escott, unsuccessful candidates. Mr. Mare was afterwards unseated, on petition, for bribery. Her Majesty Queen Victoria and the Prince Consort visited Plymouth.

1853. – Copleston Lopes Radcliffe, Mayor. Sir Roundell Palmer, Member of Parliament, in room of Charles John Mare, unseated; G.T. Braine an unsuccessful candidate. The Cottonian Library, in connection with the

Plymouth Public Library, in Cornwall-street, opened on the 1st of June; the new front and additional buildings having been erected from the designs of Messrs. Wightwick and Damant. The Bath and West of England Agricultural Society held its annual meeting and Cattle Show at Plymouth in June.

1854. – Thomas Stevens, Mayor. Plymouth adopted the provisions of the "Public Health Act," and thus did away with the old Board of Improvement Commissioners, and its Corporation became a Local Board of Health.

1855. – John Kelly, Mayor. The Church of Saint John the Evangelist, Jubilee-street, Sutton-on-Plym, erected from the designs of Mr. Benjamin Ferrey, and was consecrated in June by the Bishop of Exeter.

1856. – Francis F. Bulteel, Mayor. Hans Hansen was found guilty of wilfully murdering Charles Jacobi, his brother soldier in the Jagar regiment of the German Legion, at Maker on the 13th of March.

1857. – Richard Hicks, Mayor. Robert Porrett Collier and James White, Members of Parliament, John Hardy an unsuccessful candidate. The first tube of the Royal Albert Tubular Bridge floated, and fixed to its piers on the 1st of September. As by means of this bridge, Plymouth became connected with the Cornish Coast by a direct line of railway, the following interesting particulars of the event are worth preserving: – "Temporary docks were cut at the ends of the tube for the admission of four pontoons – two at each end. These pontoons draw about 8 ft. 6 in. of water, and were capable of sustaining a weight of 500 tons each, or 2,000 tons in the whole. As the weight of the section which they had to float is 1,100 tons, it will be seen that ample power had been provided. By means of valves, the pontoons admit water into their interiors, and having by this means been sunk to some extent, they were passed beneath the ends of the tubes. Five vessels, borrowed from the Government authorities, were moored in different positions in the river, one being placed on the eastern side, another in the centre of the stream, and a third at the western side, above the bridge; the other two being moored lower down. On board these were stationed a number of men from the Dockyard and Her Majesty's ships, with powerful crabs for the purpose of warping the tube to its position. Four more hawsers were attached to as many windlasses at different points on shore, and arrangements had been made to guide and control the pontoons in every direction as they floated onwards with their gigantic burden. The plan adopted for directing the operations of the workmen and labourers engaged was that of signal flags from a temporary platform, in the centre of the tube, which was under the immediate and entire control of Mr. Brunel. Early in the morning, the men were engaged in pumping out the water which had been let into the pontoons, in order to render them more buoyant, and as the tide rose they rose also, and thus the ponderous weight of the tube was thrown upon them. It was calculated that the tide would have risen sufficiently to float the mass soon after 1 o'clock, and at 1h. 15m. the monster tube was seen to float. Gradually it moved out, first one end and then the other, until it reached the centre. The assembled crowds saw with astonishment this huge mass moving without the slightest sound. Not a voice was heard, not a direction was spoken; a few flags waved, a few boards with numbers on them were exhibited, and, as by some mysterious agency, the tube and rail borne on the pontoons travelled to the resting-place, and, with the impressive silence which is the highest evidence of power, it slid, as it were, into its position without an accident, without any extraordinary mechanical effort, without a "misfit" to the extent of the eighth of an inch. Equally without haste and without delay just as the tide reached its limit, at 3 o'clock, the tube was fixed on the piers about 30 feet above high water, and the band of the Royal Marines, which was stationed in a vessel near Saltash, struck up "See the conquering hero comes," and then "God save the Queen," when the assembled multitude broke out into loud and continued cheers in expression of their admiration and delight. Numbers of boats immediately passed under the railway, which was some 8 feet above high water, and people touched the iron road ere it should become elevated to the height it was destined to occupy. At 5 o'clock, the tide was found to have sufficiently receded for the removal of the pontoons. The shores were knocked away, the wedges were removed, and the heavy mass rested independently on the piers, from which it was afterwards gradually raised by hydraulic pressure. For this purpose the hydraulic presses were fixed, and the first lift of the tube was made on the 25th November 1857.

1858. – James Skardon, Mayor. The second tube of the Royal Albert Tubular Bridge floated to its place July 10th. The Roman Catholic Church of Saint Mary and Boniface, in Cecil-street, opened in March. The Higher Mills destroyed by fire. The Old Mitre Tavern, in Southside-street, burnt down.

1859. – John Burnell, Mayor. Robert Porrett Collier and Viscount Valletort, Members of Parliament; James White an unsuccessful candidate.

Monday, May 2nd. – The Royal Albert Bridge opened by H.R.H. Prince Albert in person. The Mayors of Plymouth (Mr. James Skardon) and Devonport (Mr. Wilson) invited to the opening, and the next day the mayor attended the *déjuner*, the railway being on that day opened to the public. The "South Devon and Cornwall Institution for the Indigent Blind" established at Plymouth through the exertions of Mr. Gale. "May 6th. – A train ran off the railway line at Saint Germans, and the engine was buried ten feet; three men killed."

This gigantic bridge, in its completed state, which connects Devonshire with Cornwall by means of the Cornwall Railway, is shown above. The bridge consists of nineteen spans, or arches, seventeen of which are comparatively narrow, and the remaining two of immense width. These two, which rest on a single cast iron pier of four columns, in the centre of the river, span the whole width of the Tamar, no less than 910 feet – the entire length of the bridge being 2,240 feet, or 300 feet longer than the Britannia Tubular Bridge. The greatest width on the basement is 30 feet, and its highest elevation, from foundation to summit, is no less than 260 feet. The total quantity of wrought iron in the bridge is 2,650 tons; of cast iron, about 1,200 tons; of stone masonry and brickwork, about 1,700 or 1,800 cubic yards; and of timber, about 1,500 cubic feet.

1860. – William Luscombe, Mayor. New reservoir at Hartley opened , and abattoirs built.

1861. – William Derry, Mayor. Walter Morrison, Member of Parliament in room of Viscount Valletort, who this year succeeded to the title and estates of his father, the Earl of Mount Edgcumbe. Hon. W, Addington an unsuccessful candidate. Special services and general mourning on occasion of the death of H.R.H. the Prince Consort. A marble bust of Sir Joshua

Reynolds, by Behnes, commissioned by subscription, presented to the Cottonian Library. The British Archaeological Association Congress at Exeter opened in August. The Western College opened in June.

1862. – William Derry, Mayor. The Plymouth Life-boat "The Prince Consort," the cost of which was presented to the Royal National Life-boat Institution, (John-street, Adelphi) by Miss Burdett Coutts, now the Baroness Burdett Coutts, inaugurated this year. The boat, of which we give the engraving overleaf, is a 34 feet ten-oared boat, and is provided with a launching carriage and full equipments. It is kept in a substantial house, built specially for its reception, on the western side of Millbay. From the time of the establishment of this Life-boat station this year (1862), down to the time of publication, the *Prince Consort* has been instrumental in saving about 40 lives from different wrecks besides going on several occasions of imminent peril.

The Clock Tower and Bell Turret erected in George-street; its entire height 60 feet. It is constructed principally of blue and pink limestone, the quoins of light limestone, and the centre part blue, with bands of granite. There are three drinking fountains of elegantly carved Portland stone on the north, east, and west sides, and a doorway on the south. Over the fountains, on a string-course, is the inscription – "Erected 1862. William Derry, Mayor." About 15 feet up the shaft are the Plymouth Arms, cut in Portland stone. At the top is the clock, on which Mr. Derry expended, as a free gift, some £400 or more, and this is surmounted by an elegant bell turret. The architect was Mr. Henry Hall, of London; and the builders were Messrs. Call and Pethick, of Plymouth. The town expended £300 on the erection of the tower, Mr. Derry paying all additional cost and presenting the clock.

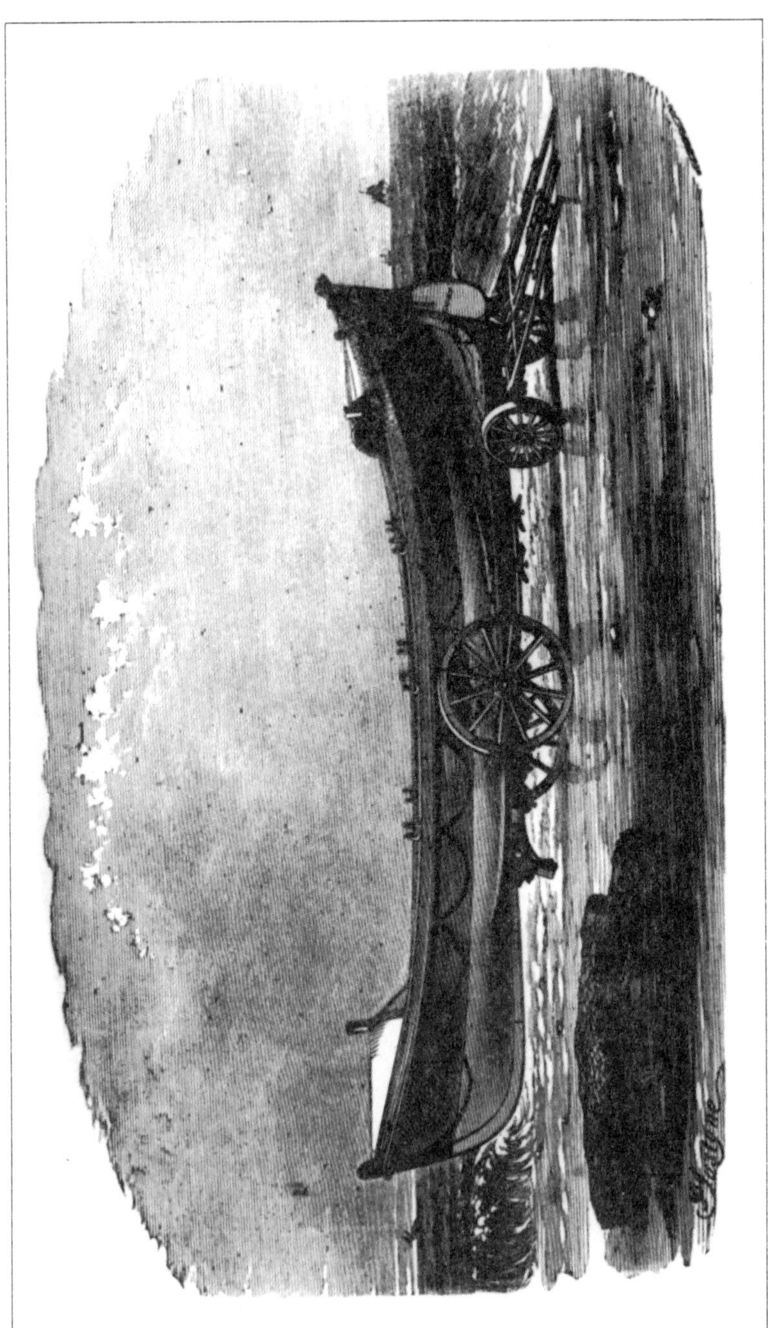

A portrait of H.R.H. the Prince Consort was this year placed in the Guildhall, at a cost of about £80. Proposal mooted for establishing an "Albert Museum" at Plymouth. Foundation stone of Sherwell Congregational Chapel, in the Tavistock-road, laid by David Derry, Esq., in September. Blondin performed at the Citadel.

1863. – Charles Norrington, Mayor. The Theatre Royal partly destroyed by fire. Mr William Cotton, the donor of the Cottonian Library, Plymouth, died January 22nd, aged 69, at 8, West Hoe-terrace.

Great rejoicing on occasion of the marriage of H.R.H. the Prince of Wales with the Princess Alexandra of Denmark. H.R.H. the Prince of Wales appointed Lord High Steward of the Borough of Plymouth, on which occasion a beautiful casket, enclosing the patent of his appointment, was presented to him. The casket was of oak, elaborately mounted in silver, with the arms, motto, etc., of the Prince and those of the Borough of Plymouth, elegantly engraved, and bore the following inscription: – "Presented to His Royal Highness Albert Edward, Prince of Wales, together with the patent of office of High Steward of the Borough of Plymouth, to which His Royal Highness was appointed by the Council of the said borough, in succession to his late Royal Father, January 14th, A.D. 1863." Robert Porrett Collier, Esq., M.P. for Plymouth, was knighted in November.

1864. – Charles Norrington, Mayor. Sir Robert Porrett Collier, re-elected on his becoming Solicitor-General. The Sherwell Congregational Chapel, in the Tavistock-road, opened. The new Albert Wing of the South Devon and East Cornwall Hospital was opened in February. The following inscription was in 1835 engraved on a plate imbedded in the foundation stone: – "The foundation stone of the South Devon and East Cornwall Hospital and Public Dispensary was laid on the 6th of August, 1835, by the Rev. John Hatchard, M.A., at the request and in the presence of the committee and subscribers, in grateful acknowledgement of the Divine favour through which they have been enabled to begin the building, and in humble reliance upon the blessing of God on their endeavours to carry the charitable objects of the institution thus commenced into effect. George Wightwick, Architect." In April, General Garibaldi, accompanied by the Duke and Duchess of Sutherland, passed through Plymouth on his way to Penquite, and was received at the railway station by the Mayor, Charles Norrington, Esq., the ex-Mayor, W. Derry, Esq.; the Committee of Reception, and other officials. A bouquet was presented to the General by the Misses Norrington and the reception was very enthusiastic. Addresses were presented to him at Penquite. Foundation of the new Wesleyan Chapel,

King-street, laid May 17th. A silver cup, bearing the inscription, "Presented by the Corporation of Plymouth to the Mayor, Charles Norrington, Esq., on the occasion of the birth of a son to him," on one side, and on the other, the borough arms, presented to the mayor. A testimonial presented to Dr. Cookworthy on his resignation of the office of senior physician to the Plymouth Public Dispensary.

1865. – Francis Hicks, Mayor. Sir Robert Porrett Collier and Walter Morrison, Members of Parliament. R. Stuart Lane an unsuccessful candidate. Sir Charles Lock Eastlake, R.A., died in December. The Royal Agricultural Society of England held its annual meeting at Plymouth, the show yards occupying nearly 30 acres of ground, being situated at the back of Pennycomequick, near the Saltash-road, and the dinner pavillion near the Hoe. The meeting commenced on the 12th of July, and closed on Friday, the 21st of the same month. The President was Sir E.C. Kerrison, Bart., M.P. On this occasion Plymouth was honoured by a visit from their Royal Highnesses the Prince and Princess of Wales, who anchored in Barn Pool, off Mount Edgcumbe, on the 18th of July, amid salutes from all the batteries. Upon coming to anchor the Earl of Mount Edgcumbe went on board the Royal yacht to meet his Royal guests, and in the afternoon a deputation from the Plymouth Corporation, consisting of the Mayor (C. Norrington Esq.), the Town Clerk (C. Whiteford, Esq.), and Messrs. H. M. Gibson, S. Jackson, J. Skardon, and J. Kelly went on board the Royal yacht to present an address from the Corporation, and were graciously received, as was also a deputation from the Corporation of Devonport. Shortly after 4 o'clock preparations were made on shore for the landing of the Royal visitors, and about 5 o'clock they landed and at once proceeded to Mount Edgcumbe House. The 2nd Devon Administrative Battalion of Volunteers including the Plymouth, Devonport, Stonehouse and Tavistock corps, were in attendance as a guard of honour to their Royal Highnesses, under the command of Lieutenant-Colonel Fisk. The following day, Wednesday, their Royal Highnesses left Mount Edgcumbe a few minutes before one and landed from the Royal barge at the Royal William Victualling Office, where they were received by the mayors of Plymouth and Devonport, and where every preparation had been made. At 1 o'clock the Prince and Princess, with the Countess de Grey and the Earl of Mount Edgcumbe, entered the first carriage, drawn by four horses, and attended by a guard of honour. The suite followed in other carriages, the mayors of Plymouth and Devonport bringing up the rear. The *cortége* then proceeded along Durnford-street, Millbay-road, past the Duke of Cornwall Hotel, the Athenaeum, Theatre, and Royal

Hotel, and so along George-street, Russell-street, York-street, and St. Michael's-terrace, to the Show Yard at Pennycomequick, the whole line of route being lined with an immense concourse of enthusiastic spectators, and the windows and house-tops lined with ladies, while triumphal arches and flags were everywhere to be seen. At the Show Yard they were met by the President of the Society, Sir Edward Kerrison, Bart., M.P.; Lieut-General Lord Templetown, Commander of the Western District; Sir W. Fairfax, A.D.C.; Colonel Mann, the Town Major; Lord Vivian, the Lord-Lieutenant of Cornwall; the mayors of Plymouth and Devonport, the Lord of the Manor of Devonport, and several members of the Council of the Society. In the Show Yard the reception was of the most hearty and enthusiastic character, and the Royal visitors, with their party, remained for some time and partook of an elegant luncheon which had been provided for the occasion. They then re-entered the carriages and proceeded direct to Saltash Passage, where, after viewing the Royal Albert Bridge, they embarked on board the *Princess Alice* – the Admiral's yacht – and proceeded down Hamoaze to the Sound, under salutes from all the ships in commission. The yacht conveyed their Royal Highnesses first to the *Magenta,* one of the French Squadron, where they were received with a Royal salute, which was returned from the Citadel. They then visited all the French, Austrian, and English vessels of war in the Sound in succession, and at about a quarter to seven in the evening re-landed at Mount Edgcumbe, under a Royal salute from the battery. In the evening the band of the Royal Marines played during dinner, and were afterwards, at the express wish of the Prince, retained for the dance, in which their Royal Highnesses took part. The party did not break up until 3 o'clock in the morning. On this day, Mr. Gale, the electrician, of Plymouth, who had discovered a process by which gunpowder can be rendered non-explosive and its combustible properties easily restored when required, exhibited experiments in the lawn at Mount Edgcumbe, before the Prince and Princess of Wales, the Duke of St. Albans, Lord Skelmersdale, Lady Skelmersdale, the Countess of Dalkeith, the Countess de Grey, Lord George Hamilton, Lady Bertha Hamilton, the Earl of Mount Edgcumbe, the Dowager Countess of Mount Edgcumbe, Mr. Cust, General Knollys, and Major Grey. The trial was first made on about one pound of the ordinary blasting powder, which within a comparatively short space of time was rendered non-explosive, and the slow match was applied. The result of the application was merely the causing the ignition of the grains of the powder which came in immediate contact with the flame, which otherwise did not have the least effect on the body of the powder, the inventor holding the vessel containing the material in his hand. The powder was subsequently made explosive without any diminution in its strength or loss in its weight, and the Prince, at the Termination, expressed himself satisfied with the experiment, and with the value of the discovery. On Thursday a large number of noblemen and ladies and gentlemen of the neighbourhood were invited to luncheon in the grounds of Mount Edgcumbe with their Royal Highnesses. The Earl of Mount Edgcumbe issued the invitations, which were rather numerous, and most select. Precisely at 3 o'clock the Royal party and suite left the Earl of Mount Edgcumbe's house, the leading steps of which were covered with crimson carpet. An open carriage was in waiting to receive them, and in it their Royal Highnesses and the Earl of Mount Edgcumbe and the Dowager Countess of Mount Edgcumbe seated themselves. The rest of the party found places in other carriages placed at their disposal. The procession then started, and proceeding along the carriage drive in front of the house, turned into the road leading to Cremyll under a long avenue of trees, at the bottom of which they sharply turned to the right to the entrance of the flower gardens of the Park; they then proceeded to within a few feet of the people who were assembled to meet them. As the Royal party entered the orangery the Marine Band struck up "God bless the Prince of Wales." About an hour having been spent in luncheon, the party broke up, and they then promenaded in the lawn of the orangery. The Prince entered into conversation with those on the ground, and the Princess, after walking in the lawn for some time, took a carriage drive, attended by the Dowager Countess of Mount Edgcumbe, to the Barn Pool and visited the fort there. During luncheon the band of the Plymouth Division of Royal Marines attended. After the Prince and Princess of Wales had driven around the Park, they proceeded to Cremyll beach, where they embarked on board the Admiralty barge and landed at the Dockyard, where they were received by the heads of the departments. The General's (Lord Templetown) carriage was in waiting, and took the Royal party to his house on Mount Wise, where their Royal Highnesses dined. About thirty-four persons of the highest rank sat down to dinner; most of them being those who had been present at Mount Edgcumbe. The reception of the party in Devonport was most enthusiastic, for notwithstanding the short notice given, the streets through which the Royal carriages had to pass were crowded. In the evening a grand ball, got up by the officers of the United Service at this port, to do honour to the French Navy now in Hamoaze, was held with the greatest *éclat* at the Royal William Victualling Yard; the presence of the Prince and Princess of Wales investing it with additional interest. The utmost anxiety was evinced to obtain tickets, and the Ball Committee did their best to oblige all so far as it lay in their power. Many were of course disappointed, but large and capacious as was the ball-room, it was not half large enough for the immense number who thought they had some claims to be in the presence of Royalty. The committee, on whom devolved the duty of the arrangements, displayed excellent taste in the fitting up of the rooms. The walls were surrounded with the flags of all nations. At the end of the ball-room was erected a throne on a slightly elevated dais, and surmounted by a canopy of flags, consisting of the Royal Standard, the French tricolour, and others. On either side was a beautiful star formed on the left of R.A. swords, and on the right a star of sea service swords. The room was lit up with 200 jets of gas, and as all the officers were in full-dress uniform, the ball-room, when full, presented a most elegant appearance. Adjoining the ball-room, and running off from the part nearest the throne at right angles, was the supper-room, in which there was a most beautiful display of everything that could gratify the eye or satisfy the palate. At about 10 o'clock the company began to assemble. A guard of honour was stationed opposite the entrance to the apartments, and the spacious front in the Royal William Victualling Yard was soon lined with carriages. The company as they arrived were received by the officer with the Prince of Wales and the party who had been dining at Lord Templetown's, drove up, and as his Royal Highness alighted the band struck up "God save the Queen." The Prince was accompanied by the Earl of Mount Edgcumbe, the Duke of Somerset, and the other Lords of the Admiralty, Viscount Templetown, Admiral Sir Charles Freemantle, and a bevy of ladies. On reaching the ball-room the Prince proceeded to the throne, where, for a time, he was the observed of all observers. The scene at this time was most brilliant and beautiful, and the whole affair passed off in the most admirable and enjoyable manner. On the following day (Friday) the Royal party remained at Mount Edgcumbe during the early part of the day, and at 3 o'clock the Prince, with the family of his noble host, unaccompanied, however, by the Princess, went on board the *Princess Alice*, the Port Admiral's steam yacht, and took a cruise up the River Tamar as far as Cothele, and returned shortly after seven in the evening. By this time it had become generally known that His Royal Highness would first proceed to the yacht, and from thence to Mount Edgcumbe in a barge. Consequently a large number of persons, chiefly ladies, had assembled at the landing stage on the beach. The Prince, on landing, was cheered, and in response raised his hat as he passed along. In the evening it was announced that the Prince and Princess had invited a select party to dine with them on board the *Osborne*, and at 8 o'clock the Prince was observed leaving the mansion, which was the occasion for additional cheering. His Royal Highness wore an evening suit, over which he had on a light walking coat, and across his breast the blue ribbon was suspended. The Princess shortly afterwards arrived in a carriage, drawn by two horses, and was accompanied by Lady de Grey and the Earl of Mount Edgcumbe. The Princess, on alighting, was warmly and enthusiastically cheered, and bowed her acknowledgments. She was then led to the barge by the Earl of Mount Edgcumbe, when the greatest eagerness was evinced by the assembled throng to obtain a glimpse of the fair guest. The remainder of the party from Mount Edgcumbe, consisting chiefly of the Royal suite, and the members of the Edgcumbe family, subsequently went on board, where they were joined by the several guests that had been invited to attend. The band belonging to the French Squadron was present and played in an admirable manner a select programme of music in the forecastle of the yacht. The dinner was of a sumptuous character, and was held in the dining saloon on the upper decks of the vessels. In the evening the yacht was beautifully illuminated, and the scene was witnessed by persons who congregated in large numbers on the eminences best calculated for seeing it to advantage. The following day the Royal visit was brought to a close.

1866. – William Radford, Mayor. This year the Cattle Plague raged to an alarming extent. Day of humiliation fixed for March 9th, when all places closed at 5 o'clock, in accordance with a notice from the mayor. The King street Wesleyan Chapel opened on the 1st of March.

1867. – William Radford, Mayor. Sir William Snow Harris, F.R.S., died at his residence in Lockyer-street, January 22nd, aged 76.

1868. – Alexander Hubbard, Mayor. Sir Robert Porrett Collier and Walter Morrison, Members of Parliament; the first election under the second Reform Act. R. Stuart Lane, an unsuccessful candidate. Soon after the election, which took place in November, Sir Robt. P. Collier became Attorney-General, and was re-elected without opposition in December.

1869. – William Luscombe, Mayor. The Rev. John Hatchard, Vicar of St. Andrew's Church, died in December. Mr. Hatchard had been for 45 years vicar of this parish, and his funeral was a very marked one. "The procession, which was conducted by a *posse* of policemen, under the direction of Superintendents Wreford and Thomas, was formed at the vicarage, in Westwell-street, at half-past 10 o'clock, and such were its dimensions that the intervening space between the vicarage and St. Andrew's Church was completely filled up. It was headed by a verger, bearing a draped mace, next to whom were the officiating clergymen, attired in surplices, namely, the Revs. H. A. Greaves, Vicar of Charles; F. L. Bazeley, H. Gibbs, Curates of St. Andrew's; P. Holmes, Mannamead; and Boyton Kirk. Following were Mr. Square, surgeon; Mr. A. Hingston, the deceased's executor; Mr. Gill, solicitor; Messrs. F. Hicks and J. W. Matthews, Churchwardens; Mr. W. P. H. White, Parish Clerk; and Mr. Fowler, undertaker. The coffin, which was of polished oak, and carried by twelve bearers, came next in order, and it was the inscription – "John Hatchard, M.A., Vicar of St. Andrew's born May, 1793, died December, 1869. The chief mourners were Commander Hatchard, R.M.; Rev. J. Alton Hatchard, St. Leonard's, Sussex; Mr. S. H. Hatchard, sons of the deceased; Rev. J. Coulthard, Dr. Bright, and Mr. W. Bazeley, Devonport, sons-in-law. Eight servants of the household came next, and following them was the Mayor (Mr. W. Luscombe), who was accompanied by the following magistrates, members and officers of the Corporation – Messrs. A. Hubbard (ex-Mayor), W. Burnell, T. H. Bulteel, G. Mennie, J. Skardon, R. Hicks, H. Brown, J. B. Wilcocks, J. Kelly, C. Norrington, R. W. Stevens, S. Jackson, T. Nicholson, S. C. Parkhouse, C. S. Skardon, W. H. Luke, R. C. Serpell, I. Latimer, J. Wills, B. Sparrow, I. Watts, J. King, T. Pollard, J. A. Page, J. Norrington, W. Auten, H. E. Hurrell, C. C. Whiteford (Town Clerk). R. E. Moore (Clerk of the Peace), T. C. Brian (Borough Coroner), C. W. Croft (Borough Treasurer), R. Hodge (Borough Surveyor), and J. Rowley (Sanitary Inspector). Several clergymen attired in their robes were present walking two deep, and amongst them were the Revs. J. E. Risk, St Andrew's Chapel; Flavel Cook, Liskeard; J. Bliss, S. W. E. Bird, St. James-the-Less; F. Bellamy, St. Mary's, Devonport; F. Courtney, Charles' Chapel; Sydney Thelwall, Charles' Church; J. Wilcocks, R. M. Blakiston, St. Peter's, Eldad; J. Fletcher, Compton; R. Gardner, St. Michael's Stoke; T. A. Bewes; T. Furneaux, St. German's; M. Dimond-Churchward, St. Paul's, Stonehouse; W. H. Nantes, St. George's, Stonehouse; W. Dunning, Torpoint; F. Barnes, Trinity; – Doyle, I. Hawker, Royal Albert Hospital; C. Coombs, Sutton-on-Plym; – Arthur, Tamerton; J. Bartlett, Millbrook; J. Burrows, Totnes; N. Proctor, R.N.; J. Yonge, D. Yonge, Newton Ferrers; and R. Lane, Wembury. The Rev. W. J. St. Aubyn, Rector of Stoke Damerel, was prevented, by illness, from attending. Then followed a long line of gentlemen, walking in fours, who attended as a mark of respect for the departed. Several shops in Bedford-street were partially closed, and the thoroughfare was completely lined with spectators. Arriving at the church, the coffin was placed in the chancel during the preliminary service for the burial of the dead. The Rev. F. L. Bazeley read the sentences, the Rev. Dr. Holmes the first psalm, the Rev. Boyton Kirk the second psalm, and the Rev. Dr. Gibbes the lesson. The procession being re-formed, as it was about to leave the church, Mr. Clark, the organist, played the "Dead March in Saul," and the subsequent part of the service was read at the vault, which was situated at the east end of the church, by the Rev. H. A. Greaves. The bells of the church were muffled, and rung a solemn knell at half-past 9 o'clock, and on the completion of the service the tenor bell intoned the number of the years of the deceased's age – 76."

1870. – Robert Code Serpell, Mayor. Sir Robert Porrett Collier, re-elected Member of Parliament on occasion of his accepting the Recordership of Bristol. After the election considerable objections were raised to Sir Robert Collier holding the appointment, and he at once resigned it.

Foundation stone of the new municipal buildings, guildhall and courts laid on the 28th of June, by the Mayor, Mr. W. Luscombe, with appropriate ceremonies.

1871. – Isaac Latimer, Mayor. Three memorable trials, of very decisive character, took place this year. The first was a court-martial, held at Devonport, to enquire into the cause of the stranding of H.M.S. *Agincourt* on the Pearl Rock, which opened on July 26th, and lasted for ten days; the second, an action for assault, brought by Mr. Nicholas Were, solicitor, against Captain Augustus S. Murray, R.A., the result being one farthing damages for the plaintiff; the third, an action for libel, brought by Mr. Isaac Latimer, proprietor of the *Western Daily Mercury*, against the *Western Morning News*, which resulted in a verdict for Mr. Latimer, with damages £400., and costs against the *Morning News* Company. The Court of Common Pleas was moved for a new trial on November 4th, but it was unanimously refused.

July 25th. – The fine colossal granite figure of Sir Francis Drake, the work of Mr. S. Trevenen, a rising sculptor, of Plymouth, raised to its lofty position on the point of the gable of the new municipal buildings. The Volunteer Drill Hall, capable of holding 10,000 people, and of drilling 800 men, with armoury, news rooms, residences for staff-sergeants, and spacious drill grounds, opened on the 31st of July, when two grand concerts were given in the building, the one in the morning, the other in the evening, the orchestra consisting of 30 clarionets, 4 flauts, 3 hautbois, 4 bassoons, 2 bass clarionets, 4 contra-bassos, 8 bombardos, 6 euphoniums, 4 alto-horns, 8 French horns, 4 Sax-horns, 8 trombones, 18 cornets, 7 trumpets, 4 fugle horns, 1 bass drum, 1 cymbal, 1 triangle, 1 tamborine, 1 Turkish crescent, 35 side drums, and 4 bag-pipes, under the conductorship and direction of Mr. Winterbottom, the bandmaster of the Royal Marines.

Chapter VIII

The British Medical Association held its thirty-ninth annual meeting at Plymouth and Devonport, commencing on the 8th August, under the presidency of Mr. J. Whipple, of Plymouth. The proceedings commenced with Council Meetings in the afternoon, and in the evening a general meeting, very largely attended, was held in the Assembly Rooms at the Royal Hotel. Amongst those present were the Earl of Mount Edgcumbe, the Mayors of Plymouth and Devonport, Dr. Sibson, Dr. Anstie, Mr. Ernest Hart, Dr. Lord, Mr. Sampson Gamgee, Dr. Day Goss, Mr. Benson Baker, Mr. Macnamara, Dr. A. P. Stewart, Dr. Wilbraham Falconer, Dr. Hextall Smith, and a very large number of members. The Mayor of Plymouth, Mr. Serpell, accompanied by Messrs. C. C. Whiteford (Town Clerk), J. Kelly, F. Hicks, I. Latimer, and A. Hubbard, attended as a deputation from the Corporation, and presented the following congratulatory address to the members of the Association, which was read by the Town Clerk: –

"To the President and Members of the British Medical Association. – We, the Council of the borough of Plymouth desire, in the name and on behalf of the burgesses, our constituents and the inhabitants at large, to offer to you our cordial welcome on this occasion of your visit to this town. It is our privilege on various occasions to offer such a welcome to distinguished guests, but we have never experienced a more real satisfaction than we now enjoy in hailing your arrival among us, and expressing our admiration and respect for the scientific and philanthropic pursuits which form the objects of your Association. The profession to which you have devoted yourselves is distinguished alike by its labours in mitigating the horrors of war, and in assuaging suffering and arresting the progress of disease in its ordinary and epidemic forms. These services to humanity rendered on the battle field, and in our hospitals and infirmaries, and in the dwellings of our poorer classes, often without regard to personal interests or personal safety, have obtained for you a deservedly large measure of the public gratitude. As constituting the Local Board of Health for this district we feel a peculiar interest in your labours in the cause of sanitary improvement, and we anticipate a valuable addition to our sources of instruction and information in the discussion which will be devoted to this all important subject. We offer you our best wishes for the success of your Association, and our willing co-operation in all that may facilitate your proceedings, and render agreeable your visit to this town and its interesting neighbourhood. – Robert C. Serpell, Mayor."

The Mayor then gave the members of the Association a hearty welcome to Plymouth, and the retiring president, Dr. E. Charlton, of Newcastle-upon-Tyne, responded in an eloquent speech, and was followed by the president, Mr. Whipple, who gave a kind of historical sketch of the town. The next day the meetings of the Association were held at Devonport, when the Mayor and Corporation attended, and an address of welcome was read by the Town Clerk. Meetings of sections were held at different public buildings in Plymouth, at which scientific papers were read. In the evening the President's Soirée was held at the Royal Hotel, Plymouth, and was attended by upwards of five hundred ladies and gentlemen. The third day was occupied by a "temperance breakfast," given at the Royal Hotel, by the National Temperance League, and in various business and sectional meetings, and in the evening a dinner at St. George's Hall, Stonehouse. The fourth, and last day, was occupied in sectional meetings, and in various excursions in the neighbourhood. The concluding meeting was held at the Royal Hotel in the evening.

The West of England Horse and Dog Show opened at Plymouth on the 8th of August, in the new Rifle Drill Hall, under the presidency of the Earl of Mount Edgcumbe. Nearly 150 horses, and over 300 dogs were exhibited, and the show remained open three says. A Luncheon, at which the Earl of Mount Edgcumbe presided, took place the first day. Prizes were, as usual, awarded in the various classes, and Mrs. Kate Radcliffe, the famous equestrian, from the Agricultural Hall, Islington, rode the horses over the stone fence twice each day. August 11th. – A meeting, to advocate the immediate suspension of the Contagious Diseases Acts was held, the Vicar of Charles presiding.

The annual meeting of the Associated Chambers of Commerce was this year held in Plymouth. The meeting commenced on the 26th September, under the chairmanship of Mr. Sampson S. Lloyd, of Birmingham, at the Royal Hotel, the Mayors of Plymouth and Devonport and a large number of members and delegates attending. The business of the meeting continued over three days, and on the second day the Plymouth Chamber of Commerce entertained the Association at a splendid banquet at the Royal Hotel. Mr. Alexander Hubbard, Deputy Chairman of the Chamber, presided, and on his right were Mr. Sampson S. Lloyd, the Chairman of the Association; Sir Massey Lopes, Bart., M.P.; Mr. W. Morrison, M.P.; Sir Edward W. Watkins, Bart.; Rear-Admiral Houston Stewart; Lieut.-Colonel Hill, Cardiff; and the Mayor of Devonport. On the left of the chairman were the Earl of Mount Edgcumbe, Mr. C. M. Norwood, M.P.; Mr. J. D. Lewis, M. P.; Mr. J. Whitwell, M. P.; Mr. Behrens, Bradford; and the Mayor of Plymouth (Mr. R. C. Serpell), and there was a large number of guests. The principal speakers were those already named.

October 7th. – A meeting called by requisition to the Mayor, was held for the purpose of considering the desirability of establishing a Free Reading Room and a Free Library for the borough, at which the Mayor (Mr. Serpell) presided. At this meeting the following resolutions were carried: – "That this meeting, being impressed with the value of higher education to all classes of the community, considers the establishment of a Free Library and Reading Rooms in Plymouth, under the provisions of the Public Museums and Library Act, 1855, desirable." "That the removal of the municipal offices from the present Guildhall, and the erection of the new hall, affords the town an opportunity of providing for the reception of a Free Library and Public Reading Room in Plymouth at a small cost." "That a memorial embodying the above resolutions, be presented to the Town Council, requesting that body to take the necessary steps to establish a Free Library and Reading Rooms under the Public Library Act, 1855, and that a committee be appointed with a view to giving effect to the opinion of this meeting on the subject." And, "that voluntary subscriptions be solicited from the town for the establishment of a Free Library, relying for its future support on the public rates, and that a subscription list be opened at once." Subscriptions were also entered into, and donations of books promised.

October 16th. – Plymouth was visited by the ex-Emperor of the French, Louis Napoleon, and the Prince Imperial and suite. The Royal party left Torquay, where they had been sojourning for a few weeks, at 10-9 a.m., and arrived by railway at Plymouth at 12-25, where an immense concourse of spectators was assembled. At the station three carriages from the Royal Hotel were in waiting. In the first the Emperor, the Prince Imperial, Prince Murat, and Sir Lawrence Palk, Bart., M.P., took their seats, and in the other carriages followed Count Clary, Count D'Avilliar, Mons. Conneau (medical attendant), and Sir Thomas Dick Lauder. The route taken was by way of the Duke of Cornwall Hotel, the Crescent, the Royal Hotel and Theatre, where the Emperor and Prince Imperial acknowledged the salutes of a small crowd which had assembled there, and so up Lockyer-street – the British and Female Orphan Asylum being pointed out to the Emperor – to the Hoe, being admitted on the Hoe through the park gates at the lodge entrance, which had been opened by Mr. J. Wills, the Chairman of the Hoe Committee. Arriving at the top of the Hoe, near the Camera Obscura, a halt was made, and here the Emperor made enquiries as to the principal points in the panorama, and, expressing his delight at the charms of the scene, proposed to get out and walk awhile. "He had, however, counted without his host. By this time the crowd from the railway station, making a short cut by way of Citadel-road, joined by contingents from the centre of the town, just made aware of the Emperor's presence, came rushing on the Hoe, and, cheering most lustily, surrounded the carriages. A walk was thus impossible; the cheers were acknowledged, and the party drove through the gates at the Citadel end, and quietly proceeded around the sea-drive towards Millbay. From Millbay the route was through Stonehouse, past the Marine Barracks, and on to the Royal William Victualling Yard, where, above the

Queen's Steps, some twenty or thirty naval and marine officers in full dress, with several ladies, had assembled. Here the Emperor and suite were received by Admiral Houston Stewart, Superintendent of the Dockyard, and by Mr. Churcher, Superintendent of the Victualling Yard; Capt. Coode, of the flag-ship, Royal Adelaide; Flag-Lieut Watson &c. From here the party embarked for Mount Edgcumbe in the Port Admiral's barge, scarlet cloth being laid from the carriage down the steps to the boat. At Cremyll beach the Earl of Mount Edgcumbe, accompanied by Col. the Hon. Charles Edgcumbe and the Hon. George Edgcumbe, received his distinguished visitors, who, in four of the Earl's carriages, were driven to the entrance of the gardens and pleasure grounds, where Lady Ernestine and the Hon. Mrs. Edgcumbe joined them. Through the Italian garden, French garden, and the wilder English garden, the Emperor walked, and found much to admire. A short stay was made on the walk overlooking Barnpool and the Sound; and from thence, the party proceeded to the house, where luncheon was served. After lunch the Emperor and the Prince Imperial were received by the Countess of Mount Edgcumbe, and for upwards of an hour enjoyed a drive around the Park, and about half past-three Cremyll was regained, and the visitors, again taking to the Port Admiral's barge, were towed by a steam launch up the Hamoaze, above the Gun Wharf, passing on their way the flag-ship, the boy's training ships, the Dockyard, the sunnery ship, and Admiral Seymour's flag-ship the *Narcissus*. Returning to the Victualling Yard, the Emperor thanked Admiral Stewart and Mr. Churcher for their kindness, and the carriages were then resorted to, and the route to the railway station was taken through the whole length of Union-street." The Royal party left by the 4-10 p.m. train. A few days afterwards Plymouth was visited by another celebrity, Sir Roger Tichborne, the claimant of the Tichborne estates, who took up his quarters at the Royal Hotel, and on the evening of the 19th, occupied a private box at the Theatre, the "observed of all observers", when every part of the house was crammed; large numbers of persons being unable to obtain admission. Blondin also this year performed at Plymouth.

We bring our Annals to a close by briefly recording four important events which followed close one upon another in the eleventh month of the year, and for which, in fact, we kept back the printing of this portion of our work. They are the following: – The appointment of Sir Robert Porrett Collier, H.M. Attorney-General, senior Member of Parliament for the borough of Plymouth, to the Judicial Bench; the elevation of Mr. Isaac Latimer to the office of Mayor of the borough; the adoption by the town of the Free

Libraries and Museums Act; and the election of Edward Bates, Esq., as M.P. for Plymouth, in room of Sir R. P. Collier, resigned.

Sir Robert P. Collier, son of the late John Collier, Esq., who was M.P. for Plymouth from 1832 to 1841, by his wife, Emma, daughter of the late Robert Porrett, Esq., was born in 1817; was educated at the Plymouth Grammar School and at Trinity College, Cambridge, where he graduated as B.A. in 1841. He was called to the bar at the Inner Temple (of which he is a Bencher) in 1843, and was made Q.C. in 1854, with a patent of precedence. He was Counsel to the Admiralty and Judge Advocate of the Fleet from 1859 till 1863, when he became Solicitor-General, and was knighted. In 1868 Sir Robert was appointed Attorney-General, and in 1870 accepted the Recordership of Bristol (having for some time held that of Penzance), which office, however, he a few days afterwards resigned at the request of his Plymouth constituents. In November of the present year Sir Robert Collier was sworn in as one of H.M. Privy Council, and a few days afterwards received his patent as one of the Judges of the Court of Common Pleas, from whence he was transferred – much controversy taking place upon the question of this elevation being an evasion of the recent Act of Parliament – to the Judicial Committee of the Privy Council. Sir Robert married, in 1844, Isabella, daughter of William Rose Rose, Esq., of Eton-place, London, by whom he has issue two sons and one daughter. He had sat as M.P. for Plymouth since 1852.

On the 3rd November a public meeting of the ratepayers of Plymouth was held in the Mechanics' Institute to consider the desirability of adopting, for the town, the provisions of the Free Libraries Act of 1855. The Mayor, Mr. R.C. Serpell, presided, and opened the proceedings. Mr. Alfred Rooker proposed, and Mr. J. N. Bennett seconded, the first resolution – "That the Free Libraries Act, 1855, be adopted for the Municipal Borough of Plymouth," which being supported by several speakers, was carried by an overwhelming majority of the burgesses; and by the whole of the mixed meeting, with the exception of one dissentient hand.

On the 9th November, Mr. Isaac Latimer, proprietor of the *Western Daily Mercury*, was elected Mayor of Plymouth for the ensuing year.

On Friday, the 17th, the writ for the election of a Member of Parliament for this borough, in the room of Sir Robert Porrett Collier, was received by the Mayor, and the Town Sergeants and Town Crier at once proceeded, according to the usual custom, to proclaim it in several places. First at the Guildhall, then at the Barbican, and amongst other places at what is called "New Tree." This "New Tree" was at the point of junction of Westwell-street and Bedford-street, but has since passed out of the knowledge of the oldest inhabitant. The writ was proclaimed by the Town Crier, in his ancient official costume – something like a parish beadle. He was accompanied by the Sergeant-at-Mace, who carried one of the maces, as his insignia of office. The antiquated ceremony excited a great deal of interest. The usual order as to the military was also issued from the Assistant-Adjutant General's office. "Tuesday next being the day appointed for the nomination, and Wednesday that for taking the poll, for the election of a member for the borough of Plymouth, the provisions of the 2nd section of 10 Vic., cap. 21, will be complied with. No soldier, therefore, within the garrison of Plymouth, Devonport, and Stonehouse, or within two miles of the Three Towns, will be allowed to go out of the barrack or quarters at which he may be stationed during Tuesday and Wednesday next, unless for the purpose of mounting or relieving guard, or for giving his vote at such election; and every soldier allowed to go out for any such purpose within the limits aforesaid shall return to his barracks or quarters with all convenient speed as soon as his guard shall have been relieved or vote tendered." The nomination took place on the 21st, the Mayor, Isaac Latimer, Esq., ably presiding as returning officer, on hustings erected in front of the Royal Hotel and Theatre, when Mr. Alfred Rooker, solicitor, of Plymouth, an advanced Liberal, was proposed by Mr. Francis Hicks, seconded by Mr. Alexander Hubbard; and Mr. Edward Bates, shipowner, of Liverpool, Conservative, was proposed by Mr. Charles T. Bewes, seconded by Mr. W. F. Moore, the show of hands being in favour of Mr. E. Bates. The polling took place next day, and at the close, at 4 o'clock, the numbers were announced as follows:–

For Mr. Bates	1753
For Mr. Rooker	1511
Majority for Mr. Bates	242

Mr Bates was therefore declared by the Mayor to be duly elected. It was computed that upwards of 15,000 persons were present at the declaration.

At the latter end of the year the small-pox broke out to an alarming extent in the town, and on the 29th November a joint meeting of the Sanitary Committee of the Local Board of Health and of the principal members of the Board of Guardians was held at the Guildhall, for the purpose of considering what steps should be taken in the emergency to enable persons afflicted with the small-pox to receive proper and immediate attention. The Town Clerk and the Clerk to the Board of Guardians were present. The subject was carefully considered, and every desire expressed by both bodies to afford accommodation to the afflicted. It was suggested that the Board of Guardians should allow a field to be used near the Workhouse, on which a temporary building might be erected, capable of affording accommodation for from 50 to 60 persons. The Sanitary Committee undertook to pay for its erection out of the funds of the Local Board of Health. This was eventually agreed to, and resolutions were passed to be brought under the consideration of the Board of Guardians. The following Board-day the subject was fully discussed, and resulted in favour of the hospital being erected.

CHAPTER IX

SITUATION — CHARACTER — STREETS — MUNICIPAL GOVERNMENT — POPULATION STATISTICS — MARKETS, FAIRS, AND SHAMBLES — ANCIENT REGULATIONS REGARDING BREWERS, BUTCHERS, AND OTHERS.

Plymouth, the oldest, and the principal and most important of the "Three Towns," comprising the "Metropolis of the West," is situated at the confluence of the Tamar and the Plym, at the extreme south-west corner of Devonshire, and divided from Cornwall only by the River Tamar. Unlike that of many towns, the origin of the name of Plymouth is involved in no obscurity. It is simply the *mouth* of the River *Plym*, at which the town lies, and its geographical position is thus (in like manner as Dartmouth, Exmouth, and other places) correctly indicated by its name. Of the two rivers upon which the "Three Towns" stand, old Michael Drayton in his *Polyolbion* thus writes: –

> Proude TAMAR swoopes along, with such a lustie traine
> As fits so brave a flood, two Countries that divides;
> So, to increase her strength, shee from her equall sides
> Receives their several rills –"
>
> *   *   *   *   *
>
> "PLYM, that claimes by right
> The christ'ning of that Bay, which beares her nobler name.
> Upon the British coast, what ship yet ever came
> That not of Plymouth heares, where those brave Navies lie
> From Canon's thund'ring throats that all the world defie.
> Which to invasive spoile when th' English list to draw,
> Have check'd Iberia's pride, and held her oft in awe,
> Oft furnishing our dames with India's rar'st devices,
> And lent us gold and pearle, rich silks and daintie spices."

The situation of the town is remarkably pleasant and commanding, and the whole district has been commended for its extreme beauty by all who have written upon the locality. Westcote, in his "View of Devonshire," 1630, says: –

Chapter IX

"And now we are ready to enter the fair Town of Plymouth, at the most south-west lip of this province. Here Tamar, in finishing his course, is to pay his tribute, and emptyeth itself into the ocean; and, coming from Hartland, hath measured the breadth of this country, and finds it by direct line and our ancient computation 35 miles at the least; but by the new measure, more; and to follow him in his pleasant vagaries, either for his own ease or country's profit, he hath doubled the measure. Now will we cast anchor and take a view of this famous haven. This so much renowned town is situated in the most south-west part of this province, which, by the River Tamar on the west, and Plym (of whom it borroweth name) on the east, is demi-insulated. But concerning the name, while the West Saxon kingdom kept his state, this haven was called Ostium Tamaris, Tamar-mouth, or Tamar-worth, as you may read in the life of St. Indractus. And in this river's commendation Alexandra Necham thus versified: –

"Leogriæ Tamaris divisor Cornubiæque,
Indigenas ditat pinguibus Isiciis."
Tamar that logers doth divide from Cornwall in the west,
The neighbour-dwellers rich serves with salmon of the best.

These two rivers united make it a most excellent and safe road for shipping, and fit to take the opportunity of the first wind to set forth either west, east, or north."

The town itself lies, for a considerable part, in a natural hollow, but it has gradually extended itself up the heights in every direction until it reaches the sea on one side, and Stoke and other surrounding places on the others. To the sea-ward is the Hoe, a magnificent, extensive, and highly elevated tract of ground, forming one of the most delightful promenades, and overlooking every part of Plymouth South with its splendid breakwater, its fortified Island of St. Nicholas, and the open English Channel beyond, with the Eddystone Lighthouse on the extreme horizon. To the left is the Citadel – one of the important fortifications of the kingdom – whose guns command the Sound, the mouth of the Channel, the estuary of the Plym or Catwater, and the mouth of the Tamar or Hamoaze; Mount Batten, with its Martello Tower; Sutton Pool, with its array of ships; Catdown, with its quarries; and Staddon Heights, Bovisand, the Shagstone, and the Mewstone. To the right lies Millbay, with its admirable pier from whence steamers depart to almost all parts of the world, its war prison, its warehouses, and its many other important features; the Great Western Docks, the Railway Stations, and the Royal William Victualling Yard at Stonehouse; and, further on, Devonport, with its Dockyards, its Gun Wharves, its batteries, its Tubular Bridge, its

Steam Ferry, and its Guardships; Mount Edgcumbe, stretching from Cremyll, at the mouth of Hamoaze, to Maker, opposite the end of the Breakwater; Kingsand, Cawsand, Penlee Point, and the Rame Head. Landward from the Hoe, to the right is the Citadel, with the Laira and the open country, as a background, stretching out towards Tavistock and Roborough; in front is the town, bounded by Stoke Damerel and the heights beyond; and to the left is the Esplanade and Elliot-terrace, with the mingled towns spreading out in every direction.

The streets of "Old Town" are mostly narrow and crooked; but many of those of the more modern parts are remarkably fine and wide and lined with elegant buildings. Much improvement has, of late years, taken place even in the worst parts of the town, under the careful management of the Local Board of Health, and the result has been that instead of Plymouth being, as was officially reported in 1853, "One of the most unhealthy (because uncleanly) towns in the kingdom," it has now become remarkably healthy and pleasant in every respect. Of some parts of the Old Town, the Government Sanitary Inspector, Mr. Rawlinson, thus reported in 1853: – "Many of the old back streets of Plymouth are narrow, crooked, and steep, with a wide-jointed rough pavement and a dirty surface-channel down the centre. The old houses are very irregularly built, both as regards their elevation and style of architecture. Originally, many houses, now in ruins, were erected as residences for the nobility and gentry of the town; but from being the abodes of those possessing wealth, they now give partial shelter to the improvident, the vagrant, the vicious, and the unfortunate. The quaint carving on the stonework looks out of place; the walls are half in ruins, the gables are shattered, and foul weather-stains of damp blotch the surface. Within, matters are even worse; the rooms are now divided and sub-divided on every floor; the staircase is darkened, its massive hand-rail and carved balusters are crippled and broken; the once firm stairs are now rickety and dangerous; the stucco-finished plastering is blackened and in holes, the dusty and rotten laths being in many places bare; the landing windows, where the space is open, have neither frame nor glass, so that the rain drives in right and left; make-shift doors lead into small spaces let off as separate tenements. The narrow space of street betwixt the houses is further contracted by rude looking poles rigged out of windows on either side, story above story, on which clothes are hung to dry. Thus a free flow of air is impeded, and an atmosphere, usually very damp, is made more so. In the same street houses may be found which were erected in Queen Elizabeth's reign, with others of more modern date; the walls are of hewn stone, of granite or limestone rubble or of brick. Some have been plastered over, and others have been covered with slates; some are plain vertical fronts, and others project at each story. Out of these streets, covered passages lead into still narrower, dirtier, and more crowded courts. In many instances the ground rises abruptly, and slippery half-worn limestone steps lead to houses more ruinous and more crowded than those fronting the street. One privy serves a whole court, and this is usually filthy; the cess-pool full, overflowing, and the foetid refuse stagnant over the surface. An external stand-pipe, the water on only for one hour in twenty-four, supplies water to an entire court with many tenants; tubs, mugs, pots, pans, and troughs being placed in the yard, on the stairs, landings, or in the filthy rooms, to absorb all the deleterious gases of the place. Within, the furniture accords with the premises; it is old, rotten, broken, and ruinous. One room serves for a family of father, mother, and children – not unfrequently grown up sons and daughters. Dogs and fowl inhabit the same apartment, and, in some instances, ten human beings."

With this state of things it might naturally be expected that in such visitations of the cholera as those which occurred in 1832 and in 1849, the proportion of deaths would be very large, and such was the fact. The deaths from cholera alone from June 15th to September 24th, 1832, in Plymouth, were 702, the cases being 1805; and in 1849 the deaths from cholera between the 4th of July and the 8th of November were 819 – this, without any reference to the adjoining towns. Since then the improvements which have been effected have tended materially to decrease even the ordinary rate of mortality in the town. In the narrow streets which characterise the old parts of the town, many fine remains of ancient domestic architecture still exist, and among these are some remarkably rich houses with over-hanging stories and enriched gables and doorways. Some of the finest and most interesting of these will be found in Notte-street (already noticed on page 66) and in St. Andrew's-street, but they exist in many other parts of the town. The principal streets are –

BEDFORD STREET, leading from George-street and Frankfort-street, to Whimple-street and Old Town street. In it are St. Andrew's Church, the Devon and Cornwall Bank and the Globe Hotel. This street has, of late years, been very considerably widened, and the buildings which now line its south side are of a majestic character. Great improvements have been effected at the east end of the street by removing some old buildings and taking away a portion of the churchyard of St. Andrew's.

GEORGE STREET, leading from Bedford-street at its junction with Frankfort-street, Russell-street and Cornwall-street, to Union-street and Lockyer-street, and to the Railway Station, the Great Western Docks, Millbay, etc. In it are the Royal Hotel, Theatre, Assembly Rooms, Athenaeum, the Baptist Chapel, and Harvey's Hotel. At the junction of these two streets with Lockyer-street and Bank of England-place is erected the Gothic Clock Tower, already described, and in the latter place is the Branch Bank of England.

UNION STREET AND UNION ROAD; a remarkably long street, leading from George-street to Stonehouse Bridge, and forming a line of direct communication between the Three Towns. In it are St. James's Hall, the Octagon, etc. Along this street, which is crossed by a bridge of the South Devon and Cornwall Railways, a tramway, or street railway, is laid down, by which means a quicker and more convenient traffic is carried on between Plymouth, Stonehouse and Devonport.

LOCKYER STREET, leading from the junction of George-street and Union-street, to the Hoe. In it are St. Andrew's Chapel, the Royal Hotel, and the Female Orphan Asylum. From this street Alfred-place leads to Millbay and Stonehouse; Windsor-terrace, to Saltram-place and the Citadel; and Princess-street to Princess-square, and so on, by Princess-place and Notte-street, to the Parade, the Barbican, Sutton Pool, etc.

WHIMPLE STREET, in continuation of Bedford-street, leads from the junction of that street with Old Town-street, to Looe-street, for the Wharves; and Buckwell-street, for Briton-side. In it are the old Guildhall, the Post-office, and the Naval Bank. From this street High-street leads down to the Parade and Sutton Pool, and Kinterbury-street to Treville-street.

OLD TOWN STREET leads from the junction of Bedford-street with Whimple-street, to Tavistock-street and Saltash-street. At the head of this street formerly stood the Conduit, erected in the mayoralty of Sir John Trelawny in 1598. It has been removed some years, and the armorial and other tablets are built into the wall of the Reservoir on North-hill.

TAVISTOCK STREET, leading from Old Town-street to North-hill, and so on to Dartmoor and Tavistock. In it are the Cattle Market and Sherwell Chapel.

NORTH HILL, from Tavistock-street, by Torrington-place, Saltash-road, Pennycomequick, Eldad and No-place, to Mill Bridge and Stoke.

COBOURG STREET, from Richmond-street to James-street and the North-road.

YORK STREET, leading with Russell-street, from Bedford-street and George-street to St. Michael's-terrace, Pennycomequick, the Cemetery and the Devonport Prisons, etc.

FRANKFORT STREET, leading with King-street, High-street and Fore-street, to Stonehouse Bridge.

TREVILLE STREET, from Old Town-street to Bilbury-street, Briton-side, etc., and so on to the Exeter-road.

SOUTHSIDE STREET, from Notte-street to the Barbican, Sutton Pool, the Pier, Lambhay Point and the Citadel.

HIGH STREET, leading from the Guidhall to Notte-street, the Parade, Sutton Pool, etc.

HOEGATE STREET, leading from Notte-street to the Hoe and the Citadel.

CORNWALL STREET, leading from the junction of Bedford-street with George-street, Russell-street and Frankfort-street, to the Market. In it are the Public Library and the Freemason's Hall.

BANK STREET, from Bedford-street to Cornwall-street and the Market.

WESTWELL STREET, from Bedford-street to Princess-square. In it are the New Guildhall and the magnificent pile of municipal buildings (which are also approached from St. Andrew's Church) and the Mechanic's Institution.

PRINCESS SQUARE, containing the Mechanic's Institution and the Grammar School, is approached from Lockyer-street by Princess-street; from Bedford-street by Westwell-street; from the Hoe by Windsor-street; and from St. Andrew's and the Guildhall by Catherine-street

THE CRESCENT and Buckland-terrace lie near the Railway Station. Near these are the Royal Eye Infirmary, the Duke of Cornwall, the Albion, and the Mount Pleasant Hotels.

PORTLAND SQUARE is approached from James-street and the Tavistock-road.

THE ESPLANADE is at the head of Lockyer-street, on the Hoe.

ELLIOT TERRACE, in a line west of the Esplanade, is approached by Elliot-street, at the head of Athenaeum-street. The Royal Western Yacht Club is in the same terrace.

WEST HOE TERRACE, overlooking the Sound, is by the seaside, and is approached from the Hoe and from Millbay-road.

Plymouth is 216¼ miles S.W. by W. from London by the old road computation, and 246½ miles by railway, and is 43¼ miles S.W. from Exeter, the county town, by road, and 52¾ by railway. it is situated in the Hundred of Roborough and Deanery of Plympton, and it is a Parliamentary and Municipal Borough, returning two Members to Parliament, and is governed by a Mayor and Corporation. It is strongly fortified, and is a seaport of considerable magnitude.

The government of Plymouth is vested in a Mayor, twelve Aldermen, and thirty-six Councillors, appointed under the Municipal Corporations' Act, 5 and 6 William IV., c.76. The Borough, for municipal purposes, is divided into six wards, viz., Frankfort Ward, Drake's Ward, Charles' Ward, Sutton Ward, Vintry Ward, and St. Andrew's Ward, each of which is represented by two Aldermen and six Councillors. The Mayor and Recorder are, by virtue of their offices, Justices of the Peace, and there are also several magistrates appointed by commission. The Corporation is the Local Board of Health, under the Public Health Act, whose provisions were put in force in 1854. Up to that time the paving, lighting, etc., was under the control of a Board of Improvement Commissioners, constituted under the Paving and Lighting Act, of 5th George IV. The town has also adopted the Free Libraries Act, and an Educational Board has been established. The Markets are the property of the Corporation, and are under their control, and they also have the management of the police force. The Water Works and water supply are also the property of the Corporation, and they likewise own the Theatre, Royal Hotel, and Assembly Rooms. The Borough, to the extent of its present limits, was first incorporated 18th Henry VI. (1440), but the constitution of the Corporation was materially changed by the "Municipal Corporations' Act" of the reign of William IV.

The population of Plymouth, according to the Census taken in April, 1871, is as follows: –

	Males.	Females.	Total.
Parish of St. Andrew	18,373	22,973	41,346
Parish of Charles	10,946	14,233	25,179
		Total	66,525

The increase of population during the present century is stated to be as follows:–

Year.	Persons.	Increase.	
		Number.	Per Cent.
1801	16,040		
1811	20,803	4,763	29-69
1821	21,591	788	3-78
1831	31,080	9,489	43-94
1841	36,527	5,447	17-52
1851	49,673	13,146	35-98
1861	62,599	12,926	26-02
1871	68,080	5,481	8-75

The above table includes the floating population for 1871

The rateable value of property in 1821 was £28,983; in 1851, £101,818; and in 1871, £169,251 10*s*. The number of inhabited houses at different periods in the present century is as follows: –

1801	1,782	1841	4,298
1811	2,099	1851	5,178
1821	2,447	1861	6,084
1831	3,472	1841	7,287

The increase in the first half of the present century, from 1801 to 1851, was 3,396 inhabited houses, and 33,633 inhabitants; and in the last twenty years, from 1851 to 1871, 2,109 inhabited houses, and 18,407 inhabitants

The Market at Plymouth is said to have been first granted to the Priory of Plympton about the year 1253, to be held on Thursdays, with a three-days' fair to be held at the Festival of St. John the Baptist. In or about 1257, Baldwin de L'Isle had, as appears from the Rolls of 42nd Henry III., a grant for a market at Sutton, to be held on Wednesday, and a three-days' fair to be held at the Feast of the Ascension. By the charter of Henry VI. the "fairs, feasts and markets" were vested in the Mayor and Commonalty, the town being then. for the first time, incorporated. In 1670 the town bushel for public measuring was set up in the Market. In the last century the market days were Monday and Friday, and continued on the Saturday, and the Markets were at that time held under the Guildhall, in the open space shown in our engraving on page 101, and in the surrounding streets.* The market having been held on the Saturday, the open space was cleaned out on Sunday mornings for the display of civic grandeur that had to take place. An halberdier, in full array and "armed to the teeth," was stationed under each archway, while the Mayor and Corporation, with mace-bearers and other officers, in their gowns, paraded backwards and forwards till they were marshalled in procession to march to St. Andrew's for Divine worship.

In 1804 the present inconvenient Market place, situated between Cornwall-street, East-street, and Drake-street, the Corn Market being at the Cornwall-street entrance, was opened; the principal market days being Tuesday, Thursday, and Saturday, although it is open every day in the week. The Market occupies an area of three acres, and contains covered vegetable, butter, dish, and poultry markets, butcher's stalls, pot market, and shops and stalls for general merchandize. There are three principal entrances, viz., from Cornwall-street, from East-street, and from Drake-street, and several smaller ones. The Market, it must be added, is totally inadequate to the requirements of the town, and calls for early removal and reconstruction. A good, lofty, well-arranged and well-ventilated Market Hall is much needed,

*Some interesting accounts of the Market Tolls will be found on p81

and is, indeed, a necessity in such a town as Plymouth; and it is much to be hoped that, as the tide of improvement has now so wisely and so strongly set in, and has already swept away the abominations at the back of Bedford-street, and erected on their site the palatial piles of municipal buildings, its waves will soon carry away the present Market sheds, and plant in their place an erection that shall be a comfort and an honour to the town.

The Fish Market – the Plymouth Billingsgate for wholesale dealers and others – is held on the Barbican, by Sutton Pool. Formerly there was an old "Fish House" at this place, which has been removed. "This old building was situated in a most singular place, as it served for a breakwater for Sutton Pool. It occupied almost two-thirds of the site of the Western Pier that now is, and the other third was the total way, nearest the Old Barbican, where vessels of large burden could enter. There was a way also on the other side, but of less depth, and the Fish House stood in the water, and surrounded by it. It was a large, square, ancient building, and towards the Sound it was quite plain. The windows and stairs were on the Pool side. This place was used for a store-house for provisions for the Royal Navy in Queen Anne's time, during the wars in her reign, and it was full when, in a dreadful storm, it was entirely washed down and all the stores lost; and in this storm many ships were wrecked, others drove on Friary Green, Old Tree Slip, etc. The painting of the old Fish House put one in mind of Noah's Ark. This singular erection has always (or its ruins) been known by the name of the Fish House, but whether it was built for the purpose of curing and storing of fish for exportation, or for its being deposited there anciently, in order to receive King's and Queen's Customs thereon, is now uncertain." The "Fish Shambles," also called the "Fish Cage," were built in 1692 in Whimple-street, near the Church passage. Closely adjoining was a guard-house.

A Yarn Market was formerly held in St. Andrew's churchyard, which, having fallen into disuse, was revived in 1651, as will be seen by the interesting Corporation order already given on page 146.

Meat Shambles appear to have existed from a comparatively early date, and they were re-erected in 1605. In 1657 new shambles were built "in the midst of Old Town-street," and until recent years shambles abutted on, and, indeed, were built into, the churchyard of St. Andrew. In the forming of the new Market place provision was made for the butchers. The following highly curious document, which is now, for the first time, printed, shows the regulations made in Plymouth, between two and three centuries ago, for the ordering of butchers, bakers and brewers: –

Chapter IX

"The Mayor commandeth in the Kinges name of Ynglond that all maner of Bakers make good brede and of good corne and a holsome for mannys body and that they make a loffe for a peny, ij lofes for a peny, and iiij loffys for a peny, and that your Brede kepe weyte. At the first tyme upon payne of a grievous amerciament: and the second tyme a grevousser amerciament: And the thirde fawte on payne of the pyllory and to forfeyte ther Brede and their Body to Pryson and thereto make a Fyne at the Mayres will, etc.

"Also that all manner of Brewers make good Ale and of goode Malte holsome for mannys Body. And that they sell a Gallon of the best in the leve for 1d. 2qrs. and when it is clere and stale in the Barrell for 1d. over. And of the Second Ale in the Kyve for iij farthinges, and when it is clere and stale in the barrell for 1d. And that they sell no Ale by Wyne measure, but only by Ale measure and Sealed. And that they sell none till the Ale Taster have tasted hyt. And soe that it be good hoelsum and able for mannys body. And that no manner of Brewsteres neither Hoggesters sell none Ale tyll they sett oute their Signe in payne of forfeyture of all together and their bodyes to pryson there to make a Fyne and Rawnson at the Mayre's will etc.

"Also that no manner of men sell no corrupte Wynes nether reboyled Wynes: nether Mellis Wynes, ne no nother but hit be good and holsome for mannys body nether sett ij pypes in one Pype Hoggeshead or Tonne to rese the price, that is to saye, first for iiij*d.* and after for vj*d.* on payne of forfeyting of all suche Wynes solde and the boddyes of the Sellers thereof to Pryson etc.

"Item. – All Bochers that bringes Fleshe to Mkett to sell bring none but hit be good and abull and holsom for mannys body. And that they bring no bull fleshe, ne Rammys Fleshe ne Cowe Fleshe that be an Calfe and the calfe be quicke, ne no other Fleshe but hit be in season and good and holsom for mannys Body; And that they bring their kydenes in their motons and their skinnys of all manner of Fleshe to Mkett on payne of all their Fleshe and their bodys to pryson.

"Also that no Bocher putt no filthe in the markett, ne bones ne blode in the Shamells on payne of imprisonment of their bodyes that so doo.

"Also that no manner of men sell lynnen clthe by no mett yardys into the tyme that they be broughte into the Gildehall and avowved by the Kinge's stondert, and sealed, on payne of prisonment of their Bodyes and forfeyten of all suche clothe so solde etc.

"Also that no man bye ne sell by no false weyth neither by the weyth that be forbidden by the Lawe, that is to saye, the sheste nether by no nother weyth but they be truly avowed by the Standerts of Wynchestire, nether bye by one and sell by another, that is to saye, to bye by greater weyth and sell by lesse, on payne of prysonement of their bodyes that such wyeth occupy and a grevous Fyne to be made at the Mayres will.

"Also that no Astler nether no nother man ofte no vocabundys nother no noyman passing ij dayes and ij nightes but he be a man of knawledge and where whence he come and whither he will, and what his busynes be in Towne, and that no man walke up and downe worken dayes to nale and to wyne but he be a man of (   ) or merchment other wayting upon any gentylman upon payne of prysonement of their bodyes and a grevous Fyne to be made at the Mayres will for yt ys suspicyous.

"Item – That no Hosteler nor Tavernner by color of their tavern or hostelry suffer no suspicious people of their lyving to ryott, accompany or logge to gether as man and a woman, but he knows verily that hit be a man and his wife, that no landoner keep in his House harlott nother strompett but voyde her away hastely on payne of a grevous amerciament.

"Also that no man forestale any vyntayle coming to the Mkett warde as Fleshe, Fyshes, Butter, Cheese, Egges, Chekins, Capons, Gese, or any other Vytale, but suffer hit to be brought to the Common Mkett place, and then that no man regrate hit, that is to saye, by hit in grete to the intent to sell it agen afore the Towne be full servyed on payne of emprysonement of their Bodyes, and a Fyne at the Mayres will.

"Also that no Hoggestars nether no other person take upon theym to bye any Fishe aborde any Bote, but suffer the fishe to be layde a lande or they make any price. And that then any Man have a part thereof that is present at the lyeng of the same pounde and pounde alike yf it life theym so beinge present to holde hit on payne of Forfeiture of the Fishe so boughte, and the byers body to prison, and there to make a grevous Fyne for his offence at the Mayres discression."

A Cloth Fair was formerly held in November. At this fair all the clothiers from Somersetshire, etc., attended with cloths and blankets, and the people saved up their money till the fair for the purchase of those commodities, the most respectable people of the town preferring to buy of the clothiers rather than of the shopkeepers. The Cloth Fair was held in Old Town-street, where the cab stand now is, and reached to St. Andrew's Church, whilst the sweetmeat and trinket stalls were placed from the Church, down Whimple-street and Bilbury-street.

The fairs now held are the first Monday in April and the first Monday in November, but although they were at one time thought much of, they have now almost died out.

CHAPTER X

RELIGIOUS HOUSES — THE WHITE FRIARS — THE GREY FRIARS — LEPER'S HOSPITAL — THE BLACK FRIARS — THE ABBEY — CHAPEL OF ST. CATHERINE — CHAPEL OF ST. MICHAEL — CHAPEL OF OUR LADY OF GRACE — PALACE COURT — ST. ANDREW'S CHURCH AND ITS MONUMENTS.

Of the ancient religious houses in Plymouth but little is, unfortunately known, and even their exact sites are, in some instances, matters of grave uncertainty. The two principal ones were the Convent of the Carmelites, or White Friars, and the Convent of the Franciscans, or Grey Friars, but there were also other minor establishments.

The White Friars was situated at the head of Sutton Pool, where the names of Friary-street, Friary-court, and White-friar's-lane still attest its locality. It was an extensive establishment, enclosed in battlemented walls, and had a lofty tower and spire. Near it stood one of the gates of the tower – the "Friary Gate" – which was taken down some years since. This convent was established in 1314. In the very beginning, however, according to Oliver, something uncanonical in their settlement had occurred, which occasioned the displeasure of Bishop Stapeldon; but at the recommendation of his sovereign, King Edward II., who was their great patron, he was induced to overlook the irregularity, and on September 28th, 1314, issued his

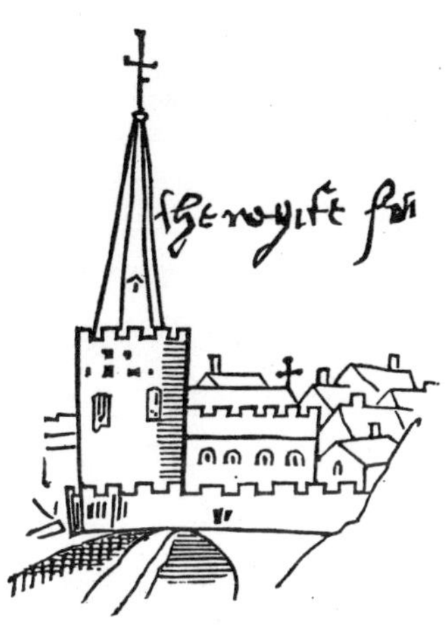

license: "*ut religiosi viri ordinis Beate Marie de Monte Carmeli in areâ suâ de Sutton nostre diocesis divina valeant celebrare,*" and that site of their convent might be dedicated by any Catholic Bishop (*Reg: fol.* 88.) Subsequently their Prior – Henry – was excommunicated by Bishop Brantyngham for presuming to absolve in a reserved case, September 17th, 1374; but he was afterwards reconciled to his diocesan (*Reg: vol.* 1, *fol.* 48.) Prior Henry, in an official deed, dated "*In domo nostra Sutton*, 30 Nov., 1376," granted to the benefactors, William Forniaux, and Joan, his wife, a participation in all the prayers and good works which shall be performed by his community. The seal attached to the deed is oval and of green wax, but imperfect. The Virgin Mother is represented standing, holding on her left arm the Divine infant, and there are two kneeling figures below. The legend is imperfect. Eleven years later the name of John appears as prior of this house (September 22nd, 1387). That this community was not allowed to perform the funerals or interments of strangers dying in St. Andrew's parish, without the consent of the vicar, is evident from Bishop Lacy's Ordinance, Nov. 27, 1438 (*Reg: vol.* III., 175-6.) On the 26th June, 1387, the Commission upon the Scroop and Grosvenor Controversy sat in the church and refectoiy of this convent. At the time of the dissolution this convent, with others, is said to have passed into the hands of the Mayor and Commonalty, and, afterwards, through several hands, and was, of course, converted to other purposes. At the close of last century its site belonged to the family of Julian, and it was used for a time as a military hospital. As late as 1830 some portions of the tower were remaining, as well as a part of the refectory and what is supposed to have been the kitchen, but these have now disappeared and only some small remains can now be traced. The following inventory of the church goods belonging to this establishment, which has been copied from the original, in the Public Record Office, for this work, by my friend, the Rev. Mackenzie E.C. Walcott, F.S.A.: –

"The Whyt Fryeres of Plummouth. M. thys Indenture makythe mencyon yt ye howse of ye Whyte Fryers in Plummowthe with all ye pertenaunce ys delyveryd to Master doctor Wegans & to James Korsewall to kepe & order to ye Kyng's use tyll hys gracs plesur be forther knowyn and thys stuffe remaynethe in ye howse.

"The Vestrie a sute of Vestments blewe sylke pryste decon & sub decon with ij copys of the same iii li; a Vestement blew saten ye decon & sub decon clothe of tynsell xxxd; a syngle Vestement of rede saten, ye crosse blewe xvs; iij olde tenacles xvjd; a clothe of blew sylke to hange before ye auter, iijs iiijd; a nother clothe for ye same of blewe damaske vs; ij ffrunts j of sylke a nother of rede velvet ijs; iij olde chessabulls xiid; j olde cheste & an olde coffer standeying in ye Vestrie xijd; a presse for Vestements viijd; a holy water stope vjd; iij stolys for chanters vjd; a sacrybell jd. the Chambers j tabull ij trustells & iiij formeys, a cupborde xvjd; ij candelsticks of tynne iiijd. an olde cheste iiijd."

Chapter X

The convent of Grey Friars was situated on the west side of Sutton Pool, in Woolster-street. It, like the White Friars, was a large and important establishment. It had a tower but no spire, as may be seen by the accompanying facsimile of a drawing of the time of Henry VIII. Its buildings closely abutted on the water. The precise date of its foundation has

not been ascertained, but it appears that on the 28th of June, 1383, a license was granted by King Richard II. to "Willielmo Cole, Thomæ Fishacre, Galfrido Couche, et Humfrido Passour," to alienate six acres of land in Plymouth, which were held of the King *in capite*, to the Friar's Minors in the same town ("*Fratrum Minorum in villa predicta habituturis*") as a site for a certain church, a belfry, and other buildings, and for the necessary habitation of the same brethren anew to be made and constructed. It is possible that the land thus conveyed might be the site of a still older establishment. The Brethren having "proceeded uncanonically in erecting their church '*in villa de Sutton juxta Plymouth*,' and obtaining its consecration by one John Berham, a Dominican, who passed himself for the Bishop of Naples, Bishop Brantyngham visited this violation of jurisdiction with his high displeasure, excommunicating the guilty parties and laying the church itself under an interdict." (*Reg: vol.* 1, *p.*221.) The last remaining parts of this convent were (with the exception of a doorway, still standing) removed in 1813, when the present Exchange was erected. A part of the site was used for many years as an inn, called the "Mitre Tavern." This inn was entered from the street through a low arched doorway, leading into a quadrangular court, having on the eastern side a cloister, supported by twisted or spiral pillars. At the end of this a staircase led to apartments formed out of the convent church; the lower part had been used as cellars for merchandize. The site of this convent was granted on November 13th, 1546, to Giles and Gregory Iseham.

The Dominicans, or Black Friars, had also an establishment in Plymouth, which is said to have been situated near Notte-street and Southside-street, where a narrow street called "Blackfriar's-lane" perpetuates its name. Probably the buildings now used as a distillery by Messrs. Coates and Co. may be a part of this religious house. In the distillery buildings are two interesting doorways belonging to the monastic establishment, and also a fine room, one part of which is now used as an office, and the other, and larger part, as a store-room, with a remarkably good and characteristic timber roof. In the lower part of the building is a room with a strongly barred window, which is said at one time to have been used as a cell or marshalsea.

Another religious house was the Leper's Hospital, (*Domus Leprosorum*) dedicated to the Holy Trinity and to St. Mary Magdalene. It was erected "*in honore S. Trinitatis ac beatæ Mariæ Magdalanæ.*" The date of its foundation would appear to have been unknown to the members of the establishment, for in the reign of Edward III., about 1370, they laid claim to immemorial existence. In that year the prior of the house sued the Prior of Plympton for a corody consisting of a daily loaf of white and black bread, a gallon of convent ale, and a mess of '*cochin des chaires*' on every flesh day, and a mess of '*cochin de peshon*' on every fish day, like a canon of the priory. The Prior of Plympton denied the corporate character of the hospital, alleging that it was a mere voluntary association of poor laymen, without convent, college, or common seal, and, therefore, incapable of suing in the name of their prior. The plaintiff replied that priors had been elected by the brethren from time immemorial. The court eventually over-ruled the plea, and adjudged that, as the defendant did not deny that there had always been such elected priors from time beyond memory, he was bound to give a more substantial answer to the complaint. We may safely infer from this reported case, that the origin of the establishment, if not really immemorial, was, at all events, very obscure. The house was recognized by Bishop Brantyngham in 1374.

The Abbey, so called, adjoining St. Andrew's churchyard, in Finewell-street, is evidently a part of the domestic buildings attached to that Church, which belonged to the Priory of Plympton. Of these remains we give an engraving on next page, copied from an original drawing by Worsley, showing it as it existed half a century ago. The building is three stories in height, and is entered by a gothic doorway, the inner arch of which has foliated spandrels, and a tympanum with an open quatrefoil. Above this is a mullioned window of twelve lights, and above this again a window of two lights. It is traditionally said that a subterranean passage from this building communicates with the crypt of St. Andrew's Church.

Chapter X

The Church, or Chapel, of St. Catherine was on the Hoe. It was, as will be seen from the subjoined facsmilie from the chart which has before been referred to, a small building, with a lofty tower. On the south side of the nave were three windows, and at the east end a large east window, the gable being surmounted by a cross. In the south side of the tower was a two-light gothic window, and above this was a projecting bell turret of wood, in which the alarm bell, to be rung to alarm the town on occasions of the approach of an enemy, and otherwise, was hung. The Church was enclosed by a wall, and near it, on the Hoe, stood a well-formed cross, raised up on steps.

Mention of the chapel is made by Bishop Brantyngham in 1370, and Bishop Stafford in 1413, as the Chapel of St. Catherine, *super le Howe juxta Plymouth*; and again by Bishop Lacy in 1425. Among other Corporation payments occurs this entry:– 1565, "Item paide for lathe nailes for mendinge the Howe Chapple, 10*d.*;" and in 1569, "Item payd for a rope for the bell upon the Hawe, £0 1s. 1d." Leland thus speaks of this chapel, of which all trace is lost except the name of Catherine-street, and, possibly, Catwater and Catdown, in the following words: – "There is a righte goodly Walke on an Hille without the Towne by south, caullid the How, and a fair Chapel of S. Catarine on it." The following curious document appears to refer to a chalice belonging to this chapel, as well as to those of some chantry chapels, etc.:–

Memorand qd. calix Sancte Katerine Et calix Bte Marie reman cum Petro Ligger.

Itm – Calix Ste Crucis reman in custod Johis Ilcombe.

Itm – Alt calix reman cum Johe Furneys.

Itm – Calix Sancte . . . . . reman cum Petro Erle.

Itm – Calix . . . . reman cum Willmo Thikpeny.

Itm – Calix Ste Marie Attewille reman cum Peke.

Memorand – That remayneth in the hands of John Paynter a Chalice of Seynt Katirin rec. of Pers Lygger.

Itm – Remayneth with John Furneys II Chalices of the Rode delyved by the hand of Willm Belde.

Itm – In the hands of John Hawkins and Willm Lewys a Chalice of Seynt Erasmus.

Md. – For to enquyre for our Lady Chalice yt remaynith with pers Lygg.

On St. Nicholas' Island, formerly called "St. Michael's Island," and now more frequently known by the name of "Drake's Island," in the Sound, formerly stood a chapel, or cell, given to Plympton Priory by Walter de Valletort, which was dedicated to St. Michael, and so gave name to the Island. In the chart so frequently referred to this chapel, or cell, is shown, and is the only building on the island, which was fortified not long after this chart was drawn. In the proceedings of the Privy Council it appears that a letter was written to the Mayor of Plymouth and his brethren, on the 28th of March, 1548, "merveilinge of their unwillingness to proceede in the fortifyinge of St. Michaelles Chappelle to be made a bulwarke, and when they allege the pluckinge down of that Chappelle to the foundation, they were answered, the same being made upp againe with a wall of turf, should neither be of less effecte or strength, nor yet of such greate coste as they intended, and, therefore, eftsones the lordes desired them like good subjects to goe in hande with that worke accordingle, as they might thereby be esteemed that they tender the Kings Ma[ties] pleasure, and their owne sureties and defense chiefeste."

Another chapel, dedicated to Our Lady of Grace, was at Quarreywell, within the boundaries of Plymouth.

Although there is literally nothing in the way of direct evidence to connect Palace Court with the ancient religious houses of Plymouth, it may, very possibly, have formed a part of the residence of the old priors of Plympton at the time when St. Andrew's was one of their possessions, and when they held a grange in the town. Palace Court, entered by an arched doorway, is situated in Catte-street, not far from the Old Guildhall, and is, at the present time, so far removed from anything palatial in appearance, or, in

fact, that is has simply become the residence – being let off in separate floors or rooms – of people of the very lowest ranks of society. It is, indeed, a place to be but once visited, and that, a visit of but short duration. Still, putting aside all feelings of disgust at the modes of living of its denizens, or of the filth and squalor of the place, it is worth a visit, and some few interesting features will repay examination – especially a carved corbel on the landing of one of the principal staircases. Of the "Palace Court," denuded of an excresene, which has been built up in the quadrangle, and so cuts off some portion even of the little amount of free air the inhabitants formerly had to breathe, we give an engraving. In the old rent-rolls of the Trelawny family are several entries relating to rents received for "the Palace" for "cellars in the Palace," and for "lofts in the Palace," which at that time belonged to the Trelawny's.

ST. ANDREW'S CHURCH, "The mother Church" of Plymouth, is no doubt an old foundation, although no portions of the present building would appear to date back beyond very late in the XIV., or very early in the XV. centuries. That the Church existed in the XIII. century is abundantly proved, and the probability is that it was founded some years anterior to that time. In 1460 the present tower was erected, although in some records it is stated, as shown on a preceding page, to have been built in 1440. It was built mainly at the expense of Thomas Yogge, a merchant, of Plymouth – he, apparently defraying all costs and charges, and the town finding the materials. Leland says:– "One Thomas Yogge, a Marchaunt, of Plymouthe, paid of late yeres for making of the Steple of Plymmouthe Cherch. The Towne paide for the stuffe." St. Andrew's, until the dissolution, belonged to, and was a prebend of, Plympton Priory, which possessed the greater part of the town, holding a courtleet, possessing the corn-mills, markets, fairs, assize of bread and beer, and rights of pillory, etc. This Prebend is stated to have been occasionally called the Prebend of St. Peter and St. Paul, at Sutton. After the dissolution it passed into the hands of the Mayor and Commonalty by the charter of Queen Elizabeth, and so remained until the passing of the Municipal Corporations Reform Act, when the advowson was sold. The matter was not, however, at all times smooth sailing for the Corporation, and they were now and then in hot water with the incumbents. One memorable instance occurred in 1637, when a dispute arose between the vicar, Aaron Wilson (whose monument stands at the east end of the south aisle) and the Corporation, respecting several alleged encroachments on what he considered his rights. The Star Chamber decree, respecting this matter, is so curious, that it is worth printing in full. It is as follows:–

At the Inner Star Chamber, the 10th May, 1637. Present – Lord Archbishop of Canterbury, his Grace, and Lord Keeper.

WHEREAS, Aaron Wilson, Vicar of the Church of Plymouth, in the County of Devon, heretofore preferred a petition to His Majestie against the Mayor and Commonalty of the Burrough of Plymouth, concerning some usurpations made by the said Mayor upon the rights and privileges of the said vicar; and, whereas, His Majestie was graciously pleased to referre the consideration thereof to the Lord Archbishop of Canterbury, his Grace, and the Lord Keeper; and, whereas, the said Mayor and Commonalty exhibited lately to the Lord Archbishop of Canterbury, as Metropolitan, for the ending certaine differences between them and the said Aaron Wilson, Vicar, concerning the said Church, his Grace being assisted by the Lord Keeper, having thereupon fully heard the said parties and their counsell concerning the said matter in question and variance, between the said Mayor, Commonalty, and parishioners, and the said vicar. After a long debate and consideration, all parties professing an unfeigned desire that all things might be settled and established in such sort as might produce an amicable end of all differences, and a perfect union amongst them for the future, it was ordered as followeth: – "And, in the first place, Mr. Glanvell, Recorder of the said towne, and Mr. Fowell, Town Clerke, they did, in the name of the said Mayor and Commonalty, humbly submit all the right of patronage of the vicarage of the said Church to His Majesty's disposall, professing the said Mayor and Commonalty were very unwilling to dispute their title there with His Majesty; yet humbly besought, in behalfe of the said Corporation, that in the now grant to be passed to the said Mayor and Commonalty, the Gramer School there might be established and some maintenance be settled upon the same; whereupon it was ordered that the Council of the said towne should attend His Majesty's Attorney and Solicitor-Generall and receive their directions how such surrender and assurance as the said Mayor and Commonalty is to make to His Majestie of the said patronage and vicarage." As touching the sundry differences between the said Mayor and Commonalty and parishioners, and the said vicar, their lordships did examine and consider the same particularly, and ordered them as followeth: – "First. Touching the incroachments alleged by the said vicar to be made by the said Mayor and Commonalty on the east side of the churchyard by building a row of shambles and other houses on parts of the churchyard, and on the west side by building of the hospitall, where the vicar had anciently an house. This was, by the vicar, waved, and disallowed by their lordships, for that there was not sufficient proofe made to make good that said pretence. Whereas it was objected that the said Mayor and Commonalty tooke from the vicar a duty of burialls in the churchyard, viz., 06s. 08d. for every coffin interred in the churchyard, and £1 6s. 8d. for every coffin interred in the Church; for as much as it was on all sides confessed that the vicar hath now for every corps buryed in the Church 1s. 4s., and the clerk 8d., and for every corps buryed in the churchyard 8d., and the clerk 4d.; and for that it is alleged that the rates lay on such as are buryed in coffins in the Church and churchyard was, by agreement of the parishioners, to prevent the great number of buryals in coffins, which were found to be very inconvenient, and were agreed to be imployed to the use of the Church. Their lordships thought fitt that the said rates shall be settled by the Bishop of the Diocese for such as are buryed in coffins, and shall be accordingly continued, but to be received by the Churchwardens, who are to be accountable for the same, for the repairs, and other uses of the Church, and that the vicar and clerk shall enjoy their severall rates for buryalls, as aforesaid, respectively.

As touching the pewes in the Church, which is alleged are sold by the Mayor to such as will give most, taking 50*s*. and £3 and more for one roome in the seat, it is ordered that the disposall of the said pewes is to remain in the vicar and churchwardens, and if they cannot agree, then the Bishop of the Diocese, or his chancellor, is to determine and order the same according to the Ecclesiasticall law; and their lordships farther think fitt that there be no seat hereafter appropriate to any house or family, yet that no seates be altered that are now settled, but as they shall become void, to be disposed of according to the former order, and that therein care be had to prefer the ablest inhabitants and householders and that the revenues and profits thereof be to the repaires and other uses of the Church, which the churchwardens and their successors are to receive and to be made accountable for, and in such manner as they are for other money received by them for the use of the Church. And as touching the pewes belonging to the Mayor, magistrates, common councell, and publick officers and their wives, that these be, from time to time, continued as they now are, without any alteration. Whereas, it is farther alleged by the said vicar, that the Mayor claimeth the right of the chancell, setts up seats therein, giveth away others (and among them the vicar's seat) selleth the rest, and taketh duties for buryalls there. The Mayor and Commonalty confess that they claim the same under the impropriator, and do employ the benefit thereof to, and for the use of the Church; and in regard thereof, are at the charge of reparation of the said chancell, and if there be any surplus, of benefit they employ it to the use of the Church, upon which consideration their lordships think fitt that the said Mayor and Commonalty shall enjoy the same accordingly. And as concerning the seats in the chancell, belonging to Mr. Hele and his wife, the same are to be restored to them, and another convenient seat to be erected in the chancell for the vicar, at the charge of the parish, and the vicar's wife is to be seated in the seat next to the Mayor's wife, being the antient seat appertaining to the wife of the vicar of that Church.

Concerning the choice of the churchwardens, it is ordered that if the vicar and parishioners cannot agree, that then the election of the churchwardens shall be according to canon, which is, the vicar choose one, and the parisioners the other.

As for the money collected for the poor at the Communion, the same is to be received by the churchwardens and to be given amongst the poor by the distributions as hath been formerly used.

Touching the clerk's wages, the same is to be collected and paid by the churchwardens as formerly.

Collections upon briefs are to be made at the Church doors as formerly, the vicar to give convenient and timely notice to the churchwardens when he receiveth any such briefs, to the end that they may gett some to assist them in the said collection.

As concerning marriages, that now be married without license or bans publickly asked in the Church, and if either of the parties to be married are strangers, that then the vicar is to have a certificate from such strangers according to the canon before he marry them.

As for the fees for marriages, with or without license, the antient fees for the same are to be set downe and regulated by the Chancellor, according to the table of fees in the office of the Archbishop of Canterbury.

And, lastly, whereas the said vicar hath commenced divers suits against some of the said parishioners for tithes of kine, milk, apples, etc., for payment whereof the said parishioners claim a custome, and a tryall is to be had between the said vicar and Nicholas Sherwill, one of the parishioners, at the next assizes. Upon that account it is ordered that the vicar shall not proceed upon any other suites for the said tithes until such time as the said tryall shall be passed; and as well the said vicar as the said parishioners shall, for such tithes, conform themselves to the judgments that shall be given upon the said tryall, except there be some just cause to the contrary.

And this their lordships order to be entered in the registry of the Bishop of the Diocese.– EDWARD NICHOLAS."

In Pope Nicholas' taxation – begun 1288, and ended 1291 – the entry is as follows: –

	Taxatio.	Decima.
Ecclia de Sutton (S. Andree Plymouth)	5.6.8	0.10.8
Vicar de eadem	4.6.8	0. 8.8

Until the year 1640 Plymouth was one parish, St. Andrew's being the vicarage, but in that year a new parish was created by Act of Parliament, as shown on a previous page.* The Church of St. Andrew is a large, fine, and commodious edifice, and being situated in the centre of the town, with its majestic tower rising above the surrounding buildings, forms a prominent object for whichever side it is seen. It consists of a nave and chancel, with north and south aisles throughout, and north and south transepts. The tower is at the west end. The north and south aisles are each separated from the nave and chancel by a series of nine obtusely pointed arches, six of which are in the nave, and three in the chancel, and these spring from clustered columns with foliated capitals. The chancel arches rise to the roof, and the division between the chancel and nave is therefore not strongly apparent. The roofs are barrel-formed, and divided into square compartments by carved wooden framework, with carved bosses at the intersections. There is no clerestory, the nave being lighted by a series of open glazed compartments in the roof. At the west end is a large organ loft and gallery,

*page 122

beneath which is the vestry, used for holding parish meetings, and in each of the transepts is a gallery supported upon two low arches, and having its front decorated with quatrefoil panelling. These galleries were put up in place of more unsightly ones, when, in 1826, the Church was repaired and its interior re-modelled from the designs of Mr. Foulston. At this time, too, the "huge three-decker" pulpit, which stood against one of the side columns, was placed under the chancel-arch and its canopy taken away and ultimately replaced by a large and hideous sounding board. This pulpit has recently been removed, and a new one, of extremely beautiful design, put in its place. The stalls for the Mayor and Corporation are placed on either side the chancel, near the chancel-arch. They are of carved oak, and bear the arms of the borough. The east window is filled with stained glass, by Ball; it represents the Ascension. The east windows of the side aisles are also filled with stained glass, as, indeed, are all in the Church, with geometric and foliated designs, some of which have groups in their upper lights. On the south side of the south aisle is a good window, the four lights of which contain figures of St. Peter, St. Andrew, St. James Major, and St. Thomas, under elaborate canopies, and figures of angels beneath; another similar window contains the figures of SS. Philip, Bartholomew, Thaddeus, and Simon. In the same aisle is a remarkably fine and beautiful memorial window of four lights, bearing the following inscription: – "This window, dedicated to the honor of God & to the memories of Zachary Mudge, Esquire, Admiral of the White, & Jane Granger, his wife. Their bodies lie interred in the churchyard of Newton Ferrers." At the top are the arms of Mudge, *argent*, a chevron, *gules*, between their cockatrices, *vert*; and the motto, "All's Well." In the two side lights at top, "They that go down to the sea in ships, that do business in great waters." "These see the works of the Lord, and His wonders in the deep." In the four principal lights are figures of the four Evangelists; over the first are the arms of Mudge, impaling Granger, with the name beneath; over the second, in the same manner, Rosdew, impaling Mudge; while in the third and fourth respectively, are Fletcher, impaling Mudge; and Mallac, impaling Mudge. Beneath the figures of the Evangelists are respectively the arms of Mudge, impaling Dickinson; Mudge, impaling Yonge and Granger; Seaton, impaling Yonge; and Burrell, impaling Prowse. One of the windows on the north side of the north aisle bears in the centre light, at its head, the arms of the Plymouth Workhouse, or Hospital or Poors Portion, which are the same as the arms of the borough, with the addition of the saltire, or St. Andrew's Cross, being charged on each limb with three bees, and a bee-hive in its centre. In the same aisle is a memorial window of four lights, which bear, respectively, the Adoration, the Crucifixion, the Descent from the Cross, and the Baptism of Christ. At the top of the window, in the central lights, are the arms of the borough of Plymouth, with the modern supporters, flags, etc.; and at the bottom the inscription – "In memory of Edmund Lockyer, Esq., born Sep. 18, 1750; died Feb. 20, 1836." "Eleanor, his wife, daughter of Francis Penrose, of Durian, Cornwall; died 1807." "Edmund Lockyer, Esq., M.D., their only son, born Oct. 28, 1782; died Dec. 3, 1816." "And Eleanor, their only daughter, wife of Admiral Sir Samuel Pym, K.C.B., died 1835." The window also bears the arms of Lockyer, impaling those of Penrose.

The Church contains many interesting monuments and tablets, the earliest of which are of quite late in the XVI., and of the early part of the XVII. century. Among them are the following: – At the end of the south aisle is an altar-tomb of black marble, bearing, besides a long inscription on the top, the following on its front:–

"Here rest the Bodys of ye Right Worpll Aaron Wilson, Dr. of Divinity, Archdeacon of Exeter, and Vicar of Plymovth, and Aaron Wilson, his son, who departed this Life, the one the 7 of July, ye other the 21 of January next following 1643."

Near this stands a beautiful bust, by Chantry, of Dr. Zachariah Mudge, sometime vicar of St. Andrew's. The bust, which cost £700, and was taken from a portrait of the vicar by Sir Joshua Reynolds, stands upon a rough pedestal, and was fixed in its position by Chantry, who came down specially to Plymouth for the purpose. The following inscription is to the memory of Dr. Mudge:–

"Zachariah Mudge, Prebendary of Exeter and Vicar of St. Andrew's, Plymouth. Born 1694, Died 1769. In private Life he was Amiable and Benevolent; In his Ministry Faithful , Eloquent, and Persuasive; Distinguished for knowledge among the Learned, and for Talent among Men of Science."

There are also tablets to Jenney, daughter of Dr. John Mudge, and wife of Richard Rosdew, of Beechwood, 1818; and to Richard Rosdew, 1837. Others in the same part of the Church are as follows:–

"Near this Place lyeth ye Body of Mr. Thomas Swanton, who dyed May 19, MDCCIII, having been Collector of Her Majesty's Customs in this Port XII years. He was ye youngest son of Francis Swanton of Salisbury, Esq., who was Clerk of ye Assize for ye Western Circuit."

"Near this place is interred the Body of Capt. Edmund Lechmere, formerly Commr. of His Majesty's Ship ye Linn, & late of the Lyme Frigot of 32 guns, on board of which he departed ys life ye 16 Jany., 1703, of ye wounds he recd. ye 15 in an Engagent. wth a French Privr. of 46 guns. From whom he protected a large Fleet of Merchants Ships all in safety, and he bravely gave ye enemie Battel & forced him to bear away with very much damage. He was in the Begining of ye Action wounded in both knees, and afterwards recd. a Musquet shot through his body, yett by neither discouraged from prosecuting the enemie with ye utmost vigour. Thus fell this Brave Man, whom his early years had (as well as by ye Constancy of his good Disciple &

prudent conduct, as by his Intrepid Gallantry in this & many other actions) rendered himself Famous in many Parts of the World; Servicable to his Queen & Country, highly esteemed by the Commander of ye Fleet, entirely beloved by ye Seamen, and universally lamented by all yt knew him. He was 3rd Son to Edmund Lechmere, of Hanley Castle, in ye County of Worcester, Esq., by Lucy, his wife, daughter of Anthony Hungerford, of Farleigh Castle, in ye County of Somerset, Esq. Anno Ætat, 47.∏

At the top are trophies of arms, nautical emblems, etc., and the arms of Lechmere; and at the bottom a sculptured representation of the engagement.

"Johes Gilbert olim Coll Wadhami in Oxon: Socius et A: M: Nuper Hujus Eccles Vicarius et St. Petri in Exon Canonicus Residentiarius. Laboribus Lassatus Obijt Anno. Ætat: Suæ 85° Annoq Domini 1722°. Et hic jacet Sepultus Mrs. Alice Gilbert, departed this Life the 20th of February, 1740. And her Sister, Mrs. Emm Gilbert, the 28th of May, 1750. Daughters of the Canon, by Whom this Monument was Erected."

Underneath is represented the Ascension; at the top is a medallion head of Canon Gilbert, who was vicar of St. Andrew's, in his robes. A very interesting monument, but one not much seen, through being on the wall of the inside of the tower, is to the memory of Captain Francis Drake, R.N., a descendent of Sir Francis Drake. At the head are the arms of Drake, with crest, mantling, etc., beautifully sculptured. The arms are *sable,* a fess wavy, *or*, charged with a crescent, *gules,* between two pole stars, *argent*; impaling, quarterly 1 and 4, *or,* a lion rampant, *gules*, 2 and 3 *sable*; crest, on a helmet, a ship under ruff, drawn round the globe with a cable rope, by a hand out of the clouds; over it the motto "Auxilio divino," and underneath it, "Sic Parvis Magna." The inscription is –

"Near this Place lyes the
Body of Francis Drake Esqr
for many years a Captain
in the Royall Navy, who
died the 26th day of Decr
Anno Dom 1729
In the 61st year of his Age.
As also the Body of Mrs
Prudence Sausure widow (his
Sister) who died the 22 day of
November 1737 aged about
90 years."

A fine upright incised slab, with cupids, foliage, death's-heads, etc., bears at the top a shield with the arms, crest, mantling, etc., of the family of Smith, of Plymouth, party per bend engrailed, two crosses patée countercharged, impaling . . . . three lions heads erased; crest, out of a ducal coronet, *or*, a demi-falcon, wings expanded, proper. the inscription, which is curious, is –

"Neere this Place Lyeth Interred Mr. Anthony Smith, late of This Towne, Merchant, who departed this Life the 15 Daye of October, 1680, in the 53 yeare of his Age, to whose Memory this White Stone was given by Mr.

> William Bowtell, of London, Merchant, and sett up in this place by Loveday Smith, Relict of the sayed Anthony. Allsoo Elizabeth, Daughter of the said Anthony."

To the family of Fownes, of Plymouth, are some interesting memorials, the earliest of which, 1589, is an upright slab in the vestibule; it bears the arms of Fownes, *azure*, three eagles displayed in chief, and a mullet in base, *argent*. Another bears the inscription–

> "Memoriæ Sacrum Prudentiæ Thomæ Founes Armigeri Uxoris Sepultæ 9 Jany 1606. Joannæ ejusdem Thomæ Uxoris, Sepultæ 24 February 1625. Julianæ Richardi Founes, Armigeri, Sepultæ 28 May 1632. Richardi Founes Armigeri., Sepultæ 4 Septembris 1633. Thomæ Fownes, Armigeri, Sepultæ 25 Aprilis 1635.

Quen vixisse semel celebrabrunt eccla leuamem
Qui tulit hospitibus pauperibusq dedit.
Marmoream q domum iduis qui struxit eenis
Quæ sit ab Anthoris nomine dicta Fovens."
Ne Careant, tenebris obducti lampade spargent
Extinctis radios, quæ micuere faces.

Another reads –

"Memoriæ Sacrum Prudentia filia natu maxima Tho: Fownes et vxor Jo: Waddon de Plymo: Armig: hic jacet, Curæ loquuntur leues ingentes stupent."

Here Lieth the Bodie of Joane late
the Wife of Master Hvmphrey Fownes of Plymouth
Marchant, who departed this Life
the Third Daie of Avgvst
in the Mairoltie of her Hvsband

O That My Wordes were now written
or graven with an iron Penne in
Leade or Stone to continew For
I Knowe that my Redemer Liveth and
That I shall Rise ovt of the Earth
in the last Daie and shall Be
Covered againe with my Skinne
and shall see God in my Flesh yea
and I my selfe shall behold Him
Not with other bvt with these same
Eyes. Anno Domini 1589."

"Here Lyeth the Body of Ivdeth the wife of Francis Amada of Plymovth, Gentel, and onely Dauvghter Vnto Hvmphry Fownes of Plymovth, Marchant, and Ioane his Wiffe, who died the xxvi Daye of Aprill 1623

Also Here Lyeth Bvried the Bodyes
of two Children of the same
Francis and Ivdeth
both named John."

"Here Rest
The Bodyes of John Fownes of Plymuth
Marchant, and Dorothy his Wife
who both departed this Life
the 5th Daye of October 1624
Beinge slaine by the fall
of a chimney
Also her ———— 69
Spectacles of griefe command
Ears and Eyes to be at stand;
Reader then amongst so many
Read, and Weepe at this is any."

A large and strikingly curious monument, bears beneath an arch supported upon pillars, the figures of a gentleman in armour, and his wife, kneeling one on each side of a lectern. Behind him are their two sons, and behind her, three daughters. Beneath this is an oblong tablet, on which, in the centre, are half-length three-quarter-face figures of a gentleman in robes, of the time of Charles I., with moustache, imperial, etc., and his son; their hands clasped, and the sons left hand on his breast. Behind the gentleman are three other sons, with hands clasped in hands; and behind the son, on a pallet, lie two chrisom children, their heads resting on a skull; and behind them again, another child. At the top of the monument, is a shield bearing the arms of Sparke, chequy, *or* and *vert*, a bend, ermine. On one side of the inscription tablet are the arms of Sparke, as before, and on the other, what have originally been the arms of Rashleigh, but have evidently been altered in the re-colouring of the tablet. Beneath the inscription is Sparke, impaling Rashleigh. At the bottom are three shields of arms, viz., Sparke, alone; barry wavy of 6, *or* and *gules*, alone; and Sparke, impaling the latter. the inscription is as follows:–

"To the lovg memory of John Sparke Esqr late of this Towne and Deborah his Wife daughter to John Rashleighe of Foy, Esqr who departed this life in expectation of a Joyful Resurrection. He March the 17th 1640 aged 66. She November ye 1 1635 aged 57.

A Father, Mother, and two daughters deere
In silent earth are sweetly lodged heere
Two still of age and two in infancye
Denotes to all both old and young must die
A vertuous life they lived amongst friendes
And crownes of Glory now for them attends.

(To John Sparke and his Wife Deborah)

I was once as thou art now
A man, could speak and goe
But now I ly in silence heere
Serve God, thou must be soe.

When death did me assayle
To God then did I crye
Of Jacob's well to newiste my
soule
That it might never die."

An extremely curious tablet, has a pediment supported by pillars; beneath this, under an arch, is the upright figure of Mrs. Jane Fowell, wrapped in a winding sheet, which is tied in the usual manner above the head. On either side the monument, outside the pillars, is a circular medallion; on one of these is represented four small half-length figures, with the names, "Henry, 4; William, 3; Edmond, 1; John, 2;" and on the other, two small half-length figures, with the names, "Ann," "Jane." At the top is a shield, bearing the arms of Fowell (*argent*, a chevron, *sable*, on a chief, *gules*, three mullets of the first) surmounted by a skull. On the spandrels, and at the bottom, are also the arms of Fowell and others, and beneath the figure, "Mors Mihi Lucrum Cubyle Sepulchram." The inscription is as follows:–

"Here resteth the body of Jane the daughter of Sr Anthonye Barker of Sunning in Barkeshire, Knt, deceased, late Wife of Edmonde Fowell of Plymouth Esq, who died the 23rd day of May, Anno Domini 1640, having issue that survived her four sons and two daughters."

Another tablet has an entablature and shield of arms, supported by two pillars on either side. In the centre, under an oval, lies the figure of a lady, habited in the dress of the period, and at her foot stands a child, holding a skull in the right hand. At the top are the arms of Goodyeare (*gules*, a fesse between two chevrons, *ermine*) with crest and mantling, and at the bottom is also a shield of arms. The inscription is –

Heer Lyeth the Body of Ivdeth late the wife of Mr Moyses Goodyeare, Merchant, Daughter of Mr Abraham Goodyeare, aged 24 yeares, who Died in Childbirth of a Sonne Dead-borne the 21st October 1642. Heer is also interred their Sonne Abraham Goodyere, aged 2 years who died the 30th September 1641.

I being Deliver'd of a Dead-borne Sonne
My Soules Deliver'd and my Labour done
His Birth-day wrought my death to sweeten this
Death is to me the Birth-day of my Bliss
Mors Natatis æternetatis.

Another tablet, to the Sparke family, is curious for its allusion to the name. At the top are the arms of Sparke (chequy, *or* and *vert*, a bend, ermine) in a lozenge, in the centre, and on one side Sparke, and on the other, barry wavy of six, *or* and *gules*. The inscription is –

"To the precious Memory of that Truly Vertuous Gentlewoman Mrs. Mary Sparke, Daughter of Jonathan Sparke of this Towne Esq who departed this Life the xxx. Day of December Anno Domini 1665

> Life's but a SPARKE, a weak uncertain breath
> No sooner kindled than puft out by Death.
> Such was my name, my frame, my fate, yet I
> Am still a living SPARKE, though thus I dye,
> And Shine in Heaven's orbe, a star most bright,
> Though Death on Earth so soon Eclipt my light."

Another has –

> "Here Lyeth Buried The Body of Mr. John Sparke who departed this Life The xix of August, Anno Domini 1603. And also of Milian His Wife who Departed The xxviii. of December Anno Domini 1583."

On a tablet bearing the arms of Carter, *azure*, a talbot passant between three buckles, *or*, in a lozenge, is –

> "In Memory of Mrs. Constance Carter, Daughter of Mr. John & Constance Carter of this Town, who dyed ye 3d of May in ye 23 year of her age and was buryed near this place 1674."

A remarkably curious and rude Egyptianesque tablet, on which are represented a female kneeling before a lectern, and three smaller figures of two of her daughters and one son, on a kind of bracket, or shelf, behind her, bears the following inscription:–

> "In memory of Elizabeth the Wife of Edward Calmady & Daughter of George Baron Esqr who died ye 3 day of February 1645, and of their children 3 here interred, to wit Edward aged 6 yeares, Elizabeth 9 yeares, and Mary 16 yeares. Mors Janua Vitæ."

At the bottom are the Calmady arms, *azure* a chevron, between three pears, slipped, *or*; and on either side is a shield of arms of their alliances. The date at the bottom, 1645.

In the south transept is a fine and elaborate tablet to the memory of George Strelley, Esq. At the top is a shield, bearing the arms of Strelley, with its quarterings, as follows:– 1st, Strelley, paly of six *argent* and *azure*; 2nd, Somerville, *argent*, an eagle displayed *sable*, armed and langued, *gules;* 3rd, Sacheverell, *argent,* on a saltire *sable,* three water bougets, of the first; 4th, . . . *argent*, a chevron between three martlets, *sable*; 5th, Vavasour, *or*, a fesse dancette, *sable*; 6th, Reding, *argent*, three boars' heads, erased, *sable*; 7th, St. Amand, quarterly: 1st and 4th, *argent*, a bend, *azure*, between a mullet in chief and an annulet in base, *gules*; 2nd and 3rd, *argent*, a bend engrailed, *sable*; 8th, Strelley impaling St. Amand, and at the bottom the arms of Strelley alone. The inscription is as follows: –

> "Erected by MRS, ANN STRELLEY, widow, daughter of John St. Amand, of Mansfield, in the County of Nottingham, Esq., in Memory of GEORGE STRELLEY, Esq., her late husband deceased who Lineally descended from Strelley of Strelley an Antient family in that County and was Maior of this Borough in the year 1667 where (after 63 years conversation in this world, Loveing mercy, doeing justice, and walking humbly with God) he peaceably (on the 16th day of February 1673) Resigned this life for an

heavenly habitation (leaveing Issue by the said Ann only George Strelley his sonn and heir) and resteth interred neere this funerall Pile in certaine hopes of a Glorious Resurrection.

Ransack this lower Orbe youle Scarcely finde
Such Peace, such Piety, in one behinde.
Diamonds have flaws (His actions were so just)
His name had none: His fame Survives his dust.
True charity and zeale adorne his Herse
And scorne the flattrys of a Poet's Verse
Non Mortuus, sed Dormit."

Under the gallery, in the south transept, are the following:–

"Sacred to the Memory of Mrs. J. Dunsterville, the amiable wife of Bathw. Dunsterville, Esqr., Alderman and Magistrate of Plymouth, his native Town. She died on the 11th day of July, 1815, aged 64 years, and is buried, with nine of her children, in a Family Grave in the higher Church Yard, which is there noticed. Bartholomew Dunsterville, Esqr., survived his beloved Wife nearly 20 years, and died on the 7th May, 1835, aged 89 years; Having been blessed in his last Moments by the Return of His Son, Col. Dunsterville, from India, after an absence of 31 years."

"Sacred to Lucy, the beloved Wife of Lieut.-Col. Dunsterville, who departed this life at Bombay, in the East Indies, December the 3rd, 1834, aged 43 years, after eighteen year's devoted to the duties of an affectionate Wife, a most fond and anxious Mother. After having visited the Ship, by which her care was to be rewarded by conveying her to her loved Children, and her native land, It was the Almighty's will to call her hence, Leaving her bereaved Husband, two Sons, and two Daughters, to feel the awful truth that, 'In the midst of Life we are in death.' "

Another tablet records the death of her husband, James Henderson Dunsterville, who became a Major-General in the Bombay Army. "He was a faithful servant of the Honorable E.I. Company for 30 years, 7 of which he was Commissary-General." He died July 12th, 1858.

An elegant tablet, with the inscription on a roll, at the top of which is an exquisitely carved sword, surmounted by the crest of Havelock, a lion rampant holding a battle axe (by Bedford, of London), bears the following inscription:–

"Sacred to the Memory of Charles Wemys Havelock, Lieutenant 66th Gookhas, and 2nd in command 12th Irregular Cavalry, the beloved and only son of Major-General Charles Frederick Havelok, Imperial Ottoman Army, and of Mary, his wife. he was killed in Action at Tigra, Oude, with Sir E. Lugard's Force, whilst gallantly leading his men, of the 12th Irregular Cavalry, in a charge against the Rebels. Born February 16, 1834. Died 11 April, 1858. 'The Blood of Jesus Christ, His Son, cleanseth us from all sin.' 1st John, chap. 1, verse 7."

On a slab, in the floor, is the following inscription to the memory of the only surviving son of the great ballad-hero Admiral Vernon, who is immortalised on innumberable medals as having taken Portobello with only six ships of the line:–

> "Here lies the body of James Vernon, Esq., only surviving son of Admiral Vernon, who, returning by sea from the south of France, was landed here dangerously ill from a bloody Flux, the 6th day of July, 1753, and dyed the 25th of the said month, in the 23rd year of his age."

One of the most important tablets is the "Citadel Monument," on which Sir John Skelton, sometime Governor of the Citadel, and his wife, Bridget Prideaux, are represented kneeling at a lectern. Of this monument we give an engraving overleaf. It bears the following inscription:–

> "Here lyeth the Body of Sr. John Skelton Knt. Lieut. Governor of this Place & Deputy Lieut of this County who by Dame Bridget Prideaux his wife had issue five Sonns and one Daughter viz John his eldest Sonn – who dyed younge. Beuill his second Sonn Groome of the Bed Chamber and Capt. of the Guardes to his present Majesty Grenuill his 3rd Sonn who dyed younge John his 4th Sonn: Charles his 5th Sonn Elizabeth his Daughter who likewise dyed younge Having loyally served his Prince Both in his Exile and since his Restoration dyed the 24th December Anno 1672.

The family to which Sir John Skelton belonged is of considerable antiquity in Cumberland and Yorkshire, its principal seat being Armthwaite Castle, which had been in the family for several generations prior to 1712, when it was sold by Richard Skelton. From time of Edward II. to Henry VIII. the honor of knighthood was held in succession by its members. Sir John Skelton was page of honor to Charles II. while in exile, and married Bridget, daughter of Sir Peter Prideaux and Lady Christian Grenvile, his wife, and granddaughter of Sir Bevil Grenvile. He was knighted and appointed Governor of Plymouth by King Charles in 1660, and made Deputy-Lieutenant of the county of Devon 1665. He died 1672. The monument was erected by Bevil Skelton, who, at the time of his father's death, was Groom of the Bedchamber and Captain of the Guard, and was afterwards knighted. He quartered the arms of Grenvile and Prideaux with his own, and married Frances, daughter and heiress of Sir Robert Lemster, of Ravely, Huntingdonshire, by whom he had an only son, who, upon coming of age, took the name of his paternal grandfather. Of the five sons named on the monument, three only arrived at maturity, viz., the 2nd, Bevil; the 5th, Charles, who held a lieutenant's commission in the French army; and the 4th, John, who settled on one of the Prideaux estates in or near the parish of Modbury. The arms as represented on the monument, were granted by Charles, as the arms of "Sir John Skelton, of Plymouth." Bevil Skelton and his brother Grenvile were named in honor of their maternal great grandfather, Sir Bevil Grenvile. Of John, fourth son of Sir John Skelton, of Plymouth, little need be said beyond the fact that he married and had two sons, John and James, and, with the sale of the Prideaux estates, the family declined, Peter Skelton, of Ermington, son of James Skelton, being the last

who held property in the neighbourhood. There are, however, several of the descendants of the family still residing in Plymouth and Devonport, amongst whom are Dr. John Skelton, of Plymouth, whose son, Dr. John Skelton, is a physician in London.

CHAPTER X

Among the other inscriptions in the Church are the following: –

"John Gandy, M.A., Prebendary of Exeter, and Vicar of this Parish. Died August the 15th 1824: aged 84. A beautiful example of the Christian Pastor, he endeared himself to his flock during the long period of Fifty six years. Devoting himself to acts of usefulness and Benevolence, he exercised the Endowments of a powerful mind in the spirit of one who knew that he was a Steward, and desired only to be found faithful. This Memorial of grateful Veneration is erected by those who esteemed his Friendship a privilege, and his Ministry a public blessing."

"To Catherine, the Wife of Admiral Sir Thomas Byam Martin, G.C.B., and Daughter of Robert Fanshawe, Esqr. She was born at Plymouth the 2nd January, 1775, and died the 25th of March 1849. Blessed be her Memory. Also to Sir Thomas Byam Martin, G.C.B., Admiral of the Fleet, and Vice-Admiral of the United Kingdom, who, during 16 years, represented this Borough in Parliament. Died 21st of October , 1854, aged 81."

"Erected By Admiral Sir T. Byam Martin, G.C.B., to the Memory of his youngest son, Lt.-Colonel Robert Fanshawe Martin, Deputy Adjutant-General of the Queen's Forces, in the Bombay Presidency. He was born at Plymouth June 19, 1805. He died at Poona, in the East Indies, July 13, 1846. A Brother Officer gives a just Epitome of his character in the following words – 'Colonel Martin was a thorough Soldier, and full of Honesty and Truth."

"D.O.M. – In this Church Yard 75 feet North of this Tablet lie the remains of Henry Falkner, late of Derby, only Son of the late John Falkner, Gent, Solicitor, of Nottingham, who died the 11th day of August, 1817,(on board the Brig Sicily, bound to Gibraltar, but driven into this Port by contrary winds) in the 31st year of his age. At the instance of Maternal Affection This Tablet is erected; but in the Hearts of all his sorrowing Relatives and Friends whilst Life is spared to them, will his Memory exist."

"Sacred to the Memory of Joseph Whiteford, Esquire, Who retiring from Professional Life in the Vigor of his Faculties, Devoted himself during many Years to the Duties of the Magistracy and the service of the Charitable, and other Public Institutions of this Town. Universally respected for the Integrity and Moderation of his Character, and beloved for the kindliness of his Disposition, He closed a long career of useful Labor and active Benevolence on the 23rd January, 1849, in the 79th year of his age. His Children, in grateful Remembrance of his unceasing Affection and Parental care, have inscribed this Tablet to his Memory."

"To the Memory of Captain Nicholas Lockyer, R.N., C.B., Who died in command of Her M.S. Albion, at Malta, February 27 Anno Domini 1847 aged 65 years. This Tablet is erected by the Officers and Ship's Company of Her M.S. Albion, and a few Shipmates, as a Testimonial of their regard and Esteem to him, their late Captain and Friend."

"Sacred to the Memory of the Revd. John Heyrick Macaulay, M.A., of Trinity College, Cambridge, late Head Master of Repton School, and formerly of the New Grammar School, Plymouth. By his accurate Scholarship, strict and impartial Discipline and unwearied Diligence, He enabled many of his pupils to attain Academic distinction. By his domestic Virtues, generous Hospitality, and high companiable qualities, He secured the devoted affection of his Family, and endeared himself to a large circle of acquaintance. To the Poor, he was a kind and liberal Benefactor: and the Regard entertained for his character, as a Christian Minister, is Recorded, where it was best known, on a worthier Monument at Repton, where he suddenly died,

December 18, 1840, aged 42 years. As a tribute to his moral, social, and intellectual worth, This Tablet has been erected by his Friends and Pupils of this Neighbourhood."

"To perpetuate the Memory of departed worth This stone is inscribed with the names of Mary Johns, who died February 2, 1792, and of Thomas Johns, her husband, who rested from the Labors of a well-spent Life May 17th, 1797, aged 67.

The mould'ring Form below to dust consigned
Was once the mansion of a polish'd mind.
A mind enrich'd with sentiment and taste,
By Virtue dignifi'd, by talents grac'd,
Fraught with each charm that gladdens wedded life,
Exalts the Mother, or endears the wife.
Nor rests she here alone, the lifeless frame
Of him with whom she shar'd a heart and name
Here shares with her the Almighty's awful doom;
Sleeps near her ashes, and partakes her tomb.
Far above human praise his Virtues rise,
Their true Memorial is beyond the skies."

"William Woollcombe, M.D., Died on the 23 of May, 1822, aged 49 years, and lies buried at Plympton St. Mary. His Humanity, Skill, and Liberality, in the discharge of his Professional Duties, were not less eminent than his general Knowledge, his sound and discriminating Judgment, and the peculiar mildness and benevolence of his Character. His Loss was deplored as a Public Calamity, in this his native place, and in the surrounding country. The numerous Friends in whose Hearts his Memory is fondly cherished, express their sincere and affectionate regret and gratitude, by inscribing this Monument with his Name."

"Near this Place Lies the Body of Philip De Sausmarez, Esq., Commander of his Majesty's Ship ye Nottingham. He was the Son of Mathw. de Sausmarez, of the Island of Guernsey, Esq., by Ann Durell, of the Island of Jersey, his wife, families of Antiquity and repute in those parts. He was born Novr. 17th 1710 and gloriously but unfortunately fell by a cannon ball Octobr 14th 1747, in pursuing two Ships of the Enemy that were making their Escape when the French were routed under the command of Admiral Hawke. Out of gratitude and affection his brothers and sisters have caus'd a Monument to be erected to his Memory in Westminster Abbey."

"Sacred to the Memory of Hugh Walker, Esq., Surgeon R.N., aged 52 of Larne, in the County of Antrim in Ireland, who on his return from a third voyage to New South Wales found his beloved Wife and (only) child deposited in the Family Vault beneath as Commemorated on the adjoining Monument, in deep affliction and agony of mind undertook his fourth voyage to that Country, from whence returning in the Ship Cumberland of London in the Month of May 1827, he together with the Captain (Carne) the whole Crew and all the Passengers are believed to have perished at Sea in the South Pacific Ocean. A small vestige of the Ship only was discovered giving too melancholy a proof of the afflictive nature of the event. 'It is not in Man that walketh to direct his steps.' 'That they may know that this is thy hand and that thou Lord has done it.' 'The Righteous will consider this and rejoice!' "

"Sacred to the Memory of Catherine, wife of Hugh Walker, Esqr. Surgeon R.N. and Daughter of the late Thos. B. Darracott, Esqr. an Alderman of this his Native Town, who died 12th September 1825, aged 51 Years, Also of Thomas Samuel their Son who Died 3rd May, 1826, aged 10 Years. Their Mortal Remains are deposited in the Family Vault of the Darracotts the Entrance to which, is close on the Inside of the Southern Door of this Church."

"Sacred to the Memory of John Yarde Fownes Esqr. (Lineal Descendant of Thomas Fownes, Mayor of Plymouth in 1620,) Who departed this life 22nd October, 1839; aged 67. Also of John Yarde Fownes, son of the above, Who died 16th January, 1839; aged 20."

"Consecrated to the Remains of Mrs. Anne Hill, wife of Captn Henry Hill, of the Royal Navy, and Daughter of the Revd. James Worsley, Rector of Gatcombe, in the Isle of Wight, who departed this life Sept. 23rd, 1800; aged 23 years.

Here let the Proud, the Volatile, and Gay,
Who bask and glitter in life's little Day,
Who follow Pleasure, thro' the maze of Fate,
And never dream of their precarious State:
Here let them pause, and read Beneath this Stone,
Lies every female Virtue, joined in one.
If Beauty ye require, a fairer form
Could never catch the Eye, or Bosom warm;
Yet, fairer still, her mind displayed thro' life,
The best of Daughters, Sisters, Mother, Wife.
Heaven view'd th' Angelic soul with fond Regard,
And snatch'd her early to a blest Reward."

"To the memory of the Revd. Thomas Byrth, D.D., F.A.S., for fifteen years Rector of Wallasey, who departed this life October 28, 1849, Aged 56 years. This Tablet is erected by his Parishioners and Friends, in token of their gratitude to God, who gave to this Parish a Teacher so earnest and eloquent, a Friend so faithful and affectionate, an Example so bright of a Christian life. He is pure from the Blood of all men, for he hath not shunned to declare unto us all the Counsel of God. The Marble Tablet on which the above was inscribed having been destroyed by the Fire which, in February 1857, burnt Wallasey Church, Cheshire, to the ground, the bereaved Widow has erected this Memorial to her beloved and revered Husband in the Church where he often Ministered."

"Sacred to the memory of Albert Edward Hutchinson late Sub-Lieutenant of H.M.S. Tartar, second son of Commander Hutchinson R.N. and Hannah his wife, who was drowned in Simons Bay on the night of the 14th February 1865 by the Swamping of a Boat. He was on his return to his Native Land, after an absence of about 4 years, when thus suddenly cut off in his 21st year, to the deep grief of his Parents, his only surviving Brother, and Sisters, by whom this Tablet has been erected to his beloved Memory. I. Corinthians ch.11, v.IX. In my Father's House are many Mansions. St. John, XIV. ch., II. V."

"This Tablet is erected by a few friends in affectionate remembrance of the Rev. Henry Eugene Flos Tracey M.A., Incumbent of the District of St. Stephen-in-the-Fields, Paddington, and to commemorate the ability and devotedness with which during four years he preached the Gospel, and performed all the duties of a Christian Minister, as Curate of St. Andrew's, Plymouth. He died at Hastings, respected, loved, and lamented, on the 8th of May aged 34 years."

"Sacred to the memory of Two beloved Sisters, whose Remains are interred near this Place; Mrs Rebecca Hirst, Widow of the late Arthur Hirst, Lieut. in the Royal Invalids, Who Died 4th April 1820, aged 84 Years. She gave by her Will, among other

Charitable Bequests, to the Vicar of this Parish, Two Hundred Pounds; upon Trust to lay out the Interest in the Purchase of Coals and Bread, to be Distributed to the Poor of the said Parish, annually for ever. Also, Mrs Sarah King, Widow of the late Richard King, of Fowelscombe in this County, Esquire, who died 17th January, 1824, aged 83 Years. She also gave by her Will, to the Vicar of this Parish, Fifty Pounds; upon Trust, to lay out the Interest thereof, in the Purchase of Coals, to be distributed to the Poor of the said Parish, annually, for ever. As a Tribute of Gratitude and Respect, this Monument is erected by their Executor, Thomas Taylor."

"Underneath Lies Buryed the Body of Mr. James Yonge, Phisitian, & Fellow of the Royal Society, who was once Mayor of this his Native Town, and dyed the 25th day of July 1721, in the 76th year of his age. And by him his Beloved Wife Jane who dyed Novr. 25th 1708 in the Sixtyeth year of her Age, after having lived near 40 years in wedlock, and born 9 Children."

"Near this Place lie the Remains of Frances Troubridge, Wife of Captain Thomas Troubridge, of the Royal Navy, who died June the XIII. MDCCXCVIII, Aged XXXVIII Years. Also in the same Grave is interred Elizabeth daughter of Captain Thomas Troubridge and of Frances his Wife. She died XXIVth April MDCCXCIV, in the Vth year of her age."

"His Parents cheerful joy and grief lies heere
Their only child like Abrams sacrifice
Whome the Almighties fatall Marshall kills
To Gods Will then did they resign their wills
Like Noah's Dove in the tempestuous seas
Of a distracted state he found no ease
His soule thene mounted like the early larke
To find a resting place in Heaven his Arke"

At the bottom is a monogram of the letters M. and W., and the date 1684.

REBEKAH'S TOMBSTONE

"To the memory
of Mrs. Rebekah Hughes, Wife 17 yeers to
Mr. G: H: Minr. of the Gospel in Plymo.
the 4th davghter to Iohn Vpton of Lvpton
Esqr. who deceasing on the 10th day of
Ivne 1661 in the 41st yeer of her
age, is interred neer this Pillar
and being dead yet speaketh

My Gold I have	Arise I shall
Now in the grave	When God doth call
Death is no pain	Look vpon me
Christ made it gain	And Godly be

Next her another
Lieth a mother,
Frances Hughes."

"Sacred to the Memory of Peter Immanuel Schow who departed this Life on the 24th of May 1842; aged 74 years 36 of which he faithfully discharged the duties of his office, as His Majesty's Danish Consul, for the Western District of England. 'The Memory of the Just is blessed.' Also Jane relict of the above who departed this life December 2 1855, aged 82 years."

"In Memory of Sir John Coode Knight, Commander of the Most Honourable Order of the Bath, Knight of the Order of St. Ferdinand and Merit, and Knight of the Order of Wilhelm of the Netherlands, Vice-Admiral of the Royal Navy, Born at Penryn, 11th February, 1779, Died at Plymouth, 19th January, 1858. Also of Elizabeth, his Wife, eldest daughter of Vice-Admiral Sir Charles Vincombe Penrose, K.C.B., who died 7 March, 1849."

"Sacred to the Memory of Sir George Magrath, Doctor of Medicine, Inspector of Her Majesty's Fleet and Hospitals, Commander of the Most Honourable Order of the Bath, Knight of the Royal Guelphic Order of Hanover, Knight Commander of the Order of the Cross of Christ of Portugal, Fellow of the Royal College of Physicians, London and Edinburgh; Fellow of the Royal and Linnean and Geological Societies, and Member of other Learned Bodies. He was born in the year 1772, and died at Plymouth, June 12, 1857. A ripe Scholar and a skillful Physician, he served his country by sea and by land for a quarter of a century. A follower of the immortal Nelson, his friend and patron, in all things he did his duty – as an Officer, with zeal; as a a Citizen, with dignity; and as a Friend, with devotion. He was distinguished by nations for his public services."

Some of the most interesting tablets in St. Andrew's Church are those to the Artist-sons of Plymouth, and to their families, and to other men whose greatness in the various walks of "the polite arts" has been their own making, and whose genius has cast such a bright and lasting halo around the locality. Among these memorials are the following:–

A beautifully *painted* tablet on panel, to the memory of Philip Pearse. On it are exquistely painted cherub's heads, winged skulls, drapery, etc., and the inscription:–

"In Memory of Philip Pearse of this Town, Painter, Who died the 16th day Feby 1724 in the 70th year of his Age, and was buried near this place. As were also 9 of his Children."

An oval tablet bearing a wreath and urn, on which are inscribed the names, "Samuel Northcote," "Mary Northcote," above which, on a ribbon, is "Christi Crux est me Lux." On the square tablet upon which rests the urn, is the inscription:–

"To the Memory of Samuel Northcote of Plymouth who died on the 13 November 1791 in the 83rd year of his age, and of Mary his Wife who died on the 3rd of September 1778 in the 67th year of her age. In this Church also are interred the remains of all those of his family who have deceased since its settlement at Plymouth about the year 1630."

Another tablet, with simple ornament, bears the following record:–

"In memory of Samuel Northcote, Elder brother of James Northcote Esq. Member of the Royal Academy of London. He was born in the parish of St. Andrew, Plymouth, and was buried there 9th May, 1813 aged 70 years. Also in Memory of Mary Northcote, who was born in the Parish of St. Andrew, Plymouth, Died in Argyl Place, 25 May 1836 aged 85 years, and was buried beside her brother James in the Church of St. Mary-Le-Bone, London."

A pretty and simple tablet records the memory of Samuel Prout, thus:–

> "In memory of Samuel Prout, Eminent in his profession as a Painter, born at Plymouth, September 17 1783, Died, deeply lamented at Denmark Hill, Surrey, February 10 1852. He was a sincere and humble Christian relying alone upon his Saviour. 'Verily verily I say unto you He that believeth on me hath everlasting Life.' St. John vi 47 verse."

In literature and science the tablets already described to Dr. Mudge, Dr. Woolcombe, Dr. Yonge, Rev. J. H. Macaulay, and others, amply testify to the interest of the memorials in this Church, and to these is added a simple, unassuming gothic tablet, in white marble, but of poor design, erected to the memory of Charles Mathews, the comedian, who, dying in Plymouth, was here buried. The tablet, which bears the name, as sculptor, of "J. Brown, Stonehouse," is thus inscribed:–*

> "Near this Spot are deposited the honoured Remains of Charles Mathews, Comedian; Born 28th June, 1776. Died 28th June, 1835. Not to commemorate that Genius which his Country acknowledged and rewarded, and Men of every Nation confessed; nor to record the worth which secured the respect and attachment of his admirers and friends; but, as an humble Tribute to his devoted, unvarying affection and indulgence as a Husband and father, this Tablet is erected in sorrowing Love and grateful Remembrance by his bereaved Wife and Son.

"BY A FRIEND.

"All England mourn'd, when her Comedian died,
A public loss that ne'er might be supplied;
For who could hope such varied gifts to find,
All rare and exquisite, in one combined?
The private virtues that adorn'd his breast,
Crowds of admiring Friends with tears confess'd,
Only to Thee, O God! the grief was known
Of those who rear this Monumental Stone;
The Son and Widow, who, with Bosoms torn,
The best of Fathers and of Husbands mourn,
Of all this public, social, private woe,
Here lies the cause – Charles Mathews sleeps below."

A tablet commemorates the death of Mr. Edward Nettleton, bookseller, of Plymouth, to whose industry and good taste is owing the collection of much of the matter which forms the foundation of this work. The inscription reads thus:–

> "To the Memory of Edward Nettleton of this Town who died February 22 1859 Aged 65 years; and in Memory of Matilda his daughter, and Wife of John Libby, who died April 11 1847 aged 24 years."

*It would be pleasant to add to these a note that suitable memorials exist in this Church (whose spacious vestibule is admirably adapted for, and should be used as, a valhallah of Plymouth worthies) to other gifted sons of the place – Sir Charles Lock Eastlake, P.R.A.; Benjamin Haydn; James Northcote (who, by the way, is stated to have left a sum in his will for the purpose of putting up a memorial to himself and his brother); Samuel Cook; Ball; John Opie; and Dr. John Kitto, one of the most profound and learned scholars of any age, and to whom not only Plymouth, in whose Workhouse he was once a poor boy, but the whole civilised world, is indebted for many works, besides his "Biblical Cyclopaedia." Cannot the town do something towards erecting simple, but lasting, memorials to these great names?

Besides these, memorials exist, among others, to the following:– John Hawkins, Esq., many years Paymaster of the South Devon Militia, 1819. Vice-Admiral Samuel Hood Linzie, 1820. William Baron, 1862, and his wife, Sarah Baron, 1867. "Frederick Bone, Esq., Paymaster, Royal Navy, a native of this town, who died on the 28th June, 1863, in the 77th year of his age. He served the office of Churchwarden of this parish for twenty-eight consecutive years." Eliza Pym, wife of the late Rev. F. Pym, vicar of Bickleigh, 1867. T. H. Rolt, Esq., eldest son of J. D. Rolt, Esq., of Broomfield, Deptford, Kent, 1866. Lieut. John Cartwright, R.N., 1865, and Helena Augusta, his wife, 1862; William Jacobson, 1866, erected by his wife, Mary Grace Furneaux Jacobson. William Copeland, Esq., of Sussex House, Fulham, 2nd son of Alexander Copeland, Esq., Gunnersbury Park, Middlesex, 1836. Eleanor, wife of Edmund Lockyer, Esq., 1807. Thomas Henry Brooke, Esq., formerly of the Honourable East Indian Company's Civil Service, Island of St. Helena, June, 1849; and Ann, his widow, September of the same year. Vice-Admiral John Manley, 1816; his son, Captain John Lampen Manley, R.N., 1817; and Elizabeth, widow of the Admiral, 1832. Miss Amelia Henrietta Dunsterville, daughter of Bartholomew Dunsterville, in 1841; and "Jana Maria Welch, her friend," 1843. Sir John Dineley, 1818. Diggory Tonkin, Esq., 1791. Mrs Mary Ann Rosdew, wife of William Rosdew, and daughter of Diggory Tonkin, Esq., 1794. Richard Rosdew, of Beechwood, 1837. Joseph May, 1766, and other members of his family. Mrs. Sarah Reynett, wife of H. J. Reynett, Esq., 1804. William Rattenbury, surgeon, 1847. Mary, "widow of General Hughes, R.M., and grandchild of Alderman Facey (who was twice Mayor of this Antient Corporation, having worthily discharged the duties thereof)," 1822. Alderman John Pridham, 1829, and Elizabeth, his wife, 1827. Charles Christopher Lockyer and William Lockyer, sons of Thomas Lockyer, Esq., of Wembury House, 1828 and 1858; and Louisa, wife of William Lockyer, 1845; "erected by Major-General Henry Frederick Lockyer, C.B., K.H. (brother of the above Charles and William Lockyer), and James Lawes Lockyer, of Wembury, their nephew, April 1860." Edmund Lockyer, Esq., 1836; "erected by the great-granddaughter, Mary Eleanor Ann Pym, August, A.D. 1855." Major-General George Elliott Vinicombe, Commandant of the Plymouth Division of Royal Marines, 1841; and his wife Dorothy, 1844. Margaret, widow of Lieutenant-Colonel George Fearon, 31st Regiment of Foot, 1841. John Sleeman King, 1846; and Jane, his wife, 1834. William Harson Bayly, aged 19, 1851; and Caroline Ann Chapman Bayly, aged 16, 1851, brother and sister; children of

William Harson Bayly, Esq., and Leah Rundell, his wife; and other of their children. And another to William Harson Bayly, 1858. James Bovey, Ensign and Quartermaster South Devon Militia, 1855; and his granddaughter, M. A. E. Matcham, 1856. A neat gothic recessed tablet to Augustus Hamilton Bampton, C.E., Borough Surveyor, 1857; "erected by a few friends: C. A. Hartley, George Wightwick, P. J. Margary, E. A. Bishop, Walter Damant." A singular slab to a member of the family of James; at the top, in an oval, are two singularly carved shields of arms, side by side, with crests and mantling. Mrs. Mary Murch, wife of Mr. Joseph Murch, of the Globe Inn, Plymouth, 1827; Joseph Murch, her husband, 1830; and to various members of their family. Lieutenant Owen Phipps, of the Roscommon Militia, 1813; erected by his brother officers. Reverend Frederick Pym, M.A., vicar of Bickleigh-cum-Sheepstor, eldest son of Vice-Admiral Sir Samuel Pym, K.C.B., by Eleanor Penrose, his wife, daughter of Edmund Lockyer, Esq., 1848. William Johnstone Macfie, 1831. Flower, wife of Philip Phillips, surgeon, and Anne Spinster Facey, 1796. Frances, wife of Capt. Thomas Troubridge, 1798, and their daughter, Elizabeth, 1794. Henry Hayne, 1797; and various members of the Hayne, White, and Lindon families, down to 1859. Jonathan Baron, 1805; and Jane, his wife, 1821. General Hughes – "This tablet, piously erected by their next of kin, Francis Annesley Hughes, in memory of a tender Father and a zealous Soldier, General Hughes, some years Lieutenant-Colonel of the Plymouth Division of Royal Marines; and of two fond Brothers, who fell in H.M. service. John, a Lieutenant R.N.; Thomas, a Captain, R.A., 1808." Mrs. Margaret Smith Clark, 1786. Mrs Jane Morshead, 1775. John Morshead, 1771. Richard Dunning, 1795. Benjamin Dunning, 1731. Mrs Elizabeth Dunning, 1754; and others to the Dunning and James families. Reader Watts, Esq., 1839; and his wife, Ann, 1837. Charles Kevern, "Assistant to the Master Shipwright in H.M. Dockyard, Plymouth," 1815; and his wife, Mary, 1810. Mrs. Ann Maxwell, widow of Archibald Maxwell Esq., 1801; and her daughter, Elizabeth Cornthwaite Maxwell, 1842; erected by their daughter and sister, Ann Gilbert Maxwell. Capt. William Williams, "late Capt. in the Company of Invalids in this Garrison," 1775; Elizabeth, his wife, 1774; and Alice, their daughter, 1779. Nicholas Jacobson, 1789; and Johanna, his wife, 1800.

There were formerly Guilds and Chantries attached to St. Andrew's Church, but of those only meagre particulars can now be gleaned. Regarding the Guild of Corpus Christi, a curious account of church ales has been given on page 63.

In the Chantry Rolls of Devon and Cornwall is the following interesting entry:–

"Plymouth – The stipendarye there. Founded by ——— Dabnone and John Paynter. To fynd a pryst to praye for the sowles of the founders, and mynystre dyvine service in the quyer in the parish churche of Plymouthe; paying unto Margaret Sommester, sometyme wyf unto Jonn Paynter, one of the sayd founders, xxiijs yerelye for her dowry, which is deue unto her during [her] naturall lyf. The yerelye value of the lands and possessions vij li xvs viijs. The almes house there called Goddeshouse. Founded by ——— For the relief of impotent and lazare peple, without any certayne nomber appoynted to be partakers of the sayd relief; forr there are at present but xiiij impotent peple relevyd sometyms there be xxti, somtyme more or less. And they have over and besyds thire mansyon house the rents of certayn lands gyven by diverse persons. The yerelye value of the lands and possessions xiiijii vijs."

The following curious indenture, 34, Henry VIII. (1543), refers to the chantry of St. John the Baptist, in St. Andrews:–

"Indenture between Thomas Chamond Esq., and the Mayor and Commonalty of Plymouth – Devisee of certain Lands for 99 years for the following uses:– To help towards the stipend of an honest Priest to serve within the parish Church of St. Andrew, there sometimes to sing Mass at the Altar of St. John the Baptist, to pray for the soul of John Taybyn (or Toybin) and his friends."

References to other Chantries and Guilds will be found in the curious extract from account of Church goods, given on a preceding page.

In 1593 "the cage of five new bells were cast for Plymouth Church in the Workhouse;" in 1708 a ring of six fine bells was presented to the Church by Colonel Jory; in 1748 these were recast into a peal of eight; in 1840, the tenor bell having become cracked in the previous year, was recast by Mears, of London. The following notice of this bell is painted on a board under the tower:–

"The present Tenor Bell was cast in London, and hung in the Tower 17th July 1840. It bears the following inscription:– This bell was Founded by Thomas Mears, of London, A.D. 1840. JOHN HATCHARD, M.A. Vicar, FREDERIC BONE, ALFRED HINGSTON, Churchwardens of St. Andrew's Plymouth. Weight, 35 Hundred 14 Pounds; Breadth, 4 Feet 11 Inches; Circumference, 15 Feet 2 Inches; Height, 3 Feet 5 1/2 Inches. The Old Tenor Bell became cracked December, 1839, and was removed to make room for the present July 1840. It bore the following inscription:– Ego sum vox Clamantis Parate. ZACH. MUDGE, Vic. Geor. Marshall, Rich. Hicks, Eccles Guard; Conflabat Stipe Publice Collata Tho Biblie 1749. Weight, 35 Hundred 45 Pounds; Breadth, 4 feet 10 1/2 inches; Circumference, 15 feet 0 1/2 inches; Height 3 feet 6 inches. Note – This Bell became cracked by being struck too near its rim, in consequence of the descent of the Clapper from long use."

On another board is this inscription:–

"The Clock in the Tower of this Church was made by Mr. Thomas Mudge, of London, A.D. 1706. The same was repaired, and four dials affixed, by Mr. Frank H. Goulding, of this town, A.D. 1857. John Hatchard, Vicar. Frederick Bone, Alfred Hingston, Churchwardens."

There are also four painted tablets of arms which are somewhat curious. One of these, dated 1619, bears the arms of the See, with mitre, mantling, etc.; another, dated 1625, has the Royal arms with crest, supporters, mantling, etc., of Charles I, with the letters C.R., each of which is crowned; a third, dated 1632, bears three shields, first Stert, *argent*, a saltire, *gules*, between four crosses pattée, *sable*, second, Hele, *gules*, a bend lozengy, *ermine*, third, Lanyon, *argent*, three sinister hands, *gules*; and the last, dated 1658, also bears two shields of arms.

The following curious ringing laws also hang in the belfry:–

"NOS RESONARE HIBET PIETAS MORS, ATQ, VOLUPTAS."

"Let awfull Silence first proclaimed be,
And praise unto the holy Trinity,
Then honour give unto our Valiant King,
So, with a blessing, raise this noble Ring.
Hark how the chirping Treble rings most clear,
And Covering Tom comes Rowling in the Rear.
Now up an end at stay, come let us see
What Laws are best to keep Sobriety.
Then all agree and make this their decree
Who Swear or Curse or in an hasty mood
Quarrell and strikes altho' they draw no blood;
Who wears his Hatt or Spurrs or turns a Bell
Or by unskillful handling marr's a peal,
Let him pay Six pence for each single crime –
'Twill make him cautious 'gainst another time;
But if the Sextons fault an hindrance be
We call from him the double penalty.
If any should our Parson disrespect
Or Wardens orders any time neglect
Lett him be always held in foul disgrace
And ever after banished this place.
Now round lett goe with pleasure to the ear
And pierce with eccho through the yielding air,
And when the bells are ceas'd then lett us Sing,
God bless our holy Church – God save the King
1700."

There was formerly a lich-gate at the entrance to the churchyard at the head of Basket-street. Here was the coffin-rest, built of stone, about five feet long, by three and-a-half in width, and covered with a slab of slate; upon this the coffins were placed while waiting for the clergyman. At one period but few persons were buried in coffins – a coffin kept by the Corporation, being let out and used for funerals. In this the body was placed, wrapped up in its shroud, and carried to the churchyard. The coffin was then placed on this "coffin-rest," the corpse lifted out and carried to the grave, and the coffin taken away to be again used.

It may be well here to say that Basket-street, just alluded to, and which has recently been removed to make room for the new municipal buildings, was lined with quaint-looking gabled houses, which had evidently at one time been inhabited by the "Dons of Plymouth." From the entry of Basket-street a flight of twelve or fourteen steps led down from the "Pig Market" – as that part was formerly called – to the entrance to the Church, and there an inn, bearing the sign of "The Old Church House Inn," stood; the site of the shops on the west side of Bedford-street being, at the same time, a timber yard.

The churchyard is said to have been enclosed in 1596, and it then occupied a considerable area. This was subsequently encroached upon, and in 1637 the vicar complained that the Mayor and Commonalty had encroached upon the east side "by building a row of shambles and other houses on parts of the churchyard, and on the west side by building of the Hospital, where the vicar had anciently an house." Some of these old houses, or others on their site, existed until 1813, when they, with many other obstructions, were removed, and the streets and roadways widened. To commemorate this a tablet was placed in the churchyard wall, facing Old Town-street, bearing the following inscription:– "Immediately in front of this wall lately stood a set of stalls called the Flesh Shambles, which narrowed the space from the opposite houses to about nine feet.

On the right hand were two houses which considerably confined the entrance to the Church; immediately in front was a building called the Fish Market, taken down on His Majesty coming to this borough in the year

1789; on the left hand, by Buckingham steps, were some miserable, loathsome Almshouses; and at the entrance of Old Town-street stood a Conduit and new Shambles, all of which, for the greater comfort and convenience of the inhabitants and persons resorting to the town have, with great liberality and public spirit on the part of the Mayor and Commonalty been removed, and the present new Market erected. To commemorate these improvements this tablet was set up 4th of June 1813." Other improvements followed these, and the row of low, unsightly houses, forming the continuation of Bedford-street, by the churchyard, were removed. Latterly the thoroughfare has been again widened; the graveyard, which was an unsightly and morbid mound, in the very centre of the town, has been, to some extent, levelled, and planted with shrubs, the high wall taken away, and a new one of granite, with chastely ornamental railings and carved gateposts, substituted. The superfluous ground, too, around the Church tower, has been removed to its original level; the four corners of the tower made good; and a fine opening from Bedford-street effected. By these improvements the tower has been restored to its original lofty proportions, and thrown open to view from almost every direction. By the time a second edition of our work is called for, we trust we may have to add that even the mound – much as it has been improved of late – on the north side of the Church has been entirely swept away, and lowered to the level of the street, so as to open out the body as well as the tower, to the view of passers by.

CHAPTER XI

CHARLES CHURCH AND ITS MONUMENTS — ST. ANDREW'S CHAPEL CHARLES CHAPEL — ST. PETER'S CHURCH, ELDAD — TRINITY CHURCH — CHRIST CHURCH — ST. JOHN THE EVANGELIST CHURCH— ST. JAMES'S CHURCH — EMMANUEL CHURCH — ST. SAVIOUR'S CHURCH — CITADEL CHAPEL AND ITS MONUMENTS — PORTLAND CHAPEL — NONCONFORMITY IN PLYMOUTH — VARIOUS DISSENTING BODIES.

CHARLES CHURCH. – As has before been stated, Plymouth was, until the reign of Charles I. comprised in one sole parish, that of St. Andrew. In 1634, the Corporation having regard to the increase of the town and the want of church accommodation, took steps for the division of the borough into two parishes, and for that purpose presented a petition to the King, praying him to give his consent thereto. In 1640, "an Act for the confirmation of His Majesty's letters patent to the town of Plymouth, and for dividing the parishes and building a new church there," was passed. By this Act which, with the petition praying for it, has already been given on pages 172 to 181, the boundaries of the parish were fixed, and all the necessary arrangements were made, and it was stipulated that "the new church to be built shall be called *Charles Church*, and the advowson to belong to the Mayor and Commonalty of the town." Shortly after this the memorable Siege of Plymouth, one of the stirring events of the civil wars, took place, and, as a natural consequence, the building had to be suspended until more peaceful times. In 1645 the work was re-commenced, and in 1657 it was completed, "though long in building, and some disturbance by a paltry pretended churchwarden, etc., yett by God's goodness carried on, we hope to His glory." In 1707 the completion of the tower, which until that time would appear to have been only twenty feet in height, was commenced, and was, with the wooden spire, completed the next year. In 1709 a peal of six bells was presented to the church by Joseph Jory, Esq., who also, in 1719, gave to it a clock and chimes. In 1735 considerable alterations were made in the church, and in

1759 a meeting of the parishioners was held "to consider a method of plaistering the church by subscription." In 1766 the wooden spire was taken down and replaced by one of stone, "the ball and vane being put up" on the 20th October. In 1815 a faculty was obtained for the erection of two galleries, and in 1828-9 the church was repaired, galleries were fixed, and a new pulpit and screen erected by Mr. Ball, the architect. In 1864 the church was restored, altered in some respects, and entirely renovated. At this time new porches were erected in place of the old external stair-entrances, new windows were added, a new reredos and altar rails put up, and the interior refitted, at a considerable outlay.

Charles Church, as it now exists, consists of a nave and chancel, with north and south aisles, and a tower and spire at its west end. It is perhaps the best existing example of a gothic building of so late a period, and some of its features and details are remarkably good. The east window is an elegant example of geomatric tracery. The roof, which is "barrel-shaped", is divided into square compartments by longitudinal and transverse ribs of wood, with carved bosses at the intersections. The side aisles are each divided from the nave by a series of three arches, rising from clustered columns, and there are galleries on the north and south sides and at the west end; the tall pulpit, with spiral staircase, stands in the centre. The altar screen, or reredos, is an arcade of nine arches, supported on marble pillars with foliated capitals. The font is a wretched foliated excrescence, totally unworthy of any church.

Many of the windows are filled with modern stained glass, of good character. The east window is of five lights, and has its head filled with elaborate geometric tracery. The lights and general portions of the window are beautifully diapered; in the centre of the rose in the head is our Saviour, and in the surrounding circles are twelve adoring angels; beneath this, at the head of the centre light, is the Agnus Dei. The window on the south side of the chancel is of three lights, and is filled with stained glass "to the memory of John Moore, Esq., J.P.;' born A.D. 1780, died A.D. 1861; By his children;" and that on the north, of a similar character is "Ad Gloriam Dei, et in Mem: Herbert Fillis, ob. x. Aug. MDCCCLXII." The windows in the aisles are filled with diapering in stained glass, and some of them bear the inscriptions – "H. A. Greaves, vicar; W. B. Cuming, P. J. Marshall, wardens, 1868."

The oldest memorials are to be found among the slabs on the floor, which, much to the shame of this parish, as well as that of St. Andrew's, are fast being worn away. Among these are memorials to Pasco Hovell, "of this Towne, Merchant," 1674, and his wife, Ann, 1659, with arms; Nicholas Curle, Merchant, 1679, and his wife, Elizabeth, "daughter of Captain John White, of this Towne, Merchant," 1671, with the arms, on a chevron, between three fleurs-de-lis, three cinquefoils, impaling, a chevron between three goat's heads erased, crest, a hedgehog, passant; and another – "Here lyeth the Body of Mary, the wife of Richard . . . . who departed this life the 5th day of December, Anno Dom 1678.

"Under this couert doth her Body lie,
Who while she lived made it her worke to die,
With Christ her life was hid, by Christ againe
She shall be Rais'd & ever with him Reigne
Lament not then her death who lives in Blisse,
The losse is only ours, the Gaine is Hers."

There are also other slabs to John Whitely, 1665; Amos Doidge, of Plymouth, Merchant, 1737, and others of his family; and others.

Among the monumental tablets on the walls are the following:–

A tablet, with cherub's heads at the sides, skulls at the bottom, and drapery, etc., to the memory of Peter Westlake, 1715. At the top are the arms of Westlake, *argent*, on a fesse, *sable*, between two chevrons, *gules*, three escallop shells, *or*; impaling *sable*, a fesse between six escallop shells, *or*. Another, to the memory of Anthony and William Durston, 1666, surmounted by shields of arms.

"In memory of Mr James Richardson many years one of this Corporation who died the 7th day of April 1772, aged 83."

"Sacred to the memory of John Cooban Esq. who was Mayor of the Borough in 1789 and 1790 and who died July 20th 1794 aged 75 years" and to other members of his family. At the top are the arms of Cooban; on a bend sinister, within a bordure engrailed, bezanty, three griffins passant; crest, a demi griffin.

A large tablet, by I. R. Veale, 1774, with arms and other devices, to John Gennys, Esq., and Christiana, his wife, daughter of Nicholas Docton, Esq. At the bottom are the arms of Gennys impaling Docton.

A small tablet, with folds of linen, and with a urn at the top –

"In memory of Elizabeth the second Daughter of the second Sir John Rogers Bart. and Relict of Rear-Admiral Charles Fanshawe. She died 27th August 1797 aged 88 years and is buried in the vault beneath."

'To the memory of George Wolfe, Esquire, Captain in the Royal Navy, and Commander of the most Noble Order of the Bath. Died January 18th 1826 aged 45. By his affectionate and afflicted wife and daughter."

A large tablet, with pillars and entablature, with "death's-head" and hour glass at bottom, and the inscription in an oval, with carved foliated frame –

"To the memory of Mr William Rowe, of this Towne, Merchant; a great Benefactor to the Poore, who died ye 27 day of December 1690. Also Frances his wife who died the 18 of December 1688." At the bottom of the inscription a death's-head and "Memento mori."

An oval tablet, with foliated frame, supported on angel's heads, etc., with the inscription:–

Moses
Georgi Vincent de Batens
in North hill præ optimæ spei
juvenis
Cornubiensi hujus Nominis surpe
Oriundi Hic imfra Recondita est
Nec annos Exegit Octodecum Augusti
23 die Anno MDCLXIII
Mathias Vincent Frater hujus
fraterrimus Mnemosynen
Hanc non minus amoris
sui Quam Mœroris
posuit February XI
Die Anno
MDCLXXXIIII

A tablet, with a small trophy at the top, and foliage, etc.–

"Descendo ducente Deo
Here rest ye Ashes of
Kane Willm. Horneck Esq.,
One of His Majesty's Engineers in Ordinary,
who died the 18th of Decbr 1752 aged 26 years.
By his Death at once his afflicted Wife lost an affectionate and faithful Husband,
his Children a tender and careful Parent, his acquaintance a hearty Friend,
the Government an ingenious and useful Servant,

the Commonwealth a worthy Member,
and the World an honest Man.
Reader, contemplate this, and fear to place
The least Dependance on the Mortal Race;
Not Strength the Young, nor Counsel saves the Wise,
The brave are Vanquished – even the good Man Dies.
Hence learn to fix thy faith on God alone,
Trust in His suff'ring Son (for both are one
None love the Father who reject the Son),
Then may thy Hopes extend beyond the grave,
"Till God shall fail to Love, or Christ to Save."

A gothic tablet, with reflected arch, crocketed and finialed –

"Sacred to the Memory of the Rev Sir Cecil Augustus Bisshopp Bart M.A. Patron of this living, who for two years faithfully and zealously preached the pure word of God in this Church. He was born the 6th of June 1821, and died at Malta on the 18th of January 1849, in the 28th year of his age, beloved and respected by all who knew him. Blessed are the dead which die in the Lord for they rest from their labours and their works do follow them. This monument was erected by his sorrowing family as a small token of the sense of their deep loss." At the bottom are the crest and motto of Sir Cecil.

A tablet, by F.A. Lege, of London–

"Sacred to the memory of James Carne D.D. five years Vicar of this Parish, who died August 14th 1832, aged 38 years; and of Charlotte Carne, his widow, who died August 18th 1832, aged 40 years. In him devotedness to his sacred calling was happily united with meekness of wisdom, and he sought the eternal interests of his flock with the prudence affection and watchfulness of the Christian pastor. He preached faithfully the great doctrines of the gospel of Christ and the Divine blessing rested upon his labours. In all his designs and benevolence his beloved wife was his most zealous and affectionate helpmate, and they were both sustained by looking unto Jesus the author and finisher of our faith. During the awful pestilence which spread mourning throughout the land, they were taken within four days of each other, from this scene of their usefulness to the rest that remaineth for the people of God. This memorial of respect and attachment is erected by the voluntary contributions of many grateful parishioners and sorrowing friends."

Above this inscription is a group representing the Doctor lying dead on a pallet, and his widow mourning over him. Above these are two urns, over which is thrown a mantle. At the bottom are the arms, crest, and motto of Carne.

A tablet, surmounted by an Obelisk, on which are the arms of Bedford, *argent*, three lions paws (?), *sable*; impaling the arms of his wife.

"To the memory of the Rev John Bedford M.A. 25 years Vicar of this Church who died 20th of April 1784 aged 47 years, and of Lucretia his wife who died the 11th August 1764 aged 55 years. The grateful affection of their children hath erected this marble."

A gothic tablet, with an admirable medallion profile portrait of Mr. Courtney at the bottom –

> "In memory of the Revd. Septimus Courtney A.M. late vicar of this Church and twenty two years a Minister of the Gospel in this parish, who died on the 7th of March, 1843, aged 63 years. Regarding the Sacred Scriptures under the teaching of the Holy Ghost as the only source of truth, he made the Glory of Christ and his redemption, the great subjects of his Ministry and while he laboured diligently in the public preaching of the Gospel, he exemplified in his life the doctrine which he taught. 'I take you to record this day, that I am pure from the blood of all men, for I have not shunned to declare unto you the whole counsel of God.' Acts XX. 26 27. This Monument is erected by his Parishioners and Congregation."

A very fine tablet, of large size, by F.A. Lege, of London, erected in 1829, and inscribed –

> "A public tribute of affection and respect to the Memory of the Revd. Robert Hawker D.D., six years Curate, and forty-three years Vicar, of this parish who died the 6th day of April 1827 aged 74 years."

At the top is a fine life-sized draped bust of the learned divine, with drapery, books, inkstand, chalice, rolls of paper, etc. At the bottom are the arms of Hawker; a hawk statant on a stand; crest, a hawk's head erased; motto, "Sincère et constanter."

Two small plain tablets, the one a –

> "Memorial to bring to remembrance Pslams 38 and 70. In memory of her beloved and affectionate Husband Thomas Hodson, Mary Glanville Hodson has invested the sum of two hundred and fifty pounds stock three per cent. annuities, in the names of Trustees, the annual Dividends whereof to be paid into the hands of the Vicar of this parish for the time being and to be by him given away in Bread to the poor thereof, on the twelfth day of December next and on the like day in each succeeding year for ever. March 10th 1829."

And the other of the same date which is similar in every way and headed in like manner shows that the same lady

> "In order to perpetuate the lively remembrance of her beloved Father Robert Hawker amongst the Poor of the Parish in whose welfare he was ever deeply interested" has likewise invested £250 the dividend of which is to be given away in Bread by the Vicar on the 13th of April for ever."

A particularly interesting tablet, surmounted by an urn, is inscribed –

> "Sacred to the memory of a beloved husband Admiral Sir Israel Pellew K.C.B. who died 19th July 1832 aged 73. This simple memorial of faithful affection is erected by his sorrowing widow who finds consolation only in the blessed assurance that 'them that sleep in Jesus will God bring with him.' Also to the memory of Dame Mary Helen Pellew widow of Sir Israel Pellew K.C.B. who died the 2nd day of Novr. 1844 aged 77 years. Also of her niece Catherine McMorrine who died at Plymouth June 17th 1855 aged 81 years."

At the bottom are the arms, *argent*, a chevron, *gules*, on a chief of the same, three mascles, *or*; at the base a wreath of laurel, *vert*. The motto "Deo Adjuvante" over the crest, a ship, the Dutton, wrecked beneath the fort of the Citadel, all proper; and "Fortuna sequatur" beneath the shield.

Another is inscribed –

"To the beloved Memory of Elizabeth wife of Sir J.H. Seymour, Bart, M.A., Rector of Northchurch, Herts. and eldest daughter of Thomas Culme, of Tothill, Rector of Northlewe and Perpetual Curate of Plympton St. Mary in this County. She Died March 6th 1841. As a record of her rare and excellent qualities, her purity of heart, firm, faith, and humble Christian hope, this tablet is inscribed by her attached and mindful husband. Blessed are the pure in heart for they shall see God."

An oval tablet, with a draped urn, and the arms and crest of Downing, is inscribed –

"To the memory of a beloved Husband, John Wall Downing (late a Lieut. in the 67th Regt. of Foot), who died shortly after his return from the West Indies, on the 26th of July 1799 aged 26 years."

An imposing monument, with sculptured figure of a seated semi-nude angel, resting on a pedestal, with urn, and holding a wreath of flowers in one hand–

"To the memory of Henry Sabine Browne, of Portland Place, London, late Captain of Her Majesty's 85th Light Infantry, who departed this life on the 24th of February, 1843, aged 34 years. Also in memory of Alice Sabine, his infant daughter buried in Montreal, Canada, where she died on the 22nd of December 1841, aged one year; this monument is erected by the Wife ! and Mother !"

"Benzonica sculp Milano."

Beneath is another tablet –

"To the memory of Compton Sabine; son of the above, who is buried in Corfu; where he died on the 2nd March, 1849, in the 7th year of his age. Also Isabel Harrt. Ann Fearon, widow of the above, and 2nd daughter of Admiral Sir J.J. Gordon Bremer K.C.B., K.C.H., who is buried in London, where she died on the 13th April 1866. This inscription is added by their daughter."

There are also two elegant gothic tablets, exactly alike, one of which is inscribed–

"Sacred to the memory of George Edward Roby Esq late Lieut-Coll of the Royal Marines. He served his country with honour and distinction for fifty years and departed this life Jany. 7th 1836. Aged 72 years. Also to Ann his wife daughter of James Norman Esq., Capt. Royal Navy, and Mother of Commodore Sir Gordon Bremer K.C.B., K.C.H., of Compton in this Parish. She lived greatly beloved and esteemed and died on the 9th day of April 1848 aged 85 years."

And the other–

"Sacred to the memory of Harriet Bremer, the beloved wife of Commodore Sir Gordon Bremer K.C.B., K.C.H., of Comptom in this parish. Pious benevolent, and excellent in all the duties of this life she was called hence March 1st 1846 aged 60 years. Also Edward Gordon Bremer Esqr. Commander in the Royal Navy, son of the above, who died April 7th 1847 aged 26 years. Also in memory of Rear Admiral Sir Gordon Bremer K.C.B., K.C.H., who died 14th Feby. 1850 aged 63."

There are also other memorials to John Nichols, 1790, and Elizabeth, his wife, 1794; to Captain William Helling Bennett, E. I. Co's Service, 1823, and Louisa, his wife, 1819; to Philip Edward Lyne, Esq., 1846; to Elizabeth Lean Culme, 1845; to George Winne, 1793, Sarah , his wife, 1807, and various members of their family, with the arms of Winne, *sable*, three eagles displayed in fesse, *or*, and the crest, an eagle displayed *or*; to Peter Symons, merchant, 1809, and others of the family, with an urn at the top and at the bottom the arms of Symons, per fess *sable* and *argent*, a pale counterchanged, three trefoils, *vert*; to William Sison, Esq., of Woodside, Plymouth, 1831; to members of the Lowgay family; to John Luscombe, K.N.L., 1864, and others of the family; to Thomas Yates, of London, 1830; to Ann Morshead, wife of Capt. Hankisson, 1766; to Joseph Moore, shipbuilder, of this town, 1829, who was for 25 years churchwarden of this parish, and his wife, 1822; to Alderman William Moore, 1867, and others of the family, with the crest of Moore; "Sacred to the memory of Edward Moore, Esq., M.D., F.L.S., etc., magistrate of this borough, who died 17th July, 1858," with the crest of the family, a Moor Hen; to John Hawker, of Plymouth, merchant, and a magistrate for the county of Devon, 1839; to George Coryndon, Esq., 1856; and Sarah, his wife, 1867; to Thomas Hodson, Esq., 1820; to Samuel Codd, Esq., of Norley House, 1835, with crest; to Dr. Thomas Stewart, 1829, and to Andrew Tracey, Esq., 1826, and Sarah, his wife, 1838; to James Moore, Esq., Mayor of Plymouth in 1848; a very elegant gothic tablet to Vice-Admiral Richard Arthur, 1854, Elizabeth Fortescue, his wife, 1853, Catherine Elizabeth Caroline Henn-Gennys, their daughter, wife of Commander Henn-Gennys, 1851, and Richard William Arthur, their son, 1832; to Samuel Brent, 1788, and Henrietta, his wife, 1784, and to Samuel, infant son of Samuel Brent, 1747; to Post-Captain James Hawker, 1786, Dorothy, his widow, 1816, Francis Hawker, 1818, Mary Frances Hawker, 1834, and Mary Frances Winne, daughter of Sir Edmund Keynton Williams, 1820, and her sisters; and to others.

In the gallery, at the west end, are some hatchments with helmets, and in the bellchamber is the following metrical version of bell-ringing laws, which, it will be seen, vary in some measure from those at St. Andrew's, given on a preceding page:–

Let awful silence first proclaimed be,
And praise unto the Holy Trinity,
Then Honour give unto our Gracious King,
So with a blessing, Raise this Noble Ring,
Hark how the chirping Treble sings most clear,
And cov'ring Tom comes rowling in the rear.
Now up an end, at stay, come lets agree
What Laws are best to keep Sobriety.
Who swears or curs'th or in an hasty mood
Quarrells or strikes, although he draws no blood;
Or wears his Hat, or Spurs, or turns a Bell

Or by unskilful handling mars a peal;
Shall forfeit Sixpence for each Single crime –
'Twill make him causious 'gainst another time.
Or any should our Parson disrespect
Or Wardens orders any time neglect
Let such 'till they relent be in disgrace
Nor dare to enter such a sacred place.
Now round lets go and when weve done let's sing
God bless our Holy Church, God save the King.
Amen.

In the churchyard, which is extremely crowded with gravestones, are many interesting memorials, among which are records of members of the families of Kitto, Prout, and other Plymouth worthies.

The land for the church and churchyard were acquired from William Warren, of Plymouth, Vinter, and Judith, his wife, who by indenture made 21 August, 1664, between himself and the Mayor and Commonalty conveyed this land on which had been 'lately made, erected and built, a decent and beautiful fabricke or structure now commonly called or known by the name of Charles Church," "not yet consecrated," "out of his true and heartie love and zeal to God his worshippe and service, and in performance of his former good intentions promises and declarations that so laudable and pious work may be the better and more duly accomplished, and the said structure or church and churchyard and with their appertenances legally consecrated." By this indenture the Mayor and Commonalty "made, ordained, constituted, and in their place putt their well beloved in Christ, Samuel Eastlake and Thomas Payne, of Plymouth aforesaid, gentlemen, their true and lawful attorneys jointly and severally to receive" possession of the same from William Warren or his attorneys. Possession was delivered up the same day by Mr. Warren, the memorandum on the deed being signed by the Rev. Francis Porter, John Harris, Junr., George Botton, Joseph Warren, Samuel Eastlake, and Thomas Payne.

The other churches in Plymouth being of modern erection, have no particular history attached to them. They are as follows:–

ST ANDREW'S CHAPEL, Lockyer-street, built in 1823, at a cost of £5,000, from the designs of Mr. Foulston. It is an uninteresting granite building, capable of accommodating upwards of 1,000 people, and has an altar-piece painted by Ball.

CHARLES CHAPEL, Tavistock-place, built in 1828 for the Rev, Septimus Courtney (and frequently called "Mr Courtney's Chapel"), from the designs of Mr. Ball, at a cost of about £4,000.

ST. PETER'S, ELDAD, formerly known as Eldad Chapel, Wyndham-place, was commenced building by subscription in 1828, as a free chapel for the Rev. J. Hawker (who seceded from the church,) and was at first called "Mr. Hawker's Chapel." After Mr. Hawker's death the chapel was licensed, and in 1850 was consecrated as St. Peter's. It is a plain, square building, without ornament, except in the chancel, which is divided from the body by a carved screen. The altar-piece is somewhat rich, with a central cross, and the evangelists on either side. At the altar are tall candlesticks, and on the sides of the chancel are stalls, etc. Over the vestry door is a painting of the Virgin and child. Adjoining are the Mission House and St. Peter's Industrial Home; and close by is the establishment of the Sisters of Mercy, founded by Miss Sellon. This establishment – the oldest existing sisterhood of the Church of England – has been established about thirty years. In 1850 the foundation stone of what is known as 'the Abbey', was laid, and it is now the head of many similar establishments in various places. Schools and a House of Refuge are attached.

HOLY TRINITY CHURCH, Southside-street, founded mainly through the exertions of the Rev. John Hatchard, was consecrated in 1843 as a chapel of ease to St. Andrew's, and made a new parish by order of the Queen in Council in August, 1851. The population (census 1871), 4,886. The church – a neat Doric building – holds 1,200, 600 sittings being free and unappropriated. The National Schools are some of the largest in the diocese. There is a fine organ by Dicker, of Exeter, containing 26 stops.

ST. SAVIOUR'S CHURCH, Lambhay-Hill, was built entirely by private subscriptions, on a site given by Her Majesty as a chapel of ease to Holy Trinity, and was consecrated 24th August, 1870. Owing to the difficulty in collecting the necessary funds no architect was employed except in laying the foundation, but the whole was designed and carried out by the vicar of Holy Trinity, the Rev. F. Barnes. The church is of the early English style; the pillars and arches are of white and red brick, and have a pleasing effect. No attempt has been made at ornamentation It accommodates 380 persons, 280 being free and unappropriated, and the remainder let at a very low rate.

CHRIST CHURCH, Eton-place, Oxford-street, was erected from the designs of Mr. Wightwick in 1845, in the perpendicular style of gothic architecture.

ST. JOHN THE EVANGELIST, Sutton-on-Plym, Jubilee-street, erected from the designs of Mr. B. Ferrey in 1854-5, is one of the prettiest of the churches of Plymouth. The altar-piece is of good design.

ST. JAMES, Citadel-road, erected from the designs of Mr. St. Aubyn in 1861, will accommodate about 800 persons.

EMMANUEL CHURCH, Compton Gifford, a gothic building, consecrated in 1870, was erected from the designs of Mr. Reid, at a cost of about £3,000.

THE CITADEL CHAPEL is situated in the Citadel, and is intended for the use of the Garrison. The original chapel is coeval with the Citadel itself, dating about 1668. It consisted, as is apparent on the original plan of the citadel, in the Royal Engineers' office Devonport, of a nave 59ft. long by 25ft. in width. It is capable of accommodating about 100 persons. The walls, considering the small size of the building, are very massive, being about 2ft. 9in. in thickness doubtless as a matter of safeguard. In 1845 the building was enlarged by throwing out the two transepts and the erection of three galleries. By this means, the chapel is now capable of accommodating about 450 persons. The east window is filled with stained glass representing the crucifixion, by Lavers and Bond, which was put up in 1868 in memory of former worshippers in the church. The altar-plate was presented by Louis Dufour Esq., who also, at his own cost, erected the statue of His Majesty George the Second on the Citadel green. The font was presented by General the Hon. Sir Henry Murray, K.C.B., to whose memory a tablet is placed in the chapel. It is said that the citadel chapel was the last building belonging to the Established Church in which mass was celebrated; the occasion being the bringing here of the body of some distinguished foreigner, when requiem mass was said.

The following monumental inscriptions* occur in this chapel:–

"Sacred to the memory of Lieut-Colonel Malcolm Macregor, 5th Fusiliers, who departed this life on the 4th January, 1847. Aged 67 years. 'For if we believe that Jesus died and rose again, even so them also which sleep in Jesus, will God bring with him.' I Thess., 4th Chap., 14th verse."

"Sacred to the memory of Colonel Alexander Brown, Royal Engineers, Obt. 6th Jul: MDCCCLIII. ÆT: LXIII. His Remains lie in the Plymouth Cemetery. More than the above was forbidden by this estimable man and excellent Officer. His loss has been deeply felt by his Family and by his Corps."

"Sacred to the memory of Jessy, wife of Colonel Calder, Commanding Royal Engineers, Western District, who died on the 13th of May, 1852. Aged 64 years. 'The Lord gave, and the Lord hath taken away, blessed be the name of the Lord.' Job, 1st. Chapter, 21st verse."

"Sacred to the memory of Major-General Patrick Doull Calder, Royal Engineers (of Aswanlee, N.B.,) who died in Guernsey, Septr. 1st, 1857, in the 70th year of his age. To the memory also of his Son, Somerville Mc.Donald Calder, Captain Royal Artillery, who died March 25th, 1857, aged 35 years, at St. Nicholas Island, Plymouth. The mortal remains of Father and Son are deposited in the General Cemetery of these towns. 'There remaineth therefore, a rest to the people of God.' Hebrews 4th, 9th."

"Sacred to the memory of William Cuthbert Elphinstone Holloway, C.B., Colonel, Commanding Royal Engineers, Western District, who departed this life in the Citadel, Plymouth, on the 4th of September, 1850. He served in the Peninsular Campaigns of

*For these inscriptions I am indebted to the Chaplain, the Rev. W. Sykes.

1810, 1811, and 1812. Was wounded in the Trenches before Badájoz and shot through the Body on the 26th March 1812; whilst storming the enemy's works. Colonel Holloway was not only distinguished for his Military Services, but for his deep and unaffected Piety. His end was Peace. 'Blessed are the Dead which die in the Lord.' Revelations, 14th Chap., 13th verse."

"Sacred to the memory of Alicia, Wife of Colonel Oldfield, of Oldfield Lawn, County of Sussex, K.H. Royal Engineers, A.D.C. to the Queen. Died 5th February, 1848. Sincerely pious, without ostentation, her trust was in the Lord. 'With the Lord, there is mercy and with Him is plenteous redemption.' Psalm 130., V.7."

"To the honored and beloved memory of General the Honble. Sir Henry Murray, K.C.B. (fourth son of David, 2nd Earl of Mansfield,) who served in Naples, Sicily & Calabria in 1806-7 accompanied the Expedition to Egypt in March 1807; and was present as an Aide-de-camp to the Honble. General Meade, at the attack on Alexandria, Siege and Storming of Rosetta, and on every other occasion when our troops were engaged. He served in Walcheren in 1809, at the landing including the Siege and Surrender of Flushing, until the Island was evacuated by the British Army. He went in Command of the 18th Hussars to the Peninsula, January 7th, 1813; was present at the crossing of the Eslar, and was badly wounded on the knee by his horse falling with him on a pointed rock; after which he commanded the Regiment in support of the 10th Hussars at the action of Marales-de-Toro. He served also in the Campaign of 1815, including the Battle of Quatre Bras: commanded the rear Regiment of the Column, on the retreat during the following day; and, at the Battle of Waterloo, he led the 18th Hussars in the brilliant charge of Sir Hussey Vivian's Brigade at the conclusion of the action. He commanded the Western District from 1842 to 1852, and after a long and severe illness, borne with the most Christian Resignation and Fortitude, died on the 29th July, 1860, deeply lamented by his Family, and all those who had known his excellent qualities.*

"Arthur Stormont Murray, aged 28 years, Son of Major-General the Honorable Henry Murray, and Captain in the Rifle Brigade, died a Soldier's Death on the 30th of August 1848, in consequence of wounds received the previous day, while leading an attack on the enemy's position at Bloom Plaats, in the Colony of the Cape of Good Hope. A career which gave promise to his country of usefulness – to himself of glory, was thus cut short; but the memory of the good and brave perish not, and the fruit of a virtuous life shed early on earth cometh to perfection in Heaven. His parents mourning over their own bereavement, yet not rebellious against the Divine will, caused this Tablet to be erected."

PORTLAND CHAPEL, in Portland-place, built in 1844, is a Free Evangelical Chapel, and, like most of the others we have enumerated, is devoid of architectural features.

NONCONFORMISTS. – The history of nonconformity in Plymouth is one of extreme interest, and one to which alone a whole volume might advantageously be devoted. Dating back far beyond the time, 1662, when the *Act of Uniformity* was passed, it may well be imagined that that arbitrary Act would cause the ejection of many ministers in Plymouth. Thus we read

*General the Hon. Sir Henry Murray was the fourth son of the second Earl of Mansfield by the Hon. Louisa Cathcart, daughter of Earl Cathcart, and married the daughter of Gerard de Visme, Esq., of Wimbledon Lodge, where he died in 1860, after being sixty years in the service. He was buried at Wimbledon, where a tablet, recounting his actions as above, and stating that this tablet "in the Garrison Chapel at Plymouth" was erected by special permission" was put up by Lady Murray in 1862.

that no less than seven ministers connected with that town were amongst those who were "persecuted for conscience sake." These were George Hughes, Obadiah Hughes, Nicholas Sherwell, Thomas Martyn, Samuel Martyn, Nathan Jacob, and John Horseman. Suffering and persecution evidently made these men brethren, and, such of them as were actually at Plymouth seemed, with their followers, to hold their meetings, in common; and, after the Indulgence, and the later Act of Toleration, founded their respective chapels and conventicles. The various denominations of Dissenters in Plymouth are the following:–

GENERAL BAPTIST (Chapels in George-street and at Mutley). The foundation of this congregation has been traced back to something like 250 years, but the earliest authentic records date only to 1648, in which year Abraham Cheare was baptized and joined the Baptist Church, of which, in the following year, he became pastor. Two years later a piece of ground was purchased in the Pig Market (Bedford-street) and a chapel founded, but Cheare was soon after twice seized and imprisoned at Exeter for three years. Having obtained liberty to visit Plymouth, he was again seized and confined for a month in the Guildhall, from whence he was, in 1665, removed to St. Nicholas Island, under an order of perpetual banishment. Here he was confined along with Hughes, Martyn, and others, and here he died. After the death of Cheare the Baptist congregation was without a minister for the space of 19 years, when, in 1687, Robert Browne was appointed, who, however, died soon afterwards, and a tomb to his memory will be seen in the George-street Chapel. He was succeeded first by a Mr. Warner, and next by a Mr. Holdenby. The next ministers were Samuel Buttall, and, after some changes, Nathaniel Hodges, but a long course of change seemed to have set in, and it was not until 1748, when Mr. Philip Gibbs became the pastor that a better time seemed to dawn upon the congregation. Through his exertions, in 1751 the chapel was taken down and a new one built. In 1781 a chapel was built at Dock, and the following year Mr. Isaiah Birt became co-pastor with Mr. Gibbs. In 1789 the congregation removed from the Pig Market to How-street, and in 1865 the old chapel was taken down. In 1790, Mr. William Winterbotham became co-pastor with Mr. Gibbs (in room of Mr. Birt, who removed to Dock), and not long after was tried and imprisoned two years for "seditious language" in two of his sermons. At the expiration of this term he returned to Plymouth. In 1800 the chapel in How-street was purchased, and in the same year Mr. Gibbs died, when Mr. Winterbotham became sole pastor until 1804, and was succeeded four years later by Mr. Ragsdale, and afterwards by Mr. Dyer and others. In 1821 Mr. Samuel

Nicholson did duty, and in 1823 became sole pastor. In 1830 How-street chapel was altered and repaired, and in 1843 steps were taken for building a large chapel in George-street, which was opened in 1845. In 1856 Mr. George Short was appointed co-pastor, and in the same year, (Mr. Nicholson dying in March,) became sole pastor till 1858. In 1860 Mr. Page succeeded him; in 1864 schools, etc., were built; and in 1868, the foundation stone of the chapel on Mutley Plain, was laid. Mr. Page resigning in 1869, Mr. Robert Lewis was appointed pastor.

CONGREGATIONALISTS. – (Sherwell Chapel, Tavistock-road, &c.) The Congregational body in Plymouth originated with the Nonconformist ejectment in 1662. In scarcely any other county in England was the effect of the Act of Uniformity so seriously felt as in Devonshire – no less than one hundred and thirty ministers being either ejected or silenced through its operation. In the immediate neighbourhood of Plymouth John Searle was ejected from the living of Plympton, and imprisoned; Mr. Pitts, from Plympton St. Mary; Robert Wyne, from Tamerton; Thomas Larkham, from Tavistock; John Quicke, a man of considerable learning from Brixton; Nathaniel Jacob, from Ugborough; Christopher Jellinger, an able and voluminous writer, from Brent; and John Hickes, from Stoke Damerell, who, when asked in reference to his large family, what he would do for them if he did not conform, answered, "Should I have as many children as that hen has chickens I would not question but God would provide for them all."

In Plymouth, during the Commonwealth, the Rev. George Hughes was the Incumbent of St. Andrew's Church, and the Rev. Mr. Porter, of Charles, then the New Church. During the incumbency of Mr. Hughes the services in both churches were conducted in the Presbyterian form, Mr. Porter having first disused the liturgual service; and Mr. Hughes during the morning service in St. Andrew's, regularly expounded the scriptures to his congregation, a folio volume being still extant containing his exposition of the book of Genesis and of the first thirty-three chapters of Exodus, which abundantly indicates his learning and piety.

Immediately after the Restoration, Mr. Porter conformed and retained his living, but on the passing of the Act of Uniformity, five ministers in Plymouth, or in immediate connection with it, were ejected or silenced. Of these, Mr. Hughes, who had held his living for eighteen years, was the most prominent. A Fellow of Pembroke College, a good scholar and a sound theologian, his influence was felt not only in Plymouth, but throughout the county, and on the king's return, he was offered a bishopric if he would conform, but declining on principle to accept the offer, was compelled, on the passing of the Act of Uniformity, to relinquish his living; and being summoned with Mr. Martyn his assistant, his son Mr. Obadiah Hughes, Mr. Nicholas Sherwell, and others, to appear before the Earl of Bath, the then Governor of Plymouth, he was sent with Mr. Martyn, in charge of two files of musketeers to St. Nicholas' Island, where he remained a close prisoner for nine months, until incurable dropsy with scurvy having ensued, he was at length permitted to retire to Kingsbridge, upon giving security in £2,000 not to reside within twenty miles of Plymouth. Mr. Hughes died at Kingsbridge in 1667, in the sixty-fourth year of his age, and a monument was erected by Mr. Crispin to his memory in the parish church, with a Latin inscription by John Howe, the celebrated Puritan Divine, who had married a daughter of Mr. Hughes – His son, Mr. Obadiah Hughes, ejected as a student from the University of Oxford, through the Act of Uniformity, on his return to Plymouth was imprisoned, but having obtained his release was ordained by Mr. Hickes and five other ministers, and for some time continued to exercise his ministry as best he could, in Plymouth and the neighbourhood, until his removal to London. Mr. Thomas Martyn, who had been educated at Oxford, and afterward became Lecturer at St. Andrew's, having been silenced and imprisoned, on his release resumed his ministry as a Nonconformist in Plymouth. His son, Mr. Samuel Martyn, well known in the Town as an occasional preacher, was also silenced and afterwards imprisoned at Exeter, and only obtained his discharge on consenting "to take the Sacrament according to the rites of the Church of England." He died in 1692.

Mr. Nicholas Sherwell, a graduate of Magdalen College, Oxford, was a native of Plymouth, and is described as having been "a gentleman who lived on his own estate, some of the richest and ablest in Plymouth, being his relations." He was imprisoned on the passing of the Act of Uniformity at the same time with Mr. Hughes and Mr. Martyn, and appears to have again suffered for his principles in 1665.

It may probably be assumed that shortly after 1662, and immediately resulting from the ejectment, two congregations were constituted in Plymouth, – the Independents before the Commonwealth, having probably associated with the Baptist Congregation, distinct reference being made to Meetings, which were held in "The Green House," in Green Street, and also at "The Old Mashalls" and Mr. Sherwell, whose opinions are believed to have been the same with those now held by the Congregational Body, was the minister of the one, and Mr. Martyn, and for a time Mr. Obadiah Hughes, of the other or Presbyterian Section. the Registers of Baptism kept by Mr. Sherwell extend from 1662 to 1692, that is to within four years of his death which occurred in 1696 – and in 1708 or as some suppose, in 1705, the present Chapel in Batter-street, was built – the Government it is said contributing to its erection in order that after the Union between England and Scotland (1707) there might be a place of religious worship for the Scotch soldiers who were then quartered in Plymouth in exchange for English Regiments stationed in Scotland, and the chapel was used for this purpose at intervals until the recent erection of the Presbyterian place of worship at Eldad – so that as late as the Crimean War, when the Highlanders then stationed in Plymouth left for Balaklava, the minister of Batter-street Chapel, as their Chaplain, preceded the Regiment to the place of embarkation.

In 1708, Mr. Enty was the pastor of this congregation, and distinguished himself by his orthodoxy, and the part he took in the Arian Controversy, which afterwards assumed such importance in the West of England.

In the other church, of which, Mr. Martyn and Mr. Obadiah Hughes are supposed to have been the ministers, either conjointly or in succession, it appears from an inscription on the Communion plate that in 1705, Mr. Nicholas Harding was the pastor. His opinions were orthodox, and he is reported to have had an influential congregation of more than seven hundred persons. On his death in 1744 Mr. Moore, who had been for some years assistant minister, became the sole pastor; but gradually adopting Arian sentiments and ultimately lapsing into Unitarianism, the great body of the people withdrew from his ministry, and united with the church in Batter-street; the congregation that remained constituting the Unitarian Body in Plymouth, which still subsists and continues to worship in the Chapel in Treville-street.

In 1760, on the death of Mr. John Moore, the then minister of Batter-street Chapel, the trustees nominated Mr. John Hanmer, as his successor, but being strongly inclined to Arianism his appointment was objected to by the congregation, and on an appeal to the Court of Queen's Bench their right of election was affirmed, and Mr. Christopher Mends whom they had selected in 1761 as their minister, was formally established in the pastorate in 1762. On his death in 1799 he was succeeded by his son Mr. Herbert Mends, who died in 1819 and whose name is still remembered in Plymouth with much respect and affection.

In the year 1845 – Mr. T. C. Hine being at the time the minister of the Batter-street congregation – it was thought by many, and particularly by Mr. Hine, that owing to the altered state of the population a removal to another part of the town, would be desirable, and the erection of a new chapel in

Courtenay-street now known as Union Chapel, was accordingly begun, the building being completed in 1848; but a considerable section of the people did not fully concur in the change and continued to worship in the Chapel in Batter-street of which Mr. W. Whittley is the present pastor. In connexion with this place of worship large and commodious School-rooms have been erected and during Mr. Whittley's pastorate the chapel, which affords accommodation for upwards of seven hundred persons, has, at a considerable cost, been almost rebuilt.

Union Chapel, of which, for some years after its erection Mr. T. C. Hine was the minister, presents an effective front elevation designed by Mr. Wightwick, and has 750 sittings. During the pastorate of Mr. C. B. Symes, who has recently left for an important ministerial appointment in South Australia, School-rooms, immediately connected with the chapel, were built by the congregation at a cost of £1800.

But independently of Batter-street and Union chapels, which are in immediate succession to the churches of the ejectment, with the growth of the population, there was a further accession to the Independent body in Plymouth during the last century. Consequent on the revival of religion under Whitfield, a large congregation had been gathered in Devonport of which Mr. Andrew Kinsman, was the minister and a chapel erected for its accommodation. In a M.S. letter from Mr. Kinsman to Mr. W. Fawcett, dated the 19th December, 1767, he writes:–

> "This last summer providence pointed out the way for an addition of ground which for the sum of £8 per annum we possess; and the Artificers in the King's Yard of every business built another addition to the meeting, of 35ft. square and three galleries. This they undertook to do gratis. So soon as the bell rung, and they came off from working for an earthly King, they came with fresh ardour, to work and build for the King of Kings. Those that were only labourers or smiths, did such work as they were able. They had a few lines which they used to repeat when carrying out the rubbish &c.,
>
> "Gilder and Carver I am none.
> But I can carry lime and stone."
>
> I don't preach to less than 14 or 1500 every sabbath afternoon. At Plymouth my suitors are large, but as there are several meeting houses with which several are connected, the increase is not so remarkable. I suppose our numbers are about 180."

This movement resulted in the erection of a chapel in Briton Side, known as first as "The Tabernacle," but afterwards, as "The Old Tabernacle," of which Mr. H. Wheeler is the minister, but in 1797, a portion of the church and congregation were desirous of opening another place of worship and "The New Tabernacle" in Norley-street, now known as "Norley Chapel," was built and afterwards enlarged, so as to afford room for about 800 persons – good school-rooms were added during the pastorate of the late Dr. George

Smith and subsequently a branch chapel opened in Mount-street. Under the ministry of Mr. Charles Wilson, owing to the increase of the necessary, it was determined by the church in Norley chapel to erect a new place of worship in the Tavistock-road. The foundation-stone of the new building was laid in 1862 by the late Mr. David Derry, and the erection completed from designs by Messrs. Paull and Ayliffe, of Manchester, in 1864, for 1250 persons. The school-rooms adjoining, which are large and handsome, and afford accommodation for 800 children, were built in 1867-8; and the cost of the entire buildings with the organ, presented by Mr. Charles Fox, a member of the congregation, amounted to £13,500.

After an interval of two years Norley Chapel, which, as recently restored, is a very commodious place of worship, was re-opened, Mr. E. B. Hickman being the present minister. The Congregationalists have therefore in Plymouth five places of worship, with their school-rooms, beside the branch chapel in Mount-street.

THE WESTERN COLLEGE at Mannamead, near Plymouth is an institution designed for the training of young men intended for the ministry in connection with the Congregational body. In the early part of the last century the extension of Arianism within the Established church and amongst dissenters, especially in the West of England, excited much anxiety, and in 1762 the Congregational Fund Board in London, established at Ottery in Devon, an institution for the education of ministerial students. Subsequently under the Rev. James Rooker, at Bridport, the Rev. Thomas Reader, at Taunton, the Rev. James Small, at Axminster, and the Rev. Dr. Payne, at Exeter, the work was continued, but in 1845, this college under the presidency of Dr. Payne and the Rev. Samuel Newth was, removed to Plymouth. Dr. Payne on his death was succeeded by the Rev. Dr. Alliott; the present Theological Professor being the Rev. John M. Charlton, M.A., with the Rev. F. E. Anthony, M.A., as Professor of Classics and Mathematics. In 1861, the present building, which is intended for the reception of nineteen students, besides any who may be non-resident, was opened, and has for many years past been very efficiently conducted. The College is maintained at a cost of about £1200 a year, partly with income derived from settled property, but mainly by donations and annual subscriptions contributed by members of the Congregational body. This institution is open to lay students of approved character on the payment of moderate fees and is affiliated with the London University, and, as the nearest Congregational Institute is at Bristol, the Western College cannot but be regarded as of great value by the Congregational body in the West of England.

UNITARIANS. – (Norley-street.) This body claims to have for its founder in Plymouth, both the Rev. George Hughes, who, as has already been stated, was ejected from the ministry of St. Andrew's; and Mr. Nicholas Sherwell, of whom also much has just been written, and whose name appears in the Registry book as having officiated both at baptisms and marriages from 1662. Entries in the same book likewise show that baptisms were also performed by the Rev. Thomas Martyn, and the other ejected ministers. It is supposed that the old chapel was erected soon after 1689, as Nathaniel Harding commenced his ministry in 1690; the earliest trust deed is dated in 1708, at which time the chapel was sold by Nicholas Jenkins to Mark Batt, Joseph Wilcocks, Nathaniel Northcott, and Joseph Fuge, as Trustees. Of Nathaniel Harding a memory exists on the Communion plate of the chapel, which bears the inscription:– "*Bought by and for the use of that church in Plymouth of which Nathaniel Harding is Pastor,* 1705."

He was succeeded by Mr. Henry Moore, in 1743, and the next minister was Mr. J. Hanmer. In 1763, Mr. John Reynell joined Mr. Hanmer, and ultimately succeeded him. After several changes, Mr. Israel Worsley became minister in 1813, and in 1832 was succeeded by Mr. W. J. Odgers, who leaving in 1853, was succeeded in 1866, by the present minister, Mr. W.

J. Frekleton. In 1832, the old chapel was taken down, and the present much enlarged one, erected on its site. In connection with this chapel is a "Fellowship Fund," commenced in 1817, for assisting in building places of worship, etc.; a "Chapel Library," founded in 1825; a "Tract Society"; a large Sunday School, to which are attached a Library and a Savings' Bank; and a "Visiting and Working Society."

SOCIETY OF FRIENDS, BILBURY STREET. – It appears from the records of the Society of Friends that their distinguishing tenets were first promulgated in Plymouth on the arrival there of John Audland and Thomas Ary about the middle of the year 1654. The former boldly preached the new doctrines in St. Andrew's Church, while the latter held forth in the Baptist meeting, in spite of the abuse of the ministers and congregations. Notwithstanding, or probably in consequence of, the strong opposition they encountered, their brief visit of four or five days duration produced a considerable effect on the minds of the townsfolk; and when, a few months later, they were followed by Thomas Salthouse, of Lancashire, and Miles Halhead, of Westmoreland, matters were found to be ripe for the establishment of regular meetings for worship in accordance with their views. Salthouse and Halhead experienced much persecution here as elsewhere. It is related that they "had several peaceable meetings at friends' houses; ministering to the people what they had seen, heard, and handled of the Word of Life, and their testimony reached to the consciences of many who flocked to hear them, insomuch that a meeting, appointed on the next first day (Sunday) at one John Harris' near the town (his house not being large enough to contain the people), was held in his garden, when the said Miles and Thomas did publish the free grace of God, which brings salvation unto all, inviting people to obey the same, and provoking them to love and good works, labouring in great simplicity and plainness for the advancement of the kingdom of Christ, to the general approbation of the hearers." At the instance of one George Brooks, chaplain of the *Nightingale* frigate, who attended this meeting, the two preachers were committed to the High Gaol at Exeter under a warrant signed by the Mayor, John Page, on a charge of disturbing the public peace; and on their trial, after six weeks incarceration, were committed for a further period of seven months for refusing the oath of abjuration. In 1655, George Fox, the founder of the Society, came to Plymouth in the course of his first visit to the West of England, in company with his staunch supporter, Edward Pyot, of Bristol, an ex-captain in the army. Fox relates in his Journal that, "after having refreshed ourselves at an inn, we went to Robert Carey's house, where we had a very precious meeting. At this meeting was one Elizabeth

Trelawney, daughter to a baronet; she being somewhat thick of hearing came close up to me, and clapped her ear very nigh me while I spoke, and she was convinced. After the meeting came in some jangling Baptists, but the Lord's power came over them, and Elizabeth Trelawney gave testimony thereto. A fine meeting was settled there in the Lord's power, which hath continued ever since; where many faithful friends have been convinced."

The early records of this body abound in cases of persecution, by fine and imprisonment, and it appears that in 1660 the High Gaol and Bridewell of Exeter contained "all the men-inhabitants of Plymouth of that persuasion." Amongst these records which have been preserved in unbroken series from 1669 to this day, the well known Plymouth names of Burnell, Collier, Cotton, Cookworthy, Fox and Hinston, are of very frequent occurrence. Until the removal of legal restrictions to the erection of Conventicles the members assembled for worship in private houses, and they rented a burial place near the Hoe, at 20s. a year. In excavating for the foundations of the modern Hoe Park Terrace, numerous remains of bodies were brought to light, and as these were believed to occupy the site of this ancient place of sepulture, they were collected by Mr. Thomas Luscombe, a member of the Society, and re-interred in the present burial ground behind the Meeting House in Bilbury Street. The site of this Meeting House was purchased in 1703, but the present structure was substituted at a later period, for the building formerly used. By a deed of 13th May, 1703, John Beare the younger, of Bearscombe [near Kingsbridge], Alice, his wife, only daughter and heir of Ambrose Hind, late of East Allington, Devon, deceased, and George Beare, of Bearscombe, gent, in consideration of four score and ten pounds and two broad pieces of gold conveyed to Henry Ceane, of Plymouth, (a Quaker) all those messuages, tenements and curtilage within the Borough of Plymouth, near a street called Bilbury Bridge, bounded on the north by a lane leading to Hampton Shute and Charles Church; and on the south by the aforesaid street called Bilbury Bridge or Street. On the 18th December, 1704, H. Ceane conveyed the premises to Trustees "to and for the only use and behoof of the people called Quakers, for a Meeting house and Burial Ground." This trust deed, we are informed by Mr. Robert Dymond, to whom we are indebted for the above particulars, has ever since been renewed from time to time, as the number of Trustees became reduced by death. The present Meeting House was erected in 1804, at a cost of about £1,200. A few years ago an adult school of about 200 scholars of both sexes, was established in the Meeting House, and in 1870 a large school room was erected in Charles street.

WESLEYAN METHODISTS. – Methodism appears to have been introduced into Plymouth about 1744, when Whitfield first visited the town, intending to embark hence for America. In 1752, Mr. Kinsman, who became minister of the tabernacle in Briton Side, to the erection of which he had largely contributed, built the first dissenting chapel, at Dock. Wesley first visited Plymouth in 1746, and at this time and till much later, preachings were held in various parts of the town. In 1779, a chapel in Lower Street, Dock, was commenced, and in 1792 the foundation stone of Wesley Chapel, in Buckwell Street (then called Mud Lane) was laid, the fittings from Lower Street Chapel being removed to it. In 1815, Ebenezer Chapel was commenced building, and shortly afterwards Wesley Chapel was closed, and at one time used by the General Baptists, under the name of Rehoboth Chapel, but again reverted to its original persuasion. In 1864, the foundation stone of the King Street Chapel (chapels at Stonehouse having in the meantime been erected) was laid by Mr. John Allen. It is a fine and spacious building, capable of accommodating a large number of persons, and has schools attached. Besides the Wesleyans, the Primitive Methodists, the Reform Methodists, the Bible Christians, the United Methodist Free Church Society, and others have places of worship.

ROMAN CATHOLIC, CECIL STREET. – The history of this body in Plymouth is but short. The first priest since the Reformation who is known to have preached in Plymouth was the Rev. Edward Williams, who, about a century ago, occasionally visited the town, but the first resident incumbent of the laborious mission of Plymouth was the Rev. Thomas Flynn, a native of Ireland, a "man of zeal and herculean strength." This gentleman preached in a room over a stable at the rear of the George Inn, at Dock, – the only place of worship then established by the Catholics. In 1803, the Rev. Jean Louis Guilbert was appointed to succeed Mr. Flynn, and in the same year Mr. Rowland Conyers, who then died, provided funds to maintain a priest in Plymouth. Mr. Guilbert, who was a French refugee, in 1763 undertook the construction of a public chapel in lieu of the room over the stable at Dock. Having obtained a central situation near the Marine Hospital, at Stonehouse, the foundation stone was laid on the 28th May, 1806, for St. Mary's Chapel, with an adjoining presbetère and school, and on 20th December, 1807, mass was celebrated in that sacred edifice. Mr. Guilbert returned to France in 1815, and died at Epinal in 1822. In 1834 the Rev. Henry Riley was appointed, and during his ministry, which lasted till 1848, when he resigned through ill health, and died in the following year, considerably enlarged and improved the chapel and the rest of the premises. In 1851 Plymouth was erected into a Roman Catholic Bishopric, the first prelate being the Rev. Dr. Errington. – St. Mary's Chapel being raised to the rank of a cathedral, and from 1853, having a chapter of eight canons attached to it. In 1856 (June 28) the foundation stone of the present cathedral was laid by the Rev. Dr. Vaughan, the new Bishop of the Roman Catholic diocese. Adjoining to, and connected with the cathedral, on one side is the residence of the Bishop, and on the other a Nunnery of the Sisters of Notre Dame, and extensive schools. The cathedral, which has a lofty tower and spire, is a cruciform structure in the Early English style of architecture, erected from the designs of Messrs. Hansom; its length is 155 feet, and width across nave and transepts 80 feet. The old premises in Stonehouse are now used as an establishment of Little Sisters of the Poor. Another Roman Catholic church is in contemplation on the east side of the town.

THE JEWS' SYNAGOGUE, CATHERINE STREET. – The first congregation of Jews is said to have been commenced in Board Hoe Lane about the middle of last century. The present synagogue was built in 1764.

PLYMOUTH BRETHREN. – This sect appears to have originated about the year 1829, and two years later Plymouth becoming its centre, it took the name of "Plymouth Brethren." The first meetings were held in Raleigh Street, and next in Ebrington Street.

CATHOLIC-APOSTOLIC, OR IRVINGITES, meet in Princess Street; the UNIVERSALISTS in Henry Street; and the FREE EVANGELICALS have a large Chapel in Portland Place; the PRESBYTERIAN Meeting is near the Catholic Cathedral. It is a large, substantial, and imposing looking building. The PROTESTANT EVANGELICAL Church is in Compton Street.

CHAPTER XII

THE GUILDHALL — CORPORATION PLATE — MACES — SEALS, ETC. — NEW MUNICIPAL BUILDINGS — CORPORATE CEREMONIES — FISHING FEAST EXCHANGE — CUSTOM HOUSE — POST OFFICE — THEATRE — ASSEMBLY ROOMS — LIBRARY — MECHANICS' INSTITUTION — ATHENÆUM — VOLUNTEERS — WATER WORKS — HOSPITAL OF POOR'S PORTION — ALMS HOUSES — HOSPITAL OF ORPHANS' AID — CEMETERY — HOSPITALS AND OTHER CHARITABLE INSTITUTIONS ETC.

The Guildhall of the Borough of Plymouth at the present time in use, but whose days for municipal honours are numbered, occupies a triangular plot of ground between Whimple and High Streets. It was erected in 1800 from the designs of a Mr. Eveleigh, upon the site of the former building, of which an engraving and some particulars will be found on page 101. The building is most inconvenient, and unworthy, in every respect, of the important town to which it belongs. The front consists of a central tower surmounted by an open bell-cote. In the base of this tower is the entrance doorway, above which is the town arms and a window surmounted by a quatrefoil light. Above this, in the upper part of the tower, is a projecting illuminated clock. To the left and right of the entrance in the basement story, are the police offices and cells, and above these are, to the left, two gothic windows which give light to the great hall, and to the right is another similar window. The building contains besides the great hall, a council chamber, chamberlain's room, town clerk's office, police library, police office, lock-up, witnesses rooms, magistrate's rooms, and other offices.

In the great hall several full length life-size portraits, and some few other interesting features, are preserved. They are the following:– Over the Mayor's seat at the west end, is the portrait, bare-headed and in robes, of George IV., when Prince Regent, by Hoppner. To the Mayor's right hand are portraits of George II. in robes, "presented by George Pridham, Esq., Mayor, 1845"; and of Queen Charlotte, seated, "presented by James Skardon, Esq., Mayor 1867." To the Mayor's left are those of Queen Caroline, wife of

George II., "presented by George Pridham, Mayor, 1845;" and of George III., seated, in robes, "presented by James Skardon, Esq., November, 1867." In the body of the hall, to the Mayor's right, is a similar portrait of William IV., standing, in naval uniform, "presented by John Burnell, Esq., Mayor, 1860;" and to his left is that of H.R.H. the Prince Consort, in his robes of state, which was purchased by the Corporation at a cost of 100 guineas. In the windows of the hall are some fragments of stained glass, probably from a former and much finer guildhall. In the east window are the arms, with supporters, etc., of James I., quarterly, 1 and 4, France and England, quartered; 2, Scotland; 3, Ireland; and the motto "Beati Pacifici;" in the same window are portions of shields of arms bearing *gules*, a chevron, *argent*, between three cinquefoils, *or;* and *or*, a chevron, *vert*, between three goat's heads, erased, *sable*. In one of the other windows are the Prince of Wales' feathers, with the motto "Ich Dien," within a garter, with the usual motto; and in the other the arms of Plymouth, *argent*, a saltire, *vert*, between four castles, *sable*, with mantling, etc. In the hall are also preserved the colour of the old volunteers.

In the Council Chamber, besides other paintings and engravings, are also some Royal portraits, and a most curious and highly valuable portrait of the great admiral, Sir Francis Drake. The painting, which is on panel, is a half-length portrait of Sir Francis, in robes, and with a ruff about his neck. In front of the head are the arms, crest, mantling, etc., of Drake and there are also the words "Ætatis suæ 53, An., 1594." Beneath, is the following verse:–

"Sir Drake, whom well the world's end knows,
Which thou didst compasse rounde,
And whom both poles of heaven ons saw,
Which North and South do bound:
The stars above will make thee known,
If men here silent were,
The Sunn himself cannot forgett,
His fellow Traveller.

Great Drake, whose shippe about the world's wide waste,
In three years did a golden girdle cast,
Who with fresh streams refresht this Towne that first,
Though kist with waters yet did pine with thirst,
Who both a Pilote, and a Magistrate,
Steered in his turne the shippe of Plymouth's state;
This little table shewes his face whose worth,
The World's wide table hardly can sett forth."

In the magistrate's room is a half-length portrait of George I. in his robes, and in the chamberlain's room are portraits of George W. Marshall, Mayor in 1782, "presented by George Pridham," and of Peter Burdwood, Common Councilman in the Corporation, painted by Soloman Hart, in 1824, presented by Mr. Skardon. There is also a remarkably curious painting of the old wooden Eddystone Lighthouse, which was destroyed in 1703, as well as several curious engravings.

The corporation plate, an insignia of office of the Mayor, consists of three splendid silver-gilt maces; two silver-gilt loving cups, or chalices; a gold chain with suspended medal; and a large silver snuff box on which are engraved the Plymouth arms with supporters, etc.

The three maces are here engraved. The largest measures 4ft. 3in. in height, and weighs $10\frac{1}{2}$lbs.; the other two measure 4ft. in length, and weigh respectively $8\frac{1}{2}$lbs. each. They are all, as will be seen by the engraving, of the same general form. Around the head of each are the following heraldic devices divided from each other by semi-figures and foliage; a rose and a thistle conjoined on one stem, surmounted by an open arched crown, between the letters A.R. (*Anna Regina*); a fleur-de-lis, crowned in a similar manner, also between the letters A.R.; a portcullis, with the same crown and letters; and a harp with the same. At the base of the large mace are, on one side, the Plymouth arms with supporters, etc., and on the other the arms of Jory; on the other two, the rose and thistle. Around it is the inscription "*Ex dono Josephi Jory Armigeri Prœtori oppidi Plymovthiani et Successoribvs svis in Sempiternvm A^o D^i* 1709." One of the smaller ones, has on the base, on the side the Plymouth arms and supporters, and on the other the date "1711," with roses and thistles between; and the other, the arms and a plain tablet alternating with the rose and thistle.

The Loving Cups, or Chalices, are shown in our engraving. The large one has, in front, the arms of the Borough of Plymouth, and at the back those of Gayer, with crest and mantling. Around the inner rim is the inscription "*The guift of St Iohn Gayer, Alderman of London, An^o Domini* 1648." The smaller one has no armorial insignia, but is of much more ornamental and artistic character than the other. It has four heads in high relief, and bears the following inscription:– "*The gift of Iohn Whit of London, Haberdasher, to the Mayor of Plymouth and his bretheren for ever, to drinke crosse one to ye other at their Feastes or Meetings. Dated ye 5th of June* 1535."

The Mayor's Gold Chain of Office, was purchased in 1803. It is 16 feet 5 inches in length, and forms a four-fold chain. Attached to it is worn suspended a large gold medal, given by the Freemen of the Borough for that purpose. A copy of the inscription on this medal, which with the chain is represented on the cover of this volume, is given on page 391. The cost of the chain and a medal will be seen by the following bill which is preserved in the Guildhall:–

Philip Langmead, Esq., London 6th June 1803
Bought of Thomas Barnard, Working Goldsmith and Jeweller, Corner of Adam Street, Adelphi, Strand,

	£	s.	d.
A Standard Gold Mayor's Chain 16 feet 5 inches long	66	0	0
A Standard Gold Mayor's Medal to hang to do., Engraved with the Arms of Plymouth on one side and an inscription on the other*	9	0	0
A Morocco Case lined with Sattin for do., with a Lock and Key	1	18	0
Paid Insurance to Plymouth on £30 value	0	12	6
	£77	10	6

The Robes of Office worn by the Mayor at the present time are a scarlet cloak trimmed with sable, and a cocked hat. Scarlet gowns were first worn by the Mayor and Aldermen in 1582. The halberdiers, mace bearers, crier, and other officers had also liveries about the same time.

There are three ancient seals belonging to the borough. The largest of these, here engraved of its full size is very elaborate in design.

The field is divided by a base-line from which rise three gothic niches with highly decorated canopies. Within the central, or principal niche, is a seated figure of St. Andrew, with nimbus, holding in his right had a cross

*This was probably a different medal from the one now worn, which is dated 1816.

saltire (or St. Andrew's cross) and in his left, a clasped book. In the niche on his right hand is an angel holding a shield bearing the cross of St. George; and in the other niche is a similar angel holding a shield bearing the arms of England (quarterly 1 and 4 France, 2 and 3 England); the whole of the ground work is filled in with gothic tracery. Beneath the base-line is a shield bearing the arms of the borough of Plymouth (a saltire, or St. Andrew's cross, between four castles) supported on either side by a lion. The inscription is "THE COMEN SELLE OF THE BOROVGH & COMENALTE OF Y^{E} KYNGS TOWNE OF PLYMOUTHE."

Another seal, which is particularly chaste and elegant in design, is here engraved of its full size. It is very sharply cut, of circular form, and bears

the arms of the borough on a shield within the inner circle. The shield is surmounted by a crown of fleur-de-lis, and the space between the inner circle and shield is filled in with gothic tracery. The inscription is as follows:– "S. OFFICII MAIORATUS BURGI VILLE DE .... DE PLYMOUTH," and it is somewhat remarkable that one portion of the inscription has, intentionally, and most probably originally, been defaced in the matrix. The third of these seals, also here engraved of its full size, is of circular form, and simply bears the arms of the borough, on a plain shield, surmounted by the date, 1595. Another ancient seal, mentioned by Oliver, is described as bearing the device of a ship, and the inscription: – "SIGILLUM COMMITATIS SUTTON SUPER PLYMOUTHE."

Plymouth of late years seems to have had a decided penchant for altering and adding to, without any real authority, its armorial insignia. Thus, one circular seal bears a shield with the arms of the borough supported by two lions rampant; the crest, a sheaf composed of seven swords, spears, and battle axes, between two flags, dexter and sinister, each bearing the Union Jack, the whole issuing from a cannon's mouth, and an assemblage of cannon balls, etc.; the motto, on a ribbon beneath the supporters, *Turris fortissima*

est nomen Jehovæ: while the present official seal (which by the way is one of those modern abominations adopted by corporations and other official bodies, a *stamp* for paper, and not a "seal" in any sense of the word) differs materially from it. This seal is circular in form, 2 1/4 inches in diameter, and may be thus described. At the base of the field are waves of the sea, upon which is the hull of a ship, having a flag of the cross of St. George at its stern. Above the hull, on a shield, are the arms of the borough (a saltire between four castles) with two lions rampant guardant as supporters, behind each of which, their tails twining around them, stands an empty beacon. The crest (if so it may be called) is as follows: a beacon of fire in the centre, between six flags, three dexter and three sinister, each charged with the arms of the borough and typifying the six municipal wards into which the town is divided; the hole issuing out of a ducal coronet. Around the seal in the inner circle is the motto "*Turris fortissima est nomen Jehovæ,*" with a lion passant guardant at the base. The outer circle bears the legend "Common Seal of the Mayor, Aldermen, and Burgesses of the Borough of Plymouth, 1835." The general design of the insignia here described was made by Lieut-Colonel Chas. Hamilton Smith, and will be pretty well understood by the accompanying official engraving of the arms. Among the other seals are a Mayor's seal, 1 1/4 inches by 1 inch, well executed, with the entire design here described, filling its whole surface, but without any lettering whatever; a circular seal 3/4 of an inch in diameter being simply a fantastically shaped shield with the arms of the borough; and a small oval seal, of much the same poor design.

Many curious events have occurred in connection with the history of the Guildhall, but these have already been detailed in the preceding part of this volume.

An admirable site for the new Municipal buildings, has been gained by the purchase and demolition of the old Hospital of Poor's Portion, the Hospital of Orphan's Aid, and premises and lands adjoining, in Westwell, Basket, and Catherine-streets. The space thus thrown open comprises an area of about 250 feet by 80 feet, and consists of the square of land behind Bedford-street, Westwell-street, and Catherine-street, and on the other by the buildings in the rear of Princess-street. On the north side of this plot the municipal offices are erected, and on the south side are the new Guildhall, the law courts, the police offices, etc. On the east the fine old tower of St. Andrew's church fitly fills up the space, while on the west the area is open to Westwell-street.

The new buildings have been designed in some degree to harmonize with the tower of St. Andrew's, the wings being treated in broad and simple masses, leading up to central features of appropriate richness and dignity; the local materials, of which the exterior is chiefly constructed, – viz., granite and limestone, – rendering such treatment desirable. The large hall which is intended to seat 2,600 persons, occupies the centre of the façade on the south side, shown in the engravings, with the proposed law courts at the Westwell-street end, and the police-court and station-house at the eastern end. The great hall is entered immediately from the public square through a deeply-recessed central double doorway and side porches, and has a nave 58ft. wide, with narrow aisles on either side, the extreme length being 146ft. The aisles open into the body of the hall, with two arcades of seven arches each, the pillars supporting which are of polished grey granite, 2ft. 9in. in diameter. The traceried windows of each clerestory follow the number of the arches below. There are seven separate doorways for ingress and egress. At the west end is an orchestra, in connection with which is a suite of ante-rooms, available for performers and others; and at the east end is a gallery for the public, to seat about 300. The hall has a semi-circular boarded roof. The internal dimensions of the police-court are 46ft. by 38ft., and adjoining are rooms for the magistrates, magistrates' clerk, attorneys, and witnesses; and in the rear, the station-house, police muster-room, reading-room, &c. Each of the courts at the Westwell-street end is 49ft. long by 38ft. wide, and there are separate entrances and rooms for barristers, attorneys, and witnesses, with distinct accommodation for the public in galleries at the ends of the courts, approached by a stone staircase in an octagonal angle tower. An important feature of this pile of buildings is the tower at the south-west corner of the group, which will be nearly 200ft. high to the vane. The council-chamber and municipal offices occupy a portion of the northern side of the public square, a space at the Westwell-street end of this side having been reserved for future public uses. This municipal structure is for the most part two-storied, the council-chamber forming the central feature, and somewhat corresponding in detail with the great hall on the opposite side. The north block includes, besides council-chamber and other municipal offices, offices for the town clerk, chamberlain, and surveyor, and apartments for the school board, &c., with strong-rooms, store-rooms, and a large vaulted muniment room. Gothic, of the early French type, is the style which has been adopted, and the details are bold rather than elaborate. The plain surfaces are executed in Cornish granite and local limestone; the moulded and enriched portions being in Portland and Mansfield stone.

On the apex of the gable of the Council Chamber is a colossal full-length statue of Sir Francis Drake, by Trevenen; and in other parts of the exterior are medallion heads of our beloved Queen Victoria, Sir Walter Raleigh, and others. There are also some very rich and appropriate armorial decorations, cleverly executed by Mr. Harry Hems, of Exeter, which add greatly to the beauty of the structure. The shields on the octagonal tower at the Westwell-street end of the municipal buildings, twenty nine in number, are arranged in a series of panels beneath the upper windows; they bear besides the royal arms, those of several Devonshire worthies, and of neighbouring boroughs. Commencing on the cant nearest to Basket-street, and terminating with that immediately over the parapet to the main front of the building, the arms are arranged in the following order: Saltash; Exeter; Launceston; Plympton; Morice; Rogers; Devonport; Earl St. German's; Earl of Morley; Duke of Bedford; Earl of Mount Edgcumbe; Earl of Devon; Sir Walter Raleigh; Trelawney; Hawkins; Strode; Slanning; Diocese of Exeter; H.R.H. the Prince of Wales; H.M. Queen Victoria; H.R.H. the Duke of Edinburgh; the Borough of Plymouth; Hele; Oxenham; Drake; Harris; Woolcombe; and St. Aubyn. In the gable of the Crown Court facing the municipal offices is a large shield, five feet high, bearing the royal arms, surmounted by a crown, and on the corresponding gable of the police court is a similar shield, bearing the arms of the Prince of Wales; on the gable of the council chamber facing towards the great Hall are shields bearing the arms of England and of the Borough of Plymouth. The entire works are being carried out from the designs and under the direction of Messrs. Norman & Hine, architects, of Plymouth. Mr. J. Pethick, of Plymouth, is the contractor, and the contract amount is £32,475.

There were formerly some curious customs connected with the corporation, to which reference may best be made in this place. One of these was "Freedom Day" which is said to have been originated in commemoration of the defeat of the invading Bretons, but its real use was the perambulating of the boundaries – "beating the bounds" – of the borough. On "Freedom Eve" it appears a glove used to be hung outside the Guildhall, and at 3 o'clock that afternoon the "Freedom Boys" assembled for the purpose of "knocking down the glove set up over the Guildhall door."

Next day, "Freedom Day," the town was in commotion through two parties of young men meeting, by mutual consent, and fighting a battle with clubs, sticks, and other weapons, generally in a field known by the name of "Freedom Field," the prize being a barrel of beer, which is said to have been provided by the Mayor. The name of the one party was "Burton Boys," (or *Breton* Boys), being the residents from Martin's Gate eastward; and the other "Old Town Boys," the residents of the other parts of the town. In 1782 the fighting was abolished "through several serious injuries having been inflicted – indeed it was quite unsafe for people to walk the streets, and genteel people would be sure, if they did not bestow a moiety on every party, to be well ducked* from the kennel. One Nickey Glubb, a well known character in Plymouth, was famous among the Burton Boys, and there is, (and has been for a number of years,) a public-house called the Burton Boys, in Exeter-street, and on the sign Nickey is painted, carrying the beer among the rude rabble. After the year 1782, the 'Freedom Boys' were changed to the children belonging to the Red, Blue, and Green Schools; to them it was a 'liberty day,' but was disgraced by a prevailing idea among them, that on this day they may rob with impunity all the fruit shops, and bakers' shops; and after having over-run the town for some time, they leave it to visit the orchards on the eastern part of the borough. On this day too the old Mayor attended by the Sword Bearer, Serjeants-at-Mace, and as many of the most respectable of the inhabitants on horseback, as choose to ride, go round the boundaries of the borough, shewing them to the mayor elect. At two o'clock, they meet in Frankfort-street, proceed down George-street to Millbay, across to Stonehouse-lane, up the road to No-Place, and to the Mill-bridge, and across it, and back to No-Place again; – thence to Mutley and come into town by Lipson turnpike, and go down by Whitecross-street, Briton-side, Tin-street, Vauxhall and Woolster streets, unto the new quay. There dismount, and walk in procession to the Lammy Point for the purpose of waiting to assist the Freedom Boy out of the boat, present him with a piece of coin, and give him a box on the ear, to remember the place and the occasion by. Then they go to the Barbican steps, and take the oldest boy out of the boat there with the like compliment. The boys after having met the mayor in or near freedom field, then go away for Prince Rock, or Catdown, and embark in boats for the lower parts of the town – latterly in only two boats; and in the Mayoralty of Mr. Lockyer, they rode around the hoe, after having been at the Lammy; then they go to partake of a cold collation provided at the Guildhall."

*They always were provided with "ducking horns," to lade up water from the street to throw over passers by.

Formerly the mayor was elected annually on St. Lambert's day, September 17th, but since the passing of the Municipal Reform Act the election now takes place on the 9th November. On the two sundays next before St. Lambert's day notice used to be given in the churches and chapels of the borough, after the reading of the nicene creed, in the following form:– "The Right Worshipful the Mayor desires the Commonalty of this Borough to meet him at the Guildhall thereof on ..... day, the 17th day of September next, at 10 o'clock in the forenoon, then and there to elect a Mayor of the said borough for the year ensuing." On the 17th, the Mayor and Commonalty being assembled in the Guildhall at 10 o'clock, proceeded at 11 in full state, with robes, maces etc., preceded by a band of music and the town flag, to St. Andrew's church, "where a sermon was preached by the Vicar on Brotherly Love, Duty of Magistrates, &c. – and to the corporation he particularly addresses himself. After the service being over, they return in full procession to the Guildhall, when the Mayor opens the business of the day, by observing the time being come for him to nominate a successor and retire from office; the Town Clerk or his Deputy reads the Bribery and Corruption Act, and then proceeds to call over a list of the Freemen of the Borough (one of the Serjeants being the Repeater). Notice being taken of those freemen who have answered to their names, the old Mayor being President or Returning Officer, still fills the chair – then one of the Freemen, (or the Mayor under the New Bye-laws), nominates one from their number (indiscriminately)* to be Mayor for the year ensuing, which must be seconded and then polled by a show of hands, and if there is not a second nominated, the Mayor returns him duly elected, and he immediately takes his place at the right hand of the Mayor; but if two should be nominated, and their respective numbers (on polling) cannot be ascertained, then a stricter poll is taken, and the freemen sworn, two, three, or four at a time, in the same manner as choosing the representatives. The Mayor must be chosen before the meeting is dissolved; – many times it has been 12 o'clock at night before he has been chosen, which is the more strange, when it is known that there is an elegant and plentiful dinner provided for those concerned in voting, by the old Mayor. Then the Chartered business of the day, as choosing, nominating or appointing" being over "they go again to church, for to pray, (as sly rogues) say, – that the dinner may be good! but that may be uppermost in their mind; but the custom was only to hear and sing the Psalm." The election "being completed, and extraordinary discussions adjourned, two hampers are hoisted upon the table, one containing buns and tough cakes, (the latter for the Commonalty) and the other sherry wine to

*But the Charter says, he ought to be able to purchase Lands, Heriditaments, &c., &c., &c.

drink the health of their chief," as Baron expresses it. The procession was then re-formed and again proceeded to St. Andrew's church, where, as has been said, the 117th Psalm was sung, the offertory collected, and prayers and collect read. Leaving the church, the procession was re-formed and proceeded to perambulate the borough.

"First went the Old Governor of the Barbican, and the two town's Corporals with White Rods; next the Constables, two and two, with their small four-square-headed maces, (in number 34,); then the South Devon Band, if in the place, or in the neighbourhood; the Standard Bearer (or sword bearer armed) with the silk flag bearing the town's arms; the three town Sergeants with their maces and cloaks; then the Mayor and Mayor elect, and the other ten Aldermen, and the Justices and Recorder, two and two in their scarlet robes, trimmed; the town Vicars and other Clergy in their gowns; the Common Council, in number 24, two and two, in their black silk gowns, The Town's Clerk and Coroner joined the procession, and lastly such Freemen as chose; and gentlemen who did not belong to the Corporation brought up the rear." In the early part of this century "the gowns and gownsmen disappeared. None of the Aldermen or Common Council were to be distinguished; the Constables went in form, followed by the band, and then the Sergeant-at-mace preceded by the colours – and then the Mayor and Mayor elect, sometimes in gowns, and sometimes without them, as suited their caprice or whims, and the Freemen generally brought up the rear; the Constables with their long staffs looking like so many Dock-Yard warders."

The Mayoralty House was in Woolster-street. It is supposed to have been the residence of John Paige, better known by the name of "Wealthy Paige," concerning whom some curious old ballads are extant relating to his ill assorted marriage, his murder, the illicit loves of his wife and George Strangwidge, and their execution. The house was large and spacious. "The great room where the Mayor's table was laid, being very large, was, during the building of the Guildhall, used as the Hall of Justice, and the rest fitted up as Prisons. The Mayor's Feast was formerly held yearly on the same day as the Mayor was chosen. It was given by the old Mayor on his leaving office, to the Corporation, Freemen, and their friends. The feast, before the building of the Guildhall in 1800, was held at the Mayoralty House, but since then was held in the rooms belonging to it, until the passing of the Reform Act. The kitchens under the Guildhall were fitted with every convenience."

THE FISHING FEAST is the pleasantest and most agreeable relic of bygone times at the present day observed in Plymouth. Long, long may the utilitarian spirit of modern times be from encroaching upon it! The "fishing feast" commemorates the bringing of the supply of water into Plymouth by Sir Francis Drake, and it therefore has an historical significance peculiarly its own. It is held in this wise: on the appointed day the Mayor and Corporation of Plymouth, and invited guests, assemble at ten o'clock in the morning at the Reservoir, in the Tavistock Road, and from thence proceed in a number of carriages and pairs to the various other reservoirs, at each of which they alight and examine the works and all matters connected with them, and then the cortege proceeds – in all this headed by the Mayor in his carriage – across Roborough Down to the Head Weir on Dartmoor, about fifteen miles from Plymouth. Here they alight, and having partaken of refreshment, assemble around the weir. The "loving cups" are then produced, and the Chairman of the Water Committee having filled the smaller one with water from the stream, hands it to the Mayor who then drinks "To the pious memory of Sir Francis Drake," the cup being handed to each person successively, and each drinking the same toast. This done, the larger cup is filled with wine, and the Mayor having drank "May the descendants of him who gave us Water never want Wine" passes the cup, and each of the assembly drinks from it to the same toast. Fish is then caught in the stream, and, later on in the day, a splendid dinner, cooked on the moor, and comprising "all the delicacies of the season" is served in a spacious tent, when toasts are drunk and the loving cups passed "cross" in accordance with the "guift" down the table. Thus the whole day is pleasantly occupied and the memory of Sir Francis Drake, and the blessing of the water which he procured, and kept alive from year to year.

THE EXCHANGE is in Woolster-street. Formerly it was on the New Quay, having been there built, evidently of timber, by John Lanyon, in 1673. An Exchange was also erected somewhat later in South-side-street. The present building was erected in 1813 at a cost of about £7,000; but since that time the open yard has been covered in with a dome, and additional offices added. In the Exchange, the Chamber of Commerce, the Board of Trade Office, a News Room, and the Local Marine Board are held.

THE CUSTOM HOUSE is on the Parade, near Sutton Pool. It was erected in 1819-20, at a cost of about £8,000, by Mr, Laing, the architect of the Custom House at London. It contains, besides the Long Room, collectors, comptrollers, surveyors, tide surveyors, landing waiters, searchers, and other offices.

THE POST OFFICE – This building was erected in 1847-8 from the designs of Mr. Oswald Arthur, at a cost of about £3,000. The first running post between Exeter and Plymouth was established in 1635, and this, and occasionally a horse post, was the only means of getting letters to the town; the time occupied was at one time nine or ten days in bringing a letter from London. The "Fly Coach," for passengers, which beat the post by several days, stopped its fifth night at Exeter and, proceeding next morning to Axminster, a "woman-barber then shaved the coach" or rather the whole of its passengers. In 1658 a stage coach set out on "Mondays and Wednesdays to Ockington and Plymouth for 50s." but about eight days was occupied on the journey. About this time letters were despatched once a week to and from Plymouth. In 1784 Palmer, the great post improver, brought to bear his scheme for establishing Mail Coaches, the first being from London to Bath and Bristol, the journey to Bristol being accomplished in fifteen hours, and from this period a better state of things was brought about, and letters received "every morning, except Mondays, from London, between ten and eleven; and go out at half-past four in the afternoon." At this time (1792) it took two days for letters to travel from London. The Post Office was formerly in Bilbury-street. The present building is far too small for the requirements of the town, and it is much to be hoped that the authorities will replace it by a larger and more commodious erection, in which proper accommodation will be provided for the various branches of the service, and where the convenience of the public will be studied.

THE THEATRE. As was the case in most corporate towns, plays and mysteries would at one time be performed in the Plymouth Guildhall, and occasionally in St. Andrew's church. Here it would be where the following companies, to whom payments were made, performed in 1561-8:–

Item to my L Bushoppe's players	...	0	13	4
Item to Mr Fortescue's players	...	0	13	4
Item to the Queen's Players	...	1	0	6
Item given to Sir Parcyvall Harts Plairs	...	0	6	8
Item to the Erell of Warwick ys pleers, the IX of June, for pleying	...	0	13	4
Item to the Queen's Players	...	1	0	0
Item to the Erell of Worsetter's pleers	...	0	13	4
Item paid to my Lord Munger's pleyers	...	0	13	4
Item paid to my Lord Hunsdon's Pleers	...	0	13	4
Item paid to Players in the Church uppon St. John is daye	...	0	6	8
Item paid to the Erle of Worcesters pleers	...	0	5	0
Item paid to Sir Harry Fortescue ys pleers	...	0	10	0

There appears at one time to have been a theatre in what is now called Hoe-Gate-street, but the one about which most is known, and which was the immediate predecessor of the present admirable building, was the "New Theatre Franckfort Gate" which took the place of the one in Hoe-Gate-street. Of this highly interesting building we are fortunately enabled to give a representation from an old engraving. It is described as a very convenient, "neat and commodious" theatre. The building itself still exists opposite the Globe Hotel, but is now converted into business premises, being at the time we write, occupied by Mr. Eyre, as an Upholsterer's shop. Some curious play bills, the original of which are in my own possession, are preserved. One of these of the year 1759 has been already been printed on page 215; as an appropriate companion to that, the following copy of the play bill of the opening night of the present Theatre in 1813 will be read with interest.

"The PUBLIC is most respectfully informed, that
The New Theatre Royal, Plymouth, will open
on MONDAY next, the 23d of AUGUST 1813
with
AN OCCASIONAL ADDRESS.
After which, SHAKSPEARE's celebrated PLAY of
As You Like It.

Jacques ... ... Mr. Hughes.	Le Beau ... ... Mr. Lambert.
Orlando ... ... Mr. Sandford.	Duke Frederick ... Mr. Edwards.
Adam ... ... Mr. Reymes.	Charles ... ... Mr. Wheatley.
Banished Duke ... Mr. Mara.	First Lord ... ... Mr. Hayden.
Amiens ... ... Mr. Congdon.	And Touchstone ... ... Mr. Bennet.
Oliver ... ... Mr. Bickerton.	Celia ... ... Mrs. Bennett.
Corin ... ... Mr. Andrews.	Phoebe ... ... Mrs. Andrews.
Silvius ... ... Mr. Weeks.	Audrey ... ... Mrs. Windsor.
William ... ... Mr. Barnes.	And Rosalind ... ... Mrs. H. Hughes.

To which will be added the FARCE of
Catherine and Petruchio

Petruchio ... ... Mr. Sandford.	Nathaniel ... ... Mr. Wheatley.
Baptisa ... ... Mr. Reymes.	Gregory ... ... Mr. Coombes.
Biondella ... ... Mr. Edwards.	Philip ... ... Mr. Libby.
Music Master ... ... Mr. Lambert.	And Grumio ... ... Mr. Bennett.
Cook ... ... Mr. Hayden.	Curtis ... ... Mrs. Wilde.
Hortensio ... ... Mr. Weeks.	Bianca ... ... Mrs. Andrews.
Taylor ... ... Mr. Barnes.	And Catherine ... ... Mrs. H. Hughes.

BOXES 4s. PIT 2s. 6d. GALLERY 1s.
SECOND ACCOUNT to the BOXES 2s. 6d. To the Pit 1s. 6d. But nothing under
FULL PRICE TO THE GALLERY
The DOORS to be OPEN'D at SIX and to begin precisely at SEVEN O'CLOCK
TICKETS to be had at the BOX LOBBY of the THEATRE
☞ Ladies and Gentlemen are respectfully requested to send their Servants to keep
Place at HALF-PAST FIVE O'CLOCK.
SUBSCRIPTION TICKETS for the SEASON, Transferable......................£5 5s.
NON TRANSFERABLE ....£4 4s.
ON TUESDAY EVENING, a PLAY and ENTERTAINMENT.
Haydon, Cobley, and Co., Printers, No 75, Market Place, Plymouth."

The present Theatre, which with the Royal Hotel, and the Assembly Rooms forms one large and imposing block of buildings at the junction of Lockyer-street and George-street, was erected at the cost of the Corporation from the designs of Mr. Foulston. They were commenced in 1811 and completed in 1813 at a cost of about £60,000. The foundation stone bears this inscription:– Theatri et Hospitii impensis Maioris et Communitatis Burgi de Plymouth. Edmundus Lockyer, M.D., Maior, fundamenta locavit 1811. Johanne Foulston, Architecta." The Theatre which forms the south-end of the pile of buildings at the junction of George-street and Athenæum-street, with entrance in the grand central portico, is one of the most conveniently arranged, most chaste and elegant, and certainly one of the best conducted in the provinces – its lesse Mr. J. R. Newcombe, having at very considerable outlay improved its interior which, originally, was very improved in its arrangements.

THE ASSEMBLY ROOMS are entered from the same central portico and also from the Royal Hotel. The ball-room is 76 feet long and 40 feet in width and is richly decorated; and there are also in connection with it supper, tea, card, and ante rooms, with lavatories, and every convenient arrangement for the comfort of visitors.

THE ROYAL HOTEL is entered by the portico in Lockyer-street and is an extremely substantial and convenient establishment. The principal apartments comprising handsome coffee, dining, sitting, billiard, and smoking rooms, are on the ground floor; the other floors comprising suites of apartments, and sitting, bed, dressing, and bath rooms, etc. The area of ground occupied by the entire range of buildings – which are 490 feet in length – is said to be 59,400 feet.

The Rules of the Assembly Rooms, at the Fountain Tavern, Plymouth Dock, in 1792, are so curious and so well illustrate the state of society at Plymouth in those days, that they are worth transcribing. The season was from the first Monday after Michaelmas week, and continued on alternate Mondays for thirteen weeks.

Rules to be observed, viz:–

I. – Subscribers to pay Ten Shillings and Six-pence each for the Season.

II. – Non-Subscribers Two Shillings and Sixpence each for Admission.

III. – Gentleman to pay One Shilling each for Tea.

IV. – A Queen to be drawn for, among the married Ladies, (Subscribers,) who is to preside for one Night only, and to appoint a Successor.

V. – The Queen's Determination, in any Dispute, to be final.

VI. – The Queen to be assisted by two Stewards, who are to be chosen by her.

VII. – The Queen and Stewards to chuse their own Partners.

VIII. – Ladies who are Strangers, are neither to draw for Partners or Places.

IX. – Ladies to be considered as Strangers only the first time of their Appearance for the Season.

X. – No Lady to Dance before Tea who does not draw.

XI. – Gentlemen who mean to Dance before Tea, to give their Names to one of the Stewards

XII. – Minuets to begin at Seven o'Clock precisely.

XIII. – Two Country-Dances only before Tea.

XIV. – After Tea the Ladies to draw for places only.

XV. – No Dances to be called for after 12 o'Clock.

The rules at the same period observed "in the Long Room at Stonehouse, to which all genteel company never fail to resort both from Dock and Plymouth," are equally curious. Assemblies were here "held in summer seasons, and on all Birth Nights and other Public Seasons."

I. – All Ladies and Gentlemen, that frequent this room are desired to subscribe.

II. – Every Thursday during the Summer Season there is a Concert and Assembly

III. – The Concert to begin at Six o'Clock in the Afternoon, and end at Eight o'Clock.

IV. – Dancing to begin at Eight and leave off precisely at Eleven o'Clock.

V. – The subscribers to pay one Shilling each on entering the Room, and the Non-Subscribers to pay Three Shillings and Sixpence for which they are to have Coffee or Tea.

VI. – No Tea or Coffee to be allowed for Entrance Money in the Room after Nine o'Clock.

VII. – If any Lady or Gentleman should omit paying their entrance, it is humbly hoped they will not take it amiss when called on for it.

VIII. – Gentlemen on Public Days are desired not to wear Swords in the Room.

IX. – The Proprietor begs that no Dogs may be suffered in the Room.

THE PLYMOUTH AND COTTONIAN PUBLIC LIBRARY – This important institution, which is one of the many buildings of which Plymouth may well be proud, is situated in Cornwall-street. It was founded in 1811 in great measure through the exertions of Mr. George Eastlake, and the foundation stone of the building was laid in that year. The building was erected from the designs of Mr. Foulston; the front thrown back from the street. This front, of which, for the sake of keeping its design on record, we reproduce an interesting engraving, was taken down in 1851 when the building was considerably enlarged, brought forward to the street, and raised another story in height for the reception of the Cottonian Library. The Library is

approached from a spacious entrance hall, from which access is also obtained to the new room, and to the staircase leading to the Cottonian Room. The Library itself is a lofty quadrangular room, 33 feet square; at each angle is a massive hollow pier with pilasters, supporting an entablature and cornice from which spring elegant segmental arches. The whole is surmounted by a vaulted dome, in the centre of which rises a circular lantern, the roof of which is supported on fluted columns, and between these columns and the coupled pilasters a passage is left. Concealed in one of the piers is a spiral staircase, which gives access to the gallery that runs round all round all four sides of the room and divides it into two nearly equal heights. The collection of books is arranged on all sides of the room, both above and below the gallery. Communicating with the Library, is the Committee room, a spacious apartment with windows to the street which also is lined with books, as is also the Law Library over it, in which, in addition to other matters, the Halliwell Collection of MSS. presented to the Library through his friend Mr. Jewitt, the author of this work, by James Orchard Halliwell, F.R.S., is placed. This collection comprises MSS. on vellum and paper, consisting of very many curious original documents arranged in volumes under counties, some curious rubricated and other ecclesiastical MSS., orders of Parliament, original manuscripts and early transcripts of curious works, the original life of Dr. Forman, etc. The Cottonian Room, erected for the reception of the gift by the late Mr. William Cotton, F.S.A., of Ivybridge, of a fine collection of books, prints, drawings, paintings, and works of Art and vertu, is a beautiful and extremely chaste apartment with an enriched coved ceiling from which rises an elegantly decorated lantern. Around the upper part of the walls of the room is a continuous frieze, selected from the Panathenaic frieze of the Elgin marbles, and especially cast at the British Museum for that purpose. The collection may in few words be said to comprise a remarkably fine series of prints, more than 5,000 in number; some original paintings by Sir Joshua Reynolds, and others; an extensive and valuable collection of books relating to the fine arts; several rare and curious early books, and illuminated MSS.; a large number of original sketches by old masters and others; some bronzes and models; and many other highly interesting objects. The collection was, by deed, presented by Mr. Cotton, the proprietors of the library undertaking to provide a suitable room for its reception, and to support it for public use; and the whole of the arrangements were carried out, and the treasures arranged in the apartment by Mr. Llewellynn Jewitt. The Cottonian collection may be viewed on application to the Librarian.

CHAPTER XII

Plymouth having recently adopted the Public Libraries' and Museums' Act, is, at the time of publication, busying itself with the founding of a Free Library for the use of its inhabitants – a movement which must be productive of immense benefit to the town.

THE MECHANIC'S INSTITUTE in Princess-square, was established in 1825; the old building (opened in 1827) was taken down and the present one erected in 1849 from the designs of Messrs. Wightwick and Damant. It contains a large lecture hall, library, class-rooms, and other necessary apartments, and is calculated to be one of the most convenient and successful institutions of its kind. The publications of the Patents Office are here deposited for public inspection.

THE ATHENÆUM of the "Plymouth Institution and Devon and Cornwall Natural History Society," is at the bottom of Athenæum-street, by the Theatre. The "Plymouth Institution" was founded "for the promotion of literature, science, and the fine arts, in the town and neighbourhood," in 1812 (as has already been fully stated) its meetings being first held in various places amongst which were the Public Library, and the Picture Gallery in Frankfort-place. In 1818 the foundation stone of the Athenæum was laid by Mr. Woollcombe on the 1st of May, and the building was completed in the following February, on the 4th of which month it was opened by an address from the Rev. R. Lampen, which has been printed in the "Transactions" of the Institution. About twenty years ago the Devon and Cornwall Natural History Society was incorporated with the Institution. The building was erected from the designs (gratuitously supplied) of Mr. Foulston, and its front is of remarkably pure and chaste character. The entrance is within a portico, the pediment of which is supported on five massive fluted columns. The building contains a lecture hall, library, museum, laboratory, vestibule, attendant's apartments, &c. The lecture hall has at one end, on a raised dais, the president's seat, supported on either side by those of the treasurer and secretary; at the opposite end is the lecturer's table. The casts of statuary which adorn the room were presented by George IV., Lord Morley, Sir Wm. Congreve, and Sir T. Byam Martin; and around the upper part are bas-reliefs from the Parthenon, presented by George IV.; there are also portraits and busts of Drake, Raleigh, Northcote, Reynolds, Woollcombe, Lieut-Col. Hamilton Smith, and others. In the museum are preserved many interesting local and other remains. Among the more noticeable are the assemblage of antiquities from the cemetery on Stamford Hill, described in the second chapter of this volume; some good examples of Roman and other pottery; some flint implements and stone celts; bone mesh rules; studs and spindle whorls; bones of extinct animals from Oreston; Roman tesseræ; Persian inscribed bricks; models of groups of Indian figures; remains of a Peruvian mummy, and other relics from Peru; and many other objects. There are also good mineralogical, botanical, and other collections.

Most of the literary, scientific, and artistic celebrities of the town and neighbourhood for the past half century have been connected with the Plymouth Institution and devoted their time and talents to its furtherance. Among those who have lectured and held office are, Mr. H. Woollcombe, Lieut-Col. Hamilton Smith, Rev. R. Lampen, Sir Wm Snow Harris, Dr. Edward Moore, Rev. S. Rowe, Mr. G. Wightwick, Mr. Cyrus Reding, Messrs. George and William Eastlake, Mr. John Prideaux, Mr. J. M. Rendell, Dr. Blackmore, Dr. Wm. Elford Leach, Mr. Pengelley, Mr., J. C. Bellamy, Mr. J. Hine, Mr. Llewellynn Jewitt, Mr. A. Rooker, Dr. Prance, Dr. Soltau, Mr. J. N. Hearder, Mr. C. S. Bate, and many others.

St. James's Hall, Union-street, is a large and well proportioned room, for concerts, lectures, public meetings, exhibitions, &c. The Albert Hall, at Eldad, is also a large and convenient building, for the same purposes.

The Volunteer Drill Hall, erected in 1871, is an enormous structure, 260 ft. long, 86 ft. wide, and 45 ft. high. It is situated at Millbay, and besides its legitimate use as a drill hall for the volunteers, is admirably adapted for monster concerts, and election and other mass meetings. Soon after its completion it was much injured by a hurricane, and up to the present time has not been restored. The history of the Volunteer movement in Plymouth and its neighbourhood is extremely interesting. "In 1759, the Militia of this county, were one of the first raised, and embodied 600 men, and when the French fleet appeared off Plymouth, with the Spanish fleet, there were two companies of Volunteers raised, one of whom fed and clothed themselves, and the other was clothed by the town, and took pay from the Government." They remained embodied the greater part of the war, and did duty over the prisoners confined in the China House, at the Round House, and Millbay Prisons. "Early in the War of 1794, there were two independent companies embodied under the command of Capt. John Hawker and Capt. Edmund Lockyer, and were composed of tradesmen only, who clothed themselves, and served without pay. They were clothed in super-fine red cloth, and faced with yellow. They wore helmets with bear skins over. After a year or two, the tradesmen began to leave it by degrees, and the vacancies were filled by workmen, and were increased to six companies, under the command of Mr. Hawker, who was then the Lieut-Colonel, and Mr. E. Lockyer, Major. They continued till the end of the war, and were on permanent duty once or twice. When they increased, they took pay, and were clothed by Government. About the year 1797, there were some more companies formed. The most respectable of the inhabitants formed themselves into three companies, called *The Plymouth Foot Association*, under the command of Major Culme, and clothed in blue coats and pantaloons, and white waistcoats, with red collars, – they clothed themselves and served without pay, and paid their drummers and fifers. The captains names were Mr. Robert Fuge, Mr. B. Fuge, and Mr. A. Hill; – they were about 190 file. These gentlemen were not regularly sized, as David sometimes took the right of a Goliath. There was another company on the same principle as the last, but they were a Rifle Company, called *the Rangers*, and were clothed in a nice green, under Capt. Julian. They were seldom above 50 file. They had a good pair of Colours. The next company was commanded by Mr. P. Langmead. They were clothed in red coats, and faced with yellow. Here, to this gentleman's honor, or the company's, be it recorded, that he clothed and paid the men of his company all the time they were embodied, without any expense to the Government. They were a fine company of men, consisting principally of brewers, and were seldom less than 70 men, sometimes 100, like brewer's horses, very stout. There were a few cavalry, under Mr. Hilley; they were chiefly butchers &c., were independent of Government, and seldom numbered above 25 or 30 horsemen. They had a neat standard, and were clothed in red and yellow, and wore helmets. The *Sea-Fencibles* were about 250, and met on Saturday afternoons, and were taught the pike exercise, with which they were armed, and also to fire the heavy ordnance. They were not clothed – were under the command of Capt. Clements and other sea officers, and composed principally of the Custom house men, and trawlers or fishermen, and some seamen; they had no drums or colours, nor non-commissioned officers, but were taught by the Garrison Artillery." At Stonehouse were two Volunteer companies, one was independent and clothed themselves, and took no pay, under Capt. Pridham, not above 50 men; the other were called Barrack Artificers, and were paid by Government, but clothed themselves, and were commanded by Capt. Scoble, whose employ they were principally in. Neither of these companies did any duty; the latter were clothed in red, and faced with yellow. At Dock there were two independent companies, under different officers, and were distinguished by being the first and second division, and so remained until the end of the war. The total numbers at the end of the war were:–

Col. Hawker's battalion	350	rank and file
Major Culme, Plymouth Foot Association	170	do.
Major Julian's Rangers	50	do.
Major Langmead's Company	100	do.
Capt. Hilley's Light Horse	30	do.
Sea Fencibles	250	do.
Capt. Pridham's Stonehouse Volunteers	50	do.
Capt. Scoble's Barrack Artificers	70	do.
Dock Volunteers	350	do.
Total	1420	

The last time they met was when peace was proclaimed when the greater part met and fired on the quay. "In the war of 1803, no sooner was the intention of Government known to raise volunteers in this town than all ranks hastened to enrol themselves. In a few days more than 700 men has enrolled themselves in Plymouth only, and at Dock about 400, all infantry. Those at Plymouth chose their commanding officer, as two names were set down for them, viz.:– John Hawker, and P. Langmead, Esqs. The greatest number were for the latter. Printed addresses were circulated, subscriptions were set on foot, and the managers of the theatre gave a night or two to the fund established for giving better clothes than was allowed by the Government. The three battalions were at first clothed nearly alike, in red and yellow; when the 2nd Plymouth changed their facings to blue, and were called the *Prince of Wales's Own Plymouth*. In the year 1807 they formed a Rifle company, who were clothed entirely in green, with black muskets. At Dock was also raised by Colonel Rawle, a battalion consisting of five companies of Artillery of 48 gunners, 4 bombardiers, 4 corporals, and 4 sergeants to each company. They were clothed like the Royal Artillery, and were called the *Duke of York's Own*, making in the two towns, four large battalions. They all went on permanent duty in their turns, but in 1807, the Plymouth only went on duty. When the first battalion was 525 men they had no band, but many drums, and were much like the 9th regiment of foot, and were a very fine set of men. The *2nd,* or *Prince of Wales's*, were more like the *3rd Lancashire Militia*, with their Grenadier caps and Rifle companies, but the men were small and more like the *Middlesex* for size. They had a good band the whole of the time, and each of the battalions had a pair of good colours. The *Dock Infantry* were about 500 men, had a good band, and a pair of colours. The Artillery and non-commissioned officers, 300. The Fencibles were 230. There was at Dock a small party of Horse, not more than 25 of the inhabitants, and none to Plymouth. Abstract of the Totals.

1st Plymouth	525
2nd do.	420
Dock	500
Artillery	300
Fencibles	230
Horse	25
Total	2000

being more by 700 men, than in the last war" When the present Volunteer movement was inaugurated Plymouth was, as usual, early in adopting it. The Plymouth Rifle Corps was formed in the autumn of 1859, being one of the first to tender its services to the government as citizen soldiers. It was officially designated the *2nd Devon (Plymouth) Volunteer Rifle Corps*, and owes much of its present prosperity to the exertions of Major Duperier, who lost no time in instructing the 150 gentlemen who so readily responded to the resolutions passed at a public meeting held in the Guildhall.

The members were drilled at first in the Corn market and paid threepence each drill to a sergeant instructor, detailed for the militia for this special duty. Each member purchased his own uniform, which consisted of shako, black leather cross and waist belts, and dark green tunic and trowsers, with black kid gloves. After a few years the braid trimmings which were worn on the tunic were dispensed with, and the sombre colour of the uniform relived by red facings. The first uniform parades, after the public swearing in of the members, were held at Cattedown, and, after the expiration of a few months, the executive obtained the Corporation Grammar School in Finewell-street, (the site of the present new Guildhall) as the head quarters of the corps. Considerable alterations were made to form a parade ground, the two large gardens being added to the playground, and the hole levelled and thoroughly metalled. The fact of the head quarters being situated in the centre of the town was one of the principal reasons of the rapid increase of numbers. Major Duperier, who was the first Commandant of the corps, was appointed Adjutant on the formation of the 2nd Devon Administrative Battalion, consisting of the Plymouth, Devonport, Stonehouse, and Tavistock corps. He was succeeded in the command of the corps by Capt. Bewes, who in April, 1861, was appointed Adjutant of the 4th Devon Administrative Battalion. Lieut-Col. Hutchinson was then appointed, but resigned after a short period; his resignation bearing date September, 1861. The next commandant was Lieut-Col. Fisk, who had just resigned the Adjutancy of the South Devon Militia, and under his auspices the corps was increased to three companies; the Cadet Corps, which was formed in 1860, was considerably augmented, and a Reading and Recreation Society was established, entertaining, during the winter season, the members and their friends with a series of Dramatic and miscellaneous entertainments – one of the popular features were the performances of the "Second Devon Lilies," adding considerably to the funds of the corps. To increase the numbers it was decided to pay for the uniform and accoutrements of fresh recruits from the funds; the annual subscription of ten shillings being also abolished. A large number of young men joined under this new system, and it was found necessary to build a drill shed by covering in the parade ground; the corps receiving government assistance in the shape of a Capitation Grant. In one corner of this shed a large concert hall was erected, affording increased accommodation for the entertainments, which were conducted on a larger scale.

For upwards of seven years Lieut-Col. Fisk devoted his entire energies and time in making the corps as attractive as possible, not forgetting to instill into the members the great importance of a due regard for discipline. Ill-health compelling him to resign the command, the Volunteers presented to him a handsome testimonial and an address signed by all the members, as a slight acknowledgement of the kindness experienced at his hands in performing the duties of what had to him been a true "labour of love." In August, 1869, Colonel Elliott accepted the command, and heartily seconded the efforts of his predecessor. Aided by many active officers and members, he succeeded in forming fourth, fifth, and sixth companies, and the old head quarters being required to give place to the new Guildhall, he obtained permission from the government authorities to erect the present head quarters in Prospect-row. The necessary alterations and improvements involved a considerable outlay, and about £500 from the funds of the corps were devoted to the purpose. The large drill shed just spoken of was also erected.

Major Duperier having resigned the Adjutancy of the Battalion on the 19th of December, 1870, Colonel Elliott was appointed Adjutant in his place and gave up his commission as commandant of the corps. He was succeeded by the present commanding officer, Major General Pickard, who had taken active steps to give the Volunteers an insight into Camp Life, having camped out with a large number of men on Maker heights, for several days prior to the annual inspection.

The following are the officers at present holding commissions:–

Lieut. Col. Commanding ... Major Gen. Pickard.
Major .... Mortimer J. Collier.
Captains .... Thomas Pitts.
" .... Thos. H. Butcher.
" .... George Browse.
" .... John Stevens.
" .... W. T. Spearman.
" .... J. T. Avery.
Lieutenants .... H. H. S. Pearse.
" .... John J. Matthews.
" .... Henry J. Hissett.
Ensigns .... Wm. J. Penn.
" .... Alfred Dyer.

Ensigns .... Jas. J. Avery.
" .... John D. Spooner.
" .... L. D. Westcott
Hon. Chaplain .... Rev. Charles T. Wilkinson, M.A.

Officers of the Battalion.
Lieut.-Col: The Right Honble. the Earl of Mount Edgcumbe.
Major: Edward St Aubyn.
Adjutant: Col. J. Elliott.
Surgeon: J. H. S. May.
Quarter-master: W. H. Luke.

The following tabular form shews at a glance the progress and efficiency of the corps from 1862 to the present date:

Year	Efficient 30s.	Efficient 20s.	Non Efficient	Total Enrolled	Capitation Grant £ s d	Alterations Added	Alterations Discd	Marks men
1862	—	—	48	113	———	39	34	25
1863	80	24	59	163	93 15 0	23	33	29
1864	71	20	61	152	144 0 0	28	39	20
1865	96	32	40	168	126 10 0	46	30	30
1866	109	19	40	168	176 0 0	32	32	23
1867	96	25	54	175	169 0 0	35	28	31
1868	188	50	26	264	322 0 0	123	34	21
1869	265	109	—	374	506 10 0	187	77	50
1870	413	147	—	560	876 10 0	246	60	30
1871	329	110	41	460	701 0 0	49	129	26

THE FREEMASON'S HALL, Cornwall-street, was opened in 1828, by the Provincial Grand Lodge of Devonshire. It contains besides the Commercial rooms, and an Auction room, a large hall, originally used for the purposes of the Order, as well as for lectures, public meetings, etc.; it is now only used for offices and auction rooms.

THE WATER WORKS. The water supply of Plymouth is one of the most complete and perfect in the kingdom, and the water itself of the purest and finest quality. Like all other towns in mediaeval times, Plymouth was dependant on its public and "holy" wells for a supply of water, but in the reign of Elizabeth, through the energy and exertion, as well as the skill and liberality, of the great admiral, Sir Francis Drake, and endless stream was brought into the borough, and made available to its inhabitants, by means of conduits. In 1589 or 1590, "the town agreed with Sir Francis Drake, to bring in the water of the River Meavy, and gave him £200 in hand and £600, for which he is to compound with the owners of the land over which it runneth, which, being in length about 25 miles, he, with great care and diligence, effected, and brought the river into the town the 24th of April, then next after. Presently after he set in hand to build six great mills, two at Widey in Egg Buckland parish, the other four by the towne; the two at Widey and the two next the towne he fullie finished before Michaelmas next after, and ground corn with them." This water course and the Grist Mills are all included in the charters of the town. The Conduits were several in number, one of the finest erected, and the last removed, being that by Old Town Gate, which was taken down in 1834, when the sculptured arms and inscriptions were inserted in the wall of the Reservoir on the Tavistock-road. It is shown in our engraving of Old Town Gate.

THE LEAT. More of a history, and more romantic interest, is attached to the water supply to Plymouth than that of any other town. Brought in by the perseverance, the energy, and the skill of no less a man than the great Admiral Sir Francis Drake, at a time, and under circumstances when so great a boon could be but little expected; continued to the present day with watchful care by the corporation; and surrounded by pleasant old customs and numberless traditions, the history of the water supply of this busy town is something more than a dry detail of a "limited" company, or of reservoirs, pipes and taps. An abstract of the history of the Plymouth Leat, drawn up by no less an authority than Mr. C. C. Whiteford, the Town Clerk of the borough, for the Government inquiry into the sanitary condition of the town gives the facts so well that I here quote it along with an extract from the report of the borough surveyor. Mr. Whiteford says:–

> "The stream from which the inhabitants of Plymouth derive their supply of conduit water is the property of the mayor, aldermen, and burgesses of the borough, and the profits derived from the supply, form a large part of the corporate revenue. The channel in which this water is brought from the River Meavy to the town of Plymouth, commonly called the Plymouth Leat, was formed about the year 1590 under the powers of an Act of Parliament 27th Elizabeth, intitled 'An Act for preservation of the haven of Plymouth.' The works were executed under the superintendence of the celebrated navigator Sir Francis Drake, who was for a long time commonly supposed to have defrayed the cost of the works out of his private funds, but the records of the Corporation show not only that he was supplied with funds by the Corporation, but that he received a valuable acknowledgement from them, in the form a lease of certain mills erected on and worked by the stream. It appears from the records of the Corporation that on the stream being thus brought to the town they proceeded to regulate its distribution for the supply of the inhabitants, which was chiefly effected by means of public conduits, erected in the streets or set up against houses and public buildings. Many of these existed until the year 1827, when they were finally closed by the Corporation. From these public conduits the bulk of the inhabitants derived their supply of water without any charge, but it is evident that from a very early date it was also the practice to afford supplies of water at the houses of the inhabitants by pipes laid for the purpose, for which the parties supplied paid an annual rent to the Corporation. The rental for the year 1608, being the first of the series which has been

preserved, contains the names of 38 parties thus supplied. Of these 37 paid a rent of 4*s.*, and 1 of 10*s.* per annum. The strictness with which the control of the water was maintained by the Corporation is evidenced by a bye-law, passed as early as 1602, by which the inhabitants were prohibited from conveying water from the great pipe into any of their houses, or otherwise without the leave of the Corporation, under a penalty of 40*l.* to be levied by distress or imprisonment of the offender. It is unnecessary to trace in detail the history of the water supply which grew with the extension of the town, and the increase of the population, but no essential change took place in its general conditions until the year 1824, when the Corporation entered into a contract with the Commissioners for Victualling the Navy for the daily supply of 400 tuns of water to the Victualling Establishment then about to be erected in the township of Stonehouse, with a further contingent supply of 80 tuns per diem to the same establishment, or to the Royal Naval Hospital in the same place. The terms of this contract were embodied in a public Act of Parliament 5th George the Fourth, cap. 49, which contained several provisions protecting the rights of the Corporation in the water, and imposing penalties for the abstraction or pollution of the stream, for which no summary remedy was afforded by the statute of Elizabeth. These powers, however, might still be beneficially extended and it would be of great advantage if the provisions of the Water-works Clauses Act 1847, (Stat. 10 & 11 Vict. c. 27), were applicable to the works. The engagements entered into by the Corporation for the supply of the above-named Government Departments, were the occasion of extensive alterations and improvement in the works. The weir for diverting the water of the Meavy into the Plymouth Leat was rebuilt and improved, the channel of the Leat was repaired, defective portions replaced, and the banks in many places raised. In Plymouth a reservoir of greatly increased dimensions was formed, to which a second was added, the public conduits were closed, the leaden pipes used for conveying the water to the houses of the inhabitants were taken up, and iron pipes laid through all the principal streets, No accurate statement exists of the costs of these improvements, which extended over several years, but the sum of 25,000*l.*, at which they have been roughly estimated, is probably not wide of the truth. The whole cost was defrayed by the Corporation out of the proceeds of their corporate estates. From this period the general supply of the town has assumed a greatly improved character. Increased care has been given to the works, and large sums have been annually expended in their extension and improvement. The income derived from the water has in like manner increased, and in a ratio greatly exceeding even that of the population, rapid as that has been. The catchment basin of the river Meavy is fully 4,000 acres, or 6 square miles, in area, and varies in altitude above the sea from 700 feet at the weir of the river Meavy, to 1,300 feet at the summit, near Prince Town. This basin is drained into the Meavy by three tributaries, the Deancombe, Wineford, and Stainlake, and their subsidiary feeders. The sides of the valleys are precipitous, and the tributaries are *torrents*, consequently a large portion of the rain falling is discharged into the river with much rapidity. In consequence of the geological conformation of the district a large portion of the rain passing through the soil is ultimately discharged into the river at the lower level. The elevation of the district, and its geographical position on the south-western margin of the island exposes it to the wettest winds sweeping off the Atlantic Ocean, consequently the rain-fall upon it is excessive. The result of 16 years observations at Goodamoor, 800 feet above the sea, and not far distant, shows an average fall of rain equal to 56 inches annually, (whilst the average of 80 years observations at Plymouth

> is only 35 inches,) of which, at least 18 inches flows into the rivers, being a proportion of about one-eighth. The quantity of water, therefore, flowing from 4,000 acres into the river Meavy would be 261,360,000 cubic feet annually, or on the average 4,439,540 imperial gallons per diem throughout the year. Or allowing for the loss of floods at least 4,000,000 gallons per diem throughout the year may be obtained from the Meavy only. But the Leat itself in its winding course of 16 miles, receives the rain water flowing from more than 2,000 acres, a large proportion of which is moor land. If over the whole course of the Leat an average of 13 inches per annum flows off the ground the supply is equivalent to an average of 1,600,000 imperial gallons per diem throughout the year. But at this time a very large proportion of water is *lost* over the weir in the winter season and during floods. It is consequently prudent to affirm that the sources of supply of the Plymouth Leat are capable of yielding 6,000,000 imperial gallons per diem throughout the year, and that allowing one-sixth part for waste and partial loss during storms, and for the wants of the country fully 5,000,000 imperial gallons per diem may be delivered into Plymouth every day equally throughout the year, if proper storeage, reservoirs, and engineering works are constructed for the purpose."

Since this time wonderful improvements have been made in the Water Supply, by the formation of new reservoirs, of the best construction and of large size, and by other engineering additions. The memory of Sir Francis Drake who

> "With fresh streams refresht this Towne that first,
> Though kist with waters, yet did pine for thirst,"

is kept alive year by year with religious care at the "fishing feasts," and a noble statue of him, on the highest point of the new municipal hall, overlooks the town to which he gave this inestimable blessing.

THE BOROUGH PRISONS are in Cheltenham-place, North-hill, near to the New Workhouse; they were erected in 1849, at a cost of £12,500, from the designs of Fuller and Gingell.

THE WORKHOUSE, near the Prisons, was built after the designs of Messrs Arthur and Dwelley in 1851. The workhouse, originally called the "Hospital of Poor's Portion" was founded in 1615, in the Mayoralty of Abraham Colman or Colmer and was vested in the corporation and endowed with lands and messuages in Plymouth; other gifts and endowments being subsequently made. In 1707-8 the corporation conveyed their rights and trust to a body of Guardians who became incorporated by Act of Parliament. The workhouse became, by authority of the Act of Incorporation, a house of correction, and the guardians in whom were vested the various corporate and parish alms-houses, seem to have possessed extraordinary powers. Some curious entries in the record of the Hospital of Poor's Portion, illustrate the state of society at the time, and also show the kind of arbitrary power exercised by the guardians. There are several such entries as the following:–

CHAPTER XII

It was ordered "that Mr. Turtliff, Mr. Collier, Mr. Smithurst, Mr. Freeman, be desired to take one or more constables with them and either suppress the Lottery and other unlawful games that shall be kept in the Great Market to-morrow or bring the persons that keep them, to this house as vagrants."

January 26 1726-7 after recounting the statutes etc., the Court of Guardians having taken into serious consideration the decay of Trade of this Town and consequent thereto the deficiency of the Poor Rates from vacant Houses and yet the increase of the Poor, and being desirous according to the example of their predecessors, some years since to discountenance and discourage all tendance of vice and immorality, as they esteem interluders, to be resolved, and it is the inviolable resolution of this Court, that in case any Players or Actors or Interludes who by the aforesaid Laws are declared Rogues and Vagabonds, shall presume to Act as such within the Borough of Plymouth, that the Constable or any of them do by virtue of the Warrant to them issued from the Governor and some other members of this corporation for apprehending all Rogues, Vagabonds and other offenders therein specified, apprehend all such Players of Interludes so presuming to Act, to committ them to be kept to hard labour till the further pleasure of this corporation therein, and that this corporation will at their own cost and charges indemnifle and defend all such constable or constables as may happen to be mulcted or prosecuted for doing their duty therein." This order is signed by the Governor and eighteen other Guardians.

March 15 1727 "That Mary Clarke be committed to Bridewell and have Six pounds of Hemp to beat every day and in default thereof to be whipt." "That no person in this House have Breakfast and Supper at once as hath letely been practised, and that such in the House as do not attend at Prayers the usual Hours Morning and Evening be Mulcted of their Breakfast or Supper and otherwise punished as the Court think fitt, and that if any sell their provisions that they be punished as the Court thinks fitt, and likewise the Buyer, if in the House." "That Diana Weymouth and her Daughter Elizabeth, be whipt, for not performing the task set them by this House."

"That John Guy who was committed to the Bridewell by the Mayor's order to Mr. John Guswell one of the Constables of this Borough to be kept at hard labour have ten pounds of Hemp to beat every day in default thereof to be whipt."

March 20 1727 John Robertson, "taken up as a vagrant beggar" and refusing to answer some questions "the Court ordered him to the Cage, to be kept at hard labour for twelve months and to beat ten pounds of Hemp every day, and in default thereof to be whipt." On the 17 of April, it was ordered however "that the Vagrant Beggar, John Robertson, be discharged the Bridewell he having entered as a Soldier with Capt. Thompson in Col. Harrison's Regiment; the Capt. being present in Court and promising to take him away with his wife and two children."

May 15 1728 "That the Examination of the Glassman, and of the Woman that mends Chairs, and also the Baker at Old Town Gate, and the man that sells Sweet Meats in Howes Lane be taken touching their Settlement."

1731 "That Mr Morshead be desired to speak with Doctor Gortley and know of him what he will have for cutting off a poor Man's Legg, and report it to the next Court" "The Treasurer to pay Mr. Gortley three guineas for cutting off John Woodcocks Legg."

This day Mr. Peter Whipple agreed with this Court to shave the poor men of this House once a Fortnight for a penny a time for each person, and to poll the Boys for Sixpence a Quarter."

In 1731, "the Court of Guardians gave leave to the Bell Founder to cast a Bell for St. Andrew's Church, in the Workhouse garden" and the next year it was ordered that the our poor shall wear badges. In 1748, on the 5th October, "leave was given to cast a set of Bells for St. Andrew's Church, in the Workhouse garden." On the 19th September, 1750, it was ordered that Bamfylde Moore Carew's settlement be taken. In 1758, a building was ordered to be erected for a Pound for beating Hemp, with a large Moorstone like that used for bruising apples, and all other things convenient for that purpose. In 1780, Mr. Justice Nicholls, was fined £2 10s. for his daughter being buried in linen, and on the 27th of August, 1787, it was ordered (what a change from 1726!) "that Players be requested to Act a Play for the benefit of the Poor." In 1814, the building was much enlarged. in 1827, the eastern side of the quadrangle was rebuilt, at a cost of £1058, and in 1833 was again considerably extended. Acts of Parliament relating to this Hospital have at various times been passed, the last, that of 1813, among other provisions declaring the House of Correction within the Workhouse available for lunatics and for other purposes. In 1849, it was resolved to erect the present new building on one of the fields belonging to the Hospital, and the site of the venerable pile with its quadrangle, its large Bridewell, its pound for hemp beating, its cells, dormitories, hall and numerous offices was eventually sold to the Corporation of the borough as a part of the site for the New Guidhall and Municipal buildings.

THE ALMSHOUSES of the Town are, or were, somewhat numerous. The oldest of these is the one to which the following entry relates:–

"Almeshouse called Gods Howse for the reliefe of impotente and lazare people with owte any certayne nomber appoynted .... there are at this present but xiiij .... somtyme there be xx[ii] sometyme more or lesse as the occayson of tyme dothe offerr ...... they have besydes theire mansyon howse the rentts of certayne lands gyven by dyverse persons. The yearly value of possessyons xiiij*l* vij*s*. There ys no jewells, etc."

This "Gods House" was probably the Almshouse whose chapel was later on used as a grammar school over which the master had lodgement provided, and other Almshouses were the "Old Church Twelves;" these founded by Col. Jory in 1703; Anne Prynne; Alice Baker, in 1660; Fownes; John Lanyon 1674; Fox 1834; Victoria 1844, by Mrs Hodson; and others. The Charities are also unusually numerous and liberal.

THE HOSPITAL OF ORPHAN'S AID was founded in 1625 by Thomas and Nicholas Sherwell as is fully shown on page 117. In a bye-law of the corporation in 1653 it is recited that the Mayor and Commonalty by reason of the populousness and increase in the Borough, the access of strangers, &c., have become much in debt and that to pay the same &c., they had agreed in consideration of £1400 (which is stated to be a part of a greater sum due from the Mayor and Commonalty to the Governors, Assistants, Wardens, and Poor People of the Hospital of Orphan's Aid) to convey to them a fourth part of the grist mills, malt mills, toll and mulcture of the inhabitants, the leat, and of all the several closes, pieces, or parcels of land which were heretofore set to Sir Francis Drake Knt., (except Sour Pool,) and also of two new grist mills then lately built &c. The building has been removed and the charity is now located in modern premises in Regent-street.

THE GRAMMAR SCHOOL appears to have been founded in the reign of Henry VII, in 1501, when a master was appointed to teach grammar to the children of the town at a salary of £10 a year, with a lodging over the chapel of the Alms-house ("Gods House") and the use of the chapel itself as a school-house. Probably another room was, in the latter part of the same century used for a school, for in 1561 an item of payment occurs "for a locke for the bulworke door and for mending the school-house door 3s. 4d." and the following year a sum was paid "for helynge stones for the schole-house." In 1572 Queen Elizabeth besides other matters granted to the corporation the annual payment due by St. Andrew's to Plympton Priory on condition of their maintaining the Grammar School and these grants were confirmed by Charles II. The corporation retain the right of nomination of a certain number of boys.

The other old schools of the town are the now united *"Hele and Lanyon's,"* the former founded in 1632, the latter in 1674, and formerly dressed respectively in red and in blue. These schools are on the Tavistock-road. The *Grey School* in Hampton-street founded in 1713 and formerly known as the "Grey and Yellow" Schools. *Lady Rogers' School* in the Tavistock-road founded in 1764. The *Public Free School* founded in 1809. *The Infant's School* in connection with the former was established in 1860; the *Ragged Schools* in 1848; and Jews School in 1867. Parish and denominational schools are abundant and admirably conducted. The education of the children of Plymouth is now under the control of a School Board, which appears to be working well for the good of the town.

THE CEMETERY, on the north side of the town, occupies a site of about ten acres of ground, and is beautifully laid out with winding paths and shrubberies. It has two chapels, and is approached from the town by the way of St. Michael's Terrace, and Pennycomequick. It was first opened in 1848, and has since then been very considerably enlarged.

THE DISPENSARY was founded in 1798, principally through the exertions of Dr. Yonge, and in 1807 the present building was erected. In one of the rooms is a portrait of its founder, by Northcote. THE SOUTH DEVON AND EAST CORNWALL HOSPITAL, in Sussex-place was founded in 1835, the building being erected from designs of Mr. Wightwick; wings, and a children's ward, have since then been added. THE EYE INFIRMARY was established in 1821, by Dr. Butter and Dr. E. Moore; a portrait of the former, by Lucas, is placed in the building. THE SOUTH DEVON AND CORNWALL INSTITUTION FOR THE BLIND, in Cobourg-street, was founded in 1859 by a blind man, Mr. J. Gale, junr., who, deeply sympathising with his fellow sufferers, went from door to door seeking out the blind and inquiring into their condition, and after finding about 80 such persons, in the three towns, and ascertaining, apportionately, the number in Devon and Cornwall, conceived the idea of establishing this Institution, and he set about canvassing for subscriptions for the purpose. He next convened a meeting of the blind, 40 of whom, as well as several clergymen and others, attended. Mr. Gale then proposed that an Institution should be established at Plymouth for the three towns, and extend its benefits to the south of Devon and Cornwall. A committee was afterwards formed, premises taken, and a number of blind persons admitted and taught useful trades. Ultimately the Prince Consort became its patron, and many legacies were added to its funds.

THE FEMALE PENITENTIARY was established in 1808, but after many vicissitudes, was closed about the year 1832, when the property belonging to it was sold off. A few years later the institution was re-formed, this time in Wyndham-place, and soon afterwards, removed to Mill-lane, and, next, to Hampton House, which was purchased for the purpose. It is now one of the best and most useful of institutions of its kind, and is of incalculable benefit to the class for whose reclamation it is intended. There are also other institutions of a similar character in the town. THE FEMALE ORPHAN ASYLUM, Lockyer-street, established in 1834, and the building erected in 1841, maintains, educates, and trains about 70 orphan children, and is supported by voluntary subscriptions. Besides these there are Temperance Societies, with a Temperance Hall in Raleigh-street; Soup Societies; a Sailor's home, in Vauxhall-street; a Mendicity Society; and various other benevolent and useful institutions, as well as many important charities.

CHAPTER XIII

MANUFACTURES, ETC. — PLYMOUTH CHINA AND EARTHENWARE — BELL FOUNDING — WOOLLEN TRADE — OIL MILLS — SALT — SAIL CLOTH — SOAP-WORKS — SUGAR REFINERIES — DISTILLERIES — STARCH AND BLACK LEAD — BISCUITS — IRON FOUNDRIES — PATENT CANDLES — NEWSPAPERS — HOTELS — DILIGENCES — COACHES — RAILWAYS — TRAMWAYS — GAS ETC.

The manufactures, past and present, of Plymouth, are very varied, and some are of great importance. There is not, nor has there every been, any distinctive manufactory connected with the locality, and many which have at one time or other flourished and increased have ultimately died out and become extinct. Leaving Ship-building out of question, the principal manufactures now carried on are Soap Works, Sugar Refineries, Chemical Works, Distilleries, Starch and Blue Works, Soda Works, Patent Candle Works, Paper Staining, Black Lead Works, Rope Makers, Pipe Makers, Gunpowder Mills, &c., and in addition to these there formerly were China Works, Earthenware Works, Oil Mills, Woollen Cloth Weavers, Serge Weavers, Sail Cloth and Canvas Weavers, Fellmongers, Salt Refiners, Bell Founders, and others.

Some little information regarding some of the trades of Plymouth from about 1650 to 1680 is to be gathered from the traders tokens issued at that period. Taking twenty-eight known varieties of these tokens there appear among the owners to have been besides five or six uncertain ones, probably merchants one Cooper, two Mercers, ten Vintners or Innkeepers, one Tallow Chandler, three Grocers, one Bookseller, one Draper, one Apothecary, and the Postmaster. These traders tokens are as follows:–

1.–	*Obv.*	ABRAHAM APPELBEE	A ship in full sail
			A
	Rev.	OF PLYMOUTH	A M
2.–	*Obv.*	ELIZABETH BYLAND	The Coopers Arms
	Rev.	OF PLYMOUTH 1667	E B between two stars
3.–	*Obv.*	NICHOLAS COLE	A full blown Rose
	Rev.	OF PLYMOUTH 1665	N C

4.–	*Obv.*	JOHN COOKE	Shield bearing the arms, a chevron between three pears
			C
	Rev.	IN PLYMOUTH	I M
5.–	*Obv.*	HENRY CLARKE	A Lion rampant
			C
	Rev.	OF PLYMOUTH 1667	H M
6.–	*Obv.*	HENRY DAVIS	HALFE-PENNY
	Rev.	OF PLYMOUTH 1669	H D with true lovers knot with flowers for terminations
7.–	*Obv.*	BENIMIN DVNNING	A Castle
	Rev.	IN PLYMOUTH 1666	B D
8.–	*Obv.*	MARGARET EATON	The Apothecaries Arms
	Rev.	IN PLIMOVTH 1655	M E
9.–	*Obv.*–	GRACE ELLIOTT	The Mercers Arms
	Rev.	OF PLYMOVTH	G E
10.–	*Obv.*	IVDITH FORD 1669	
	Rev.	OF PLYMOUTH	I F
11.–	*Obv.*	IOACHIM GEVERS	A Castle
			G
	Rev.	OF PLYMOUTH 1656	I A
12.–	*Obv.*	CHRISTOPHER HATCH	A Swan
			H
	Rev.	OF PLYMOUTH 1658	C R
13.–	*Obv.*	MICHAEL HOOKE GROCER	The Grocers Arms
			HIS
	Rev.	IN PLYMOUTH 1667	HALF-PENNY
14.–	*Obv.*	IAMES IACKSON AT THE	The Sun
			I
	Rev.	SUNN IN PLYMOVTH 1651	I G
15.–	*Obv.*	WM MOUNSTEVENS 1670	
			M
	Rev.	OF PLYMOVTH	W P
16.–	*Obv.*	SAMVELL NORTHCOTT	S N
	Rev.	POSTMA IN PLYMOVTH 1653	
17.–	*Obv.*	ROGER OLIVER 1663	Arms, a chevron between three trees, each on
	Rev.	IN PLYMOTH MERGER	R O a mount
18.–	*Obv.*	EDWARD PATESON	The Drapers Arms
			P
	Rev.	IN PLYMOVTH	E A
19.–	*Obv.*	JOHN PAYNE	A Pelican in her piety
	Rev.	IN PLYMOVTH 1656	I P
20.–	*Obv.*	SIMON PAYNTER OF	Four Castles, two and two
			P
	Rev.	PLYMOVTH 1657	S A
21.–	*Obv.*	RICHARD PERRY 1658	A man making candles
			P
	Rev.	IN PLYMOVTH	R D
22.–	*Obv.*	HENRY PIKE AT THE THREE	Three Cranes
	Rev.	CRANES IN PLYMOVTH	Hp conjoined
23.–	*Obv.*	THO. PIKE AT YE 4	The arms of the borough of Plymouth; a saltire between four Castles
	Rev.	CASTLES IN PLYMOTH	P T 1657
24.–	*Obv.*	WILLIAM REEPE 1666	
			R
	Rev.	OF PLYMOVTH	W P

25.–	*Obv.*	WILLIAM TOM GROCER	Arms of the family of Tom; three bucks heads couped; crest; a Cornish Chough
	Rev.	IN PLYMOVTH 1667	HIS HALF-PENNY
26.–	*OBV.*	WILLIAM WARREN	*A Fleece W T
	Rev.	IN PLYMOVTH 1656	W W I
27.–	*Obv.*	WILLIAM WARREN	A Fleece
	Rev.	IN PLYMOVTH	W W between four cinquefoils
28.–	*Obv.*	WILLIAM WEEKS	A book closed and clasped
	Rev.	IN PLYMOVTH	W *W S*

Of Tokens of a later date there have also been one or two struck at Plymouth, and these again throw some little light upon the trades of the town. These are;

Obv. PLYMOUTH HALFPENNY A man at work at a loom
Rev. SAIL-CANVAS MANUFACTORY, 1796 A girl, seated at a spinning-wheel
Edge. PAYABLE AT SHEPHEARD HAMMET & CO.

Of this token no less than ten varieties are known. Another, although more strictly a medal than a token, may be classed with this. It was struck to commemorate the visit of George III. to Plymouth, and was issued both of copper, and plated:–

Obv. GEORGIUS III. REX Laureated bust of the king to the right; a small D beneath the bust
Rev. VISITED PLYMOUTH AUGUST 1789 Oval shield of arms under a draped canopy

About the time of the issuing of these later tokens there appear to have been (according to a "Directory" of 1783 quoted by Burt) the following businesses carried on in the town in that year.

Linen Draper	1	Brewers	4	Ship Chandler	1	Cabinet Makers	5
Corn Factor	1	Silversmiths	3	Sail Makers	4	Earthenware and Glassmen	2
Rope Makers	2	Braziers	2	Ship Builders	7	Tallow Chandlers	3
Coach Maker	1	Chemists	3	Block Makers	2	Surgeons and Apothecaries	10
Ironmongers	3	Grocers	9	Wine Merchants	2	Physicians	4
Merchants	11	Curriers	2	Brush Maker	1	Tobacconists	2
Attornies	11	Baker	1	Tanner	1	Confectioner	1
Gunsmith	1	Hat Maker	1	Cheesemonger	1	Notary Public	1
Salsemen	2	Auctioneers	2	Carpenter	1	Marble Cutter	1
Bagmaker	1	Cutler	1	Brokers	4		
Barrister	1	Printer	1				

So that at that time there would not appear to be any actual manufacture carried on in the place. During the present century, however, many manufactures have sprung up, and Plymouth can now boast of producing goods of one kind or other which are not only supplied throughout the kingdom, but are exported in large quantities. Some of the principal manufactures of the place, past and present, will now be noticed.

*This William Warren was the owner of the land on which Charles Church and Church-yard were built and formed.

THE PLYMOUTH CHINA WORKS – These works, whose productions are now ranked among the most rare and valuable of any, were established by William Cookworthy, of Plymouth – a man whose name deserved the highest honour among ceramists as the discoverer of the two great native materials for the art, kaolin and petuntse. William Cookworthy was born at Kingsbridge, on the 12th of April, 1705, his parents being William and Edith Cookworthy, who were Quakers. His father was a weaver, and died leaving his family but ill provided for, in 1718. Thus young Cookworthy, at the age of thirteen, and with six younger brothers and sisters – for he was the eldest of the family of seven – was left fatherless. His mother entered upon her heavy task of providing for and maintaining her large family with true courage, and appears to have succeeded in working out a good position for them all. She betook herself to dressmaking, and her little daughters were taught to aid her. In the following spring, at the age of fourteen, young Cookworthy was apprenticed to a chemist in London named Bevans; but his mother's means being too scanty to admit of his being sent to the metropolis in any other way, he was compelled to walk there on foot. At the close of his apprenticeship he returned to Plymouth, not only with the good opinion, but with the co-operation of his late master, and commenced business in Nutt-street, as wholesale chemist and druggist, under the name of Bevans and Cookworthy. Here he gradually worked his way forward, and became one of the little knot of intelligent men who in those days met regularly together at each other's houses, of whom Cookworthy, Dr. Huxham, Dr. Mudge and the elder Northcote were among the most celebrated. Here he brought his mother to live under his roof, and she became favourite among the leading people of the place, and was looked up to with great respect by the lower classes whom she benefited. In 1735 Cookworthy married a young Quaker lady of Somersetshire, named Berry. This lady, to whom he seems to have been deeply attached, lived only ten years after their marriage, and left with him five little daughters, and Cookworthy remained a widower for the remaining thirty-five years of his life.

In 1745 his attention seems first to have been seriously directed to experimenting in the manufacture of porcelain – at all events, in May of this year the first allusion to the matter is made in his letters and papers and this casually, as follows in:–

"I had lately with me the person who hath discovered the china-earth. He had several samples of the china-ware of their making with him, which were, I think, equal the Asiatic. 'Twas found in the back of Virginia, where he was in quest of mines; and having read Du Halde, discovered both the petunse and kaulin. 'Tis the latter earth, he says, it is the essential thing towards the success of the manufacture. He is gone for a cargo of it, having bought the whole country of the Indians where it rises. They can import it for £13 per ton, and by that means afford their china as cheap as common stone ware. But they intend only to go about 30 per cent. under the company. The man is a Quaker by profession, but seems to be as thorough a Deist as I ever met with. He knows a good deal of mineral affairs, but not *funditus*."

The death of his wife which took place a few months afterwards took his attention away from business and he retired to Looe for a time. On his return he took his brother Philip, who had lately returned from abroad, into partnership, and carried on the business under the style of "Wm. Cookworthy & Co." This arrangement enabled William Cookworthy to devote himself to the scientific, which his brother took the commercial, part of the concern. Left thus more to the bent of his scientific inclinations, he pursued his inquiries relative to the manufacture of porcelain, and lost no opportunity of searching into, and experimenting upon, the properties of the different natural productions of Cornwall; and it is related of him that, in his journeys into that county, he has passed many nights sitting up with the managers of mines, obtaining information on matters connected with mines and their products. In the course of these visits he first became acquainted with the supposed wonderful properties of the "Divining Rod," or "Dowsing Rod," as it was called by the Cornish miners, in the discovery of ore of various kinds. In the magic properties of this rod he was an ardent believer, and he wrote an elaborate dissertation upon its uses, which has been published. His journeys into Cornwall, however, were productive of much more important results than the fabulous properties of the divining rod, for it was in these journeys that he succeeded in discovering the materials for the manufacture of genuine porcelain. The information given him by the American in 1745 had never been lost sight of, and he prosecuted inquiries wherever he went. After many searchings and experiments, he at length discovered the two materials, first in Tregonnin Hill, in Germo parish; next in the parish of St. Stephen's; and again at Boconnoc, the family seat of Thomas Pitt, Lord Camelford. There is a kind of traditionary belief that he first found the stone he was anxious to discover, in the tower of St. Columb Church, which is built of stone from St. Stephen's, and which thus led him to the spot were it was to be procured. At this time he lodged at Carlogges, in St. Stephen's parish, with a Mr. Yelland, and was in the habit of going about the neighbourhood with his "dowsing rod," in search of mineral treasures. This discovery would probably be about 1754 or 1755. Having made this important discovery, Cookworthy appears to have determined at once to carry out his intention of making porcelain, and to secure the material to himself. To this end he went to London to see the proprietors of the land, and to arrange for the royalty of the materials. In this he succeeded;

and ultimately Lord Camelford joined him in the manufacture of china, and, as appears from a letter of that nobleman to Polwhele, the Cornish historian, the two expended about £3,000 in the prosecution of the work.

The experiments on the Cornish materials having been quite satisfactory, Cookworthy established himself as a China manufacturer at Plymouth, his works being at Coxside, where some parts of the buildings still exist and are known as the "China House," although now used for a very different purpose – that of ship building. In 1768, William Cookworthy took out a patent for the manufacture of "a kind of porcelain, newly invented by me, composed of moorstone or growan, and growan clay." The patent was dated 17th March, 1768, and contained the usual proviso that full specification should be lodged and enrolled within four months of that date. This important specification, which I have examined and printed in extenso in another work, was duly enrolled, and from about this period a marked improvement was discernible in the productions of the manufactory, which, however, was not destined to continue long in existence as it was not a *commercial* success. Coal, which was abundant in Staffordshire, and other localities, was entirely wanting at Plymouth, and the "firing" of the kilns had to be done with wood. The clay and the stone Cookworthy had within easy distance, but coal was wanting; his material was difficult and expensive to make, and therefore he was unable to keep pace with other manufactories, and to compete with them. Add to this that he was far from being a young man – being then in his seventieth year – it is not surprising that he should determine on giving up the works, especially as Lord Camelford, (one of his partners,) says nearly £3,000 had been sunk in their prosecution. On the 6th of May, 1774, therefore, William Cookworthy, for considerations set forth in the deed of assignment, sold the business and patent-right to Richard Champion, merchant, of Bristol, a connection of Mr. Cookworthy's by marriage, who had been connected pecuniarily with the works at Plymouth, and they were transferred to that city. The works having been transferred to Bristol, were carried on by Richard Champion, who, having incurred considerable expense without a proportionate return, petitioned for a further term of fourteen years patent-right to be extended to him, which was accordingly done by Act of Parliament passed in the session which commenced the 29th of November in the same year (1774). Thus ended, after the brief period of fourteen years from its first experimental formation to its close, the manufacture of porcelain in Plymouth – a manufacture which was an honour to the locality, a credit to all concerned in it, and which has given it, and Cookworthy its founder, who died in 1780, an imperishable name in the ceramic annals of this country.

The early examples of Plymouth China are, as might naturally be expected, very coarse, rough, and inferior, but they evidence, nevertheless, considerable skill in mixing, though not so much, perhaps, in firing. They are remarkable for their clumsiness as well as for their bad colour, their uneven glazing, and their being almost always disfigured by fire-cracks – if nowhere else almost invariably on the bottom. The decorations at first were principally (as were those of other manufactories) blue; the original blue being of a heavy, dull, blackish shade, but gradually improving until on some specimens it attained a clear brilliance. To this Cookworthy, who was a good chemist, paid considerable attention, and he was the first who succeeded in this country in manufacturing cobalt direct from the ore. The blue for his porcelain, he of course prepared for himself, and it is said, with great probability, that some of the painting in this colour was done by his own hand. The plain *white* porcelain is one of the notable features of Plymouth China. The pieces are mostly salt-cellars, pickle-cups, toilet, and other pieces formed of corals, shells, and other marine objects beautifully, indeed exquisitely, modelled from nature and grouped together with consummate skill; busts and figures, and various other articles, were also produced in white. The later productions consist of dinner, tea, breakfast, toilet and other services; mugs and jugs; trinket and toilet stands; busts, figures and groups; birds and animals; "Madonnas" and other figures after

foreign models; candle-sticks, and a variety of other articles. Some of these were exquisitely painted in brilliant colours with birds, groups, flowers, and other decorations, by Saqui, Bone, and other artists employed at the works. That Cookworthy endeavoured to procure good artists is evident by the following advertisement, in 1770:– "China Painters wanted, for the Plymouth new invented Patent Porcelain Manufactory. A number of sober, ingenious artists, capable of painting in enamel or blue, may hear of constant employ by sending their proposals to Thomas Frank, in Castle-street, Bristol." Among the busts and statuettes are an admirable bust of George the Second, after the statue by Ruysbrach in Queen's-square, Bristol; Woodward, the actor; Mrs. Clive; a Shepherd; a Sheperdess, etc., which show that excellent modellers must have been employed.

The mark of the Plymouth China is usually painted in red or blue on the bottom of the piece, but it does not occur on the white examples. The mark is the chemical sign for tin or mercury, and was doubtless chosen by Cookworthy, the chemist, to denote that the materials from which it was made, and which he had discovered, were procured from the Stanniferous districts of Cornwall. The form of the mark, naturally, is found to vary in different examples, through the different "hands" by which it was painted on. In one or two instances the mark was incised in the soft clay before glazing; but these instances are very rare. The following are varieties of the mark from different specimens:–

Besides these it is necessary to name especially a mark which occurs on a pair of small sauce-boats belonging to Mr. W. Skardon. These are embossed and painted with birds and flowers in colours, and upon each is the mark:–

Mr.
Wm Cookworthy's
Factory Plym^o.^
1770

On an example belonging to Dr. Ashford, is much the same mark:–

Mr.
Wm Cookworthy's
*Factory Plym^o.^*
1770

Another curious example, has, on the bottom, "March 14th, 1768, C.F." and on another part the Plymouth arms and the word "Plymouth," etc.

Among the finest known examples of Plymouth China are a pair of splendid covered vases of hexagonal form, with festoons of raised flowers, and richly painted with butterflies, &c., in the possession of Mr. Francis Fry, F.S.A. These I have engraved in the "Art Journal," and in my "Ceramic Art."

In Lord Mount Edgcumbe's possession too, is a pair of vases of very similar character (but more nearly resembling Mr. Fry's specimens of Bristol,) on which the Plymouth mark has, at a later period, been added. Many good examples of this ware still remain in the hands of families resident in Plymouth and its neighbourhood and in the cabinets of most collectors. The accompanying engravings show some characteristic examples of this famous porcelain.

The manufacture of China-ware having ceased in Plymouth in 1774 this useful and elegant art was lost to the town. Some years later rough common brown and yellow earthenware was made here. In addition to these, manufactories of fine "Queen's Ware," and painted, printed, and enamelled war, were established in 1810. The proprietors of the various potteries, in 1815, were Mr. Fillis, Mr. Algar and Mr. Hellyer. Mr. Wm. Alsop, also, later on (who made coarse ware near the Gas Works), built a manufactory for fine earthenware of the ordinary commoner quality, but afterwards removed to Swansea, his works passing into the hands of Messrs. Bryant, Burnell, and James. Subsequently Mr. Alsop, returned from Swansea and formed a Limited Liability Company. At his death a Mr. Bishop from the

Staffordshire pottery district took the management, but the manufacture died out, and about 1863 the plant was sold off and the place disposed of to the Gas Company. The Mark used by this company was the Queen's Arms, with the words "P.P.COY.L. (Plymouth Pottery Company Limited.) Stone China." The quality of the ware was of the commonest description of white earthenware, blue printed in various patterns. There is at the present time a manufactory of common brown ware, carried on by Mr. Hellyer.

WOOLLEN MANUFACTURE, formerly a staple trade of the place, but now extinct, was introduced by a Mr. Shepherd, from Northampton, towards the close of the seventeenth century, and continued for three or four generations in his family. Mr. William Shepherd, grandson of the introducer "seems," says Burt in his admirable Review of the Commerce of Plymouth (1814), "to have been one of the greatest benefactors ever possessed by the port; for, besides keeping regularly at work six or seven looms in private houses in Plymouth, and the business done immediately under his own eye at the manufactories, he had branches of the trade at Ashburton, Totnes, Buckfastleigh, Tavistock, and other places within a circuit of 25 miles, which altogether employed 4,000 men, women and children, to whom he paid every week from £1,200 to £1,500 for wages." Of these about 1,800 persons were employed in Plymouth and adjacent places, about 800 of whom were spinners, 600 washers, spoolers, warpers, and tuckers, 300 weavers, and the remainder woolcombers. After computing his annual profits at Christmas he invariably divided a tenth part of them among the poor. He assisted, by occasional loans, tradesmen of good character; delivered frequent lectures on religious and social subjects to his workpeople; and "became their human father and friend on all occasions." Mr. Shepherd having established a line of six coasting vessels at Plymouth, besides others at Ashburton, Bristol, etc., forwarded his goods to London for the East India Co. "The baizes and cloths manufactured from coarse wool, not disposed of at Plymouth or in its neighbourhood, were shipped for North America. On the breaking out of the first American War the trade began to decline, and gradually died out." In 1783 the woolcombers organised a grand procession on the ratification of peace. The Messrs. Shepherd also carried on the business of Fellmongers – the making of leather for gloves, small-clothes, and other purposes – Neats-foot Oil makers, and Glue makers.

BELL FOUNDING. This was a trade formerly carried on in Plymouth, but not of long duration. The only Founder of whom any record remains was Ambrose Gooding, who flourished from 1717 to 1750. Twenty six bells cast by him remain in Devonshire at the present day. These are Tetcot, on which his name, "A Gooding, 1717," appears in full; Sherford, on one of which appears his name "Ambrose Gooding, of Plymouth," and on another his mark, a Bell between the initials, A and G, with the date 1728; Welcombe on one of which appears

"A Gooding cast us all fower
For this new builded tower – 1773;"

and on another the initials and Bell as before; Dartmouth, on one of which is "Ambrose Gooding, of Plymouth, cast us all, 1732; on another "A. Gooding, Founder, 1742;" and on another the mark of a Bell and "A. Gooding, 1732;" Holne, where "A. Gooding cast us all five, 1743," and other ways of putting his name occur; South Tawton; Paignton; Churchstow; Ringmore; Charlton; Thurlestone; and Berry-Pomeroy – this last being the latest date, 1750. These are all the bells (twenty-six in number) which are known to be his casting now remaining in Devonshire, but others exist in adjoining counties. It is a curious fact, and one that illustrates well the truism that "a prophet hath no honour in his own country" that while Ambrose Gooding, the Plymouth Bell Founder, was casting so many beautiful and sonorous bells for surrounding parishes, he was not permitted to cast those for his own. In 1749, Thomas Bilbie, of Chewelstoke and Cullumpton, cast the old peal of eight for St. Andrew's Church, Plymouth, having obtained permission, as had been before done, to found them in the old Workhouse-yard. These bells bore respectively the following inscriptions 1st bell T B 1749; 2nd T B 1749; 3rd "T. Bilbie 1749;" 4th "T. Bilbie, Fecit 1749;" 5th quite plain; 6th "Thomas Bilbie cast us all;" 7th "Thomas Bilbie, cast all wee;" 8th "Ego Sum Vox Clamantis Parate. Zach Mudge, Vicar. George Marshall, Richard Hicks, Eccles Guard." This last Bell was re-cast by Thomas Mears, of London in 1840. The trade of Bell Founding seems to have begun and died out with Ambrose Gooding.

LINSEED OIL MILLS formerly existed here, but the trade has long since been discontinued.

SALT appears to have been made at Plymouth as early as the reign of Queen Anne, when it was classed among those privileged by that sovereign. The works appear to have been in Lower-street, and in Briton-side, but although very productive and lucrative in the early part of this century, have long been discontinued.

In 1814, when Burt issued his "Report," the principal trades in the town were: – Tallow Chandlers, of which there were six in Plymouth, one in Stonehouse, and seven or eight in Devonport; the trade was both home and export. Block and Pump makers; Anchor Smiths; Shoe Makers; Saddlers; Brush Makers, who did a good export trade; Nail Makers, now discontinued; Earthenware Makers, already spoken of; Paper Makers; Brewers; Coach Makers; Upholsterers; Marble Masons, who worked the native marbles; Dyers, who, besides the usual branches of their trade, dyed the blue and green serges made in Plymouth; Writing Slate and Slate Pencil Makers, by whom a large home and export trade was carried on, and who by their excellent machinery, produced two slates per minute; Millers; Varnish and Pitch Makers, carried on by Mr. Saunders and Mr. Nicholls; Ivory Black Makers, commenced by Mr. Briggs; Tobacco and Snuff Makers – the Tobacco being cut by horse power, and the Snuff by the same method, or by hand; Tobacco Pipe Makers (Mr. Taylor, in Market-street, and Messrs Burnell, in Briton-side), a trade which is still carried on; Straw Plaiting, carried on by Mr. Tozer and Mr. Bigg; Tanners, there being at that time five tan-yards, belonging respectively to persons of the names of Tanner, Martin, Crews, Dove, and Branscombe and Son; Ship Builders; Rope Makers, there being fourteen rope-walks in the Port, belonging respectively to the following names, Dunsterville, Rodd and Co., Ellis, Bath, Hammett and Stevens, Nicholls, Norris, Gill, Thatchel, Tendre, Chubb Alder and Johnson, Rowe, and Peak and Bond; Sail Makers, of which there were several; Curriers and Leather Cutters; Fellmongers or Tawers; Timber Merchants; Canvas Makers, (Mr. Peter Welsford, and Messrs. Hammett Prance and Co.,) who produced brown and bleached sail cloths, Poldavies, bagging wrappering, corn sacks, and bed sacking; and a White Serge manufacturer, (Mr. Codd,) the last remnant of the Woollen trade of the town already alluded to.

The first Sail Cloth, or Canvas manufactory in Plymouth, was established in Westwell-street, by Mr. Jardine, and was continued there by Mr. Welsford. Another firm, Shepherd, Hammett, and Co., afterwards Hammett, Prance and Co., built the Frankfort Barracks for the same purpose, but sold it to Government, and erected another near the King's Mill, outside Old Town Gate. These are seen in the engraving on another page, of Old Town Gate, beyond the archway and conduit. Later still Mr. Byron Aldham carried on a similar manufacture, (along with flax-spinning,) in Mill-street, and this is still continued.

At the present time, Plymouth can boast within itself of having, besides all the ordinary trades and businesses, many very important manufactories, which as they become more and more developed, cannot fail to be of immense benefit to its inhabitants. These are the Sugar Refineries, Soap

Works, Starch Works, Patent Candle Manufactories, Chemical Works, Biscuit Makers, Cement Works, &c., &c.

THE SOAP WORKS are among the more important manufactures of Plymouth and have become, in fact, one of the staple trades of the place. This manufacture was introduced in 1818 by Mr. Thomas Gill, and the works erected at Millbay. Afterwards they were carried on by a company called the "Millbay Soap Alkali and Soda Company." The Soda and Alkali works were built about 1830 but are now discontinued, the very large premises being devoted to the manufacture of soap. The works which are under the management of Mr. John Rice, are situated at Millbay and occupy the entire area of ground from the Millbay barracks and the line of railway into the Docks; the line passing close to the buildings for loading and discharging. They are the most extensive and important works of the kind in the West of England, and indeed are among the largest in the kingdom, and the machinery and general business arrangements are of the most modern and complete description, and enable, by a skillful arrangement, about twenty tons of soap per hour to be run into the frames. Household soaps of every kind, are produced in large quantities as are also those for manufacturing purposes, for silk throwsters and other trades. Toilet soaps, in all sizes and shapes of tablets, etc., are also produced in every variety and of high quality. The speciality of these important works is the "Millbay Soap," a fine pale yellow production whose bars are specially marked with the arms of Plymouth and the name of "Millbay."

The "Victoria Soap Company's" works are also situated at Millbay, near the floating dock. The "Victoria" Company was established on these premises in 1858, by Mr. F. A. Morrish, and, in 1863, purchased the "West of England Soap Company" which had been founded by Messrs. Bryants and Burnells, and removed their plant, &c., from the Sutton-road. These works, at the exhibition of 1862, were awarded the medal for excellence of quality of their household yellow and of soaps for manufacturers' use. The great speciality however, of the Victoria works is Toilet Soap, which is produced in great quantities, and of every conceivable kind, and of the very finest qualities. These, and the household soaps, are exported in considerable quantities, and a good home trade is also done; many tons being despatched weekly to one place or other.

The "Imperial Soap Company," also at Millbay, is of much less extent, and produces the ordinary classes of household and toilet soaps, for the home markets.

Sugar Refinery. The manufacture of Sugar was carried on in Plymouth in the early part of last century. One of these works was on the eastern side of Sutton Pool, the other on the old Exeter-road, where an old round building, often mistaken for a fort, was in use about 1750 "for grinding canes, and worked contrary to the modern principle by a horizontal instead of a perpendicular wheel." These however died away and in 1838 the present refinery was established by Mesrs. Bryant and Burnell, by whom it was carried on until 1856 when it merged into a company, established under the Limited Liability Act, under the title of the "British and Irish Sugar Refining Company, Limited" and is under the management of Mr. G. H. Brown. The works are situated in Mill-lane, where they cover a very extensive area of ground. The site includes a portion of that of the old Frankfort Barracks, and also a part of the gardens of Sir Francis Drake, whose residence in Saltash-street was immediately contiguous. The business done by this company has been, from its commencement, on an extensive scale, its produce being distributed through the Midland and Southern districts of England and throughout Ireland, and it has of late been considerably increased. Over 10,000 tons of Sugar are imported annually by which the Customs' receipts of the port are much increased, in fact some few years ago, when the Sugar duties were much higher than now, this company alone contributed about one half of the entire customs' receipts of this port. Employment is given to nearly 150 hands, and about 120 tons of coal per week are consumed in the works. The machinery and business arrangements are of the most complete and admirable kind.

Distilleries. "Plymouth Gin" is so well known far and wide, and is made and drank to such an extent that distilling must be included among the staple trades of the town. The principal distillery is that carried on in the name of "Coates and Co.," by Mr. Hawker, in Southside-street, on the site, as has already been stated on page 310, of an ancient religious house, probably belonging to the Black Friars. The premises, which are extensive, and fitted with the most modern appliances, contain many interesting remains of the old buildings. A large quantity of spirit is produced at this distillery, and is sent to all parts. There are two other, but smaller, distilleries in the town; and there are likewise some extensive breweries.

Starch and Black Lead Works, &c. The business of Starch making was introduced by the late Mr. E. James, in 1843, who, in that year commenced the manufacture of Wheat Starch, but shortly afterwards, it being discovered that a larger percentage, and a finer quality could be produced from Rice, he obtained a license from the patentee and continued to make the Rice Starch until the expiration of the patent. Since then many improvements in the patent have been effected by Messrs. James, who are now among the most successful manufacturers of Starch. In the course of time the firm assumed the style of "Burnard James and Sons," and various articles were added to the manufacture of Starch, viz.: – some of the other laundry requisites, such as "Ball Blue," and some of the numerous Alkaline detergent preparations, sold under the names of "Washing Powders," "Soap Powders, &c." The packing of every description of Plumbago, or Black Lead, for household purposes, has also been added, for the most part in the form of solid blocks, compressed by the aid of machinery. For most of these productions the firm has received medals from various International Exhibitions. Messrs. James and Sons' works are in Sutton-road, and another Starch manufactory, that of the Plymouth Starch Works Company, Limited, is carried on in Russell-street.

CHEMICAL AND ARTIFICIAL MANURE WORKS also flourish in Plymouth, and, commercially speaking, have been very serviceable to the town. ROMAN CEMENT manufactories also give employment to several persons.

BISCUIT MANUFACTORY. – This was established towards the middle of the present century by Mr. George Frean and is now carried on by Messrs. Serpell & Co.

IRON FOUNDING. – These works, established by Mr. Mare, were afterwards carried on by the "Plymouth Foundry and Engine Works Company, Limited" in Frankfort Square and Millbay, but are now closed.

PATENT CANDLE WORKS. – These works, belonging to the "New Patent Candle Company, Limited," are in Sutton Road, where they cover a large area of about 20,000 feet of ground. Wax, sperm, and composite candles, as well as night lights and other goods, are produced in large quantities, entirely for the home trade.

NEWSPAPERS. Plymouth has had its Printing Press ever since the close of the seventeenth century – a Mr. D. Jourdaine, having set one up in 1696 or thereabout – and its newspaper from the first part of the eighteenth – a Mr. E. Kent, in Southside-street, having then started "the Plymouth Weekly Journal or General Post." This paper had but a short life, commencing in 1721 and being discontinued in 1723. Towards the latter part of the century "the Plymouth Chronicle" was started by another of the same name in 1808. This was discontinued in 1818 and shortly afterwards two new papers, the "Journal" and the "Gazette" were started; the latter continuing only about a year, and the former being the precursor of the present "Western Daily Mercury." In 1820 the "Plymouth, Devonport and Stonehouse Herald" was commenced; a few years later the "Western Times" and in 1831 "the Plymouth, Devonport and Stonehouse Advertiser" was started and continued for twelve months, ultimately merging into the "West of England Conservative and Plymouth, Devonport and Stonehouse Advertiser." In 1836 the "Plymouth, Devonport and Stonehouse News," was started and continued to be published for about six months, and the next venture the "Plymouth Times" started in 1842 has also long ceased to exist. In 1844 a new venture the "South Western Standard," was set afloat and issued for a month or two. In 1852 the "Plymouth Mail" was commenced and ten years later was incorporated with the "Western Morning News." In the same year the "Western Beacon" was issued for a few months. In 1856 the "Plymouth Stonehouse and Devonport Standard" was published for a short time. In 1860 the "Western Morning News," and in the following year the "Western Weekly News," were commenced and in 1869 the "Western Daily Standard" was started first as a daily and afterwards as a weekly, but was of short continuance. The newspapers published at the present time in Plymouth are "*The Western Daily Mercury*" (daily) established under its present name as a daily paper in 1860 (as the successor of the "*Plymouth and Devonport Journal*" which was first commenced in 1817); its proprietor is Mr. Isaac Latimer, Mayor of Plymouth 1871, and the publishing office is in Frankfort-street. "*The Western Morning News*" (daily) established in 1860; it belongs to the "Western Morning News Company Limited" and its publishing office is in George-street. "*The Plymouth Devonport and Stonehouse Herald*" (weekly) first published as a full priced weekly in 1820, but now simply a small advertising paper; it is published in George-street. "*The Exeter and Plymouth Gazette and Daily Telegram*" (daily) although not printed in Plymouth, is supplied there. "*The West Country Lantern*" established in 1871 and published at Treville-street. "*The Thunderbolt*," also established in 1871 and published in Ebrington-street. "*The Western Globe*" established in March 1872, and published weekly at one halfpenny in Flora-street.

In periodical and local literature, Plymouth has had its full share; and many of the serials to which it has given birth, are of high standing and considerable excellence. Of these, however, it is scarcely necessary to speak.

HOTELS. In 1792, Plymouth contained several Inns for the accommodation of Strangers, viz.: – the Prince George and London Inn, in Foxhole-street; the Fountain Tavern, near Smart's Quay; the Pope's Head Inn, in Pike-street; the King's Arms, at the bottom of Exeter-street; the Bristol Inn, in Old Town, and Globe Tavern, at Frankfort Gate." In 1814, there were "124 innkeepers publicans, and victuallers;" in 1843, there were 171; and in 1852, 263. At the present time there are considerably more. The principal hotels now, are the following:–

The "ROYAL HOTEL," at the corner of George-street and Lockyer-street, (Already described on pages 279 and 377) and connected with the Assembly Rooms and Theatre.

The "DUKE OF CORNWALL" Hotel, belonging to the "Plymouth Hotel Company – Limited," nearly adjoining the railway station at Millbay, erected from the designs of Mr. C F. Hayward, F.S.A., is one of the most elegant buildings in the West of England. It contains about 150 rooms, and the whole are fitted up with every modern appliance for ease and comfort.

The "GLOBE" is at the junction of George-street and Frankfort-street, and facing directly up the whole length of Bedford-street. This is one of the oldest established hotels in the town, and is centrally situated and excellent in its internal arrangements.

"HARVEY'S HOTEL," at the corner of George-street and Lockyer-street, facing the Royal Hotel, and fronting down Bank of England-place, is built on the site of the house of the late Sir George Magrath.

The "ALBION", by the Railway Station, and "CHUBBS" in Old Town-street, are large and commodious establishments.

TRANSIT. – Carriages plying for hire appear to have been introduced about 1775, and, towards the close of that century, "Dilligences" were to be found upon the Stand "at the end of the Old Town, Plymouth," and that in Fore-street, Dock, from 9 a.m,. to 9 p.m. in summer, and till 8 p.m. in winter, for the conveyance of passengers backwards and forwards between those two places. A few years later the Stands for "Dilligences" were at the Fish Market, and by Frankfort Gate. The fares were curious and are worth preserving. Some of them were as follows:–

Between any place in Plymouth, Plymouth Dock or Stonehouse, and any other place within the same town (except Coxside and the Victualling Office at Plymouth*)

One or more ... ... 1s.

Between any place in Plymouth, and Bound's Cove, the Citadel, the Victualling Office, Coxside, and Tothill:–

One, Two or Three ... ... 1s. 6d.

Four ... ... 2s. 0d.

Between any place in Plymouth, and any other place within the Parishes of St. Andrew's and Charles:–

One or more ... ... 3s. 0d.

Between Frankfort-Stand in Plymouth, and any place in Plymouth Dock, not exceeding in distance the stand in Fore-street:–

One, Two or Three ... ... 1s. 6d.

Four ... ... 2s. 0d.

Between Frankfort-Stand in Plymouth, and any place in Plymouth Dock, not exceeding in distance the stand in Fore-street:–

One, Two or Three ... ... 2s. 0d.

Four ... ... 2s. 6d.

Between Frankfort-Stand in Plymouth, and any place in Stoke or Morice town, by way of Pennycomequick:–

One, Two or Three ... ... 2s. 6d.

Four ... ... 3s. 0d.

Between Frankfort-Stand in Plymouth, and any other place in the Parish of Stoke Damerel:–

One or more ... ... 3s. 6d.

Between Frankfort-Stand in Plymouth, and any place in Stonehouse, in the direct road between Plymouth and Plymouth Dock:–

One ... ...1s. 0d.

Two or Three ... ... 1s. 6d.

Four ... ... 2s. 0d.

*The Old Victualling Office under the Citadel.

Between Frankfort-Stand in Plymouth, and any other place in Stonehouse, not exceeding in distance the Southern end of Durnford-street:–

One, Two or Three ... ... 1s. 6d.
Four ... ... 2s. 0d.

Between Frankfort-Stand in Plymouth, and any other place in Stonehouse, exceeding in distance the Southern end of Durnford-street:–

One, Two or Three ... ... 2s. 0d.
Four ... ... 2s. 6d.

Between any place in Plymouth, beyond Frankfort-Stand (except Coxside and the Victualling Office) and any of the places above-mentioned, an additional 6d.

Between Coxside, Tothill, the Citadel, and the Victualling Office, and any of the places above-mentioned, an additional 1s.

No Hackney Coach was allowed to carry more than six passengers, nor Chaise more than four, and every driver was entitled to 6d. extra for every fare. Besides these "Diligences" for conveying people from place to place, "Sedan Chairs" were much in vogue, the regulation of 1790 settling the fares "for carrying" any person to or from any destination in the town; the general charge being 6d. for short distances, with 3d. for every quarter of an hour's attendance.

STAGE COACHES at that time lumbered their heavy, weary way from Plymouth to various parts of the country, carrying three inside and one outside passengers; a Passenger "Diligence" carrying six inside and four outside passengers; a "Balloon Coach," a "Long Coach," and a "Mail Coach," carrying four inside and two outside passengers, conveyed passengers to and from Exeter, and waggons conveyed goods.

At the present day Cabs and Omnibuses in abundance, with the latest improvements in "Hansoms" have done away with the "Diligences" and "Chairs" of those times; the South Devon Railway has annihilated the "Balloon" and "Long Coaches" ; and the new Tramway is doing its best to supersede even pedestrianism on the connecting line of the Three Towns.

THE SOUTH DEVON RAILWAY, was opened to Laira in 1848, and to its present station 1849; the Tavistock Branch in 1859; the Cornwall Railway in the same year. The first of these (from Plymouth to Exeter by way of Plympton, Ivybridge, Totnes, Newton for Torquay, Teignmouth, Dawlish, Starcross, and Exeter), places Plymouth in connection with the entire railway system of the kingdom. The second opens out an important Devonshire district, and the last places Cornwall in direct communication with the rest of the kingdom. The joint station is at Millbay, but is quite unworthy so great an undertaking and so important a locality. Schemes of extension and enlargement, are, while we write, being considered, and there seems every probability of these being carried successfully out.

GAS. In 1770, as shown on page 221, Plymouth was first lit with Oil; 250 Oil Lamps being ordered to be procured, 200 of which were to be mounted and the other 50 kept as a reserve. In 1823, a company for manufacturing and supplying the town with Oil Gas was incorporated; and two years later the "United General Gas Company" was formed; these two companies becoming incorporated in 1832. The Gas Works were at Millbay, and consisted of 44 retorts arranged in six groups of 5 each, and two of 7 each, consuming in all 222 bushels of coal per day. In 1845 the "Plymouth and Stonehouse Gas-light and Coke Company" was incorporated by Act of Parliament and still supplied those towns with Gas of excellent quality and at a very moderate rate.

CHAPTER XIV

THE CASTLE — TOWN WALLS — GATES — CONDUITS — DUCKING STOOL — THE CITADEL — THE FORTIFICATIONS AND DEFENCE OF PLYMOUTH — THE HOE — ST. NICHOLAS OR DRAKE'S ISLAND — THE BREAKWATER — THE BREAKWATER FORT — THE EDDYSTONE LIGHTHOUSE — MOUNT BATTEN.

Plymouth formerly possessed a Castle, and was enclosed with walls in which were a number of gates. The CASTLE appears to have been quadrangular in form, with a round battlemented tower at each angle, and a central keep. It had battlemented walls running from it to the west, while below it, to the east, was the Barbican, with its Fort and chain, enclosing and guarding the Haven, or Sutton Pool. From the four towers, at the angles of this "Castell quadrate," the arms of the Borough of Plymouth – a Saltire, or St. Andrew's Cross (from St. Andrew, the patron Saint of the Church) between four Castles, – are said to have been derived, and the coincidence in form between the four Castles, on the old seals of the Borough as engraved on page, 367 and those on the old chart of the haven, etc., at the time of Henry VIII. here engraved, is particularly striking.

The Castle has disappeared many years, and only some very slight remains are to be seen at the present day. Its locality, however, is perpetuated in the name of Castle-street. The Barbican, shown in the engraving, had a Fort on one side, and a strong wall on the other, and from one to the other of these, as Risdon says, "it was chained over when need requireth" – the chain is shown in the sketch. The other fortifications at the time of the making of the chart appear to have been a wall with towers and other strong work, studded with cannons, along the sea-front of the Hoe; and a platform, or breast-work, on the summit of the Hoe, seaward of St. Catherine's Chapel. These will be seen on our facsimile plate of the chart.

At the time of the siege of Plymouth, in 1643, the town appears, from the curious plan of which we give a facsimile, to have been strongly fortified; the walls commencing at the castle (whose four towers are marked) and running round, and enclosing, the whole of the borough; that side, next the Hoe being of double strength. Starting from the castle, the names of the different points on the walls, as shown on the plan, are Spur, Drawbridge, St. George, Charles Forte, Terrour, Drawbridge, Spurr, Resolution Forte, Maidenhead, and Eastgate. The outworks which were all triangular with ramparts and trenches to connect them together extended from Stonehouse by "New-worke" at Eldad, "Pennicomequick," "Mawdlyn" at North-hill, "Holiwell" near the present Workhouse, Lipson, and Lipson Mill Works, to the Laira, with other outworks at Prince Rock, Cattedown, Fisher's Nose, and other places.

The GATES in the town walls appear to have been several in number, but the last of these, (and indeed, with only a small exception, every trace of the old walls) has disappeared. FRANKFORT GATE, or as it is called on an old map "West Gate," stood where the Globe Hotel now stands but was taken down in 1783.

The following inscription commemorating the taking down of this gate, is fixed to the wall of the Globe Hotel:–

> "Near this place formerly stood Frankfort Gate, which, with others, formed the principal entrances into the Town, then enclosed by a wall, erected for the greater protection thereof, by the Mayor and Commonalty, under the authority of the Charter of Henry the VI. But, in course of years, this mode of defence ceasing to be of any effect, the gate was taken down in 1783, and the streets and avenues adjoining considerably widened and improved. This tablet was put up by order of the Mayor and Commonalty, 4th of June, 1813."

There was formerly a horse pond outside this gate, which was filled up, levelled, and planted with two rows of trees, in 1752. FRIARY GATE, which adjoined the White Friars (the locality still known as "the Friary") was taken down in 1763, and on the 4th of June, 1813, a tablet commemorative of the fact was put up by the Corporation in same manner as was done at Frankfort Gate.

OLD TOWN GATE or North Gate, at the head of Old Town-street was rebuilt in 1759, and taken down in 1809. Of this gate we give an engraving, from a curious old painting. Through the archway the conduit is shown as is also the sail cloth factory. ST, MARTIN'S GATE, in Briton-side, is said to have been removed in 1789. GASKING (or Gascoigne) GATE, in Gascoigne-street, was removed in 1768; COXSIDE GATE, or "East Gate," "which is to be shutte every night," was built in 1589, and removed in the early part of the present century; it stood near Jory's Alms-houses. The BARBICAN GATE, or "South Gate," as its name implies, stood at the Barbican just by the old Fort; it was built in 1602 and removed in 1830. The HOE GATE, the last of its race, is shown in the engraving on the following page. It was built in the sixteenth century, and rebuilt about the middle of the seventeenth. In 1657 it was leased by the Corporation, and subsequently passed out of their hands. It ultimately came into the hands of Mr. T. W. Fox, who, it is much to be regretted, caused its destruction in 1863 – the materials being then sold by him by auction, despite strong expressions of public opinion to the contrary, for the paltry sum of forty-four pounds.

At most of the old gates as well as in other parts of the town, Conduits formerly stood for the supplying of the inhabitants with water. Thus, at Old Town Gate, Martin's Gate, and East Gate, Conduits were placed as well as at Foxhole Quay, on the Parade, Vauxhall-street, Notte-street, Bilbury-street, at the Shambles, Briton Side, and other places. On special occasions, some of these Conduits were made to run wine instead of water – a hogshead being emptied into them for that purpose.

The conduit of Old Town Gate was quadrangular and bore on its front the Royal arms and those of Plymouth with inscription tablet; these are now built in the wall of the reservoir on the Tavistock road, and an inscription stating that it was erected in the mayoralty of Sir John Trelawny, in 1598, runs around its top. A portion of an inscription from another conduit – I believe that of St. Martins – is in possession of Dr. Stewart; it bears the words "Redigit" and "Drake" the remainder being lost.

Not far from the Barbican, was formerly, a Ducking Stool, in which unruly women were "ducked" in the Pool. This instrument of obsolete punishment, which is here engraved, is still in existence, and belongs at the present time to Dr. Stewart. It is much to be hoped that the learned doctor will present it to the town as the nucleus of a free museum.

Chapter XIV

The Citadel, which through its formidable character, and its commanding situation, took the place of the other fortifications, was planned in the middle of the seventeenth century; its entrance gateway, here engraved, bearing the date of 1670. It was built on the highest point of the Hoe, on the site, probably, of the old "platforms" named in the town records, and to it also, the Castle gave place. Since its first formation considerable alterations and improvements, as well as additions, have been made, and it is now one of the most important and effective strongholds in the west.

The Citadel is entered by crossing a drawbridge and then passing through a gateway shown in the engraving. Over the archway are the sculptured arms of Grenville, and on either side, between the pilasters are boldly carved military trophies; above these, on the next stage are more than equally fine trophies, and in the centre a niche, which formerly held a statue of King Charles II., but now holds a pile of cannon balls; above this are the Royal Arms, with supporters, crest, matling, etc., and these are again surmounted by two crowns on obelisks, and a central globe; and on the sides are respectively, a lion and a unicorn holding shields bearing the cross of St.

George. On entering, to the front is a wide promenade, having to its right the Governor's range, and to the left the guard-house; further still are the barracks, the orderly-rooms, the magazines, the chapel, and the other necessary buildings forming so important a stronghold; there is also a statue of King George II. Commencing at the left of the entrance gateway the principal features of the fortifications are the Prince of Wales's curtain; William's range; Prince of Wales's bastion, in which is the tennis court; Prince Edward's curtain, with range of barracks; Prince Edward's battery; the mess room; Prince Henry's demi-bastion, with swivel rifled-ordnance of the finest construction; the ramparts; Cumberland battery; the tiers of fortifications down to the sea-side; old saluting battery; King Charles' curtain; King Charles' battery; King George's curtain; King George's bastion; and the Prince of Wales's curtain. Of late years many alterations and improvements have been made in the Citadel and its strength and usefulness much increased. Of the garrison chapel some account has been given on a previous page.

The present Defences of Plymouth have for their object the protection of the Dockyard and Steam Fitting-yard of Devonport, so that our fleet might fit out in safety, and in case of an unsuccessful engagement might run in to the Hamoaze securely and refit; they have also for their object an entrenched camp for our armies, so that an enemy landing anywhere in the west would hesitate to march on for London or to leave Plymouth in his rear without first endeavouring to take it.

The Defences therefore consist of land and sea works, and these again of outer and inner lines. The land Defences being supplemented by an army lying within the outer works, the sea Defences being supplemented by a carefully designed system of submarine mines and by the assistance of such floating batteries and fire-boats as might be available for the harbour defence.

It will not be necessary to enter into a detailed description of the land defences and works which consist generally as follows:–

Inner Line. The town of Devonport is surrounded by a bastioned *enciente*, which though in itself insufficient to protect the Dockyard, on account of its proximity, would, nevertheless, serve as an interior retrenchment for a garrison to defend to the last, after the army had been beaten and the Outer Line had been broken through and captured. Plymouth Citadel, a bastioned work, detached and complete in itself, though as old as the time of Charles II., might still prove very useful in a similar way to hold out to the last. The Citadel which, as has been stated, is situated at the east end of the Hoe, on high ground, commands the Sound, and so forms part of the sea Defences, and it has a good command over the town of Plymouth.

Outer Line. This consists of a series of detached forts on the German system, *i.e.*, the ditches are flanked in themselves by Capiniers of counterscarp galleries, and the ramparts do not necessarily follow the lines of the ditches. They are placed at about 3 miles from the town of Plymouth, though some are at a much greater distance, and extend from Tregantle on the sea at Whitsand Bay, right round the three towns to Bovisand on the east side of the Sound. These works can easily be connected by parapet and ditch, at any time, on very short notice by the army, or even the garrison inside, should such a course be thought necessary or desirable. The first part of this line takes up the position between the sea and the river Lynher, and two very large forts, Tregantle on the sea, and Scraesdon, at Antony, on the Lynher, occupy the position in very commanding situations. The next portion of the Outer Line of Land Defences, which should occupy the ground between the Lynher and Saltash, and defend the Albert Railway Bridge, for want of money, has not been executed, and as this is the most vulnerable point, the omission is the more important. The Royal Engineers propose to place these forts in advance of Saltash, taking up the line opposite Scraesdon on the Lynher and extending to above Saltash on the Tamar, with a strong *tête de pont* at the Albert Bridge, and it is needless to say that unless Parliament see fit to grant the money, the huge expenditure in the Land Defence of Plymouth is lost to the country, for with the break in the line at Saltash, the most vulnerable point, the other land works are useless, no line being stronger than its weakest point. On the other side of the Tamar where strong Garrisons would lie in Devonport and Plymouth and would be backed by the inhabitants, the position is occupied by a series of smaller Forts, extending from Ernsettle, above the Albert Bridge, to Crown Hill Fort, a very large work, the most advanced in the north of Plymouth, and occupying a most commanding situation, flanking the line on either side. Beside the interior flank defence of ditches by Capiniers, the works flank one another, and take up the ground between. From Crown Hill Fort there is another series of Forts, extending to the river Plym or Laira, on the east side of Plymouth, where Fort Efford, a large work on most favourable ground, looks frowningly down, like a second Ehrenbreitstein, on the town, the railway, and the high road to London. The Laira itself carries the defence down to Turnchapel, though money is still wanted for a *tête de pont* at Laira Bridge. Just above Turnchapel, on the side of the river opposite Plymouth, stands Fort Stamford, with its gorge resting on the Laira, and having some guns looking out into the Sound, but mainly directed landwards to oppose an enemy advancing from the eastward; above Stamford is the large work of Staddon, on the highest ground in the neighbourhood, capable of containing a large garrison and supplies, and commanding all the country around; the gorge resting on the Sound. From Staddon a continuous line of ditch and rampart, broken by two or three open works, runs down to the Sea Defence of Bovisand Battery at the entrance of Plymouth Sound.

The Sea Defences are also of two lines; an outer and in inner.

Outer Line. To commence with the Outer Line. – This line consists of three main works, which defend the entrances to the Sound. The Breakwater, a mile long, forms the southern boundary of the Sound, which is entered by a deep water passage between the land and the Breakwater on either side. These passages are called respectively the East and West Passages. The West Passage is defended by Picklecombe Battery on the land, and the Breakwater Fort, behind the centre of the Breakwater, supplemented by the fire that could be obtained by various smaller works on Maker Heights and behind Cawsand; the East Passage is defended by Bovisand Battery (already mentioned) on the land, and the Breakwater Fort again behind the centre of the Breakwater.

These works are the most formidable that have yet been built. Picklecombe Battery is a treble tier of arched casemates, perfectly bomb proof; the lower tier is appropriated as magazines; the other two are for guns, with sleeping accommodation for the men in rear. The piers and arches are of the most massive granite masonry in the front, and brickwork in cement in rear, while the fronts of the casemates, between the piers and arches, are fitted with iron armour, through which the guns fire. There are 21 guns in each tier. The lower tier of guns, with the exception of two flank guns which look along the shore, are of 10 inches calibre or 18 ton guns (450 pounders); the upper tier, with the exception also of two flank guns are of 9 inches calibre, or 12 ton guns (300 pounders); the flank guns are 7 inches, or 7 ton guns.

The shields are composed of three iron plates each 5 inches thick, and having spaces of 5 inches between them, which spaces are filled with brickwork in asphalte; port holes are cut in the plates for the guns to fire through, and heavy iron frames are placed round the 5 inch spaces where the port hole passes through them. The plates are backed by four massive beams, 5 inches thick and 16 inches wide, with teak between them, which run from top to bottom of the shield. The whole is securely bolted together, by 3 inch bolts, with spherical nuts and coiled washers on Lieut. English's principle.

The Fort at Bovisand is similar, except that there is only one gun tier of casemates and there are 23 guns; half 10 inch, or 18 tons, and half 9 inch, or 12 tons. The backing of the shields also is different, instead of large and long iron beams, there is an iron frame-work rivetted together and filled with Portland cement concrete. The magazine accommodation is in a series of casemates below the gun floor as at Picklecombe.

The Breakwater Fort is situated at the centre, and 80 yards from the Breakwater, and quite distinct from it. The foundation is in the Shovel Rock, 37 feet below low water level, and is built up solid to high water level; the difference of tides is about 15 feet, so the solid portion is 52 feet high. The plan of the Fort is an eclipse, whose major axis is 150 feet, and minor axis 120 feet. The masonry of which these foundations are built is very massive; the external work is granite, in large blocks, and the internal work is composed of blocks of cement concrete, every block being laid by the diving-bell.

At one foot above high water mark are the floors of the magazine, and the solid foundation ceases. The granite exterior wall is, however, carried up 18 feet thick all round, and the magazines are well arched over and made bomb proof. At the level of the top of the magazine, which is 16 feet above high water mark, is the gun floor, and here the Fort differs from any previously constructed, for the wall of the gun floor is formed entirely of iron armour and backing, through which the guns fire. The iron wall is composed of one thickness of 5-inch iron plates, then 6 inches of concrete, next two thicknesses of 5-inch planks, then one inch of iron concrete, and, finally, the backing consisting of iron beams and teak, 12 inches deep and 5 inches wide, placed alternately all round, except where the port-holes occur, and here an extra 5-inch iron plate is placed above and below the port to compensate for the backing, which necessarily must be there omitted. The iron wall is on a batter of 1 in 11, and, standing on a base plate, leans at the top against a stronger plate attached to girders radiating from the centre of the Fort; these girders being themselves supported by transverse girders, the ends of which at the front rest on hollow iron piers, filled with concrete between the parts and at the rear in the masonry pier of the casement where the men live. Arches are turned between the girders, over arch plates, and concrete filled in over the arches to make them bomb proof, and the whole is asphalted over to exclude the wet. The port holes are the smallest that can be made, being for muzzle pivoting guns. The guns are 10 inch, or 18 tons, and there are 18 of them, the Fort having a fire all round. Over the tier of 18 ton guns two turrets will be fixed, each containing two 25 ton guns, or 600 pounders.

These three forts forming the outer line, have iron armour, which cannot be penetrated by any projectile or gun as yet invented or designed, while the guns they carry, can, with the greatest possible ease, pierce the armour of any ship as yet constructed.

The Inner Line consists of a casemated battery, similar to Bovisand, for nine inch guns, on Drake's Island, to act against any ship rounding into the Channel, and to support the outer line; there is also a very powerful open earthwork on the top of Drake's Island, armed with five 25 ton guns, 600 pounders, *en barbatte*, which would command the Sound inside the breakwater. The Channel between Drake's Island, and Stonehouse is enfiladed by a battery, with iron shields, in Mount Edgcumbe, while it receives direct fire from the Eastern and Western King's Redoubts and the Citadel. The iron shields for the Inner Line are not yet provided. Every preparation has been made for laying down submarine mines, at a day's notice, in all the channels and passages; the mines are composed of gun cotton and are fired by electricity through cables.

The Works about Plymouth have been generally directed at the War Office, and carried out in their details by the following Royal Engineer Officers.

North and North-east Land Defences	Major Cox and Major Fowler
Staddon Line and Bovisand Battery	Lieut. Col. Moggridge
Breakwater Fort and Picklecombe	Capt. Vetch and Capt. Tracy

The Hoe, of which notices have already been given, is a lofty eminence overlooking the whole of the Sound on the one side, and the town and surrounding country on the other. It is converted into public grounds for the free and unrestricted use, day and night, of the inhabitants, and forms one of the most delightful and inviting, and at the same time invigorating and healthful, promenades in the kingdom. The Hoe is covered with soft closely-cut grass, and laid out in paths, with shrubberies on its town side and beneath the cliffs; and along its centre, running in a line from the Citadel on the one hand, to West Hoe on the other, is a broad gravelled promenade, where the townspeople and visitors, in fine weather, assemble in thousands to enjoy the sea breeze and the splendid scene around them. On the East side of the Hoe a public carriage drive is formed from the town at Saltram Place, down to the cliffs and so along by the sea to West Hoe Terrace and Millbay;

and on the sea-side of the cliffs, winding paths and flights of steps, with innumerable alcoves, recesses, and seats are provided for the comfort of the public. Public bathing places, both for ladies and for gentlemen, are constructed below the Hoe, but there are no bathing machines or conveniences of any kind to induce visitors to come to the town for sea-bathing. Baths, now closed, were, a few years ago, erected at West Hoe, and it would be very desirable near this spot to form a good bathing place, and so give Plymouth the advantage of becoming a watering place. A project has recently been set on foot for the erection of a promenade pier under the Hoe, and, no doubt, this would add much to its attractiveness to visitors, and give the town advantages it does not now possess.

Few towns on the English coasts possess so fine and so attractive a promenade, or so magnificent and elevated a plot of open public ground as Plymouth does in its Hoe; and few towns could have done more, of late years, towards improving its features and rendering it attractive than it has. Much, however, yet remains to be done before it is all that can be desired for the convenience of the inhabitants and the comfort and pleasure of the visitor. Of these the forming of a commodious bathing place and the establishment of machines, as has just been said, would be one of the most important, and doubtless will, ere long, be effected. The want of sea bathing naturally deters visitors from remaining more than a few days in the town, and drives them to other places where it can be had, and where they take up their abodes for a more extended period.

ST. NICHOLAS, OR DRAKE'S ISLAND, in the Sound, on which formerly, as has been shown, existed a chapel, was two centuries ago fortified, and these fortifications have, of late years, been very considerably increased, strengthened and improved – its guns commanding every surrounding point. The island is connected by a sub-marine ridge of rock, called "The Bridge," with the main land at Mount Edgcumbe, so that the passage on that side is dangerous for any but small craft; larger vessels having to make the circuit of the eastern end of the island. The landing place is opposite the landing place under the Hoe, and is vaulted and well sheltered by cannon.

THE BREAKWATER. This stupendous piece of work, one of the most gigantic, and certainly the most substantial and effective, erections of its kind, is situated on the Sound, in a line between Bovisand Bay, on the east, and Cawsand Bay, on the west, and it is about three miles from Plymouth. The construction of the Breakwater for the shipping was first suggested by Admiral Earl St. Vincent, in 1806, and surveys of the sound were in those years made by Mr. Rennie and Mr. Whidbey, who recommended the forming of a detached mole, or embankment, on the Shovel and San Carlos Rocks, with shore projections, to be from time to time lengthened. In 1811, fresh schemes were propounded, but the original scheme was determined to be carried out. The depth of the water over the rocks or shoals spoken of, was found to vary from eight to ten fathoms, and it was proposed to raise upon them a solid structure, rising ten feet above low water mark, and to make it thirty feet in width on the surface, with a base width of about 210 feet. This it was proposed to effect by sinking rough masses of stone, as torn from the quarry in masses of from half a ton to ten tons each, with a large quantity of rubble and smaller stones, and it was correctly calculated that these would naturally find there proper position and angle by the force of the water and their own specific gravity, and would grout themselves together into a solid mass. Upon this plan the works were commenced and carrried out; a large quarry for the purpose of supplying the material – now universally known as "Breakwater Marble" –being opened at Oreston. In 1812, wharves were built, rails laid down, and vessels and machinery provided, and the line of the intended works marked out on the surface of the sea, by mooring chains and buoys. The first stone was laid on the 12th of August, 1812 (the Prince Regent's birthday), and the work fairly commenced in the centre of the proposed line. The trucks were laden at the quarry, taken down to the wharf, and at the same time run on board the vessels, which were fitted with lines of rails for the purpose, and had windlasses for raising the loaded trucks and tilting platforms for discharging the loads. By the end of the first year, no less than 43, 789 tons of stone had been thrown in, and here and there the blocks were perceivable above the water; and it was shortly afterwards determined to make the height twenty, instead of ten feet above low water mark. In 1817, a considerable part of the erection was displaced by a violent gale, the slope being by its force altered from one in three, as intended by the engineers, to one in five, and the whole much consolidated and improved. Despite this strong warning and practical lesson, however, the authorities continued to build on in their own idea, of a slope of one in three, until 1824, when another terrific gale occurred, which displaced the greater part of the work, and again asserted, even more significantly than before, its right to a slope of one in five. This time the engineers were satisfied that their theory was wrong, and they left the slope as the sea and the storm had fixed it, and removed the centre thirty-six feet nearer shore; and from that day to this, the stupendous work has remained "firm as a rock," and is likely to endure for countless ages.

The form of the Breakwater is a line of three thousand feet in length, with an arm at each end, kanting off an an angle of 120 degrees towards the shore, to the length of one thousand and fifty each – thus making in all an immense barrier of considerably more than a mile in length. It is calculated that considerably over four millions of tons of stone were used in the rough forming of the barrier, in addition to nearly three millions of granite, etc., used for facing and paving the surface; the cost of the former being at the rate of about 1s. 10d., and of the latter about 2s. 8d., per foot. The largest number of workmen employed at any one time in its erection, is stated to have been 765; and its entire cost has been considerably over a million and a half sterling.

At the west end of the Breakwater is a beautifully constructed and admirable Lighthouse, containing oil room, store room, dwelling and sleeping apartments, and watch room, and surmounted by a magnificent lantern of the best construction; its lights being red to seaward, and white from anchorage ground. At the east end is a Beacon, and in the centre, as well as at the west end, a landing place. The surface is composed of massive square blocks of granite, firmly embedded and fastened together, and forming a fine promenade. On one of these blocks of granite is cut the inscription "Prince Wm. Henry Duke of Clarence, Duchess of Clarence, July 17th, 1827," commemorative of the visit of these illustrious persons to the breakwater works.

In the centre of the breakwater, but at some distance from it on its inner shore side, an artificial island has been recently formed, upon which is built a circular fortress, called the "Breakwater Fort," strongly armed with Armstrong guns, and forming the best and most important work of its kind in the kingdom. The position of this fort, already described while speaking of the fortifications of Plymouth, is indicated in our engraving.

Between the shore and the eastern end of the breakwater, a clear passage, a mile in width, is left for shipping, and at the opposite end is a similar passage, of greater width; and the area of water enclosed by it, is about 2,000 acres. Opposite its west end, at Mount Edgcumbe, is a grand fortress "Picklecombe Fort," and opposite its east, or Bovisand end, is another admirable fort, so that with the other strongholds which have been fortified, the Sound is well secured, and the approach of an enemy to the towns of Plymouth and Devonport, with the Dockyard and the shipping in Hamoaze, rendered perfectly impossible.

The Eddystone Lighthouse lies about fourteen miles from Plymouth, and its light may be distinctly seen with the naked eye, in a direct line over the west end of the Breakwater from the Hoe. The first lighthouse erected on the Eddystone rocks was built by Mr. Henry Winstanley, of Littlebury, in Essex, a London mercer, who commenced his useful work in 1696, and completed it in 1700. This remarkable building, which was of stone and wood, and deficient in every element of stability, although recased to the thickness of four feet, and raised in height to 100 feet, was of polygonal form, which rendered it peculiarly liable to be swept away by the waves in any tempest, from whatever quarter it might arise; whilst its peculiar form at the top, with overhanging roofs and cornices and other projections, and cranes, vanes and any other appliances, rendered it a fit object for the fury of the wind to play against. In form, it was much like a Chinese Pagoda, and was gaudily painted outside with representations of suns and compasses and other devices, and with mottoes of various kinds, such as "*Post tenebras Lux*," "*Pax in Bello*," "*Glory be to God*," etc. In the interior the fittings were lavishly ornamented; there was a kitchen, with all necessary convenience and accommodation for keepers; a state-room,. splendidly carved and gilded; a noble bedroom, also finely gilded and painted; and at the top were large wooden candlesticks, etc. So certain of the strength of this fantastic erection was its builder, that he openly expressed a wish that he might be in it during the greatest storm that ever blew under the face of heaven, to see its effect and to shew that those who had remonstrated with him on its construction were wrong. This almost impious wish was fearfully fulfiled, for, having gone to the lighthouse in November 1703, the "Great Storm," as it is called, which passed over the country, carrying with it death and devastation in every direction, arose, and lighthouse and occupants were swept together into the sea. Winstanely thus lost his life, and not a vestige of him, or of his building, or of those with him, remained, with the exception of a piece of chain which the fury of the waves had firmly wedged into a cleft in the rock

In July, 1706, the second lighthouse on the Eddystone rocks was commenced, and was completed in 1709. It was constructed by Mr. John Rudyerd, a silk mercer, of Ludgate Hill, London, member of the old Staffordshire family, of Rudyerd in that county He saw the errors into which Winstanely had fallen, and endeavoured to avoid them. Instead of a polygon he choose a circle as the outline of his building; and in place of stone, except interposed strata of moor-stone above the base, he constructed it entirely of wood; its extreme height being 92 feet. The first and temporary light was exhibited on the 28th July, 1708, and the whole of Rudyerd's plans and calculations were proved to have been correct. Years passed on, storms arose, the waves dashed over and around it wildly, but it remained firm and unshaken, even through the dreadful tempest of 1744. What wind and water could not do was, however, soon after fearfully accomplished by fire – the lighthouse being burned down in 1755. On the morning of the 2nd of December, in that year, at about 2 o'clock, the light-keeper then on watch, went into the lantern, as usual, to snuff the candles, when he found it full of smoke, and on opening the door into the balcony, a flame at once burst forth. His companions being asleep in bed, it was some time before he could obtain assistance, and then their united efforts in bringing up water from the sea were of no avail, for the upper man had to endeavour to throw each bucket full about four yards higher than his own head – a feat, even in time of such imminent danger, not easily accomplished. While standing thus, looking upwards to watch the effect of the water he had thrown, a quantity of melted lead fell upon this man, Henry Hall, by name, which covered his head, face, and shoulders, as well as his clothes, and burned him frightfully – but not only this – a quantity of the molten metal, falling into his open mouth, ran down his throat, and made its way into his stomach, producing an intense internal burning sensation. The men were thus compelled to retreat to the lower rooms, and so downwards, from room to room, until at length they had to take refuge in a hole in the rocks. Early next morning the Lighthouse was discovered to be on fire, by some Cawsand fishermen, who immediately proceeded to the spot, and after much difficulty, succeeded in bringing off the wretched men, and landing them at Plymouth. Here the moment he set foot on land, one of the terror stricken men, who had evidently lost his reason through fright, ran off, and no tidings were ever afterwards heard of him. The poor man, Henry Hall, who was 94 years of age, lingered some days, when he died, and after his death, a mass of lead, weighing nearly half-a-pound, was taken from his stomach. Of this singular circumstance, the following account was sent to the Royal Society by Mr. Spry, who attended him:–

> "On the 4th of *December*, 1755, at 3 in the afternoon, *Henry Hall*, of *East-Stonehouse*, near Plymouth, aged 94 years, of a good constitution, and extremely active for one of that age, being one of the three unfortunate men, who suffered by the fire of the Lighthouse at *Eddy-stone*, nine miles from *Plymouth*, having been greatly hurt by that accident, with much difficulty returned to his own house, I being sent for to his assistance found him in his bed, complaining of extreme pains all over his body; especially in his left side, below the short ribs, in the breast, mouth and throat. He said likewise, as well as he could, with a hoarse voice, scarce to be heard, that melted lead has run down his throat into his body."
>
> "Having taken the proper care of his right leg, which was much bruised and cut on the tibia, I examined his body, and found it all covered with livid spots and blisters; and the left side of the head and face, with the eye, extremely burnt; which having washed with linnen dipt in an emollient fomentation, and having applied things used in cases of burning, I then inspected his throat, the root of his tongue, and the parts contiguous, as the uvula, tonsils, &c., which were greatly scorched by the melted lead. Upon this I ordered him to drink frequently of water-gruel or some such draught; and returning to my own house, sent him the oily mixture, of which he took often 2 or 3 spoonfuls."
>
> "The next day he was much worse, all the symptoms of his case being heightened, with a weak pulse; and he could scarce swallow at all."

"The day following there was no change, except that, on account of his too great costiveness, he took six drachms of manna dissolved in an ounce and half of infusion of senna, which had no effect till the day following; When just as a clyster was going to be administred he had a very foetid discharge by a stool."

"That day he was better till night, when he grew very feverish."

"The next day, having slept well the preceding night, and thrown up by coughing a little matter, he was much better."

"He began now to speak with less difficulty, and for three or four days to recover gradually; but then suddenly grew worse; his pulse being very weak; his side, which grew worse daily from the first, now reddened a little and swelled; to which I applied the emplaster of gums. But all methods proved ineffectual, for the next day being seiz'd with cold sweats and spasms in the tendons, he soon expired."

"Examining the body, and making an incision thro' the left abdomen, I found the diaphragmatic upper mouth of the stomach greatly inflamed and ulcerated, and the tunica in the lower part of the stomach burnt; and from the great cavity of it took out a piece of lead of the shape and weight here described."

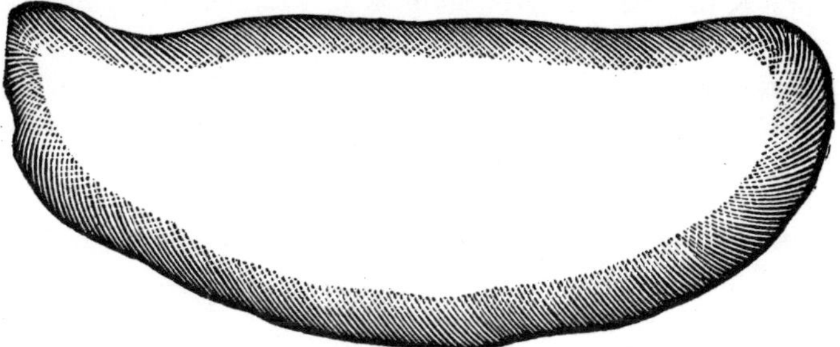

"The exact Figure of the Lead, which weighed 7 Ounces, 5 Drachms, and 18 Grains."

"It will perhaps be thought difficult to explain the manner, by which the lead entered the stomach. But the account, which the deceased gave me and others, was, that as he was endeavouring to extinguish the flames which were at a considerable height over his head, the lead of the lanthorn being melted, dropped down before he was aware of it, with great force into his mouth, then lifted up and open and that in such a quantity, as to cover not only his face, but all his cloths."

"Some gentlemen of the faculty imagining that the degree of heat in melted lead was too great to be borne in the stomach, without immediate death, or at least much more sudden than happened in this case, and thence doubting of the truth of the above narrative, Mr. Spry made experiments in the sight of many creditable witnesses, to evince the obsolute possibility of his assertion, by pouring down melted lead, in considerable quantities, into the stomachs of living dogs and fowls, some of which not only survived, and eat heartily afterwards, but absolutely recovered of the injury; and others he opened, and showed the consolidated lead in their stomachs. At the time of writing his last account, Mr. Spry had a dog with lead in his stomach, which he intended to keep, to prove how long he might live."

Thus ended the second lighthouse – an edifice of excellent construction, and built with much skill; and one that, but for the fire, might have stood for years against the raging of the waves and tempest. At the time of its building, Louis XIV. was at war with England, and a French privateer took the men at work on the rock and carried them off as prisoners. When Louis heard of it he immediately ordered them to be set at liberty and their captors to be put in their place, declaring that, though at enmity with England, he was not at war with mankind. The men were brought back and at once resumed their work.

The third, and present Lighthouse, was commenced building in August, 1756, and on the 1st of June, 1757, the first stone was laid. Mr. John Smeaton, for an account of whom, see page 233, was the architect of this splendid erection. Taking nature, in her provision against wind and storm, in the form of the trunk of the oak tree, as his model, and planning a system of dovetailing his blocks of stone together, and also of dovetailing the lower courses into the solid rock itself, so as to form, as it were, roots to his gigantic stone tree, Smeaton commenced his great work, cutting each stone to its proper shape, and fitting them together in a workyard, at Millbay. The foundations were commenced on the 6th of August; granite being adopted for the exterior casing, and Portland stone for the internal parts. In the following June, the windlasses, etc. were fixed, and the first stone laid, and in September, the first entire circular course was set. The entire stone-work was completed on the 23rd of August, 1759 and on the 12th of October, the light first burned in the lantern and has, without intermission, sent forth its cheering and warning light every night for one hundred and thirteen years. The storms of 1762 and 1817, which would have washed

away any ordinary erection, left the Eddystone unscathed, and it is as firm at the present day as when he left it. The plan of dovetailing, by which Smeaton sought successfully to engraft the structure upon the rock and to make it, in fact, a part of the rock itself will be best understood by the accompanying engravings. The first shows the face of the rock as dovetailed down its sloping side for the first course to be fitted into. The second shows the system of dovetailing when the structure had reached its twenty-third course – the faint lines showing the positions of the stones of the next, or twenty-fourth course. The third shows the system when the building had reached its twenty-ninth course. The lantern is octagonal, and of copper, and is set in grooves in the stone, firmly fastened with lead and with bars of iron.

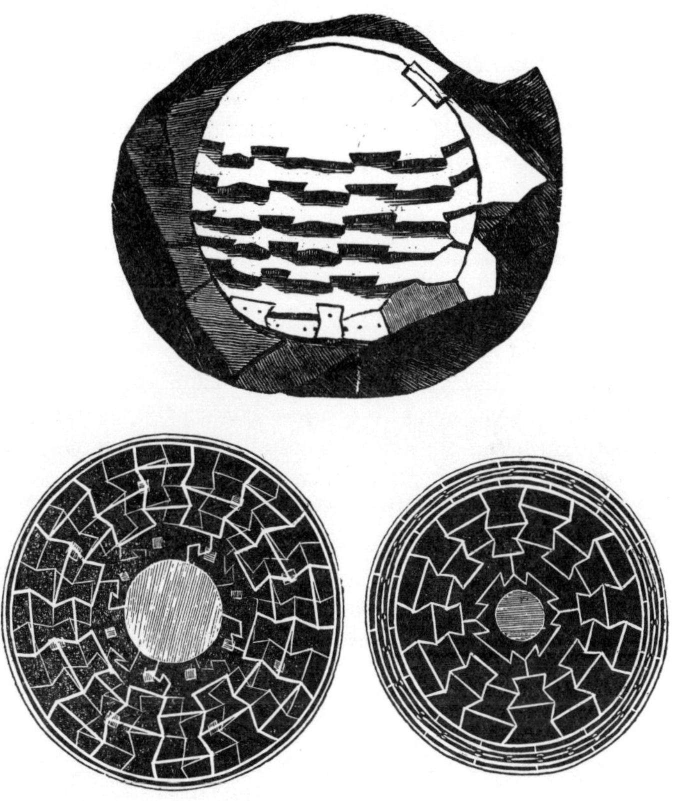

This building, which has given to the name of Smeaton an imperishable fame, bears round the upper store-room the truly appropriate inscription "EXCEPT THE LORD BUILD THE HOUSE THEY LABOUR IN VAIN THAT BUILD IT. – *Psalm* cxxvii," and on the last stone set up, being that over the door of the lantern on the east side, "24th AUG., 1759. LAUS DEO." The entire time actually occupied in building was 111 days and 10 hours; there being in the three years which were occupied over the work, a considerable time when no operations could possibly be carried on upon the rock.

The Eddystone Lighthouse, it is well to record, was adopted as a background of the figure of Britannia, on the reverses of the copper coinage of this country, by George II., and has so remained to the present day. Thus Plymouth is commemorated on every penny, halfpenny, or farthing of the bronze coinage, in common daily use, by every individual in the kingdom.

MOUNT BATTEN is a bold rocky promontory, projecting into the Sound, at the entrance to Cattewater. About seven-eights of this neck of land are surrounded by water, and, from its summit, some of the most charming views of the neighbourhood – embracing both sea and land – are obtained. The Town on one hand, with its shipping, its Citadel, and other attractions; on another, the open fields on Staddon Heights; on another Cattewater and the Laira; and on the South, the Sound, with Drake's Island and the wooded heights of Mount Edgcumbe, are all full of beauty and of interest. On the summit of the Mount is a fine old Martello tower, built in the reign of Charles II., on the site of a fort thrown up for defence of the town during the "Siege of Plymouth." This tower, which is circular in form, and is built of the limestone of the district, is two floors in height, the upper having a vaulted roof. It has embrasures for ten guns, and in 1717, was mounted with six pieces of ordnance; eight others lying in the bay, near at hand. On one side is an arched doorway, surmounted by a well designed and boldly executed piece of sculpture, bearing the arms of Plymouth, surrounded by the characteristic ornament of the period.

On Mount Batten, several Celtic coins have at one time or other been discovered, as detailed in the early part of this volume.* The principal discovery was made in 1832, in the process of quarrying, when they were found in the head-soil. At this time, five gold, and eight silver coins were discovered and a short account of them was given in the *Archælogia*. Since then others have been discovered, several of which are now in my own cabinet. Among these is the fine gold coin, here engraved.

*see page 20

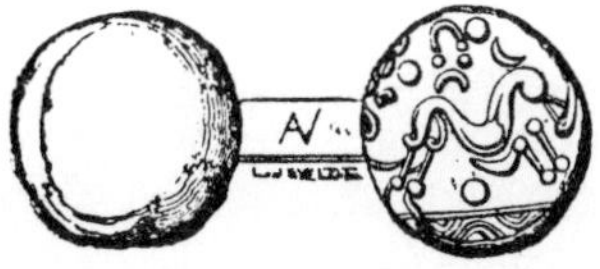

It has one side plain and convex, and the other, which is concave, bears a horse galloping, to the right, above the back of which is a reversed crescent and a horse-shoe shaped figure, terminated with pellets derived from the arms of victory, and pellets, etc., and over its head are a crescent and an annulet, while beneath is a pellet. Among the others in my possession, are the bronze coins here engraved. Some of these, especially the first two, bearing on one side the usual horse, and on the other, the rude copy of a laureated bust, are highly interesting.

The others, also here re-introduced, are equally curious and interesting, and are in a fine state of preservation. The finding of these coins shows that Mount Batten, now rapidly disappearing through the constant quarrying which is carried on, was inhabited by the Ancient Britons, who doubtless found it a valuable stronghold.

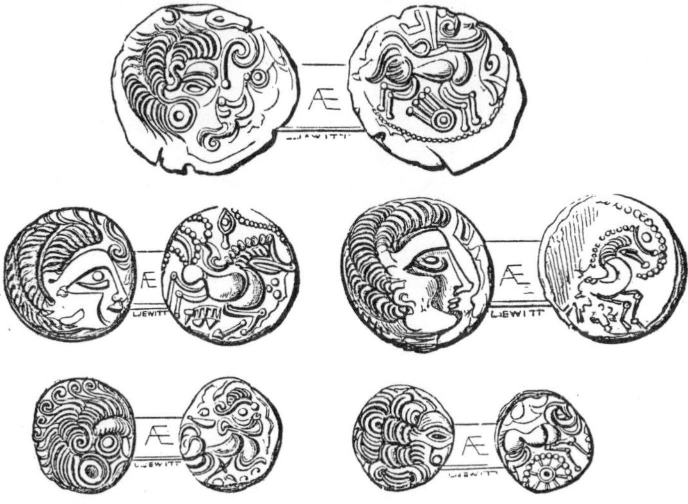

At present, Mount Batten forms an admirable and valuable shelter for the shipping in Cattewater, by protecting the vessels from the Southerly gales. It is much to be feared however that in process of time, as the elevation is removed by quarrying, that an injurious effect will be felt on the shipping, and that the mercantile interests will regret the removal of this natural barrier.

Near this is Turnchapel, a small village lying on the banks of Cattewater, at which vessels of tolerably large size were formerly built. Here, in 1810, the *Armada*, 74 guns, was launched, as was also at a later date, the *Clarence*, likewise of 74 guns. Not far from Turnchapel is Hooe Lake, on the banks of which lies the picturesque and charming little village of Hooe, a favourite resort of parties from Plymouth, during the summer fruit season. Higher up Cattewater is Oreston with its famous quarries. From these quarries the whole of the stone used in the construction of the Breakwater was procured; the land, about twenty-five acres in extent, having been purchased by order of the Duke of Bedford for £10,000. The rocks are of beautifully veined limestone, of various colours, and so hard as to be capable of taking a very high polish. It is usually known as "Breakwater Marble," and is much used for chimney pieces and other ornamental work. The pavements of many of the streets of Plymouth, are formed of this beautiful material, and have, especially in wet weather, a very striking effect.

During the working of these cliffs in 1812, at the depth of sixty feet from the summit, and twenty-five from the margin of the sea, a cavity, or nodule of clay, was discovered about twenty-five feet in length, by twelve square, in the midst of which were found several bones of the rhinoceros, in a more perfect state, and containing less animal matter, than any fossil bones that have been dug out of rock or earth. Other bones of the wolf, hyaena, elephant, deer, cow, horse, etc., have also been found. The arrangements with tramways, quays, cranes, and other appliances, for getting the stone for the Breakwater and for its transit, were on a gigantic, and at that time, remarkable scale. The quarries are still very extensively worked.

CHAPTER XV

MOUNT EDGCUMBE — THE HOUSE AND GROUNDS — THE GARDENS — THE FAMILY OF EDGCUMBE — CAWSAND — MAKER — SALTRAM — THE HOUSE AND GROUNDS — COLLECTION OF PICTURES — FAMILY OF PARKER, ETC.

Standing on the Hoe at Plymouth with the grand expanse of the Sound in front and the Channel beyond, the spectator sees, to his right, the wooded heights of Mount Egcumbe, skirting the water from Hamoaze to Cawsand; and in the distance, beyond Cattewater, those of Saltram, on his left. To these two noble piles, and their equally noble owners, attention must briefly be called. The mansion at Mount Edgcumbe was built about 1550, but has been so much altered since that time that its outward and inward character has been greatly changed.

It is square in general form, and originally had a circular tower at each angle; these, however, have been rebuilt of octagonal form, and additions have been carried out in different directions. The principal internal feature is the

Great Hall, in the centre of the building, which has a minstrel's gallery, with an organ, and other attractions, and is a noble room; the remainder of the house is, as such a home ought to be, elegant but not stately, and designed more for substantial comfort than showy receptions. The front faces down a grassy slope to the sea, and thus has a charming prospect always before its windows; it forms a striking object from the mouth of the Tamar, as shown in our engraving. In the house are preserved several fine old paintings, including many family portraits, by Sir Joshua Reynolds, Sir Peter Lely, and others; full-length portraits of Charles II., James II., Prince Rupert, and William III.; portraits of Charles I., the Duke of Monmouth, and many others; and several valuable pictures by old masters. Among the latter ten or twelve Vanderveldes, grace the several apartments. Of these some are stated to have been painted by the artist at Mount Edgcumbe. Of one, which formed the subject of correspondence between Sir Richard Edgcumbe and the artist, the original and amended sketches hang beside the picture. The portraits by Sir Joshua Reynolds are of individuals of three generations, and those by Lely are in his best style.

The grounds of Mount Edgcumbe, many miles in extent, are full of natural beauties, and these have, to some extent, been aided by art. Still, art has done but little, for it was here unnecessary to do much; this delicious peninsula has been so richly gifted by nature, that, perhaps, efforts to enhance its attractions might have lessened instead of augmenting them. Hill and dell, heights and hollows, pasture slopes and rugged hillocks, succeeded each other with a delicious harmony rarely to be seen elsewhere. Everywhere Nature has had its own sweet will; even the laurel hedges have risen thirty feet in height; the lime trees grow as if they had never been trimmed; while the slopes, from the hill-heights to the sea-rocks, appear as sheen as if the scythe had been perpetually smoothing them. Here and there, pretty and pleasant shelters have been provided for visitors who throng hither for health and relaxation; "look-out" seats are provided on many of the hill-tops; and the deer and the rabbits have free pasturage in the noble Park that occupies a space of many hundred acres between the harbour and the sea. The gardens are prettily laid out; enriched by rare trees, with several summer-houses in pleasant nooks, where cedars, magnolias, cork trees, and other trees, supply shade and shelter from rain and sun. Art has here been aiding Nature, but its influence is felt rather than seen; those to whom the "grounds" owe much seem to have been ever mindful that their profuse and natural luxuriance needed few checks of the pruner and trainer. The name of one of these benefactors is recorded – a votive urn contains a tablet to the

memory of that countess "whose taste embellished the retreats, herself the brightest ornament" – Countess Sophia, who could not have found on earth a home more lovely than that which, in 1806, she was called to leave for one still more perfect and more beautiful.

The great charm of Mount Edgcumbe, however, consists in the five-mile drive through the Park, along a road that everywhere skirts the harbour or the sea, It is perpetual hill and dell; a mimic ruin, intended as a view tower, and answering its purpose well, is the only object remarkable on the higher grounds, if we except Maker Church, which contains many interesting memorials of the Edgcumbe family; but down in some of the dales, are pretty "lodges," where the keepers and gardeners reside, and where simple "refreshments" of milk and hot water are provided for the crowds who visit the domain. One of these, "Lady Emma's cottage" (Lady Emma being the first Countess of Mount Edgcumbe, wife of George, first Baron and Earl of that title), is charmingly situated in one of the most lovely of the dells of this domain, surrounded by soft grassy turf, and overhung by lofty trees; the cottage itself is completely embosomed in creeping plants, and has a rustic verandah exquisitely decorated with fir-cones and other natural productions, so disposed as to give considerable richness to the effect of the building. The little valley in which it stands, hollowed out with great regularity by nature, and sloping gently down towards the sea, is one of the sweetest spots on the whole estate. The footway winds round the upper part of the valley, and at the head of the dell is a spacious alcove composed of Gothic fragments, called the "Ruined Chapel," from which a glorious view is obtained.

In the grounds the most famous points for the attraction of visitors are "Thomson's Seat;" the "Temple of Milton;" a recess, called the "Amphitheatre;" a charming alcove, the "White Seat," which commands a splendid prospect; "The Arch," which overlooks the Sound; and the "Zig-Zag Walks," which lead down along the cliffs and through the wood, and are the favourite resorts of visitors.

The Gardens are three in number, and called respectively the "Italian," the "French," and the "English" gardens, in each of which the special characteristics of planting and arrangement of those countries are carried out – the conservatories, fountains, orangeries, terraces, &c., being, in each instance, built in accordance with the tastes of the three kingdoms.

Indeed, it is difficult to convey an idea of the grandeur, beauty, and interest of the views from every portion of the Park; they are perpetually varied as the eye turns from sea to shore, and from shore to sea; each one of

C P. NICHOLLS

them enhanced by ships at anchor or in full sail; while boats of all forms and sizes are continually passing to and fro.

The family of Edgcumbe, to which this domain belongs, is one of the oldest in the County of Devon; the name being derived from their original possession of Eggescomb, Edgcomb, or Edgcombe (now called Lower Edgcumbe), in the parish of Milton Abbots, in that county. From this family and this place, the noble family of the Earls of Mount Edgcumbe is descended as a younger branch. In 1292, Richard Edgcumbe, was Lord of Edgcumbe, in Milton Abbots, and he was direct ancestor, both of the present representative of the main line, who is twentieth in direct lineal descent, and of the present enobled family, as well as of the branches settled in Kent and elsewhere. In the reign of Edward III., William de Eggescombe, having married Hilaria, sole daughter and heiress of William de Cothele, of Cothere, or Coteel, in the parish of Calstock, in Cornwall, a fine old Cornish family, became possessed of Cothele and the other estates, and removed into Cornwall. Here at Cothele, he and his descendants resided for several generations. Richard Edgcumbe, great grandson of William de Edgcumbe and Hilaria de Cothele, is said to have built the greater part of the grand old residence of Cothele, as it remains at the present day. This Sir Richard was, as Fuller says, "memorable in his generation for being zealous in the cause of Henry, Earl of Richmond, afterward King Henry VII. He was, in time of King Richard III., so hotly pursued, and narrowly searched for, that he was forced to hide himself in his wood, at his house, in Cuttail, in Cornwall. Here extremity taught him a suddain policy, to put a stone in his capp and tumble the same into the water, whilst the rangers were fast at his heels, who, looking down after the noise, and seeing the capp swimming therein, supposed that hee had desperately drowned himself, and deluded by this honest fraud, gave over their further pursuit, leaving him at liberty to shift over into Brittany. Nor was his gratitude less than his ingenuity, who, in remembrance of his delivery, after his return built a chappel (which still remains) in the place where he lurked, and lived in great repute with prince and people." After thus cleverly misleading his pursuers, Richard Edgcumbe crossed the Channel in a small ship, to the Earl of Richmond, in Brittany, with whom he afterwards returned to England, and was engaged in the battle of Bosworth Field, in Leicestershire, where King Richard was killed.

At Bosworth, Richard Edgcumbe received the honour of knighthood from his victorious leader, Henry VII., was made comptroller of his household, and one of his Privy Council, and had the castle and lordship of

Totnes, in Devonshire – forfeited to the crown on the attainder of John Lord Zouch for high treason – conferred upon him by that monarch, with many other honours and dignities, and large extents of land, including those of Sir Henry Bodrugan, who had likewise been attained for high treason. He also held, as he had previously done, the offices of recorder and constable of the castle of Launceston, and constable of Hertford, etc. In 1488 Sir Richard was sent into Ireland, as Lord Deputy, by his royal master, to take the oaths of allegiance of the Irish people, embarking at Mounts Bay in the *Anne of Fowey*, and attended by other ships, and a retinue of five hundred men. He died in 1489, at Morlaix, while holding the appointment of ambassador to France. He married Joan, daughter of Thomas Tremaine of Collacombe, by whom he had issue.

His son, Piers Edgcumbe, was sheriff of the county of Devon, 9th, 10th, and 13th Henry VII. and 2nd Henry VIII. "At the creation of Prince Arthur he was one of the twenty individuals who were made Knights of the Cross of St. Andrew." He, with others, was "appointed to review and array all men at arms, archers, and others, who were to accompany Sir Thomas D'Arcy in his expedition against the Moors and infidels." He was one of the expedition into France, 5th Henry VIII., and for his distinguished gallantry at the sieges of Tournay and Thurovenne, and at the battle of Spurs, he was created a knight-banneret. Sir Piers Edgcumbe was married twice: first to the daughter and heiress of Stephen Durnford, by his wife the heiress of Rame; and, second, to Katherine, daughter of Sir John St. John, and widow of Sir Griffith Ap Rys, by whom he had no issue. By the first of these marriages, Sir Piers Edgcumbe acquired the manors and estates of the Durnfords, including that of West Stonehouse (now Mount Edgcumbe). He had issue by her, three sons, Richard, John, and James, and three daughters, Elizabeth, Jane, and Agnes (or Anne). Sir Piers Edgcumbe died in 1539, and was succeeded as heir by his eldest son, Richard Edgcumbe, who was knighted in 1536.

This Sir Richard Edgcumbe built the present family mansion on a part of the estate which his father had acquired by marriage with the heiress of the Durnfords (who had inherited it from the ancient family of Stonehouse or Stenhouse), and gave to it the name of "Mount Edgcumbe." He was sheriff of Devon 35th Henry VIII. and 1st Queen Mary. He married first a daughter of Sir John Arundel, by whom he had no issue; and, second, Winifred Essex, and by her had, besides other issue, a son, Piers, or Peter, who succeeded him. Sir Richard Edgcumbe, who kept up a fine establishment, and at one time entertained at Mount Edgcumbe the English, Spanish, and Netherlands admirals, died in 1561. Piers (or Peter) Edgcumbe, who was member of Parliament, and was also sheriff of Devon 9th Elizabeth, married Margaret daughter of Sir Andrew Lutterell, by whom he had five sons and four daughters, and was succeeded by his eldest son, Richard. Piers Edgcumbe died in 1607, and on his tomb his honours are thus set forth:–

"Lief Tenant to my Queen long Time,
And often for my Shire a Knighte;
My Merit did to Creddit clime,
Still bidinge in my Callinge rights;
By Loyalty my Faith was tryede,
Peacefull I liv'd, hopeful I diede."

His son, Sir Richard Edgcumbe, knighted by James I., was member of Parliament for Totnes, for Grampound, and for Bossiney; he married Mary, daughter and heiress of Sir Richard Coteele, or Cottle, of London, and by her, who died eighteen years before him, had issue, two sons, Piers and Richard, by the eldest of whom, Piers Edgcumbe, he was succeeded. This gentleman distinguished himself by his devotion to the royal cause; he "was a master of languages and sciences, a lover of the king and church, which he endeavoured to support in the time of the civil wars to the utmost of his power and fortune." Sir Alexander Carew and Major Scawen, for holding communication with Piers Edgcumbe, who held a colonel's commission in the king's army, were beheaded. He married Mary, daughter of Sir John Glanvil, and died in 1660, being succeeded by his eldest son, Sir Richard Edgcumbe, who had been knighted during his father's lifetime. He was also a member of Parliament. He married Anne Montague, daughter of Edward, Earl of Sandwich, by whom he had issue, two sons, Piers, who died young and unmarried, and Richard; and six daughters. He died in 1688.

To this time, for several generations, it will have been noticed, the inheritors of the estate alternated, in name, between Piers (or Peter) and Richard. This succession of name was now broken by the death of Piers, the eldest son. Richard Edgcumbe, soon after coming of age, was chosen M.P. for Cornwall, and continued to sit for various places until 1742. In 1716 and 1720 he was one of the Lords Commissioners of the Treasury, and in 1724 was Vice-Treasurer, and Paymaster of the Taxes, etc. In 1742 he was created BARON EDGCUMBE of Mount Edgcumbe, and was afterwards made Chancellor of the Duchy of Lancaster, one of the Privy Council, and Lord-Lieutenant of Cornwall. His lordship, by his wife Matilda, daughter of Sir Henry Furnese, had issue, three sons, Richard, Henry (who died an infant), and George; he died in 1758, and was succeeded in his title and estates by his eldest son, Richard (second Baron Edgcumbe), member of Parliament for various places, one of the Lords of the Admiralty, who was afterwards appointed Comptroller of his Majesty's Household. He was a man of great talent, and is thus spoken of by Horace Walpole in his "Royal and Noble Authors:" – "His lordship's skill as a draughtsman is said to have been such as might entitle him to a place in the "Anecdotes of English Painting," "while the ease and harmony of his poetic compositions give him an authorised introduction here." … "a man of fine parts, great knowledge, and original wit, who possessed a light and easy vein of poetry; who was calculated by nature to serve the public, and to charm society; but who unhappily was a man of pleasure, and left his gay associates a most affecting example how health, fame, ambition, and everything that may be laudable in principle or practice, are drawn into, and absorbed by, that most destructive of all whirlpools – gaming." His lordship, dying unmarried in 1761, was succeeded by his brother George as third baron. This nobleman who had sat in several parliaments, and held various public offices (among them the Lord Lieutenancy of Cornwall), and was Vice-Admiral of the Blue, married Emma, only daughter and heiress of John Gilbert, Archbishop of York, by whom he had issue an only son, who succeeded him. His lordship was, on the 17th February, 1781, created, in addition to his title of Baron Edgcumbe, *Viscount Mount Edgcumbe and Valletort*; and in 1789 he was further advanced to the dignity of an earl, by the title of *Earl of Mount Edgcumbe*. Dying in 1795, he was succeeded by his only son, Richard, as second earl, who also held the office of Lord-Lieutenant of Cornwall. This nobleman married Lady Sophia Hobart, daughter of John, second earl of Buckinghamshire, and by her had issue, two sons, Ernest Augustus, and George, and two daughters. His lordship died in 1839, and was succeeded by his eldest son, Ernest Augustus, as third earl, who (born in 1797) was Aide-de-Camp to the Queen, and Colonel of the Cornwall Militia. He married Caroline Augusta, daughter of Rear-Admiral Charles Fielding, who still survives him, and is an extra Lady of the Bedchamber to the Queen. By her his lordship had issue two sons: viz., William Henry and Charles Ernest, and two daughters, of whom Ernestine Emma Horatia is still living. The earl died in 1861, and was succeeded by his eldest son as fourth earl.

The present nobleman, William Henry, fourth earl of Mount Edgcumbe, the noble owner of Mount Edgcumbe and of the large estates concentrated in the family, was born in 1832. He was educated at Harrow, and at Christ Church, Oxford, where he became B.A. in 1856, and sat as M.P. for the borough of Plymouth from 1859 to 1861, when by the death of his father, he entered the Upper House. His lordship is an extra Lord of the Bedchamber to H.R.H. the Prince of Wales; is Lieutenant-Colonel of the 2nd battalion and Captain Commandant of the 16th corps of Devon Rifle Volunteers; and is a Special Deputy Warden of the Stannaries, etc. He married in 1858 the Lady Katherine Elizabeth Hamilton, fourth daughter of the Duke of Abercorn, and has by her issue one son, Piers Alexander Hamilton, Viscount Valletort (born 1865), and three daughters, Victoria Frederica Caroline, Albertha Louisa Florence, and Edith Hilaria. The arms of the Earl of Mount Edgcumbe are *gules*, on a bend, *ermines*, cottised, *or*, three boars heads, *argent*; crest, a boar statant, *argent*, gorged with a wreath of oak, *vert*, fructed, *or*; supporters two greyhounds, *argent*, gutte de poix, and gorged with collars, dovetailed, *gules*.

Forward along the coast from Mount Edgcumbe is CAWSAND, a noted fishing village, beautifully situated in a bay to which it gives its name, and forward still is Penlee Point, where a convenient alcove gives rest to the pedestrian while he enjoys the beauty of the scene before him; and, further still, the Rame Head, on which are the remains of an ancient oratory.

SALTRAM.

Passing up Cattewater, and so on up the Laira – the two names by which the estuary of the river Plym is called – is the Laira Bridge, and, near it are the RACE COURSE on Chelson Meadow, and Saltram, the seat of the Earl of Morley.

The LAIRA BRIDGE was built at the expense of the first Earl of Morley, who also at his own charge embanked the Laira. In 1807, Lord Morley engaged Mr. Alexander, a successful engineer, to survey and report on the practicability of erecting a bridge across the estuary. The report of Mr. Alexander was to the effect that in consequence of the unfavourable nature of the bed of the river, the erection of such a structure would (if at all practicable) be attended with enormous expense. The idea of a bridge was, therefore, abandoned, and his lordship being proprietor of the ancient ferry between Oreston and Cattedown, established an improved ferry boat which was called a "flying bridge." By means of this ferry boat, which was open at both ends for the purpose of admitting waggons, carts, carriages, and other vehicles with their horses attached, as well as cattle of all descriptions, and passengers, a regular communication was established between Plymouth on the one side and Wembury, Brixton, Yealmpton, and other places on the other side. It was impelled across the water from side to side by means of a strong iron chain, stretched across the channel and passing over trucks in the boat which were made to revolve by means of two winches. The service of this "flying bridge" sufficiently proved its utility to the public, but it was liable to interruptions through bad weather and spring tides. In 1822, Mr James M. Rendel, the eminent engineer, then a young and almost untried man, having projected a suspension bridge across the Tamar, at Saltash, which, however, was never constructed, was desired by Lord Morley to consider the practicability of erecting a suspension bridge across the Laira. Mr. Rendel prepared drawings which were approved, and in 1823, an Act of Parliament was obtained empowering its erection. Subsequently, however, circumstances occurred to occasion the abandonment of the site first proposed, and the one on which the present bridge is built being unfavourable to the erection of a bridge on the principle of suspension, the original intention was relinquished. In 1824, another Act of Parliament was therefore obtained, by which the Act of 1823 was repealed, so far as related to the suspension bridge, and the powers extended to meet the requirements for the erection of the present bridge. Of this bridge, which is extremely elegant in its proportions, the accompanying engraving gives a representation from Mr. Rendel's own drawing. It is five hundred feet in length, and consists of five elliptical arches, the centre one, with a span of 100 feet, the two next, of 95 feet each, and the two outer ones of 81 feet each. The roadway is twenty-four feet in width, and it is twenty-two feet above highwater of the spring tides. The masonry is of limestone and granite; the bridge itself of iron; the foundation and the masonry being executed by Mr. Johnson, of the Plymouth Granite Works, and the iron-work by Mr. Hazeldine, of Shrewsbury.

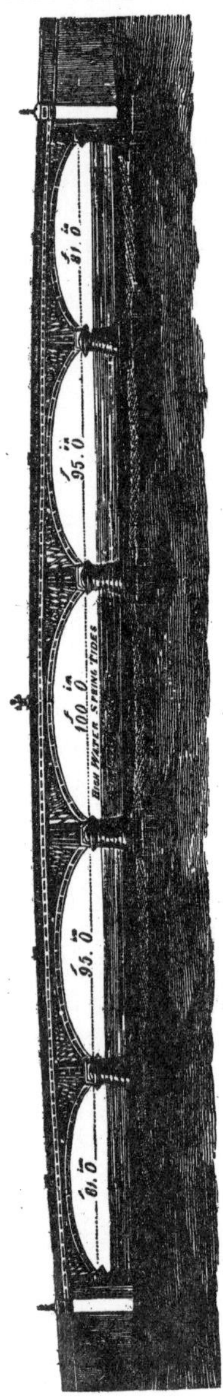

The works were begun on the 4th of August, 1824; the first stone laid by the Earl of Morley, on the 16th of March, 1825; and the bridge was opened on the 14th of July, 1827, when H.R.H. the Duchess of Clarence (afterwards Queen Adelaide) with her suite, passed over it. The following inscription is carved on a block of granite at the north end of the bridge:–

HUNC PONTEM
SENATUS AUCTORITATE SUSCEPTUM
NOVAS ET COMMODAS VIAS
RECLUDENTEM
JOHANNES COMES DE MORLEY
STRUENDUM CURAVIT
OPUS INCHOATUM, A.D. 1824;
ABSOLUTUM, A.D. 1827.
J. M. RENDEL, ARCHITECT.

CHELSON MEADOW, near Laira Bridge, was almost entirely recovered by the embankment of the Laira by the Earl of Morley. It is used as a race-course, being first opened for that purpose in 1826. The course is a mile and a half. The work of embankment was commenced in 1806, and completed in 1817, at a cost of nearly £10,000; the quantity of land reclaimed being 175 acres, and valued at about £20,000

SALTRAM, in the reign of Charles I., belonged to, and was the residence of, Sir James Bagg, of Plymouth, but, having been forfeited to the crown, became the property of Lord Cartaret, and afterwards of Mr. Wolstenholme, from whom, in 1712, it was purchased by George Parker, Esq., who owned the neighbouring place, Boringdon. The present house was built in the early part of last century by the grandfather of the first Earl of Morley, and Lady Catherine Parker, but has since been materially altered and added to; among the additions being a portico, erected from the designs of Mr. Foulston. The house has no architectural pretention, but it is nevertheless a noble residence, and its rooms are peculiarly elegant. Among the Art-treasures in the various apartments are the following paintings:–

Galatea (of Raphael)	*Copy of Domenichino.*	Holy Family	*Guido.*
Cattle	*Cuyp.*	Bacchanalians (valued at 3,000 guineas)	*Titan.*
Madonna and Child	*Sasso Ferrato.*	Sir Thomas Parker	*Janssen.*
Flight into Egypt	*G. Poussin.*	Queen Elizabeth	———
Marriage of St. Catherine	*Corregio*	Place of St. Mark, Venice	*Canaletto*
Spanish Figures	*Palamedes.*	Sea Piece	*Vandervelde.*
Soldiers in a rockyscene	*Salvator Rosa.*	View of Naples	*Ricciarelli.*
St. Anthony and Christ	*Caracci.*	Two small pictures	*Albano.*
St. Catherine	*Guido.*	Charles XII.	———
Sir Joshua Reynolds	*Kauffman.*	Appollo and Daphne	*Albano.*
Tribute Money	*Caravaggio.*	Marquis of Lansdowne	*Sir J. Reynolds.*
Landscape	*Wouvermans.*	Phaeton	*Stubbs.*
Adoration of the Shepherds	*Carlo Dolci.*	Sigismundi	———
Madonna and Child	*Andrea del Sarto*	Landscape	*Wilson.*

Landscape	*Berghem*	Decapitation of St. Paul	*Guercino.*
Bolingbroke Family	*Vandyke .*	Cattle	*Rosa de Tivoli.*
Three Female Figures	*Rubens.*	Animals	*Snyders.*
Game	*Snyders.*	The Assumption	*Sabbatini.*

The ceilings of the saloon and dining-room were painted by Zucchi; and the house contains many other specimens of art, among which is a bust of the Earl of Morley, by Nollekens, and casts of Psyche, a Faun, and a Hebe, by Canova. The grounds and gardens are very extensive and extremely beautiful, and the whole domain is full of lovely spots and of grand prospects.

The family of Parker is of considerable antiquity in Devonshire, having been seated for several generations at North Molton, when one of them, Thomas Parker, married the heiress of Frye, of Frye's Hall, in Hatherleigh. John Parker, his son and successor, married the heiress of Ellicott of Bralton, and was succeeded by his son, Edmund Parker, who married the heiress of Smythe of Essex. Edmund Parker was, in turn, succeeded by his son, John Parker, who, in the reign of Queen Elizabeth, marrying the heiress of Mayhew, or Mewe or Boringdon, became possessed of that patrimony. By this marriage, also, the Parkers became possessed of the barton of Woodford, and other places. On attaining the Boringdon estates the Parkers removed there from North Molton, and, ultimately, in the building of Saltram House, made that their residence. This Edmund Parker, Esq., who was High Sheriff for the County of Devon, in 1575, died in 1610, and his descendant, John Parker, Esq., who was member of Parliament for Devonshire, was, in 1784, created Baron Boringdon, of Boringdon, Devonshire. He married, first, in 1763, Frances, daughter of Dr. Hort, Archbishop of Tuam, who died the following year, without issue; and, second, in 1769, the Hon. Theresa Robinson, second daughter of Thomas, first Lord Grantham, by whom he had one son, his successor, and one daughter, Theresa, married to the Hon. George Villiers. His Lordship died in 1788, and was succeeded by his son the Hon. John Parker.

This nobleman, who was born in 1772, was married twice, first to Lady Augusta Fane, second daughter of John, Earl of Westmoreland, which marriage was dissolved in 1809, the lady afterwards marrying the Rt. Hon. Sir Arthur Paget; and, second, in 1809, to Frances, daughter of Thomas Talbot, Esq., of Wymondham, by whom he had issue his son and successor, Edward Parker. In 1815 his lordship was advanced to the dignities of Viscount Boringdon of North Molton, and Earl of Morley. It was to this peer, who died in 1840, that Plymouth is indebted for the Laira Bridge, the Embankment of the Laira, and other public improvements.

Edmund, second Earl of Morley, was born in 1810, and in 1842, married Harriet Sophia, daughter of Montague E. Parker, Esq., of Pentillie Castle, by whom he had issue one son, who succeeded him; and one daughter. He died in 1864.

The present peer, Albert Edmund Parker, third Earl of Morley, Viscount and Baron Boringdon, was born in 1843, and succeeded his father, Edmund, second Earl of Morley, in 1864. His lordship, who was educated at Eton and at Balliol College, Oxford, where he became B.A. in 1865, is a deputy Lieutenant for Devonshire, and in 1868, was appointed a Lord in Waiting to the Queen.

The arms of the Earl of Morley are *sable*, a buck's head caboshed, between two flauches, *argent*; crest, a cubit arm couped below the elbow, the sleeve *azure* cuffed and slashed *argent*, the hand grasping a stag's attire, *gules*; supporters, dexter, a stag, *argent*, collared, *or*, pendant from the collar a shield, *vert*, charged with a horse's head couped *argent*, bridled, *or*, sinister, a greyhound, *sable,* collared, *or*, pendant from the collar a shield, *gules*, charged with a ducal coronet, *or*.

ADDENDA TO ANNALS

1872. – This year the Congress of the National Association for the promotion of Social Science was held at Plymouth, and passed off with considerable *eclat*. The Congress commenced on the 11th of September, and continued until the 18th. On the 11th an inaugural address was delivered by the President, Lord Napier and Ettrick, in St. James's Hall, and special service was held at St. Andrew's Church. Meetings of various sections were held daily at St. James's Hall, the Athenaeum, the Assembly Rooms, the Royal Hotel, the Mechanic's Institution, the Guildhall, etc. In the evening of the 12th, the Mayor of Plymouth, Isaac Latimer, Esq., held a reception at the Assembly Rooms, which were specially devoted for the occasion: the company being one of the most brilliant assemblages ever held in Plymouth. The same day his worship entertained at dinner, the Right Hon. Lord Napier and Ettrick, K.T., the President of the Social Science Congress, George Woodyatt Hastings, Esq., President of the Council, H.W. Acland, Esq., M.D., F.R.S., J. H. Kennaway, Esq., M.P., Presidents of Sections, Edwin Pears, Esq., General Secretary, Walter Morrison, Esq., M.P., Professor Hodgson, Edward Burkett, Esq., R. N. Fowler, Esq., M.P., Dr. Waddilove, Edward Jenkins, Esq., author of "Ginx's Baby," the Mayor of Devonport, Admiral Kennedy, Sir Robert Torrens, and others. On the 14th, a Garden Fête was given at Mount Edgcumbe. On the 15th special services were held at most of the Churches and Chapels of the three towns. On the 16th the Congress was removed to Devonport where its meetings continued to be held until the 18th, when various excursions were taken. The Congress is said to have been the most successful ever held.

A movement was set on foot, for the restoration of St. Andrew's Church, and Sir Gilbert Scott was called in to prepare a plan, and give a report. The estimated cost is about £7,000. During the year a monument to the Rev. John Hatchard, for forty five years vicar of the parish, was put up in this church. It is from the design of Sir Gilbert Scott, and bears an admirable bust, by Mr. H. H. Armstead, and an incised group, emblematical of Mr. Hatchard's labours during the prevalence of cholera in the town.

In October a testimonial of plate was presented to Mr. Alfred Rooker, by his friends and supporters at the late election.

In November Mr. Alderman John Kelly, was elected Mayor for the ensuing year, and Honorary Colonel of the 2nd Administrative Battalion of Volunteers.

INDEX

INDEX

INDEX

INDEX

INDEX

INDEX

INDEX

SUBSCRIBERS 1873

A

Arthur, Edward, Mr.
Alger, W. H., Mr.
Allen, Joseph, Mr.
Alger, Oswald, Mrs.

B

Burnell, John, Mrs.
Bennett, E. G., Mr.
Bewes, Rev. T. A.
Boger, Deeble Esq., J. P.
Briggs. Thomas, Mr.
Bayly, John, Mr.
Brown, Eldred R., Mr.
Bate, Charles Spence, F.R.S., F.L.S.
Blight, T. R., Mr.
Bulteel, F. F., Mr.
Burnell, W,. Mr.
Bewes, Charles T., Mr.
Bastard, B. J. P., Esq., J.P.
Body, Walter, Mr.
Bickford, Mr.
Bates, Edward, Esq., M.P.
Bovey & Co., Messrs.
Bowden, Frederic J., Mr.
Bayly, Robert, Mr.
Barnes, rev., F.
Brian, T. C. Mr., Coroner

C

Call, B., Mr.
Carew, W. H. Pole, Esq., J.P.
Collier, Mortimer J., Mr.
Colley, J. L., Mr.
Cudlipp, J. S., F.S.S., Mr.
Cranford, Robert, Mr.
Cuming, W. B., Mr.
Collier, Sir Robert P.
Collier, W. F., Mr.
Cleverton, F. W. P., Mr.
Cross, Henry, Mr.
Clarke, Samuel, Mr.
Crewdson, W. D., Mrs.
Collier, A. B., Mr.
Calmady, V. P., Mr.
Champion, Lieut, R.M.L.I.

D

Dyer, Alfre, Mr.
Derry, W., Mr.
Davies, Edward. Mr.
Dymond, T. R., Mr.
Derry, David, Mrs.
Dawson, Ralph, Esq., J.P.
Davidson, J.B., Mr.
Dawe, J. E. E., Mr.
Davy, Thomas Hyne, Mr.

E

Elliott, J. J., Esq., J.P.
Edmonds, John, Mr.
Essery, W., Mr.
Ellis, Robert, Mr.
Evers, H. Mr., L.L.D.

F

Fuge, Miss
Farley, Mrs.
Feather,m Henry, Mr.
Fortescue, W.C., Mr.
Fowler, F. S., Mr.
Fortescue, J. F., Mr.
Fitz-Gerald, Lt.-Col.

G

Govett, P. Herbert, Mr.
Gill, Rev. W.
Grigg, Mark, Mr.
Goulding, F. H., Mr.
Greaves, Rev., H. A.
Gale, Dr.
Gliddon, Mr.
Grepe,. W.S., Mr.

H

Hingston, Alfred, Esq., J.P.
Hutchinson, Capt., R.N.
Hill, Richard, Mr.
Hare, J., Mr.
Hingston, J. T., Mr.
Harris, W. H., Mr.
Harris, A. S., Mr.
Hawker, James, Mrs.
Hingston, Mrs. C.
Hooper, John, Mr.
Holmes, Peter, D. D., F.R.A.S.
Hicks, Francis, Mr.
Hine, James, Mr.
Harper, Thomas, Mr.
Hawken, Silas, Mr.
Hawker, W. H., Mr.
Herron, Frederick, Mr.
Hatchard, rev. J. Alton
Hellyer, J., Mr.
Holberton, W., Mr.
Hill, Richd., Jun., Mr.
Hems, Harry, Mr.
Hingston, C. ALbert, M.D.
Healey, E., Mr.
Higman, F. Mr.
Howland, H.J., Mr.

J

Jago, Dr.
Jonas, Rev. J.G.
Jago, Edward, Mr.

K

Kelly, J. Esq., Mayor of Plymouth
Keys, I. W. N., Mr.

L

Lopes, Sir Massey, Bart., M.P.
Latimer, Isaac, Mr.
Luce, Mr.
Littleton, T., Dr., M.B., Lond.
Libby, John, Mr.
Luscombe, Henry, Mr., Vice-Consul for Spain
Luscombe, W., Esq., J.P.
Lewin, W. Mr.
Lee, C. K., Mr.
Lewis, J. D., Esq., M.P.
Liscombe, R., Mr.
Luke, A., Mr.
Luke, Alfred, Mr.
Luke, W. H., Jun, Mr.
Lampen, Miss.

M

Mount Edgcumbe (Dowager Countess of)
Mount Edgcumbe, Earl of
Morrison, Walter, Esq., M.P.
Matthews, W. E., Esq., J.P.
Moore, Rev. Joseph
Marshall, W., Mr.
Moore, R.E., Mr.
Matthres, J. W., Mr.
Morris, George, Mr.
Mudge, A., Mr.
Mennie, George, Esq., J.P.
Marshall, Edred, Mr.
Morrish, Francis, A., Mr.
Moon, James, Mr.
Matthres, Chas. M., Mr.
Mead, William, P., Mr.
Maynard, Henry, Mr.

N

Norrington, Charles, Esq., J.P.
Newton, J. B., Mr.

SUBSCRIBERS 1873

O

Officers Library, Royal Marines
Oriston, Thos., C. E., Mr.
Oldrey, Robert, Mr.

P

Plymouth Public Libraru
Plymouth Institution
Prideaux, Walter, Mr.
Prideaux, Charles, Mr.
Parlby, Rev. Hall
Phillips, W. R., Mr.
Pridham, George, Mr.
Prance, W. H., Mr.
Popham, Radford & Co.
Pearse, Samuel, Mr.
Polkinghorne, E., Mr.
Pearse, Thomas, Mr.
Picken, S., Jun., Mr.
Pethick, John, Mr.
Pardon, B., Mr.
Pode, Stephen, Mr.
Pitts, Thos., Jun., Mr.
Page, J. H., Mr.
Picken, Miss.
Peck, Mrs.
Page, Mrs.
Palmer, W. J., Mr.

R

Rodda, Richard, Mr.
Rooker, Alfred, Mr.
Rogers, J. P., Mr.
Risk, rev., J. E.
Radmore, W., Mr.
Richardson, Mrs. T.
Radford, W., Esq., J.P.
Rowe, J. Brooking, Mr.
Ryall, R., Mr.
Ralph, A., Mr.
Rawlings, W., Mr.
Rorie, Goerge, Mr.
Rice, John, Mr.
Roach, S., Mr.
Rogers, Rev. E.
Raddall, Warne, Mr.

S

Stewart, Sir Houston
Strode, major
Skardon, Jmes C., Mrs.
Skardon, James, Esq., J.P.
Skardon, W., Mr.
Skardon, Charles S., Mr.
Spink, M., Rev.
Spence, Charles, Mr.
Square, Miss.
South Devon & Cornwall Library Society, per Mr. Blewett.
Spender, edward, Mr.
Saunders, W., Mr.
Shelley, John, Mr.
Spooner, N. A., Mr.
Seargeant, L. J., Mr.
Skelton, John, M.D., M.R.C.S.
Skelton, Dr. R.
Saunders, John A., Mr.
Steadman, Mr. H.
Sparrow, Benjamin, Mr.
Square, Elliott, Mr.
Stephens, Robert, Mr.
Stevens, Thos. Jones, Mr.

T

Trebry, Miss.
Trelawney-Collins, Rev. C. T.
Taylor, Mrs.
Tanner, Charles, Mr.
Tubbs, C. F., Mr.
Trist, Major, J.P.
Thomson, Michell, Mr.
Trevena, Mr.

W

Woodhouse, Mr. H. A.
Whiteford, C. C., Mr.
Waddington, R. E., Mr.
Wills, Miss.
Watts, Elias, Mr.
Whiteford, Miss.
Woods, W., Mr.
Widger, J. A., Mr.
Wills, Joseph, Mr.
Whiteford, H. Mr.
White, W. H. P., Mr.

Y

Yonge, Capt.

SUBSCRIBERS 2001

Linda, Shams, Omar and Khaled Badran, Plymouth

Pat and Rosamund Barrow, Ilfracombe

Vivien Bond, Plympton

Stephen Bowles, Bideford

Graham and Pat Brooks, Eggbuckland, Plymouth

Wendy Brown, Plymouth

Peter Budd, 12 Furland Close, Plymstock, Plymouth

Sue, Robbie and Joseph Burns, Liverpool

Jennifer Capern, Higher Clovelly

Nicholas Casley, Peverell, Plymouth

John and Rachel Challenor, Plymouth

Steven Francis Clark, Stoke, Plymouth

Derek Deacon, Peverell, Plymouth

William Dewhurst and Norma Finn, Bideford

Christopher John Edgcombe, Cambridge

David J L Gabbitass, Wolferstans, Deptford Chambers, 60/64 North Hill, Plymouth

Edward Gaskell, Appledore (2 copies)

Louella (Liddy) Gaskell, Appledore

Natalie Gaskell, Bideford

Bridgett, Lorna and Leslie Gilbert

Sam and Teresa Gordon, Stoke, Plymouth

Terry and Sue Guswell, Plymouth

Reg & Sylvia Hamley, Paul & Isabelle, Claire & Mike, Plymouth

John Penwill Hodge and Pamela Trudie Hodge

Frederick James Lacey

Lazarus Press, Bideford (10 copies)

Joyce M. McDermott, Lipson, Plymouth

Alan Michael and Josephine Maud, Plymouth, Devon

David John Morris, Stoke, Plymouth

Roderick Murphy, Stoke, Plymouth

Nicholas Nickleby Bookshop, Bideford (20 copies)

Michelle Marie Ninnim

Roy and Barbara Parsons, Millbridge, Plymouth

Plymouth City Council Archaeology Service

Quay Gallery, Appledore, North Devon

Andy and Shirley Roberts, St Judes, Plymouth

Ronald Roberts, Roborough, Plymouth

Rods Books, Barbican, Plymouth (2 copies)

John Ruth, Saltash, Cornwall

Janet Schreyer, Stoke, Plymouth

Ernie Stanton, Mainstone, Plymouth

Stuart Road Primary School, Palmerston Street, Stoke, Plymouth

Albert C. Symons, Mount Gould, Plymouth

Norman Sydney Trethowan

Alasdair Walker, Plymouth

Gretchen Wallace, Raleigh, North Carolina, USA

Ann Westcott, Appledore, North Devon

Westwell Publishing, Quay Gallery, Appledore

Saul Whitford, Park Farm, Sortridge

Beryl Scott Whittington, Plympton, Plymouth

Simon Wilson and Diane Williams, Crownhill, Plymouth

Derek Wingett, Crownhill, Plymouth

David Young, Oxford

Various subscribers who wish to remain anonymous